The United Nations and a Just World Order

STUDIES ON A JUST WORLD ORDER

Richard Falk and Saul H. Mendlovitz, General Editors

†*Toward a Just World Order*, no. 1, edited by Richard Falk, Samuel S. Kim, and Saul H. Mendlovitz

†*International Law: A Contemporary Perspective*, no. 2, edited by Richard Falk, Friedrich Kratochwil, and Saul H. Mendlovitz

†*The United Nations and a Just World Order*, no. 3, edited by Richard A. Falk, Samuel S. Kim, and Saul H. Mendlovitz

†*Toward Nuclear Disarmament and Global Security: A Search for Alternatives*, no. 4, edited by Burns H. Weston with the assistance of Thomas A. Hawbaker and Christopher R. Rossi

†*Culture, Ideology, and World Order*, no. 5, edited by R.B.J. Walker

†Available in hardcover and paperback.

STUDIES ON A JUST WORLD ORDER, NO. 3

The United Nations and a Just World Order

edited by Richard A. Falk,
Samuel S. Kim, and
Saul H. Mendlovitz

Westview Press

BOULDER • SAN FRANCISCO • OXFORD

Studies on a Just World Order, No. 3

Copyright © 1991 by Westview Press, Inc.

Published in 1991 in the United States of America by Westview Press, Inc., 5500 Central Avenue, Boulder, Colorado 80301, and in the United Kingdom by Westview Press, 36 Lonsdale Road, Summertown, Oxford OX2 7EW

Library of Congress Cataloging-in-Publication Data
The United Nations and a just world order : edited by Richard A. Falk,
   Samuel S. Kim, Saul H. Mendlovitz.
       p.   cm.—(Studies on a just world order ; v. 3)
   Includes bibliographical references.
   ISBN 0-86531-240-0. ISBN 0-86531-250-8 (pbk.).
   1. United Nations.   2. International organization.   I. Falk,
Richard A.   II. Kim, Samuel S., 1935–   .   III. Mendlovitz, Saul H.
IV. Series.
JX1977.U42563   1991
341.23—dc20   90-28785
                                                                          CIP

Printed and bound in the United States of America

∞   The paper used in this publication meets the requirements
     of the American National Standard for Permanence of Paper
     for Printed Library Materials Z39.48-1984.

10   9   8   7   6   5   4   3   2   1

Contents

Preface   xi
Credits   xiii

General Introduction   1

Section 1
The Role of Social Movements   13

1. Dilemmas of Antisystemic Movements,
    Giovanni Arrighi, Terence K. Hopkins,
    and Immanuel Wallerstein   16

2. Party and State in Our Times: The Rise of
    Non-Party Political Formations, *Rajni Kothari*   29

3. The Peace Movement: A Comparative
    and Analytical Survey, *Nigel Young*   46

PART ONE
CHANGES AND CONTINUITIES

General Introduction   67

Section 2
A Normative and Structural Overview   83

4. The United Nations in Historical Perspective:
    What Have We Learned About Peacebuilding?
    Chadwick F. Alger   87

5. The United Nations, Lawmaking, and World
    Order, *Samuel S. Kim*   109

6. Developments in Decision Making in
    the United Nations, *Johan Kaufmann*   125

Section 3
Diverse Perspectives   137

7. The Management of Power in the Changing United Nations, *Inis L. Claude, Jr.*   143

8. The Functional Approach to World Organization, *David Mitrany*   153

9. World Peace Through World Law: Two Alternative Plans, *Grenville Clark*   163

10. On the Prospects of Global Governance, *Georgi Shakhnazarov, A. Bovin, and G. Tunkin*   166

11. No Development Without Peace, No Peace Without Development, *Mohammed Bedjaoui*   178

12. A Statement Made by Premier Zhao Ziyang at the UN General Assembly for the Commemoration of the 40th Anniversary of the Founding of the United Nations, *Zhao Ziyang*   184

13. Realities and Guarantees for a Secure World, *Mikhail Gorbachev*   188

14. Prospects for a New Era of World Peace, *Ronald Reagan*   198

PART TWO
THE UNITED NATIONS
AND WORLD ORDER VALUES

General Introduction   207

Section 4
The United Nations and International Peace and Security   213

15. The Nuremberg Principles   220

16. The United Nations and the Resolution of International Conflicts, *Raimo Väyrynen*   222

17. Relationship Between Disarmament and Development: An Overview of United Nations Involvement, *Preparatory Committee for the International Conference on the Relationship Between Disarmament and Development*   240

18. Toward an Alternative Security System,
    Robert Johansen   252

19. Building a Permanent and Globalist Peace
    Movement, *Nigel Young*   276

Section 5
The United Nations and the World Economy   281

20. The Declaration on the Establishment of
    a New International Economic Order   288

21. The New International Economic Order
    and the Basic Needs Approach, *Johan Galtung*   292

22. The World Bank: A New Role in the Debt Crisis?
    Cheryl Payer   307

23. Towards a Development Strategy and Action
    Programme for the South, *The South Commission*   319

24. Role of People in the Future Global Order,
    Chadwick F. Alger   327

Section 6
The United Nations and Social Justice   345

25. The Universal Declaration of Human Rights   351

26. Global Human Rights and World Order,
    Samuel S. Kim   356

27. The United Nations and Human Rights, 1945–1985,
    David P. Forsythe   377

28. The Nairobi Forward-Looking Strategies
    for the Advancement of Women,
    Adopted by the World Conference
    to Review and Appraise the Achievements
    of the United Nations Decade for Women   392

29. A Crime of Silence: The Armenian Genocide,
    Permanent Peoples' Tribunal   403

Section 7
The United Nations and Ecological Balance   419

30. The Stockholm Declaration   427

31. What Happened at Stockholm, *F. H. Knelman*   433

32. On the Problem of "the Global Problematique":
    What Roles for International Organizations?
    John G. Ruggie   447

33. The World Charter for Nature   467

34. Towards Common Action: Proposals for
    Institutional and Legal Change, *The World
    Commission on Environment and Development*   471

                        PART THREE
              THE UNITED NATIONS AND THE FUTURE

General Introduction   497

Section 8
The United Nations at a Crossroads   501

35. Secretary-General Pérez de Cuéllar's
    1988 Report on the Work of the Organization   504

36. The Future of the United Nations System:
    Some Questions on the Occasion
    of an Anniversary, *Marc Nerfin*   519

37. A Successor Vision: The United Nations of
    Tomorrow, *UN Association of the USA*   535

38. Towards Comprehensive Security Through the
    Enhancement of the Role of the United Nations,
    Vladimir Petrovsky   542

39. The Establishment of a World Authority:
    Working Hypotheses, *Silviu Brucan*   546

40. Openings for Peace and Justice in World
    of Danger and Struggle, *Richard A. Falk*   550

41. Struggles for a Just World Peace: A Transition
    Strategy, *Saul H. Mendlovitz*   565

Bibliography   573
List of Acronyms   585
About the Book and Editors   589

Preface

Never has it seemed more relevant and urgent to reflect upon the United Nations. The Gulf War has put the organization, even if temporarily, at the very center of our hopes and concerns about the shape of a new world order to come in a post–Cold War era. Our initial impetus was to redo the United Nations volume in the Strategy of World Order series, which seemed quite out of date a decade ago. However, during the course of writing this book, neither the world order nor our perceptions have remained frozen in time, easily recorded in an objective, factual manner. The world has undergone a tremendous upheaval: an upheaval of myths, regimes, and ideologies. The firm ground of the Cold War and of deterrence thinking has collapsed, leaving the future of global relations nebulous and challenging. Will we lapse into the familiar and destructive pattern of power politics, or Pax Americana? Or will we take advantage of the opportunities that lie before us and build a new foundation based on a broader conception of security and interdependence? The role of the United Nations in this new world order is crucial; where we go from here depends upon our aspirations and our goals.

Initially, Donald McNemar, while on the faculty at Dartmouth College, was the third collaborator. We wish to acknowledge his contributions, which have remained relevant to our thinking through these years. He did some important, preliminary writing on the place of the United Nations in the wider setting of world politics as well as on the character and evolution of the organization itself. When Don left scholarly life to become headmaster at Andover, we sought and found a willing Samuel S. Kim. For the last six years or so, Sam has prodded us to the limit of his considerable prodding ability, but even his stimulus has not proved sufficient.

Rather than exhibit our insecurity by setting forth excuses, it seems more in keeping with the enterprise itself to celebrate our timing as evidence of a "feel" for the subject matter. Until the last few years, the United Nations was experiencing a long downward pull in stature and performance, especially here in the United States. Who, after all, would want to celebrate an organization presided over by Kurt Waldheim? The presence of Waldheim as secretary-general was a deliberate expression by leading governments of the low esteem they had for the United Nations.

Now, happily, with Javier Pérez de Cuéllar at the helm and with the superpowers, especially the Soviet Union, again supportive and constructive, it is quite possible

xi

to portray the United Nations in generally, although not invariably, positive terms. Such matters of assessment will be dealt with throughout this book, starting with the General Introduction.

Here, primarily, our intention is to acknowledge some debts. Richard Falk and Samuel Kim wish, especially, to thank the Center of International Studies and its director, Henry Bienen, as well as the Peter B. Lewis Fund for supporting their research on the United Nations. Saul Mendlovitz wishes to thank the World Order Models Project and the World Policy Institute for providing auspices and logistical capabilities needed over the years. He wishes to express his appreciation to Dean Peter Simmons, Rutgers Law School, for research funds and for creating a congenial structure in which to do his work.

Beyond our institutional debts are some of a more personal character. As so often in the past, we were greatly helped by June Garson's overall intelligence and various human, secretarial, and administrative skills. Additionally, Philomena Fischer gave us valuable assistance, particularly in relation to gathering and coordinating the materials.

Our largest debt by far, however, is owed to Lester Ruiz, who stage-managed all aspects of the last steps of this undertaking. Lester has been more than a coordinator and a friend; he has been, as always, an intellectual collaborator of the highest quality.

We also want to thank Westview Press for its patience and continuing interest in the world order approach to international relations. We are particularly grateful to Miriam Gilbert, Jennifer Knerr, Libby Barstow, and Cheryl Carnahan for their editorial role in relation to the book.

Without delving into substance, let us express merely a hope: that the expansion of the scope and significance of United Nations activities in the years ahead will date this collection of materials at the earliest possible time. Although we write within a world order framework that adopts a positive view of the United Nations, we would feel greatly encouraged if by the year 2000, readers could look back on what we have done and marvel at our editorial caution.

Richard A. Falk
Samuel S. Kim
Saul H. Mendlovitz

Credits

The selections in this book are from the following sources. Permissions to reprint are gratefully acknowledged.

1. Reprinted from Giovanni Arrighi, Terence K. Hopkins, and Immanuel Wallerstein, "Dilemmas of Antisystemic Movements," *Social Research* 53 (Spring 1986), pp. 185–206. Reprinted with permission.
2. Reprinted, with notes deleted, from Rajni Kothari, "Party and State in Our Times: The Rise of Non-Party Political Formations," *Alternatives* 9 (Spring 1984), pp. 541–564. Reprinted with permission.
3. Reprinted, with notes deleted, from Nigel Young, "The Peace Movement: A Comparative and Analytical Survey," *Alternatives* 11 (April 1986), pp. 185–217. Reprinted with permission.
4. Adapted, with notes deleted, from Chadwick F. Alger, "The United Nations in Historical Perspective: What Have We Learned About Peacebuilding?" (Hakone, Japan: UN University Global Seminar on International Organizations, September 1985).
5. Excerpted, with notes deleted, from Samuel S. Kim, "The United Nations, Lawmaking, and World Order," *Alternatives* 10 (1985), pp. 643–675. Reprinted with permission.
6. Reprinted, with notes deleted, from Johan Kaufmann, "Developments in Decision Making in the United Nations," pp. 17–32 in Jeffrey Harrod and Nico Schrijver, eds., *The UN Under Attack* (London: Gower, 1988). Reprinted with permission.
7. Reprinted, with notes deleted, from Inis L. Claude, Jr., "The Management of Power in the Changing United Nations," *International Organization* 15:2 (Spring 1961), pp. 219–235. Reprinted by permission of The MIT Press, Cambridge, Massachusetts, and the author.
8. Reprinted, with notes deleted, from David Mitrany, "The Functional Approach to World Organization," pp. 149–166 in A *Working Peace System* (Chicago: Quadrangle Books, 1966).
9. Excerpted from Grenville Clark, "Introduction," pp. xv–xvii in Grenville Clark and Louis B. Sohn, *World Peace Through World Law: Two Alternative Plans*, 3d ed., enlarged (Cambridge: Harvard University Press, 1966). Reprinted by

permission of the publishers. Copyright © 1958, 1960, 1966 by the President and Fellows of Harvard College.

10. Reprinted from Georgi Shakhnazarov, A. Bovin, and G. Tunkin, "Dialogue: On the Prospects of Global Governance," *Alternatives* 14 (April 1989), pp. 245–257. Reprinted with permission.

11. Reprinted from Mohammed Bedjaoui, "No Development Without Peace, No Peace Without Development" (the address delivered by Ambassador Bedjaoui as chairman of the Group of 77 to the 36th Session of the UN General Assembly, as reprinted in *IFDA Dossier* 27 [January/February 1982], pp. 55–62). Reprinted with permission.

12. Reprinted from Zhao Ziyang, "A Statement Made by Premier Zhao Ziyang at the UN General Assembly for the Commemoration of the 40th Anniversary of the Founding of the United Nations," *Beijing Review* (November 4, 1985), pp. 15–17.

13. Reprinted from Mikhail Gorbachev, *Realities and Guarantees for a Secure World* (Moscow: Novosti Press Agency Publishing House, 1987), pp. 3–16.

14. Reprinted from Ronald Reagan, "Prospects for a New Era of World Peace" (an address before the UN General Assembly, September 26, 1988, as reprinted in U.S. Department of State, Bureau of Public Affairs, *Current Policy* No. 1109, pp. 1–5).

15. The Nuremberg Principles are reprinted from *Yearbook of the United Nations 1950* (New York: United Nations, 1951), p. 852.

16. Excerpted, with art and notes deleted, from Raimo Väyrynen, "The United Nations and the Resolution of International Conflicts," *Cooperation and Conflict* 20 (1985), pp. 141–171. Reprinted by permission of Norwegian University Press (Universitetsforlaget), Oslo, Norway, and the author.

17. Excerpted, with notes deleted, from Preparatory Committee for the International Conference on the Relationship Between Disarmament and Development, "Relationship Between Disarmament and Development: An Overview of United Nations Involvement," UN Doc. A/CONF.130/PC/INF/5 (February 4, 1986), pp. 2–13.

18. Excerpted, with notes and art deleted, from Robert Johansen, "Toward an Alternative Security System," World Policy Paper No. 24 (1983), pp. 15–43. Reprinted with permission.

19. Excerpted, with notes deleted, from Nigel Young, "Building a Permanent and Globalist Peace Movement," *Alternatives* 11 (April 1986), pp. 185–217. Reprinted with permission.

20. The Declaration on the Establishment of a New International Economic Order is reprinted from General Assembly Resolution 3201 (S-VI), GAOR, 6th Special Sess., Supplement No. 1 (A/9559), pp. 3–5.

21. Reprinted, with notes deleted, from Johan Galtung, "The New International Economic Order and the Basic Needs Approach," *Alternatives* 4 (March 1979), pp. 455–476. Reprinted with permission.

22. Reprinted, with notes and art deleted, from Cheryl Payer, "The World Bank: A New Role in the Debt Crisis?" *Third World Quarterly* 8 (April 1986), pp. 658–676. Reprinted with permission.

23. Reprinted from The South Commission, "Towards a Development Strategy and Action Programme for the South," *IFDA Dossier* 66 (July/August 1988), pp. 43–51. Reprinted with permission.

24. Excerpted, with notes and art deleted, from Chadwick F. Alger, "Role of People in the Future Global Order," *Alternatives* 4 (October 1978), pp. 233–262. Reprinted with permission.

25. The Universal Declaration of Human Rights is reprinted from General Assembly Resolution 217A(III), December 10, 1948.

26. Excerpted, with notes deleted, from Samuel S. Kim, "Global Human Rights and World Order," *The Quest for a Just World Order* (Boulder, Colo.: Westview Press, 1984), pp. 195–214.

27. Reprinted, with notes deleted, from David P. Forsythe, "The United Nations and Human Rights, 1945–1985," *Political Science Quarterly* 100 (Summer 1985), pp. 249–269. Reprinted with permission.

28. Reprinted, with notes deleted, from The Nairobi Forward-Looking Strategies for the Advancement of Women, adopted by the World Conference to Review and Appraise the Achievements of the United Nations Decade for Women: Equality, Development, and Peace, Nairobi, Kenya, July 15–26, 1985, pp. 5–16.

29. Reprinted from Permanent Peoples' Tribunal, A *Crime of Silence: The Armenian Genocide* (London: Zed Books, 1985), pp. 211–227.

30. The Stockholm Declaration on the Human Environment is reprinted from *Report of the United Nations Conference on the Human Environment, Stockholm, 5–16 June 1972* (New York: United Nations, 1973), pp. 3–5.

31. Reprinted from F. H. Knelman, "What Happened at Stockholm," *International Journal* (Winter 1972–1973), pp. 28–49. Reprinted by permission of *International Journal*, which is published by Canadian Institute of International Affairs.

32. Excerpted, with notes deleted, from John G. Ruggie, "On the Problem of 'the Global Problematique': What Roles for International Organizations?" *Alternatives* 5 (January 1980), pp. 517–550. Reprinted with permission.

33. The World Charter for Nature is reprinted from General Assembly Resolution 37/7 (October 28, 1982), Annex.

34. Reprinted, with notes deleted, from The World Commission on Environment and Development [Bruntland Commission], "Towards Common Action: Proposals for Institutional and Legal Change," *Our Common Future* (New York: Oxford University Press, 1987), pp. 308–343. Copyright © World Commission on Environment and Development, 1987. Reprinted by permission of Oxford University Press.

35. Secretary-General Pérez de Cuéllar's 1988 Report on the Work of the Organization is excerpted from UN Doc. A/43/1 (September 14, 1988), pp. 2–22.

36. Reprinted, with notes deleted, from Marc Nerfin, "The Future of the United Nations System: Some Questions on the Occasion of an Anniversary," *Development Dialogue*, the journal of the Dag Hammarskjöld Foundation (1985:1), pp. 1–25.

37. Reprinted from United Nations Association of the USA, "Executive Summary," *A Successor Vision: The United Nations of Tomorrow*, Final Panel Report (New York: UNA of USA, 1987), pp. i–x. Reprinted with permission.

38. Reprinted from Vladimir Petrovsky, "Towards Comprehensive Security Through the Enhancement of the Role of the United Nations," UN Doc. A/43/629, Annex (September 22, 1988), pp. 1–6.

39. Excerpted, with notes deleted, from Silviu Brucan, "The Establishment of a World Authority: Working Hypotheses," *Alternatives* 8 (Fall 1982), pp. 209–332.

40. Reprinted from Richard A. Falk, "Openings for Peace and Justice in World of Danger and Struggle," *IFDA Dossier* (November/December 1987), pp. 17–35. Reprinted by permission of *IFDA Dossier* [62] (International Foundation for Development Alternatives, 4 Place du Marché, 1260 Nyon, Switzerland).

41. Reprinted, with notes deleted, from Saul H. Mendlovitz, "Struggles for a Just World Peace: A Transition Strategy," *Alternatives* 14 (July 1989), pp. 363–369. Reprinted with permission.

The United Nations and a
Just World Order

General Introduction

THE UNITED NATIONS AND THE CRISIS OF MULTILATERALISM

As the United Nations (UN) turned forty in late 1985, it seemed at the time to have few friends left and little reason for celebration. Never before in its turbulent history, not even during the 1964 crisis, was there such a global chorus about a crisis of multilateralism afflicting the world organization. In the shadow of another cycle of superpower rivalry during Cold War II (1980–1986), the UN's image as an irrelevant and spent talkshop reached a climax. Yet this disenchantment may have served as a blessing in disguise, as a great teacher of the reality principle, confronting the United Nations with the Grotian moment of decision—the danger of breakdown or the opportunity of breakthrough. The year 1987 produced no breakthroughs but what Secretary-General Javier Pérez de Cuéllar called "the growing commonality factor in international affairs." For the first time in recent years, 1987 witnessed some constructive efforts to strengthen the role and character of the United Nations as the world organization.

More dramatically, in 1988 the United Nations demonstrated its usefulness, even its indispensability, in relation to a series of difficult regional conflicts. To varying degrees, UN auspices and diplomacy facilitated a formal agreement to arrange for Soviet withdrawal from Afghanistan, to resolve the Iran-Iraq War, to promote discussions about future arrangements for Kampuchea, and to secure the independence of Namibia and the phased withdrawal of foreign forces from southern Africa. Such a record of achievement represented a peak performance for the United Nations and even elicited praise from the previously antagonistic Reagan presidency. Much credit for this turnaround in performance and perception has deservedly been given to the secretary-general of the organization, Javier Pérez de Cuéllar of Peru, who exhibited energy and perseverance without antagonizing member states. Symbolically at least, this turnaround in public perceptions reached a dramatic focus when UN Peacekeeping Forces were awarded the Nobel Peace Prize in 1988.

The UN crisis and resurgence is a natural incident of an institutional life cycle that reflects varying pressures in international life. With the membership explosion of the 1960s, and especially since the entry of the People's Republic of China and the two Germanys in the early 1970s, the United Nations became the first truly

1

global organization in all of human history. Yet near-universal membership has also amplified contending voices, visions, and expectations about the nature and role of the United Nations. By and large, the organization seems to have become just marginally useful enough for the old member states (and major financial contributors) not to abandon it or walk away but not useful enough to command their priority concern and support. In recent years, what emerged as a UN crisis can be understood mainly as a crisis of *national* policy in the *global* organization, especially pertaining to the United States. The contending images of the UN today stem from the paradoxical position it occupies—it is neither as helpful as its young members would wish nor completely irrelevant, as some of its senior members claim, even in relation to various particular conceptions of national interest.

Another part of the identity crisis stems from a certain linguistic confusion about the character of the United Nations as a whole. Objections to the "United Nations" by Western countries, particularly the United States, are mainly directed at the activities of the General Assembly, a principal organ of the United Nations but only one of six such organs. It is mainly in the General Assembly that the antagonistic claims of Third World countries have been asserted as demands, but it should be appreciated that these demands are expressions of political and normative sentiment, not binding decisions. Also, within the other organs of the United Nations these pressures can be resisted far more easily. The United Nations *system* consists of six principal organs of the United Nations as well as a host of subsidiary organs and committees or commissions, including sixteen specialized agencies and two quasi-specialized agencies (General Agreement on Tariffs and Trade—GATT; International Atomic Energy Agency—IAEA). This UN system as a family of separate but affiliated international intergovernmental organizations (IGOs) should also be distinguished from the UN Charter, which is a multilateral treaty among the member states of the United Nations establishing the constitutional framework for its overall undertaking and premised upon a somewhat idealistic interpretation of the future of international society as agreed upon at the end of World War II.

THE UNITED NATIONS AND THE PAST

Evaluating the UN performance today is a confusing and contradictory enterprise, especially in the United States. The United Nations has often been saddled with a series of undue expectations that have inevitably turned into disappointments when not satisfied. Such a process restricts our understanding because it tends to overlook the actual pattern of achievements and potentialities. Two main sets of disappointments are worth mentioning:

- The United Nations was established to override the balance-of-power war system, yet its peacekeeping role has never been developed with such capacities in mind and, in fact, has been seriously diminished over the years; and
- The United Nations was established to sustain a common allied front against aggression, yet bloc voting and ideological rivalry have frequently paralyzed or politicized the organization when warfare breaks out, as was the case during the Iran-Iraq War (1980–1988).

In some respects, the Iraq-Iran War, which continued for more than seven years—almost as long as World Wars I and II combined—epitomizes the UN's limitations. Iran was a victim of a large-scale armed attack by Iraq but was not supported—even normatively—by the United Nations because many governments intensely disliked the Khomeini regime in Tehran or were hostile to both belligerents. The two superpowers initially claimed that they favored neutrality, but directly and indirectly they began providing arms to both sides. China, Israel, and several European countries joined in the global game of arms trade, some selling arms simultaneously to both Iran and Iraq. Indeed, all five permanent members of the Security Council have sold arms to both sides, earning higher profits as the magnitude and persistence of the fighting increased. As concerns rose in 1987 that Iran might overwhelm Iraq, that the war might spread throughout the Gulf region, and that world oil supplies might get tighter, a diplomatic insistence on imposing a cease-fire and an arms embargo gained support, and the United Nations was enlisted in the process. Such a pattern suggests both the marginality of the United Nations to a situation of ongoing warfare and the limits of its politics of collective legitimation; it also indicates, however, the UN's importance in promoting an end to the fighting by helping to arrange a cease-fire.

When a superpower is directly involved, the United Nations normally plays a restricted role, ministering in some way in a situation of superpower overextension. The Soviet military intervention in Czechoslovakia and Afghanistan and the U.S. military intervention in Central America and, earlier, in Indochina have largely proceeded without UN involvement. One qualification needs to be made, however. The main judicial organ of the UN, the International Court of Justice, did pronounce against the U.S. role in helping the contras, but the U.S. government thus far has ignored this decision. In fact, none of the Big Five in the Security Council has been willing to submit its claims to use force to the normative discipline of international accountability, seeking to the extent possible to avoid even a debate as to its propriety under the UN Charter. However, this disregard can be overstated. When a conflict is stalemated, even the superpowers can take the initiative in encouraging a major UN role, as the Soviet Union did late in the Afghan War. Recent proposals by the Soviet Union promote the possibility of a greatly expanding UN review of member governments' actions.

It is important to identify what is appropriate to expect from the United Nations at this stage of world politics. Many commentators are disappointed by the United Nations because they apparently believe that the organization was put on trial as the collective security system in the years after World War II and failed, that the revival of old-style geopolitics took place in reaction to the inability of the United Nations to act effectively in conflict situations.

But this type of interpretation is seriously misleading and encourages a deprecating assessment of the organization. The Soviet Union and its bloc ideologically distrusted the United Nations from its inception in 1945. With respect to the capabilities and authority of the United Nations, they took a minimalist stand in the ideologically and politically inspired determination not to endow the organization with a commanding voice in world politics. The West, particularly the United States, was ambivalent in the early years. The dominant Western preoccupation in this period

was to avoid an encouragement of Soviet expansionism comparable to the appease-
ment at Munich and elsewhere during the late 1930s, which was widely regarded
as having sharpened Hitler's appetite for aggressive war. Dean Acheson and George
Kennan, the main architects of postwar thinking in the 1940s, both believed in
the overwhelming importance of keeping the West prepared to meet a Soviet
challenge, especially in relation to the future of Europe. They believed that such
preparation consisted mainly of being ready for war and of developing an active,
effective coalition among the non-Communist liberal democracies. This reigning
Cold War perspective was formalized as the doctrine of containment. In this
geopolitical setting, the United Nations was viewed as essentially diversionary—
not harmful if conceived mainly as a forum to mobilize world opinion but potentially
dangerous if treated as a substitute for military strength and alliance politics.

Thus, the logic of avoiding war—and of checking Soviet expansion—by preparing to fight it was not consistent with the logic of the UN Charter based on a
collective security regime of support for the rules of international law, or with the
political expectation that developed during World War II in which the Soviet-U.S.
wartime arrangements against fascism would persist after peace was restored. Initially,
Westerners were uncertain as to whether the wartime anti-Fascist alliance could be
sustained in peacetime. Given the veto power lodged in the Security Council and
isolationist sentiments in the United States, it was obvious that the United Nations
could not be an effective political actor unless a political consensus between the
United States and the Soviet Union persisted. When this consensus completely
collapsed by 1947, the only remaining issue was what to do with the United
Nations.

As the Cold War got underway, the United Nations initially looked like a willing
instrument of Western interests, especially during the Korean War (1950–1953)
in which action taken in defense of South Korea was fought beneath UN flags but
was otherwise operationally conducted as if it were wholly a U.S. war. Even when
the U.S. diplomatic stature enabled it to control most of the votes in the General
Assembly and the Security Council during the early 1950s, official documents
show that U.S. policymakers considered the United Nations at the time primarily
in terms of "its usefulness to us in the event of general war, its usefulness to us
during a twenty or thirty year period of a war of nerves." Usefulness needs to be
understood here as a source of ideological support, not as a peacemaking actor.

Both the United Nations and the United States have changed considerably in
the past four decades, moving in divergent directions. The United Nations in 1990
is, in many respects, quite different from the vision of its U.S. founding fathers in
1944–1945; it evolved through its first decade mainly as an instrument of Pax
Americana. The global political and systemic context in which the UN operates
has shifted from a period of allied unity in the early postwar era to an extended
Cold War, to a period in which many of the dominant issues on the world agenda
moved from an East-West to a North-South axis, to a period of general and
precipitous decline of the UN's organizational role during Cold War II, and, finally,
to a period of impressive revival under the sunshine of an emerging period of
renewed Soviet-American détente.

Between 1968 and 1988, aside from the early Carter years (1976–1978), the
U.S. government mounted a continuous attack on the United Nations as inefficient

and ineffectual and, worse, as a "dangerous place" of opposition to democracy and freedom, a citadel of anti-Zionism, and a virtual outpost of Third World Marxism and Soviet geopolitics. In a sense, Senator Barry Goldwater's voice from the extreme Republican right in reaction to the People's Republic of China's entry to the UN in October 1971 became the virtual mainstream voice a decade later: "The time has come to recognize the United Nations for the anti-American, antifreedom organization it has become [sic]. The time has come for us to cut off all financial help, withdraw as a member, and ask the United Nations to find a headquarters location outside of the United States that is more in keeping with the philosophy of the majority of voting members, some place like Moscow or Peking."

Milder versions of this hostile attitude led the U.S. government to interpret its host country obligations during 1988 in a manner that offended virtually the entire UN membership. For instance, the failure to grant Yasir Arafat a visa to enable him to participate in the General Assembly debate on Palestinian issues in New York forced a rescheduling of the debate in Geneva at considerable added expense to the organization. Similarly, the Nicaraguan leader, Daniel Ortega, cancelled plans to attend the General Assembly because his delegation was denied a sufficient number of visas and travel restrictions were so stringent that Ortega would not have been able to visit the residence of the Nicaraguan ambassador to the United Nations. Such behavior goes beyond policy discretion. By treaty, when the UN established its headquarters in New York, the U.S. government obligated itself unconditionally to allow entry to all seeking such entry for official UN business.

Despite this massive governmental assault and a misinformation campaign by the mass media, a 26 percent gap between the policy preferences of the general public (49 percent) and those of the American elite (23 percent) revealed a somewhat surprising level of persisting popular support for strengthening the United Nations. U.S. oppositional politics at the UN is also reflected in its voting record in the General Assembly.

In contrast, some of the social and political forces in the world that had formerly discounted the significance of the United Nations have recently stepped out from the shadows of skepticism and disbelief. In the post-Mao era, especially since 1982, the Chinese image and strategy of world order, as made manifest in the United Nations, have discernibly shifted from a vision of continuous revolution to a more task-oriented functional theory of multilateralism. Instead of registering complaints and grievances, China now takes an instrumental approach—all the organs and agencies of the UN system are regarded as vehicles to help the Chinese more rapidly reach the promised land of modernity. In a world of growing complexity and interdependence, international organizations in general and those that make up the UN system in particular are now perceived by China as useful instruments of multilateral cooperation. A corollary of this rising learning curve is the growing tendency to conceptualize Chinese and world interests and responsibilities in mutually complementary terms. What is good for China is good for the UN system, and what is good for the UN system is also good for China.

More remarkable in this regard is the sudden and dramatic reversal of Soviet attitudes in the Gorbachev years. Early in the history of the organization, the Soviet Union adopted a minimalist damage-limitation stand, relying heavily on its

Security Council veto power to confine UN operations within narrow bounds and a strict construction of the Charter principles and procedures. The United Nations was perceived by Moscow through ideological lens as a political instrument for promoting Western interests, as an extended arena of U.S. hegemony, as an invisible collaborator in the Western selective security system, and as a congenial adversary of Soviet priorities in the world economy. But by the second half of the 1980s under Gorbachev, especially since 1987, the Soviet Union has become a remarkably forthcoming member of the UN, breathing life into the organization, even proposing serious consideration of a new vision of a comprehensive global security system. Gorbachev's statement about the United Nations, "Realities and Guarantees for a Secure World" (Selection 13), expresses a very positive attitude by the Soviet government toward the organization. Reinforced by the constructive role of the UN in resolving regional conflict, Gorbachev's Soviet Union has given the organization a renewed sense of relevance.

Governments of the non-Western world, the so-called Third World, often emerged assertively from the decolonizing process of the postwar era. The changed composition of the UN membership undoubtedly contributed to disenchantment with the organization on the part of First World countries. The new members of the United Nations from Asia and Africa, together with those from Latin America, put forward new demands and claims through the global politics of collective legitimation and delegitimation, evidently enjoying access to global prime-time and prime-arena. These countries believed that their united front through the Group of 77 could generate shifts in global policy, especially in relation to developmental issues.

Aside from escalated militancy on how to resolve the Arab-Israeli conflict and the anti-apartheid struggle, the Third World pushed hard, first in the United Nations Conference on Trade and Development (UNCTAD) on development issues and, during the 1970s, in the General Assembly for the establishment of a New International Economic Order (NIEO). This push was considerably buttressed at the time by the successful use of oil power by the Organization of Petroleum Exporting Countries (OPEC), as well as by the U.S. perception of the threat from the Third World. By the 1980s it had become evident that NIEO was a paper tiger, and the world economic order had rejected the NIEO trajectory of structural reform favorable to the South on matters of trade, money, and investment. The collapse of the eleventh Special Session convened in 1980 to rejuvenate the North-South dialogue signified, temporarily at least, the collapse of NIEO politics in the United Nations. By the turn of the decade, one of the most eloquent champions of the Third World pronounced NIEO politics to be "this strange environment of formal motions without actual movement."

What this new circumstance suggests is that the symbolic domain of UN debates is not to be confused with the power structures of wealth and influence that shape and control the international economy. The evolution of NIEO politics suggests that the rich North may temporarily acquiesce in the normative claims of the poor South for socioeconomic justice, but that effective patterns of resistance will emerge to reinforce existing structures of power and influence within the global political economy. It has also become apparent that the united front of the Third World is more symbolic and rhetorical than substantive. The non-Western world is very diverse in actuality and lacks cohesion; cleavages between rich and poor, small and large, coastal and land-locked, left and right, and democratic and authoritarian emerge to make any claim of a unified "movement" seem like a bizarre mixture of hype and wishful thinking. At the same time, deconstructing the symbolism of the Third World as an independent force can be just as misleading, if carried too far, as the earlier claims on behalf of its negotiating solidarity. The General Assembly, or a global conference sponsored under its auspices, as the primary global arena for non-Western countries exhibits at this time both the cleavages and the affinities, and it is this complex, shifting political environment that expresses the global reality in North-South relations.

A built-in institutional momentum has carried the UN system as a whole along a more self-reliant trajectory, pushed by the increasing pressures of global interdependence characteristic of modern life. It is along these more globalist functional lines of evolution that we currently find the greatest hope and the most potential for shaping and realizing world order values. The organization has been notably successful in normative activities, setting standards in the fields of human rights and environmental policy as well as providing guidelines for other functional issues of shared global concern. Further, the conflict between the power of expertise and the power of numbers often creates a storm of political controversy even in the functional domains of world politics. Ironically, since the mid-1970s, the United States has championed such political attacks in several specialized agencies (e.g., the International Labour Organization—ILO; and the United Nations Educational, Scientific, and Cultural Organization—UNESCO) in the name of depoliticization and, more recently, as a justification for its defiance of a World Court judgment that ruled U.S. policy toward Sandinista Nicaragua to be in violation of international law. Law and politics—functional expertise and political control—have always coexisted as the two sides of the same coin in the authoritative formulation and allocation of values in IGOs. The novelty of the current controversy arises less from alleged politicization than from the normative shift of politicization from an East-West to a North-South axis. The UN crisis in its institutional sense, then, as Marc Nerfin reminds us (Selection 36), "is largely a Northern expression of a felt challenge to the old order and a reflection of the North's unwillingness to accept that change is necessary."

A summary of the evolution of the United Nations can be conveyed by stages of development, accompanied by the realization that such generalizations miss some cross-cutting tendencies. Nevertheless, a dominant character of the organization can be discerned at each given stage. In the initial stage, from 1945 to the early 1960s, the activities of the organization reflected domination by the United States and its Western-led coalition of states. During the second stage, from the early 1960s to 1972, the advent of Third World states and the process of decolonization placed emphasis on the General Assembly. From 1972 to 1978, the most characteristic UN activity involved global consciousness-raising around problem areas— the environment, population pressure, food shortages, human settlement, and various categories of oppression—carried on within conference formats. The fourth period in UN history, from 1978 to 1986, was characterized by a pervasive mood of geopolitical fatalism, expressed in the form of Soviet indifference, U.S. hostility, and Third World ineffectuality and disillusionment. Starting in 1987 a new period was initiated based on renewed hopes and buoyed by Soviet enthusiasm, U.S. selective support, and a dynamic secretary-general who constructively involved the organization in the resolution of troublesome regional conflicts.

THE UNITED NATIONS AND THE STATE SYSTEM

A fuller realization of the potential of the United Nations as a global institution is hindered by the restrictive base of representation. Despite the opening line of the Preamble, "we the peoples," the Charter grants status as members in full standing only to states represented by governmental delegates. A rare exception to this has involved granting an observer status to the Palestine Liberation Organization (PLO), an aspiring candidate state. This has caused considerable political fallout and has hurt the public image of the United Nations in some areas, especially in the United States. The organization does not have an independent financial base; its operations depend precariously on the political priorities and attitudes of seven member states (France, West Germany, Italy, Japan, the USSR, the United Kingdom, and the United States), who contribute over 70 percent of the UN budget. The UN's current financial difficulties are symptomatic of the deepening conflict between First and Second World money power and Third World voting power. Even at the assessment rate of 25 percent of the total UN budget, the U.S. annual dues amount to only about 72 cents per capita per year, but this proportion of the overall budget remains sufficient to work as a virtual financial veto in overriding many decisions of the overwhelming majority. The current 160 member states chronically complain about this financial hegemony, but they will not contribute more.

In this volume, we take the position of "the peoples of the United Nations" more seriously than in the past, and we view observer status, which is open to international nongovernmental organizations (INGOs), as a wedge that breaks into the statism of the organization. We would go even further and endorse ideas about creating a possible Third Chamber that consists of an Assembly of Peoples chosen by direct popular election (Selection 36). Democratizing forces within civil societies and transnational social movements currently seem to be the best vehicles for world order system transformation. Recently, some social movements have come to regard the United Nations as a more promising political arena than was previously believed. Earlier, movements concerned with social issues had generally regarded the United Nations as an exclusive framework of, by, and for governmental delegates, whose global rhetoric was a means of gaining distance from the actual struggle taking place throughout the world. It is encouraging that some of these movements now invoke the United Nations as a multilateral and humanist alternative to statism and increasingly resort to UN-sponsored norms and standards to legitimate their normative claims at the national level.

At the same time, we accept the possibility that some states at some periods on various issues are capable of being positive, progressive actors. We do not hold a dogmatic, deterministic antistatist outlook. If China promotes demographic stability, India food self-sufficiency, Argentina human rights, the Soviet Union political perestroika, the United States ozone protection, and Sweden common security, these governments enhance the world order performance of their states and, in the process, the world order performance of the United Nations as well. Conversely, by resorting to force—overt or covert—in international conflict situations, adopting repressive political measures, imposing economic austerity on the poor, and neglecting the environment, states play negative roles in world political life.

While the United Nations operates primarily as an instrument and extension of the state system, at the same time it frequently functions within this framework as a global standard setter, communication network, consciousness-raiser, mobilization system, and legitimator. The UN works at a crossroads between mutually contradictory and countervailing trends of the world historical process—universalism and heterogeneity, globalism and nationalism, integration and fragmentation. These forces inevitably pull and push the organization in opposite directions.

THE UNITED NATIONS AND THE WORLD-ORDER APPROACH

Understanding and evaluating the United Nations as an evolving political actor in world affairs is the main purpose of this volume. As part of the Studies on a Just World Order series, which taken as a whole evaluates the overall world order performance of social actors in relation to each other over time and across issue areas, the present volume is also based on this world order approach. Normatively, this approach is premised on an overall commitment to shaping a just and humane world order based on the values of peace, economic equity and well-being, social justice, and environmental quality. By norms, we refer to constraints on behavior that arise from various sources of authority (especially law and morality); by values, we refer to preferred goals of action that also bear on the selection of means to attain these goals. Analytically, this approach can be described as world order realism. It attempts to steer a course between the Scylla of realist cynicism and the Charybdis of idealist sentimentalism. Our hope is to reflect the dialectics of the United Nations—a creative tension between limitations and possibilities.

In this volume, then, we proceed from the premise of world order realism to comprehend the contradictory and dialectical forces confronting the United Nations. Tension between geopolitical rivalry and world order values would not exist if the member states' foreign policies were firmly anchored in the principles and objectives of the Charter. The logic of statist tradition and practice shapes the behavior of most states, especially the leading ones. Most governments are generally guided by a short-term calculus of narrow and selfish interests.

From a world order perspective, the United Nations does not necessarily become better because it is becoming bigger. The understanding and appraisal of its performance in all instances are keyed to wider concerns about world order values and prospects for nonviolent system transformation.

Of course, a full empirical procedure of inquiry would be elaborate and tedious. Specifying normative achievements by quantitative measures (e.g., percentage of disputes referred to the United Nations) can be useful as an indicator of trends but is seldom conclusive. Causal connections are almost impossible to establish because correlation does not demonstrate causation. In social science research, even if data sources are assumed to be uncontaminated, most reported correlations between independent and dependent variables have been uniformly small and repeated correlations between specified variables extremely rare. At times, the numbers game in social science research becomes an expression of a programmed inability and unwillingness to acknowledge a political position of support for the status quo. "In many societies," warned the late Roy Preiswerk, "those who agree with the established power and values stand a good chance of being considered as scientists, while those who disagree and demand social changes are easily discredited by the label of 'ideologues.' "

The effort here is to grasp the United Nations as a world order actor and to interpret its role as a positive or negative force in world politics at various stages and in various domains since its inception in 1945. We are also concerned with encouraging and identifying paths of development for the organization that are more receptive to the needs and aspirations of the peoples of the world than has been true in the past. As noted, we emphasize the distinction between "we the peoples of the United Nations" as identified in the Preamble of the Charter as the UN's constituting authority and the actual membership, which is composed of governments that are often unresponsive even to the claims and grievances of many of their own citizens, much less to the global interest of the various peoples in the world. The plight of indigenous peoples highlights the contrast between using "peoples" rather than "governments" as the unit of analysis and assessment.

The United Nations has by now clearly established its presence in world politics. But the significance of this presence continues to be controversial and confusing. Perhaps reassessing the origins, evolution, contributions, and prospects of the United Nations, both those of its central political organs and its various functional agencies, can help us evaluate the organization. Radicals on the right contend that the world would be a better place without the United Nations. Centrists contend that the United States can better serve its national interests by using the United Nations in a selective manner or, as Thomas Franck puts it, by becoming skilled at geopolitical hardball within the arena of the United Nations. In contrast, world orderists evaluate the organization's performance in terms of world order values and explore how the United Nations can and should be seen mainly as part of a wider social movement to create a global peace and justice system premised upon human solidarity and ecological harmony.

Although we seek to keep these lines of debate open throughout this book, our particular effort is to depict a world order perspective. In this regard, we do not inquire into whether the United Nations of 1990 can somehow become a useful instrument for a neoconservative U.S. foreign policy. Our main concern is with the enhancement of the power and authority of the United Nations to meet the challenges of international political life in the 1990s and beyond.

In the end, we rely upon world order values to answer ethical questions about the quality of human life, problems of shared global concern, and long-range developments. We are also concerned with whether the United Nations can be conceived of as a world order actor that can, in part or in stages, challenge the statist structure of international society by fostering human solidarity, by educating peoples on the perils of persisting international anarchy and the benefits of coop-erative regimes, and by protecting the autonomy of civil society through the promotion of human rights and through finding more space to facilitate the growth of transnational democratic social forces.

THE UNITED NATIONS AND THE FUTURE

We are convinced that some degree of global institutional restructuring is essential for the fuller realization of the UN's potential as a world order actor. While there is no general agreement about the exact shape of institutional reform or about how enhanced institutions and procedures would operate or how they would come into existence, various ideas, models, and proposals of "how to move from here to there" will be considered. Part Three more fully addresses this question.

UN approaches to alternative futures may be divided into two broad schools of thought—system reforming and system transforming. These two schools are differentiated basically by the magnitude and rapidity of change. The reformist school accepts the current political and social realities as constraints on change and suggests that the development of international organizations will occur within a relatively narrow range of expanded and altered functions for the United Nations. This school advocates gradual and cumulative reform of select organs of the UN system.

The system transformation school argues that such reformist steps are simply inadequate in light of the gravity and scale of contemporary problems and, furthermore, that more drastic system change can be made feasible through global consciousness-raising and political mobilization. Great system transformations have occurred abruptly in the past, although in retrospect it is always possible to find antecedent conditions and explanations to show that the change was less cataclysmic than it appeared at the time. It is important to recall that all great transformations in the course of human history have been preceded by the emergence of new conceptions of reality, by an alternative worldview that shifted the overall understanding of the world historical process. It is equally significant to appreciate that most past reorderings of international society have taken place *after* major wars. A crucial question still remains: Will the next system transformation come about through the shock effect of cataclysmic events, or can we find ways to intervene in history to facilitate a nonviolent and nonapocalyptical system transformation?

Contemporary analysis of global authority structure occurs in an atmosphere in which progressive social forces favor decentralization and smallness, and distrust centralization and bigness, which are associated with destructive tendencies of technology and bureaucracy. An emphasis on participatory democracy and "small is beautiful" perspectives has forced a reassessment of the *traditional* world order thinking of "world peace through world law." Any future structure of global authority must be forged out of a creative interplay between centralization and decentralization. Certain system-wide problems such as the global environmental deterioration and militarization may require a buildup of centralized authority, but other issues such as social justice and human governance may be better resolved through decentralization. A dialectic between centralized and decentralized authority provides the basic dynamic for a desirable constitutional base for world order.

Our deepest commitment, aside from survival, is to the achievement of humane governance at all levels of social organization from the family to the planet taken as a whole. This desired authority structure would be attentive to human needs, antagonistic to the current war system, and empowering of participation by peoples in global arrangements. The construction of future governing structures will have to draw upon the UN experience but also be sensitive to wider contemporary social forces and movements and their fears and hopes.

The Role of Social Movements

INTRODUCTION

From a learning perspective, we emphasize the place of the United Nations system (the totality of its existence—i.e., principal organs, specialized agencies, main activities, Charter vision) in an ongoing global process to establish a transformed system of world order potentially capable of realizing world order values associated with peace, economic well-being, social and political justice, and environmental quality. As an active project the establishment of an institutionally rooted web of globally oriented institutions is a byproduct of the two world wars in this century: the League of Nations taking shape after World War I, the United Nations after World War II.

These "experiments" in global organization were exclusively constituted by the representatives of states. Within this setting, leading states have played especially prominent roles. As already suggested, these power-centers of the world have been consistently reluctant to transfer any significant portion of their capabilities to a global organization or to invest these undertakings with any conviction or commitment. The League was perceived largely as a concession to Woodrow Wilson's insistence that an alternative to the balance of power was needed to avoid the occurrence of ever more destructive general wars. Wilson's vision was reinforced by world public opinion that seemed to demand a peacemaking international innovation. The United Nations emerged after 1945 out of "the failure" of the League to prevent World War II and the broad consensus that a world order consisting of rival centers of state power would likely generate yet another world war within the century.

And yet, as suggested in the General Introduction to the book, the United Nations can by now be regarded as a facade behind which geopolitics proceeds in a more or less uninhibited form. Sovereignty at the state level remains the main organizing framework for all forms of management of conflict in the world system.

Still, the use of the United Nations as a global forum in an age of information revolution suggests an evolution of complex political realities that are independent of the will of its initial architects or its membership. A certain momentum has accompanied the life history of the United Nations, leading the main states, including the two superpowers, to wax and wane in their relation with the organization. Despite these vagaries of global geopolitics, certain continuities and cumulative

13

tendencies are also evident. The normative and institutional landscape of international life grows more complex and elaborate over time as new topics and challenges are addressed. Institutions grow and proliferate, accumulating experience and records of accomplishment. Persisting far more than four decades has by itself, beyond the cavil of critics, established a weight and assured presence for the United Nations.

At the same time, the unfulfilled potential of the organization remains a depressing reality. How to build the UN's capabilities—implementing procedures in the area of human rights, peaceful settlement of disputes, and in relation to environmental issues—seems to posit continuing challenges for the future. It seems, at present, also daunting to figure out ways to ensure the financial solvency of the organization as well as to obtain constructive participation of the United States. In the near term, as well, it seems very critical to increase the role of the United Nations in forging more effective responses to a variety of environmental problems.

This opening section attempts to encourage an unconventional orientation toward the study of the United Nations—namely, that this global institutional presence needs to be conceived of as *an element* in a wider social movement for the realization of world order values. In this regard, the United Nations is looked upon less as the outcome of governmental policy at the state level than as one expression of social movements committed to promoting drastic global reforms. We do not claim that the United Nations has served as an appropriate instrument of such a revisioning undertaking, nor do we admit that the organization has been captured by statist tendencies at work in international relations.

This opening section considers the significance of the intellectual and political context of social movements. The initial selection by Giovanni Arrighi, Terence K. Hopkins, and Immanuel Wallerstein examines the overall "antisystematic" character of contemporary social movements and regards this phenomenon as a generally hopeful development. The article only discusses the United Nations in passing, but its value is that it provides the tools that enable us to conceive of the organization as the nexus between systemic and antisystemic politics. The central expression of this dilemma, as these authors conceive it, pits dominant states that control the world economy against the vast periphery of states and peoples that are controlled and exploited. Antisystemic possibilities arise from movements of states and peoples that challenge this structure. To the extent that the Third World has emerged from colonial subordination, it has lent weight to antisystemic forces, but to the extent that the core capitalist countries have perpetuated this dominance by way of new instruments of control, systemic forces have repulsed the challenge. How this "dilemma" is eventually resolved will bear heavily on the orientation and the character of the UN's role in the world.

In the second selection, Rajni Kothari explores the changing forms of politics within the confines of territorial boundaries, especially the rise of new forms of popular or democratic participation in the face of declining confidence in the capacity of the state or conventional political parties to be vehicles for value realization. Although set in the rich experience of India where the hopes for reform have gradually shifted since the period of independence from the center to the grassroots, Kothari's interpretations are valuable in almost any political setting. Significant for our purposes is that even in Third World countries, the commitment and growth of world order values may have more to do with activist tendencies in civil society than with the orientation and policies of such formal entities as state and party. Kothari's essay helps us to locate the United Nations on a different sort of political terrain than that which is generally presupposed when the contributions of international organizations are studied and appraised.

The final selection in this section is an analysis of the peace movement by Nigel Young. What strikes one at once is the relative insignificance of international institutions generally and the United Nations in particular in the activity of peace movements. Much of the historical role of peace movements has been to oppose government policy with respect to war or preparations for war. The ideas of disarmament, nonviolence, and peaceful settlement of disputes have been relatively prominent in earlier peace militancy. Perhaps, however, the greater complexity of international life, the instantaneous transmission of news images on a planetary scale, and the need for central guidance capabilities to protect the global environment will move the United Nations nearer the center of future peace movement work.

Our concern is how these developments alter the situation and role of the United Nations, an aspect of evolving a world order realism that is appropriate for the 1990s. Do these social forces establish a more hopeful setting within which the various actors and activities of the United Nations take place? Is the context more propitious for the realization of world order values? Why? Why not?

1. Dilemmas of Antisystemic Movements

Giovanni Arrighi, Terence K. Hopkins,
and Immanuel Wallerstein

Opposition to oppression is coterminous with the existence of hierarchical social systems. Opposition is permanent, but for the most part latent. The oppressed are too weak—politically, economically, and ideologically—to manifest their opposition constantly. However, as we know, when oppression becomes particularly acute, or expectations particularly deceived, or the power of the ruling stratum falters, people have risen up in an almost spontaneous manner to cry halt. This has taken the form of revolts, of riots, of flight.

The multiple forms of human rebellion have for the most part been only partially efficacious at best. Sometimes they have forced the oppressors to reduce the pressure or the exploitation. But sometimes they have failed utterly to do so. However, one continuing sociological characteristic of these rebellions of the oppressed has been their "spontaneous," short-term character. They have come and they have gone, having such effect as they did. When the next such rebellion came, it normally had little explicit relationship with the previous one. Indeed, this has been one of the great strengths of the world's ruling strata throughout history—the noncontinuity of rebellion.

In the early history of the capitalist world-economy, the situation remained more or less the same as it had always been in this regard. Rebellions were many, scattered, discrete, momentary, and only partially efficacious at best. One of the contradictions, however, of capitalism as a system is that the very integrating tendencies that have been one of its defining characteristics have had an impact on the form of antisystemic activity.

Somewhere in the middle of the nineteenth century—1848 is as good a symbolic date as any—there came to be a sociological innovation of profound significance for the politics of the capitalist world-economy. Groups of persons involved in antisystemic activity began to create a new institution: the continuing organization with members, officers, and specific political objectives (both long-run and short-term).

Such organized antisystemic movements had never existed before. One might argue that various religious sects had performed analogous roles with an analogous organization, but the long-run objectives of the religious sects were by definition otherworldly. The antisystemic organizations that came into existence in the nineteenth century were preeminently political, not religious—that is, they focused on the structures of "this world."

SOCIAL MOVEMENTS AND NATIONAL MOVEMENTS

In the course of the nineteenth century, two principal varieties of antisystemic movements emerged—what came to be called respectively the "social movement"

16

and the "national movement." The major difference between them lay in their definition of the problem. The social movement defined the oppression as that of employers over wage earners, the bourgeoisie over the proletariat. The ideals of the French Revolution—liberty, equality, and fraternity—could be realized, they felt, by replacing capitalism with socialism. The national movement on the other hand defined the oppression as that of one ethnonational group over another. The ideals could be realized by giving the oppressed group equal juridical status with the oppressing group by the creation of parallel (and usually separate) structures.

There has been a long discussion, within the movements and among scholars, about the differences between these two kinds of movements. No doubt they have differed both in their definitions of the problem and in the social bases of their support. In many places and at many times, the two varieties of movements felt they were in direct competition with each other for the loyalty of populations. Less frequently in the nineteenth century, but sometimes, the two varieties of movements found enough tactical congruence to work together politically.

The traditional emphasis on the differences of the two varieties of movements has distracted our attention from some fundamental similarities. Both kinds of movements, after considerable internal debate, created formal organizations. As such, these organizations had to evolve a basic strategy to transform their immediate world in the direction in which they wished it to go. In both cases, the analysis was identical. The key political structure of the modern world they each saw to be the state. If these movements were to change anything, they had to control a state apparatus, which pragmatically meant "their" state apparatus. Consequently, the primary objective had to be the obtaining of state power.

For the social movement, this meant that, despite the internationalism of their ideology—"workers of the world, unite!"—the organizations they created had to be national in structure. And the objective of these organizations had to be the coming to power of the movement *in that state*. Similarly, for the national movement, the objective came to be state power in a particular state. To be sure, the jurisdiction of this state was by definition what the national movement was about. Sometimes such a movement sought the creation of an entirely new state, either by secession or by merger, but in other cases this "new state" might have already existed in the form of a colonial or a regional administrative entity.

The fact that the two varieties of movements defined the same strategic objective accounts for their sense of rivalry with each other, particularly when a workers' movement sought to obtain power in an entity out of which a given national movement was seeking to detach a zone in order to create a new state.

The parallel objectives—obtaining state power—led to a parallel internal debate on the mode of obtaining state power, which might be defined in polar terms as the legal path of political persuasion versus the illegal path of insurrectionary force. This has often been called reform versus revolution, but these two terms have become so overlaid with polemic and confusion that today they obscure more than they aid analysis.

In the case of the social movement, it should be noted, this internal debate culminated in the period between the First and Second World Wars in the existence of two rival and fiercely competitive Internationals, the Second and the Third, also known as the conflict between Social Democrats and Communists. Though both the Second and Third Internationals asserted that they had the same objective of socialism, that they were movements based in the working class and on the left, and even (at least for a while) that they assumed the same Marxist heritage, they rapidly became vehemently opposed one to the other, to the point that their subsequent occasional political convergences (the "popular fronts") have seemed at best tactical and momentary. In some sense, this has remained true right up to the present.

If one looks at the geography of the movements, one quickly notices a historic correlation. Social-democratic movements have become politically strong and have "come to power" (by electoral means, to be sure, and then in alternation with more conservative parties) almost only in the core states of the world-economy, but in virtually all of them.

Communist parties, by contrast, have become politically strong primarily in a certain range of semiperipheral and peripheral zones, and have come to power (sometimes by insurrection, but sometimes as a result of military occupation by the USSR) only in these zones. The only Western countries in which Communist parties have been relatively strong for a long period of time are France, Italy, and Spain, and it should be noted that Italy and Spain might well be considered semiperipheral. In any case, the parties in these three states have long since shed any insurrectionary inclinations.

We are therefore in the 1980s faced with the following political history of the modern world. Social-democratic parties have in fact achieved their primary political objective, coming to power in a relatively large number of core states. Communist parties have in fact come to power in a significant number of semiperipheral and peripheral countries—concentrated geographically in a band that runs from Eastern Europe to East and Southeast Asia. And in the rest of the world, in many of the countries, nationalist—sometimes even "radical nationalist" or "national libera-tion"—movements have come to power. In short, seen from the vantage point of 1848, the success of the antisystemic movements has been very impressive indeed.

THE UNFULFILLED REVOLUTION

How are we to appreciate the consequences? In gross terms, we can see two consequences that have moved in very different directions. On the one hand, these movements, taken collectively as a sort of "family" of movements, have become an increasingly consequential element in the politics of the world-system and have built upon their achievements. Later movements have profited from the successes of earlier movements by moral encouragement, example, lessons in political tactics, and direct assistance. Many concessions have been wrested from the world's ruling strata.

On the other hand, the coming to state power of all these movements has resulted in a very widespread sense of unfulfilled revolution. The questions have run like this. Have social-democratic parties achieved anything more than some redistribution to what are in fact "middle" strata located in core countries? Have Communist parties achieved anything more than some economic development for their countries? And even then, how much? And furthermore, has this not been primarily to benefit the so-called new class of a bureaucratic elite? Have nationalist movements achieved anything more than allowing the so-called comprador class a slightly larger slice of the world pie?

These are perhaps not the questions that ought to be asked, or the manner in which the issues should be posed. But in fact these are the questions that have been asked, and very widely. There is little doubt that the resulting skepticism has made deep inroads in the ranks of potential and even active supporters of the world's antisystemic movements. As this skepticism began to take hold, there were a number of ways in which it began to express itself in ideological and organizational terms.

The period after the Second World War was a period of great success for the historic antisystemic movements. Social democracy became firmly ensconced in the West. It is less that the social-democratic parties came to be seen as one of the alternating groups which could legitimately govern than that the main program of the social democrats, the welfare state, came to be accepted even by the conservative parties, if no doubt begrudgingly. After all, even Richard Nixon said: "We are all Keynesians now." Communist parties, of course, came to power in a whole series of states. And the post-1945 period saw one long process of decolonization, punctuated by some dramatic, politically important armed struggles, such as Vietnam, Algeria, and Nicaragua.

Nonetheless, by the 1960s, and even more by the 1970s, there began to occur a "break with the past" with the rise of a new kind of antisystemic movement (or movements within the movements) in world-regional locales as diverse as North America, Japan, Europe, China, and Mexico. The student, Black, and antiwar movements in the United States, the student movements in Japan and Mexico, the labor and student movements in Europe, and the Cultural Revolution in China, and as of the 1970s the women's movements did not have identical roots or even common effects. Each one was located in political and economic processes shaped by the particular and different histories and by the different positions in the world-system of the locales in which they arose and worked themselves out. Yet, by world-historical standards, they occurred in the same period and, moreover, they shared some common ideological themes that clearly set them apart from earlier varieties of antisystemic movements.

Their almost simultaneous occurrence can largely be traced to the fact that the movements of the late 1960s were precipitated by a common catalyst: the escalation of the anti-imperialist war in Vietnam. This escalation posed an immediate threat to the established patterns of life and to the very lives not only of the Vietnamese but of American youth as well, and the war posed a clear threat to the security of the Chinese people. As for European youth and workers, while no immediate threat was posed to their lives and security, the indirect effects of the escalation (world monetary crisis, intensification of market competition, etc.) and the ideological spillovers from the movements in the United States, from the Cultural Revolution in China, and from the struggle of the Vietnamese people soon provided enough reasons and rationalizations for rebellion.

Taken together, all these movements and their Vietnamese epicenter were important in disclosing a basic asymmetry in the power of systemic and antisystemic forces on a world scale. The asymmetry was most dramatically exemplified on the battlefields themselves. Following the precedent of the Chinese war of national liberation, the Vietnamese showed how a national liberation movement could, by shifting the confrontation with conventional armies onto nonconventional terrains (as in guerrilla warfare), erode and eventually disintegrate the social, political, and military position of cumbersome imperial forces. From this point of view, the other movements (particularly the U.S. antiwar movement) were part and parcel of this asymmetrical relation: to different degrees and in different ways, they showed how the shift of the confrontation between systemic and antisystemic forces onto nonconventional terrain was strengthening the latter and hampering/paralyzing the former.

The outcome and implications of the combined and uneven development of the antisystemic movements of the 1960s and 1970s must be assessed at different levels. Locally, the Vietnam war had a very "conventional" outcome: the coming to state power of a "classical" antisystemic movement, and the subsequent strengthening of the bureaucratic structure of this state. Assessed from this angle, at the national level the outcome of the Vietnamese national liberation movement did not differ significantly from the earlier kinds of antisystemic movements (national and social). Globally, however, the Vietnam war was a turning point in disclosing the limits of military actions in coercing the periphery into a hierarchical world order.

These limits and their recognition were the outcome not only of the confrontation on the battlefields but also, and possibly more so, of the movements unleashed elsewhere in the world-system. It was the nature of these other movements that most clearly marked a departure from, and a counterposition to, earlier patterns of antisystemic movements. To varying degrees, the Cultural Revolution in China, the student movements in the West, Japan, and Mexico, and the "autonomist" workers' movements in Europe took as one of their themes the limits and dangers of the establishment and consolidation of bureaucratic structures by the movements themselves, and this was new.

The Cultural Revolution was largely directed against the bureaucratic power of the Communist party and, whatever its failures from other points of view, its main achievement has been precisely to have prevented, or at least slowed down, the consolidation of party bureaucratic power in China. The student and youth movements that cropped up in the most diverse context were generally directed not only against the various bureaucratic powers that tried to curb and repress them (states, universities, parties, etc.) but also against all attempts to channel them toward the formation of new, and the strengthening of old, bureaucratic organizations. Although the new workers' movements generally ended up by strengthening bureaucratic organizations (mostly unions), nonetheless the protagonists of these "new" movements showed an unprecedented awareness of the fact that bureaucratic organizations such as unions were bound to develop interests of their own that might differ in important respects from those of the workers they claimed to represent. What this meant, concretely, was that the instrumental attitude of unions and parties vis-à-vis the movement was matched and countered to an unprecedented extent by an instrumental attitude on the part of the movement vis-à-vis unions and parties.

The antibureaucratic thrust of the movements of the 1960s and early 1970s can be traced to three main tendencies: the tremendous widening and deepening of the power of bureaucratic organizations as a result of the previous wave of antisystemic movements; the decreasing capabilities of such organizations to fulfill the expectations on which their emergence and expansion had been based; and the increasing efficacy of direct forms of action, that is, forms unmediated by bureaucratic organizations. On the first two tendencies, nothing needs to be added to what has already been said concerning the successes and limits of the earlier movements, except to point out that the reactivation of market competition under U.S. hegemony since the Second World War had further tightened the world-economy constraints within which states acted.

As for the increasing efficacy of direct forms of action, the tendency concerns mainly the labor movement and was rooted in the joint impact of two key trends of the world-economy: the trend toward an increasing commodification of labor power and the trend toward increasing division of labor and mechanization. In the previous stage, labor movements came to rely on permanent bureaucratic organizations aiming at the seizure/control of state power for two main reasons. First, these labor movements were largely at the beginning of expression of artisans and craft workers who had been or were about to be proletarianized but whose bargaining power vis-à-vis employers still depended on their craft skills. As a consequence, these workers had an overwhelming interest in restricting the supply of and expanding the demand for, their skills. This, in turn, required trade-union organizations oriented to the preservation of craft work roles in the labor process, on the one hand, and to the control over the acquisition of craft skills, on the other. Like all organizations that attempt to reproduce "artificially" (i.e., in opposition to historical tendencies) a scarcity that affords monopolistic quasirents, these craft or craft-oriented unions ultimately depended for their success on the ability to use state power to restrain employers from profiting from the operations of the market. The artificial (i.e., nonmarket) restraints were twofold: state rules about workers' pay and conditions; state legitimation of unionization and collective bargaining.

The second and more important reason for the previous reliance of labor movements on permanent bureaucratic organizations aiming at state power was related to the question of alliances and hegemony. In most national locales, the struggle between labor and capital took place in a context characterized by the existence of large strata of peasants and middle classes which could be mobilized politically to support antilabor state policies and economically to enhance competition within the ranks of labor. Under these circumstances labor could obtain long-term victories only by neutralizing or winning over to its side significant fractions of these strata. And this could not be achieved through spontaneous and direct action, which often had the effect of alienating the strata in question. Rather, it required a political platform that would appeal to peasants and middle strata and an organization that would elaborate and propagandize that platform.

By the 1960s, radical changes had occurred from both points of view in core regions and in many semiperipheral countries. The great advances in the technical division of labor and in mechanization of the interwar and postwar years had destroyed or peripheralized in the labor process the craft skills on which labor's organized power had previously rested. At the same time, these same advances had endowed labor with a new power: the power to inflict large losses on capital by disrupting a highly integrated and mechanized labor process. In exercising this power, labor was far less dependent on an organization external to the workplace (as trade unions generally were) since what really mattered was the capacity to exploit the interdependencies and networks created by capital itself in the workplace.

Moreover, the increased commodification of labor had depleted the locally available strata of peasants that could be effectively and competitively mobilized to undermine the political and economic power of labor. As for the middle strata, the unprecedented spread and radicalism of the student movements were symptoms of the deepening commodification of the labor power of these strata and of the greater difficulties of mobilizing them against the labor movement. (This process was reflected in a large literature of the 1960s on the "new working class.") It follows that the problem of alliances and hegemony was less central than in the past and that, as a consequence, labor's dependence on permanent bureaucratic organizations for the success of its struggles was further reduced.

As we have seen, for many persons the conclusion to be drawn from this analysis is that the antisystemic movements have "failed" or, even worse, were "co-opted." The change from "capitalist state" to "socialist state," for many who think in these terms, has not had the transforming effects on world history—the reconstituting of trajectories of growth—that they had believed it would have. And the change from colony to state, whether by revolution or by negotiation, has lacked not only the world-historical effects but also, in most instances, even the internal redistribution of well-being so prominent in the programs of these movements. Social democracy has succeeded no better. Everywhere it finds its occupancy of state power merely a mediating presence—one constrained by the processes of accumulation on a world scale and the twin requirements of governments: burying the dead and caring for the wounded, whether people or property. To the chagrin of some, the applause of others, the one coordinated effort toward a world revolution, the Comintern/Cominform, collapsed completely under the disintegrating weight of continuing state-formation at all locations of its operations—its historical center, its loci of subsequent success, its other national arenas of strength, its points of marginal presence. Without exception, all current Communist parties are concerned first with domestic conditions and only secondarily if at all with world revolution.

THE TRANSFORMED HISTORICAL GROUND

We, on the other hand, contend, as we said, that from the vantage point of 1848 the success of the antisystemic movements has been very impressive indeed. Moreover, that success does not dim in the least when viewed from the vantage point of today. Rather the opposite. For without such an appreciation, one cannot understand where the nonconventional terrain opened up by the most recent forms of antisystemic movement has come from historically and where therefore the movements seem likely to go in the historical future.

At the same time, however, the antisystemic movements are of course not the only agencies to have altered the ground on and through which current and future movements must continually form and operate. Those they would destroy, the organizing agencies of the accumulation process, have also been at work, owing partly to an "inner logic," partly to the very successes of the movements and hence to the continually transformed historical ground which that "logic" has as its field of operation and contradiction. Above all, the ongoing structural transformation of the capitalist world-economy has in effect opened up the locations in its overall operation where the process of class struggle is proving formative of the sides in conflict and polarizing in the relations so formed.

In the course of the twentieth century, indeed defining it, a massive sea change has been occurring in the social relations of accumulation. In a sentence, the relational networks forming the trunk lines of the circuits of capital have been so structurally transformed that the very workings of the accumulation process appear as historically altered. It is this ongoing transformation that has continually remade the relational conditions of both the organizing agencies of accumulation (by definition) and those in fundamental struggle with them, the antisystemic movements, and so have continually remade as well the relational character of that struggle itself and hence the nature of the movements defined by it. To retrace the steps: the life cycles of the various movements have been a part of and have helped to form the structural shift; hence the relational struggles defining the movements as antisystemic; hence the movements themselves and the trajectories that make them antisystemic. We depict the ongoing transformation here by outlining three of its faces in the form of structural trends.

In one guise the transformation appears as simultaneously an increasing "stateness" of the world's peoples (the number of "sovereign states" having more than tripled during the twentieth century) and an increasingly dense organization of the interstate system. Today virtually the whole of the globe's nearly 5 billion people are politically partitioned into the subject populations of the 160 or so states of an interstate system which contains a large number of formal interstate organizations. This might be called the widening of stateness. The deepening of stateness is another matter. Here essentially we have in mind the growing "strength" of state agencies vis-à-vis local bodies (within or intersecting with the state's jurisdiction). Measures of this are of many sorts, from the voluminous expansion of laws and of agencies to enforce them, through central-government taxes as growing proportions of measured domestic or national product, to the structural expansion of kinds of state agencies, the geographical spread of their locations of operation, and the growing proportion of the labor force their employees form. Moreover, like international airports around the world, and for analogous if deeper reasons, the organizational form of stateness (the complex array of hierarchies forming the apparatus of administration) has everywhere virtually the same anatomy, the differences from place to place being on the order of variations on a theme. They are variations that no doubt matter a great deal to the subjects of state power, but, world historically, they are nonetheless only variations and not qualitative departures in form.

One final point should perhaps be noted here. Much has been made of the extent to which, following the accessions to power of social and/or national antisystemic movements, a marked increase in the structural "centralization" of the state has occurred, that is, a marked increase in what we're calling here the deepening of stateness. And, examining the trends in state formation within the jurisdictions severally, one at a time, one does see that. However, watching the overall trend in state formation in the modern world as a singular historical system, over the course of the twentieth century, one would be hard put to attribute the overall trend to any such "internal" processes or, for that matter, even to the interrelated successes of the particular social and national movements construed collectively as but particular emanations of a singular complex historical process of the modern world-system. For even in locations where, seen in that way, the world-historical process has been manifestly weakest (the movements least apparently successful), the structural trend in state formation is no less apparent than elsewhere.

Of even more importance here, in some ways, is the still far greater growth in the density of the interstate system. Just using the simplest of assumptions, and reasoning purely formally from the fourfold increase in the number of states, there is a sixteenfold increase in their relations with one another. But that of course barely scratches the surface. The kinds of specialized relations among the states of the interstate system have expanded nearly as much as the kinds of internal state agencies. Added to this are over a dozen specialized United Nations agencies (in each of which most states are related as members) and a very large number of regional international organizations (such as OECD, OPEC, ASEAN, COMECON, NATO, OAU, etc.). If one goes beyond the existence of the voluminous set of interstate relations to the frequency with which they're activated, via meetings, postal mail, cable, telephone, and now, increasingly, electronic mail, the density of the interstate system's relational network today is probably several times greater than the comparable density of the official intrastate relational network of the most advanced and centrally administered country of a century ago (say France).

One result is an enmeshing within each state's operations of the "internal" and "external" relational webs and processes to such an extent that the distinction itself, except perhaps for border crossings of people and goods, begins to lose substantive force (in contradiction to its nominal force, which is increased with every treaty signed, every package assessed duty by customs, every postage stamp issued). Hence, to a degree and extent never envisioned by the successful social and national movements when they eventually gained state power, both what a state's agencies administer internally and how they do so is increasingly determined, to use a Weber pairing, not autonomously (as befits sovereignty) but heteronomously (as befits what?).

A second result, and one of no less importance to our subject—the current and future terrain on, through, and against which present and future antisystemic movements are and will be operating—is the degree to which virtually all inter-relations, among peoples in different state jurisdictions, have become dimensions of their respective states' relations with one another. This is not just a matter of travelers obtaining passports and visas and passing through emigration and immigration authorities, or of packages having to be sent with export and import permits and be duly processed, etc. These interstate procedures, which daily reannounce the borders of the respective jurisdictions of each constituent state, are but mediations of the movement of people, goods, and capital, and have been practiced for a rather long time.

The "openness" or "closure" of a state's borders to such movements, however, we note parenthetically in passing, has always been less a matter of that state's policies "toward the world" than of its location in the hierarchical ordering inherent in the capitalist world-economy's interstate system, a location determined not merely by academicians but by demonstrated or creditable relational strengths, practical conditions effected by ruling classes. Rather it is a matter of the interstate system's appropriating all manner of direct and circuitous relations among people of different countries (state jurisdictions)—whether religious, scientific, commercial, artistic, financial, linguistic, civilizational, educational, literary, productive, problem-focused, historical, philosophical, *ad infinitum*—such that they all become, at the very least, mediated, more often actually organized, by the counterpart agencies of different states through their established or newly formed relations with one another. The effect is to subordinate the interrelations among the world's peoples not to *raisons d'état*, a practice with which all of us are all too familiar, but to *raisons du systéme d'états*, a practice with which most of us are all too unfamiliar.

There is, we should briefly note, a set of consequential historical contradictions being formed through this recreation of all varieties of social relations into networks within either inter- or intrastate frameworks. Many kinds of communities—in the sense of communities of believers/practitioners—form in a way "worlds" of their own in relation to, in distinction from, and often in conflict with all others, that is, those who are not of their community, who are nonbelievers/practitioners, hence nonmembers. These are often large, encompassing worlds: the Islamic world; the scientific world; the African world (or, in the United States today, the Black world); the women's world; the workers' or proletarian world; and so forth. It is far from evident that such communities of consciousness can even persist, much less grow, within the structurally developing inter- and intrastate framework. The kind of contradiction noted here marks even more so the popular peace and environmental movements, but that is because they are perforce, in today's world, state-oriented, whereas the communities of consciousness we have in mind elaborate themselves independently of stateness (hence, however, in contradiction to it and to interstateness rather than through them).

DIVISION OF LABOR, CENTRALIZATION OF CAPITAL

We have dwelt at length on but one face of the ongoing structural transformation of the capitalist world-economy, that seen through a focus on the plane of the interstate system and its constituent units, the states and their relations with one another. We have done so for two reasons. One is the seemingly enduring disposition, on the part of historical social scientists, to carry forward—all evidence to the contrary notwithstanding—the liberal ideological distinction between "state" and "economy," or "state" and "market" in some versions, as if these were fundamental theoretical categories. The other is the equally prevalent, although apparently less impermeable, disposition to imagine—again, all evidence to the contrary notwithstanding—that the capitalist world-economy has evolved rather as an onion grows, from a core of small and local beginnings through successively larger rings until the outer peripheral skin is formed, all in virtue of the self-expansion of, in this view, capital through its increasing subordination of labor.

We turn now to much briefer observations on two other faces of the transformation. A second face is in the organization and the structuring of another plane of the capitalist world-economy's operation, the axial division of labor. This is the complex of interrelated production/transportation processes that is so ordered that the surplus value created in the course of production and transportation is, historically, disproportionately appropriated at the organizing centers of the multiple and more or less lengthy chains or networks of dependent production processes. The relational patterns this ordering entails are thereby reproduced and, for still additional reasons, their reproduction has cyclically deepened the differences in productive capacity between the organizing center or core portions of the axial division of labor and its increasingly peripheralized portions. In the twentieth century, the underlying transformation has effected some truly massive alterations in the constituent relations of the complex core-periphery axis and hence in the mapping of their respective global zones, the results of which—generally rendered as if the result of state policies—are broadly known. Of more immediate interest is the extraordinary growth in recent decades of a long-standing agency of the organizing center or core of the socialization of production, hence of labor, on a world scale, namely, what is currently called the multinational or transnational firm. In a sentence, many relations among materially dependent production processes that had been exchange relations, or if newly formed could have been under other conditions (and so of, or potentially of, market-organized networks of commodity flows), became transformed into (or, if new, formed as) intrafirm relations. The elemental arrangement—centralizations of capital, as firms, entrepreneurially organizing geographically extensive and technically complex (for the time) chains of related production operations—is hardly new. It was, after all, what distinguished the chartered merchant (sic!) companies of the seventeenth and eighteenth centuries from other capitalized operations. But in recent decades this "elemental arrangement" of the capitalist world-economy has been increasingly constituted on a scale, in a form, of both organization and production that is historically original. The transnational corporations' reconstruction of the world-scale division and integration of labor processes fundamentally alters the historical possibilities of what still are referred to, and not yet even nostalgically, as "national economies."

A third face of the ongoing structural transformation we are sketchily addressing here shows itself, so to speak, in the massive centralization of capital of the postwar decades. Slowly, haltingly, but more and more definitely, the central agency of capitalist accumulation on a world scale, a world ruling class in formation, is *organizing* a relational structure for continually resolving the massive contradictions increasingly apparent between the transnational corporations' control over, and hence responsibility for, the interrelations *among* productive processes and the multiple states' control over, and hence responsibility for, the labor forces these production processes engage, more or less sporadically.

This structure being organized is basically a sort of replacement, at a "higher level" of course, for the late lamented colonial empires, whose demise the national movements sought and the new hegemonic power, the United States, required. Through those arrangements, and such cousins of them as the Chinese concessions and the Turkish capitulations, the axial division of labor had been furthered and, subject to the very system's structural cycles, assured. The twentieth century's thirty-years war (1914–45), insofar as it was about those arrangements, resolved the question of hegemonic power (a United States vs. Germany fight, it was then understood) but left for invention the means of its exercise and, with that, the perpetuation of both the axial division of labor and the necessary multiple sovereignties, through which the interstate system and hence the relations of hegemony operated.

The invention was a long time in coming and seems to have emerged fully only after, as we said earlier, the narrowness of the limits of great-power military force had finally been established by the Vietnamese for all to see. Crudely put, what seems to have been going on, by way of a structural replacement of the colonial empires, has been the simultaneous growth in massive centralizations of capital *and* a sort of deconcentration of capital (called deindustrialization in present core areas of the axial division of labor). The massive centralization has as its agencies quite small *ad hoc* steering committees of consortia, each composed of several hundred banks, working in close relations both with central banks and with international agencies, notably the IBRD, the IMF, and the BIS. The centralization here is at the money point in the circuit of capital, and the borrowers are not directly capitalist entrepreneurs but are instead states, which in turn use the more or less encumbered credits to work with transnationals, operating with undistributed surpluses, in various "development" projects, which, as they are realized materially, amount to what's called by some "Third World industrialization" and results in precisely the "deindustrialization" of heretofore core areas.

This face of the transformation does suggest reconsidering the theoretically presumed concatenation of centralization and concentration of capital. But even more it suggests reconceptualizing the *fundamental* nature of the accumulation process as it's framed through the idea of the circuits of capital. For when the indebted *states* run into trouble, one of the agencies of this arrangement, the IMF, steps forward with austerity plans, the gist and substance of which amount to lowering the costs, now internationally reckoned, of the daily and generational reproduction of the labor forces of (within?) each of the countries.

The arrangement is not *per se* historically new—one thinks of the Turkish capitulations, for example—but it is far more massive and, as a structural array of processes of the world-system, far more frequent in occurrence and far more telling in its implications for the structuring of the accumulation process as such.

Together these three facets of the ongoing structural transformation of the modern world-system, all of which reveal, to a greater or lesser extent, the structural surround of the state power seized or occupied by antisystemic movements in the course of the twentieth century and indicate the degree and kind of reconstitution of terrain with which present and future movements of a like sort have to contend. They indicate as well—though this is not here a central concern of ours—the anachronism of the contents we give to the concepts with which we commonly work. The dilemmas of the antisystemic movements are thus in some measure the unintended product of a sort of false consciousness on the part, not of toadies nor even of hairsplitters, but of the most engaged of the intelligentsia.

There remains a matter to end on here—to raise as a sort of coda—for nothing before has directly prefigured it. This is the ongoing transformation of communications networks. The *Communist Manifesto* observes: "And that union, to attain which the burghers of the Middle Ages, with their miserable highways, required centuries, the modern proletarians, thanks to railways, achieve in a few years." It is now nearly a century and a half since that was written. That sentence has lost none of its force. But it must be understood contemporarily. In the United States, in the 1960s, what effected the interrelation of the 150 or so Black demonstrations and the even more numerous public forms of the antiwar movement was television, which is why the commanding officer of the Grenada operation (Grenada: less than half the size in territory and people of an upstate New York county) correctly, from the U.S. government's point of view, decreed there was to be no accompanying news coverage of the invasion. The kind of concern flagged in the *Manifesto*, the material means of unity among those geographically separate, remains central. The means themselves, and the very form of their materiality, have been fundamentally transformed. More and more antisystemic movements will find their own cohesion and coherence forged and destroyed by the newest of the means of mediating social relations.

Where then are we? We are massively, seriously in the urgent need of reconstructing the strategy, perhaps the ideology, perhaps the organizational structure of the family of world antisystemic movements, if we are to cope effectively with the real dilemmas before which we are placed, as the "stateness" of states and the "capitalist" nature of capitalism grow at an incredible pace. We know this creates objective contradictions for the system as such and for the managers of the status quo. But it creates dilemmas for the antisystemic movements almost as grave. Thus we cannot count on the "automaticity" of progress; thus we cannot abandon critical analysis of our real historical alternatives.

2. Party and State in Our Times: The Rise of Non-Party Political Formations

Rajni Kothari

PARTICIPATION, DEVELOPMENT AND THE STATE

'Participation' is the crowning concept of the liberal paradigm of progress, equality and democracy. It is shared by a variety of occidental schools of thought, including those avowedly opposed to liberalism. It was only with the dawn of the age of mass politics—and, still later, with the entry of poor, 'backward' societies into the global political process—that its innate paradoxes and contradictions came out into the open. With the advent of 'development' as a doctrine of doing good to all, both academic and political interest in the value of participation soared high. However, by the end of the sixties, it had become clear that to participate in development was a prerogative (of some) though proclaimed as a right (of all); it was denied in particular to the 'masses', the people, the poor, in whose name 'development' took place.

THE MYTH OF PARTICIPATION

The myth still persists—above all, among the 'masses' themselves. It has been propelled by two powerful streams of thought, populist politics and populist economics, one perfected as an art of arousing faith among the masses in their benefactors and the other developed as an expertise in legitimizing such a faith. Both have co-existed with popular misery, degradation and destitution. Herein lies the central paradox of all: the more the misery, the more the faith in populism. And the key slogan of populism—whether of populist politics or of populist economics—has been participation.

The more the economics of development and the politics of development are kept out of reach of the masses, the more they (the masses) are asked to 'participate' in them. For they are told that it is for them that 'development' takes place. If poverty still persists or at times gets worse (a fact that is smartly woven into the rhetoric of populism) it is because of extraneous factors such as corruption (a 'global phenomenon'), lack of adequate capital (deliberately denied us by world financial agencies), soaring price of oil and the world economic recession, the arms race (again, externally fanned) and, of course, the destabilizing policies of outside powers. But the ruling elite is, we are told, determined to stand up to the challenge, keep pressing for more resources, more technology, more SDRs, both to stave off the 'painful transition' and to take the economy to a higher plateau of performance— in productivity, in availability of goods and services, and in the well-being and prosperity of the masses. If only the opposition would let us, if only there were fewer agitations and more order. The politics is all right, the basic model is all right,

29

too; all we need is people's cooperation and respect for law (participation) and less conflict and, some (especially the economists) would add, less politics.

Here lies the second major paradox of this age of participation: an increase in the intensity and volume of populist rhetoric which is, however, fashioned to depoliticize, in an increasing manner, the people, the development process, and indeed the operation of the political system itself. So that growing numbers of a powerless populace get marginalized, both from an organized economy and from organized politics, and become dependent on one or a few dominant individuals and their authorized agents—the techno-bureaucrats, the regional satraps and their bully-boys, the skilled experts in communication and mass media. (I shall argue a little later the opposition parties endorse the same political style: an increase in populist appeal alongside a decline in people's role in politics.)

And yet, the symbols of 'people's participation' are by no means given up; they have only been reduced to rituals of a plebiscitary democracy—the Leader going out to the people at regular intervals, 'meeting' them in the thousands (across a heavily guarded barricade), becoming 'one' with them and asking for their loyalty and their votes—making party organizations or other institutional linkages with the people redundant. Personalized appeals and charismatic techniques are used instead to instil in more and more people a sense of threat to their community/religion/ nation.

Here lies the third paradox of participation: the more the people and their representative organizations are stripped of power and authority, the more direct becomes the relationship between the ruler and the ruled; and the more isolated and marginalized and oppressed a people, the more dependent they become on the centre of power. Participation gets translated into clientage; small crumbs are thrown off the national 'cake' during (or just before) an election, and promises of more to come are made. Increasingly, the poor and the helpless get trapped into this closed pyramid of participation. With this, participation—like development—becomes a legitimization of centralized governance, dismantling of intermediate structures, a regime of law and order, and repercussion.

ROLE OF THE STATE

These new mutations in meaning systems are directly related to the nature and role of the state in our times. Four interrelated processes are at work. First, the conception of autonomy of the state that was viewed as an instrument of transformation (both by the elite that came to power after independence and by radical groups) is under decline, in part simply due to the proven incapacity of governments to perform, but also largely by deliberate design. The dominant elite having used state intervention in the economic and social spheres for a quarter century after independence, having developed a wide enough production base for supporting their life-style, and having extracted the surpluses needed for political survival and manipulation, see no need for an extended role for the state, because such a role would have had to become more distributive and mass-oriented. The state is now perceived as an agent of the technological modernization, with a view more to catching up with the developed world and emerging on the world and regional scenes as a strong state (hence the vast sums spent on armaments) than coping with the pressing, often desperate, needs and demands of the poor.

Second, in respect of the relationship between the state and civil society one finds that in a period of economic stagnation and political instability (the former growing from the refusal of the ruling elite to expand the internal market which would have required redistributive policies, the latter from the consequential mass discontent and turmoil), the coercive nature of the state increases. There is a growing demand for unity and consensus—not in the form of an organic expression of civil society but in the form of compliance with whatever happens to be the ruling orthodoxy, dissent from which is considered unpatriotic. And as this happens, the political process gets limited to agents and emissaries who, in the course of time, become less interested in playing a mediative role and more in becoming a law unto themselves, increasingly pressing in service the police and paramilitary forces, on the one hand, and local mafias and hired hoodlums, on the other.

Third, even the bearers of state power, viz. those in control of the *government* (as distinct from the state), including the supremos of power by virtue of their charisma and wide popular appeal, seem to be losing out, wielding authority that is no longer based on their own power and volition, and increasingly becoming pawns in the hands of forces beyond their control. In large parts of rural India (as well as vast tracts of the growing cities and industrial conglomerations) government is on the decline, its mediating and ordering roles being replaced by direct rule of local landlords and hegemonical castes. This has synchronized with the growing penetration of commercial interests into rural hinterlands and tribal habitats, the rise of ill-bred contractors as new managers of money power, and the still more spectacular ascendancy of the newest of the *nouveau riches* (the dealers in illicit liquor and gambling dens), all protected and endorsed by a new breed of corrupt local politicians (or their henchmen), bureaucrats and policemen.

Fourth, such a sharp decline in the rule of law and the authority of the governing elite has made secular power as such, and the state as its institutional embodiment, vulnerable to new attacks from old forces that were thought to have been put on the defensive. A notable example of this is the resurgence of so-called new fundamentalisms of religious sects (which are nothing but perversions of old civilizations), such as the Vishwa Hindu Parishad and supposedly 'cultural' organizations like the Rashtriya Swayamsevak Sangh (RSS) and the Jamaat-e-Islami. Alongside this are communalist and sectarian appeals *within* secular politics, thanks to the desperate struggle for survival on the part of ruling individuals and cliques. All this deflects attention away from the politics of socio-economic transformation, and gravely affects both the institutional framework and the finer subtleties and decor of the political process.

Alongside this backlash from the 'grass-roots' of society, as it were, are other new forces at work which also serve to undermine the autonomous political role of the state, or even its minimal role as mediator in social strife and convulsions for the sake of a larger cohesion. Thus, beneath the outer veneer of planned economic development there has emerged a new breed of highly connected middlemen and professionals (in the guise of liaison officers and management officials) who are contributing to the increasing alienation of public goods by private individuals as well as to growing lumpenization of the production process under the impact of naked corruption and open subversion of prevailing mechanisms of administrative and judicial control and accountability. Complementary to the massive increase in what is known as the 'informal' or 'unorganized' sector of the economy is a very rapid expansion of this criminal sector of the economy, which is recording probably the highest rate of growth with no holds barred.

Together, the two processes have led to one consequence: withdrawal from organized politics is accompanied by a withdrawal from the organized economy. While as a percentage of gross indicators this may not register in a big way (though I have serious doubts regarding the coverage of economic activities outside the formal sector in official statistics), its impact on the political process and on the role of the state is quite serious. In turn, it accentuates the growing vacuums in the structure of the state, reinforces the depoliticization of the people, increases their sense of insecurity and isolation, and makes them dependent on charismatic individuals (or look for a new savior).

With all this, the role of the state in social transformation has been seriously undermined; 'development' has led to a striking dualism in the social order; and 'democracy' has become the playground for growing corruption, criminalization, repression and intimidation of large masses of the people whose very survival is made to depend on their staying out of the political process, and whose desperate economic state incapacitates them from entering the regular economic process as well.

INTERNATIONAL CONTEXT

These developments receive sustenance and support from, and are indeed encouraged by, the international system. All the pathologies touched upon above—exclusion of millions of people from the organized economy and acceptance of their impoverishment and destitution as both natural and inevitable, withdrawal of basic resources from the countryside (forcing those who lived by them to migrate to cities already full of filth and squalor), depoliticization of the public realm and the rise of techno-bureaucracies, and increase in both the range and intensity of coercion by the state—are made worse by a new breed of entrepreneurs in the service of the global *status quo* which is undermining the role of the state even as it was earlier conceived by the national bourgeoisie. As the world capitalist system enters its terminal phase between the twin pincers of an unprecedented arms race and the unsatiated monster of technology bent on a new international division of labour that dispenses with an organized proletariat, the struggle over life-styles and resources is entering its most desperate phase.

Politically, this has led to the cooptation of Third World regimes and their being armed with enough flows of capital, technology and armaments to keep them and their modern middle-class base afloat and to protect them from social turmoil and the demands of large hordes of the poor and the destitute. In return, what is taking place is a reverse transfer of natural resources and raw materials, of food-stuff and feed, as well as of manufactured consumer goods that rely on labour-intensive and polluting technologies, all at continually depressed prices. This is achieved by ordering and disciplining the working classes in the Third World (with the collusion of the local bourgeoisie) so that both the quantum and the structure of production are regulated to suit the requirements of world capitalism. The much denied 'conditionalities' accompanying otherwise unjustified loans from the IMF and the World Bank are basically meant to bail out corrupt and incompetent regimes.

The North-South rhetoric, the philosophy of self-reliance and delinking, the resolutions on a new international economic order, have all been mastered by this universal union of elites and affluent classes, cutting across nations and ideological pretences, and putting into cold storage 'alternative' strategies of basic needs, national self-reliance, minimum standards of health and nutrition for all, and an increase in employment and participation in the production process.

Struggle for Survival

The world scenario is beset by a gigantic battle for survival—survival of achieved life-styles versus survival of life itself, survival of corporate (economic *and* political) power structures versus survival of states and cultures in large parts of the Third World, survival of peace and dignity for millions versus survival of structures of dominance and monopoly for ruling elites. In such a world, highly defensive and increasingly desperate at both ends of the power rope, democratic politics must suffer a big dip, technocracy and the managers of strife replacing popular politicians and the bulk of the people everywhere being asked to stay away from politics. It would be in their own interest to do so, they are told. Provided they do so and are not carried away by radicals of all types, their welfare and prosperity will be taken care of.

Turbulence

Are the people accepting such a withdrawal from the political process? Fortunately not. All over the world there is evidence of a turbulent consciousness among large sections of the deprived who had for long believed in both the grace of God and the grace of Caesar but have for some time now realized that there is no grace (or "compassion" or "mercy") among the mighty and that only through struggling against them can anything be had. In India this is particularly evident, arising partly out of the revolution in norms generated over decades by the adoption of a formerly democratic polity in a society based for centuries on the principle of inequality, partly out of a shaken faith in the theology of development that had successfully made its way into the thinking and belief systems of the people throughout the fifties and sixties, and partly out of the sheer weight of indignities, violence and deceit experienced by the poor and the dispossessed. All this is greatly reinforced by disillusionment with successive governments representing different parties thoughout the seventies in each of which a believing people had put its faith. There is discontent and despair in the air—still highly diffuse, fragmented and unorganized. But there is a growing awareness of rights, felt politically and expressed politically, and by and large still aimed at the state. Whenever a mechanism of mobilization has become available, this consciousness has found expression—often in the teeth of very heavy odds (including intimidation, persecution and repression) and against a constellation of interests that are too powerful and complacent to shed (even share) their privileges. At bottom it is an expression of resentment against a paradigm of society that rests on deliberate indifference to the plight of the impoverished and the destitute who are being driven to the threshold of starvation—by the logic of the paradigm itself.

ALL-ROUND CRISIS

Failure of the System

The crisis in India has laid bare the failure (and irrelevance) not just of government, but of organized political parties, trade unions and other traditional forms of opposition to the ruling elite. What we face in India is the failure and default of the system, not merely of its governing structure. It is a system based on (a) a formal parliamentary democracy operated through party competition that is getting increasingly desperate and violent; (b) a mixed economy composed of a large state sector and a large corporate sector, both of which have failed to generate opportunities for the people and have, instead, survived by draining resources from the countryside; (c) an agrarian and forest economy that has ceased to produce more food and has, instead, become pulverized by the onslaught of commercial interests and corrupt politics; and (d) a science-and-technology establishment so devoid of internal dynamism and so thoroughly dependent on imported ideas and technologies that even the initial euphoria of self-reliance has given way to the rhetoric of interdependence. All this is further buttressed by a military establishment that, apart from making ever new demands on the country's resources, is also increasingly called upon to perform police functions (spelling terror in some parts of the country), and a judiciary and a press, which, driven to intervene in a period of growing repression (of the poor, the ethnic minorities, the women and the social activists who happen to be working among these stata), are in effect becoming mechanisms of defusing discontent and preventing confrontation.

It is a failure of the system in a much deeper sense. First, in the sense that the established instruments of the system—the state legislatures, the Parliament, the Planning Commission, the executive—are simply unwilling or unable or both to handle a considerably changed agenda of tasks; to respond to people's expectations or cope with a scenario of deepening conflict, violence and vandalism. Second, it is a failure that the established opponents of the ruling elite—opposition parties, trade unions, peasant organizations, left-wing intellectuals—cannot cope with. Third, it is a failure from which a very large section of the people stands to benefit. As argued already, large sections of the middle class (which, in absolute numbers, is massive in India) have succeeded in utilizing the state to provide them with a production base that can sustain their parasitic life-style; and these have been joined by the numerous lumpen elements that are finding employment at the lower rungs of an ever growing bureaucracy and in a political process that increasingly relies on mercenaries.

Crisis of Theory

Above all, the failure of the system is embedded in a crisis of theory. The liberal conception of the market as the arbiter of interests broke down long ago. The social democratic theory, based on a positive and benevolent role of the state and on a conception of equity based on welfarism, is also of not much value in the absence of high growth rates and massive state surpluses (as well as an honest and efficient state apparatus).

Nor does the more radical school of thought—viz. Marxism—provide a clear enough guide to action in a society very different from the one it was posited on. The cutting edge of a predominantly agrarian society is not the same as that of an industrialized one: a working class progressively growing in number and solidarity. In the former, on the contrary, a combination of political and economic factors structurally inhibits both. Stagnation in the rural economy (that provided employment in agriculture and village crafts) and devastation of ecology (that provided the poor a source of sustenance) together cause, on the one hand, a phenomenal growth in the population living on the verge of starvation and, on the other hand, a steep decline in the number (both proportionally and absolutely) of those who can find work. The trend in the organized, industrial, sector of the economy is the same, thanks to a technology that seeks to prove itself by progressively making human labour irrelevant. This sector cannot absorb even a small fraction of those who flock to cities in the vain search for jobs; it reduces the number of those already employed. This much for the numerical growth of the working class. As for solidarity, short work is made of it by the fragmentation of trade unions and the growing strife (often violent) *within* the lower strata of society, and by the assiduously inculcated depoliticization that prevents the aggregation of local confrontations between the exploiter and the exploited into national and international formations.

The fact of the matter is that models and ideological doctrines evolved in a different cultural context and historical condition are of little use in a social and political environment where poverty takes totally new forms and where the linkage between 'progress' and 'poverty' has become organic and almost irreversible. Hence also the total irrelevance of all theories of participation. Indeed, as one reviews the overall scene, one is struck not only by the steep decline in leadership and moral values but also by this poverty of theory as a guide to action. The result is an intellectual and moral vacuum which is then filled by populist rhetoric on the one hand (taking the place of theory) and coercion and corruption on the other (taking the place of politics). And charisma covers up the two so that there is hardly any sense of failure or crisis, at least among the ruling class.

EMERGENCE OF NON-PARTY FORMATIONS

Political and Ideological Context

This is the larger context in which we have to discuss the broad theme of people's movements and 'grass-roots' politics and, as part thereof, of the phenomenon of non-party political formations. To recapitulate and enlarge upon the argument already made. It is a context where the engines of growth are not moving, the organized working class is not growing either in number or in strength, the process of marginalization is spreading, technology is turning anti-people, development has become an instrument of the privileged class, and the state has lost its role as an agent of transformation, or even as a mediator in the affairs of civil society. It is a context of massive centralization of power and resources, centralization that does not stop at the national centre, either, and makes the nation-state itself an abject onlooker and a client of a global 'world order'.

It is a context in which the party system, the organized democratic process and the regular bureaucracy are in a state of atrophy, and are being replaced by a new set of actors and a new 'order'. The new order is manned by a class of professional managers and of experts in the art of injecting corruption in the higher rungs of the economy and the polity, and by hoodlums and fixers at the lower reaches of the economy and the polity. It is a context in which revolutionary parties too have been contained and in part coopted (as have most of the trade unions); in which therefore the traditional fronts of radical action—the working class movement and the militant peasantry led by left parties—are in deep crisis; in which there appears to be a growing hiatus between these parties and the lower classes, especially the very poor and the destitute who are not amenable to the received wisdom of left politics; and in which, on the other hand, there is a massive backlash from established interests in the form of legislative measures aimed against the toiling classes and a steep rise in repression and terror perpetrated both by the state and by private vested interests.

And all this against the backdrop of growing international pressures and 'conditionalities' that herald an end of self-reliance, and that seek, on the one hand, to integrate the organized economy into the world market and, on the other hand, remove millions of people from the economy by throwing them in the dustbin of history—impoverished, destitute, drained of their own resources and deprived of minimum requirements of health and nutrition, denied 'entitlement' to food and water and shelter—in short, an unwanted and dispensable lot whose fate seems to be 'doomed'. A veritable scenario of Triage!

Role of 'Grass-Roots' Activism

It is with the plight of these rejects of society and of organized politics, and also, ironically, of revolutionary theory and received doctrines of all schools of thought, that the 'grass-roots' movements and non-party formations are concerned. They have to be seen as part of the democratic struggle at various levels, in a radically different social context than was posited both by the incrementalists and by the revolutionaries, and at a point of history when existing institutions, and the theoretical models on which they are based, have run their course, when there is a search for new instruments of political action (the existing ones having become either complacent or weary and exhausted), and when large vacuums in political space are emerging, thanks to the abdication of its role by the state and the virtual collapse of 'government' in large stretches of the Indian land mass.

The non-party formations spring from a deep stirring of consciousness and an intuitive awareness of a crisis that could conceivably be turned into a catalyst of new opportunities. They are to be seen as a response to the incapacity of the state to hold its various constituents by dint of positive action, to its growing refusal (not just inability) to deliver the goods, and to its increasingly repressive character. They are to be seen as attempts to open alternative political spaces outside the usual arenas of party and government (though not outside the state), as new forms of organization and struggle meant to rejuvenate the state and to make it once again an instrument of liberation from exploitative structures (both traditional and modern), in which the underprivileged and the poor are trapped.

They are really to be seen as part of an exercise in redefining politics at a time when unremitting attempts are being made to narrow down its range, and finding a political process different from electoral and legislative politics (which has thrown large sections of the people outside the process of power), different also in respect of the basic conception of the function and goal of political activity. They see political activity not merely (or even mainly) as an essay in capturing state power, but as a comprehensive process of intervening in the historical process.

Redefining Politics

Theirs is an attempt to redefine the very content of politics. In the new definition, issues and arenas of human activity that were not so far seen as amenable to political action—such as people's health, rights over forests and other community resources, even such deeply personal and primordial issues as are involved in the struggle for women's rights—fall within the purview of political struggle. In a number of grass-roots movements launched by the non-traditional left—for instance, Chipko (a people's movement to prevent the felling of trees in the foothills of the Himalayas), the miners' struggle in Chhattisgarh (a predominantly tribal belt in Madhya Pradesh), the Ryot Coolie Sangham (an organization of landless activists in Andhra Pradesh), the Satyagraha led by the Raiyat Sangha (a peasants' organization in Kanakpura in Karnataka against the mining and export of granite), the Jharkhand Mukti Morcha (a movement for regional autonomy in the tribal belt of Bihar and Orissa)—the struggle is not limited to economic and political demands, but extends to cover ecological, cultural and educational issues as well. Nor is it limited to the external enemy; it includes a sustained and long-drawn-out campaign against more pervasive sources of economic and cultural ruin—such as drunkenness, despoliation of the environment, and insanitary habits—evocative of the original conception of *Swarajya* as a struggle for liberation, not just from alien rule, but also from internal decay.

In sum, the phenomenon of 'grass-roots' activism is to be seen as part of an attempt to kindle faith and energy in anti-establishment forces in a variety of settings at a time when general drift and loss of elan are common, and when the suffering masses are scared of confrontations with the *status quo* and are, in fact, likely to walk into the trap both of populist rhetoric (in the modern sector) and of authoritarian patriarchy and patrimony (in the traditional arena), when the need, on the other hand, is for people with will and creativity to be ready to wage a sustained struggle, not just against a particular local tyrant, but against the larger social system.

New Roles

Not everyone involved in popular movements sees it exactly like this. Many of them are too preoccupied with immediate struggles to be able to think in wider terms; others are suspicious of both abstractions and aggregates; and, in any case, the conditions for concerted and consolidated action informed by an adequate theory are just not there. And yet, there is enough evidence to suggest that underlying the micro movements is a search and restlessness for both a more adequate understanding of the forces at work and a more adequate response to them, a certain conviction that available ideologies are inadequate to provide these, and enough experience that the existing instruments of formal politics—parties, elections, even the press and the judiciary—cannot be expected to cope with the crises they are in, and those they work among are in. In one area after another, where we in Lokayan have had dialogues with activists working among the dalits (the untouchables), the landless and the bonded labour, the tribals and various other segments of the rural poor that have been uprooted and forced to migrate to the cities, we found that none of the existing parties, including those that mouth radical slogans, really cared for these inchoate and unorganized and, on the whole, muted and suffering masses. Hence the need for a new genre of organization and a new conception of political roles.

It is in answer to this need that the phenomenon of non-party political formations (as distinct from non-political voluntary agencies working on various development schemes) has surfaced. In part these formations are performing roles previously performed by the government or by opposition parties and their front organizations (now defunct due largely to their abdication of their responsibility to the weak and the exploited). In part they are performing new roles called for by the new context of the human condition as described in this paper—a condition of profound marginalization of millions of people, and the social and moral vacuum created by the indifference and apathy of the system. And in part they are providing new linkages with segments of people's lives that had hitherto remained isolated and specialized: culture, gender and age, technology, ecology, health and nutrition, education and pedagogy; they are bringing into the political process issues that have been deleted from the agenda of organized parties, whether in or out of power. Finally, some (so far only a few) of them are also seeking to link experiments at micro and regional levels to the macro political situation, partly by similar struggles at so many micro points and partly by the sheer impact of example and will on wider public opinion. The more organized effort of joining up horizontally and vertically and building a more cohesive and comprehensive macro formation is, of course, not yet in sight despite being widely recognized.

On the whole, though, it would be a mistake to think of these action groups, either logically or empirically, as one has thought of political parties. As I see it, their role is neither antagonistic nor complementary to the existing parties. It is a role at once more limited (in space or expanse) and more radical—not competing with parties but taking up issues that parties have failed, or are unwilling, to take up; coping with a large diversity of situations that governments and parties are unable (or, again, unwilling) to cope with; coming face to face with issues that arise from not merely local and national but also international forces at work. The individual effort itself is, by and large, expressed in micro terms, but it deals with conditions that are the creation of larger macro structures. The non-party formations are therefore to be viewed as part of a larger movement for global transformation in which non-state actors, on the one hand, and non-territorial crystallizations, on the other, are emerging and playing new roles, taking up cudgels against imperialist forces (some of which, too, are in the form of non-state actors, e.g. the TNCs).

Global Struggle

Interestingly, the struggle against new forms of global hegemony and exploitation is being pushed further and further down on the agenda of most governments of the Third World (which, of course, make appropriate noises from the UN and NAM platforms) as also of most political parties, including the parties of the left (which routinely pass fiery resolutions). In point of fact, at any rate in India, when it comes to issues of international affairs and foreign policy, these parties find ingenious arguments for supporting the official line; having been in effect coopted by the ruling party (thanks largely to the increasingly anti-revolutionary stance of the Soviet Union and China), they are always on the defensive. Even in respect of joining issues with corporate interests and the global economic, financial and military establishments, this role is performed less and less by governments and parties (the various 'Internationals' having long lost their elan) and more and more by non-party, non-state actors while the nation-states, of whatever political hue, are being sucked into the global *status quo*, including the capitalist world market, despite all the rhetoric of a new international order.

This large scenario of decline, and even cooptation, of the traditional arenas of progressive and revolutionary action—within the state system as well as within individual nation-states—provides the most relevant reason for the emergence of the non-party political process. Another reason is that other political actors (such as the state, the party and party-like organizations, the larger NGOs and voluntary agencies operating outside the political process) who are expected to stem the rot are themselves in the grip of torpor while, on the other hand, the sentries of the global, regional and national *status quos* are on the offensive. The flip side of this development can be seen in the wobbliness of governance, in the depoliticization of politics, in the crisis in the enterprise of knowledge (social sciences, for instance, having become social irrelevancies), in the stark bankruptcy of ideas among the traditional carriers of intellectual ferment.

Challenge of Multidimensionality and Fragmentation

Part of the problem lies precisely in this wide array of problems, demands and oppressive structures. The diffusion and fragmentation are not all born out of conflicts of ideas and personalities; they are in a way built into the very process of transformation. The traditional institutions of the state, parties and voluntary agencies are unable to deal with it. Nor is there as yet any certainty that the non-party formations will succeed where others have failed. The problem is how to inject new energy and confidence in the very large section of the young and the concerned, how to rekindle the creative impulse which is bound to be there in an age of turmoil and stirred consciousness, how and with what vision and agenda to arm them so that they can occupy the new spaces created by this general state of exhaustion and drift and defeatism, and, above all, how to come forward with a new strategy of transformation at a time when it is clear that the old-style revolution is not on the cards; when, instead of the working classes of the world uniting, it is the world's middle classes that are becoming conscious of their 'independence'; when the production process as traditionally known has been almost wholly preempted by this class; and when the struggling masses are not an organized working class but a disorganized and 'doomed' non-class.

It has to be a strategy that builds from the here and now, empowers the people and inspires new confidence among the activists all the way along, so that they can discard old ideologies and work towards a new crystallization through the very process of struggle and survival (mere survival calls for struggle). Any long-drawn-out and sustained struggle for a brighter future entails survival—of the people at large, of activists, of the resilience of democratic institutions. It is a struggle to which are hitched not merely immediate goals but the much larger goal of sustaining and strengthening the democratic process and making it an instrument of the poor and the destitute. On it also depends rejuvenation of mainstream structures, transformation and politicization of the state and its liberation from the stranglehold of imperialism and, through all this, the realization of a truly indigenous and authentic culture that is rooted in the people of India. As D.L. Sheth has said in a recent paper of his, there was never any question of the 'grass-roots' character of the people; it is the forces that are uprooting them that one has to contend with.

There is no ground for romanticism, not even for unguarded optimism in this regard. No one with any sense of realism and any sensitivity to the colossal power of the establishment can afford to be an optimist, either for these movements or for any other transformative process at work. And yet one needs to recognize that something is on, that it is serious. That it is genuine, and that it is spread over so many places. That it is weak, fragmented, lacking in resources and infected by various kinds of personal, organizational and cognitive crises must also be recognized. And recognizing both the promise and the problems, it should be recognized that there is urgent need to strengthen these movements and other relevant levers of transformation and survival. The least that can be done is not weaken them or dismiss them either out of ignorance and complacency or out of doctrinal intransigence and narrow definitions of the historical process. For what is called for, and is in some cases underway, is a new genre of political activity carried out at so many levels and in so many settings, transcending conventional battle-lines and firmly digging in, not fleeing from the scene of action like the traditional political parties, without, at the same time, indulging in histrionics or waiting for charismatic messiahs (who are usually short-lived and leave behind a lot of debris).

OTHER FORMATIONS

Occasionally such formations are combinations of non-party and party-*like* organizations brought about in the course of dealing with a situation of growing despair and disenchantment with the *status quo*. Thus, the movements for regional autonomy and decentralization, intended to extend the avenues of political participation closer to the people, conducted in an idiom and mode of communication that people understand, and around issues that intimately relate to them, have taken the form of what are called 'regional parties'. They have dramatically emerged on the Indian scene of late. While it is too early to assess their significance, they do represent strong expressions of the will of the people and their rejection of the ruling establishment (not just in the region but on the national plane). The 'regional' phenomenon in India combines in itself a rejection of the authoritarianism of the centre, of the dominance of the metropoles (and their imperial patrons), of the cultural hegemony of bourgeois cosmopolitanism and of the political economy of corruption unleashed by an elite unsure of itself, of also (though this perception is not yet there) the chauvinist drives of the dominant national elite. The assertion of regional feelings should be understood as part of the larger democratic struggle. By insisting on taking the political fulcrum closer to the 'grass-roots' the regional formations provide local responses to national crises—in a way not unrelated to impulses that move the large variety of micro movements led by wholly non-party groups.

The rationale and historical specificity of the non-party character of the regional formations is of course clear. All the same, given their political nature (which is lacking in various development oriented voluntary bodies), they must take cognizance of other large and powerful upsurges that give expression to mass discontent with the establishment and signify a search for alternatives to the *status quo*. In as much as they ask for reordering the distribution of power in favour of the lower reaches of society, they batter down the system as a whole. The upsurge in Assam, Jharkhand, the tribal north-east, Andhra Pradesh, Kashmir (though here it is of a different sort), and even West Bengal and Karnataka (where parties that are otherwise 'national' have decided to join forces in the demand for regional autonomy), all represent a churning at the bottom of society in a territorial and 'nationality' sense, though unfortunately still not in a social sense. They raise issues of language and culture and dignity and self-esteem; they emphasize mass education, employment and ecology preservation; above all, they battle against the drainage of power and resources from the localities to the centres. These are too important happenings in an otherwise highly centralized and oppressive and corrupt state to be ignored by the 'grass-roots' activists.

Furthermore, these newest types of upsurge and political formations (there is considerable variety among them despite a common thrust) display two characteristics that make them relevant to the non-party activists: they stride across the party and non-party spaces, and thus provide a broader political space to the struggle for transformation. And they operate in the space between the actual grass-roots and the national and international levels. It is the task of the activists working among the very poor and deprived to instil a social purpose in this new generation of party-like formations and to make them vehicles for classes and categories of people that have been deserted by both the government and the opposition.

The key question, however, is: Will the Telugu Desam of Andhra, the National Conference of Jammu and Kashmir, the leaders of the Assam and Jharkhand movements, and other proponents of 'regionalism' and decentralization pave the way for a greater say of the people in policy-making and, with their help, correct the course of development policies and constitutional functioning? Or will they too, like opposition parties, having risen on the crest of mass discontent, ignore the masses? On the answer to this question will depend the response of non-party activists, though to an extent the answer depends also on the activists, especially on their ability to link horizontally with regional stirrings and instilling in them the need for fresh thinking on a series of policies affecting the mass of the people.

ROLE OF HISTORY

We may conclude on perhaps the most basic issue that faces the grass-roots phenomenon, namely, the micro-macro, macro-micro dynamic. Two related criticisms are levelled against the non-party action groups and movements. First, that they do not represent any basic change in the political process and are to be looked upon as at best a transition to a period when left parties will once again resume their revolutionary role and capture state power. Second, that to the extent they do succeed, their success is limited to local situations; the transformations they provide are far short of being macro, i.e. national or international. Both these arguments are plausible and, in a period of self-doubt and soul-searching, carry conviction even to the activists. I reject them both.

Issue of Organizational Forms

The whole question of new forms of organization and expression of politics needs to be located in the larger context of a world in transformation. They need to be understood as part of a whole range of attempts at redefining the content of politics on the part of hitherto peripheral and marginalized strata of a large number of societies. They need to be seen as expressions of new stirrings of consciousness engulfing large masses of the people, a new conception of rights and responsibilities, an urge to find new creative spaces in what is fundamentally a conflict-ridden social situation, in which all avenues of participation have been appropriated, driving a staggeringly large number of people to the wall to wage a ceaseless struggle for survival in an increasingly inequitable world.

Above all, non-party formations should be seen in relation to the startling incapacity of regimes and power structures (parties, unions, development agencies) to cope with new aspirations, on the one hand, and aggrandizements, on the other. They need to be seen as a response to a multiplicity of agonizing stimuli: a growing hiatus, and the consequent vacuums, in existing institutional frameworks; a felt crisis in human arrangements in the wake of new stirrings and sufferings; a situation of growing conflict between pressures for enlargement of the range of politics and equally (and in some ways more) powerful pressures for its contraction. (Depoliticization, as argued already, also includes withdrawal from organized economic activity.) The non-party political process has emerged at a time of a new and different phase in the structure of world dominance, a change in the nature and role of the state in national and sub-national settings, and a drastically altered relationship between the people and what we (half in jest and half in deception) call 'development'.

Viewed in this manner, the rise of the non-party political process has to be seen not as transient occurrences answering to contingent situations (or *ad hoc* expressions of some intriguing behaviour on the part of a few romantics), but rather as a historical phenomenon playing a specific social role and occupying a specific political space—a role and a space not suddenly appearing from nowhere, but born of the problematique of the human condition in contemporary national and international—and local—settings. If the received political theory and ideological constructs cannot explain the phenomenon, so much the worse for the theory and the ideology! They should be recast to enable them to see reality as it is, and to explain it rather than wish the inconvenient thing away. Just as our understanding of the nature and range of politics needs to be redefined, so does our understanding of revolutionary change. If the assumption that history (a secular euphemism for destiny) has invested a particular class within the capitalist system (viz. the organized working class) with the sole prerogative of overthrowing the system has been empirically proved wrong, the theory that the essence of the revolution is violent change and the inheriting of the mantle of power by the revolutionary vanguard (of course, with a view to ushering in a new era) has proved pernicious, especially for the organized working class itself. Today's oppressed will need to wage their struggle from *outside* the existing structure, not just to dethrone the ruling class and 'smash' the state and take it over, but to redefine the whole concept and structure of politics with a view to empowering the masses for transformation at and from the very bottom of society—the 'grass-roots'.

There can be no assurance that the new actors will be better able to cope with the crisis we are in, but there is no denying that they are not a freak phenomenon but have systemic characteristics. Hence the need to take cognizance of the phenomenon and, to the extent it is found to reflect a new phase in human transformation, to respond to it with both theory (to provide a clear insight into the symbiotic existence of injustice and oppression in all spheres of life—political, economic, social, cultural—and on all levels—local, regional, national, global) and praxis (to explore new forms of action).

Our analysis, so far drawn mainly from the Indian experience and its global context, suggests that the phenomenon has a more general relevance in the form of responding to a historical situation, though without doubt local contexts and parameters greatly vary. It is my view that these variations are going to be far more important in shaping the world we live in, including the prospects of survival, than presumed external 'universals'. And therein—this is strictly personal view—lies hope.

THE MICRO-MACRO DYNAMIC

I might as well spell out the implications of this position in respect of both empirical prognosis and social theory. 'Global problems, local solutions' is not a mere cliche. We know enough about the deep dualism of the world we live in to be able to say that there are no exclusively global solutions to global problems. As life in personal and communal spheres and at local, sub-regional, regional and national political levels becomes uncertain, vulnerable and dangerous under the impact of forces beyond one's control, the way to redemption will be through working out 'local solutions' to 'global problems' (though even this may not work). Enough has been said in this paper to suggest that those who work for local solutions are not bereft of a macro perspective, a global vision. Such a perspective and such a vision are by no means the monopoly of either the global intellectuals or the global managers of power. In fact, there is reason to think that it is the latter who are being purged of perspective and vision.

Understood in this dynamic way, and in the specific case of the politics of transformation, 'macro' and 'micro' are only differential expressions of the same process. Not polar opposites in some pyramidal structure, but in coexisting contexts in a mesh of variations and diversity, each autonomous and all interrelated. At what point in this vast space will the macro permutations take off is difficult to say. It could conceivably be only through the capture of state power, either by a 'smashing' operation or by recourse to the ballot box. But these are not the only forms of affecting state power. Indeed, in a period when the arena of politics is sought to be extended to ever new processes and contours, limiting the range of politics to representative institutions and capture of state power (which in reality amounts to no more than the succession of one overthrown regime by another) is to contribute to depoliticization, which really means freezing the *status quo* and unwillingly endorse the growing of the world's middle class to banish politics from the world. For what is involved is far more basic: a dogged confrontation between transformation and backlash, between the scary scenario of destitution and brutalization (through the restriction of the role of politics) and sustained struggles for a better order (through the occupation of critical spaces in an expanding horizon of the role of politics).

It is a horizon that extends far into the (as yet) unknown. All over the country— and elsewhere—there is evidence of new forms of both political and cultural stirrings that are expressed in a vast variety of experimentations: a new wave of energy that provides powerful portrayals of the human condition in films and theatre and arts and literature; women everywhere taking up causes that are not limited to their own struggle for equality; young school and college boys and girls (till recently finding themselves rootless and alienated) marching for the rights of the tribals and the forest people. In all this, and a lot more, there is material for building a new society and polity on the ruins of the old, releasing new creative urges of the people to come into their own and take charge of their lives.

The challenge is how to sustain these new creative impulses and make them the harbingers of revolutionary change. History suggests that it is precisely when the struggling forces of change are pushed to the wall by the *status quo*, either out of panic or in sheer self-defence, that the will and the desire for change are heightened and the process of consciousness seeks organized expression. As existing organizations disintegrate or lose their relevance, self-activity of the people finds expression, spurred by a new understanding of the historical process and new visions provided by some intervening individuals, be they intellectuals or young activists or a new breed of politicians. Such self-activity will start occurring essentially at 'local' and regional sites and from there, given will and effort, reverberate throughout the wider political space.

Theoretically, this will call for a new review of ideological positions that continue to locate 'vested interests' in local situations and liberation from them in distant processes—the state, technology, revolutionary vanguards. The relevant 'macro' positions then would inhere in political entities that transcend both the very micro and the very global. We do not yet know what these entities will be, how far they will partake of state-like features and how far they will take on new forms and content and style. These are questions pertinent to the discussion of both the non-party political formations and other emergent or likely forms; they are equally pertinent to the discussion of alternative approaches to the contemporary human condition, and to a consideration of the relationship between forms of organization and ideological content. A considerable agenda of theoretical research appears to be on the cards.

3. The Peace Movement: A Comparative and Analytical Survey

Nigel Young

This paper deals with the peace movement as it grew over two centuries in the industrial societies as a social formation fundamentally concerned with the problems of war, militarism, conscription, mass violence, and the ideals of internationalism, globalism and non-violent relations between people. Therefore it does not incorporate the contemporary concerns of the South with hunger, development and related repression, nor the linkage of peace, democracy and human rights. Yet the peace movement *has*, to varying degrees, incorporated these concerns and, it will be argued, as it becomes more global and species-death more of a reality, these issues become more explicitly part of the peace programme of people's struggles everywhere.

The idea of peace is probably as old as humanity. But secular or political movements for peace—what we call peace movements—are not more than two hundred years old, and have evolved largely in the western and northern countries. Those peace movements with religious orientations are older and have arisen in many different periods and in all parts of the globe. In this paper, the peace movement refers to social or political movements which consciously, explicitly or implicitly, concern themselves (or are defined) as part of the "peace movement", or are overtly opposed to war, militarism or the organized use of violence.

Before the first modern mass movements against war emerged in the late nineteenth century, there existed a myriad of peace sects and traditions (almost all religious) which included peace and the renunciation of war as a principle or goal. The history of anti-war sentiments or peace ideas, actively expressed in the resistance to war by various sects and groups from the early Christian period onwards, is thus much older than even the first secular peace groups in Europe (*circa* 1815). In many countries, ethnic and other groups have opposed specific wars and conscriptions on political or cultural grounds without necessarily being "anti-war" *per se*, or without having any conscious orientation to peace or peace movements. Although such groups were widespread in the nineteenth and early twentieth centuries, they are not included in this survey as peace or "anti-war" *movements*. Equally, many broad religious movements and churches, such as Buddhism, have concepts of peace as part of their doctrines without as a whole ever becoming part of an active peace movement. They too are marginal to this discussion except when a section self-consciously creates or becomes a peace or war-resisting church, such as the Unified Buddhist Church in Indo-China after 1960, or Hinduism which clearly contributes elements to the Gandhian movement without ever itself being a "peace movement" or tradition. Furthermore, one has to distinguish between peace and anti-war *movements* as broad, amorphous, and sometimes ephemeral social phenomena, and the specific peace *traditions* expressed in often small but prophetic groups providing ideas, initiatives and motivation for the entire peace movement.

AIMS AND OBJECTIVES

One purpose of this paper is simply to lay out the historical sequence of these traditions so that their goals, social bases, strategies and their interrelationships in the great periods of anti-war feeling can be examined: 1890–1914, 1916–21, 1930–39, 1957–63, 1965–70 (Vietnam), 1979–86. Another is to ask why these coalitions fell apart—why do peace movements rise and fall? As can be seen in Figure [3.]1, the history of the peace movement is a history of peaks and troughs. A further objective of the paper is to analyse the objectives and aspirations of anti-war movements both immediately before and during the emergence of mass warfare after 1800. In so doing, one can assess the degree to which the sects and minority traditions follow the upturn of mass peace movements, or conversely, initiate and inspire them.

In order to gauge the growth of peace programmes, the movements will be analysed in relation to certain larger ideological or religious traditions to show the impact of intellectual trends of the period: socialism, liberalism, internationalism, etc. The constituencies mobilized around such ideas are themselves significant. If the peace movement is more than the sum of its organizational parts, how is it made up? What is its popular appeal? Some attention will be paid in each case to the social bases of recruitment into the various peace groups, and the degree to which they are related to the oppressed or agents of social change. In this regard, two phenomena have prominent impact on different social groups in different countries and, indeed, on the peace and anti-war movement itself: more recently, the threat of mass destruction by nuclear war; and earlier, the impact of the almost universal introduction of compulsory male conscription by 1915.

Before one can judge this historical peace movement as a whole in terms of its achievements or goals, its impact on state and society and its success or failure, one has to ask a prior question. In what sense can one talk of *the* peace movement as a continuous global or unitary social phenomenon? It is arguable that there is no such thing as a single peace movement but a variety of peace traditions: religious pacifism; Liberal Internationalism; the women's peace movement; anti-conscriptionism; conscientious objection; socialist anti-militarism; Social Internationalism; the peace fronts associated with the Comintern; radical, secular pacifism; anarcho-pacifism; Gandhian non-violent revolution; unilateral nuclear pacifism of parts of the nuclear disarmament movement; the transnational anti-war New Left of the 1960s; and the ecologically inspired movements of the seventies and the eighties. Each has made a contribution, sometimes in coalition, sometimes as separate sects or sub-groups. Yet, at times a peace movement has arisen that is more than the sum total of these traditions or the organizations that represent them. At such times, it has attracted a mass base.

Certainly, there have been moments of popular activity on issues related to war and peace when various strands and traditions, immensely diverse in character and often contradictory in their stance, have joined in broad coalitions with the politically

48

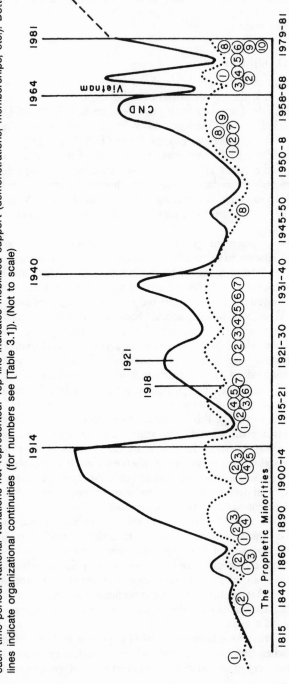

FIGURE [3.]1 The mass peace movements. An impressionistic diagram of peace cycles based mainly on data on the British peace movements—but incorporating other European and North American sources. Waves indicate support as *relative*/ratio of population, at each time period. National variations *not* represented. Top line indicates mobilized support (demonstrations, memberships, etc.). Dotted lines indicate organizational continuities (for numbers see [Table 3.1]). (Not to scale)

TABLE 3.1

A typology of peace traditions (some examples/organizations)

1. Religious Peace Traditions	Religious Pacifism, Society of Friends (Quakers), International Fellowship of Reconciliation, Pax Christi, Unified Buddhist Church of Vietnam
2. Liberal Internationalism	League of Nations Associations, Peace Councils, Peace Society, World Disarmament Campaigns, Union of Democratic Control
3. Anti-conscriptionism	(Single issue lobbies) No Conscription Fellowship, War Resisters' International
4. Socialist War-resistance	War Resisters' International, CGT (France)
5. Socialist Internationalism	Second International
6. Feminist Anti-militarism	WILPF, Women's Peace Party, Women Strike for Peace, Women for Peace
7. Radical Pacifism	War Resisters' International, No More War Movement, Gandhi's Congress, Movement for a New Society
8. Cominternationalism	World Peace Council; Peace Committees, Mouvement de la Paix
9. Nuclear Disarmament	Campaigns for Nuclear Disarmament, SANE, "The Hibaksha", Freeze, END
10. The "new peace movement" (?)	The Greens (?)

These categories are neither exhaustive nor mutually exclusive—some are much larger, more continuous and important than others—some of the sub-segments e.g. of religious traditions are themselves continuous parts of the peace movement (Quakerism). The anarchist anti-war tradition is arguably distinct, but it overlaps with anti-conscriptionism; socialist war resistance; radical pacifism; feminist anti-militarism; and the new peace movement and was also involved in socialist internationalism and nuclear disarmament; and certain religious peace tendencies (Catholic Workers, Radical Quakers, Tolstoyans). This shows the hazards of such classification.

mobilized. But these minority traditions which coexist within the broader peace movement for much of the period, have distinct histories and successes and failures. Their impact on the larger peace movement accordingly must be analysed separately: some, for example, *grew* during World War I when the peace movement generally receded. Prophetic minorities and peace sects are able to survive periods of war and movement decline—and even flourish. Yet at other times these divergent fragments have had little or no contact with society or one another, and have all but disappeared from the historical scene; they have fought bitter feuds or retreated into alternative strategies, of even emigration and escape. In other words, the history of peace movements, as with so many other social movements, is one of discontinuities and diversions.

TOWARD A TYPOLOGY OF PEACE MOVEMENTS

The overall approach of this paper is typological [see Table 3.1]. I have attempted to break down the peace movement into its constituent elements developed over the past 180 years (and some which precede the first modern peace movements). A set of "ideal-type" clusters of ideas and strategies has emerged sequentially with differing goals and methods and varying degrees of salience and influence, both within and beyond the peace movement.

Some would claim to have achieved some of their stated goals, most have not. Clearly they have achieved moments of great social significance and political leverage; as well as moments of paralysis, impotence, and near terminal despair. Above all, there is a markedly cynical character both in the rise and decline of mass public support on peace issues and in the dominance and subordination of different religious, ethical or ideological strands within the peace movement. This explains some of the volatility and most of the discontinuity in peace action.

These strands, crystallized in certain sects or organizational forms, often work alone but have also worked within broad coalitions—"The Peace Movement"— often fusing and interpenetrating one another. When the mass base falls away, sectarianism and fragmentation occur as in 1914, 1930, 1939, 1963 and 1970, and the traditions are maintained by small groups or prophetic minorities until the next surge of mass support. In Europe in 1914 and the United States in 1917 (as in 1939 and 1942), the prophetic minorities remained even after war mobilization. Political sects and religious groups sustained anti-war or anti-militarist positions even when these lacked any real popular support, but certain traditions such as the feminist peace movement of the early twentieth century seemed at times on the point of extinction.

Since the nineteenth century, the number of these strands has increased. One result is the evidence of the peace movement expanding its programme, but another is an increase in the inner contradictions within its coalitions over strategy, goals and methods. Understanding these developments is hindered by the lack of systematic knowledge and analysis of the peace movement: its history, social character, political strategies and ideologies, and social base. There are many excellent monographs and detailed studies, but what is really needed is some holistic approach to appreciate and gain strength from the variety and richness of peace movement traditions. Many peace efforts in the 1980s are seen as novel, but often they are not. For example, few know of the internationalist, feminist, anti-militarism of 1914–16 on which research is now being done, or of the massive anti-war feeling among the armies in Europe in 1916–20.

But, before analysing the mass popular peace movements 1880–1914, 1920–36, and 1957 and beyond, it is necessary to examine the growth of the constituent parts of these movements as they had developed mainly during the nineteenth century. By the 1890s, a number of major peace traditions had emerged with their own clear organizational expressions, some of them dating back to the early nineteenth century or even before. Co-operation and contact between the various wings and strands were often minimal; their visions, strategies and social base differed widely.

The Religious Peace Traditions

The religious tradition is certainly the oldest of the major peace strands and predates the growth of the concept of a peace movement—that is, as a largely secular and political force independent of churches or the representatives of states. The tradition of religious pacifism was associated with individual witness and with principled war resistance of an absolute kind. Later, conscientious objection to military service was claimed as a right as conscription spread, usually invoking both a universalistic ethic and moral critique of war, and was often rooted in a communal religious base. In some cases these collective values had led to a withdrawal of the group from the world into monastic contemplation or quietist and retreatist sects, and this continued to play a role even in the twentieth century. In other cases these groups were forced into confrontations with state and military authorities, rebellion, emigration, or were persecuted and repressed to the point of extinction.

Peace ideas, if not absolute pacifism, in Christianity, as in other major religions, certainly predate the era of the European religious Reformation. They can be found in the less orthodox social undercurrents of the Catholic Church and monastic movements which in some sense precede both the Anabaptist revolt and the cosmopolitan humanism of Erasmus. But it was out of that crucible, and the extensive warfare of the seventeenth century, that one group emerged that has played a virtually continuous role on peace issues both in England and elsewhere, including being a witness against war since the English Civil War: the Quakers.

The Society of Friends, or "Quakers", merit analysis despite their small numbers. They have had an influence on the sustenance and growth of the peace movement for more than 300 years in the English speaking countries and beyond that is truly remarkable and quite out of proportion to their size. Indeed, their activities also justify analysis since they combined a number of root elements which were to remain a key part of the broader movement as it grew. The Quakers draw together a number of strands found in other and earlier religious peace traditions for their particular contribution to peace visions, symbols, strategy and social organization (even within later secular movements).

The first element is the desire not merely to oppose but to actively resist war, both collectively and through individual witness or non-co-operation with military service. The second element is believing in the ultimate possibility of the abolition of war through non-violent unarmed relations between peoples and groups as well as individuals. This Utopian vision is based on non-violence or non-resistance as both an ethical principle and an ultimately practical basis of order. The third element is a religious notion of universalism—unit as people under God or in the spirit. It stressed the ultimate identity of all human beings, using it as the basis of a moral critique of war as a collective crime against the species by itself. This led to a transnational loyalty beyond states and national borders which characterized most religions but had special meaning for peace churches. The fourth element is a belief in the necessity for social and structural change. Peace and human fairness and compassion are perceived to be linked; an unequal world or society leads to violent conflict and death. Intrinsic in this idea is that change in the individual and the community is possible.

As will be seen later, these four dimensions of Quaker peace ideology were to pass into many of the traditions and movements which followed. This intimate relationship perhaps explains why Quakers are able to relate to so many of them, even those which are secular like the liberal or socialist movements.

Liberalism and Internationalism

The second core dimension of peace activity, to search for means of preventing war, was usually through the reformed behaviour of states: peace plans, treaties and proposals, negotiations, or international law and arbitration between all groups and peoples. This search developed further in the concepts of civil disobedience, mediation, conflict resolution, and then non-violence. In the 1890s, there was a great surge of support for such initiatives, the origins of which date back earlier than the Peace of Westphalia (1648). Elite plans and proposals for peace and disarmament had emerged even before the Quakers took them up and became widespread in European ruling circles during the carnage of the Thirty Years War (1618–48). The Quakers (for example, Penn) adopted some of these ideas in America and combined them with ideas of positive peace and a non-violent social order (Woolman) and international harmony to parallel the more cosmopolitan and visionary ideas of the Enlightenment humanists. The ideas of Liberal Internationalism thus gave the peace plans of the seventeenth and eighteenth centuries a broader base in organized popular opinion and political pressure: public opinion on war began to coalesce and to matter.

The first peace societies were formed in the early nineteenth century. Preventing war through international organization was closely linked to the third fundamental dimension—universalism, whether religious or humanistic, the cosmopolitan ethic that sprang from both the Enlightenment and earlier religious ideals of a universal or transnational church—that was to remain basic in peace movement activity and thought. With the growth of socialism, a new form of this internationalist ethic emerged to complete a peace perspective based on the relativity of national boundaries and frontiers and the ultimate limitation of the sovereignty of states.

These developments did not provide a united strategy or ideology for the early modern peace movement, but it did lay the foundations for a simple lowest common denominator of action and aims: namely, the survival of the species, the eventual elimination of war, and the basic unity of human society. It was this common platform that spurred the long delayed but deeply rooted reaction to the arms race in the early twentieth century.

Liberal Internationalism has often been termed "pacificism" since it aims to avert war but never renounces its use, or participation in it, as absolute *pacifists* do. This distinction did not become clear until 1914 when the peace movement shattered—split between its "pacifist" and "pacificist" wings. The latter and more numerous segment was willing to support the war in most cases. The liberal internationalists had formed the International Peace Bureau (1892), associated with the great peace conferences at The Hague, and agitated for a League of Nations (after 1920, supporting it through the League of Nations Unions). They also stressed civilian democratic control of war (via the Union of Democratic Control in Britain) with protection of civil liberties, as against military autocracy.

What hindered the liberal internationalist dream were the geopolitical developments which preceded the 1914–18 war. After the American and French revolutions, Europe witnessed the spread of nation states, mass conscripted armies, and industrial bases for militarism and imperial expansion. One of the key intellectual debates in the peace movement was between a non-conformist, free-trade liberalism that saw global capitalism as creating a new war-less world, and socialism which saw instead in capitalism the creation of a highly militarized, exploitative and centralized state system of enormous destructive capacity. Nobel's peace prize symbolized this basic ambiguity.

Emergence of the Modern Peace Movement

In the wake of the butchery of the Napoleonic wars, these ideas jostled each other in a somewhat unresolved and kaleidoscopic scatter of peace societies and pressure groups. Whilst many of them remained religious in character, the secular ideas of the *Aufklärung*, the development of modern ideological formulae, began to play a more dominant role. The idea of a "workers' strike against war" was heard for the first time. With the French revolution and the *levée en masse*, the reality both of the "peoples' army" and the ambiguities of the French "wars of liberation" in Europe soon became apparent. The latent dilemmas of violent social change were answered in part by Utopian and communitarian views of social change without violence, or at least without resort to arms. From now on the peace movement would be divided over the ethics and issues of "just wars", whether by progressive states or progressive oppositional groups. In the 1860s, the peace movement and indeed pacifists such as Quakers found themselves divided over a war that could emancipate black slaves in 1863. Time and time again in the nineteenth and twentieth centuries, this pattern would be repeated. The peace movement would divide over whether a war was "just" or "progressive", whether the evil to be overcome was any greater than the injustice and violence of the war or violence apparently needed to succeed, and whether military service—the "democratization of the means of violence" by conscription—might itself be a progressive phenomenon.

One can term these nineteenth century groups "modern" not because they were secular since they overlapped with religious nonconformity, but because they sought to organize public opinion in society either to create new institutions—like the Interparliamentary Union (IPU), the Red Cross and the Postal Union—which would have a bearing on peace, or to pressure existing politicians and structures to change their ways or introduce new policies or institutions. Although reformists, they inevitably paved the way for the new socialist oriented peace and anti-militarist concern which aimed to mobilize peoples to create a new war-less world society—even if it meant the violent overthrow of the old order. As the public became more involved in war through conscription, the killing of civilians, and new communications, so too did organized opinion on war grow.

Conscription and War Resistance

The peace movement's third major tradition of anti-conscriptionism was often linked to liberal issues of civil rights or the liberty of the individual. But it also coincided with religious nonconformity such as Quakerism in witness against war (conscientious objection), and with socialist resistance to war especially by left labour unions (the CGT in France). But even before modern conscription began in France in 1793, war and military service had in many countries at different times been opposed by the poor and the illiterate: inarticulate peasants and crafts people;

persecuted religious sects and communities; emigrants and immigrants. Whilst not formally part of the peace movement, these people constituted a vast reservoir of discontent that was drawn into religious and political activity by certain intellectual currents in socialism (for example, Anarchism and Syndicalism) and the charismatic anarcho-pacifism of Tolstoy in the Slav countries. A substantial following had developed by 1900, influencing Gandhi and millions of religious pacifists in Tsarist Russia.

From early Christian times, many religious communities desired to resist war, or at least to distance the religious group and the individual from the institution of war and the performance of military service. This constituted one of the moral and political foundations for the more modern "civic right" of conscientious objection, a claim which secular liberal internationalists, socialist war resisters, members of other churches (including other peace sects) and international organizations came to support in different ways, at different times, and to different degrees. By the twentieth century, it was being claimed as a basic human right. During the 1914–18 war, this element was to prove of crucial importance in sustaining the peace movement and anti-conscriptionism in wartime, and in building the new anti-war movements at the end of the war. However, as will be seen, these nonconformist inspirational roots did not produce a single or uniform socialist response to war and conscription. Socialists were deeply divided over the progressive character of conscription and the justification of progressive war.

Socialism and the Peace Movement:
Militarism and Anti-Militarism

Socialism coincided with the fourth element in the inspirational roots of the peace movement: the necessity for social and human change, that war is linked to problems of economic injustice and political repression, to the selfishness of narrow élites, of powerful ruling groups, and national and imperial as well as racial chauvinsim. Marxists and non-Marxists alike continue to be divided over the role of the nation state as an apt vehicle for socialist change, on the necessity for revolutionary violence, and the desirability of socialist participation in existing capitalist governments. And by no means were all socialists anti-conscriptionist or internationalist (or even anti-militarist). It is no wonder then that all the debates and proclamations of the Second International came to nothing in 1914, despite the rhetoric of the Stuttgart Resolution of 1904.

The socialist peace tradition can be best broken down into two main dimensions: "socialist war resistance" (as typified by the CGT in France), and "Socialist Internationalism" that was partly taken over by "Communist Internationalism" after 1917.

Socialist war resistance opposed, through direct grass roots actions like the Barcelona Strike of 1909, militarist governments, conscription, and war preparations which they perceived to be integral aspects of capitalism, imperialism and class rule. Whilst some Marxists such as Liebknecht and Luxembourg may be identified with this first dimension, it was mainly non-Marxist socialists, anarchists and syndicalists (often from outside the Second International) who organized this proletarian anti-conscriptionism (usually through the labour unions) into an anti-war movement. In the period before 1914, socialist anti-militarists like Keir Hardie in Britain, Karl Liebknecht in Germany and Domela Niuwenhuis in Holland tried to link their socialist critique to the idea of practical war *prevention*. If the organized producers, now numbering tens of millions in Europe, could strike in unison across national frontiers against war, then the militarists and nationalists, generals, emperors, tsars and capitalist-backed governments would be immobilized by mass non-co-operation. Anti-militarist strikes did take place before and, also, after 1914; the dream of a general strike of workers of all countries against war did not die with the August mobilizations, but led on to other political action during the war and after.

In the anti-war opposition from 1880–1918, one can distinguish the existence of a socialist, Marxist anti-militarist tradition. Admittedly Marx himself contributed little to this argument, particularly for those revolutionary Marxists like Liebknecht and Luxembourg who were among the socialists who most resolutely opposed the war in 1914–1918. Liebknecht had opposed the idea prevalent amongst many socialists that conscription created a "people's army". Rather, he argued, it created "an army against the people" and could not be an instrument for socialism. Luxembourg questioned whether progressive national wars between the increasingly militarized states were possible any longer, though Lenin advocated nationalist "wars of defence". (Marx had established a tradition of seeking to establish the more "progressive" of mililtary antagonists in each war, one that many Marxists continued to follow.) Luxembourg, however, was far more critical than Lenin of the effect that revolutionary war could have on revolution itself, and believed that opposition to violence was (like freedom and democracy) essential to socialism.

Yet the Marxist anti-militarist tradition, despite the courageous sophistication of Leibknecht and Luxembourg, was always a weak one. The rich socialist anti-militarist tradition was overwhelmingly non-Marxist and often anti-Marxist. Niewenhuis, Proudhon, Herve, Keir Hardie, Debs, De Ligt, and the mass syndicalist anti-militarism before 1914 often found themselves opposed by the Marxists in the Internationals. Marxists supported the expulsion of libertarian anti-militarists, and Marxist support for the Stuttgart Resolution was actually a tactical shift in emphasis from practical steps to *prevent* war. The basic problem was not the horror of war but who was fighting whom. Indeed, since Engels campaigned for conscription, war as an institution has been discussed little within Marxist theory.

Socialism was divided between its anti-militarist and militarist traditions. Since the Russian Civil War, the latter has predominated. In the 50 years before that, a heroic anti-militarist tradition had evolved, and at the turn of the twentieth century appeared to be in the ascendant. Socialist anti-militarism preceded Marxism, and was often in tension with it during this crucial half-century. However, the national mobilizations of August 1914 and the military consolidation of the Russian state after 1918 reversed that relationship and made socialist militarism the key factor in world politics.

Revolutionary socialists like Lenin and Luxembourg also saw in the war a new chance to organize the mobilized producers against their officers and rulers as war weariness grew. At the Zimmerwald Conference, the notion of revolutionary defeatism was born, turning the armed conflict between states into a conflict between classes—a war within a war. In a number of European countries, and a number of armies, the idea grew that peace would have to be made by attacking those ruling groups responsible for war (Peace through Revolution). Later in the war, in the French and British armies, massive mutinies occurred; by 1917, the mood in the Russian army and, by 1918, the German army had gone beyond mutiny to revolutionary discontent and mass desertion.

But part of the reason for the failure of 1914 was due to that other socialist peace tradition, Socialist Internationalism, and its inability to act in a practical transnational way. Unlike socialist war resistance, it was a movement of intellectuals, party leaders and organizers, not so rooted in popular movements and local communities [see Table 3.2]. Moreover, it was more closely linked to the sentiments of national parties and union leaders. Like the socialist war resisters, it indulged in the rhetoric of war prevention and anti-militarist strikes, and it was much less convinced than liberal internationalists about the possibilities of agreements between existing states.

On the other hand, Socialist Internationalism took the nation state for granted and was largely wedded to advancing within that framework. In 1914, one socialist party after another succumbed to the call for national unity and voted war credits. Only a minority of socialist anti-militarists and internationalists defied this debacle. When the socialist movement might have become more fundamentally anti-militarist given the appalling experiences of 1914–19, it turned in the opposite direction because of the perceived need to defend the Russian revolution. The revolutionary tradition had become militarized as well as "state-" and nation-centred.

The Twentieth Century Peace Movement: A New Beginning

Despite the hardships and traumas of 1914–22, a number of peace traditions went through a period of renewal. Several key international peace organizations such as Women's International League for Peace and Freedom (WILPF), the International Fellowship of Reconciliation (IFOR) and War Resisters' International (WRI) emerged. Moreover, a new form of integral pacifism was born that was largely secular (and often socialist) in character. It drew on all the previous traditions and was more radical than pre-1914 pacifism, linking international war resistance, anti-conscription and civil libertarianism with schemes of Utopian social (if not always socialist) change. These changes were to be brought about by the new non-violent direct action techniques of Gandhi that were publicized by Rolland and others in Europe after 1918, rather than by the violent class war still advocated by many socialist anti-militarists. In many countries, branches of the War Resisters' International were formed which expressed this radical synthesis, both socialist and anti-conscriptionist, forged during the war and now related to minority strands (conscientious objection, feminism and libertarianism).

In charting the sociology and history of the peace movement, two of its major peaks in terms of mass public support occurred before and after the first (1914–18) "Great" European war. From the late 1880s until 1914, and from the 1920s until the mid-1930s, one can talk of a mass peace movement certainly in Europe and the United States (as one can again in the 1960s and 1980s). The situation of the western peace movement as it reached its first peak of support between

TABLE 3.2

The nation state frame and the detachment of war resistant groups

Social Group	Communal Base	Transnational Orientation
Peasants	Tribe Village Kinship system Church (religious sect)	Cross frontier "Pan-isms" and itinerant and nomadic groups
Emigrants/ Immigrants	Rural village Urban village Ethnic ghettos Migrant subculture	Non-national territoriality Cross-national experience Dual nationality
Religious (e.g. Protestant/ non-Conformist sects)	Religious community Rural setting Social isolation	Migration/spirituality A-political, non-national orientations (universalism)
Unincorporated Workers	Isolated occupations industries. Labour camps, working class subcultures	Transnationalist/Internationalist ideas (migration) "Solidarity" actions
International Socialists	Political cells and organizations Trade unions (syndicalists) Working class communities, co-operatives and Bourses du Travail	Conferences (Internationals) Speaking tours, etc. Exile Contact in war situation or by migration

Specific Examples of These Groups in Varieties of War Resistance

Conscientious objectors	Religious sects, peace churches, Socialist Internationalists, Libertarians and secular pacifists Anarchists	As above As above As above
Non-co-operators and non-registrants (Absolutists)	Anarchists, socialists (Transnational theory) Peasants Some sects (Witnesses) Absolutist pacifist	As above As above Migration
Deserters	No specific social category, may form communities in exile Ethnic minorities (e.g. national groups)	Foreign service Travel Migration (As peasants above)
Émigrés from draft or conscription	Young people Religious groups Peasants, political objectors	Cross national borders— may re-emigrate

58 The Role of Social Movements

1890–1900 reflects, as we have shown, its prior origins and the development of peace groups and organizations in which some initiated this impressive growth and others jumped on the bandwagon of an emergent peace movement.

Both Socialist Internationalism and anti-militarism suffered near terminal defeat in 1914, but socialist war resistance had continued (sometimes illegally) in many belligerent countries. In fact, certain new peace traditions emerged as understanding of the nationalist mobilizations grew. During the war, these various traditions overlapped, coexisted and fused, or were renewed. War resisters in prison included religious pacifists, anti-conscriptionists—in Britain where conscription was introduced in 1915–16, they were organized into the No Conscription Fellowship, an organization headed by Fenner Brockway, Bertrand Russell and Clifford Allen—and socialist anti-militarists of various hues.

A major new force was feminist anti-militarism. Even before 1900, a new transnational women's peace movement had begun to assert an identity of its own. It created groups and brought together Marxist, socialist, anarchist and liberal women, feminists and non-feminists, those involved in the suffrage movement and those from Christian backgrounds, all united by the ideals of a distinctive role for women on the issue of peace and female unity across national boundaries even in wartime. Inspired by women such as Adams, Pankhurst, Jacobs, von Suttner, Schwimmer, Eastman, Luxembourg and Goldman, by 1914, these women had created a feminist peace tradition in its own right. The war-time meeting at The Hague of over 1,000 women (some from the United States) in 1915 that founded WILPF exemplified this new transnational movement.

The secular pacifism of the war years grew in the 1920s into movements like the No More War Movement in Britain (and later the PPU of the 1930s), and Liberal Internationalism regrouped in organizations such as the League of Nations Union and the German Peace Society. Protestant religious pacifism was now co-ordinated by the International Fellowship of Reconciliation with Quakers continuing in key roles. Small numbers of Catholic pacifists were also now grouping in Pax Christi. As for socialist anti-militarists and internationalists, they submerged themselves in the broader peace coalitions (and in Britain the ILP). Socialist Internationalism tended to merge either with social democracy, Liberal Internationalism and the League, or else identified with the socialist militarism and the geopolitical interests of the Soviet Union after 1920.

As communism retreated to its Russian base, a new internationalism, that of the Comintern, dominated by the Russian state, occupied the vacuum left by the Second International, and played a leading role in the mass peace fronts emerging in the late twenties and thirties. With the domination of the pro-Russian communist parties and the rise of fascism in Italy and Germany, the independent socialist anti-militarist tradition became a minority one. Comintern nationalism practised effective "entryism" in the peace movements of the twenties and thirties, but switched to anti-fascist rather than peace activity. However, it did establish national peace committees, later linked to the World Peace Council, which played significant roles.

By 1932, the peace movements in Italy, Germany and Russia had already been crushed or had disappeared. In Japan, it was harassed. But in the United States, Britain, the Netherlands, and to some extent in France and Scandinavia, mass peace movements still thrived.

TWO PATHS OF EVOLUTION
IN THE MODERN PEACE MOVEMENT

The European peace movements gathered strength during the arms race that led to the war of 1914–18. In its wake, a new mass movement based on revulsion at the nature of the conflict arose. But by the 1930s the peace movement was focused on the renewed arms race and the rise of fascism. However, a fundamental divide had opened up after 1918. One tendency was to organize public opinion to reform the world system of nation states either through a League of Nations, or hegemony by an enlightened power or powers. The other tendency was to stress increasing claims against the state system associated with extra-parliamentarist strategies of social change: extension of the rights of conscience, resistance to conscription, civil disobedience and anti-militarist direct action (radical non-violence and transnational and subcultural identification).

In the short term, both these tendencies in the peace movement were doomed to failure given the context of national rivalries and the nascent period of political autocracy. Indeed the peace movements in this period achieved few manifest victories. The establishment of the League, the creation of a new socialist state, the Kellogg-Briand Pact, the widespread acceptance of peace propaganda, all could not arrest the drift towards militarization and the war of 1939.

The latent effectiveness of the peace movement in preventing even worse militarist excess is impossible to measure. All that can be claimed is that the peace movement evolved new perspectives from the disaster of 1914, maintained a moral critique of war, accumulated new peace traditions and acquired (but only temporarily) a new mass base. It failed to halt the arms race after 1930, as it had failed after 1900, and failed in most of its other stated goals. Also, several key peace traditions suffered dramatic discontinuities.

Still, ideas and organizations were created in these three decades which remained alive and active later. They provided links to strategies for peace and disarmament in the later years of the twentieth century, when a broad coalition of peace constituencies—like that which grew in the years 1900–14—re-emerged to form the contemporary movement.

The Peace Movement as a Global Movement

The rise of fascism and the cataclysm of the 1939–45 war led to another profound disjuncture in the peace movement. Peace organizations and ideas remained, but not a peace movement. Indeed, this period from the growing protests against civilian bombing in the 1940s until the rising tide of concern in the mid-fifties is the longest single caesura in the two hundred year history of the peace movement. It can be best explained by the partial relegitimation of war in the face of fascism, East and West, and by extension in defending liberties against autocracy by force of arms. In the period before and after the war of 1914–18, it is plausible to argue that the silent majority became sceptical of war as an instrument of politics and that almost all nation states were considered quasi-legitimate. Ironically the subsequent democratization of a number of states and the establishment of socialism in one country led to a more widespread legitimation of war by socialism and liberalism through expanding communications and literacy. The anti-fascist fronts of the thirties laid the groundwork for the "just war" theory of World War II. The silent majorities before and after 1945 supported the war alliances: the "unjust" stereotype of war from 1918 was replaced by a grudging acceptance of big battalions, and apostasy from pacifism and anti-militarism lasted beyond 1945. This is the only way to explain the delayed reaction to nuclear weapons (in Japan there are 'some specific circumstances). The state system itself shared in the general legitimation of the peace of the victors despite the bloc bifurcation and the new arms race. This acceptance of a "just nuclear peace" was paralleled by the shift of liberation movements to anti-colonial war in Asia and Africa.

During this hiatus, perhaps for the first time, it was events, movements and ideas outside the white western and industrial countries that became significant in the peace movement. Gandhi's movement to liberate India came to fruition in 1947 through an overwhelming non-violent social movement that linked itself explicitly to peace. The first use of atomic weapons took place on an Asian country, Japan, whose earlier peace movement had been shattered by fascist militarism. A new peace movement arose that was partly inspired by the witness of the atomic victims, the "Hibakusha". In many countries, peace became identified again with social justice, the end of racial and colonial oppression. Many countries tried to follow India's example, some, like Gandhi, through non-violent or peaceful means. The repression of Indo-Chinese independence led to a global anti-war reaction. Nuclear testing in the Pacific was responded to by transnational peace voyages. There were international protests in the French Sahara. The movement of non-aligned states emerged after Bandung with great portents, and involved mostly less developed states. Tanzania and Cuba were hailed as new models of development.

So far the peace movement has largely been analysed as a phenomenon developing in the western or Christian countries, in the industrial democracies, or the English-speaking world. But it is also arguable that Gandhi's movement, the response to Hiroshima and Nagasaki, and the influence of socialism—first Russian, then Chinese and other more indigenous forms—on liberation movements such as the Indo-Chinese began to shift the locus of the peace movement to a more global plane. Rising radiation levels throughout the world due to nuclear testing by several countries, especially in the Pacific, had led to a global outcry. Certainly the emerging peace movements of the northern hemisphere were beginning to find new echoes and counterparts in the South. Also, human or civil rights came to be seen as integral to peace, as in the massive US movement for black social justice associated with Martin Luther King and its advocacy of non-violence, and which linked itself to struggles in black Africa.

The lack of opposition against the growing atomic arsenal of the United States provided a vacuum for the World Peace Council to step in with its Stockholm Peace appeal in 1950, a move that gained mass support despite its aligned origins given the US monopoly of the genocidal weapons. Most of the old peace traditions had survived by the late 1950s, when the upsurge of public opinion against nuclear arms grew in Europe, North America, Australasia and elsewhere, but it can be argued that the then "nuclear pacifism", such as that of the British Campaign for Nuclear Disarmament (CND), while drawing on the old traditions was actually itself a *new type*—reflecting the drastically altered character of war and weaponry. By 1965, US involvement in Indo-China and the repression of the non-violent movements there forged an international coalition.

[*   *   *]

The Changing Context in the West

The position of the peace movement is now almost unrecognizable from that of the mid-1970s. The official centre of gravity, of conventional wisdom, has moved towards the peace movement's platform: in a small way this is shown in Europe by the dramatic move in moderate opinion from 40 per cent to 60 per cent against "cruise", Pershing and Trident, between 1981 and 1983. Such shifts give much greater "democratic" legitimacy to civil disobedience and direct action. Moreover, the non-violent compaigns shift the focus back from the negotiations table to communal grass roots action from where the long term visions and strategies spring. At Greenham, in international camps, with mass confrontations, transnational debate and dialogue, the peace movement has made a strategic leap from communal base to global strategy.

Across the Atlantic, the issues of the American peace movement such as the Nuclear Freeze Campaign are difficult to integrate within the new European peace movement because they represent a substantial step back for almost every peace group. That the US movement is also concerned to prevent further Vietnams in Latin America is also a key difference. Of course, there is much activity in the United States on NFZ's and the MX, on SDI, on "first strike", or "first use", on deployment in Europe that is complementary to the European movement.

To some degree, the two movements understand each other's different contexts. Tactical differences in the short-term do not necessarily disguise the fundamental solidarity of the long-term vision. In parts of the movement, there does exist a somewhat unstable peace alliance between religious pacifists (including Quakers), nuclear pacifists, pro-Moscow peace fronts and old style communists, but it fails to grasp the real political issues. The danger is that simple, national campaigns like those against deployment or for the freeze could reproduce the mistakes of the past and founder on leadership splits. For many countries, the pressures against "going it alone" will be massive internally and, from the United States, externally. Only broad internationalist stances with an alternative foreign and defence policy, can sustain such moves. But while "alternative defence" commissions and other groups have worked feverishly to provide such policies and to help educate public opinion for such options, the peace movement has largely shunned such platforms for a variety of reasons. Thus the emergence of the European Nuclear Disarmament movement has a distinctly independent and cross-national character more reminiscent of pre-1917 internationalism. Its great danger remains that it too will be a Eurocentric movement, a movement of European leaders, parties and intelligentsia rather than of community and grass roots impulses.

THE EBB AND FLOW OF MASS PEACE PROTEST

At this point it is possible to make some estimate *not* of the success of the peace movement in terms of goals, but in terms of popular mobilization at given periods over the last 150 years. Despite successive defeats in which the movement was reduced to prophetic minorities, it revived, and with it further traditions accumulated. Using such world-wide data as the reported size of demonstrations and anti-war strikes, the circulation of peace newspapers, numbers arrested for anti-militarist activity, organizational memberships of peace groups, and the overall number of "war resisters", legal conscientious objectors and draft evaders, it is possible to come to some quantitive (*not* qualitative) estimate of numerical peace movement strength in each period.

Of course, such data is highly problematic. The "troughs and peaks" in numbers appear at different times in different countries: the peace movement was very large in America and Britain *after* 1932, at the very time it was being crushed in Germany, the Soviet Union, Japan, Italy and elsewhere. Gandhi's movements in India (1917–46) has a profile quite different from peace movements in the West. The 1950s anti-nuclear movement in Japan emerged some years before the first western ones, as did its second wave in the 1970s. The Dutch movement was stronger in the early 1920s than in the 1930s. And in the 1970s, Greenpeace Pacific activity had little western support.

The profile in this paper is based mainly on historical evidence from the northern and western movements and the English-speaking areas, and even so cannot reflect all variation or depth or quality of participation accurately. For example, 6,000 conscientious objectors ("subjects") willing to face imprisonment *may* have more impact on a society than 600,000 organized ("objects") demonstrators. A number of sources show also that the decline in the peace movement in 1939–40 (for some countries in 1914–18) was neither as sudden, dramatic nor complete as conventional wisdom once held. The external environment shifts so dramatically, however, that in a period of war mobilization a peace movement can *seem* to "disappear" when it may only be "underground", or as in the case of pacifism in Britain between 1939–41, continue growing organizationally.

Nevertheless, it can be seen that there is a tendency for peace movements to gather greatest strength before wars—at the time of accelerating arms *races* rather than after wars (1918 being one major exception). However, the *new* peace *traditions* tend to emerge during or immediately after wars (1815, 1915, 1920, etc.). What such a profile does not show is the degree of feeling, new ideas, or commitment expressed in each period. In some periods, for example, the United States in the thirties or the Soviet-backed movements, one gets the impression of large numbers mobilized but which are of superficial segmental commitment, or segmental attachment. In retrospect, size of mobilization is an unsatisfactory indicator of either effectiveness or success, as the popular mass movements of the 1930s or the 1950 Stockholm Appeal indicate. One can measure effectiveness because in most cases the peace movements made explicit a particular objective or goal: some sought to abolish war (pacifism or pacificism); some opposed particular wars on liberal or socialist grounds; some aspired to limit or prevent war by negotiated disarmament, international law and peace treaties; and some opposed specific dimensions of armaments and war (such as conscription). In some cases, such as with the socialist movements, anti-war movements fused with movements for social change to abolish the war-making society and associated institutions. These and a number of later peace movements (for example, the Gandhian) had positive as well as negative objectives of peace; not only did they wish to create a non-violent or more just, equitable and harmonious society, they also linked with Utopian and communitarian movements.

With peace movements, as with other social movements, the results of public activity are always ambiguous. Like other great social change or social protest campaigns, they have both latent and manifest consequences. They may actually prolong the wars they aim to stop. They may alienate public opinion. Their relative success or failure always depends on other independent or external factors, not just the degree or level of activity achieved. This has always been one of the weakening illusions of peace movements: the structural and historical context of the deeply humanist abolitionist movement against slavery, for example, was just as, or more, important than, the efforts of the abolitionist campaigns themselves. Moreover, the abolition of slavery left or even produced *new* evils, and involved the injustices and carnage of a terrible civil war that split the American peace movement and virtually destroyed it, whilst racist oppression soon grew in virulent forms.

A further variation of this critique is the theory of "cycles" or of political "generations". For each wave of the peace movement, commitment appears inevitably cyclical: a theory involving "cycles of protest" argues that movements have an inherent limit, such as the length of time people will devote energy and resources to a single issue or movement unless institutionalization takes place. Generational explanations stress the span of youthful involvement from 17 to 25, roughly the years of compulsory military service for males. These years may be relatively free of social ties and commitments and thence can be spent in radical movements where risks may be taken in social protest. Youth involvement in peace politics is undoubtedly a generational experience, as transient as military service in most countries—a few intense years and it is over. A movement that can institutionalize youth involvement, however, can capture a generation. The attendant danger of such a development is inflexibility and dogmatism, an introverted, "retreatist" sectarianism, where the generational experience is frozen into dogma and slogans which are damaging to the peace movement. Thus people "drop in", and out, of anti-war and other movements in large numbers—but may and do return ten or twenty years later. Evidence of the two phases of nuclear opposition shows recruitment from both the new younger age groups and the earlier generation. The cycles may vary from three or four, to ten or even fifteen years, but the time span appears to be getting progressively shorter. Without success, and after a few years, fatigue, cynicism and despair may predominate; or people may turn to other issues.

Another factor often cited to explain failure has to do with social class. It has been typically argued that peace movements have drawn from too narrrow a social base to succeed (for example, that they have been "middle class"). The Marxist charge that much *individualist* pacifism was originally "petty bourgeois" had some truth. Equally, Liberal Internationalism or "pacificism" was overwhelmingly middle class and "respectable" or professional (male, white and middle-aged most of the time also). Yet other peace traditions, like anti-conscriptionism, have appealed in *all* countries and to all classes. Socialist anti-militarism was overwhelmingly working class and Socialist Internationalism represented both the labour aristocracy and the independent intellectuals. Equally many fundamentalist peace sects have been found amongst the very poor, the peasantry, and ethnic minorities.

What is true is that only in rare periods has a really broad social coalition been forged. This issue of "coalitions" and why they fell apart is also related to whether peace movements have too narrow or too wide a programme. Are they single-issue (or single-war or -weapons) movements, or broad ideological and programmatic movements with manifestos for social change? The temporary coalitions of the mass peace movements have usually included both tendencies, as does the current anti-nuclear movement. As a result, basic splits are likely on tactics, methods, goals and alignments. They occur most when the specific, concrete successes sought are lacking—for example, if a movement fails to prevent a new weapons system from being deployed, having pledged to do so.

The "lowest common denominator" movement aims to avoid such splits by demanding consensus on two or three simple demands that cut across other allegiances, religious or political: "Refuse the Missiles", "No Visits of Nuclear Armed Ships", "End the Draft", "No to Napalm", "Ceasefire Now", "Troops Home", "No Nuclear Weapons on Our Soil" and so on. Yet these movements can easily be co-opted or defused by alternative policies or conventional weapon systems. Or temporary delays can allow the movement to subside (as may be an official tactic in Europe). Either way, the coalition can still fall apart, even if the aims or goals remain narrow. The obverse is not much better. A diffuse general programme of peace has often been successful in mobilizing broad masses, but unsuccessful in making any political impact. It is often a more visionary *element* in a diffuse coalition—for example, the Greens in Germany, draft resisters in the United States, women's peace camps in England—who provide the most dynamic thrust or represent the symbolic leading voice for the movement.

There is also a sociological approach which dismisses much peace protest at the grass roots as "expressive" or millennial rather than "instrumental" or pragmatic; as being not really about war or nuclear weapons, but a channel of expressing personal or social alienation. Whilst such an argument tends to be conservative and can be abused, it would be wrong to dismiss the possibility that latent motivations for involvement in peace politics exist, especially among the prophetic minorities. Certainly the division between the "blind activists" of the grass roots and the "pure theorists" in the leadership can produce charge and counter-charge of impure (or anti-intellectual) motivation. Certainly the lack of a strategy for popular political change can compound such frustrations, and movements that are reactive rather than creative fall victim to this type of introversion and in-fighting, especially when success does not come as quickly as is hoped.

A general problem for social and political movements in opposition has been that of participation in government through individual co-optation or group incorporation. Individuals can be manipulated and bought off; protests can become ritualistic; an élitist leadership may not wish to lose its prestige, its organization, its money or its position. The elevation of leaders into any national establishment or parliament can weaken and discourage the grass roots who feel betrayed; or raise false hopes that are quickly shattered as has happened wherever local peace movements have looked to established leaders and politicians within the structure of the state.

As a result, several of the peace traditions analysed have displayed a deep ambivalence or distrust about operating within the state system—or attempted to transcend it. This was most marked before and after World War I, and again in the 1980s. Movements in this situation can become a safety valve, rather than a challenge to the war-making system. A clear case is where conscientious objection is drawn into the actual machinery of the war effort as in the United States during World War II; or where socialist MPs vote for war credits (World War I) or nuclear bases (after 1963 in Britain), having been previously pledged to oppose them.

Peace movements can of course be repressed and severely harassed—leaders jailed, even killed. The American anti-war movement of 1917 was virtually destroyed physically by police raids, arrests and vigilante action (1917–20), and the leaders were given long terms in prison. The civil disobedience campaign in Britain was badly shaken by long-term imprisonment of a few of its leaders (1961–62). The South Vietnamese Buddhists were attacked, imprisoned and killed by both sides (1965–75). The independent peace movements in the USSR and Eastern Europe, and the peace movement in Turkey, have recently suffered similar setbacks. In Nazi Germany and other fascist countries, a number of peace leaders were executed; similarly with some pacifists after the Russian Revolution, and in Japan before the Second World War. But this does not provide a general explanation of the failure of peace movements. Surveillance, the limitation of human rights and censorship *are* key issues for peace movements, but do not constitute a sufficient, only a contributory, cause of decline.

Of course the role of media suppression or opposition is equally crucial; adverse conditions can pre-empt the emergence of peace movements, as in many developing countries. However, the experiences of the last peace movement since the "conspiracy of silence" of the late fifties are that the movement can have an impact on the communications systems of some societies and that such media are not permanently monolithic. The censorship and bias attending the peace movement, and which culminated in the banning of a major anti-nuclear film in Britain in 1965, was countered especially in the Vietnam years by a number of alternative strategies. The movement first established its own media or was reported in an alternative media (reaching over two million people in the United States for example). This had an impact on the dominant media itself by outflanking its newsgiving function, but also trained individuals who would later "enter" the more established networks and presses. The diversity of roles and functions at different levels proved after the Indo-China experience that there was always potentially another voice. As a real alternative, the movement's media was limited, but as a lever on existing channels it was significant.

Finally, but not least important, is the sense of *impotence* or paralysis that sets into many movements. This is the feeling of social despair, that nothing can be done, that the problem of war is beyond human control. Despondency and cynicism, even suicide or other forms of self-destruction, are common responses to the weakness and sense of failure that accompany many peace and social change movements as they enter their "troughs" or suffer major defeats. Among other solutions, this has led to a self-conscious attempt at "empowerment" based on the therapeutic politics of group affinity and solidarity.

[*   *   *]

PART ONE

CHANGES AND CONTINUITIES

General Introduction

The United Nations today is quite different from that envisioned by the founding framers in 1945. An overview of the record to date seems essential for understanding *where*—and *why*—the distance between promise and performance has been a fluctuating process over the years. There is need to conceptualize the development of the United Nations as an organic part of the world historical process rather than as a set of fixed institutional landmarks. We should reflect upon this world historical process to capture a more realistic baseline for our periodic assessment of the possibilities and limitations of the organization in our collective journey toward a more peaceful and just future world. A world order transformation is possible only if and when there is a close reciprocal conjunction between objective historical conditions and subjective global human endeavor.

The relationship between the UN and the global political context may be characterized in a variety of ways, ranging from the national power perspective that the UN simply mirrors, or even amplifies and distorts, realpolitik realities to the globalist idealpolitik perspective that the UN through its multilateral conference diplomacy serves as a complex and multilayered political system of contemporary international relations with specialized structures and processes capable of managing the global problems and in the process exerting a considerable influence in the shaping of the systemic environment. Should the UN be studied and understood mainly as a marginal instrument of foreign policy used and misused by states only to obtain their own narrow advantages? Or should the UN also be understood as an independent actor that serves as a teacher of systemic learning influencing the behavior states in world affairs?

The linkage between the world organization and the member states has always been ambiguous. Contrary to the popular belief, the founders did not achieve a clear mandate on a new world public order or a well-defined vision and role of the organization. Instead, several competing images of a postwar world order found their way into the UN Charter. The Security Council represented a significant expression of a condominial world order based upon the continuation of allied wartime consensus and collaboration among the Great Powers. The Big Five, in principle, were authorized to deal definitively with any threat to international peace and security in defense of the new status quo established by the victorious Allies. At the same time, such condominial aspirations were tempered with the more traditional statist claims by assuring that the Charter would preserve state autonomy, independence, and sovereignty and uphold the juridical equality of states regardless of size. The General Assembly, although lacking enforcement powers, was endowed with the more general functions of deliberating and recommending policy on an open-ended list of emerging global problems. The Economic and Social Council (ECOSOC), together with the specialized agencies, embodied a functionalist notion of seeking world order by attacking the root causes of war (poverty, ignorance, disease, human abuse) and by incrementally building a social and economic foundation for a warless world.

In a sense, the Charter system, as originally conceived, was more an expression reactive to the trauma of the past than a visionary blueprint for a future world order. It reflected the conceptualization of the causes of war and the conditions of peace as it emerged from the ashes of World War II. The regulation of armaments was not attempted. There was also a presumption that the major threats to world order would emanate from well-defined cases of international aggression. Hence, the major "peace-loving" powers—that is, the victorious Allies of World War II— assumed a special responsibility for maintaining the international peace. Such power to deal with the immediate causes and outbreaks of war was more centralized and more favored. On the other hand, the power to deal with the underlying causes of war was more diffused and less favored. It can be said that the Charter of the world organization embodied an indeterminate mandate in an atmosphere of ambivalence appealing to both statist instincts and globalist aspirations at the San Francisco Conference.

The UN can best be understood as an institutionalized response that drew on the experience and precedents of the League of Nations, but that attempted to learn from and move beyond the League's experience to create a more effective international political order. It was designed to overcome the League's failings in a number of ways, especially the ability to organize a response to the aggressions of the 1930s that led directly to World War II. First, the League reliance on absolute unanimity among members was abandoned. Under the UN Charter, collective action would require unanimity only among the powerful—the victorious Allies of World War II. There was no assumption that the Big Five would always remain united. Rather, the veto merely ensured that no Security Council policy would be authorized if it were vigorously opposed by any of the great powers. The veto was a mechanism for expressing and constraining, but not overcoming, the condominial conception of world order.

A second major shift of emphasis was the recognition that the UN was a globalist rather that a Eurocentric organization. The League's headquarters had been in Europe, and its prime movers, after the U.S. rejection, had been European states. The decision to locate the UN headquarters in New York City was believed likely to ensure active U.S. participation and thus was viewed as critical to the organization's success. More significantly, under the League, the Assembly had been viewed as a secondary organ, meeting from time to time but not making important, binding decisions. The UN's globalist outlook is reflected in the structure and functions envisioned for the General Assembly. The General Assembly was endowed with a broad—albeit still ambiguous—mandate, was expected to meet regularly, and embodied the principle of state equality (one state, one vote). Its increased stature and scope reflected the new realization that future problems would be global in nature and would thus require a broader base of representation.

The UN also differed from the League in its greater emphasis on economic and social objectives. Whereas the League had focused primarily on military and political questions, by 1939 the importance of economic and social issues was recognized, highlighted by the influential Bruce Commission. By April 1945, when the San Francisco Conference was convened, the notion that economic development and social justice were vitally important for ensuring peace became acceptable. The Charter spoke out not only of maintaining peace but also of promoting "social progress." And the grand design of the "United Nations system" incorporated a wide array of functional organs, such as the Economic and Social Council, the Trusteeship Council, and a multitude of specific functional specialized agencies.

A fourth shift in focus was the adoption of a political role for the secretary-general. Under the League, it had never been clear whether the secretary-general was to be a spokesman for the organization or merely a glorified clerk at the service of member states. The Charter established the Secretariat as one of the six principal organs, and this body was to undertake the administrative support service for the organization. However, the individual at its head—the secretary-general—was also expected to take personal initiatives in the resolution or abatement of international conflicts. The secretary-general has emerged not only as the chief officer of the organization but also as a global spokesperson who, depending on his capabilities and stature, has exerted a strong influence in his personal capacity, especially in peace and security settings. To be sure, this highest UN executive must remain sensitive at all times to the desires and priorities of the member states, but he is nevertheless in a unique position to present issues from a global perspective.

Did the founding fathers feel they were making a decisive break with the past, or did they simply view the new institution as tinkering with the previous Concert of Europe and League of Nations systems? There is a sense in which the Charter can be seen as charting, or at least enabling, a system-transforming path. The incorporation of phrases such as "we the peoples of the United Nations," the provisions on human progress, the possibility of transnational military forces for the organization, the power of the secretary-general to bring to the attention of the Security Council any matter that in his opinion may threaten international peace and security, and the granting of one vote to each member state in the General Assembly can all be interpreted as endowing the organization with a measure of "implied power" for the assumption and evolutionary expansion of its role as a supranational actor.

On the other hand, the UN's actual performance over the years does not support the transformation thesis. Rather, the overall record generally indicates that the UN has functioned primarily as a supplement to the state system in which the state actors still remain dominant in world affairs. What factors might account for this enduring gap between promise and performance? According to one interpretation, the Charter represents aspirations that were not expected to be implemented immediately but that were intended as long-term objectives toward which states should strive. Another explanation is that the founders expected a new world order to evolve, but that their hopes were dashed by the collapse of the wartime alliance and the onset of the Cold War. The first explanation suggests that the founders were not serious about their ideals, while the latter argues that they were prepared to take a radical step but that possibilities for transformation afforded by their handiwork were subverted by the superpower rivalry.

Perhaps a more plausible alternative explanation is that the founders represented a series of uneven mixtures between statist and globalist outlooks and that the constitution they produced reflected these divergent views and expectations. Of the founders, the Soviet Union, led by Stalin, was undoubtedly the most statist of the victorious Allies in 1945 and, was also the most suspicious about the threat to its sovereignty that might be posed by the new world organization. But, in fact, the European states—England and France—were only a half-step behind, and they did not have the Soviet problem of anticipating hostile voting majorities in the United Nations. The emphasis on state sovereignty, the safeguards against inter- ference in domestic jurisdiction, and the right to use force in self-defense limited the role and function of a supranational organization and suggested the persistence of statist norms. At the same time, the Charter also reflected the globalist outlook in the provisions by which the organization was mandated to preserve peace and promote human well-being, implying the development of some kind of global governance that would, if operative, truly transform international society.

The tension between these assumptions and approaches was not resolved at the founding conference in San Francisco. Instead, elements of each were embodied in the Charter for posterity to resolve. The Charter language is indeed ambiguous about whether it is transforming the state system into a supranational organization or simply facilitating the interaction of sovereign states. Because of their ambivalence, the founders built into the UN the potential to move in either direction, setting the new organization afloat in the sea of postwar global politics.

While the UN has not catalyzed any fundamental change in the state system, the organization has proved resilient in the domain of global low politics. The major concerns as well as the procedural emphasis of the UN have fluctuated to accord with the changing claims of the changing membership. At times the Security Council has predominated and at other times, the General Assembly. On occasions, the secretary-general has been a prominent international presence; on other occa- sions, he has not. An unforeseen array of peacekeeping operations has been developed as a politically more acceptable alternative to bridge the growing gap between what should be done in theory and what can be done in the practice of collective security, given the strength of context and considerations. All the changes have occured without major revision or amendment of the Charter. Formal change has only occurred three times, and then peripherally: once to enlarge the membership of the Security Council and twice to enlarge the membership of the ECOSOC.

While member states have shied away from proposals to reshape the UN, they have been receptive to informal adjustments through broad interpretations of the

Charter, such as the ruling that a permanent member of the Security Council can exercise its veto power only by casting a negative vote, not by absence or abstention. Other adjustments, such as the Uniting for Peace Resolution, which allows the transferring of security issues from the Security Council to the General Assembly if the former cannot act, have both reflected the will of the dominant majority and enabled the United Nations to adapt itself to the changing patterns of world politics. In a central respect, the Cold War rivalry between the two superpowers led to pressures to bend the organization in partisan directions and also posed obstacles to effective action in most war-generating situations. Persisting statism notwithstanding, the organization's ability to transform its agenda and modus operandi has at least helped to keep the UN relevant and useful enough to keep all its members as active participants. To date, Indonesia's brief withdrawal from the UN in 1965 is the only instance of defection by a member, but Indonesia quickly renewed its participation, making its conduct an exception that validates the norm.

During forty-five years of checkered developments, the United Nations has come to conjure up many divergent images in the eyes of its beholders. Indeed, the organization has a serious identity crisis today, as it has become all things to all nations. No consensual master concept or hegemonic leadership exists to provide direction and establish the role of the world organization. Instead, the lot of the organization is that the old U.S. hegemony, while not quite dead, no longer prevails, and the Third World challenge mounted so vigorously in the 1970s has dissolved. There are some recent signs that the cacophony of conflicting voices and visions of the UN's future may be giving way to a renewed quest for common grounds and for a new era of renewal and reform. The UN as a world historical process may be divided into six periods of postwar international politics keyed to the global political context in which the UN operates. Each period reflected and effected different modes of response from the world organization.

ALLIED UNITY (1945–1947)

The initial period of Allied unity and concert was one of the most successful periods in the UN-style management of international conflict. It may be more accurate to characterize this period as—and attribute its success to—unchallenged U.S. hegemony in the world organization. The Soviet Union chose not to invoke the veto during this period. As a result, the UN was able to build the support of its membership for quasimilitary operations in the abatement of conflict in the Balkans (UNSCOB), Indonesia (UNCI), Palestine (UNTSO), and Kashmir (UNMOGIP).

In low politics, too, this period witnessed the first big wave of restructuring with the establishment or revamping of functional intergovernmental organizations under the hegemonic leadership of the United States. Taking advantage of its military, economic, and ideological supremacy and of Soviet absence from most international regimes, the United States by and large succeeded in formulating the new norms and rules for the specialized agencies, including the three pillars of the postwar world economic order: the International Monetary Fund (IMF); the International Bank for Reconstruction and Development (the World Bank); and the General Agreement on Tariffs and Trade (GATT).

COLD WAR CONFLICT (1948-1960)

By 1948, the possibility of Allied unity and cooperation had been shattered beyond repair. NATO was formed in that year; in August, the UN Military Staff Committee brought its operation to a close, and the enforcement provisions of the Charter (Chapter VII) became a dead letter. The efforts to turn a wartime alliance into an international collective security regime were aborted by the growing conflict between the United States under Truman and the Soviet Union under Stalin. The outbreak of the Cold War, with each side viewing the other as an enemy to be checkmated in every arena including the UN, forced the organization to adapt to an environment very different from the one envisaged by the drafters of the Charter.

By late 1940s, then, the UN was already drawn into the Cold War confrontation between the two superpowers. Many of the issues that dominated the UN in the 1950s concerned military matters. On June 27, 1950, the Security Council voted, in the absence of the Soviet Union, that North Korea's invasion of South Korea was a breach of international peace and called for a cessation of the fighting, asking all UN members to help in the implementation of this resolution. The resulting UN operation was staffed and directed primarily by the United States. The Uniting for Peace Resolution, shifting authority to the General Assembly in the event that the Security Council was paralyzed by a veto, was a continuing effort by the United States to make the UN function, presuming a coincidence between priorities in Washington and the outlook of UN majorities.

Even the question of UN membership became a Cold War issue. Each side refused to permit applicant states from the other camp to join, fearing a shift in the balance of votes with the organization would adversely affect the overriding East-West rivalry in global politics. Finally, in 1955 a package deal was arranged that provided for sixteen new states to join. The membership has expanded subsequently and, with the exception of the long-contested Chinese representation issue, without serious restrictions concerning ideological balance.

Questions of military action seized the Council again in 1956 when fighting erupted in the Middle East. On this occasion, the United States and the Soviet Union took the same position—that France and Great Britain should withdraw from the occupied territory. Troop withdrawal was then accomplished under the auspices of a UN peacekeeping force. The Suez Crisis proved to be a turning point from collective security to peacekeeping. At the same time, the Soviet Union sent its troops into Hungary to put down a rebellion. Although this case was also brought before the Security Council, Soviet opposition prevented the organization from even sending a team of investigators to the scene. Thus, on those rare occasions when the superpowers took similar positions, peacekeeping was possible.

Although the UN agenda included items relating to economic and social welfare during the Cold War period, there was much greater emphasis on issues of peace and security. Pressure for ending colonialism was building in the UN debates, but the East-West split made it clear that the UN was in no position to launch new efforts in colonialism or development, which required cooperative action by the great powers for authorization or financial support. In a period when ideological struggle was viewed in zero-sum terms, the major powers chose to run their aid programs outside the organization so as to maintain control and exert maximum leverage. During these years, the UN did moderate some military conflicts and generally exerted a constructive influence in an ideologically divided world; however, the organization failed completely to provide an effective mechanism for maintaining international peace and security. This undertaking was discharged, as previously, by ascendent geopolitical forces, especially the two superpowers.

GROWING THIRD WORLD MAJORITY (1960–1972)

The 1960s witnessed some moderation between East and West and saw the rise— in numbers and importance—of Third World member states. Both changes were reflected in the way the UN operated and in the issues with which it dealt. Following the Cuban missile crisis of 1962, where the two superpowers faced each other at the nuclear brink and seemed mutually frightened by the experience, their relations moved progressively toward coexistence, détente, and rapprochement. Direct confrontation and efforts to control or to influence other nations to participate in bloc politics gave way to an acceptance of a standoff and a greater willingness to limit conflict for allegiance to the modalities of peaceful competition. Coinciding with improved East-West relations were the rapid rise of newly independent states and the concomitant expansion of membership in the United Nations. With the granting of independence to former colonies, beginning in the late 1950s and continuing throughout the 1960s, UN membership grew in waves from the original 51 to 160 in 1990.

The Declaration on the Granting of Independence to Colonial Countries and Peoples ("Decolonization Declaration"), adopted on December 14, 1960, marked a new chapter in UN history. The organization now had 100 member states, the majority of which had recently won their independence. The dominant concern of these new states was to reorient the UN toward their problems of decolonization, development, and depolarization (nonalignment). With the gradual disappearance of an automatic U.S. majority in the General Assembly, the Third World now had the votes to control the agenda and to pass resolutions, even if the organization was still dependent on the great powers for financial resources.

Therefore, in the 1960s the focus of UN activities began to shift to Third World concerns. No longer content to act as a buffer between the superpowers, the Third World emerged as a global actor with interests and goals of its own and viewed the UN as the logical place for pursuing them. As the Decolonization Declaration indicated, one primary concern of the Third World was independence for the remaining colonial territories. Through their active participation in the UN, the ex-colonies were able to put additional pressure on the colonial powers to dismantle what remained of their overseas empires. Accompanying the drive for independence was a push for development assistance, as shown in the establishment of a series of subsidiary organs (United Nations Conference on Trade and Development—UNCTAD; United Nations Development Programme—UNDP; and United Nations Industrial Development Organization—UNIDO) focused on a world development policy in the mid-1960s.

Similarly, in the field of peace and security, the UN focused more and more on questions of concern to the Third World. The Congo operation from 1960 to

1964, the most massive peacekeeping operation yet mounted by the UN and the UNFICYP, while justified on the basis of preserving peace, was closely linked both to the Cold War and to efforts to prevent the rise of blatant forms of neocolonialism.

The problem of striking a balance between peace and decolonization was also highlighted by India's invasion of the then-Portuguese colony of Goa in December 1961. India justified this use of force on the grounds that colonialism constitutes permanent aggression. In support of India's contention, Third World states argued that colonialism was such an injustice that it overrode the normal prohibition against the use of force. The Security Council debated the question but took no action, and India effectively ended Portuguese control of Goa by annexing the territory to India. China could as easily have annexed Macao and Hong Kong, but it did not do so because it benefited from the existence of capitalist windows to the world economy.

The responses of the great powers to growing Third World dominance included increasing emphasis on the Security Council where they had the veto, more restricted financial support for the organization, and rising skepticism about the organization's relevance to their own interests. This Third World ascendency also eroded public support for the UN, especially in the United States. By the early 1970s, the U.S. ideological hegemony in the General Assembly had collapsed. Even in the Security Council, where the drama of high politics is played out, the U.S. found itself isolated on key symbolic issues involving the Arab-Israeli conflict and South Africa, and became dependent on its veto to block decisions it opposed.

During the Nixon years, the United States argued that the UN had been reduced to an arena for propaganda contests and had lost its capacity to improve international relations due to the irresponsible actions of the Third World majority. Despite efforts to cut its proportion of the UN budget, vetoes on resolutions on South Africa and Israel, and verbal downgrading of the organization, the United States nevertheless did continue to see some role and relevance for the world organization in the Middle East as well as in functional issue areas such as the environment, drugs, technology, and health.

GLOBAL CONSCIOUSNESS-RAISING
AND BARGAINING (1972–1980)

The United Nations Conference on the Human Environment, held in Stockholm from June 5 to June 16, 1972, established a path-breaking model for the global politics of consciousness-raising and norm-setting through UN-sponsored multilateral conference diplomacy in the 1970s and beyond. The pattern and precedent established by the Stockholm Conference are for the General Assembly to convene a multilateral conference on an issue or problem of global concern and to formulate or reformulate a set of principles, to adopt a comprehensive program of action, and to create or revamp an institution to put into effect whatever the member states agreed to do.

The 1970s saw a new constellation of forces in the international system favorable to global consciousness-raising and bargaining: the Soviet-American détente, expanded bargaining power of the Third World acting as the Group of 77, and a series of global economic crises coupled with growing awareness of the global character of the human predicament. This resulted in a period of bargaining on both an East-West and a North-South axis about such issues as disarmament, trade and development, the law of the sea, and other related social and functional issues.

Perhaps the most novel feature of UN politics during this period was that for the first time in the history of international relations, the hitherto forgotten two-thirds of humankind, taking advantage of its overwhelming power of numbers, took the normative initiative in transforming the agenda of global politics. Taking its cues from the 1972 Stockholm Conference but launching its first salvo in 1974 with the Sixth Special Session of the UN General Assembly on Raw Materials and Development, the Group of 77, as the Third World's caucus in global group politics, turned the General Assembly (or a multilateral conference sponsored by the General Assembly) into the central platform for projecting its will as the wave of the future. Under the auspices of the General Assembly, about twenty global conferences were held in the 1970s to establish new norms or transform old ones on practically all of the problems related to human well-being—the environment, food, population, women, human settlement, water, the law of the sea, desertification, trade, science and technology, industrialization, employment, primary health care, disarmament, and agrarian reform.

Such normative initiatives on the part of the Third World might have been hollow victories had it not been for increased awareness that the rich industrialized states were dependent on the poor Southern states for the raw materials (and also, increasingly, for markets) to continue their lifestyles and economic growth. The Third World not only achieved control of the UN agenda but also got the assurance of the majority to adopt its positions and the economic leverage (the so-called "threat from the Third World") to force the issues of its dominant concern on the agenda of UN politics. Thanks to the U.S. defeat in and retreat from Vietnam, a reluctant but general willingness emerged in the U.S. foreign policy of the 1970s to adapt itself slightly to the decline in U.S. hegemonic power and to growing global interdependence. At the same time, this period witnessed a precipitous decline in UN efforts to manage international conflicts and disputes, especially those involving two or more nonaligned member states.

COLD WAR II (1980–1986)

With the revival of another cold war, Cold War II, in 1980 in the wake of the seizure of U.S. hostages in Iran and the Soviet invasion of Afghanistan at the end of 1979, the UN once again encountered fresh attempts by both superpowers to accelerate the arms race and to beef up their declining intrabloc solidarity. The impact of this global geopolitical environment, still dominated by the superpowers, was immediately felt in UN politics. If the first Special Session on Disarmament (SSOD-I) convened by the General Assembly in 1978 succeeded in revamping and revitalizing the Disarmament Commission as the UN's *deliberative* body on disarmament and the Committee on Disarmament as the UN's *negotiating* body, SSOD-II in June 1982 was a failure. Even the modest peacekeeping operations in southern Lebanon (UNIFIL) became helpless spectators in the face of Israel's invasion in 1982. When Iraq committed aggression against Iran in September 1980, the UN turned a deaf ear.

By 1980, both proponents and opponents agreed that NIEO had become an exercise in rhetorical posturing without actual movement. In the latter half of the 1970s, it became increasingly clear to the North in general and the United States in particular that the "threat from the Third World" was a paper tiger. Far from becoming a vanguard, OPEC refused to link oil to NIEO global bargaining, serving a heavy blow to the Third World's leverage as the collective Southern trade union. Much of the petrodollar surplus was recycled or invested in European and U.S. commercial banks. With the threat from the Third World thus diffused, the North hardened its anti-NIEO posture, as evidenced by the communiqués issued by successive annual economic summits of the seven leading market industrial countries.

The collapse of the eleventh Special Session of the General Assembly, convened in September 1980 to revive global North-South negotiations, was another testimonial to the disarray of NIEO politics. The session bogged down in conflict over the forum in which global negotiations should take place and the mechanisms for implementing any eventual agreements. The Third World advocated an integrated approach through the UN, linking policy measures in several key sectors, while the United States, the United Kingdom, and West Germany insisted on a decentralized approach through the specialized agencies and the continued compartmentalization of negotiations along sectoral lines. This was more than a procedural squabbling. The purpose of the Northern strategy was to shield the cockpit of the capitalist world system (i.e., the IMF and the World Bank), the last stronghold of anti-NIEO resistance, from the "tyrannical majority." Much of the talk about the UN crisis during this period centered on the crisis in such South-dominated institutions as UNCTAD, UNESCO, and the General Assembly; little was said about the IMF or the World Bank, which served as the shield for the Northern fiscal and monetary interests.

The demonstrated capacity of the Third World to dominate the agenda of the General Assembly was at the heart of U.S.—and to a lesser extent Soviet— disenchantment with the United Nations. Even during this period of Cold War II, the United States and the Soviet Union formed an unholy alliance in advocating budgetary frugality for the organization in the name of enhancing fiscal integrity and administrative efficiency and in opposing initiatives to confer legislative character on acts by the General Assembly or on any Charter review of the unanimity principle.

The so-called Reagan Doctrine established a high water mark of global unilateralism and official lawlessness in its rollback strategy of restoring *la belle epoque* of Pax Americana. The Carter administration's "damage-limitation" strategy was discarded as being too weak and passive. Instead, the Reagan administration displayed its military muscle in defiance of Charter constraints by invading Grenada (1983) and bombing Libya (1986). As well, in this period the U.S. government adopted a mixture of demolition and withdrawal strategies, made manifest in its withdrawal from UNESCO, its unilateral withdrawal from the compulsory jurisdiction of the World Court in disputes with any Central American state, its rejection of the UN Convention on the Law of the Sea (a product of protracted negotiations involving all three previous administrations), and its linkage of bilateral aid programs to the recipients' foreign policy behavior in general and General Assembly voting behavior in particular.

In spite of all the talk about hegemonic decline, it is a sad commentary upon the deep structure of the world organization that U.S. brinkmanship still had such a consequential impact upon the financial and political viability of the "United" Nations. The hidden agenda of the Kassebaum-Solomon Amendment (August 1985) was not so much UN "reform" as a unilateral amendment of the UN Charter to insinuate the "weighted voting" formula into the General Assembly budgetary process.

A NEW ERA OF MULTILATERALISM (1987-   )?

Ironically, the Reagan administration, by posing the greatest challenge and threat to multilateralism yet, provided the United Nations with a Grotian moment. The fortieth anniversary of the United Nations in late 1985 was a time for reflection on and reappraisal of the challenge by the Reagan administration via the Heritage Foundation that "a world without the United Nations would be a better world." The designation by the General Assembly of 1986 as the International Year of Peace at a time of unparalleled crisis of multilateralism stimulated serious reflections on the role of the United Nations in maintaining international peace and security. These reflections and reappraisals involved not only member states but also scholars, research institutes, and international nongovernmental organizations (INGOs). China even responded with the convocation of a founding conference of peace research.

Both the changes within and without the United Nations in 1987–1988 facilitated a transition from Cold War II to a new era of multilateral cooperation. Perhaps more than any other single global actor, the Soviet Union under Mikhail Gorbachev and his "new thinking" in foreign policy has been responsible for bringing about a global season of peace and for ushering in a new era of great-power consensus on UN peacekeeping operations. Gorbachev embarrassed and even shamed Reagan by reversing traditional Soviet hostility to the UN as a global peacekeeper. The new concepts of global interdependence and a comprehensive world security system (see Selections 13 and 38) have been followed up, to a greater extent than most people had expected, by paying Soviet back dues on peacekeeping operations, by ending the old anti-Charter Soviet practice of secondment for its citizens in the Secretariat, by accepting International Atomic Energy Agency (IAEA) inspection of its civilian nuclear reactors, by supporting for the first time the renewal of the UNIFIL mandate, by withdrawing Soviet troops and checkbooks from several hot spots in the Third World, by dismantling SS-20 missiles (via the INF Treaty), and by reducing Soviet naval activities in the Pacific.

Even before the announcement of the awarding of the 1988 Nobel Peace Prize to the UN peacekeeping forces, the Soviet Union had put forward several proposals for ensuring "comprehensive security in military, political, economic, ecological, humanitarian and other fields" and for giving the United Nations an enhanced role "in the maintenance of global peace and in the solution of global problems." This new Soviet conception of a comprehensive global security system includes the proposal for a UN naval peacekeeping force as well as the proposition that the member states routinely earmark some of their armed forces for UN peacekeeping operations, thus establishing a standing UN army. These changes in Soviet global policy did not by themselves cause the end of U.S. hostility, but the U.S. attitude began to moderate in 1987, culminating in a more forthcoming position by the United States on several UN issues in 1988 (see Selection 14).

The Gorbachev revolution is part of the general rise in systemic learning throughout the world. Superpower Détente III (1987–   ) reflected and effected this universal shift from the high costs of unilateralism to the benefits and possibilities of multilateralism in order to gain more breathing space for putting domestic houses in order. The eight-year-long Iraq-Iran War is a reminder that there are no easy winners in modern war. It has become easier to avoid losing a war than to win it, even if one side is militarily superior. War has become easier to terminate through the United Nations than through continuous fighting or exhaustion. Security Council Resolution 598 (July 1987) is a turning point for the revival of UN peacekeeping, for it embodied for the first time in UN history the unanimity of the Big Five on such a topic (the five permanent members actually submitted an unprecedented joint draft resolution), leading to the establishment and deployment of a UN Iran-Iraq Military Observer Group (UNIIMOG) a year later to observe the UN-imposed cease-fire not only on the border between Iran and Iraq but also in the upper Persian Gulf, around the Shatt-al-Arab Waterway. In effect, this latest UN peacekeeping operation is its first maritime mission. The active leadership of the secretary-general in this case was greatly assisted by the unanimous support from all five permanent members for his efforts to implement Security Council Resolution 598; such support is also unprecedented in UN history.

The conclusion of the Geneva Accords in April 1988 and the establishment of the United Nations Good Offices Mission for Afghanistan and Pakistan (UNGOMAP) represented the first instances of the superpowers becoming coguarantors of an agreement negotiated under the auspices of the secretary-general. Historically, a cold-war conflict such as this was beyond the political reach of UN peacekeeping. It is plausible to regard the 1979 Soviet invasion of Afghanistan as having ushered in Cold War II and the 1988 Geneva Accords as marking the end of Cold War II. In the process, a new chapter in the evolution and expansion of UN peacekeeping has opened. In August 1988, Morocco and the Polisario Front agreed to a UN peace plan to end their thirteen-year-old war in Western Sahara. Even South Africa now wants to be part of the global solution and has accepted the UN plan for the transition of Namibia to independence (Security Council Resolution 435 of 1978), which includes obligations for Cuba to withdraw its troops from neighboring Angola. And the UN is poised to arrange the withdrawal of Vietnamese troops from Kampuchea and to preside over a complex and difficult transition process to peace.

Although peace seemed to be breaking out all over in 1988, the deep normative and structural problems (and the underlying causes of war) persist. Premises of unbridled nationalism and statism remain. Generalized combat fatigue may be replaced by generalized peace fatigue. UN peacekeeping is reactive, not anticipatory or preventive, as it is the court of *last* resort. "A primary fact of the present world situation," as Secretary-General Pérez de Cuéllar reminds us in his bullish 1988 annual report, "is that while the power to destroy the Earth is concentrated in a few hands, the power to make and strengthen peace is widely dispersed." Even the great-power consensus on UN peacekeeping seems fragile. The recent U.S. shift in attitude and policy toward the United Nations shows a turn toward selective multilateralism. The United States supports the UN's involvement in the prevention of chemical warfare and horizontal nuclear proliferation but not in other arms control and disarmament issues; in the termination of the Iraq-Iran War but not in the Arab-Israel conflict; in Namibia but not in Central America. The UN's Third World majority has been tempered by pragmatism in recent years, to be sure, but it still remains a primary and enduring fact of UN politics that non-Western priorities cannot be wished away by the great-power consensus. Now that the United Nations is back in the limelight after years of concerted assaults and is receiving credit for the management of this global epidemic of war-weariness, a danger of rising expectations exists, inducing renewed disappointment with the role and capacity of the United Nations.

As already noted, the United Nations started with an indeterminate potential for system maintenance, reform, or even transformation. Which path has the UN actually taken in its forty-five-year history? Has the UN made a difference in world politics? Has it made any significant contribution toward resolving the chronic security dilemma in a world of conflict-oriented states? What has really changed because of the UN, and what has remained essentially the same in spite of the UN?

The most notable contribution of the United Nations is the crucial role it played as the collective midwife for the birth of new nations and their acceptance as member states in the world organization. The list of dependent territories dropped from 64 in 1962 to 19 in 1988. As a result, the underdogs acting as a collective global actor came to exercise the dominant role in global normative politics. If the first big wave of normative activities, which occurred during the reconstruction period of 1944–1948, was dominated by the United States, the second big wave of normative activities, in the 1970s, was dominated by the Group of 77. Possibly, the Soviet Union captured the normative crown for the 1980s.

Reflecting the changing UN membership and global realities, international norms have not only grown at an unprecedented rate but have also expanded into such hitherto-uncovered areas as internal war, the environment, technology transfer, and transnational corporations. The state system is being penetrated by all kinds of UN-sponsored international norms. If we put the questions of legal validity and practical potency aside, the UN has served as a magnet for drawing attention to the forces and ideas emanating from the previously forgotten two-thirds of humankind.

Yet the rapid growth and proliferation of international norms cannot be accepted as evidence of system transformation. This is not to underestimate the power of international norms but to suggest that these changes—mostly soft norms—have not been sufficient to cope with the global security problematique generated by the exponential trends in collective violence, demographic explosion, weapons technology and spread, resource depletion, human rights abuses, and environmental degradation.

There is also a sense in which these normative changes have served as an escape from real problems or real solutions—rhetorical victories without substantive or structural impact.

In comparing normative and structural changes, we notice that norms tend to be adopted or revised, but then neutralized or even vitiated. Only when a given norm recurs in global politics without disturbing the existing distribution of power and privileges is it likely to have a behavioral impact by changing the expectations and attitudes of state actors. The UN has not been successful in bringing about a structural change in the international system. The history of NIEO politics suggests that the North may acquiesce in the normative claims of the South, provided no attempt is made to translate such claims into a new structure of power and influence in the keystone international economic organizations.

The Third World was far too diverse, even antagonistic an assemblage of states to have fully utilized its power of numbers in the enhancement of UN effectiveness as the world organization. Easy issues were emphasized to avoid the appearance of disunity: a preoccupation with the world's "easy" cases (Chile, Israel, and South Africa). Also harmful were the frequency of double standards on questions of the use of force and human rights, and a failure to make use of the Uniting for Peace Resolution in the face of paralysis in the Security Council. Further, the overkill approach to pressing global problems through the passage of rhetorical resolutions merely widened the gap between the UN's normative promise and its political performance during the period of Third World dominance. By passing one resolution after another that it has neither the will nor the capacity to implement, the Third World has cheapened the currency of UN resolutions as behavioral norms of state behavior. Even in its home turf of NIEO, the Third World's habitual demands for global economic reform (and its manifest inability and unwillingness to reform its own domestic and social systems) have lacked moral and practical credibility. The Third World has attacked the superpower arms race, while often at the same time busily engaging in the global arms trade and emulating the great-power style of geopolitics in its own quest for power and status in regional politics. In short, the Third World has not demonstrated any collective capacity to provide credible world order leadership on matters of UN politics. Herein lies another major source of the UN crisis—a crisis of multilateralism on the part of its dominant majority.

A gap has always existed between the UN as a normative aspiration and the UN as an effective global actor. But we have observed that during Cold War II, this gap widened to the point where the UN could no longer muddle through as it had in the past. One crucial challenge was posed by Maurice F. Strong: Will the non-great power majority of the UN membership take the initiative in remaking the UN by exercising the responsibility that must accompany its overwhelming majority?

From the vantage point of 1990, the UN seems to have made an unexpected and exhilarating, yet still precarious, transition from decay to renewal by way of superpower détente and great-power concert. The deep underlying structural causes of the crisis of multilateralism—and indeed of global structural disorder—are as entrenched as ever, but a sense of realism is now emerging among the Big Five that the UN still provides the most useful safety valve and the most widely accepted last-resort machinery for the abatement of explosive tensions arising from geopolitical rivalry and ideological confrontation in troubled spots of the Third World. It also serves as an indispensable setting within which to fashion a response to global environmental challenges. Yet, Gorbachev's constructive and sensible reform proposals for strengthening the United Nations in the common quest for a more comprehensive global security system have not produced enthusiasm in any quarters. Even in this period of restored confidence, the United Nations is asked once again to be essential without being given the tools or the resources to be effective.

A Normative
and Structural Overview

INTRODUCTION

The principal purpose of this section is to provide a back-into-the-future assessment of the United Nations as a potential agent of world order transformation. A ubiquitous Chinese aphorism—"past experience, if not forgotten, is a guide for the future"— serves to justify establishing a concrete empirical baseline from which scenarios of alternative futures can be projected and contrasted with the extrapolations of the present. Before we can diagnose the conditions of the present human predicament and prescribe preferred futures, we believe, there is need to reflect upon the historical circumstances that have been transmitted from the past. The forty-five-year performance of the United Nations as the world organization provides a point of departure.

Unfortunately, few of us have been able to escape swings of emotion, perception, and even fashion in our images and assessments of the United Nations. To be sure, part of the confusion stems from the erratic twists and turns of the United Nations itself and the turbulence of the global setting within which it acts. But a greater part of the problem seems to lie in our narrow nationalistic and temporal frameworks. The multilateral crisis is, in essence, a crisis of *national* security transmitted to and magnified in the surrounding of this *global* institution. At the same time, we need to view the United Nations as a *process* in a longer historical perspective. The United Nations is an institutional expression of a governing process at the international level at a given time in the world historical process—a process of communicating, coordinating, regulating, and organizing among international actors on issues of common concern or interest in a decentralized state system. It is a developing process of seeking to fashion a common framework for multilateral cooperation in the absence of a supranational Leviathan. The United Nations as a global intergovernmental organization with universal membership is particularly sensitive to the flow of world forces. It is a global mirror—and a stage—for all the contending and contradictory forces of creativity and destruction that both effect and reflect the world historical process. It is, as well, a global social laboratory for testing the outer possibilities and limitations of overcoming existing global structures of violence, inequity, exploitation, and oppression.

As with any social system, the United Nations as an international social system has a *structure* of power relations that defines the rights and responsibilities of its members and the institutional setting within which the authoritative allocation of values for international society takes place. A structure-oriented approach may explain why a gap persists between the UN's normative promise and its modest performance, between its extravagant claims and its limited capabilities to translate such claims into a global reality. A normative transformation is a necessary but certainly not a sufficient condition for world order transformation. In comparing normative and structural changes in the development of the United Nations, it can be said that norms tend to be more easily established or revised and more easily neutralized or vitiated. Yet when a given norm recurs in global politics without disturbing the existing distribution of power, it does change the expectations and attitudes and eventually the behavior of the member states.

On the other hand, any social structure tends to be rigid, resistant to adaptation and change, and easily repaired or reproduced for system maintenance. The rise and fall of the Third World–led New International Economic Order (NIEO) politics is a good example of how the rich and powerful may acquiesce in the normative claims of the poor and weak, provided such claims are not translated into a structural change. Much structural disorder in the United Nations General Assembly today may be explained by the conflict—and a poor fit—between the normative power of the Southern majority and the material power of the Northern minority.

The promise of a world order transformation, as we understand it, arises from some basic normative and structural changes in the existing international order. The UN's potential role in these challenges can be usefully assessed by reflecting upon its performance during the first forty-five years of its existence.

We begin this section with an essay by Chadwick F. Alger, prepared and presented at the UN University Seminar in Japan in September 1985. Alger sees the United Nations of today as a product of a long world historical process and as a natural outcome of the tendency of humans to extend their contacts and activities to the greatest reach possible. Within such a long-term world historical perspective, Alger presents a balanced and multilayered analysis of the evolution of the United Nations, its contradictions (e.g., the coexistence of state equality and great-power hegemony), and its failures and successes in responding to human aspirations and needs. For the first time in human history, the United Nations made it possible for the "representatives from all parts of the world, from a diversity of religious, philosophical and ideological persuasions, [to draft] standards for human relations intended to have universal validity."

Clearly, this is a normative and political accomplishment of a high order. The United Nations also served as a political arena wherein the global dialectics on the meaning of "development" could be worked out. This was more than an empty rhetorical exercise. Alger discerns a growing consensus on six themes emerging from the UN-sponsored global dialectics on development: (1) the value of life, (2) certain basic human needs, (3) autonomy and self-reliance, (4) equity, (5) participation, and (6) ecological balance. Yet, the deep underlying structure of the UN system makes it difficult to be responsive to *peoples'* needs worldwide. As a "trade union of states founded to preserve the system of states," the United Nations is hampered by the contradictions between its basic structure and the tasks it is called upon to perform. In the end, Alger calls for greater flexibility in defining and changing the bases of representation in order to make the UN system more responsive to human needs growing out of a dialogue among representatives of local, state, and global organizations.

In the second selection, written in 1985 in commemoration of the fortieth anniversary of the United Nations, Samuel S. Kim explores the possibilities and limitations of UN lawmaking as an agent of normative transformation. In this analysis, international law is redefined in a teleological sense as an enabling, positive instrument for expressing and directing the evolving common aspirations and goals of a global community. With the entry of new actors, issues, and demands, Kim argues, the international lawmaking process now takes place primarily in political forums with universal membership. The domain of morality and law and that of interest and power have now become virtually conterminous.

The most remarkable change is that for the first time in the history of international relations, the hitherto-neglected Third World states have come to play a dominant role in UN lawmaking. Yet no fundamental structural change has occurred to accompany these normative advances, widening in the process the disjuncture between the assertion of normative claims and the level of institutional capabilities. In spite of all the changes and advances, contemporary international law still remains more neo-Westphalian than post-Westphalian. For the most part, Kim concludes, contemporary international law is still an expanded and revised supplement of, not an alternative to, classical sovereignty-centered international law. Like Alger, he, too, sees the basic challenge ahead in terms of seeking a better linkage between UN lawmaking and the voices of the unheard and the unrepresented by opening up more and more channels of communication and contact with the nonstate social actors and forces struggling at the periphery of the present international system.

The last selection in this section written by Johan Kaufmann, a former permanent representative of the Netherlands to the United Nations, draws our attention to the unforeseen developments in UN decisionmaking. Both internal and external factors have brought about changes in the modes of UN decisionmaking, such as various modes of nongovernmental organization (NGO) participation, especially in the preparation of draft human rights resolutions and conventions, the rise of operational programs, the implementation of UN-sponsored global issue-specific conferences, and the changes in the mode and pattern of voting procedures. The bloated structure of the UN system is notably lacking in any central organ dealing with human misery. Kaufmann examines with detachment various ways of, and approaches to, improving UN decisionmaking, including "the management route" and "the restructuring route." While he is in favor of the NGOs associated with all decisions in the implementation process, he is skeptical about Marc Nerfin's proposal for greater NGO participation in actual legislative processes.

Kaufmann calls for more research into the cultural, psychological, and semantic constraints of international cooperation. "Even if there were to be considerable improvement in both the management of UN decision-making processes and in the structure of the UN system," he warns, "it remains doubtful whether international co-operation would gain very much in the absence of a real will to accept the consequences of such co-operation, namely the diminishing of national sovereign powers." His seems to be a counsel for prudential incrementalism based on the insider's (Secretariat's) perspective that nothing is fundamentally wrong with the UN system in its normative and structural design. What is most wanted is the political will of the member states to rely less and less on their individual security systems and more and more on the UN system as the instrument of multilateral cooperation and governance.

All of the selections suggest or imply that the United Nations is not stagnant, but that its response curve lags behind the functional requirements of multilateral cooperation in an interdependent but fragile world. None of these selections anticipated the dramatic turnabout of the Soviet Union in the Gorbachev years. Gorbachev's advocacy of a "comprehensive global security system" centered in the United Nations is as sweeping as it was unexpected. A number of wide-ranging UN activities, including peacekeeping, ecological security, the role of the World Court, and the universal realization of human rights and fundamental freedoms, are incorporated as mutually interdependent parts making up the integral whole of the global security system.

In sum, Gorbachev calls for nothing short of a normative and structural transformation of the United Nations in the quest for a comprehensive global security system. This provides the United Nations with a historical opening to augment its role in human affairs. It is also a clear and continuing challenge to the United States to respond and reciprocate. In reading the selections of this section against a backdrop of this rare and unexpected historical call from the Kremlin, and the absence to date of much reciprocation from the White House, we realize that the United Nations cannot evolve very far beyond its present reality without support from *both* superpowers. Given the locus of the organization in the United States and the U.S. role in the world economy, it is indispensable for the United States to throw its support at this stage behind efforts to strengthen the UN along the lines proposed by Gorbachev.

4. The United Nations in Historical Perspective: What Have We Learned About Peacebuilding?

Chadwick F. Alger

Forty years ago today a war-weary world awaited the fulfillment of the hopes created by the San Francisco Conference of April–June 1945. As expressed in the opening words of the UN Charter drafted at San Francisco: "We the peoples of the United Nations" are determined:

> to save succeeding generations from the scourge of war, which twice in our lifetime has brought untold sorrow to mankind, and

> to reaffirm faith in fundamental human rights, in the dignity and worth of the human person, in the equal rights of men and women and of nations large and small, and

> to establish conditions under which justice and respect for the obligations arising from treaties and other sources of international law can be maintained, and

> to promote social progress and better standards of life in larger freedom.

Spurred by the ghastly ruins of World War II all fifty states represented at San Francisco had ratified the Charter by December 27, 1945, making possible the first meeting of the General Assembly on January 10, 1946.

Have these hopes been fulfilled? Some would reply with an emphatic "no." They would point to the Korean War, the Vietnam War, the Iran-Iraq War, and fighting in Afghanistan, Nicaragua, the Middle East, Cambodia, and many other places. They would remind us of violations of human rights by military regimes throughout the world, of Apartheid in South Africa, and of the slight progress in the status of women worldwide. They would draw our attention to worldwide urban squalor and rural poverty while nuclear stockpiles soar and military expenditures consume resources that could serve human needs.

Others would have a different response. They would point to lives saved by UN peacekeeping operations in the Middle East, Cyprus, the Congo and elsewhere. They would note that millions have experienced better standards of life because of UN programs. They would remind us of the remarkable capacity of the United Nations to take on new tasks and to create new organs to deal with them, such as UNCTAD, UNDP, UNIDO, UNEP, UNITAR and the UNU. While they would acknowledge worldwide violations of human rights, they would emphasize that the standards applied in measuring these violations have for the most part been debated, negotiated and promulgated by UN bodies. And they would draw attention to the virtual universal membership in the UN of the states of the world, forty years after its founding, as a remarkable achievement in a world where violence, poverty and injustice is so rampant.

As we reflect on the achievements of the UN in its first forty years, obviously both views have something to offer. In many respects the United Nations has failed.

These failures must be recognized if we are to continue intelligently the pursuit of the goals of the charter. On the other hand, the successes of the UN must be recognized too. Most important, its continuing existence offers hope and opportunites that could not exist in its absence. With all its weaknesses and failures, the UN still is evidence of the worldwide influence of visions of what a better world could be like. The UN is a daily reminder that the states of the world deem these visions significant enough to pursue them through debates and negotiations and to devote at least some of their resources toward their fulfillment.

THE UN IN HISTORICAL PERSPECTIVE

While it is fitting that we recognize the fortieth anniversary of the United Nations, it would be inaccurate to assume that the United Nations was completely a product of the San Francisco Conference. The stage on which the drafters of the UN Charter performed was a product of a long historical process through which human inquisitiveness, restlessness and acquisitiveness produced ever increasing contacts among human settlements, across ever longer distances. The results of this historical process presented opportunities at San Francisco evolving out of growing experience in peaceful cooperation among peoples. But there were also constraints produced by tendencies toward wars of increasing geographic scope with weapons of rapidly increasing destructive power.

If we look back in time from San Francisco, we readily see that the United Nations is a child of the League of Nations. It incorporates important institutional developments of the League, such as an international secretariat and the growth in importance of economic and social activities during the relatively brief history of the League. The United Nations Charter also reflects efforts to gain from League failures, as in procedures for deployment of military forces by the Security Council in response to aggression. While the requirement that no permanent member of the Security Council vote against such deployment has been an overwhelming restraint on the use of this power, nevertheless, the unanimity required in the League was more stringent than the 9 votes out of 15 required in the United Nations.

The League too was not wholly a product of its founding conference, the Paris Peace Conference of 1919. Inis L. Claude considers the century bounded by the Congress of Vienna (1815) and the outbreak of World War I (1914) as the "era of *preparation* for international organization." He discerns three prime sources of the League of Nations. First, the League Council evolved out of the Concert of Europe created by the Congress of Vienna, convoked to create a new Europe out of the ruins of the Napoleonic Wars. Through the Concert of Europe the great powers made themselves the self-appointed guardians of the European system of states. The Concert of Europe met sporadically, some thirty times, before World War I to deal with pressing political issues. While smaller staes were sometimes present at Concert meetings, the Concert was dominated by the powerful. The League Covenant provided for a Council with explicit authority, with the continuity of regular meetings and with membership of both large and small states.

Second, the League also evolved out of the Hague System, instituted by conferences in 1899 and 1907. The League borrowed extensively from procedures for the peaceful settlement of conflicts codified by the Hague System. And the League reflected the Hague System's response to growing demands for universality, i.e. that all states take part in international conferences. In the words of the president of the 1907 Hague Conference, "This is the first time that the representatives of all constituted States have been gathered together to discuss interests which they have in common and which contemplate the good of all mankind." The notion of universality meant not only the inclusion of smaller states but also participation by states outside Europe.

Third, the League also evolved out of international bodies founded in the Nineteenth Century, often referred to as public international unions, to deal with common problems that transcend national boundaries. These included the Rhine Commission, established by the Congress of Vienna in 1815, and the Danube Commission, established in 1848. Other examples are the International Telegraphic Union (1865), the Universal Postal Union (1874), and similar organizations dealing with health, agriculture, tariffs, railroads, standards of weight and measurement, patents and copyrights, narcotic drugs and prison conditions. Through these organizations states acknowledged that problems were emerging that required periodic conferences where collaborative decisions would be made, to be implemented by secretariats on a day-to-day basis. The League borrowed extensively from this practice.

If we probe deeper into the past we find, of course, that the forces that fostered the antecedents of the League also had more distant beginnings. It is important to take note of these because we sometimes tend to forget them when we emphasize more recent forms of "interdependence." The "Industrial Revolution" in the Eighteenth Century dramatically changed the technology of transportation, communication and manufacturing. This in turn fostered the need for international organizations to deal with problems created by more rapid transportation and communication and by growth in international marketing, in importing of raw materials and in the international interdependence of labor.

Some might say that humanity was placed on an irreversible path toward the League and the United Nations even earlier, in the late Fifteenth Century, when Europeans began a pattern of worldwide exploration that eventually led to extensive empires in Africa, Asia and Latin America and to Western domination of the world. William McNeill dates the "closure of global ecumene" as 1500–1650: The result was to link the Atlantic face of Europe with the shores of most of the earth.

What had always before been the extreme fringe of Eurasia became, within little more than a generation, a focus of the world's sea lanes, influencing and being influenced by every human society within easy reach of the sea.

European-based Empires eventually led to the creation of a worldwide system of states. In its early years the United Nations was deeply involved in the creation of independent states out of former colonial empires. Much present activity in the United Nations is concerned with the efforts of these new states to transcend their economic dependence on the West. In a fundamental sense the conditions that fomented demands for a New International Economic Order and for a New

International Information and Communications Order have their roots in the "closure of global ecumene" in 1500–1650.

Of course, the creators of "global ecumene" were not the first builders of empires, they were preceded by the Roman, Greek, Persian, Mongol, Inca, Han, and many others. And the "global ecumene" was preceded by the closure of the "Eurasian ecumene" in the period 500 B.C. to 200 A.D. (or perhaps earlier), "[when] the consolidation of a Kushan empire forged a link between Parthia and China, completing a chain of civilized empires that extended all across Eurasia, from the Atlantic to the Pacific." Across this vast ecumene McNeill describes exchange in art, religion, migration of useful plants and animals, the spread of disease, some technological exchange and trade. For example, "cotton, sugar cane and chickens, all first domesticated in India, spread to both China and western Eurasia during this period, while China contributed apricots and peaches, perhaps also citrus fruits, cherries, and almonds to Western Eurasia. In exchange, the Chinese imported alfalfa and a number of vegetable crops, as well as the Iranian great horses."

Thus we see that humankind has long had tendencies to travel, migrate, exchange, borrow and dominate, and to invent ever new technologies to broaden the geographic scope of these activities. This has produced a growing number of international organizations, some 365 international governmental organizations (IGO) and 4615 international non-governmental (non-profit) organizations (INGO) by 1984. At least 31 of the IGOs and 397 of the INGOs were global in scope. The autonomous organizations that comprise the United Nations system alone account for 18 of the global IGOs. While the UN system was not a necessary descendent of the "first ecumene," it can be viewed as a natural outcome of human tendencies to extend their contacts and activities to the greatest distance possible, thus creating the need for permanent international organizations that facilitate cooperation and problem-solving.

THE ACHIEVEMENT OF UNIVERSALITY

In growing from 50 members to 159 members since its founding the United Nations has successfully attained universality. The only states not ratifying the UN Charter, other than a handful of very small ones who choose to remain outside, are North and South Korea and Switzerland. And even these states are members of many agencies of the UN system. In achieving universality the United Nations overcame the earlier exclusion of numerous states that fought the United Nations coalition in World War II and also admitted many states that were carved out of former colonial empires in Africa, Asia, Latin America and Oceania. Not only were these new states admitted to the United Nations simultaneous with acquisition of independence, but the United Nations played a significant role in their relatively peaceful independence process. Even before independence, future leaders of new states, such as Julius Nyerere, testified before the Fourth Committee of the UN General Assembly and spent many months politicking for independence in the lounges and corridors of UN Headquarters.

Now that virtual universal membership of states has been achieved, there is a tendency of some to emphasize its drawbacks, particularly the fact that all states, despite great disparities in size, have one vote in UN bodies. These disparities are very great. UN members range in population from China, with one billion people, to thirty-three members with under one million people. They range from Kuwait's per capita GNP of $22,500 to some seventy-five members with per capita GNP of under $1,000. They range from the worldwide reach of missiles, ships and aircraft of the two superpowers to numerous states with little more than local police forces. Despite the fact that all states have one vote, there are countervailing factors. The two superpowers, China, France and the United Kingdom, have a veto in the Security Council. The wealthy benefit from weighted voting in the World Bank and the IMF. And consensual voting procedures have become more frequent, recognizing that majorities that do not take into account the wishes of the wealthy and militarily powerful may not be able to implement decisions. Also, it cannot be denied that states with military and financial power use their influence to win the votes of others. And countries with great wealth and many trained people have far greater capacity to represent their interests in UN politics through the assignment of large numbers of people to UN bodies.

Whatever the difficulties of universality under conditions of one vote for each state, general acceptance that all states have a right to sit at the conference tables of humankind is a significant achievement for the United Nations. Those who worked for universality in the late 19th century would be stunned were they to wander into the UN General Assembly (or the plenary of any UN agency) and see an Assembly of 159 members, 51 from Africa, 35 from Asia, 35 from the Americas, 31 from Europe and 7 from Oceania. The same would be true of founders of the League and founders of the UN itself.

Thus, as compared to the Nineteenth Century, and even the mid-Twentieth Century, the UN system of today has extended participation in world affairs in that virtually all of the states of the world are directly represented in its deliberations. Certainly elements of the old Concert notion of rule by the powerful still remain—in the Security Council, in superpower negotiations outside the UN, and in a variety of economic and financial bodies within and outside the UN. Nevertheless, significant progress toward universal participation has been made.

SELF-DETERMINATION AS A CONTINUING CHALLENGE

Growing universalism in international organizations has been a product of two trends. On the one hand, it has been increasingly accepted that all existing states should directly participate in international organizations dealing with worldwide problems. On the other hand, the growing acceptance of self-determination for peoples has produced more states, first by dissolution of empires in Europe and adjacent territories (the Austro-Hungarian and Ottoman Empires) and then by dismantling of European overseas empires after World War II. The end of overseas empires was heralded in the United Nations by the overwhelming passage of the Declaration on the Granting of Independence to Colonial Countries and Peoples on December 14, 1960. In this great milestone of human progress paragraph 5 declared:

Immediate steps shall be taken, in trust and nonself-governing territories or all other territories which have not yet attained independence, to transfer all powers to the peoples of those territories, without any conditions or reservations, in accordance with their freely expressed will and desire, without any distinction as to race, creed or color, in order to enable them to enjoy complete independence and freedom.

Pushed aside was the great fiction of colonialism that people in the remaining colonies had to be taught how to be independent before it would be appropriate to grant them independence. For the most part, remaining overseas empires crumbled before the growing worldwide sentiment reflected in the declaration.

Despite tremendous advances in this century, self-determination is still a significant challenge to the United Nations. This should not be surprising because self-determination is a perpetual, dynamic process. Human settlements grow and change, as do relations among them, and the make-up of larger collectivities that these relations create. The territorial entities that comprise humankind have always been changing. This is reflected in the fact that today there are many territorial groups around the world, within single states and spanning state lines, that aspire to greater autonomy and even independence. These groups are to be found within every continent, within most states of any size, and even in some that are relatively small. Much of the conflict and violence in the world today is fomented by dissatisfactions created by thwarted autonomy and independence movements. It is unlikely that much of this violence can be diminished without some responsiveness to the goals of these movements.

The present inability of the United Nations to come to grips with the inevitable continuing fulfillment of self-determination was foretold in paragraph 6 of the Declaration on the Granting of Independence to Colonial Countries and Peoples:

Any attempt aimed at the partial or total disruption of the national unity and the territorial integrity of a country is incompatible with the purposes and principles of the Charter of the United Nations.

While recognizing the presumed political necessity of this statement, there is deep irony in the acceptance of states created by colonial powers by a Declaration of Independence to Colonial Countries and Peoples. Of course, one could argue that peaceful change requires one step at a time and that any effort to redraw state lines might have indefinitely delayed the representation of colonial peoples in the United Nations. But it would seem that the time has now come for the United Nations to begin to deal more creatively with a new generation of self-determination aspirations. This will certainly be difficult because the UN is a trade union of existing states who tend to band together to preserve the status quo. But this is nothing new. The same conservatism that put the prerogatives of states above the aspirations of peoples held back self-determination movements in the past. Yet, in the end, the pursuit of peace, and world opinion, overcame the tendencies of states to preserve the status quo.

Perhaps constructive change will come as the people of the world, and even leaders of states, assess more critically the role of states in the present world. Sovereignty, in the sense of independence from outside forces, has declining significance in the world. Sovereignty of states in this sense is to a large degree a myth—a myth shared by both those who wish to hold existing states together against unwilling self-determination movements and those who are fighting to create new "sovereign" states. The kind of "sovereignty" people need in today's world is control over factors that influence their daily lives, such as unemployment, poverty, pollution and the threat of nuclear annihilation. This does not require independence, in the sense of separation from the rest of the world, but opportunity for participation in decisions that affect the daily lives of people everywhere. These include decisions made in a diversity of UN agencies that deal with a panoply of global issues.

Perhaps the next breakthrough in self-determination will reflect the fact that a single kind of entity, the territorial state, is not able to adequately represent all interests in world assemblies. It will be recognized that different kinds of territorial groups require different kinds of access to world bodies, and that it is not necessary for all to be present everywhere. For example, Alaska and Siberia might in the future be represented in a new UN Economic Commission for the Pacific, and perhaps even in the Second Committee of the General Assembly. But they might continue to be represented by the United States and the Soviet Union in the Disarmament Commission and in the First Committee of the General Assembly.

CREATING STANDARDS
FOR HUMAN RELATIONS WORLDWIDE

The close observer of the United Nations can easily become cynical about the seriousness of United Nations efforts to set standards for human relations on this planet. The United Nations system has filled volumes with high sounding declarations and covenants, with debates about progress in their achievement and with charges and countercharges by states who persistently assert that other states commit gross violations of these standards. At the same time, despite the plethora of standards that would elevate the quality and longevity of human life, the daily news is full of reports on war, famine, malnutrition, repressive regimes, poverty and preventable sickness.

While most would wish for more rapid progress in implementation of human rights standards drafted under UN auspices, it would be a tragic mistake to underestimate the significance of what has been achieved. Future historians will recognize the Twentieth Century as that period in history when, for the first time, representatives from all parts of the world, from a diversity of religious, philosophical and ideological persuasions, drafted standards for human relations intended to have universal validity. Before this time specific groups and traditions enunciated principles for human relations that were intended to be universally valid, such as those found in Buddhism, Christianity, Communism, Islam, Judaism, Socialism, Syndicalism, etc. The difference that the Twentieth Century has brought is an effort, largely under UN auspices, of people from a diversity of traditions to find common ground by together defining values for humankind. Building on the UN Charter, which expressly mentions human rights seven times, the General Assembly approved the Universal Declaration of Human Rights.

Although the Declaration [. . .] is not a binding legal instrument, it has had an impact on the constitutions of many countries. Particularly those of the newly emerging nations have "accepted the Declaration either in whole or in part, as their basic laws." The Declaration has also inspired numerous international conventions now in force. Among them are conventions on elimination of racial discrimination, elimination of slavery, abolition of forced labor, against discrimination in employment, against discrimination in education, the political rights of women and consent to marriage. But the most sweeping effort to implement the Declaration has been the "World Bill of Rights," i.e. the International Covenant on Economic, Social and Cultural Rights and the International Covenant on Civil and Political Rights, both adopted by the General Assembly on December 16, 1966 and now ratified by over fifty countries.

Universal ratification of these conventions is likely years away. Actual implementation in countries that have ratified may be long into the future. But this acknowledgement should not prevent recognition of these conventions as significant landmarks in defining global standards. They give people everywhere standards against which to judge their condition and instruments which can be used in justifying efforts to improve human conditions. It is a mistake to look to a single institution, such as a world court, or even to judicial bodies alone as means through which evolving global values will be further defined and implemented. This will come through a diversity of means, in a variety of settings, international, national and local. Not insignificantly, both the Convention on Economic, Social and Cultural Rights and the Convention on Civil and Political Rights assert that:

the individual, having duties to other individuals and to the community to which he belongs, is under a responsibility to strive for the promotion and observance of the right recognized in the present Covenant.

These rights also continue to be further defined and extended in the great global assemblies that are a hallmark of our age—as in special UN conferences on topics such as Human Environment, Population, Food, Women, Human Settlements, Water, Desertification, World Development, Disarmament and Law of the Sea. These debates reflect the fact that new technologies for transportation, communication, production, distribution and killing have spilled across the entire globe— creating a vast array of linkages among the countries, societies, cities and even villages of the world. These linkages have threatened values and have thereby spawned global issues with respect to environment, energy, food, population, arms, human rights, economic interdependence/dependence, development, etc. Debate on these issues can be viewed as a value clarification process which is defining standards for life on the planet.

Perhaps the most significant aspect of pursuit, in the United Nations, of standards for quality life for all on the planet is the growing understanding of the various dimensions of quality of life, how deprivation across these dimensions varies in different parts of the world and the relations between the dimensions. In other words, one can obtain insight on the contribution of the United Nations not only by microscopic examination of achievements with respect to a specific right, such as right to food or right to vote, but also by taking a macro view of the entire enterprise. This enables one to understand the relationships between right to food and right to vote, why some people emphasize one and different people the other, and why in some circumstances these rights may have to be acquired simultaneously.

Toward this end it is helpful to take a sixty-five year perspective on the development of global standards in the League of Nations and the United Nations. Examination of the League Convenant reveals one overwhelming concern—*peace*. Contracting parties agreed "not to resort to war" and agreed to utilize a variety of approaches to avoidance of war: judicial settlement, pacific settlement, reduction of armaments and collective security. The United Nations Charter too gave priority to peace. The first sentence of the Charter addresses the problem of the "scourge of war." Based on League experience, judicial settlement, pacific settlement, and collective security are once again applied as approaches to peace, but regulation of armaments is barely mentioned.

While there is no doubt that peace was still the highest priority for the founders of the United Nations, human rights, self-determination and economic and social issues were given a prominent place in the Charter. The second clause of the UN Charter refers to *human rights* and the theme is mentioned seven times in the Charter, although the League Covenant ignored human rights. UN concern is probably a result of overwhelming human rights violations by the Axis Powers, before and during World War II. The Declaration of Human Rights was approved only three years after the founding of the UN. Significantly, fifteen of the rights enumerated in the document refer to civil and political rights, those that tend to be given priority in the industrialized countries of the West. Only six address economic and social rights.

Another difference between the UN Charter and the League Covenant, is the prominence given by the Charter to *self-determination*, i.e. procedures for moving nonself-governing territories and trust territories toward "self-government." League concern for dependent peoples had been limited to territories seized from defeated states in World War I.

Yet another difference between the League and the UN is the prominence given to *economic and social issues*, including the creation of an Economic and Social Council. To some degree this reflected the fact that the League too had become increasingly involved in economic and social activity. Importantly, the fourth clause of the Preamble of the UN Charter emphasizes the promotion of "social progress and better standards of life in larger freedom."

A GLOBAL DIALECTIC
ON THE MEANING OF DEVELOPMENT

When in the early years of the United Nations the prime goal was peace, economic and social cooperation tended to be viewed as avenues for "functionalism"—i.e. cooperation on economic and social issues that would provide background conditions facilitating peace. For the most part this cooperation took place through multilateral efforts to develop standards. Prominent examples are the international labor standards conventions of the ILO which reach back to the early days of the League. But the entry of a multitude of new states into the UN in the early sixties stimulated a dramatic transformation of the goal of economic and social activities to one of *development* in the Third World. Over the past thirty years the pursuit of development through UN programs has generated a global dialectic on the meaning of the term.

We will identify six stages in this dynamic process: (1) *national development* of Third World countries emerged as a goal in response to the disparity between wealth possessed by people in the industrialized countries of Europe and North America, and the poverty of people in Africa, Asia and Latin America. An initial approach was "aid" in the form of technical assistance, loans and sometimes grants of capital. It was assumed that this "aid" would set in motion a process of growth which at some point would enable national economies to "take off" and develop, similar to what had taken place in the industrialized countries in North America and Europe. Growth was measured by national GNP, that is, the national aggregate production of goods and services. Although some countries developed according to this criterion, overall this strategy failed in that at the end of two UN Development Decades, the sixties and seventies, the gap between the Third World and the industrialized world had increased. Not only was the rich-poor gap growing, but "aid" was increasing the indebtedness of the Third World to industrialized countries. Indeed, increasingly "aid" is largely consumed in paying off past loans.

In response to the growing gap, criticism was directed to the character of the international economic system, i.e., the ways in which the poor countries are dependent on the rich countries. A New International Economic Order was proposed in order to eliminate dependency and create (2) *international economic equity.* While national development remained as a value to be pursued, policy makers in the Third World increasingly turned to equitable relations with industrialized countries as the means that would make this possible and as a value to be pursued for its own sake. The Declaration on the Establishment of a New International Economic Order (NIEO) at a Special Session of the UN General Assembly on 1 May 1974 was a culmination of years of Third World frustration at the lack of responsiveness by industrialized countries to their piecemeal demands for change. The twenty enumerated principles of the Declaration on the Establishment of a New International Economic Order include these seven:

1. Just and equitable relationship between the prices of goods exported by developing countries and the prices of goods imported by them,
2. Measures to promote the processing of raw materials in the producer developing countries,
3. A Generalized System of Preferences for exports of agricultural primary commodities, manufactures and semi-manufactures from developing to developed countries,
4. Sovereignty of every state over its national resources and all economic activities,
5. Access on improved terms to modern technology and the adaptation of that technology to specific economic, social and ecological conditions in developing countries,
6. An international code of conduct for transnational corporations,
7. Strengthening cooperation among the developing countries.

Criticism of the NIEO continued the dialogue on the meaning of development. [. . .]

Instead of a NIEO, Johan Galtung, and others, advocate (3) *self-reliance* (or autonomy), not based on the modelling effect of "bridging the gap," but based on the basic needs of the local society in the context of local culture and experience. Self-reliance can have several applications: self-reliance of the entire Third World, self-reliance of regions in the Third World, or self-reliance of individual societies.

Still another clarification of the meaning of development has come as a result of the failure of Third World development programs to improve the living conditions of most people presumed to be the beneficiaries of these programs. Critics of both national development strategies and NIEO assert that development programs must provide (4) *basic human needs* for food, water, clothing, shelter, education, health and transportation. Increased GNP, industrialization, foreign aid, increased exports, national autonomy and national self-reliance might help to satisfy these needs but they should be treated as means—not as ends in themselves. This emphasis has stimulated yet another reformulation of development thinking, reorienting attention from national development statistics to the condition of people in the poorest sectors of societies—away from the GNP piled up in Westernized sections of capital cities, and other cities, and out to the urban shantytowns and rural villages of Africa, Asia and Latin America.

Emphasis on basic human needs has provoked yet another clarifying question: Who shall define basic human needs? Many reply that it can only be the people themselves, with an emphasis on grassroots (5) *participation* in the definition of needs. Increasingly then, *human* development is seen as the goal of development, i.e. full opportunity for fulfillment of the potential of the individual human being. All other forms of development—such as economic development, industrial development, national development—are viewed as means toward this end. Thus, the success of development is to be measured not in GNP, energy produced or consumed, or quantities of hospital beds, TV sets or even food produced. These may contribute to human development, but whether they do or not can only be determined by measuring the actual quality of life of people, particularly for those in the most deprived sectors of societies.

Increasingly the importance of balance in the relationship between human beings and the non-human environment—(6) *ecological balance*—has become a part of the great development dialogue. The global dialectic on environmental issues is moving global debate on economic issues to a new plane, making symmetric debate between the industrialized and Third World more possible in several respects: (1) The notion of *overdevelopment* has undermined the assumption that the industrialized world is a model for the Third World. (2) It is no longer assumed that all of the major changes in pursuit of development must be made in the Third World. If industrialized countries are overdeveloped, they must change too. (3) The basic philosophy underpinning the industrialized world has been shaken—the view that it is the mission of human beings to dominate and conquer their environment with ever-expanding technological competence has been seriously challenged. Now non-Western values that view human beings as a part of nature, and that expect human beings to fit into the whims and cycles of nature, have become a respected part of global dialogue.

This great global dialogue over the meaning of development that has been in process since the early 1960s can be interpreted in a variety of ways. It can be viewed as a typhoon of words and documents created by highly paid and overfed people who talk while the gap between them and the poor of the world grows ever wider. But one can also discern, underlying the cacophony flowing out of debates in the UN system, as well as experience in UN field programs, a growing consensus on certain themes. Obviously different observers would select different themes. I sense that these six themes have a growing consensus behind them:

1. The value of *life* in the sense of staying alive.
2. The value of all people acquiring certain *basic human needs*, no matter who they are and no matter where they live.
3. The value of *autonomy* and *self-reliance* for the human collectivities with which people choose to identify themselves.
4. The value of social structures that insure *equity* in relationships among these collectivities.
5. The value of *participation* by all people in decisions that affect their interests.
6. The value of *balance in relationships between people and the non-human environment* that conserve this environment.

Viewed from a historical perspective that begins with the League Covenant, the basic values on which the system of states base their common efforts have extended from preoccupation with peace to vital concern for an array of values. This has been brought on partly by the expanded membership of the United Nations. But it has also been fostered by growing knowledge that reveals the relationship between peace, in the sense of silencing guns and bombs, and peace in the sense of availability of basic needs, self-reliance, equity, participation and ecological balance. From this perspective some would assert that the great and ongoing debate over the meaning of development has been in reality a clarification of the various dimensions of peace.

GROWTH OF THE UNITED NATIONS SYSTEM

As UN membership and UN agendas have expanded, the United Nations system has grown from a collection of some half dozen organizations at its founding to some thirty today. This growth has been responsive to a variety of factors. Some agencies were needed to fill out the competence of the system to deal with the full array of governmental issues that transcend national boundaries, such as the World Health Organization, the International Civil Aviation Organization, and the World Meteorological Organization. Others were in response to the emergence of new issues on international agendas, such as the UN Environmental Program, the UN Center for Human Settlements Habitat and the International Atomic Energy Agency. Still others reflect the influx of Third World members who were dissatisfied with how existing agencies were dealing with issues important to them and pushed for new organizations to focus on these issues. These include the UN Conference on Trade and Development (UNCTAD) and the UN Industrial Development Organization (UNIDO).

The some thirty organizations comprising the United Nations system today are normally divided into two groups. Those that have been created by the General Assembly include UNRWA, UNCTAD, UNICEF, UNCHR, UNITAR, UNDP, UNEP, UNU, Habitat, UNFPA, and the joint UN/FAO World Food Program. . . . Those that have been created by separate international treaties among states include: IAEA, GATT, FAO, UNESCO, WHO, IDA, IBRD, IFC, IMF, ICAO, UPU, ITU, WMO, IMO, WIPO, UNIDO and IFAD. Although independent agencies, these organizations are required to submit annual reports to the Economic and Social Council (ECOSOC) of the UN. An exception is IAEA which reports to the General Assembly. The headquarters of this diverse array of activities are scattered across several continents. The greatest concentrations are in New York and at the expanded former headquarters of the League of Nations in Geneva. Other headquarters are in Europe (Vienna, Paris, Rome, London, Berne), North America (Washington and Montreal), Nairobi, and Tokyo.

Of course, UN activities are not limited to the headquarters of agencies. There are Regional Economic Commissions for Africa (Addis Ababa), Europe (Geneva), Latin America and the Caribbean (Santiago), Asia and the Pacific (Bangkok) and Western Asia (Beirut). Many UN agencies are involved in implementing economic development programs in countries of Africa, Asia and Latin America. There are five peacekeeping operations responsible to the Security Council: the UN Truce Supervision Organization Palestine, the UN Military Observer Group in India and Pakistan, the UN Peacekeeping Force in Cyprus, the UN Disengagement Observer Force on the Golan Heights, and the UN Interim Force in Lebanon. And there are over a hundred UN information offices around the world.

One of the continuing issues on the agenda of the General Assembly, the Economic and Social Council (ECOSOC), and numerous UN agencies is how to coordinate this far-flung network of activities. Prime points of coordination include ECOSOC, given the responsibility by the Charter to coordinate economic and social activities of the UN system. Another point for coordination is the Administrative Committee for Coordination (ACC), a body composed of the heads of UN agencies, meeting twice a year, with the Secretary General of the UN as a chairperson. The regional economic commissions attempt to coordinate UN programs in geographic regions. Efforts are made to coordinate the development activities of various UN agencies within single countries, largely through Resident Representatives of the UN Development Program. Finally, the most recent effort has been creation of a Director General for Development and International Economic Cooperation as the second ranking official of the United Nations Secretariat, under the Secretary General. The purpose in creating this post was to provide a center for leadership and coordination of all activities in the economic and social fields in the UN system. Some would say that member governments too should be a point of coordination in that each government should develop national policies for the array of UN agencies that neither encourage duplication of effort nor contradictory policies for different agencies.

The approaches of different states to UN organizational issues reflect different interests, and offer opportunities to advance those interests in the UN system. For example, the wealthy industrialized states tend to prefer to deal with global economic and social policy in piecemeal fashion in the context of specific agencies. They do not see need for macro changes in the world economic system and would prefer to see micro adjustments made by technical specialists in agencies such as ILO, FAO and WHO. Also, these states talk a great deal about the need for greater "effectiveness and efficiency" and the need to eliminate "waste, mismanagement and duplication." Significant here, as the largest financial contributors (both assessed and voluntary), they wish to keep the costs down.

When a more macro approach is needed, the Western industrialized countries prefer to deal with macro global economic issues in the context of IMF and the World Bank where voting is based on monetary contributions. On the other hand, Third World countries pushing for a NIEO see the need for fundamental changes in world economic relations to be made through Global Negotiations in the context of the General Assembly, where each member has one vote. Not surprisingly, a prime goal of Third World countries is to revise voting procedures in the Bank and Fund.

[*   *   *]

The conflict produced by contending approaches to reorganizing the UN system is helpful. We should expect this conflict to continue for some time. After all, our experience with a single system of organizations for dealing with a vast array of global problems is in its infancy. It would appear that some proposals, although not explicitly so, may be too influenced by practice in single states. Others may be primarily fostered by a compulsion for neatness. Actually, what is needed are institutions that are most responsive to the diverse and conflicting interests of the people of the world. Likely the system that will emerge will be different than anything we have yet seen. Fortunately the UN system offers a vast laboratory for experimentation. With a cost of some four billion dollars per year, despite some obvious cases of inefficiency and waste, the UN system is still a remarkably cheap laboratory, at least when compared to the hundred times greater military expenditures of the members of the UN.

UN DECISION-MAKING

[. . .] Joint decision-making by states with sovereignty (at least in legal terms) has always presented problems in international organizations. Recognizing the facts of sovereignty, the League Covenant required unanimous decisions. The UN Charter departed from this tradition by requiring a ⅔ majority in the General Assembly on "important questions" and a simple majority on others, including matters of procedure. The Security Council requires 9 of 15, or three-fifths. Of course, on substantive questions the Charter requires "the concurring votes of the [five] permanent members" of the Security Council. The work of the Security Council has been greatly facilitated by an interpretation of this clause to mean that abstention or absence of a permanent member does not prevent passage of a resolution.

One of the most significant contributions of the UN has been to make multilateral diplomacy an ordinary occurrence. This has been accompanied by the development of written and unwritten procedures for calling meetings, for electing officers, for public debate, for private negotiations, and for relations with press, IGOs and INGOs. Much of this activity is judgment, they "may well come to be regarded as the most important 'common law' development . . . within the Constitutional framework of the Charter." Thus, the participants at headquarters of UN agencies have evolved new procedures and permanent institutions for exchanging views, debating and reaching agreement. It is a shortcoming of most works on international relations and international organizations that they barely mention these developments.

Much attention has been given by the media in the West to so-called "automatic voting majorities" through which Third World majorities can pass resolutions that sometimes cannot be implemented because these majorities do not include the states with the power and resources required for carrying out the resolutions. Certainly this is a problem in UN bodies. On the other hand, approaches have been developed to deal with this problem that merit more attention than they receive. Actually voting in most UN bodies is the exception rather than the rule. A high percentage of decisions are taken by consensus. Often a consensus reflects the fact that a resolution is non-controversial. On the other hand, elaborate procedures have been developed, through UN practice, for bringing consensus out of deeply conflictual situations.

Some do not realize that UN decision-making is a multi-layered process in which the public debate is only the tip of the iceberg. Certainly the public debate is indispensable. Here public declarations are made that are targeted to a variety of audiences—perhaps the press, the public at home, the opposition at home, or even the home government that must be insured that instructions were explicitly carried out. The public debate is also useful in highlighting different viewpoints and in revealing which states share these views. But a consensus, or even two-thirds of the votes, can often not be achieved by public debate alone. This may require negotiations, carried out by a few representatives of significant points of view, in a more intimate setting outside the public arena. Here mediators schooled through vast experience in UN decision-making often make a consensus possible.

Skilled chairpersons of public meetings know how to orchestrate a dialogue between the public and private arena—prodding the private negotiations when useful, playing for time for private negotiations when it is needed by allowing seemingly useless public statements to go on and on and . . . Often the whole process is monitored and creatively helped by members of the secretariat who have not only vast background in the subject matter but who have acquired also a feel for where an eventual consensus might be pulled out of a seemingly impossible array of conflicting viewpoints.

The United Nations Convention on the Law of the Sea, completed in 1983 after a decade of negotiations, can be examined for insight on what has been learned about decision-making in the UN system since the drafting of the Charter. In 1980 Elliott Richardson, former head of the U.S. Delegation to the Third United Nations Conference on the Law of the Sea, called this decade-long conference "the most significant single event in the history of peaceful cooperation and the development of the rule of law since the founding of the UN itself."

In the Assembly of the International Sea Bed Authority (ISBA), as in the UN General Assembly, each member has one vote and decisions on issues of substance require a two-thirds vote. The Council also requires a two-thirds vote but has a more stringent requirement of three-quarters for nominations to the Governing Board of the Enterprise, the seabed mining arm of the Authority.

The attainment of consensus in the ISBA Assembly is facilitated by provisions for a five-day delay on issues of substance, which can be required by one-fifth of those voting. The Council has more elaborate procedures. A consensus is required for actions that would (1) protect less developed countries who are land based mineral producers, (2) for rules for seabed mining, (3) for rules for sharing profits from mining by the Enterprise and (4) for amendments to the treaty. A consensus is defined as the absence of formal objection. If a consensus is lacking, a Conciliation Committee is created that is required to report to the Council within fourteen days. If no consensus has been achieved, the Conciliation Committee must report the reasons.

The treaty also provides for the representation of specific interests on the Council. This reflects further development of provisions in the UN Charter for the representation of both big powers (permanent members) and smaller powers on the Security Council and of governing powers and non-governing powers on the Trusteeship Council. Half of the thirty-six member council of the ISBA is to be composed of representatives from states having specific interests: Four from states with the largest investment in the seabed, four from states who consume over 2% or import over 2% of minerals mined in the seabed, four from states exporting minerals mined in the seabed, and six from less developed countries with these special interests: landlocked, large population, major importers or potential producers of minerals mined in the seabed or least developed. The other eighteen members are to be apportioned so as to insure equitable geographic distribution of council membership.

The treaty also breaks new ground in procedures for dispute settlement that evolve out of the trying experiences of both the League of Nations and the United Nations and attempt to build on this experience. All adherents to the treaty are required to accept third party settlement. But disputing parties have five options from which to choose: (1) voluntary conciliation, (2) the International Court of Justice, (3) binding arbitration, (4) special arbitration tribunals and the Law of the Sea Tribunal. There are annexes to the Treaty that spell out in great detail procedures to be followed in all but the International Court of Justice whose jurisdiction and procedures were set forth in the Statute of the International Court of Justice, established by the UN Charter.

Innovative are the four special arbitration tribunals that can be utilized for disputes involving fisheries, marine science research, navigation and environment. These tribunals offer lists of experts from which a panel for hearing a specific dispute can be chosen. The Law of the Sea Tribunal provides for twenty-one members chosen from the principle legal systems. For specific seabed disputes, three members, agreed to by the parties, can hear the dispute. If the parties cannot agree, the President of the Sea Bed Disputes Chamber (made up of eleven members of the Tribunal) appoints the members.

The point we are trying to make is not that these provisions of the LOS Treaty will necessarily all improve on UN Charter procedures for representation for attainment of consensus and for dispute settlement. Rather, the significance is to underline the value of the UN as a laboratory for development of improved procedures for decision-making and dispute settlement. It is to be regretted that there are states who are inhibiting the rapid establishment of the new institutions called for by the treaty. They would permit significant new experiments in the UN laboratory for the improvement of multilateral governance.

PEOPLE, STATES AND THE UNITED NATIONS

It is challenging to speculate on how humanity might organize itself to deal with a staggering array of global problems were it to start from scratch. It would seem unlikely that the present state system would again be established as an intermediary between the people of the world and world organizations charged with devising solutions to an array of global problems, such as violence, poverty, resource scarcity, pollution and deprivation of human rights. The ideology of the system tends to wall people off from the UN. The ideology asserts that a small politico-military elite in each state will take care of "foreign affairs," including relations with the UN. The ideology assumes that "foreign affairs" requires very special competence and experience not possessed, nor attainable, by "ordinary people"—only a small elite can define the "national interest." This ideology, widely accepted by the people themselves, even in the democracies, inhibits participation and thus prevents most people from learning about "foreign affairs." As a result most people in the world know little about the UN system and its vast array of activities. And, cut off from the people, it is difficult for the UN to be responsive to peoples' needs worldwide.

As the UN attempts to deal with global problems, there are contradictions between its basic structure and the tasks it is called upon to perform. It is fundamentally a union of states founded to preserve the system of states. Its relationships with the peoples of the world are normally carried out through state officials who naturally wish to preserve the prerogatives of states, including their own positions in the state system. Compounding the difficulty is the fact that UN officials have often received their training and early experience in the foreign affairs establishments of states, and often look forward to returning to these establishments. The elitist traditions of these institutions inhibit the development of longterm dialogue with people for assessing needs, defining solutions and acquiring the widespread legitimacy that permit implementation of programs.

The point here certainly is not that state officials are necessarily less concerned about serving peoples' needs than are UN officials. Rather the point is that state officials tend to be trapped in "foreign affairs" establishments with traditions that inhibit their responsiveness to these needs, particularly when international cooperation is required. The consequences of these traditions are dramatically revealed by the fact that these state politico-military bureaucracies devote 100 times more to military expenditures than they contribute to UN programs.

Pointing out the difficulties presented by the state system as a mediator between the UN and the people of the world does *not* mean that the interests of people should not be represented in the UN through some kind of territorial aggregations. And it does *not* mean that the UN should necessarily become some kind of centralized world government. But we are suggesting that it would be useful were there greater flexibility in defining and changing aggregations to be represented. And it is necessary that the traditions of the state system be transformed with respect to participation of people in "foreign affairs."

Of course, the state system has not been impervious to change in ways that do permit wider participation. Obvious is the great growth in International Nongovernmental Organizations (INGOs), from 176 in 1909, to 832 in 1951, to 4,615 in 1984. These figures include only permanent organizations, with rotating headquarters and officers and with membership and financial support from at least three countries.

In this century the involvements of nongovernmental organizations, both national and international, with IGOs has been increasing. ILO, founded in 1919, was a trailblazer in its tripartite form of representation, including labor and management, as well as national governments, in its deliberations. The League Charter charged members "to encourage and promote the establishment and cooperation of duly authorized voluntary national Red Cross organizations" (Article 25). The United Nations Charter provides that "The Economic and Social Council may make suitable arrangements for consultation with non-governmental organizations which are concerned with matters within its competence" (Article 71). In pursuit of this clause, some nongovernmental organizations may speak before the Council and many others have observer status. UNESCO has a similar arrangement under Article XI of the UNESCO Constitution.

In the early years of the UN there was a tendency for many INGO observers at the UN to perceive their role as limited to communicating information about the UN to their members, and developing support for the UN within their countries. But through the years INGOs, and some of their national counterparts (NGOs) present at the UN, have taken a more assertive role in UN politics. INGO and NGO representatives attending UN meetings increasingly lobby with state representatives for specific proposals and also propose to them resolutions for UN bodies. And through their national organizations they coordinate this effort with pressure on national governments. The significance of these efforts was recognized when Amnesty International was awarded the Nobel Peace Prize. An example of the influence of INGOs is the successful campaign against infant formula marketing practices in the Third World that led to the creation by the World Health Assembly of standards for marketing infant formula.

Important in the increasingly active role of INGOs in the UN system has been the creation, and growing activity, of coalitions of INGOs and NGOs represented at headquarters of UN organizations. A prominent example is the Conference of Non-Governmental Organizations in Consultative Status with the UN Economic and Social Council (CONGO), active in Geneva and New York. Dramatic evidence of the growing importance of nongovernmental organizations has been their participation in special UN conferences on global issues. On these occasions they have published their own newspapers, and have run their own conferences concurrently with the interstate UN conference. In a major departure from tradition, representatives of INGOs were permitted to address the plenary of the Second UN disarmament Conference. Also reflective of a new style of nongovernmental participation was the successful activity of Canadian organizations at the World Food Conference in Rome. Through a telephone network in Canada they brought pressure on the Canadian government in Ottawa to authorize Canadian government representatives in Rome to increase the Canadian pledge for food aid.

Despite the remarkable transformation that has taken place in the political style of some nongovernmental organizations active in the UN system, their influence is still very limited. A limiting factor is the fact that INGOs tend to be federations of national organizations and national organizations involved in UN issues often do not have strong grassroots participation in their activities. This is because the ideology of the state system has tended to inhibit grassroots involvement in global issues. There is a tendency for the "foreign" policies of national NGOs to be made by a small elite in the national headquarters of the organization. In turn, it is this small elite that represents the organization at the UN and in an INGO. Thus, to some degree the ideology of the state system is reflected in nongovernmental participation in that system. For the most part there are not organized avenues through which the grassroots can have access to the UN system. This access tends to be centered in national governments and in a small cosmopolitan sector of each society that has developed interest and competence in world affairs and are pioneering in new avenues for nongovernmental involvement.

Despite deeply ingrained traditions of the state system that inhibit "ordinary people" from participating in global issues, there are growing signs of transformation. Amnesty International has local chapters in a multitude of cities working for the release of specific political prisoners. Anti-Apartheid legislation, calling for disinvestment in corporations doing business in South Africa, has been passed by provinces, cities and towns, and also by universities. Increasingly people from many cities and towns are visiting Nicaragua, the Middle East, South Africa, the United States, the Soviet Union, and other countries in order to see for themselves the actual conditions contributing to international conflict, tension and arms races. In effect, there has emerged, although in small scale, a "people's foreign service." In the Western industrialized countries a "development education" movement is producing growing insight on the relationship between lifestyles in these countries and quality of life in the Third World. Cities, towns and provinces are declaring themselves nuclear free zones. Churches are challenging the policy of states by offering sanctuary for those who are faced with deportation, although they fear their lives may be in danger if they return to their country of origin.

Much of this activity is centered in the industrialized countries but there are parallel tendencies in the Third World. Fishermen from countries of Southeast Asia have joined together to prevent destruction of their fishing grounds by polluting industries. No longer do people accept as inevitable the sale of land vitally needed for food production to transnational corporations. Increasingly it is understood that the acquisition of local self-reliance requires comprehension of the involvement of the local community in the global political economy. There is even a gradual awareness of common interests between consumer groups and the "Greens" in the industrialized countries and self-reliance movements in the Third World.

Some scholars in both industrialized countries and the Third World perceive transformation potential in these developments. Two Swedish economists, Mats Friberg and Bjorn Hettne, see a worldwide "Green" movement emerging that rejects "mainstream development thinking" in which "the state is always seen as the social subject of the development process." Instead, from the Green perspective, they see that "the human being or small communities of human beings are the ultimate actors. The state can at most be an instrument of this ultimate actor." They believe that the "Green project" necessitates "stronger institutions on the global and local level," and de-emphasis of the state.

Writing out of experience with the grassroots Lokayan movement in India, D.H. Sheth perceives a "new mode of politics arising across regional, linguistic, cultural and national boundaries. It is inclusive of peace and anti-nuclear movements, environmental movements, women's movements, movements for self-determination of cultural groups, minorities and tribes, and a movement for reassertion of non-Western cultures, techno-sciences and languages." He discerns that this new politics is "not constricted by the narrow logic of capturing state power." Rather, Sheth discerns the need for new insight on micro-macro linkage. He concludes: "It is the dialectic between micro-practice and macro-thinking that will actualize a new politics of the future."

At this point it would be very difficult to prophesy where growing transformation in micro-macro linkage will lead us. One reason is that the idea that informed, purposeful action at the grassroots could shape global politics is so new to us. Indeed, the prevailing ideology of the state system has long made this possibility *unthinkable*. Yet transformations in the technology for human contact worldwide are producing new possibilities. Up to now these technologies have largely been under the control of states and corporations, but new visions for grassroots participation are suggesting ways in which many local places can be dynamic nodes in global affairs.

Growing transformation in the participation of the grassroots in world affairs is offering significant new potential for state officials and UN system officials grappling with global problems. But this potential can only be utilized if these officials take a more open-ended view of the global system in which states and the UN system are actors. States and the UN deserve much credit for providing the world with new standards for human relations on the planet. Now they must permit the state system and the UN system to adapt in ways that are necessary for the fulfillment of these standards. A new world system, with far greater participation from the grassroots could be emerging. The effective engagement of the grassroots is vitally necessary if an array of global problems are to be solved.

By underlining the significance of grassroots participation for a future world system competent to handle global problems, we do not wish to imply that grassroots movements necessarily have better solutions, nor that local leaders are more dedicated to the fulfillment of human development than are state or UN officials. All have an indispensable contribution to make from their territorial perspective. But it is necessary for all to permit a world system more responsive to human needs to grow out of a dialectic between representatives of local, state and global organizations.

SCHOLARS IN THE WORLD COMMUNITY

The United Nations has always been inhibited from fulfilling its programs and goals because the scientific talent of the world is largely at the service of large corporations and powerful states. Much of this talent is engaged in the development of military technology and in the development of products for corporations. Even research that is focused on "foreign affairs" and global problems tends to concentrate on state interests and contributes little to knowledge needs of the UN system. In particular, in research on global problems there is a glaring neglect on the programs and potential of UN organizations.

The United Nations system has, nevertheless, made important contributions to the development of worldwide scientific communities. Vital has been the support of UNESCO for the establishment of world organizations for individual scientific disciplines. This has also led to the creation of a union of worldwide association in the physical and natural sciences, the International Council of Scientific Unions (ICSU). There is a similar union of international social science organizations, the International Social Science Council (ISSC). ICSU has fomented a number of worldwide collaborative efforts, such as the International Geophysical Year and International Years of the Quiet Sun. The ISSC has developed multidisciplinary issue groups on peace and on technological change, youth and employment.

Because of limited resources, the UN lags far behind states and corporations in its ability to acquire the services of scientists. Nevertheless, through small contracts, consultations and conferences, organizations such as WHO, FAO, ILO, and others, have attempted to bring relevant knowledge to bear on UN problems. A shortcoming, of course, is that these scientists spend most of their time working on problems defined by states, corporations and foundations. Sometimes these problems are defined in ways useful to the UN, but often they are not.

The creation of UNITAR and the UN University are significant efforts through which the UN has attempted to establish separate research institutions, parallel to those created by many states. Among the contributions of UNITAR have been efforts to improve evaluation of UN development projects, future studies and studies of the role of nongovernmental organizations in the UN system. An important program has been training for new delegates to United Nations bodies. Most have been trained in the practice of diplomacy in the traditional diplomatic system and require training in multilateral diplomacy, particularly in the customary practice and rules of procedure for specific UN bodies.

The UN University has given the UN system additional capacity to bring relevant knowledge to bear on UN problems and to make scholars cognizant of these problems from a global perspective. The UN University has been particularly creative in developing sustained worldwide working groups and networks of scholars who work together in defining problems and proposing solutions appropriate to the UN context. As with all UN knowledge acquisition activities we have been describing, the UNU is severely constrained by its limited financial resources. For the most part scholars involved in UNU projects are making available to the UNU knowledge generated out of projects sponsored by other institutions. Nevertheless, the sustained work together by scholars coming from different traditions is pointing the way towards common solutions that take into account different cultural and ideological perspectives. And involvement in UNU is broadening the global perspective of participating scholars.

Whether working in the context of the UN system or outside, the greatest challenge for scholars is to help IGOs, INGOs, states, aspirant states and more local communities to develop visions that illuminate ways in which a diversity of actors can collaborate in the development of a world system more responsive to human needs. These visions would draw heavily on potential already revealed in transformation taking place—in local movements, in the style of INGO activity and in the UN system. But this will require that more scholars overcome the constraints that the ideology of the state system imposes on their perception and vision.

CONCLUSION

In conclusion, a forty-year review of the UN inevitably evokes disappointment that war, poverty and gross violations of human rights are still very prominent factors in human life on Earth. On the other hand, in many ways the UN now has potential far beyond that available at its founding. Because virtually all of the states of the world are members, it is far better equipped to deal with major world problems. It has available an array of standards for human life on the planet, incorporated in declarations and conventions, and experience in trying to implement these standards. Growth in the UN system has kept pace with the growing agenda of global problems that humanity must deal with through worldwide collaboration. Over the past forty years the UN has evolved new approaches for decision-making and conflict settlement out of the UN laboratory of experience. There is a growth of grassroots interest and concern in global issues that can offer new potential for mobilizing support needed for global approaches to pressing problems.

The UN of 1985 offers a hope and a challenge. The hope is in the fact that the UN definitely demonstrates that humankind is learning how to deal with common problems that transcend state boundaries. The UN is a tremendous advancement on the League of Nations. This offers hope that human beings may yet be able to channel in peaceful ways their penchant to extend their interests and activities to all parts of the globe and beyond. The challenge is that we may not be learning fast enough to keep up with our ever increasing competence to span the world and space beyond.

5. The United Nations, Lawmaking, and World Order

Samuel S. Kim

THE CHANGING IMAGE AND REALITY

Like the proverbial elephant and six blind beggars, international law too has suffered diverse perceptions and misperceptions. In troubled times when legality seems inapplicable to so many violent transgressions in international political life, international law has the extraordinary burden of defending its *raison d'être*. It is a revealing commentary that after three and a half centuries, international law is seldom referred to in many contemporary works on international relations, and the few that do have to grapple with the fundamental question of its existence: Is international law really law?

The more prevalent popular belief is that international law is not really law, or that even if it is, its principles and norms are being honored more in their breach than in their observance. This perception of international law as irrelevant or impotent derives largely from the fact that only the violations and alleged violations become media events. In recent years, international law has also received bad publicity because support and respect in its traditional strongholds, especially the liberal United States, have been steadily eroding. Indeed, it is commonplace nowadays to hear and even faddish to say that international law, as a behavioral guide in international relations, is in an absolute and precipitous decline.

Nowhere are these popular notions more clearly manifested than in the record of the Reagan administration for global unilateralism and official lawlessness. As represented by its first United Nations Ambassador Jeane Kirkpatrick, the administration has taken the position that international law should not be regarded as "a suicide pact" and that "unilateral compliance" with the UN Charter's principles of non-intervention and non-use of force may make sense in some isolated instances but hardly constitute a sound basis for U.S. foreign policy. This general disregard for international norms has, paradoxically enough, forced the Reagan "law-and-order" administration to rationalize its direct contraventions of the U.S. Constitution in defying the UN Charter, a treaty of the highest order.

Still, that even a superpower cannot really do without international law in the promotion of its egoistic interests is reflected by mainstream voices of concern and criticism. On April 12, 1984, the American Society of International Law, which is noted for its pro-business, anti-communist jurisprudential conservatism, voted overwhelmingly to deplore and urge rescission of the administration's decision to unilaterally and illegally withdraw from the jurisdiction of the International Court of Justice (ICJ) in disputes with any Central American state for the next two years. In the seventy-year history of the Society, this was the first time it had cast a critical vote on U.S. foreign policy. More to the point, the centralist *New York Times* characterized Washington's disappearing act at The Hague as "illegal, deceptive, and dumb."

But extrapolating about international law from the practices of one superpower in decline is to miss the context of a larger global reality. The nature of international law, or at least the general perception of it, has changed considerably since the Peace of Westphalia. As the normative foundation of the Westphalian international order (1648–1945), classical international law has long been perceived as a juridical expression of the ideological and cultural hegemony of the politically dominant Western societies during the heyday of colonial expansionism. The Third World was able to challenge it only collectively, as a global actor in the UN lawmaking process. The resulting "new" or "contemporary" international law, spawned by the UN's legislative process, has gradually come to be directed for the protection of the weak against the interventionary pressures of the strong. Indeed, the Third World has proved increasingly aggressive and innovative. The case of *Nicaragua v. United States of America* is a measure of the new willingness of a socialist David to challenge a capitalist Goliath in the principal judicial organ of the United Nations. Post-Mao China's "great legal turn outward" is another reminder of the changing nature of contemporary international law.

THE RELEVANCE OF INTERNATIONAL LAW

An uncynical and unsentimental world order approach to the relevance of international law calls for a dialectical analysis that will capture both the limitations and possibilities of law and lawmaking in international society. With international society divided by competing ideologies and interests, law or lawmaking is useful in a great variety of communicating and coordinating functions. International law acts as a socialization process to develop a common frame of reference for clarifying and regulating international life, rather than as a coercive instrument of crime and punishment. By participating in the lawmaking process the members of international society form collective norms, rules, and patterns of permissive behavior. As David Hume once noted, "it is only a general sense of common interest," which is mutually expressed and known to both, that "produces a suitable resolution and behavior." It is this "convention without the interposition of a promise," Hume argues, that structures social expectations and restrains human behavior.

The absence of a formal government or a formal enforcement machinery does not *ipso facto* negate the influence of law. Even in a domestic polity with centralized authority the state does not—and cannot—mobilize its enforcement power at the tail of every law. For the most part, legal rules are followed not because of police power or its threat but because of customary social habits or self-interest. The repeal of the prohibition (18th) amendment to the U.S. Constitution is a case in point. Indeed, Karl Deutsch has actually suggested a 90:10 formula for law compliance. Compliance habits, the invisible partner of government, do more than 90 percent of the work; and laws too divergent from the customary social habits of more than 10 percent of the population are virtually impossible to enforce. In a decentralized international system, therefore, enforcement costs without habitual widespread compliance will be prohibitively high.

Since compliance is largely a sociological problem, and not a legal one, how state actors actually behave is no less significant than any agreements (or implementation machinery) to which they might solemnly bind themselves. It is possible to have "law" without sanctions or even without legislative or enforcement machinery, but it is difficult to imagine law without norms and obligations. In addition, not every violation of a legal norm in a treaty *ipso facto* nullifies the treaty. For that to happen, the breach has to be "material," that is, of such gravity as to obviate the central purpose of the agreement. In fact, Emile Durkheim discovered "law" precisely in its breach: an action that shocks the collective community conscience is a crime, and law exists when "a sentiment, whatever its origin and end, is found in all minds with a certain degree of strength and clarity." Hence, when international norms lose validity and effectiveness as behavioral control, it is not because they failed to crystallize into "binding" law or lack enforcement machinery but because they are no longer perceived as serving the mutual interests of most states under changed conditions.

Rule following and norm compliance may not be worse in international society than it is in domestic society. Given the high frequency and incidence of domestic social systems ruptured by civil strife since 1945, the stability of the international legal order which is sustained by an elaborate and complex web of laws regulating routine transactions in international commerce, travel, and communications compares quite well with that of domestic legal order. Most nations, contrary to popular misconceptions, comply with most norms and rules of international law most of the time, guided by invisible though compelling calculations of perceived self-interest, whether on the basis of reciprocity, retaliation or reputation. [. . .]

The positivist/realist conception of legal norms and rules as a negative instrument of mutual restraint and abstention fails to capture the whole picture. Legal norms and rules are also positive enabling and empowering instruments in the conduct of foreign policy. Indeed, the expansion of international law from an essentially negative code of rules of abstention to positive rules of cooperation (or what Wolfgang Friedmann called "international law of co-operation") is one of the salient structural features of contemporary international law. As will be shown later, contemporary international law develops primarily through a legislative, not a judicial, process. Thanks to the quick mobilization of human expectations and capabilities by advances in global communications, unprecedented possibilities for global norm-making and culture-developing processes now exist. As a result, more and more "soft" laws have evolved through new and informal sources ("law-in-action") in tandem with the slower development of "hard" laws through traditional, formal sources ("law-in-book").

Of course, with its complexity, diversity, and proliferation in source and type, contemporary international law performs multiple functions in different levels with varying degrees of normative control and effectiveness. At the highest level of legal principles, contemporary international law is the embodiment of the collective moral judgment of humankind. But the problem here is the lack of clarity and coherence, or situation-specific criteria. By and large, contemporary international law in the domain of "high politics" shows these abstract and general characteristics. And because it lacks specificity, international law can be more easily stretched, that is to say, it is prone to be a flexible fig leaf or a propaganda instrument rather than a context-specific normative control. At the more prevalent functional level, however, contemporary international law is made up of regime norms and rules requiring specific behavior or outcome in given situations. In the domain of "low politics," international law bears the feature of each rule having its own specificity (delimited scope). Compliance is aided by the clarity and coherence of the rules, as well as because it is not a zero-sum game. Noncompliance here is much less common because a particular rule either applies to a particular situation or does not; one cannot stretch a specific rule too far without breaking it.

Beyond the empirical "law-as-fact" approach, there is need for a normatively grounded process conception of international law or lawmaking as an authoritative allocation of values as well as an affirmative instrument of goal pursuit, one that links law and politics as organic parts of the collective, cumulative process of norm generation. In international politics, as in domestic politics, the domain of morality and law and the domain of interest and power are coterminous. This teleological conception projects the development of international law as satisfying certain basic social needs in a decentralized international system. Hence, international law must be defined more broadly and realistically not only as a negative instrument of restraint—a codified set of rules and procedures—but also as an enabling positive instrument for expressing and directing evolving common aspirations and goals of the global community. Contemporary lawmaking must be considered also in terms of its capacity to meet the requirements of a just world order, but it is equally important to eschew a talismanic conception of law, as exemplified in the "world peace through world law" approach. Law is only one among several problem-solving and value-realizing instruments that facilitate the pursuit of a world order.

FROM AN "OLD" TO A "NEW" INTERNATIONAL LAW

To retain its relevance, international law must minimally satisfy two competing and, at times, conflicting requirements: continuity and stability, and reformist adaptation and change. Indeed, they represent the basic antinomy of the global lawmaking process. First, international law is expected to capture and codify the actual practice of the states (the law-in-action) to make the games the actors play more simple, stable, and predictable. These are the "rules of the game" and this is what "codification" entails: seeking clarity, order, and predictability in the relationships among international actors (subjects). The second task of lawmaking may be subsumed under the "progressive development of international law." This is the more challenging task of progressively remolding and reshaping global reality (Durkheim's "reality *sui generis*") in response to the changing demands and requirements of the global community. The long-term relevance and viability of international law largely depends upon the progressive development and adaptation of norms and rules in response to changing international conditions. In sum, international lawmaking must be a dynamic catalyst in shaping a new global consensus to bridge the gap between what *is* and what *ought* to be in the human condition.

Cultural relativists have often dismissed prematurely the normative potential of law or lawmaking in a multicultural world. It is wishful thinking, they argue, that a normative order can be achieved through the application of Western ideals of international law and organization. But this *a priori* assumption about the unfeasibility of establishing common norms and rules among the world's different cultures does not sit comfortably with the history of postwar UN lawmaking. International law and morality are not only possible in a multicultural world, as Terry Nardin claims, but also well-suited to deal with the difficulties created by such cultural and ideological diversity. Nardin maintains that "the evidence accumulated through historical and anthropological study suggests the existence of certain striking moral similarities among otherwise dissimilar societies," and that "many of the conflicts between Western and non-Western states concerning international law can be explained by the different situations and interests of each, without resorting to the idea of a cultural gap."

Postwar international lawmaking witnessed two discernible cycles. The first occurred during the "reconstruction" period of 1944–48, with the establishment and revamping of functional international regimes under the hegemonic leadership of the United States; the second came in the 1960s and 1970s under the revisionist challenge of the Third World. Over the last two decades, international law and international organization have increasingly become complementary aspects of an essentially Third World-led movement, with far-reaching consequences on all main arenas, procedures, and authoritative decisions of world community lawmaking.

Perhaps not surprisingly, world community lawmaking has taken place primarily in the United Nations or in special or ad hoc committees and plenipotentiary diplomatic conferences established or convened under the auspices of the United Nations General Assembly. Although denied formal "legislative" power at its inception, the General Assembly was nonetheless endowed with an ambiguous— and thus flexible—mandate in Article 13 (1) of the UN Charter, to initiate studies and make recommendations for the purpose of "promoting international co-oper-ation in the political field and encouraging the progressive development of inter-national law and its codification." Increasingly, the General Assembly has interpreted its ambiguous mandate expansively, and has thereby become the principal catalyst and sponsor of the international lawmaking process. While it lacks coercive power, under Third World dominance the General Assembly has engaged in "legislation by resolution" as the most expeditious and flexible means of responding to com-munity needs and pressures. The General Assembly is a highly condensed global network and, accordingly, it provides a sensitive barometer to evaluate innovations and trends in the development of contemporary international law and to assess their implications for world order.

The multiple and ever increasing pressures and demands of the new states, of technological change, cultural diversity, complex interdependence, and the democ-ratization of global negotiations have brought about a steady decline in the role and influence of traditional sources (Article 38 of the Statute of the ICJ) and lawmaking organs. The malaise afflicting the ICJ, the International Law Commission (ILC), and the Sixth (Legal) Committee is indicative of the recent stagnation and decline of "old" international law.

The International Court of Justice

The contribution of the ICJ to the progressive development of international law or the judicial settlement of disputes between state actors has been surprisingly modest. From the beginning the Court had the image problem of being a misconceived clone of the discredited League of Nations. Article 38 of the ICJ Statute was copied verbatim from Article 38 of the 1920 Statute of the Permanent Court of International Justice, and when the "new" Court met, it adopted the Rules of Court of its predecessor without any substantial change, seemingly looking backward to *la belle époque* for judicial continuity. In addition, the Court's physical and psychological remoteness from the realities of global politics in Geneva and New York, its sluggishness to institutional and procedural reform and adaptation, its domination by Western or Western-trained international lawyers (until recently), coupled with the general lack of enthusiasm for judicial legislation as a solution for social problems in the non-Western world, have all contributed to the progressive decline of the Court's significance in the international lawmaking process.

Of course, neglect begets neglect. During its first thirty-six years (1946–82), the Court handed down only eighteen advisory opinions (an average of 0.5 per year) and disposed of only forty-eight contentious cases (an average of 1.3 per year)—less than two cases a year, representing a marked decline both quantitatively and qualitatively in comparison to its League of Nations predecessor. Most of these cases came to the Court during its first twenty years, before the infamous *South West Africa* cases of 1966.

In both political and teleological terms, the Court's decision in the *South West Africa* cases was a self-inflicted disaster, from which it never fully recovered. By a bare majority of one (determined on the second, tie-breaking vote of the Court's president), the complaint against South Africa was dismissed on the technical ground of an insufficient legal interest on the part of Ethiopia and Liberia. Fairly or not, this judicial decision was perceived by many in the Third World as a contemporary variant on the racist majority opinion of the U.S. Supreme Court in *Dred Scott v. Sanford* (1857). Through Resolution 2145 (XXI), passed on October 27, 1966, by a vote of 114 to 2 with 3 abstentions, the General Assembly, in effect, countermanded the ICJ's decision by declaring South Africa's League of Nations mandate to administer South West Africa (Namibia) to be forthwith "terminated." With this act, the trust territory reverted back to the direct responsibility of the United Nations itself.

In a judicial volte-face five years later, the Court in the *Namibia* advisory opinion (1971) rectified the error of its 1966 decision. The *Namibia* opinion reflected a more dynamic, intertemporal conception of international law, seen not as a static, self-contained body of principles but as an evolving set of norms that "has to be interpreted and applied within the framework of the entire legal system prevailing at the time of the interpretation." However, this opinion was too little, too late for the Court to regain credibility.

In the *French Nuclear Tests* cases filed by Australia and New Zealand, the Court had a rare opportunity to rule on the legality of atmospheric nuclear tests. Yet the Court refused to bite the nuclear bullet, again on a narrow procedural pretext. In two final judgments (read *non*judgments) delivered on December 20, 1974, the Court declared that the issue had become moot with the unilateral declarations of the French government to terminate further atmospheric nuclear tests in the South Pacific. Once again, judicial conservatism prevailed over the newer demands of judicial legislation for the progressive development of international law.

What little the Court has contributed to the progressive development of international law is largely due to a number of dissenting opinions in contentious cases and several important advisory opinions: *Reparation for Injuries Suffered in the Service of the United Nations* (1949); *Reservations to the Convention on the Prevention and Punishment of the Crime of Genocide* (1951); *Certain Expenses of the United Nations* (1962); and *Legal Consequences for States of the Continued Presence of South Africa in Namibia (South West Africa)* (1971). Because the capacity of the ICJ to develop international law through contentious cases is greatly limited by the consent principle and the prevailing reluctance of many states—the U.S. repudiation of the ICJ in 1984 is the most dramatic illustration—including many of the forty-seven states that accepted the ICJ's compulsory jurisdiction to submit their disputes to international adjudication, the advisory opinion (reference jurisdiction) is the most promising path for the Court to participate in the UN lawmaking process. Since the early 1970s, however, neither the General Assembly nor the Security Council nor the Secretary-General has shown much inclination to make use of the Court's reference jurisdiction as part of UN lawmaking, despite the advantages of a process unhampered by the veto or consent principle.

But the ICJ cannot remain immune long from the changing political context and systemic pressures of UN global politics. In the first half of the 1980s, early signs of role reversals appeared, with First World states becoming progressively more disenchanted and Third World states becoming progressively more daring with the Court. The Third World's new political awareness and sophistication, shown in the politics of electing the ICJ judges in the General Assembly (most notably in the surprise election of Mohammed Bedjaoui, the brilliant and radical Algerian candidate in 1982, and of Prof. Ni Zhengyu in 1984, the first PRC jurist) and Nicaragua's first round "victory" (1984–85) against the United States in the Court, are psychologically and symbolically significant for the global underdogs. International law is a double-edged sword.

Still, the prospects of judicial activism in the international lawmaking process seem rather bleak. Since the 1966 debacle the Court has been fragmented by doctrinal division and drift among the individual national judges. The majority of the Court has shifted perceptibly from a positivistic, self-limiting role to a more self-consciously legislative path. But the shift has also widened the zone of judicial incoherence. Increasingly, the opinions of the Court are so seriously fragmented by multiple authorship that it is difficult to decipher the common ground of decision even in cases decided by near unanimity.

As in many other international organizations, fragmentation and politicization processes have proceeded in tandem in the Court. The Court relented to these pressures in *Delimitation of the Maritime Boundary in the Gulf of Maine Areas (Canada/United States)* (1984), setting a dangerous precedent by creating a five-judge special chamber. By selecting five judges—actually only three judges since the United States and Canada each added their national judge—exclusively from the West and by having this narrow, self-serving choice rubber-stamped and legitimized by the fifteen-judge ICJ, the United States and Canada moved their politicization game from word to deed. Yet "politicization" has been the pretext for the United States' unilateral withdrawal from the Court's jurisdiction in *Nicaragua v. the United States*, or for that matter from UNESCO.

The International Law Commission

The decline of the ILC is perhaps more surprising. Established by the General Assembly in 1947 as a permanent subsidiary organ to carry out the Charter mandate (Article 13), the ILC is composed of prominent jurists chosen not as representatives of their governments, but as persons of recognized competence in international law. The selection process gives due consideration to representing the main forms of civilization and the principal legal systems of the world. The ILC was expected to do path-breaking preparatory work on the progressive development and codification of international law, for which the UN Charter gives no criteria.

From the outset, the main discussions in the General Assembly made a clear distinction between codification and progressive development, a distinction embodied in the ILC Statute. Codification is "the more precise formulation and systemization of rules of international law in fields where there already has been extensive state practice, precedent or doctrine;" progressive development was defined as "the preparation of draft conventions on subjects which have not yet been sufficiently developed in the practice of States." A favorite activity of nineteenth-century international lawyers, codification has a static *status quo* bias. It is the quest for a set of established precedents and rules, to be canonized as (customary) international law. Progressive development is more dynamic; it is a continuing adaptive, open-ended process of forming an alternative body of norms and rules. The traditional legal norms prevailing at the end of World War II were inherited from a Eurocentric colonial era, and do not reflect the interests and traditions of a much broader, pluralistic international community. The mandate for the progressive development of international law provides the potential for adjusting and adapting the international legal order to gradually shift from the sovereignty-based Westphalian legal order toward a more community-oriented social order.

Yet by its own evaluation, the ILC has in practice made no distinction between the rules of international customary law that it codifies and the rules it formulates for a progressive development. Rather, it deliberately limited itself to those topics and state practices deemed "ripe" for codification conferences. The list of the ILC's accomplishments gives one a sense of *deja vu*; it maps familiar terrain from the Convention on Special Missions (1969), through to the Vienna Convention on the Succession of States in Respect of Treaties (1978). Indeed, that the protection of the diplomatic bag has occupied the center stage of the ILC in recent years is a revealing commentary.

The Commission's excessive preoccupation with legally "ripe" and politically "safe" issues is responsible for the proliferation of ad hoc or special bodies to formulate new norms and rules of international law. Because the ILC's image is that of an expert, elitist body deeply anchored in traditional sources and closely wedded to a static conception of UN lawmaking, the Third World majority in the General Assembly has come to shun it—and its parent supervisory body, the Sixth Committee—and seek alternative means for the progressive development of international law. As early as 1959, the General Assembly had set up the Committee on the Peaceful Uses of Outer Space as the focal point of UN lawmaking on outer space, producing five multilateral treaties. Instead of turning Arvid Pardo's 1967 proposal for the right to the common heritage of mankind over to the ILC, the

General Assembly created the Committee on the Peaceful Uses of the Sea-Bed and the Ocean Floor Beyond the Limits of National Jurisdiction. And to develop the principles and rules of international law relating to the New International Economic Order (NIEO), the General Assembly entrusted UNITAR with the task of preparing an analytical study in 1980. Beyond these reminders that the ILC has lost its credibility as the principal agent for the progressive development of international law, resorting to these special committees has forced the Sixth Committee to consider and comment upon the reports of these special committees.

Diversification of the Sources of Lawmaking

With the entry of these new actors, new issues, new demands, and new aspirations into the UN lawmaking process, traditional sources have been supplemented and even superceded by more informal and innovative sources. The international lawmaking process now takes place primarily in political forums with universal membership, where participants can transform both criteria and contents of contemporary international law as the collective expression of new global situations. This process relies heavily upon multilateral diplomacy and global bargaining to produce normative declarations and multilateral conventions.

International custom in the traditional sense has lost its relative importance as a source of contemporary international law. By definition, an international custom must satisfy the requirements of long duration, settled practice, and wide acceptance (*opinio juris sive necessitatis*), all of which are difficult to reconcile with the fast rhythm and heavy demands of a rapidly changing, increasingly interdependent, and technological world. In this context, the slow and vague evolutionary process of customary international law cannot be countenanced; the so-called "instant customary law" is a legal non sequitur. The status of customary international law plummeted even further with the entry of the Third World into the international normative process. As could be expected, the new states refused to be bound by the customary rules of past state practice in which they had played no lawmaking role. Indeed, the Third World views much of customary international law as merely codifying the wills and practices of colonial and neocolonial actors, lending credence to the Soviet theory that the sources of international law are based on the coordination and consent of the manifest wills of states of different social and economic systems.

The postwar period witnessed phenomenal growth in the role and importance of international treaties and conventions at the expense of customary law. In an increasingly interdependent world, the utility of bilateral treaties is declining while multilateral treaties have become "the main device in the legal regulation of relations between States." Since the end of World War II, some 200 multilateral treaties have been concluded under the auspices of the United Nations.

Yet the practice of multilateral treaty-making, especially through plenipotentiary diplomatic conferences, is now in trouble. It entails an agonizingly slow process of working out an unending series of compromises on the principles, norms, and procedures so that a given convention is acceptable to as many member states as possible. The ratification process is equally slow. For example, the process of completing two major human rights conventions took almost three decades: the politics of drafting consumed two decades (1947–66), and ratification a third (1966–76). In the ILC, the time lag between the initial exploration of a topic and its completion as a draft convention is generally seven to ten years, and it usually takes another six to eight years for a convention to be ratified and enter into force. In spite of this protracted process of compromise, the reservations attached to multilateral treaties have multiplied along with the number, variety, and scope of such treaties. The ratification record is not encouraging either: the UN Secretary-General's recent report on the status of multilateral treaties deposited with the United Nations list many as having fewer than thirty states as parties.

In large part, this is because the whole process is neither economical, efficient, nor effective. The number, form, and scope of multilateral treaties have grown unchecked, and the snail's pace of treaty-making conferences strains the resources of member states, especially small Third World countries whose governments find it difficult to have their legal experts away for more than six weeks. Treaties are increasingly shackled with unilateral reservations. Lawmaking plenipotentiary conferences, with the possible exception of the Third United Nations Conference on the Law of the Sea (UNCLOS III), have never commanded the universal attendance of a General Assembly session. A vicious cycle has developed between slow tempo and decreasing participation. As a multilateral lawmaking conference drags on, the number of participants declines. This widens the gap between original expectations and a final convention, increasing both reservations and holdouts.

To enhance the efficiency, if not also the certainty, of the law-developing process, the General Assembly has increasingly resorted to normative resolutions as a more speedy and flexible means of formulating and catalyzing community expectations on a wide range of global problems. For the Third World, this strategy has amounted to a passion. Because of its flexibility, its speed, economy, and efficiency, and above all because it crystallizes the collective will of the global community, the General Assembly resolution holds a special attraction for Third World states.

The demonstrated capacity of these global underdogs to control and dominate the resolution-making and consensus-generating process to legitimate their claims and interests is at the heart of American and Soviet disenchantment with the General Assembly. Faced with the Third World's dominance in the global politics of collective legitimation and delegitimation, the Soviet Union and the United States (often joined by the United Kingdom) have formed an unholy alliance in opposing any legislative character for the General Assembly or any Charter review of the unanimity principle in the name of enhancing fiscal integrity and administrative efficiency.

There is a good deal of sterile debate as to whether resolutions, even if called charters or declarations, can be accepted as a new source of international law or of legal obligation. However, the heated debate over whether resolutions are "binding" or not obscures the crucial and powerful effect of some normative resolutions in mobilizing public opinion and disarming initial opposition. In response to this influence, some states accept, or at least acquiesce in, resolutions whose contents and terms they would not otherwise accept in a multilateral treaty. The litmus test of the General Assembly resolution is its substantive character and its influence on the behavior of international actors.

Almost twenty years ago, Richard A. Falk pointed out that "the characterization of a norm as *formally binding* is not very significantly connected with its *functional operation* as law." A more recent study has shown that the behavioral (implementation) record of binding resolutions is only marginally better than that of nonbinding ones. Even domestic and international courts have relied upon various legal instruments (including General Assembly resolutions) as sources of laws and obligations for states and individuals, a practice that further blurs the distinction between binding and nonbinding norms and thus helps legitimate General Assembly resolutions as a *source* of law. In *Filartiga v. Pena-Irala* (1980), the U.S. Court of Appeals, Second Circuit, declared that General Assembly resolutions on human rights "specify with great precision the obligations of member nations under the Charter." And in its advisory opinion on Namibia in 1971, the ICJ upheld General Assembly Resolution 2145 of 1966, which, in terminating South Africa's mandate in Namibia, reaffirmed the Assembly's previous Resolution 2074 (XX) condemning apartheid as a crime against humanity. In theory and practice, then, the general trend is clearly toward a qualified acceptance of the various functions that General Assembly resolutions play in the global lawmaking process.

Of course, not all resolutions are equal; some are more important than others in the progressive development of international law. Generally, a resolution capped by the term "declaration" plays a more significant role. According to a memorandum prepared by the UN Office of Legal Affairs and submitted to the Commission on Human Rights in 1962, a "declaration" in UN practice "is a solemn instrument resorted to only in very rare cases relating to matters of major and lasting importance where maximum compliance is expected." To the extent that the expectation of compliance is justified by state practice, the memo further notes, "a declaration may by custom become recognized as laying down rules binding upon States." Many declaratory resolutions, including the Universal Declaration of Human Rights, the Resolution on Permanent Sovereignty over Natural Resources, and the Declaration on the Granting of Independence to Colonial Countries and Peoples, were harbingers of this law-crystallizing process, expressing authoritative and legitimate allocations of common interests or values for the world community (*opinio juris communis*). The authority and legitimacy of this lawmaking process stem from the General Assembly being the only available global forum with universal membership and the competence to discuss any matters of international concern, where member states can seek a fit between national and common interests as a way of expressing the general will and of translating this will into law.

Some resolutions serve as an important first statement of new rules and norms of international law to be further refined and embodied in multilateral treaties. A number of times, the General Assembly itself has engaged in treaty-making by resolution. Some resolutions serve as trial balloons to test norms and principles through state practice before they are firmly codified in a multilateral treaty. A series of related resolutions is a good indication of general community interest in a subject or problem. Other resolutions are merely rhetorical quick fixes, with negligible practical effect upon the problems or state policies to which they are addressed. The legal/political status of a given resolution depends on such attributes as the peremptory language, supportive weight, and frequency of subsequent recitation, as well as on a number of situational intervening variables during the UN law-declaring or lawmaking process. In the final analysis, however, the normative potency of a given resolution depends on how it affects state practice.

[*   *   *]

CONCLUSION

The postwar international system witnessed a dramatic, if somewhat uneven, development of international law with two big waves of normative cycles. The most remarkable change occurred during the second when, for the first time in the history of international relations, the hitherto forgotten two-thirds of humankind played a dominant role in UN lawmaking. Classical international law as the expression of the will of the great powers had served primarily the interests of the rich and the powerful. The greater distribution of normative power has enhanced the prospect of establishing a nonhegemonic international legal order.

Many of the normative initiatives for the progressive development of international law have originated from the new states of the Third World. A few examples may suffice: the 1963 initiative of Bolivia, Brazil, Chile, Ecuador, and Mexico for a nuclear-free zone in Latin America; China's pronouncement and popularization of the nuclear no-first-use principle in 1964; Malta's (Arvid Pardo) proposal for a "common heritage of mankind" regime for the oceans in 1967; Mexico's (Luis Echeverria) leadership for the formulation of the Charter of Economic Rights and Duties of States in 1972; Algeria's (Houari Boumedienne) initiative in January 1974 calling for the Sixth Special Session of the General Assembly to inaugurate the NIEO process; and Nicaragua's lawsuit against the United States in the ICJ in 1984. Both in terms of participants and subject matters, the frontiers of contemporary international law have been expanded to the extent that one can now speak of a "global law."

Taking advantage of its overwhelming numerical majority, the Third World caucus in global group politics (the Group of 77) turned the General Assembly into the central global forum for projecting its will as the *opino juris communis* and as the wave of the future world. In the process, the General Assembly and the special lawmaking committees and conferences authorized by it have served as a functional equivalent for a global parliament. The explosion in the membership of the United Nations, which began in 1955 and culminated in 1971 with the entry of the People's Republic of China, has transformed both the institutional setting and the policy agenda of multilateral diplomacy. The rising Third World dominance has not only destroyed the automatic pro-Western voting machine in the General Assembly but also dealt a lethal blow to the early U.S. expansive, liberal conception of the Charter and of the General Assembly lawmaking mandate.

Law and politics have always emerged indistinguishably in the authoritative formulation and allocation of values for the global community. The current novelty lies not so much in the sudden rise of politicization in international organizations, as the United States often claims, as in that politicization has shifted from a pro-American to an anti-American bias, and from an East-West to a North-South axis.

This shift also accounts for the general decline and desuetude of such principal conservative legal organs such as the ICJ, ILC, and the Sixth Committee in the international lawmaking process. UN lawmaking has now become a quintessentially politicized process, taking place primarily in the General Assembly or in the special committees or conferences under its supervisory auspices.

But in spite of all these lawmaking advances and some incremental adaptations of international economic regimes to Third World development needs, there has been no fundamental restructuring of the global political economy to meet the NIEO demands of justice, equity, and individual and collective self-reliance for the Third World. One of the most salient paradoxes of the postwar era is the widening disjuncture between extravagant normative claims and modest institutional capabilities. The development of NIEO politics to date demonstrates that the powerful may acquiesce in the normative claims of the weak for socioeconomic justice, provided these claims are not implemented within the structure of power and influence in international institutions. The transformation of international economic regimes remains devoid of any substantive content. Continued Third World dependency and poverty is the order of the day.

The democratization and politicization of the international lawmaking process has brought about a greater diversification in the sources, arenas, and contents of contemporary international law. As a result, the domain of "soft law," emanating from informal and nontraditional sources, has been greatly expanded. A multitude of diverse, pliable, and closely related norms with varying degrees of authoritativeness compete without the benefit of an ultimate judicial determination. International lawmaking has become coextensive with the global politics of collective legitimation and delegitimation, blurring the distinction between "law" and "politics."

Traditional customary and treaty laws are too problematic, take too long to make or to crystallize, and have too short a life span in an era of revolutionary change. The growing scarcity of resources, advancing technology, exploding population, and conflicting claims have provided the impetus for more flexible ways of regulating international society and filling in the normative vacua in the global commons without meeting the requirements of overly tidy multilateral treaties. The international normative process codified by customary and treaty law now represents only the tip of the iceberg. Lawmaking has been most extensive—and compliance is most consistent—in those domains remote from states' security interests, such as the developing international economic law, trade law, environmental law, humanitarian (*jus in bello*) law, and outer space law.

The move toward collective UN lawmaking has been helped by a gradual shift from the formal procedure of registering state wills and consent through recorded voting to an informal procedure of "consensual" decision making. Consensus, characterized by the absence of any formal voting or of any expressed opposition, has now become the dominant mode of decision making in practically all the law-developing and lawmaking bodies, with the obvious exception of the ICJ. Since the mid-1960s, some fifteen international organizations and conferences have adopted consensus as their *modus operandi*. The chief catalyst for consensual decision making was the establishment of UNCTAD and its organization of the member states into four global interest groups (A, B, C, and D) in the mid-1960s.

Since then it has become increasingly difficult to articulate and aggregate competing interests without resorting to the consensual procedure. As dramatically demonstrated by the decade-long bargaining for the establishment of a global ocean regime at UNCLOS-III, UN lawmaking has become a function of interest-group politics. In this context, consensus is another name for the consent of the major interest groups. The international lawmaking process has shifted from the "sources of law" to the consensual mode of global bargaining and decision-making.

With the entry of so many actors, new issues and new pressures, UN lawmaking has become diffused and fragmented. The present organization of international society, made up of states of unequal economic and military power and diverse cultural traditions and geopolitical interests, is the most serious structural constraint on international law. As a result, contemporary international law lacks coherence, clarity, and certainty in content and direction. By itself, contemporary international law cannot bear the burden of the quest for a just world order.

There is growing awareness of the need for a more comprehensive, system-wide process to restore credibility and cohesion to the progressive development and codification of international law. Contemporary international law is showing evidence of an identity crisis. What is its real name? Is it "transnational law" (Philip Jessup), the "common law of mankind" (C. Wilfred Jenks), "world law" (Percy Corbett, Grenville Clark, and Louis Sohn), "international law of welfare" (B.V.A. Roling), "the international law of co-operation" (Wolfgang Friedmann), "the evolving international law of development" (Oscar Schachter), or "international law of human dignity" (Myres S. McDougal, Harold D. Lasswell, and Lung-chu Chen)?

This lack of coherence reflects the "reality *sui generis*" of international society in an era of system transition. Two mutually contradictory and countervailing trends of the world historical process—universalism and heterogeneity, globalism and nationalism, integration and fragmentation—are pulling and pushing UN lawmaking into divergent directions. This complex and confusing global reality renders itself to conflicting interpretations and conclusions about the total systemic impact of the postwar international lawmaking process. From an optimistic and sanguine perspective, Oscar Schachter concludes "that the structure of the state system is being fundamentally transformed and that the treaty regimes in their diversity and multiplicity are evidence of this transformation." More dialectically and soberly, Richard A. Falk sees the general decline of international law as evidence that our civilization is at a Grotian turning point, from which "there can either be a breakdown or a breakthrough." More often than not, it seems to me, the tensions between contradictory pressures are papered over, not resolved, by the compromised coexistence of globalist principles at a high level of generality and of state practice at the operational level of international life. Yet the interpenetrative osmosis between the two levels of law cannot be gainsaid.

The creation of a universally based normative order still seems seriously constrained by dominant statist interests and the structure of the present world order system. Although UNCLOS-III was launched in response to normative pressures to manage the global commons on the basis of shared community interests, it ended with the triumph of dominant (coastal) state interests. The common heritage of mankind, according to the original Maltese conception, was something that could be *shared and used but not owned.* But what emerged from UNCLOS is more like real estate which is *owned* by mankind or by all states in the name of mankind. In practical terms, the common heritage of mankind has been squeezed out from all sides by the 200-mile exclusive economic zones, covering one-third of the oceans' waters and bed and preempting over 90 percent of the oceans' fish and oil. Yet what little area left for the International Seabed Authority to regulate, an area of relatively little economic importance, was characterized by *New York Times* columnist William Safire as a "great rip-off" of the rich nations by the poor ones. The whole notion, declared President Reagan's special representative to UNCLOS-III, "is inimical to the fundamental principles of political liberty, private property, and free enterprise." When international legal scholars talk about the "legal breakthrough" in UNCLOS, ironically enough, they mean this emaciated "common heritage of mankind" in the Convention devoted to the seabed and the mining and development of their mineral and other resources. Given the serious ideological split between the United States (joined by the United Kingdom and West Germany) and the Group of 77, the current depressed prices for copper, nickel, cobalt and manganese, the undeveloped technology of deep seabed mining, and the unsettled legal and financial issues, however, the prospects for the global deep seabed regime coming into operation are rather bleak.

The great advances and innovations in UN lawmaking during the second wave of normative cycles have gone a long way in enhancing the formal and symbolic equality of all states, big or small. But there is a danger in uncritically accepting quantitative ephenomenal change as evidence of system-transforming change. The proliferation of nonstate actors—some 750 NGOs now have UN "consultative status"—is insufficient evidence of a state-diminishing (system transforming) development, for progressive nonstate actors still struggle at the periphery of the system. As it is now constituted, the United Nations accords preferential treatment to statist claims and interests over human interests. Since the mid-1970s, only those NGOs with the least political relevance and impact have succeeded in gaining consultative status. As a result, UN lawmaking leaves little space for the voices of the oppressed or for global *human* interests. The structure of UN lawmaking still allows the interests, views, and values of the *dominant* elite classes in national and international societies to prevail. The political will and normative energy to create an alternative just and humane world order are more likely to emanate from those who bear the brunt of the present oppressive system of world order.

Even in the most "democratic," "representative," and "globalist" General Assembly, which plays the central role in UN lawmaking, the voices of "we the peoples of the United Nations," in whose name and behalf the UN Charter was promulgated, remain largely unrepresented and unheard. To rectify this representational anomaly and to empower the peoples of the world to hold their "princes and merchants" accountable for the consequences of their actions in the world organization, Marc Nerfin advances an imaginative proposal for a three-chamber General Assembly with the Prince Chamber representing the governments of the states, the Merchant Chamber the economic powers (transnational, multinational, national or local, belonging to the private, state or social sectors), and the Citizen Chamber representing the people and their associations.

At its fortieth anniversary, the United Nations stands at a crossroads. The old system of international order has already been discredited beyond redemption and an alternative system of a more just and humane world order is not yet in the offing. In the final analysis, contemporary international law is an expanded and revised supplement of, not an alternative to, classical international law. For the most part it is still a state-centric system anchored in such principles as state sovereignty, state equality, state responsibility, and state rights maintained by and for states. In short, contemporary international law is not so much a post-Westphalian system as it is a neo-Westphalian system. The basic challenge ahead is to seek a better interface between UN lawmaking and the voices of the unheard and the unrepresented by opening up more and more channels of communication and contact with the non-state social actors and forces struggling at the periphery of the present world order system.

6. Developments in Decision Making in the United Nations

Johan Kaufmann

HISTORICAL BACKGROUND

For better understanding of the current situation it is indispensable to return to the events and thoughts surrounding the establishment of the United Nations. Both in the political and in the economic area the founders of the United Nations were anxious to avoid repetition of what happened in the period between the two World Wars. In the political sphere, the system laid down in the UN Charter was based on the assumption of a unity concerning ends (and presumably also means) among the five permanent members of the Security Council. East-West rivalry, starting as early as the Yalta Conference and continuing into the Cold War has played havoc with this idealistic set-up. While in the opinion of most observers even the present functioning of the United Nations in dispute settlement is distinctly superior to that of the League of Nations, there can also be no doubt that the hopes of the founders that the Security Council would deal rapidly and efficiently with most, if not all, international conflicts have not been fulfilled.

In the economic sphere, the UN Charter was perhaps equally as innovative as in the part dealing with peace-keeping. The errors of the years of the Great Depression, such as protectionist 'beggar-thy-neighbour' policies, which had led to much misery and unemployment, were to be avoided by a new system that could be described as one of collective economic security, somewhat parallel to that of collective political security. It is remarkable that agreement was reached, given the fact that there were important differences of views between the Americans, the British, and the Russians. In the negotiation for the creation of the Bretton Woods Organizations (IMF, IBRD) it had become apparent that the United States wanted to have a set of clear rules which would more or less automatically provide for an orderly international financial system. The British, under the impact of their great wartime physical losses, aimed at a system that would tend to provide financial assistance beyond that which would seem to follow from automatic rules. Keynes, the main negotiator for the British, wanted to insert in the rules of the International Monetary Fund (IMF) a proviso that would ensure action by creditor nations. He had in mind, of course, the United States and the prospect—which was the strong belief of many at that time—of a permanent dollar storage. At the same time, the British did not want a system that meant too much interference with autonomy in economic decisions, specifically the presumed need to maintain discriminatory trade arrangements, such as the imperial preference system, over an extended period of time. Keynes' proposal for action in the field of commodities (an essential part of the still-born International Trade Organization) fitted into this approach, and anticipated the later problems of developing countries.

The idea of a central economic role for the United Nations (Chapters IX and X of the Charter) had not fallen from the sky. The United States had proposed at the Dumbarton Oaks conference a small co-ordinating body for economic and social matters to be subordinate to the General Assembly. The British and Russians did not like this proposal. The British, interestingly, believed that economic and social matters should come generally under the Security Council; they were against bringing economic and social problems under the general United Nations. At San Francisco the small states obtained the upgrading of the Economic and Social Council (ECOSOC) to a 'principal organ of the United Nations'. Chapters IX and X on International Economic and Social Co-operation and the ECOSOC make impressive reading, even today. The all-embracing language of Article 55 concerning, *inter alia*, the promotion of economic and social development together with the right of initiative for ECOSOC in Article 62 made it possible to engage in important work. Indeed, in the early years that is precisely what ECOSOC did, for example, by initiating the early studies on national and international measures for full employment, measures for international economic stability, and measures for the economic development of underdeveloped countries. These were groundbreaking initiatives and were imbued by a spirit of genuine international co-operation.

The Charter assumes that a 'conference approach' to international economic matters could be combined with a negotiating formula. The key phrase in this connection is Article 56 of the Charter: 'All Members pledge themselves to take *joint* and separate action in co-operation with the Organization for the achievement of the purposes set forth in article 55' (author's emphasis). Joint action is, of course, not conceivable without negotiations within a conference framework. In the course of the years, debate and negotiation became increasingly entangled in a manner which was unconstructive. The assumption of the Charter has, however, been fulfilled to a degree which the optimists will surely qualify as 'considerable' and the pessimists see as 'disappointing'.

OLD AND NEW ACTORS WITHIN THE UN SYSTEM

The system laid down in the Charter was also based on the assumption that only governments participate in decision making at the United Nations. Moreover, according to the rules of the General Assembly which are based on the Charter, governments were presumed to be voting and acting individually. An exception to this overwhelming role of governments was the right of initiative given to the Secretary-General, under Article 99 of the Charter, to bring any matter threatening international peace or security to the attention of the Security Council. It soon became apparent that actors additional to individual governments were to make their appearance: firstly, governments started to function as groups which conceivably could be seen as a part-way step towards the joint action by all member States prescribed in Article 56 of the UN Charter. The continuance of the Cold War and the formation of North Atlantic Treaty Organization (NATO) and the Warsaw Pact intensified the early habit of bloc voting, based on group positions of NATO and Warsaw Pact countries respectively. The United States and its allies, being numerically superior, regularly outvoted the USSR and its allies. The automatic majority was not considered as any kind of tyranny by those in the majority. Group positions were officially sanctioned for electoral matters, as, for example, the election of the president and the vice-presidents of the General Assembly. For many important matters *ad hoc* coalitions were formed. This was typically the case for certain economic matters. Thus the establishment of the UN Special Fund in 1958 was possible, the scope of which was determined by a more manageable problem ('pre-investment') than the ambitious set-up of Special United Nations Fund for Economic Development (SUNFED) because a group of like-minded countries, including Brazil, India, Yugoslavia, Denmark and The Netherlands was able to negotiate a compromise between extremists on both sides, that is, the United States which (wishing to eliminate competition with the World Bank and the IMF from an institution like the United Nations where the United States did not control the votes) rejected the idea of any organization bearing a resemblance to SUNFED and certain developing countries which insisted on the need for a full-fledged Capital Development Fund. The early existence of the phenomenon of group acting in UN decision making should be remembered because the impression is sometimes created that this is something new since the formation in 1964 of the Group of 77 developing countries and of the Non-Aligned Movement.

Another unforeseen development was that the secretariat (or rather specific parts of the secretariat) started to play a role in decision making (separate from the powers given the Secretary-General in the UN Charter). Especially in the economic sector the UN secretariat became active in promoting certain ideas, sometimes by peddling fully elaborated draft resolutions among state delegations. Some of these delegations were eager to co-operate with the secretariat, for a variety of reasons, in order, for example, to secure secretariat backing for their own initiatives. To the degree that the secretariat, especially in the early years, was the originator of needed international activity, this practice is quite acceptable. If, however, it leads to biased origins of decision making, contrary to the consensus principle, it cannot be considered as positive.

Similarly, chairmen have assumed tasks beyond the formal powers foreseen in the General Assembly rules of procedure. It has become normal practice that a presiding officer mediates in a conflict situation. In the Security Council such a role of the President is of course considered normal. Another group of new actors was soon constituted by the Non-Governmental Organizations. In accordance with the ground-breaking Article 71 of the UN Charter on arrangements for consultation with Non-Governmental Organizations (NGOs), the ECOSOC formally recognized NGOs from an early date and gave them status in terms of the right to submit or receive papers, the right to make written or oral statements, etc. In the General Assembly no similar arrangements exist, at least not formally. Yet, especially in the field of human rights, NGOs were active from an early date, and often played a far from negligible role in decision making and in negotiations, particularly by preparing draft resolutions. There is little doubt that the role and involvement of the private sector will gradually increase. It is desirable that in each important UN undertaking the provisions made for the participation of NGOs should be examined to see if improvements could be made. Indeed the United Nations Charter was based on the co-operation of the peoples of the United Nations. However, as Alger has pointed out, many of the 4615 international NGOs have limited influence because they do not have strong grassroots participation in their activities, their policies being made by a small elite in their national headquarters. In some cases specialized agencies and other UN bodies have considered certain NGOs which have voiced constant criticisms, as an 'irritant'.

The private sector has gradually assumed a variety of modes of participation in the UN decision-making process. In many specific negotiations the private sector actively participates, as in the case of the cocoa negotiations under the auspices of UNCTAD. In the case of the Commission on Transnational Corporations, representatives of the private sector are formally incorporated; representatives of the trade unions and universities are appointed as expert advisers, who individually or as a group may be consulted by the executive director of the UN Centre on Transnational Corporations or by the Commission itself.

The above remarks were based essentially on the United Nations but in the broader UN system various specialized agencies have different modes of decision making. In the World Bank and the IMF the size of participation in the share capital determines the weight of each participant's vote. In the International Labour Organization (ILO) the long-established tripartite system admits employers and trade unionists as full participants in decision making.

In all three cases just mentioned, the World Bank, the IMF and the ILO, decision-making procedures are distinctly more efficient, in terms of time needed and resources spent, than in the United Nations. Annual conference time is considerably shorter than the near-interminable General Assembly. Both the World Bank and the ILO have a procedure for selecting draft resolutions to be dealt with at each annual conference which avoids the plethora of resolutions discussed in the UN General Assembly.

Other developments which have had an impact on UN decision making as conceived in the UN Charter have been:

- The rise of operational programmes; these have been particularly associated with the World Bank group, UN Development Programme, UN International Children's Emergency Fund (UNICEF), and others. The governing bodies of these programmes function very much by consensus method.
- The method of holding 'global conferences' under UN auspices; the first and still probably the most important example of the new series of world conferences is the Stockholm Conference on the Environment held in 1972. It paved the way for permanent machinery in this field (UN Environment Programme, with a secretariat in Nairobi). These conferences have performed a public relations and educational function in areas such as habitat, food, population, and water. However, plans of action, almost ritually adopted, have been only partly implemented, if at all. Yet in many conferences, various government departments have gradually brought their practices and, in some cases, their national legislation into conformity with the recommendations of global UN conferences. It would, however, be useful to have each new proposal for a world conference under UN auspices preceded by rigorous analysis of costs and expected benefits (indeed to have such analysis for all proposals calling for new activities).
- The significance of the voting pattern has changed. The number of abstentions is much larger than in early UN years. If one is in favour one can declare a yes vote or abstain, if one is against one declares a no vote or abstains, and some

argue that it does not matter how one votes. Hence, the number of 'explanations of votes' has risen strongly.

• The more subtle use of procedural and parliamentary tactics. Opponents to a motion or proposition have a wide choice of such tactics which include referring to some other body ('ping-pong game'); log-rolling, stirring up opposition, and tabling amendments and/or alternative proposals in the hope of creating confusion, with the result that all proposals are referred to the next session, or to a subsidiary body. Of course, these tactical moves are not essentially different from what occurs in normal parliamentary practice. Yet their abundant use in UN diplomacy comes as a surprise to those who had hoped for idealistic international co-operation.

CHANGED ENVIRONMENTAL ELEMENTS

Not only have the impact and composition of actors in UN decision making changed, and their tactics evolved, but also a number of modified environmental elements have put their stamp on decision making and non-decision making in the United Nations. Among these elements the following should be noted (the order does not necessarily indicate their relative importance): increased membership, the rise of nationalism, changed attitudes of the superpowers, change in the level of confidence in international organizations, repetitive debates and politicization.

Increased Membership

The membership of the United Nations has more than tripled from the original number of 51 founding members. This has meant that procedures have become more cumbersome and time-consuming. According to an old adage it is difficult to negotiate effectively with more than seven in a room. The drawback can be, and has been, overcome by operating in small groups which report back to larger groups. But perhaps more importantly, the new member States come mostly from cultures which were not necessarily accustomed to the Western democracy type of decision-making processes. The new members from Asia and Africa were not used to making decisions by majority vote. They were more familiar with group caucusing followed by consensus, with often a naturally dominant position of the older or the wiser members of the group. Once in the United Nations they quickly grasped the essence of the voting system and some of them probably believed that the original members would abide by the consequences of majority decision making which they had earlier devised. The pressure for a New International Economic Order was linked to the hope of developing countries that even though UN decisions are not binding, majority decisions made in the United Nations would have a convincing impact on the defeated minority. They soon realized that in sensitive economic or political matters the majority cannot impose its will on the minority, especially if the minority includes important economic powers. The sixth and seventh special sessions of the General Assembly (1974 and 1975) on the New International Economic Order reflected this ambiguous situation with both sides having to adjust to what was, in fact, a novel situation, both in terms of the political power configuration and in view of the professed objective to negotiate about a great variety of delicate economic matters within a severely limited timespan.

Rise of Nationalism

The internationalism which inspired the founding fathers of the United Nations has been widely substituted by a rampant nationalism. In a certain sense the United Nations has reinforced nationalism because countries which have just acquired independence react nationalistically when it is suggested that powers should be handed to some international body. Let me recall a relevant comment: '. . . Where we should be dealing with all-embracing economic, political and social problems, we discuss minor trade objectives, or small national advantages. . . We must substitute, before it is too late, imagination for tradition; generosity for shrewdness; understanding for bargaining . . . wisdom for prejudice. . .'. These words are not from some vague starry-eyed world reformer but from the hard-boiled Bretton Woods negotiator for the United States in 1944, Harry White. What has happened is that many states prefer to live with some international conflict, possibly because it is the only rallying element in an otherwise difficult domestic situation. In addition, the vagaries of economic life have produced new conflict situations.

Changed Attitude of the Superpowers

The attitude of the two superpowers vis-à-vis the United Nations is, of course, of great importance. In the case of the USSR there was never much evidence that it was willing to accept supra-national guidance by the world organization. The United States in the early years of the United Nations was distinctly positive about an important role for the organization, a point of view made easier by the majority on which the United States could normally count. Even after the advent of the Cold War when the superpowers were less than ever inclined to take conflicts in which they were themselves involved to the United Nations, the United States proposed bold initiatives through presidential addresses in the General Assembly: President Eisenhower's 'atoms for peace' address to the General Assembly of 1953 which resulted in the creation of the International Atomic Energy Agency (IAEA), and President Kennedy's speech in the General Assembly of 1961, which led to the adoption of the innovative comprehensive resolution on the first UN Development Decade. The mood is now distinctly different. In the economic field the governments of the main industrialized nations are disinclined to take initiatives in the United Nations because there are many alternative organizations in which there is less risk of 'politicization'. In the political area the near-automatism with which each superpower can expect a veto from the other in the Security Council every time its vital interests are deemed to be involved, has had the expected result: the superpowers continue to keep conflicts in which they themselves are involved outside the United Nations.

This lack of idealism and low priority of multilateral arrangements is exemplified by the attitude of the United States towards the new Law of the Sea Treaty: its objections are not so much against the detailed provisions of the treaty but rather a general doctrinaire aversion against giving even limited powers to world institutions. Yet one sees that both the IMF and the World Bank have regained United States favour in as much as they are deemed indispensable actors in dealing with debt and other problems of developing countries (although in this case it is the autonomy of action of these latter countries, not of the United States, which is affected).

The Confidence Factor

Confidence in international organizations generally and in the United Nations and UN Educational, Scientific and Cultural Organization (UNESCO) in particular has suffered. Stories about the poor performance of the secretariat are popular with governments and with the media; success stories receive little notice. This lack of confidence is related to:

a)   Presumed or real declining efficiency of certain international secretariats. 'Presumed or real' because what counts is the impression left with major contributors. If they believe that efficiency has decreased, this belief becomes then an autonomous factor in the attitude of a country vis-à-vis the organization in question.

b)   The view, again rightly or wrongly, that a secretariat is biased. This was typically what happened in the case of the UN Conference on Trade and Development (UNCTAD): the United States and other Western countries believe that the reporting and recommendations by the secretariat are inclined towards the views and interests of developing countries, and do not sufficiently take into account the actual facts of a problem or situation.

c)   Changed voting power, as a result of which the United States and other Western powers are regularly out-voted by the new majority.

Repetitive Debates

The tendency, particularly marked in the General Assembly, to engage year after year in repetitive debate and adoption of the same—often unimplementable— resolutions (on the substance of which there is frequently disagreement) concerning subjects like the Middle East and the problem of apartheid, has harmed the image of the United Nations in certain, especially Western, circles.

Politicization

What is commonly called politicization is not a new factor in UN decision making but is in some of the specialized agencies. The concept of politicization is ambiguous. It seems to cover three types of events:

a)   the predominance of political debate in an organization, combined with the presumed use by certain governments of such debates for their own political advantage;

b)   the rise in the technical specialized agencies of debate on political issues and the consequent introduction and eventual adoption of resolutions on such political issues;

c)   the exaggerated emphasis—contrary to the organization's Charter—on certain particular objectives or activities by the executive head of an organization (sometimes combined with arbitrary or nepotistic rule also in staff appointment matters, and mismanagement generally).

Politicization is also reflected in the habit of making speeches for 'domestic consumption'. Politicization of UNESCO was presumably the main reason why the United States withdrew. The Soviet bloc countries accuse the ILO of being involved in a different kind of politicization: 'Since their elaboration in 1919 the ILO's basic concept and structure have remained essentially unchanged. The Organization virtually ignores the fact of admission of socialist and developing countries to its membership. By following its old course, the ILO in effect serves the interests of only one socio-political system, that of capitalism, in an attempt to impose its will and ways on other States'.

IMPROVEMENTS IN UN DECISION MAKING

There seem to be two direct ways to implement possible improvements:

• the management route; by adopting certain presumed improvements in the decision-making process,
• the restructuring route; by endeavoring to streamline and simplify the organizational set-up of the United Nations and the system of specialized agencies; the term restructuring is sometimes used for this type of exercise.

Improving the Decision-Making Process (the 'Management Route')

Over the years a lot of suggestions and proposals have been made to improve the decision-making process in the United Nations, both in several of the organizations and in numerous private conferences, such as those sponsored by the Stanley Foundation.

Recently, a meeting of former Presidents of the General Assembly made recommendations concerning the rationalization of the procedures of the GA. They recommended, for example, that items which are 'no longer relevant' should be eliminated from the General Assembly's agenda and that the General Committee should 'scrutinize the draft agenda more closely'. I doubt whether in the absence of a complete change of spirit among member States this can be realized, since a feeling of general tolerance, indeed perhaps nonchalance, appears to dominate about the question of acceptability of agenda items. The assembly presidents also recommend a reduction of documentation, specifically that 'the General Assembly should not automatically, upon the conclusion of an item, request the Secretary General for the submission of a report'. Presumably, a reduction in documents can only be achieved by severe self-restraint shown by governments, and by trying to eliminate some of the periodic reporting which is no longer necessary.

There are, no doubt, other possible improvements that could be made in the decision-making process of the General Assembly and other UN agencies:

- Too much time is now spent on speech-making. As a result less time is available for negotiations. An effort could be made to restrict debates rigorously. As at the ILO and the World Health Organization (WHO), statements in general debates at the General Assembly could be limited to 15 minutes. In agencies like UNCTAD, an effort should be made to separate speech-making and negotiation, somewhat along the lines of the procedure at the IMF and the World Bank.
- It has become general practice for the secretariat to put up a 'statement of financial implications' for any new proposal requiring study or action. It might be worth considering, in addition to this, a statement of 'cost-effectiveness' or of 'cost-benefit'. In other words, one should look at not only the expected costs, but also, and especially, at the expected benefits. If such an assessment were system- atically undertaken, it could become an important factor in restoring confidence in the United Nations as an organization which will only engage in new activities that are really useful.
- The worst period for engaging in group negotiations may be over. This period was exemplified by the well-known dichotomy in UNCTAD: the Group of 77 was unified concerning a set of maximum demands, and the Group of developed countries (Group B) settled for a minimum response, followed by difficult negotiations between the two groups whose negotiators had to go back for each modification to their group as a whole. Negotiations in small contact groups without a rigid mandate have demonstrably given optimal results. This is how the UN Special Fund in 1957/58 and the complex, far-reaching issue of the Law of the Sea Conference were negotiated. The technique of 'small *ad hoc* fire brigades' should be used more often and earlier in the negotiating process.
- It might be worthwhile to endeavour to improve the 'definition-making' process. Various terms, including 'peace', 'racism' and 'imperialism' have been used in the United Nations in a loose manner. Certain resolutions using these terms have had a negative impact in the United States and elsewhere. Ideally, the United Nations could establish a 'Committee on Definitions' to which controversial texts could be referred, with—if necessary—a long delay in voting and possibly the Sixth (Legal) Committee of the General Assembly could be given a task in this respect. However, such a committee does not belong to the realm of practical possibilities. Alternatively, the International Court of Justice could be approached more often for an advisory opinion on some concept or definition in a draft resolution. What is needed is a face-saving and time-gaining procedure in an otherwise intractable situation.

Streamlining the Organizational Structure of the United Nations and the Specialized Agencies (the 'Restructuring Route')

A better and more streamlined structure would make an important contribution to more efficient decision making. It would avoid the duplication which causes both loss of time and resources. In the United Nations, restructuring efforts (the last occurred in 1979 after the report of the Group of 25) have not yielded many results. The creation of the post of Director-General for Development and Inter- national Economic Co-operation has added to, rather than diminished, the com- plexity of the UN organizational set-up. The UN telephone directory, which still serves as the United Nations' organization chart, lists the Director-General for Development and International Economic Co-operation immediately after the Secretary-General and his office. He is presumed to be, but not officially recognized as, the number two in the secretariat. When the Administrative Committee for Co-ordination was, in the absence of the Secretary-General, to be chaired by the then newly-appointed Director-General, the heads of the specialized agencies protested: in their view, in the absence of the Secretary-General, the most senior Director-General of a specialized agency should preside. The streamlining of ECOSOC especially by holding shorter subject-oriented sessions as recommended by the restructuring resolution of 1977 no. 32/197 has hardly materialized. There is probably 're-structuring-fatigue' in the United Nations slightly comparable to aid and other fatigues. Yet some simple steps could improve the situation. Thus, combined sessions of ECOSOC and the UNCTAD Board for the many items which overlap in their respective agendas could be a modest step towards greater efficiency in the economic and social field and towards a restoration of confidence in ECOSOC. If this were successful then some of the subordinate bodies of ECOSOC and UNCTAD could also be de facto merged.

Ideally, ECOSOC should assume the role of an economic security council, ready to deal both with any situation requiring immediate attention in the economic field and with the long-term problems of poverty in developing countries. Thus, the arrangements and structure for dealing with the emergency needs of Africa could perhaps have been created more smoothly if ECOSOC could have met and acted quickly, just as the Security Council is supposed to do in political crisis situations. Yet the Organization created to deal with the food emergency in Africa (UN Office for Emergency Operations in Africa, OEOA) is functioning well, showing that, despite constitutional constraints (between the United Nations and individual governments), the United Nations could respond efficiently to an emergency.

Also, ECOSOC could revive an economic policy committee, along the lines of a similar committee which it created in the early years. Such an economic policy committee could look at the overall world economic situation (somewhat like the Economic Policy Committee of OECD) in relation to the economic situation in its member countries. An alternative would be to 'upgrade' the existing Committee for Development Planning (CDP) (including a change of name). Not much use is now made of the CDP, which is a pity since in the earlier period it played, for example, a key role in drafting the strategy for the Second Development Decade. In any transformation of the CDP into an Economic Policy Committee the question will arise whether the members should be independent experts, as is the case at present, or high government officials in charge of economic policy (as at the OECD Economic Policy Committee), or perhaps a mix of government officials and independent experts, which is done in the UN Commission on Transnational Corporations.

In the political field, if efforts to reduce the number of repetitious resolutions were successful, the Special Political Committee of ECOSOC could probably be dissolved and its remaining business taken back by the First Committee. Similarly, the Second (Economic) and Third (Social and Humanitarian) Committees of the

General Assembly might eventually be merged if they could eliminate repetitious items and structure their consideration of various programmes in such a way that, in line with the biennial budget concept, each programme is considered only once every two years.

It is tempting to reflect on a different set-up of specialized agencies and other similar UN organizations. Each agency has more or less active support by specific bureaucracies in the various capitals of the world. That being the case, ideas for streamlining or merging must be considered, at this time, as unrealistic. Yet one could conceive of more integrated clusters of specialized agencies and certain UN organs dealing with related subjects:

i) Food and Agricultural Organization (FAO), WHO, ILO, IAEA, UN Industrial Development Organization (UNIDO), and other parts of the United Nations deal with basic natural or human resources. A joint advisory council, for whose composition different formulae are conceivable, could result in better co-ordination and co-operation than is the case at present. For example, the UNIDO, after several years as a UN branch, became a specialized agency, yet the opportunity to merge with either the ILO or with FAO lapsed unnoticed.

ii) The World Bank, IMF, UNCTAD and General Agreement on Tariffs and Trade (GATT) deal with trade and finance. The strong link between the worlds of trade and finance is one of the re-discovered revelations of today. A joint advisory council for trade and finance matters might be constituted serving the agencies in this field. An eventual merger of UNCTAD and GATT, although at the same time preserving the autonomy of GATT, should be considered.

iii) Almost every agency deals in one way or another with human resources. The UN Development Programme (UNDP) prides itself on being specialized in the development of human resources. An inter-agency advisory board on human resources, possibly chaired by the Administrator of UNDP, could lead to a better co-ordinated approach to the human side of economic and social development.

There are also some notable absences in the present structure of the UN system:

Energy. While energy in all its respects is of undeniable importance, the subject is dealt with by a great many organs. The International Atomic Energy Agency deals, of course, with nuclear energy; other aspects of energy are the object of activities in the UN Secretariat in New York in the regional commissions, and—strangely—in an institution like UN Institute for Training and Research (UNITAR), which has set up an efficient data bank covering a gap felt by private business for tar sands oil. A single agency for energy would be logical, although a careful cost-effectiveness analysis should prevent any premature decision. A World Bank energy affiliate could also be considered.

Human Misery. The United Nations would seem a logical place to have a central office dealing with the various calamities which can befall mankind: physical disasters, other emergencies such as those resulting from civil war, human rights violations, refugee problems. There is a UN High Commissioner for Refugees, a

UN Disaster Relief Office, of limited size, and also an Human Rights Division. Efforts to create a UN High Commissioner for Human Rights have failed. Would it not make sense to set up a single Office, headed by a (High) Commissioner to deal with all aspects of human misery? There is, in relation to famine in Africa, a cluster of agencies working together under the auspices of the UN Office of Emergency Assistance to Africa. This cluster includes UNICEF, World Food Programme, International Fund for Agriculture Development (IFAD), International Development Association (IDA) and the World Bank, and could be the precursor of a more permanent mechanism.

Research and Fact-Finding. There are, probably, too many UN research institutes. Some of them, like UN Research Institute for Disarmament (UNIDIR) and WIDER (World Institute for Development Economics Research) have been founded thanks to the generosity of a single government. The UN University and UN Institute for Training and Research overlap in certain respects. A streamlined set-up of research institutes in the United Nations, and ideally in the UN system as a whole, would also assist in providing a better flow of reports and facts to the decision makers. Better fact-finding is generally needed, as stressed by the Secretary-General in his Annual Report 1985.

CONCLUSIONS

All these possible attempts to reduce UN inefficiency or suboptimal decision making are bound to fail if there is a lack of real will for international co-operation, and willingness to accept supranational guidance in certain situations (there will, of course, always be escape-clauses). To achieve this co-operation for such a specific purpose it will be necessary to engage in research into the cultural, psychological and semantic constraints of international co-operation.

Even if there were to be considerable improvement in both the management of UN decision-making processes and in the structure of the UN system, it remains doubtful whether international co-operation would gain very much in the absence of a real will to accept the consequences of such co-operation, namely the diminishing of national sovereign powers.

The question arises whether deeper insights into the widespread resistance to yielding parts of national power to a supranational authority are needed. The answer would seem to be in the affirmative. This unavoidably seems to mean research into the cultural and psychological barriers to international co-operation. Is there something like a psychopathological personality of nations? Do nations feel persecuted, or claustrophobic, and hence say 'no' to many proposals tending to diminish their already uncertain powers? Do the largest powers have a 'large power complex' making them indifferent to the needs of smaller countries? There has been little systematic research into these matters, even though the individual negotiating styles of particular nations have been researched.

Diverse Perspectives

INTRODUCTION

The complexity of the world makes generalizations difficult. The United Nations operates within and is part of this complexity. As well, the context shifts as a result of changes, especially in the short run, arising from the differing perspectives of the political leadership in the main states. Consider the dramatic shift in the Soviet approach to the United Nations in the post-Brezhnev era, as well as the impact of the U.S. approach in the early, anti-UN Reagan years. Consider also the interplay between U.S. and Soviet attitudes that produced a more positive overall attitude toward the organization as one expression of moderating superpower relations in the later Reagan years, apparently mainly a consequence of Gorbachev's successful diplomacy of conciliation.

As the UN system evolved out of the constitutional framework of the Charter, many potential lines of development were (and remain) plausible. Even the quality of leadership within the United Nations is an important variable. A dynamic secretary-general (e.g., Hammarskjöld, Pérez de Cuéllar) enhances the performance of the organization, whereas an ineffectual secretary-general (e.g., Waldheim) diminishes it.

The main point is that the UN system is an intensely political arrangement. State actors shape its behavior to a considerable extent, by their actions both in the world and within the organization itself. The political will of principal actors largely sets the boundary of what is possible at a given time on a particular UN issue. Most important have been the orientations of the governments of the two super-powers. The United Nations, its main organs, and even its specialized agencies, should be considered significant *arenas* in world politics. To the extent that power and information have become conflated in a global setting in which wars settle little by way of geopolitical conflict, the United Nations provides a series of platforms for debate and for the dissemination of ideas, hopes, grievances, and sheer propaganda—a valuable resource for governmental leaders even if they are otherwise skeptical about the values of peace, justice, and ecological stability. That is, we no longer have to be idealists to take the United Nations seriously, although idealists continue to believe in a stronger United Nations as an international goal.

A central contention of this book is that the UN organization is what its membership makes it, not much more or much less. We do not deny that world

137

public opinion and the quality of the UN civil service, especially within the Secretariat, can help or hurt the character of UN performance in various domains. For example, the leadership of James Grant, the executive director of UNICEF, has given that program more stature and greater budgetary resources than it would otherwise have received.

To expect the organization to transcend the geopolitical rivalries of its membership is naive, but to suppose that even unilaterally minded governments do not find the United Nations to be an important policy arena from time to time is to embrace a reductionist view of international relations (as power dynamics) that no longer accurately describes the character of political behavior at the global level.

In this section, we consider the manner in which diversity among theoretical perspectives and policymakers influences our understanding of how the organization operates and how it might be improved over the short and long terms. There is a basic split between understanding the United Nations as an *arena* for the interplay of contemporary political forces and as a framework capable of *moderating* or even *transforming* the state system in directions associated with the realization of world order values. Both roles challenge the United Nations to perform constructively, but the geopolitical perspective fits the organization into the world, while the global reform perspective aspires to regulate the anarchic forces and destructive tendencies by increasing the UN's capacity to act more independently of geopolitical pressures, more in the spirit of its own Charter, and more in the direction of world order values. We emphasize, in this section and elsewhere, a *teleological* conception of the United Nations—that is, a political entity with a *telos*, or end, in view. At the same time, we acknowledge that the delimitation of this *telos* and the means of its attainment are currently obscured by a diversity of perspectives. A consensus has not yet emerged.

The first part of the section provides some representative accounts of the true character of the United Nations as an organization seeking to realize Charter goals and world order values in a domain dominated by sovereign states. In the opening selection, Inis L. Claude, Jr., depicts with admirable conceptual clarity the central ideas of balance of power, collective security, and world government. He locates the United Nations in relation to each of these organizing notions and gives stress to the continuing preoccupations with balance of power considerations. Such a stress explains why the United Nations is limited in function and capability, disappointing those who expected a collective security system to emerge from the Charter and disillusioning in a more definitive way those who held the utopian conviction that the United Nations would evolve over time into a full-blown world government. In reading Claude, we can benefit from his realist worldview, but we can also be constrained by its definitive tone.

The second selection, by David Mitrany, suggests an alternative path against the background of a realist reading of the world. Mitrany is concerned with finding openings within statism for a different sort of world order—that is, one capable of sustaining peace over time. In this search, Mitrany has creatively tried to find some intermediate political terrain between a view that overlooks the dominance of sovereign states and one that is fatalistic about this dominance and its rigidity. He sees international institutions as valuable arenas for technical, nonpolitical cooperation, and he regards such cooperation as a cumulative process with the capacity, in time, to erode conflict formations.

Mitrany's outlook, sampled in this selection, has given rise to a functionalist approach to international institutions within and beyond the United Nations. It is currently influential in a series of ways in academic circles, especially on the part of neofunctionalist and neorealist social scientists who have studied the nature and development of international regimes. The main distinguishing feature of this Mitrany-based thinking is not to accept as a given the futility of a frontal assault on the role of state sovereignty or on the war system as such, but rather to explore the openings within this established framework for the expansion, under various conditions, of opportunities for international cooperation. The question we should pose for ourselves is whether these functionalist lines of thinking create any basis for a genuine prospect of the transformation of world politics. It should be appreciated that governments and their agents remain the exclusive sources of social action. Democratic forces and movements from below tend to be ignored, or even repudiated, by the functionalist school, whose central contention is to get governments to cooperate on technical matters outside the spheres of political controversy. Such cooperation is important given the complexity of the world, but does it add up over time?

Our third selection is a short excerpt from Grenville Clark's introduction to the Clark/Sohn proposals for a greatly enhanced United Nations. These proposals were avidly promoted as a form of feasible world government that would benefit all sectors of international society as well as create the structures of disarmament and peacekeeping needed to avoid the recurrence of general warfare. Such a constitutionalist vision of the future never caught on with either diplomats or the public. It is important to understand why their vision did not catch on, as what Clark and Sohn favor seems adapted to widely endorsed goals of survival in the nuclear age. Perhaps in the new setting of the 1990s, their somewhat drastic view of global reform is becoming politically relevant.

To support this possibility, we include a short debate discussion among Soviet scholars and government policymakers. Each of these individuals is a known and respected figure in Soviet political life. Georgi Shakhnazarov is a principal assistant to Gorbachev and a leading political scientist; A. Bovin is a leading journalist, influential in party circles; and G. Tunkin is the most prominent Soviet jurist. The discussion itself is an expression of doubt about whether current global challenges can be solved within the confines of the state system.

Even if they are not utopian from these normative and futuristic standpoints, do such "visions" help us here, acting in the world as it is? How do visions facilitate change? What is the role of the political imagination?

When we shift our focus to consider the diversity of perspectives associated with the current policy outlook of the main state actors in the UN process, we can only glimpse the tips of icebergs. There are so many diversities: through time, across space, depending on agenda domain (war/peace, human rights, the environment, development). Nevertheless, during the course of UN history, certain policy perspectives have been ascendant at various stages. At first, the United States, with its focus on the Western alliance, set the tone of UN operations, and the Soviet

Union pursued a policy of damage limitation, protecting itself behind a curtain of resistance associated with sovereign states. By the 1960s, the newly decolonized states had joined the United Nations, and they began to make their presence felt, especially in the General Assembly. In this period, as the Cold War unfolded and East-West tensions ebbed and flowed, the Soviet Union began to discover the UN as an arena of geopolitical opportunity, and the United States discovered that the organization was evolving in a manner that was eroding its earlier degree of control.

As the 1970s unfolded, both superpowers were more or less isolated on key Third World issues. The Soviet Union was more in line with UN sentiments on symbolic issues such as self-determination for the Palestinian people or mandatory sanctions against South Africa, but the United States, although formally isolated, was diplomatically and economically engaged in global policy processes associated with UN activities. In the 1980s, as we have suggested, these issues sharpened, and many sharp edges have been softened: the Sino-Soviet conflict is muted, the East-West conflict seems on the way toward being made marginal, and the North-South confrontation lacks credibility. The big patterns for the United Nations in 1990 are: Will the United Nations respond positively to the push by the Soviet Union to strengthen UN capabilities? Can the United States generate a positive diplomacy that responds to Gorbachev in a manner that allows the organization to become more effective? Can the Third World reassert its concerns to help the United Nations fashion a consensus on what can be done to alleviate indebtedness without cutting off the supply of capital?

The selections in the second half of this section seek to enable us to grasp the policy debate on the United Nations as it currently seems to be proceeding. We cannot be confident that this policy debate will remain stable, but the attitudes of particular actors toward the UN role at a given stage also disclose more abiding structural factors. Mohammed Bedjaoui, now a judge on the World Court and formerly Algeria's ambassador to the United Nations, explicates his conviction that development and peace goals are inextricably linked. Such a position is widely supported as conventional wisdom in such Third World frameworks as the Non-Aligned Movement and is generally resisted by many governing elites in the First World who stress the separability of these issues, thereby reducing development concerns at a global level to a matter of charity or altruism—that is, the rich, out of a sense of conscience or compassion, help the poor to develop. Bedjaoui's perspective insists that there can be no world peace without sustainable Third World development and that this reality is central to the ordering activities taking place in international life, including especially the United Nations.

Next, we include a short selection from Zhao Ziyang expressing a Chinese endorsement of the United Nations within its larger concern about resisting the hegemonic ambitions of both superpowers. China has experimented over the years with various blends of cooperation and confrontation with both the United States and the Soviet Union. To some extent, China has responded to the enticements of Gorbachev's efforts to build a more positive relationship, but the basic drift of Chinese policy in the post-Mao years has been to adapt Western methods to the imperative of modernization. It is uncertain whether official Chinese tactics of repression, mounted with fury in response to the May–June 1989 demonstrations, will have the effect of isolating China on the world stage in the years ahead, but for the present there is likely to be a chilly response to any Chinese attempt at a leadership role within the United Nations framework.

A very influential statement by Mikhail Gorbachev is next. This statement was published in Pravda in 1987 and was the earliest major expression of Gorbachev's "new thinking" in relation to Soviet foreign policy. It calls for strengthening the United Nations in the peace and security area, an emphasis that contributed to the revitalization of the organization. These ideas became part of a wider process of a reorientation of Soviet foreign policy during the Gorbachev years and helped overcome the unfavorable view of Soviet international behavior that had taken hold after the Soviet Union mounted its massive military intervention in Afghanistan beginning in December 1979. The credibility of Gorbachev's statement is enhanced by its compatibility with subsequent Soviet initiatives, perhaps most dramatically the Soviet withdrawal from Afghanistan and the loosening of its grip on Eastern Europe. Gorbachev conveys how the Soviet Union's position on world order issues has developed in a decade, an almost unbelievable turnabout that was not anticipated. More concretely, Gorbachev's proposals seem to strengthen the UN capability to act effectively, especially in peacekeeping settings. The Soviet leadership also seems prepared to support plans to give the organization greater financial independence and to expand the capabilities of the World Court to play a more consistent and influential role in relation to international disputes. Of course, the durability of Gorbachev and the current outlook of the Soviet government cannot be taken for granted, although the scale and scope of the Soviet reorientation are impressive. Soviet regression to its earlier stance of minimal and hostile participation would not be less unexpected than its moves in the opposite direction under Gorbachev. At the same time, a deepening economic crisis in the Soviet Union, together with a variety of ethnic nationalisms, makes the political future of the Gorbachev approach precarious.

These proposals are significant for their own sake but also because they challenge other governments, especially that of the United States, to reciprocate. There is also a new general mood of optimism about the role and growth potential of the United Nations. Rather than the slow dissipation of hopes that had occurred during the organization's first four decades, there has been a rebirth of higher expectations since 1987. Gorbachev's globalist stance is certainly responsible for this rebirth, but so are the success of the secretary-general in relation to regional conflicts and a deepening sense that global-scale problems can only be coherently addressed within the frame of a universal international organization. Also helpful has been the apparent reversal of official U.S. thinking, which seemed from 1987 to 1990 to again be supportive of an effective United Nations.

The final selection in the section is an excerpt from Ronald Reagan's farewell address to the United Nations. As with the Chinese affirmation, and in contrast to Gorbachev's concrete proposals, Reagan's upbeat remarks are rather vague and abstract. At the same time, Reagan's proposals are notable as an expression of U.S. support for a positive and constructive attitude toward the role of the organization.

Such an outlook is important in helping to overcome the UN's financial crisis and to build public support for the organization in the United States.

In sum, the theoretical and policy perspectives suggest the most relevant lines of diversity operative at present. Especially in light of Gorbachev's glasnost diplomacy, an overall short-run consensus emerged in the late 1980s that seems to subordinate the interplay of diverse and antagonistic policy approaches to the United Nations.

7. The Management of Power in the Changing United Nations

Inis L. Claude, Jr.

I.

The central problem of our time is to achieve the effective management of the power relations of states. The world is constituted as a system of independent but interdependent states—independent in authority but interdependent in destiny. States are units of power. While power is a complex conception, for present purposes it may be construed in the narrow sense of force. Physical ability to kill, to damage, or to coerce, is the particular aspect of power which serves as the focus of this article. States are characterized by the possession, in varying degrees, of this capacity to damage or destroy each other. This power may be used in competitive struggle, producing destruction on a massive scale. It may be used unilaterally, producing enslavement and degradation of its victims. In short, both survival and freedom, both sheer existence and the higher values that enrich existence, are implicated in the problem of power. The national interest of every state, and the common interest of all men, in the preservation and development of civilization are threatened by the paroxysms of violence which states are capable of unleashing. Hence, the primacy of the task of controlling the use of force by states, of managing the power relations of states, cannot seriously be questioned.

I use the term, *management,* to convey the conviction that the problem of power is here to stay; it is, realistically, not a problem to be eliminated, but one to be managed. At all levels of society, human beings inherently possess and inexorably retain the capacity to do physical violence to each other. The task of socialization is not to abolish power, but to control its exercise. At the level of collectives, I take it as a basic postulate that there will always be human groups—if no longer national states, then other social sub-divisions—which will be capable of damaging each other. They cannot ultimately be deprived of this capacity. Given brains and brawn, men can contrive instruments of lethal warfare, be they clubs or hydrogen bombs; given human social instincts and skills, men can contrive to organize their violence as the clash of collectives. The issue will never be whether power exists; it will always be whether power is subjected to effective management.

My emphasis upon the concept of management of power carries with it the specific implication that disarmament is not the key to the problem of international violence. In the literal sense, the notion of disarmament would seem to suggest reliance upon the unattainable ideal of eliminating the potential of states for violence. Most actual disarmament efforts are, of course, more modestly conceived; they aim at checking the arms race and securing the adoption of systematic programs of arms limitation or reduction. The value of such achievements, if they should prove possible, might be considerable. They might, by restricting the distribution of certain types of weapons and limiting the quantitative levels of power accumulation, prevent the power situation from becoming inherently unmanageable. Thus, that brand of disarmament which is more accurately characterized as arms control may be an essential prologue to, or accompaniment of, any effective scheme for the management of power in the contemporary world. Whether or not disarmament can be attained, however, the basic problem will remain that of establishing and maintaining reliable control over the exercise of power. Even if all existing weapons were destroyed and production of armaments totally suspended, the capacity to devise instruments of terrible power would remain a permanent potentiality; man cannot unlearn what he knows about the means of creating power. My basic criticism of the disarmament motif is that it tends to foster an emphasis upon abolition of power as the key to peace and security, whereas it seems to me that the problem is more realistically defined in terms of the necessity of bringing the exercise of power by states under effective and reliable control.

The theory of international relations, if one may apply that term to a literature which is more a thing of shreds and patches than a seamless garment covering our understanding of the processes of international relations, contains three basic concepts which may be regarded as relevant to the problem of the management of power: balance of power, collective security, and world government. These concepts have not been defined with care, used with precision, or made to serve as bases for systematically elaborated theoretical structures; at best, they stand as rudimentary snippets of theory which have been used more for polemical than for analytical purposes. Each of them has attracted its quota of advocates and detractors, who have tended to treat the concepts competitively rather than comparatively. In short, balance of power, collective security, and world government are not terms which designate well-developed and generally understood bodies of doctrine. Nevertheless, they do represent the leading ideas regarding the problem of the management of power in international relations, and they figure as the focal points of contemporary discussion and controversy concerning this problem.

It is, of course, hazardous to try to establish definite meanings for terms which have customarily been used so loosely and inconsistently as these. Recognizing that others may exercise the right to invest them with meanings different from mine, I nevertheless venture to suggest that these three concepts can, with considerable justification derived from the literature of the international relations field, be taken as characterizing disparate systems of relationship among states— systems related to each other as successive points along a continuum and differing most fundamentally in the degree of centralization of power and authority which they imply. In this view, balance of power represents the extreme of decentralization, a kind of *laissez-faire* arrangement in the sphere of power politics. It suggests a scheme within which individual states, separate units of power and policy, operate autonomously, without subordination to a central agency for the management of power relations. Singly or in combinations reflecting the coincidence of interests, states seek to influence the pattern of power distribution and to determine their own places within that pattern. In such a balancing system, the constituent states function as coordinate managers of the power situation.

Collective security falls next in line along the scale of centralization, representing an effort to deal with the power problem by superimposing a scheme of partially centralized management upon a situation in which power remains diffused among national units. It involves a centralization of authority over the use of force, to the extent that states are deprived of the legal right to use violence at their own discretion. In its ideal form, it calls for an international organization with authority to determine when a resort to force is illegitimate and to require states to collaborate under its direction in suppressing such use of force.

Finally, world government takes its place at the opposite end of the scale from balance of power, suggesting the creation of an institutional system involving a monopoly of power, comparable to that alleged to exist in a well-ordered national state. In this scheme, both the possession of the instruments of force and the control of policy concerning their use are presumably centralized in an institution superior to the state.

Unfortunately, the differences among these concepts have more often than not been exaggerated and mis-stated. The case for adoption of one or another has often been argued as if a choice had to be made between totally dissimilar systems, one offering hopeful prospects for order and security, and the other leaving the world mired in hopelessness. In fact, the differences among them are far from absolute and are perhaps less interesting and significant than the similarities—to the analyst, if not to the propagandist. Having plotted them along a common scale, I would suggest that they tend to slide into each other, developing points of approximation or overlap, rather than to maintain fixed distances of separation. Both balance of power and collective security are deterrent schemes in that they rely upon countervailing power to frustrate the ambitions of powerful aggressors; moreover, the two systems are heavily dependent upon sets of prerequisite conditions which are similiar in important respects. One can argue, for instance, that the balance system requires the diffusion of power among a number of major states so that no single state will control such a large fraction of the world's power resources as to make the task of counterbalancing it inordinately difficult; the same requirement can be cited for a collective security system, to avoid the possibility that any state will be invulnerable to the pressure of collective sanctions. Thus, a global power configuration marked by bipolarity is equally unfavorable to the operation of a balance system or of a collective security system. One can demonstrate that a successful balance system requires that national policies be adaptable to contingencies that may arise rather than rigidly fixed, so that old friends can be resisted when they endanger the stability of the system and former enemies can be supported when the exigencies of the power situation so require. A similar flexibility of policy, involving the capacity to switch the foci of friendship and enmity, is essential to collective security.

On the other hand, the ideal scheme of collective security is not wholly unlike that of world government. It involves a concentration of authority in a central organ giving that organ a government-like quality that can be ignored only if one dogmatically denies, as many proponents of world government do, that there are many shadings of gray between the "black" of essential anarchy and the "white" of actual government. Moreover, a scheme of world government which undertook to maintain order on a global scale by methods comparable to those used within limited boundaries by national governments would, in fact, involve reliance upon intricate and delicate processes of balancing the power of constituent units of the society. The proposition that government is a matter of exercising a literal or virtual monopoly of power over a society, rather than of presiding over a balancing process, is largely a myth, even though totalitarian dictators have sometimes gained considerable success in translating it into reality. The point is that the typical enthusiast for world government wants a system which has more in common with the balance of power system than he customarily realizes or admits.

Despite these and other points of similarity which might be cited, there are characteristic differences among the implications of the concepts of balance of power, collective security, and world government, sufficiently important to justify the proposition that they designate alternative patterns for the ordering of power relations among states. The balance of power concept allows states to maneuver freely in a competitive world. Its typical institutional expression is a set of flexible alliances within which recurrent shifts of alignment take place; its promise of order lies in the expectation that competing power urges will somehow balance and thereby cancel each other, producing deterrence through equilibration. Collective security looks to a general international organization, presiding over a collaborative, rather than a competitive, arrangement. It purports to inhibit any aggressor by making virtually all the other states the *ad hoc* allies of any state that suffers attack; thus, it promises deterrence through the mobilization of a preponderance of power against any member of the system which threatens its peace and order. World government relies upon neither the interplay of competitive states nor the collaboration of states organized to uphold the principle of order; it promises to deprive states of their standing as centers of power and policy, where issues of war and peace are concerned, and to superimpose upon them an institution possessed of the authority and capability to maintain, by unchallengeable force so far as may be necessary, the order and stability of a global community.

These are not necessarily the only conceivable patterns for the management of power in international relations. They are, however, the patterns which have become the common currency of intellectual transactions concerning world affairs in the twentieth century. Whether any of these patterns has been, or can be, or should be, fully realized in actuality is not at issue here. They constitute the standard list of theoretical alternatives; they are the intellectual pigeon-holes in constant use.

With this introductory statement of the categories which, however poorly defined, dominate contemporary thinking about the problem of ordering international relations, we can turn to the questions to be considered in part II [. . .] of this article: 1) what was the nature of the system for management of power in international relations envisaged by the founders of the United Nations; and 2) what is the nature of the system which has in fact taken shape during the period of operation—and alteration—of the United Nations, from 1946 to 1961?

II.

It has been widely assumed and frequently asserted that the United Nations was originally intended and expected to function as the institutional manager of a full-fledged collective security system, capable of bringing collective force to bear against any aggressor. In most instances, this assertion is made in the context of a discussion of the failure of the United Nations to realize that ideal. Sometimes the founders of the Organization are convicted of idealism; they should have known better than to expect the United Nations to be effective as an instrument of collective security. Sometimes an objective analysis of the changes which have occurred in the setting within which the Organization operates is presented as explaining the failure of the collective security scheme; thus:

The great-power split, together with the admission of large numbers of African, Asian, and European neutralist states, has almost destroyed the collective security functions that were to be the organization's principal reason for existence.

More often, the Soviet Union is pictured as the villain in the piece; by abusing the veto power and obstructing the creation of the enforcement mechanism envisaged in Article 43 of the Charter, it has frustrated the realization of the promise of collective security. Whatever the explanatory argument, the essential point in such statements is that the United Nations was intended to be, but has failed to become, the directing mechanism of a universally effective collective security system.

Why has it been so generally assumed that the establishment of the United Nations represented an effort to institutionalize collective security in the postwar world? An attempt to answer this question must precede an assessment of the validity of the assumption itself.

In the first place, it may be suspected that this interpretation of the United Nations experiment was reached by the processes of elimination and deduction from a preconceived definition of the purposes of general international organization. Was the new world order designed as a balance of power system? Certainly not. Participants in the creation of the United Nations were too emphatic in their criticism of reliance upon balance of power, and too insistent in their assertion that they were creating a system better than balance of power, to permit that interpretation. True, they did not whip the balance of power as vigorously and persistently as their Wilsonian ancestors had done a generation before, but that was presumably because they thought it uneconomical to spend their time in flogging a dead horse. In any case, the United Nations was essentially a new version of the League of Nations, and it was well understood that the latter organization had been conceived by men who repudiated the balance of power system and aspired to introduce an alternative system. If the projected scheme were not a balance of power system, was it then a world government? No, it was clearly much more modest than that. If proof were needed, one could refer to the Moscow Declaration of October 30, 1943, in which the major powers of the anti-Axis coalition had declared the purpose of "establishing . . . a general international organization, based on the principle of the sovereign equality of all peace-loving states," or to President Roosevelt's decisive assertion that:

We are not thinking of a superstate with its own police forces and other paraphernalia of coercive power. We are seeking effective agreement and arrangements through which the nations would maintain, according to their capacities, adequate forces to meet the needs of preventing war and of making impossible deliberate preparation for war and to have such forces available for joint action when necessary.

Only one of the standard categories remained. If the United Nations were not designed to implement the concepts of balance of power or world government, then who could doubt that it must be an experiment in collective security? This conclusion must have come easily to men who stressed the resemblance of the new Organization to the defunct League. The original general international organization had been dedicated to the effectuation of collective security. It was natural to assume that the second edition was dedicated to the same purpose.

Secondly, it must be noted that the entire process of planning and formulating the United Nations Charter was dominated by the theme: "We are going to create a collective security system, and this time we are going to make it work." The United States planners were preoccupied with the necessity of providing the new Organization with an enforcement mechanism which would enable it to effectuate the collective security principle by coercive means which had been denied to the League. In the opening sessions of the San Francisco Conference, a long procession of speakers reiterated the proposition that statesmen had gathered to create a world organization which could and would maintain the peace, by force if necessary. A typical expression of the prevailing viewpoint was provided by Joseph Bech, speaking for Luxembourg, who declared that the peoples of the world

would not forgive their leaders if they returned to a policy of balance of power, which would inevitably result in a race for armaments heading straight for another war. The protection of peace can only be insured on the basis of collective security.

Moreover, the end of the conference was marked by exultant speeches proclaiming the initiation of a real collective security system. Joseph Paul-Boncour of France declared that "the international organization will no longer be unarmed against violence. . . . That is the great thing, the great historic act accomplished by the San Francisco Conference. . . . " The venerable Jan C. Smuts said of the Charter:

It provides for a peace with teeth; for a united front of peace-loving peoples against future aggressors; for a united front among the great powers backed by the forces of the smaller powers as well. . . . And it provides for central organization and direction of the joint forces for peace.

Thus, the assumption that the creation of the United Nations signaled a new effort to institute a universal collective security system was encouraged. In view of the circumstances, it is hardly surprising that this interpretation gained general acceptance. Nevertheless, it is fundamentally incorrect, as a careful analysis of what the world's statesmen did at San Francisco and a more extensive review of what they said about their handiwork, will indicate.

The crucial element in the analysis is an understanding of the import of the veto rule which enables any of the five permanent members of the Security Council to block decisions on substantive matters in that organ—including the determination that aggression has taken place, the designation of the guilty party, and the decision to resort to sanctions, military or otherwise, against the aggressor. Such decisions, be it noted, are fundamental to the operation of a collective security system. The veto rule clearly gives each of the great powers the capacity to prevent the operation of the United Nations enforcement system against itself, against any state which it chooses to support and protect, or in any other case in which it prefers not to participate or to have others participate in an enforcement venture under United Nations auspices. The veto provision, in short, renders collective security impossible in all the instances most vital to the preservation of world peace and order, and problematical in cases of lesser importance.

It will not do to say that the founding fathers of the United Nations went home from San Francisco with the blissful assurance that they had formulated a beautiful system of collective security, only to be rudely shaken later by the discovery that the system was spoiled by a devilish Soviet Union which insisted upon taking seriously its right to use the veto power. In the first place, logic denies the probability that the veto was regarded as an obstructive capability that would never be used and would therefore never interfere with the operation of collective security. It is difficult to believe that the major powers worked as hard as they did to secure acceptance of the veto provision, in the conviction that it would be superfluous; this grant of a special power to a dissenter reflects the assumption that there will be dissent, not that there will be unity. The veto provision was not inserted in the Charter in a fit of absentmindedness. It was adopted with full awareness, and deliberate intent, that any of the major powers might use it to block collective action. Its insertion can only be interpreted as a declaration that the United Nations should not and could not be drawn into any attempt to implement the principle of collective security in opposition to a great power.

We need not rely solely upon logical analysis of the provisions of the Charter for evidence that the original United Nations scheme involved a repudiation of the ambition to construct a collective security system which would be operative in the type of case most critically relevant to the issue of global war or peace. The records of the San Francisco Conference show that the participants were thoroughly aware of the fact that, in adopting the veto provision, they were renouncing that ambition. The United States declared that the veto rule "meant that if a major power became the aggressor the Council had no power to prevent war." An Indian spokesman warned against the delusion "that the proposed Organization could prevent wars between the great nations or even between small nations, if the great powers were divided in their sympathies." The general understanding of the import of the veto rule was expressed by a delegate from New Zealand, who said that it made collective security impossible. This interpretation of the limits of the system contemplated in the Charter was stated explicitly by Secretary of State Stettinius in the hearings on the Charter.

As I have intimated, a case can be made for the proposition that the founding fathers of the United Nations engaged in some misrepresentation of their product; they did not *always* qualify their praise of the projected Organization with explicit acknowledgment of its deliberately contrived incapacity to function as a collective security agency in cases involving great-power aggression or great-power support of aggressors. Realistically, one should not have expected that they would stress this important limitation of the new Organization. We have, after all, a working understanding that statesmen are not expected or required, any more than advertisers of soap or cigarettes, to put their worst feet forward. However, the accusation that the United Nations was "oversold" by its creators and sponsors has often been made too loosely and without adequate consideration of all the evidence.

The sober truth about the built-in restrictions on the capability of the United Nations as an organ of collective security was frequently and prominently stated. There is, indeed, ample evidence that this limitation was widely understood within the interested United States public. The National League of Women Voters was only one of many groups which revealed this understanding in public statements soon after the San Francisco Conference; in a memorandum inserted in the record of the hearings on the Charter, this organization stated the view that:

If a great power becomes an aggressor, the United Nations Organization will not be able to act, and the situation will have to be handled outside the Organization. This is because we are still in the experimental stage of collective security, and world opinion has not yet developed to the point where nations are willing to delegate sufficient authority to an international organization to make it capable of coercing a great power.

The Senate Committee on Foreign Relations proved itself both cognizant of and eager to encourage public understanding of the inherent limitations of the United Nations when it took care to point out, in its report on the Charter, that:

neither this Charter nor any other document or formula that might be devised can prevent war, and the committee would be performing a disservice to the public if its action with respect to the Charter should indicate any such opinion on its part.

The committee held that the creation of the new Organization "will at best be a beginning toward the creation of those conditions of stability throughout the world which will foster peace and security."

The evidence leads me to the conclusion that the formulators of the United Nations Charter deliberately refrained from attempting to create an organization which would undertake to control the use of force by great powers or states supported by them, through the operation of a collective security system. They acted on the assumption that such a venture could not succeed, and ought not to be attempted. In this fundamentally important sense, the establishment of the United Nations represented the repudiation of the idea of collective security, not an unsuccessful effort to institutionalize its application.

What then was the nature of the scheme for management of power in international relations which the Charter set forth? The answer can be found only if we emancipate ourselves from the rigidity of the categories of balance of power, collective security, and world government.

The influence of the collective security orientation is evident in many of the provisions of the Charter. Aggression is prohibited, though left undefined; in principle, states are deprived of the legal right to use force against each other at their own discretion, in pursuit of their unilaterally defined interests and purposes. The legitimacy of resort to international violence is made subject to the determination of an international body; an effort is made even to hold states accountable to an international body in their invocation and exercise of the right of defensive action. Moreover, the principle is asserted that any illegitimate use of force in international relations is properly a matter of concern to all Members of the United Nations. The Security Council is expected to be equipped, through agreements to be concluded with Member States, with military forces constantly ready for action at its decision; it bears the responsibility for taking action to uphold peace and security and has a general authority to command the assistance of all member states—except that their obligation to provide military units is limited to the commitments which may be stated in their agreements with the Security Council.

In its restriction of the right of states to resort to force, its espousal of the principle of collective action to repress illegal violence, and its provision for an organ to preside over the arrangements pertaining to the use of force, the UN scheme exhibits some of the essential characteristics of a collective security system. It should be noted that it is incomplete, in that the acceptance by states of an operative obligation to put force at the disposal of the Security Council—and, consequently, the equipping of the Council to perform its enforcement role—is postponed; on this score, the Charter registers merely an agreement to agree. Nevertheless, the scheme clearly reflects the intention to create an international enforcement mechanism capable of functioning in cases which do not involve a conflict of interest and will among the great powers. It might be described as a design for a collective security system applicable only to situations of relatively minor importance as far as maintenance of the general peace is concerned. The framers of the Charter contemplated a system in which the great powers would bear the major responsibility for providing United Nations enforcement potential, with supplementary contributions by lesser states, for the purpose of dealing with aggressors acting without the support or sympathy of any of the major powers. The great powers, it should be recalled, persistently spoke at San Francisco of the "unanimity rule," not the "veto rule," thereby emphasizing the positive hope that the Security Council would be able to act decisively against aggression insofar as its permanent members could achieve unanimity in supporting such action. There was no middle ground in this arrangement. Either an act of aggression would be committed by a minor state with all the major powers ranged against it, in which case collective suppression of the misdeed would be a relatively simple matter, or it would be committed by a major power or its protégé, in which case the United Nations would be debarred from attempting collective suppression. Although the applicability of the United Nations enforcement scheme to the control of the defeated Axis powers of World War II was excluded, it was provided that this limitation might be removed at the request of the victorious allies.

The key prescription of the Charter for dealing with the potential crises of greatest international importance—those involving antagonism among the great powers or aggressive action undertaken or sponsored by one or more of the great powers—is to be found in Article 51, with its recognition of "the inherent right of individual or collective self-defense" in response to armed attack. This provision may be interpreted as a declaration that it is incumbent upon states to take the necessary measures, outside the structure of the United Nations, for dealing with the more crucial threats to peace and security which might arise. The framers of the Charter were saying, in effect, that they saw no possibility of implementing collective security safely and effectively against major powers, and that some device other than collective security would have to be improvised if a major power should go on the warpath. They did not, as has often been suggested, assume that no such problem would arise; in this respect, they were hopeful but not smugly confident. Rather, they asserted the conviction that it was impossible to construct a collective security system adequate to deal with such a problem, if it should arise. The advice implicit in Article 51 is that states should establish alliances—combinations for collective self-defense—for dealing with the actuality or threat of attack by powers exempted by the veto rule from the impact of the projected United Nations enforcement mechanism.

In this vitally important respect, the Charter contemplates what is in essence a balance of power system. This was no doubt an unhappy choice for the founding fathers. Their ideological bias clearly ran not toward collective security. Their sense of realism, however, impelled them to acknowledge that they could see no way to devise a workable alternative to the balance of power system for dealing with aggressive threats posed directly or indirectly by great powers. It should be noted that the balance of power system, involving the freedom and responsibility of states to look to their own position within the international configuration of power, does not have to be adopted; it exists, until and unless an alternative arrangement for managing the power relationships of states is put into effect. Failing even to formulate—much less to put into effect—a more centralized scheme for handling conflicts in which major powers might be competitively engaged, the creators of the United Nations left states to "do what comes naturally" in such situations: that is, to develop the power and policy, individually and in alignment with others, for coping with security threats presented by dangerously powerful antagonists.

The original scheme of the United Nations for the management of power on the international scene may thus be described as one which left the balance of power system intact for cases of major importance to global peace and order, and provided for a collective security system to be applicable in cases of relatively minor significance. The Charter endorsed the *ideal* of collective security in unqualified terms, but envisaged its application in severely limited terms. It limited the legal right of states, great or small, to engage in the unfettered maneuvering which has been traditionally associated with the operation of a balance of power system, and reflected the hope that the political processes of the United Nations would inhibit the tendency of states to abuse their strength under the pretext of protecting their relative power positions. In the final analysis, however, the Charter acknowledged that the new Organization could not relieve states of the necessity of attempting on their own to match power with power, as the means of attaining security within the context of great-power rivalry. The scheme of the Charter was a curious amalgam of collective security, dominant in ideological terms, and balance of power, dominant in terms of practical application. The concept of world government, insofar as it figured at all in the consideration of the San Francisco Conference, was viewed as a distant ideal.

[*   *   *]

8. The Functional Approach to World Organization

David Mitrany

It seems to be the fate of all periods of transition that reformers are more ready to fight over a doctrine than to pull together on a problem. At this stage I only ask to be given credit for the claim that I do not represent a doctrine or a dogma; I represent an anxiety. At home when we want change or reform we state our objectives in such terms that all may see how we propose to attain them. When it comes to the international world, where we are faced with old and stubborn habits of mind and feeling and political dogma, where the change we have in mind must close one of the heavy tomes of history and open up a new one, it seems that nothing will do but the perfect goal and winged results.

When we compare the general mood of 1919, when everybody was eager to get back to the old order of things, with the mood of 1948, only one generation later, when the need for an active international society is almost universally taken for granted—then we are surely justified in regarding the change as progress indeed. For without such a change in outlook all schemes for international peace, as in past centuries, would remain but noble dreams. Yet even with this change present schemes may likewise remain noble dreams if they are beyond the reach of the ways and means of practical everyday government. "Government is a practical thing," Burke wrote to the sheriffs of Bristol, and one should beware of elaborating political forms "for the gratification of visionaries." Vagueness in this difficult transition will merely produce vagueness in popular sentiment. If the new popular receptiveness to the idea of international organization is to ripen into an informed public opinion, it must now be fed with a diet of hard facts and with proposals that are visibly practicable, so that it may know how to press and support governments in the pursuit of a positive international policy. The task of experts in this field, whether individuals or groups, is to pass now beyond fine appeals and ideal formulas. There has already been too much pleading and too little thinking. How otherwise explain why, with such broad good will and a sense of urgency, so little has been fulfilled?

The general outlook is promising. When we come to examine present trends more closely two stand out above all—the trend for national self-government and the trend for radical social change. The intensity of the two trends varies in different parts of the world, but everywhere they tend to merge into one political current. Even in Europe, where there is little room left for new state-making, the transformation of society is taking place on a national basis; while in the Middle East, in Southeast Asia, in Africa, and elsewhere, the new states are an expression of social revolution as much as of political revolution.

From the international point of view there is a danger in this. Such social nationalism, or national socialism, is actually bringing about a regression. The modern political trend has led increasingly to the splitting up of the world into independent states. The idea of national self-government, the guiding principle of the peace settlement of 1919, is still strongly at work in the Middle East, in Southeast Asia, and in Africa; while at the same time modern economic life, with its extensive division of labor, has tended to weld peoples and countries socially together. It is that living unity which is in danger of being bruised and battered by the new conception of the planned welfare state. It is not my business to discuss whether this trend is desirable or inevitable, but merely to establish that these are the conditions from which our international house-building has to start. We are favored by the need and the habit of material co-operation; we are hampered by the general clinging to political segregation. How to reconcile these two trends, both of them natural and both of them active, is the main problem for political invention at this juncture of history.

Speaking broadly, ideas and schemes for international organization can be considered under one of three categories: (1) a general and fairly loose association, like the League of Nations and the United Nations, (2) a federal union, and (3) a system of functional arrangements. Whatever our personal inclinations, we have to look at these alternatives against the conditions of the time, and with the ultimate end of international government in mind.

Both the League of Nations and the United Nations, as their names imply, have been based upon national separateness. They could be taken as loose associations for certain specified and limited joint ends, or as clubs making joint action easier if needed and if approved according to their constitutional provisions. But the United Nations cannot, and neither could the League, prescribe action to its member states, much less take action on its own authority.

Our short but tense experience since the creation of the United Nations has shown that such a loose arrangement is inadequate in its scope and uncertain in its working. Hence, no doubt, the widespread interest in the federal idea in a variety of forms. Federalism is one of the great inventions of political theory. It came to us from the New World and has been adopted in a number of places, especially in newer political groupings. It has served admirably where a number of adjacent and related provinces or countries, while retaining a substantial separate identity, wanted to join together for some important common purpose. Federation has been the political equivalent of a company with limited liability. Habitually a federal union rests upon a number of similar elements—a degree of close kinship or historical relationship, and a will to unity—but with them also a clear intent by the parts to manage many of their social affairs separately. How does all this apply to the international scene?

We have been presented with a choice of proposals for international federation. Some advocate, variously and vaguely, European federation or Western federation or democratic federation; others, more ambitiously, world federation. The fact that there are so many differing and overlapping proposals shows that they are not impelled by any inherent force of kinship or sense of unity into the suggested groupings. Any of them may be desirable, but we have no proof that any of them is desired. There is no evidence of the will to unite. Indeed most of these ideas, even that for European federation, have been pressed upon peoples who themselves have shown no lively signs of wishing to take the initative. Alternatively, they have been urged to federate so as to be better able to stand up to other antagonistic political groupings. The advice may be sound, but it is an argument for a new nationalism, not for a new internationalism. Hitherto federation has indeed merely created a new and larger political unit which in the process did bring peace within the group, but it has not been proved that its creation necessarily contributed also to peace between it and other groups. The prospect of two powerful federations, for instance, facing each other across Europe, is not a comforting one. It would not check the more disturbing of the present general trends, that toward political division; it would change the dimensions of nationalism but not its nature.

But let us for the sake of argument take the most hopeful view as to the will of the states to unite in wider political units, and leave aside for the moment the negative kind of peace that this would represent. The main question is really this—whether some kind of international federation under present conditions would strengthen the trend toward the social integration of international life, making of it a general and positive foundation for peace. A federation comes into being for certain specific ends; a federation unites, but it also restricts. It rests on a rigid division of powers and functions between territorial authorities which formally have equal status, and that division is usually and necessarily laid down in a written constitution, provided with an armory of safeguards against its being easily tampered with. In a volume of essays on federal planning, Professor Wheare grants that federal government is by its nature conservative and legalistic. Every attempt to give the central government some new function or power has to knock long at the massive and rusty gates of the constitution. The efforts of the Canadian government to change the fiscal arrangements of the federation have been blocked so far, in spite of long discussion and patent need. In Australia repeated efforts for concerted economic and social action have been similarly balked, and the recent decision to nationalize the banking system shook the political structure and temper of the country. Even in such a dynamic country as the United States the sin of uncon-stitutionality has often bedeviled efforts at social reform—such as the prohibition of child labor in factories—and killed or maimed most of the original New Deal measures. The now universally admired and imitated TVA experiment had to sustain some forty legal suits or more on grounds of unconstitutionality before it was allowed to settle down to its great work.

It is curious how those who urge the use of the federal idea internationally have neglected this central characteristic of its working. Jefferson, politically wise beyond a man's measure, foresaw the dangers of a rigid constitution and wished to provide for its periodical revision every ten years. Such a provision, for just such a term, was part of the old Austro-Hungarian federal arrangement, the so-called *Ausgleich*, with the result that every term became a crisis which brought with it a threat of dissolution—causing the irrepressible Viennese wits to speak of it as *"Monarchie auf Kündigung."* And yet such an entrenched restraint is not unreasonable. New functions and new powers granted to the supposedly co-equal central authority, however beneficent the social purpose for which they are claimed, must have politically a cumulative effect; and a sufficient number of such additions would before long permanently change the balance upon which any federation is estab-lished. As Professor Alexander Brady points out, it took almost twenty years of difficult negotiations to find a basis for the federation of Australia and the reluctance to see it changed is therefore understandable. To come into being at all an international federation would have to start with a very narrow common denominator and with very rigid arrangements as to form and functions, and the reluctance to allow these to be lightly disturbed would be correspondingly all the greater.

In an international federation every adaptation, every amendment would have to run the gauntlet of jealous argument between countries newly come together and differing in their political background. Even in agreed common matters the pace can only be that of the slowest member of the group; issues which divide deeply must be shunned. But in our time conditions, needs and problems are apt to change rapidly. Either the constitution would have to be continuously adapted or the difficulty of such adaptation would hobble the life and government of the federation. Can such a rigid instrument then be made to fit the present revolutionary mood which, whatever we may think of it, is surging throughout the world? People have been puzzled that the most revolutionary of all governments—one whose ideology stands for world unity and the withering away of the state—has on every possible occasion and at the United Nations insisted on the strict observance of national sovereignty. The explanation can be found in a recent article on sovereignty by Professor I. D. Levin, a leading Soviet jurist, who uses the very argument adumbrated above: that in a revolutionary situation any and every people must be free to transform its social organization as it wills, without external interference or complications. Professor Levin is obviously right in assuming that this would not be possible under some rigid and comprehensive form of political association. If a federal house cannot be half free and half slave, neither can it be half capitalist and half communist. Every attempt at some fundamental change in one part would put in jeopardy the continuance of the whole; for the alternatives would appear to the legalists as disruption and to the reformers as stagnation.

A federal system has many virtues. But in form and working it is a combination of rigidities: rigid in its framework, whether geographical or ideological; rigid in its constitution, which has to be formal and unchallenged; rigid in its general life, because of the limits and obstacles the constitution places in the path of fresh common action. If under present conditions of political nationalism an international federation would be difficult to achieve, under present conditions of social revolution it would be even more difficult to maintain. Its only prospect would be either to limit it to the lowest common denominator as regards membership—such as the Benelux or a Scandinavian group—or to restrict it to the lowest common denominator as regards federal functions and powers. And if a dynamic federal grouping is not possible, a federal grouping so limited in membership or so restricted in its activities would be meaningless as a contribution to the problem of world unity.

The main central functions of federations have always been common defense and foreign policy. These indeed, with a common budget for their purpose, Mr. Lionel Curtis considers sufficient to start the world federal arrangement which he has advocated so eloquently and devotedly. But is this not again neglecting the historical perspective? Not only are the number of functions which need joint action apt to change; their character is apt to change even more rapidly. A hundred or even fifty years ago, defense and foreign policy absorbed only a limited part of the total life of the community. Now between them they control material resources and the organization of industry, manpower and training, and even education and opinion, and sweeping controls of trade as of fiscal and financial policy.

Federation, to sum up, was born in times of enthusiasm for formal constitutions; now we are in a pragmatic mood that scorns rigid bonds and restrictions. Federalism was meant to put into the hands of central authority the least possible functions of common life; now the run of political life can only mean leaving in the hands of the individual authority the least possible functions of local life. It was born when in general the scope of government was limited, whereas now we live feverishly and somewhat precariously under limitless planning and controls. If a world union were to try to do all those things for political security and for social security which present trends demand—and inevitably they would have to be done through the instrument of a central authority—it would all end in the paradox that the federal idea would be proclaimed only to be stripped of all the meaning and virtue of a federation.

Thus to expose the difficulties of the federal idea does not come from any inclination to be destructive. It is rather the outcome of a conviction that in this stubborn international field we cannot hope to make progress by propounding schemes with a pleasant symmetry without regard to the rough and shifty terrain on which they have to be grounded. In looking at the federal idea against present conditions and needs, I have really been trying to draw attention to the sociological framework within which any effort toward international government would have to work. Shaped as it is both by the will for national distinctness and by the need for social integration, that framework would be difficult to construct simply by changing the dimensions of our traditional political instruments. We must rather look for a new political device, and the device best suited to construct that framework out of the present historical material would seem to be the functional idea—not new as an invention but new in its application.

The functional approach has indeed been used a great deal even in established federations—in particular very successfully in America by the New Deal, with the TVA scheme as its outstanding example. Two circumstantial points arise here. If, it may be argued, existing federations have been able to carry through great reforms in this way, does not this break the argument that the federal idea would prove a drag to international social action? Though plausible at first sight, the point does not stand up to closer examination. Existing federations can sometimes get around formal federal divisions only because they are old-established federations. Generations of common life and experience have welded their component parts into a society with a common outlook, with common problems expressed in the programs of national parties. In their case a common central government has come to be taken for granted, with state or provincial governments more on the level of local administrative bodies. The significant exception of Quebec within the Canadian federation proves indeed the need for such common background. In most cases the problem, therefore, was not so much a matter of creating a common policy as of consolidating a line of similar or identical policies. Yet in times of crisis even in such old-established federations the joint national activities were expanded not by changing constitutional arrangements but rather by circumventing them. In no case has there been any deliberate change in the formal hierarchy of power. Federal governments have simply taken upon themselves many new tasks, with tacit national consent, and in that way acquired new powers by functional accretion, not by constitutional revision. In the United States the only attempt at constitutional change during Roosevelt's presidency—to increase the membership of the federal Supreme Court—was also the only issue on which he was utterly defeated; and yet its effect would have been relatively marginal compared with the revolutionary impact of the New Deal as a whole.

America has used the functional approach also in starting new lines of association with neighboring states, not only in the close wartime arrangements with Canada, a matter of expediency, but in permanent measures. The Alcan Highway has created a strip of international administration running from the United States through Canada to Alaska; the arrangement with Mexico for the development of the Rio Grande has turned a river frontier into a joint enterprise of common benefit; and Pan-American developments are likely to follow the same line. Experiments such as these have a particular lesson for the wider international problem. There is a simple lesson in the sheer fact that they can be made; but there is a more significant lesson in that the United States found it easier to complete the Alcan arrangement with Canada and the Rio Grande arrangement with Mexico than to set in motion its own TVA scheme. The first two were made with sovereign countries prepared to pool their resources and to relinquish that part of their sovereignty necessary for a specific joint functional undertaking. The TVA experiment affected federal units which were reluctant to part with any of their share of power and which therefore tried hard to maintain the original balance laid down in the federal Constitution.

A more extreme example was the insistence of the Australian government, against American reluctance, on the inclusion in the San Francisco Charter (1945) of some form of international undertaking to work for "full employment"—an "obligation" meant to give the Australian government the right to take internal social action which would otherwise be beyond its constitutional powers. That was indeed a striking and novel way of overcoming federal obstructions by courting international obligations. (The incident also illustrated how the content of foreign policy is changing.) In the United States and other federations, necessary nationwide action has been possible in the face of constitutional obstacles because there existed an old and live sense of national unity. A new international federation would have no such ingrained sense of unity, and constitutional barriers would obstruct all the more impassably at every corner. And as we have seen, even those old federations have at times found it easier to make functional arrangements with foreign states than within their own community.

The truth is that by its very nature the constitutional approach emphasizes the individual index of power; the functional approach emphasizes the common index of need. Very many such needs cut across national boundaries; not a few are universal, and an effective beginning for building up an international community of interest could be made by setting up joint agencies for dealing with these common needs. And this is both an urgent and an opportune moment for such positive steps in international government. The emergence of so many new national states will complicate politically our difficulties, but socially this multiplication might be put to the service of international unification. For if these new and mostly undeveloped states are to achieve a healthy social foundation for their political independence they will need many things which are beyond their means and experience; and, as in the case of the Marshall Plan, such needs could be used deliberately and insistently to set up lines for joint international action.

The universal popular demand for social security could likewise be turned into a channel for international unity. Everywhere the new nationalism is a peculiarly social nationalism. As in the nineteenth century, many a people wants to have its own national house, but unlike the earlier nationalism it is especially intent upon a new form of social life within that house. There is much to be said for one solid international block of flats, but as long as people choose to live in detached national houses we could at least go a long way toward establishing a sense of community by supplying them with joint social and other services. Only in some such way is there any prospect, for instance, of mending the breach in the political unity of the Indian continent and of restoring there an awareness of the unity of natural common interests; whereas any suggestion for political reunion between India and Pakistan would make even proposals for practical common action suspect. Again, this seems the only possible hope of mending the division between Arabs and Jews and, indeed, of building some true unity among the Arab countries themselves, along the path so admirably mapped out by the Middle East Supply Center during the Second World War. In the Danubian region, in spite of much ideological fraternizing, a mere reference by the Bulgarian Communist leader, M. Dimitrov, to a federal link-up at once brought a rebuke from Moscow and little response from his neighbors; but those same countries are apparently working on a scheme for a Danube Valley Authority.

Much could be learned from an examination of the structure and working of the wartime functional arrangements, or of the work of the International Labor Organization in giving a common direction to policies of social improvement without encroaching on state sovereignty. The French, Belgian, and British governments are now working out lines of co-operation for their African territories, ranging from sanitation, irrigation, and soil conservation to the common use of communications and other services, with a view to co-ordinating economic, educational, and administrative policies.

It is not only in the fields of government and economics that the functional approach can bring relief. In a noteworthy sermon the Archbishop of Canterbury boldly admitted that all schemes of reunion between the English churches had failed because, he insisted, they had tried a doctrinal reunion. He called for a different, a more humble but practical approach through the exchange of ministers and pulpits. "It is because I fear stalemate," said Dr. Fisher, "that I venture to throw out this suggestion—Can we grow to full communion with each other before we write a constitution?" The evolution of the Flemish problem in Belgium is also instructive. During the First World War the political separatist movement created a bitter reaction in the country and almost led to civil strife. Since then, by gradual, quiet changes, the Flemings have obtained complete autonomy in education—the University of Ghent is now completely Flemish and that of Liège completely

French—and almost as wide autonomy in the administration of the Flemish area. In addition, there has grown a close cultural association between the Belgian Flemings and Dutch institutions and activities. No constitutional provision has so far legalized this evolution, while on the other hand talk of political separation has died out among the Flemings.

Earlier in this essay I pointed out, as one proof of the weakness of the federal idea, the many varieties of schemes competing for public support. There are as many, if not more, schemes for functional experiment. Does that not show a similar fragility of conception? Perhaps nothing brings out more clearly than this question how different in essence is the federalist from the functional approach. Under the federal idea the several schemes are mutually exclusive: A state could not be in both a European and a Commonwealth federation, or in both a European and some general democratic federation. Functional schemes, on the other hand, are at best complementary, each helping the others; at worst, they remain independent of each other. Any such scheme can be started at any time, whether the others are accepted or not, and any one may live and prosper even if others fail and are abandoned. In our politically ever-changing times, functional arrangements have the invaluable virtue of autonomous existence and likewise of autonomous development. A scheme started originally by a few countries for transport, for example, could later be broadened to include new members or reduced to let reluctant ones drop out. Moreover, such schemes can vary in their membership; countries can take part only in activities in which they have an interest, not in others, whereas in any political union such a divided choice would obviously not be tolerable. Functional "neutrality" is possible; political "neutrality" is not. The requirements of an international federal authority for the conduct, for instance, of a common foreign policy would always have to be a matter of political bargaining. The requirements of a functional authority for the needs of the clear-cut task entrusted to it—for example, in charge of oil or aviation—would at any given time be a matter of factual audit.

These characteristics of the functional approach therefore can help to mitigate the obstinate problem of equal sovereignty. Under this idea it is not a matter of surrendering sovereignty but merely of pooling as much of it as may be needed for the joint performance of a particular task. Under such practical arrangements governments do not need, as in political schemes, to safeguard their right to equal voting, but can allow a special position to those countries with a particular responsibility for the task concerned—in keeping with the whole trend of modern government. Twentieth-century government means less a division of powers than an integration of functions. Administration and administrative law are its characteristic tools, and such functional arrangements would simply mean giving international range to administrative organs and jurisdiction, in accordance with the nature of each task. They would also be in harmony with the social philosophy of our time. As a former head of the FAO said of his particular responsibility: "Here in this world food plan we have the means whereby the nations could begin to cooperate on something which would do none of them harm and do all of them good." Insofar as governments have only the welfare of their own peoples at heart there can be no reason why they should not allow such organizations to go to work;

and if the organizations are successful and their number grows, world government will gradually evolve through their performance. From the point of view of normal daily life, to quote the late Professor Hobhouse, "the life of a community may be regarded as the sum of the functions performed by its members"; conversely, the performance of a number of common functions is the way to create a normal community. If one were to visualize a map of the world designed to show international economic and social activities, it would appear as an intricate web of interests and relations, crossing and re-crossing political divisions—not a sullen map of isolated states but a map pulsating with the beneficent intercourse of everyday life. And it is this which is the natural basis for international organization. The task is to bring that map, which is already functioning as a reality, under the control of some form of joint international agencies. Then the political dividing lines would in time be overlaid and blurred by that web of joint relations and administrations.

A close association of states can be either comprehensive or selective. Clearly the first is the ideal—all countries working together for the common good. But if it cannot be comprehensive, if it has to be selective, it is better that it be selective on lines of common activities rather than of exclusive groups. Whereas any one country may join a particular activity, a set group cannot help being exclusive; and, in the words of Dr. Johnson, "such is the disposition of man, that whatever makes a distinction creates rivalry." Seen in this light, the functional approach implies not merely a change of political device but a change of political outlook. It should help to shift the emphasis from political issues which divide to those social issues in which the interests of the nations are plainly akin and collective; to shift the emphasis from power to problems and purpose.

In all societies there are to be found both harmonies and disharmonies. It is largely within our choice which we pick out and further. Since the end of the Second World War we have had many a brutal illustration of this truth at peace conferences and at meetings of the United Nations, at which the new international life was supposed to be born. Therefore we must begin anew, with a clear sense that the nations can be bound together into a world community only if we link them up by what unites, not by what divides. In the second place, ways and means to that end must be fitted to the purpose in hand. They have to be adequate, but they also must be relevant; and if they are to be relevant they must start from the conditions which we find around us. They must avoid reaction but also avoid Utopia. We can ask our fellowmen to look beyond the national state; we cannot expect them to feel themselves at once members of a world state. During his first months as President, Jefferson wrote to a friend that he realized how short he would fall of achieving all that reason and experience justified. But "when we reflect how difficult it is to move or inflect the great machine of society, how impossible to advance the notions of a whole people suddenly to ideal right, we see the wisdom of Solon's remark, that no more good must be attempted than the nation can bear."

In our case, and in our time, what the nations can bear varies according to the nature of the load. Taken by and large, they seem as yet unable to bear much interference with their political independence, but they can bear quite a lot of it when it comes to practical economic and social action. The distinction gives a first guiding line for peaceful international action. The next question is how such economic and social action should be organized so as to lead the nations toward international community and international government. In our own countries we are becoming accustomed to putting nearly all such action into the hands of the central government. Are we ready to follow the same course in the international sphere? If we are, a federation, with its restrictive constitutional machinery, would hardly be the proper instrument. A federation leaving those social and economic activities in the hands of its national members would, in this respect, be little more than a replica of the United Nations. If, on the other hand, those activities were to be entrusted to a central international authority, with effective power and means, that authority will be no less than a full-fledged world government. The larger social and economic tasks will, of necessity, have to be performed jointly and to be controlled centrally. The true choice, therefore, is not between the present competitive nationalisms and a lame international federation; the choice is between a full-fledged and comprehensive world government and equally full-fledged but specific and separate functional agencies.

9. World Peace Through World Law: Two Alternate Plans

Grenville Clark

[. . .] The fundamental premise of the book is identical with the pronouncement of the President of the United States on October 31, 1956: "There can be no peace without law." In this context the word "law" necessarily implies the law of a world authority, i.e., law which would be uniformly applicable to all nations and all individuals in the world and which would definitely forbid violence or the threat of it as a means for dealing with any international dispute. This world law must also be law in the sense of law which is capable of enforcement, as distinguished from a mere set of exhortations or injunctions which it is desirable to observe but for the enforcement of which there is no effective machinery.

The proposition "no peace without law" also embodies the conception that peace cannot be ensured by a continued arms race, nor by an indefinite "balance of terror", nor by diplomatic maneuver, but only by universal and complete national disarmament together with the establishment of institutions corresponding in the world field to those which maintain law and order within local communities and nations.

A prime motive for this book is that the world is far more likely to make progress toward genuine peace, as distinguished from a precarious armed truce, when a *detailed* plan adequate to the purpose is available, so that the structure and functions of the requisite world institutions may be fully discussed on a world-wide basis. Consequently, this book comprises a set of definite and interrelated proposals to carry out complete and universal disarmament and to strengthen the United Nations through the establishment of such legislative, executive and judicial institutions as are necessary to maintain world order.

UNDERLYING PRINCIPLES

The following are the basic principles by which Professor Sohn and I have been governed.

First: It is futile to expect genuine peace until there is put into effect an effective system of *enforceable* world law in the limited field of war prevention. This implies: (a) the complete disarmament, under effective controls, of each and every nation, and (b) the simultaneous adoption on a world-wide basis of the measures and institutions which the experience of centuries has shown to be essential for the maintenance of law and order, namely, clearly stated law against violence, courts to interpret and apply that law and police to enforce it. All else, we conceive, depends upon the acceptance of this approach.

Second: The world law against international violence must be explicitly stated in constitutional and statutory form. It must, under appropriate penalties, forbid

163

the use of force by any nation against any other for any cause whatever, save only in self-defense; and must be applicable to all individuals as well as to all nations.

Third: World judicial tribunals to interpret and apply the world law against international violence must be established and maintained, and also organs of mediation and conciliation,—so as to substitute peaceful means of adjudication and adjustment in place of violence, or the threat of it, as the means for dealing with all international disputes.

Fourth: A permanent world police force must be created and maintained which, while safegarded with utmost care against misuse, would be fully adequate to forestall or suppress any violation of the world law against international violence.

Fifth: The complete disarmament of all the nations (rather than the mere "reduction" or "limitation" of armaments) is essential for any solid and lasting peace, this disarmament to be accomplished in a simultaneous and proportionate manner by carefully verified stages and subject to a well-organized system of inspection. It is now generally accepted that disarmament must be universal and enforceable. That it must also be complete is no less necessary, since: (a) in the nuclear age no mere reduction in the new means of mass destruction could be effective to remove fear and tension; and (b) if any substantial national armaments were to remain, even if only ten per cent of the armaments of 1960, it would be impracticable to maintain a sufficiently strong world police force to deal with any possible aggression or revolt against the authority of the world organization. We should face the fact that until there is *complete* disarmament of every nation without exception there can be no assurance of genuine peace.

Sixth: Effective world machinery must be created to mitigate the vast disparities in the economic condition of various regions of the world, the continuance of which tends to instability and conflict.

The following supplementary principles have also guided us:

Active participation in the world peace authority must be universal, or virtually so; and although a few nations may be permitted to decline active membership, any such nonmember nations must be equally bound by the obligation to abolish their armed forces and to abide by all the laws and regulations of the world organization with relation to the prevention of war. It follows that ratification of the constitutional document creating the world peace organization (whether in the form of a revised United Nations Charter or otherwise) must be by a preponderant majority of all the nations and people of the world.

The world law, in the limited field of war prevention to which it would be restricted, should apply to all individual persons in the world as well as to all the nations,—to the end that in case of violations by individuals without the support of their governments, the world law could be invoked directly against them without the necessity of indicting a whole nation or group of nations.

The basic rights and duties of all nations in respect of the maintenance of peace should be clearly defined not in laws enacted by a world legislature but in the constitutional document itself. That document should also carefully set forth not only the structure but also the most important powers of the various world institutions established or authorized by it; and the constitutional document should also define the limits of those powers and provide specific safeguards to guarantee the observance of those limits and the protection of individual rights against abuse of power. By this method of "constitutional legislation" the nations and peoples would know in advance within close limits what obligations they would assume by acceptance of the new world system, and only a restricted field of discussion would be left to the legislative branch of the world authority.

The powers of the world organization should be restricted to matters directly related to the maintenance of peace. All other powers should be reserved to the nations and their peoples. This definition and reservation of powers is advisable not only to avoid opposition based upon fear of possible interference in the domestic affairs of the nations, but also because it is wise for this generation to limit itself to the single task of preventing international violence or the threat of it. If we can accomplish that, we should feel satisfied and could well leave to later generations any enlargement of the powers of the world organization that they might find desirable.

While any plan to prevent war through total disarmament and the substitution of world law for international violence must be fully adequate to the end in view, it must also be *acceptable* to this generation. To propose a plan lacking in the basic essentials for the prevention of war would be futile. On the other hand, a plan which, however ideal in conception, is so far ahead of the times as to raise insuperable opposition would be equally futile. Therefore, we have tried hard to strike a sound balance by setting forth a plan which, while really adequate to prevent war, would, at the same time, be so carefully safeguarded that it *ought* to be acceptable to all nations.

It is not out of the question to carry out universal and complete disarmament and to establish the necessary new world institutions through an entirely new world authority, but it seems more normal and sensible to make the necessary revisions of the present United Nations Charter.

10. On the Prospects of Global Governance

Georgi Shakhnazarov, A. Bovin, and G. Tunkin

"Questions of Theory": The World Community Is Amenable to Government

Georgi Shakhnazarov

It is common knowledge that the rate of progress—economic, scientific, technical, and social—in the 20th century has been much higher than during the previous century. However, even against this dynamic backdrop, the frenetic kaleidoscope of events and the sharp twists and turns that have abounded in international life of the past decades look perplexing. Mercilessly overturning dogmas and prejudices, life is presenting theoretical thought with ever new puzzles and categorically dictating the need for creative renewal.

The beginning of such a renewal was laid by the foreign policy concept put forward by the 27th Congress of our party. It is based on the fundamental ideas of the interconnection and interdependence of the present-day world which represents a specific entity. This [is] the result of the internationalization of world economic ties, the all-embracing nature of the scientific and technological revolution, the fundamentally new role of the information and communication media, the state of the planet's resources, the general ecological danger, and the strident social problems of the developing world which affect everyone. However, the main factor is the emergence of the problem of survival of the human race since the existence of nuclear weapons and the threat of their use have called into question mankind's very existence.

I

Essentially, the concept of interdependence is nothing but the development of one of the fundamental ideas of Marxism-Leninism—that of the internationalization of mankind's economic activity and of all social activity—applied to the conditions of our time.

An indispensable and most important consequence of this process must be the enhancement of the degree to which the world is amenable to government [*mera upravlyayemosti mirom*]. The first to broach this subject, as is usually the case, were philosophers, albeit in rather vague terms such as global spirit, global wisdom, and so forth. Then came the science fiction writers. Scientists took over from them—after Hiroshima and Nagasaki, many scientists came to the conclusion that

166

henceforth only a world government [*mirovoye pravitelstvo*] could save mankind from perishing.

The hope that the creation of a centralized international authority would help to prevent a world war was nurtured with the foundation of the League of Nations and the conclusion of various agreements, which contributed to the gradual transformation of international law into an integral system. However, the peak of this current of political thought which was referred to as mondialism (from the French word "le monde"—the world) dates back to the fifties and sixties.

It must be admitted that during the fifties, the theoretical and practical Soviet foreign policy attitude to the idea of mondialism was unequivocally negative. There were serious reasons for this. Most of the advocates of world government [*mirovoye pravitelstvo*] were categorically opposed to sovereignty, declaring this principle to be all but the source of all evil. This was happening at the very moment when dozens of former colonies and semidependent states were freeing themselves from imperialist bondage. It goes without saying that in this light, encroachments on sovereignty appeared doubly reactionary.

There was another, no less important circumstance. At that time the United States held absolute sway in the capitalist world. It had a considerable advantage in economic, political, and military terms in the global correlation of forces. The idea of world government [*mirovoye pravitelstvo*] was bound to end up as nothing other than the legalization of the domination of the world by US capital.

Over the more than two decades that have elapsed since then, the situation in the world has drastically changed. In terms of the capitalist world, a serious redistribution of might between the United States on the one hand, and West Europe and Japan on the other hand, has taken place. While retaining its position as the leader of the capitalist world, the United States can no longer claim absolute supremacy.

Assessing the changes on a world scale, it is necessary, above all, to bear in mind the attainment by the Soviet Union of military-strategic parity with the United States, the general growth of the socialist countries' economic might and political influence, and appreciable progress and consolidation of the political positions of the developing countries and the nonaligned movement, and other factors.

In short, one of the main arguments against world government [*mirovoye pravitelstvo*] has disappeared. As for the second argument, this obstacle could also be removed if the implementation of the idea could be divorced from encroachments on sovereignty. Is this possible? Is there not an objective contradiction between sovereignty and world government [*mirovoye pravitelstvo*]? This contradiction does exist, but the point is that the concept of an interconnected, interdependent world provides the key to its solution. It is a question of building a new international political order based not on the denial of sovereignty and national independence of states (this remains a reactionary demand to this day) but on the basis of taking account of and coordinating their interests. As is known, it is the balance of interests of the various states that forms the core of the concept of the world as an entity, which was put forward by Mikhail S. Gorbachev.

II

There can be no doubt that the world community is managed [*upravlyaytsya*] by the joint efforts of its members. Were it otherwise, trains would not cross borders, pirates would rule the waves, planes would constantly be colliding in midair, and the air waves would be a confusion of voices. Furthermore, the world would long ago have ceased to exist. It would have been consumed in a nuclear war.

In order to exercise management [*dlya upravleniya*], there must be law and a government [*pravitelstvo*]. In our time international law has become so widely developed that its norms are used to regulate [*reguliruyutsya*] many spheres of international life. There is no government [*pravitelstvo*] yet, but there is every basis for talking about the beginnings of one—the numerous international organizations headed by the United Nations which perform, albeit with limited powers, the most diverse administrative and managerial [*administrativ-no-upravlencheskiye*] functions.

How is one to assess the level of governability of the world [*stepen upravlyaye-mosti mira*] that has been achieved—is it sufficient, does it fully correspond to mankind's existing needs? There can be no simple answer to that question.

For understandable reasons, international administration [*upravleniye*] has made the greatest progress in the sphere of transport, communications, and trade, and on a broader scale, in the international division of labor. In other words, we are talking about the traditional exchange of material and spiritual assets, as well as the maintenance of public order by joint efforts. It goes without saying that in this area of activity, too, one which has long been regulated by joint norms and rules; there is a need for constant renewal. But the existing international mechanism makes it possible to pose and resolve these questions quite flexibly.

It is far more difficult with international relations as regards so-called universal and global problems. For example, whereas one can speak of a certain degree of governability [*upravlayemost*] or, rather, the regulation [*regulirovaniye*] of states' actions on a bilateral, group, or collective basis in the spheres of health care, education, the organization of emergency aid for the victims of natural disasters, and the struggle against crime, areas such as the joint protection of nature have still not become the object of mankind's general concern despite their vast significance to humanity.

This claim may be disputed. But what has been achieved can only be assessed more or less soberly by measuring it against the scale of the problem. The latter is so great that there is every justification for placing it on a par with the danger of nuclear war. In such a system of coordinates, there is no justification yet for speaking seriously either about manageability [*upravlyayemost*] or even about any effective joint struggle to save man's environment.

The situation is the same, if not worse, with another equally formidable global problem: the gap between the economically developed countries and the underdeveloped countries. This problem is by no means beyond the scope of international cooperation. There are quite a few regional and world aid problems in existence, although the insignificance of these efforts and their failure to measure up to the true need is demonstrated by the fact that in the eighties, the gap between the economically developed and the underdeveloped countries began to widen again.

But until recently, perhaps the most difficult problem was that of war and peace. Once again there are more than enough good intentions to be seen. However, one must recognize the extremely low, indeed paltry degree of governability [*upravlyayemost*] in this sphere, which is of vital importance for mankind. The subject of special anxiety is the steadily increasing pace of the arms race which, if continued, threatens to destroy all of mankind's hopes for the future and doom him to inevitable catastrophe.

The degree of danger also determines the degree of our general satisfaction with the fact that it is thanks to the persistent efforts of the Soviet Union—and we can say this with a clear conscience—and thanks ultimately to the prudence of both sides at the recent Soviet-US summit, that it proved possible to halt the train of the arms race on at least one track and then agree on ways to derail it. However slight the percentage of weapons liable to destruction at present, the mere fact of that destruction enables one to speak of a significant increase in the degree to which the questions of war and peace are amenable to management [*mery upravlyayemosti voprosami*], primarily because solutions have been found to many of the concrete, extraordinarily complex problems that necessarily accompany the disarmament process.

But however great and incontrovertible the significance of the two (intermediate- and short- [as published—*"malyy"*] range) nuclear missile "zeroes" is, it is of course too soon to say that the questions of war and peace have reached the required degree of manageability [*upravlyayemost voprosamil*]. The militarist forces' activeness and their desire to be compensated with interest for the destruction of the intermediate- and shorter-range missiles by other means of mass destruction give an idea of the obstacles still to be overcome.

III

The success of future work for peace conclusively depends on success in further boosting the degree to which the world is amenable to government [*upravlyayemost mirom*]. Hitherto almost every step on this path was taken at the cost of great efforts and was only possible as a result of a prior cataclysm. The Caribbean crisis of 1962, which brought the world to the brink of nuclear war, encouraged the establishment of a "hot line" between Moscow and Washington and the adoption of a number of other "preventive" measures. The Chernobyl tragedy provided a powerful impetus for cooperation in the sphere of the management and control [*upravleniye i kontrl*] of the development of nuclear energy. The appearance in the world or the awakening from dormancy of the AIDS virus—this scourge of the 20th century—gave rise to sharp intensification in cooperation among medics.

What can be done to ensure that henceforth the need for cooperation and joint control [*upravleniye*] of the course of events does not have to be proved by dangerous incidents and to ensure that constructive political thought preempts and prevents crises? That is the ultimate question. Now that the first success has been achieved with regard to abandoning the arms race, it is important not to lose the momentum, for every major agreement creates favorable preconditions for progress in other spheres also. To put it more simply: more peace means more development, more joint concern for nature, more security for nuclear power stations, and more chances to be rid of epidemics, and so on.

Hence the need to take advantage of the "momentum" created in order not to grow slacken off but proceed further. This approach prevailed in Washington, where it was agreed in the wake of the Treaty on the Elimination of Intermediate- and Shorter-Range Missiles to reach an accord on a 50% reduction in USSR and US strategic offensive armaments.

The possibility of stepping up the measure of world governability [*mera upravlyayemosti mirom*] to meet mankind's requirements depends on many factors, and above all, on the readiness of all participants in the world community to put common human interests above any others.

The socialist world is well prepared to resolve such a task. The idea of internationalism has been enshrined in the very nature of our system. But we would be acting against our conscience if we did not add that, along with our society's splendid internationalist properties, there are also negative phenomena making themselves felt, these being associated with long-standing "rose-tinted propaganda," which has inspired the conviction that our country is always unreservedly right in its actions in the international arena. It is perhaps especially intolerable that in defiance of the Leninist tradition in literature, especially within the historical novel, attempts have been made to reappraise from chauvinistic positions the fundamental class assessments of certain events in the prerevolutionary past and depict in a justificatory, or even eulogistic, tone individual episodes in the oppressive and aggressive policy of czarism and that of the rulers of the states that constituted the Russian Empire.

Of course, genuine Soviet socialist patriotism has nothing in common with blind nationalism. For nothing ennobles the people and does it credit in the eyes of other peoples like the ability not only to take pride in the glorious deeds of one's forefathers and work good deeds oneself but also to judge one's history objectively and acknowledge one's mistakes honestly and with fortitude.

In short it is a question of learning to look at oneself from outside and seeing not only one's merits but also one's weaknesses and endeavoring to get rid of them.

Human rights are a subject of particular complexity for international regulation [*uregulirovaniye*]. The question of human rights, that is, ultimately the status of the individual in a particular society essentially falls within the compass of internal affairs. Making it a subject of international regulation [*uregulirovaniye*] by general voluntary consent would entail a breakthrough to another level of world governability [*upravlyayemost mirom*].

Of course, this is by no means a task that could be resolved by any one agreement. I think this is quite a lengthy process during which political principles and legal norms for cooperation must be elaborated. Our attitude toward it is obviously predetermined by the fact that Marxism-Leninism sees the provision of conditions for the comprehensive development of the individual as the ultimate goal of the socialist, communist transformation of society.

Furthermore, participation itself in such a process enables the practice itself to be improved. Lenin, as is well-known, deemed it essential to take account of criticism emanating from the enemy camp if there was even the slightest element of truth in it. By rectifying its shortcomings, broadening the zone of social justice, and enriching the rights of the individual, socialism will prove its total superiority over capitalism.

But discussions on human rights can and must, naturally, unfold on an equal footing. At the moment, this is not happening and here the hypocritical nature of Western speculations on this topic and the desire to make propaganda capital from it are being exposed. Indeed, if the United States and other imperialist states take the human rights charges they have levelling as applying to themselves as well—and sooner or later this is unavoidable—then they will have to tackle in earnest many acute social problems that are inevitably concomitants of capitalism.

Thus we have a right to draw the conclusion that the sphere of world governability [*upravlyayemost mirom*], despite all its contradictoriness, is slowly but steadily expanding. This process is for the good of mankind. It can only be given the requisite dynamics by peoples' common efforts. However great the role of ruling political parties' and governments' constructive initiative may be, these very initiatives can only become reality if they are accepted and supported by the international public and become the expression of general human will.

The English political specialist E. Mortimer writes: "If the 18th century were French, the 19th English, and the 20th American, then won't the 21st be Japanese? In all events, the transition to a new hegemony will take several decades. At least it will as long as we live in a multipolar world. But how will we be able to govern [*upravlyat*] it, taking into consideration the fact that the existence of nuclear weapons excludes the traditional process of recording changes in the geopolitical balance—namely war? Truth to tell, we have no idea."

The English author has reached an impasse because his thought cannot break free of the old logic's limitations. At the same time, it is not the next powerful hegemony that is becoming increasingly perceptible in the future but a "world concert" playing a melody of peace and cooperation without a conductor.

World Community and World Government. Reaction to "The World Community Is Amenable to Government"

A. Bovin

The need for purposeful global government of the world community is becoming increasingly apparent. G. Shakhnazarov, corresponding member of the USSR Academy of Sciences, is right to draw this to our attention. But the main thesis of his article (*Pravda* 15 January), basically, as far as I understand, that it is time to return to the idea of a "centralized international authority," a "world government," raises doubts.

Let us look at G. Shakhnazarov's train of thought and line of argument. He recalls that in the fifties, Soviet foreign policy theory and practice were entirely opposed to "mondialism." In the first place, its supporters categorically rejected sovereignty. In the second place, in conditions where the United States had a considerable economic, political, and military advantage in the worldwide correlation of forces, the idea of a world government was bound to result in a legalized form of world domination by US imperialism.

Now the position of the United States has changed fundamentally. So "one of the main arguments against a world government has gone by the board." But what about the other main argument, the other obstacle? This obstacle can be removed if a world government is based not on a denial of sovereignty but on a "balance of interests" of different states, taking these interests into account and coordinating them.

Let us stop there for a moment.

If one goes by common sense and accepted usage, government presupposes that the governing systems have the right to issue "commands" that are compulsory for those whom they govern. Therefore, government is impossible without limitation (or self-limitation) of the "sovereignty" of the governed. G. Shakhnazarov appears to acknowledge this. At any rate, he writes about the "objective contradiction between sovereignty and world government." But, in my view, he considerably oversimplifies the situation when he carries the discussion into the area of balance of interests.

In this area equal partners build their relations on a mobile basis of mutual compromises that changes with time. One could only talk about the presence of a governing center, an "international authority" in a case where the steady, constant balance of interests enabled the members of the world community to delegate some of their rights (their sovereignty) to that center, that is consider its decisions (within limits defined by the balance of interests) binding on themselves and compulsory. As for the current and foreseeable (at least in the medium term) level of balance of interests, it is scarcely so steady as to be able to take the weight of a world government.

But let us follow the writer further. He points out quite rightly that "to govern you need law and a government." Let us leave aside the issue of law as a secondary issue in this context. But what about government? "There is no government as yet," we read, "but one can definitely say that the rudiments exist. . . ." The "rudiments" are the numerous international organizations headed by the United Nations. Assessing the "degree of governability of the world" with the aid of the aforementioned "rudiments," the writer of the article claims that government is farthest advanced in the sphere of international division of labor and also in the sphere of "maintaining public order through joint efforts." As regards the government of global problems, the situation is "much worse" and "worst of all" in the case of the government of issues of war and peace.

Let us analyze this.

Can the United Nations and, in particular, other international organizations be regarded as the "rudiments" of a world government? In purely abstract terms, or, at the other extreme, in the sphere of international journalism, they probably can. But in the scientific plane? Not a single state would carry out (nor does it) a decision by the United Nations or an international organization if it considered it contradictory to its interests. The activity of the United Nations, the experience accumulated by numerous international organizations of cooperation and coordination of interests, and the potential for trust that is increasing as a consequence—

all this in principle can be seen as the gradual establishment of conditions in which the creation of the "rudiments" of a world government is conceivable (only conceivable!).

What and whose "joint efforts" to maintain "public order" is he talking about? I cannot guess. Although, I suppose, there are UN troops in a number of regions of the world maintaining order there. The claim about "far advanced" government of "international division of labor" is also dubious. What does he have in mind? CEMA? The Common Market? The General Agreement on Tariffs and Trade? Like several other organizations, they influence—in varying degrees—international division of labor. But on the whole, at the global and regional levels, it continues to be at the mercy of elemental, ungovernable forces, primarily those of the market and competition.

Thus, to my mind, the idea of a world government, even "rudimentary," today and, apparently, in the near future as well, lacks a sufficiently sound basis. And the article essentially admits this. The last sentence says: In the future a "world orchestra" performing "without a conductor a melody of peace and cooperation" will become more and more clearly discernible. Precisely, without a conductor.

An observation of a more general nature: When elevating general human interests, one should not forget, it seems to me, that **class** interests continue to exist alongside general human interests and that an integral world is inseparable from a world torn by contradictions. If we forget about this, we will find ourselves in a sociopolitical vacuum in which the contradiction between socialism and capitalism disappears, in which peaceful coexistence is dissociated from the class conflict, and in which, as we have just seen, the "rudiments" of a world government already exist.

I know how nice it is to soar in the pure air of abstraction. But I prefer to remain in closer contact with reality, both social and political.

Mechanism of the Secure World: Discussing the Theses of the Central Committee of the Communist Party of the Soviet Union

G. Tunkin

The security concept put forward by CPSU and based upon the international law grounds attracts an ever growing attention of scientists, politicians and broad public throughout the world. As it is stated in the Theses of CC of CPSU for the 19th All-Union Party Conference, the influence of realities of the contemporary world and possible modifications of a number of objective factors allow to believe that a consolidation of security of states would be to a greater extent shifted from the sphere of the military potentials ratio to the sphere of politics, privacy of rights and general human morality in observing international obligations.

What could an efficient international mechanism of regulation really be under conditions of the existence of, on the one hand, an ever increasing interconnection and interdependence in the world and, on the other hand, the existence of sovereign states belonging at the same time to different socio-economic systems? Is it possible?

In the contemporary international life there are two kinds of regularities having a direct relation to this question. On the one hand, it is an internationalization of the economic and other aspects of the life of the society what even Marx and Lenin wrote about. It is a process of the growth of an interconnection and interdependence of states, the emergence of global problems on the resolution of which the very existence of the human civilization is dependent. First of all, the question is on a liquidation of the nuclear war threat and also on a preservation and rational utilization of environment. That is on problems which cannot be resolved by separate countries and require their collective actions.

This regularity of development of the contemporary society manifests itself, in particular, in an intensification of a conscious coordinated international regulation expressed first of all in a rapid progress of the international law and international organizations and in the growth of their role in the international life, the fact that is correctly defined by some scientists as "the growth of manageability of the world". The term "management" sometimes stirs up objections because it is usually associated with the existence of a system issuing commands. That's why some people prefer to use the term "regulation" accepted by the way in the international-law literature.

When proceeding from this regularity only, which is inherent to a majority of supporters of the world state in the West, then the way for establishing the world government is open. However, there are other regularities of development of the society which act in another direction. First of all and in general, it is an existence of sovereign states and two socio-economic systems different by their class nature.

Is the establishment of the world government conceivable in the existence of sovereign states? G. Shakhnazarov in his article published in the newspaper "*Pravda*" on January 15, 1988, admits that there is an objective contradiction between the sovereign and world government. Therefore he believes that "the concept of the entire interdependent world gives the key for its resolution. The question is on the building up of a new international political order not on the basis of a negation of the sovereignty and independence of nations (such a claim remains to be reactionary up to now), but on the basis of an observance and coordination of their interests." Certainly, the reference to the coordination of interests does not resolve the question completely which consists of the problem on what mechanisms should be for coordinating those interests, but the term "coordination" means much.

Here, first of all, the term "government" is frightening, and not without grounds. The concept "government" relates to the state. But in the article of "*Pravda*" it was said not about a formation of "the world government," but on the establishment of a "new international political order."

It seems that in the foreseeable future the question could be only on an international organization possessing a number of authorities similar, but not equivalent, to those possessed by governments in states.

As for the sovereignty of states, then it is not absolute and does not mean an unlimited freedom of actions. When preserving attributes of sovereignty, the states may restrict the freedom of their actions with agreement concluded on the basis of voluntariness and equality of rights. The progress of the international law was going on just along this way. Thus, for example, in the 19th century the international law acknowledged "the right of the state for a war" which was considered to be the most important attribute of the state sovereignty. On the basis of an agreement, the states gave up this right, and a prohibition to resort to wars in relations between states has become one of the basic principles of the contemporary international law (the Paris Pact of 1928). This principle turned into a broader principle of a non-utilization of force or threat of force after the adoption of the UN charter. The sovereignty of state is realized within the frameworks of the international law the norms of which are formed as a result of the concordance of the will of states.

While remaining sovereign ones, the states can provide international organizations created by them according to treaties with broad powers in international affairs. Including also supernational powers the nature of which is reduced to an adoption of resolutions compulsory for member-states by the international organization.

It seems to us that the opinion dominating in our science and meaning that the best form of the international organization is an organization without supernational powers is outdated. If the mankind managed to escape a nuclear self-annihilation then the progress would go along the way of imparting certain supernational powers necessary to maintain the international peace and security to the international organization.

At the same time such an organization would be an inter-state organization by its nature, but not the world government. In this connection, it cannot but be noted that the United Nations Organization has already acquired the supernational and superstate powers to a certain extent, the Article 25 of its Charter has the provision that "the Organization member-states, in accordance with this Charter, agree to obey the resolutions of the Security Council and carry out them."

Therefore, as we believe, the existence of sovereign states does not exclude an establishment of an efficient international organization possessing superstate powers and functions in certain problems.

As for the difference of socio-economic systems, it is not a less important circumstance which should be kept in mind. You know, side by side with the general human interests there are still class interests. The question is how to ensure a priority of the general human interests that is urgently dictated by realities of the nuclear and space era.

Is the existence of different socio-economic systems an insuperable obstacle in this way? Yes—for the establishment of the world government and the world state. The existence of different social and ideological systems may create difficulties also for the formation of an efficient international organization, but in this case that obstacle is surmountable. Having transfered their prerogatives to the international organization, the states would continue to remain sovereign ones, the problems of the socio-economic order would still relate to the exclusively internal competence of states, and the international organization could not interfere with them.

What is to begin with? As a matter of fact, the beginning has been commenced. There are the international law and the universal international organization for preserving the international peace and security—that is the UN.

In the West there are not a few sceptics which contend that the contemporary international law and the UN are not suited for the nuclear and space era because they were formed in general even prior to the emergence of nuclear weapons. In developing countries there is a certain proliferation of the concept that the contemporary international law needs a radical change because it was formed before the emergence of new states constituting a majority of the international community.

It is hardly possible to agree with such concepts. The contemporary international law contains the necessary minimum of principles and standards the strict observance of which by states is necessary for the secure world. At the same time, it is not developed enough in those spheres of the international-law regulation which relate to new vital problems appeared before the mankind during the last decades. First of all they include problems of the international peace and security in their new meaning, of an accelerated development of less developed countries, of the protection and rational utilization of environment, and a number of others.

The matter is especially poor in the international law in the sphere of problems of securing peace. Such is the wide-spread opinion which is correct in general, but not quite exact. And this inaccuracy leads to practical mistakes in many cases. The international law contains still a few standards restricting the arms race: several multilateral and bilateral agreements and treaties. The first in the history treaty on a nuclear disarmament—the INF Treaty which has come into effect recently—is of the greatest importance.

But in the contemporary international law there is a principle of a non-utilization of force or a threat of force which has a fundamental importance for the creation of the secure world. An emergence of this principle was a true revolution in the international law which made a step forward for the entire epoch. The policy of force practiced during centuries became illegal because of this. Certainly, it should be acknowledged that the absence of a quite authoritative international mechanism reduces the efficiency of this most important principle.

When speaking on the international law as the main means of a normative regulation in the interstate system one should not forget that in the interstate system, side by side with the international law, a number of other special standards are functioning, in particular, standards of recommendation, resolutions of international organizations, political standards, international moral standards. Having no legal obligatoriness they nevertheless exert a certain influence upon the behavior of states.

When speaking on the necessity of an international mechanism for the establishment of the secure world, Mikhail S. Gorbachev wrote: "The United Nations Organization is called to be such a mechanism by the idea and by its origin. We are convinced that it is capable to accomplish this role."

For this purpose in view, first of all it is necessary to raise the efficiency of the UN on the basis of its Charter where enormous potential opportunities are contained. In the interstate system there are a lot of other international mechanisms in the form of universal and regional international organizations. In short, as G. Shakhnazarov noted, "the sphere of manageability of the world is gradually but undeviatingly expanding in spite of all its contradictory character."

The proposals on the problem of the universal international security system put forward by the Soviet Union and other Warsaw Treaty Organization member-states are aimed at the introduction of a new vivifying stream into existing mechanisms of the international regulation, to create new necessary mechanisms, to make them to be more efficient means of the international regulation, to create new necessary mechanisms, to make them to be more efficient means of the international regulation. It is suggested to achieve this by realizing broad international measures in political, military, humanitarian and other spheres.

Certainly, difficulties in the way are enormous. The reconstruction of thinking is necessary in the entire world. The following measures are necessary: a refusal from the concept dominated through centuries according to which relations between states are based on force and first of all on armed forces; an adoption of the concept put forward by the Soviet Union according to which relations between states in the rocket and nuclear era, in spite of existing contradictions, should and could be based upon negotiations and agreements that is upon the international law; a refusal from the policy of interference with internal affairs of other states; a recognition and maintenance of the peaceful coexistence of states independently on their socio-economic systems. All this is declared with the entire definition in the tenth section of the Theses of Central Committee of CPSU for the 19th All-Union Party Conference.

Of course, the movement forward along the way towards the creation of the efficient international mechanism of the secure world is possible only under condition of a further growth of the activity of the peoples directed at the liquidation of nuclear weapons and at every kind of consolidation of the international order.

11. No Development Without Peace, No Peace Without Development

Mohammed Bedjaoui

The general debate which inaugurates each session of this Assembly provides us with an opportunity to take stock of past activities. Through the dynamic of contrasting views, it prompts us to permit the collective ambition necessary for great works to prevail and to take shape in reality. This year we are again brought face to face with the gravity of the situation and the dangers it implies.

Against a heavily darkened international horizon, sources of concern seem legion. Disquiet has struck deep roots in man and society. Wherever we turn we see distress for some, anxiety for others, destitution for most. It is a global crisis the world is facing.

That crisis stems from the free rein given conflicting power relationships. It is deepening the gap between well-being for the few and want for the immense majority of mankind. The disorder prevailing in world affairs and the absurdity of the present system of international economic relations are apparent.

But in order to muster the strength and will to act, one must first understand.

It is true that the mind boggles when we announce to an indifferent world that before two decades elapse we shall have to support, employ, feed two billion people—in more graphic terms, the equivalent of 2000 cities of one million inhabitants. But reason itself fails us when we look at the other side of this picture: the fact that, should things go on as they are, those two billion people will face inexorable death before two decades are over. Have our understanding and conscience grown so numb that we can no longer react to an inconceivable present masking this terrifying future?

In 1980 fifty million human beings perished from hunger. Although it gave rise to no general surge of indignation, this was surely a holocaust on a planetary scale. The Second World War took five years to reach similarly macabre results. Non-assistance to peoples in peril may indeed be the proper term to use when more than 500 billion dollars are earmarked yearly for worldwide military expenditure, while the report *Global 2000* of the Carter Commission informs us that the amount of grain necessary to eliminate malnutrition in the world could be purchased for the price of five submarines.

In the year 2000 some one billion people will be living beneath the threshold of absolute poverty, a scholarly euphemism which falls far short of expressing everything this subhuman condition implies.

The external debt of the Third World corresponds exactly to the amount spent yearly on arms by a human community seemingly unable to conceive of its future save through an unfathomable fascination with destruction or through an irresistible urge to collective suicide. The salient fact is that this growing burden of indebtedness is not the logical outcome of economic development, but rather the result of the servicing of the debt, which will exceed the astronomical level of 100 billion dollars in 1981.

Should not an effort be made to explain how, misleading appearances notwith-standing, the industrialized nations receive from the proletarian nations nearly seven times what they invest through "reverse aid"?

Skyrocketing interest rates heavily penalize our fragile economies. A trade war without quarter is being waged against our exports. The restructuring of world industry remains at the discretion of transnational corporations, subject to the dictates of their strategies and profits. In this unequal contest, the Third World countries are not even successful in putting an end to abuse. The international monetary system proceeds to demolish what our arduous labours build.

At a time when the framework of world affairs is revealing its structural weaknesses, it is a healthy sign that importance should at last be accorded to international economic relations.

This coming to grips with the problems has the merit of envisaging development and peace not only in their casual relationship but as elements of a close-knit dialectic which makes them mutually necessary. There is no development without peace or peace without development. Peace and development will be the two distinguishing features of the emerging picture of the new international order so fervently desired by the international community.

In singling out the inequities upon which the present system of international relations rests, the Third World has put into true perspective the fact that development is the new name of peace. Under-development, like war, is not foreordained. Under-development is the product of an organized system of domination and exploitation. That system runs directly counter to the hopes for prosperity harbored by two thirds of mankind. It is a denial of their legitimate right to development.

It is a system which breeds insecurity even for those who have built it, a system which breeds frustration and alienation, a system of dominance which is the negation of peace.

I have said that there cannot be peace without development. But development has its rules, and those are certainly not the rules of the market economy which have recently gained the limelight.

It is cause for concern that the philosophy of international economic cooperation seems to be losing ground. The new concepts emerging in the general approach to the problem of development are troublesome in many respects. Praise is being lavished on the virtues of bilateralism, for ulterior motives which we are well aware of. A veritable campaign is being orchestrated to promote the concept of indivi-dualized cooperation tailored to strategic considerations. Similarly, the merits of free interplay of market forces are being touted now as means both to restore growth and to ensure development.

Is there any need to recall that the present world crisis—a structural crisis if ever there was one—is precisely the result of the unchecked, unpredictable dealings of these private interests? Likewise, in a system characterized by unequal oppor-tunities and resources for development, the free play of market forces breeds dependence and fosters underdevelopment.

The laws of the market and of competition are the playthings of the world's big capital interests and of the transnational corporations. The facile glorification of these laws is mystification. Liberalism is a doctrine well suited to the powerful and the strong. The free, spontaneous, and beneficial operation of natural market laws is a grim illusion.

The realities are there to see. The market economy is at the end of its tether. It disregards the complexities of economic interdependence and the deep aspirations of mankind for more freedom and humanity. The world economy is not a random flux of things and objects. By their anachronistically untrammelled character, the natural laws of the market spell their own doom, just as they have brought about the end of growth itself, the liberal concept of growth which alienates man both as producer and as consumer, and which degrades his social surroundings and natural environment.

To allow private interests in the world economy free rein is to allow them to develop according to their own rationale, the rationale which compels them to acquire ever greater power—the very negation of international cooperation. We are thus being asked to allow the lives of billions of men, the future of our planet, to become the stakes in the game of chance of *laissez-faire* liberalism, in this grand worldwide casino where the majority of the earth's inhabitants are being despoiled. Even the winners in this dubious undertaking can hope for only a Pyrrhic victory. For ultimately, our entire planet will be the loser in this vast game with marked cards.

Need I say that we are also wary of the eagerness with which we are urged to create appropriate political and material conditions in our countries to host transnational corporations? Are these corporations truly the harbingers of development, as we are being assured? One may at least be allowed some doubts. The countries of the Third World, having long endured exploitation by a system which dealt with them as marketable commodities, are keenly aware that the transnational corporations today are unlikely to change their nature, disregard the profit motive, and set out in pursuit of their own extinction.

We are being reminded nowadays of the virtues of self-reliance. Self-reliance is a part of us—no doubt the most demanding part. It is through self-reliance that we express our identity and take into our hands the aspirations of our peoples. It is also, as we know, the only avenue towards building nationhood. But what impact can be expected of national development efforts when the international context thwarts them and cancels out their effects through the merciless laws of a global jungle?

We must face a paradox. Is not the free play of the so-called natural laws of the market likely to lead to exacerbated feelings of frustration among the hungry masses of mankind? The paradox is that these laws institutionalise anarchy and engender violence. The paradox is that, under the guise of fighting human alienation, they themselves become the very fabric of violence. They are not, therefore, the appropriate remedy for our problems. One does not fight anarchy with anarchy. One does not combat violence by fostering still more violence.

The crisis of the world economy is in fact so far-reaching that a rehabilitation of the laws of the market as a panacea for its ills becomes ludicrous.

The imperative of development is a pressing one. Surely it calls for more than a mere glorification of the merits of *laissez-faire*. As against this vain rehabilitation [of] an anachronistic liberalism, our preference is for responsible dialogue.

The global negotiations are an integral part of such a dialogue. It is a dialogue which we want, which we believe in. It is, in our view, both a condition for and a means to orderly endeavour for the common good.

The imperative need for this dialogue derives not only from the world crisis. For mankind, the dialogue also represents a renewed stake in the future, an act of faith. Its success is hence a matter of historical necessity. It is a means to the consolidation of peace.

In this context, we regret that the global negotiations have not been launched. We reaffirm our adherence to these negotiations because we believe in their merits. The global negotiations can, through the dynamic of concerted action, make possible a structural reorganization for the benefit of all.

There can be no development without peace.

While development must be adopted as the very goal of a steadfast quest for peace, the improvement of the international political climate clearly constitutes an essential stage.

It is true that, in the last two decades, international relations have gone through a qualitative evolution perceptible in a relative detente between power blocs and major strides in peoples' liberation. But the fact remains that solid foundations for the building of peace have not been laid. Persistent expressions of the spirit of confrontation and the spread of hotbeds of tension through the Third World are rooted in the very logic of the system, which generates crisis even while trying to contain it this side of a general conflagration.

The politics of spheres of influence, interventionist doctrines based on so-called vital interests, the opening or reactivation of military bases, the formation or deployment of rapid deployment troops—all are part of a persistent desire to use Third World countries as the terrain of a global strategy aimed directly against those countries' independence and their legitimate aspiration to peace.

The resurgence of gunboat diplomacy and the feverish search for power-bases are being accompanied by a standstill in disarmament field of arms control. Moreover, the pursuit of an increasingly sophisticated technology of death has just given birth to a new weapon of mass destruction about which we are told, to our astonishment, that it is designed to kill men while leaving equipment intact. The production of the neutron bomb casts a raw light upon the tragic absurdity upon which technological civilization is embarked: worship of objects and disdain for life.

This initiative is reminiscent of the spirit behind the concept of "security through vigilance". It can only feed the spiralling arms race and further slow down the effective pursuit of the major objective of general and complete disarmament, the ultimate and absolute guarantee of the principle of non-resort to force.

The deteriorating international political climate is inherent in the logic of the system, even if the phenomenon of detente prompted some transitory belief, through its promises of indivisibility, in a spreading momentum of peace extending its benefits into ever-widening spheres of international relations.

Detente failed to generate such a dynamic, particularly in the Third World, thereby revealing all its historical limitations.

The geo-strategic partitioning of the Third World into surrogate-states and terrains of aggression tends to perpetuate the subjugation of peoples. The attempts to distort the nature of the Palestinian, Namibian, and South African problems are designed to contain the advance of peoples' liberation movements by involving them in an East-West context which is external to them.

In the Middle East, the deterioration of the situation resulting from Camp David has entered a crucial phase. Current events provide countless examples of the aggressiveness of the Zionist entity against the Palestinian people and other peoples of the region. Repeated aggressions against ravaged Lebanon, which has been subjected to a criminal process of dismemberment, the bombing of peaceful nuclear facilities in Iraq, the unrestrained repression of the populations of the occupied Arab territories—all reveal the full depth of a very strange concept of peace which aimed, from the outset, only to liquidate the Palestinian cause and to bring under foreign sway the whole of the Middle East. In this regard, the strategic co-operation which has just been formalized is charged with peril for this long-suffering region.

Until the Palestinian people are enabled to exercise their national rights, until a true process of peace is undertaken, with the full participation of the PLO, its sole legitimate representative, any attempt at a solution, which would disregard the origin of the crisis and focus only upon its effects, will be doomed to failure.

In Southern Africa, the Pretoria regime, by its practice of *apartheid*, by its illegal occupation of Namibia, and by its acts of aggression against neighbouring States, is doing grave injury to the United Nations, undermining their foundations and defying their authority.

The Eighth Emergency Special Session clearly strengthened international consensus regarding the need for immediate independence for Namibia on the basis of strict application of resolution 435 of the Security Council, in its entirety. That consensus must prevail. It must bring about the independence of Namibia, which will be the crowning achievement in the heroic struggle of its people under the guidance of SWAPO, its sole authentic representative.

That same fight must go on against *apartheid*, the most unacceptable system for the dehumanization of man.

Other open or potential crises are awaiting solution. Whether it be Afghanistan, the conflict between Iraq and Iran, Korea or Cyprus, frank dialogue constitutes the ideal framework for the pursuit of political solutions through which the right of everyone to live in peace can be made a reality in conformity with international law.

Within the framework of the tireless efforts exerted by the Organization of African Unity, the 18th Summit of the Organization laid down the elements of a just and definitive settlement of the question of the Western Sahara.

By deciding to organize and conduct a general and regular referendum of self-determination by the people of the Western Sahara and to work for the achievement of a cease-fire, and by establishing an implementation committee for this purpose, the African Heads of State sought to complete the decolonization of this territory. This desire to restore its original impetus and carry to a successful conclusion a course of events which had been interrupted may be seen in the specific mechanisms which the implementation committee defined, such as the creation of an impartial interim administration, the establishment of an international peace-keeping force, and the declaration of a cease fire by the parties to the conflict through negotiations under the auspices of the implementation committee.

The direct responsibility and authority of the implementation committee in the conduct of the process, together with the participation of the United Nations in its completion, constitutes the best guarantee of its regularity.

A tribute is due to the Organization of African Unity and to the Heads of States who are members of its implementation committee for their worthy efforts to seek a solution which will enshrine the freely expressed will of the people. Algeria, whose position on this matter is that of the OAU and the United Nations, can only reaffirm its willingness to assist the two belligerents, Morocco and the Polisario Front, in entering into negotiations in good faith with a view to achieving a cease-fire that may create the necessary dynamic for the restoration of peace.

Peace is a precondition of development. It is not always, however, a sufficient condition. Peace and development must be indissociably embodied within a clear-sighted and ambitious vision of a fraternal future for mankind. It is precisely the vision of the world the Movement of the Non-aligned brings to the international community.

This year the Non-aligned Movement is celebrating its twentieth anniversary. Its universal message is clearly understood. It brings to mankind its aspirations for peace and progress. It invites us all to dedicate ourselves through democratic dialogue to developing rationally a new political and economic world for our times.

This undertaking has as its bywords peace and development. It requires that present unjust, war-engendering structures in international relations give way to an equalitarian system built by all and for all. It tends to promote an international order which may be an authentic work of universal civilization and an expression of man's collective intelligence in search of the common good.

This debate which the Third World has advanced today has acquired the dimensions of a historic dialogue. It is a dialogue which carries the seeds of an era of universal peace, a peace which may enable every people to come into its own and make a human planet of this earth.

12. A Statement Made by Premier Zhao Ziyang at the UN General Assembly for the Commemoration of the 40th Anniversary of the Founding of the United Nations

Zhao Ziyang

Forty years have passed since the birth of the United Nations.

In world history it is rare for a political international organization to have such enduring vitality like that of the United Nations whose universality and importance grow with the passage of time. Despite twists and turns and its present weaknesses, the United Nations is irreplaceable in the historical mission it shoulders and the impact it exerts on the world. Today, we may say that the world needs the presence of the United Nations as much as the United Nations needs the support of the world. We are holding this august session to celebrate its birthday for the very aim of reaffirming the purposes of the United Nations and strengthening its functions in the hope that it will better play its due role.

It is the common aspiration of mankind to build a world of peace and security, prosperity and development, and equality and co-operation. The purposes and principles of the Charter of the United Nations are the very reflection of this aspiration. All peace-loving countries and peoples have made unremitting efforts, and the United Nations has done a great deal of work under complicated and difficult conditions in order to realize these lofty objectives.

Over the past four decades, tremendous changes have taken place in the world, but they fall far short of our expected goals. Though no new world war has broken out, regional hot wars and the East-West cold war have been on and off. The colonial system has disintegrated, but there have been repeated encroachments upon others' sovereignty and armed conquests. All countries, big or small, should be treated as equals, yet power politics remains operative in international relations. Though the system of apartheid has been universally condemned, the perverse acts by the South African authorities are being intensified. While the wealth created by mankind has multiplied, there is a widening gap of wealth between the North and the South. The arms race has swallowed up an enormous amount of wealth and resources, whereas millions upon millions of men, women and children in some developing countries are suffering from starvation and diseases and struggling for their very existence. In a word, our present world is still fraught with contradictions, confrontations, turbulence and conflicts. There are many factors of insecurity and causes for anxiety.

The decision of the United Nations to take "United Nations for a better world" as the theme of the commemoration of the 40th anniversary of its founding accords with the aspiration and desire of the people of all countries, irrespective of their colours. There are bound to be different explanations as to what kind of world can be regarded as a better world. According to the purposes of the UN Charter, a better world cannot be built without peace and development, and it calls for equality and co-operation among nations. These are its fundamental requirements.

The Charter of the United Nations has made it clear in its very first sentence: "We the peoples of the United Nations" are "determined to save succeeding generations from the scourge of war, which twice in our lifetime has brought untold sorrow to mankind. . . ." Regrettably, however, the four postwar decades are years of East-West confrontation and spiralling escalation of the arms race. The international situation remains turbulent and the danger of war lingers on. In order to safeguard international security and prevent war, the East and the West should remove confrontation, ease the atmosphere and develop their relations. All countries, whether different or similar in social system, should coexist peacefully. Every country should recognize the right of the people of any other country to choose a social system as they think fit. No country should harm the security of any other country on the excuse of safeguarding its own. In international relations, no country should resort to the threat or use of force as a means to push its own policies. International disputes which are likely to lead to conflicts constitute a hidden danger for world peace and are sources of turbulence. The parties concerned should seek just and reasonable solutions by negotiations or other peaceful means. As an organization for maintaining world peace and safeguarding international security, the United Nations ought to play an active role in this respect.

At present, all the peace-loving countries and peoples are faced with a common task, namely, to check the arms race. We are opposed to the arms race, be it conventional, nuclear, on ground or in outer space. Neither "deterrent force" nor "balance of terror" can ensure peace. On the contrary, they are bound to give rise to spiralling intensification of the arms race. There is every reason to ask the two superpowers that possess the largest nuclear arsenals to take the lead in drastically reducing their nuclear armaments so as to create necessary conditions for the complete prohibition and thorough destruction of nuclear weapons. Like many other countries, China pays close attention to the forthcoming summit meeting between the United States and the Soviet Union. It is hoped that in conformity with the demands of the people of the world, they will really abandon their attempt to seek military superiority and reach agreement through negotiations which is conducive to world peace and, furthermore, translate it into action.

A fundamental change has taken place in the pattern of the post-war international relations owing to the rise of the third world and the development of the Non-aligned Movement. The days when a few big powers could dominate the world are gone once and for all. The peace forces have outgrown the factors making for war. So long as all the peace-loving countries and peoples unite and work together, world peace can be maintained and a new world war averted.

Another important problem and major historical challenge facing mankind is whether or not common development and prosperity can be attained throughout the world, just like whether or not another world war can be averted. As a result of the heavy burden left over from the prolonged colonial rule and of the existing inequitable international economic order, most developing countries have yet to lift themselves from poverty and backwardness. Revitalizing the economy of the developing countries and tapping the potentials in these vast areas with three quarters of the world's population will contribute significantly to the growth and prosperity of the world economy as a whole. This not only requires arduous efforts on the part of the developing countries to vigorously develop their national economies and actively strengthen South-South co-operation, but also calls for the restructuring of the international economic order and the promotion of North-South dialogue and co-operation. In spite of the exploratory efforts made at the Cancun Conference four years ago, no global North-South dialogue has been launched up to now, and no significant change has taken place in the current North-South relations. The United Nations should address this important question seriously and take effective measures in regard to finance, money, trade, debt and assistance so as to promote better North-South relations. This will be most helpful to the economic growth of both the North and the South and to the maintenance of world peace. We hope that more developed countries will join the developing countries in making their due contributions to this end.

Equal rights of nations, large and small, constitute the fundamental principle of the UN Charter as well as the cornerstone of the United Nations Organization. These equal rights should not be interpreted merely as the rights to speak and to vote in the United Nations. They should include the right of every nation to inviolability of its sovereignty and independence, and to non-interference in its internal affairs. In this regard, the present state of the world is not satisfactory. There are still attempts to impose one's will on small states in disregard of their rights. What is worse, acts of invading and occupying others' territories and trampling upon their sovereignty have not yet ceased. The universality and efficacy of the United Nations lie in the equality of all its members. Only when the weak are free from being bullied by the strong and the small nations are respected by the big powers can the United Nations play its full role and world peace and stability be maintained.

As one of the founding members of the United Nations and a permanent member of the Security Council, China is clearly aware of its responsibility and obligations. We have always abided by the purposes and principles of the Charter of the United Nations, supported its activities in maintaining world peace and promoting international co-operation and stood for the strengthening of its functions and status in world affairs. China is a developing socialist country belonging to the third world. We have always supported the people of all countries in their just struggles to maintain peace and safeguard their sovereignty and independence and to oppose imperialism, colonialism, hegemonism and racism. We will, as always, make unremitting efforts for the just cause of peace, development, equality and international co-operation.

China loves peace and needs peace. It is essential to have an international environment of durable peace and stability in which to eradicate its prolonged backwardness and turn it into a modernized socialist country with Chinese characteristics where there will be prosperity for all. Pursuing an independent foreign policy of peace, China considers itself duty-bound to oppose hegemonism and safeguard world peace. China hopes to live in harmony with its neighbours and all other countries and wishes to see peaceful coexistence among all countries. China's initiative in cutting the size of its military force by one million has once again demonstrated its firm stand against the arms race. China does not set up military bases or station troops abroad, nor does it seek hegemony or interfere in the internal affairs of other countries. It steadfastly pursues a policy of opening to the outside world and engages in reciprocal and mutually beneficial economic and technological exchanges with countries in the north and the south, the west and the east in the interest of common progress. China will always remain a reliable friend and partner to all countries that work for world peace and promote international economic growth.

The United Nations has traversed a long course, but it is still faced with arduous tasks. All the member states and the peoples of all countries must continue their tremendous efforts to build a better world of peace, development, equality and co-operation. Let us work together in compliance with the purposes and principles of the UN Charter to attain this lofty goal.

13. Realities and Guarantees for a Secure World

Mikhail Gorbachev

The 42nd session of the United Nations General Assembly opened a few days ago. That fact led to this article.

Objective processes are making our complex and diverse world more and more interrelated and interdependent. And it increasingly needs a mechanism capable of discussing common problems in a responsible fashion and at a representative level. This mechanism needs to be a place of mutual search for a balance of differing, contradictory, yet real, interests of the contemporary community of states and nations. The United Nations Organization is called upon to be such a mechanism by its underlying idea and its origin. We are confident that it is capable of fulfilling that role. This is why in the first days of autumn, when vacation time is over and international political life is rapidly gathering momentum, when an opportunity for important decisions in the disarmament field can be discerned, we in the Soviet leadership deemed it useful to share our ideas on the basic issues of world politics at the end of the 20th century. This seems all the more appropriate since the current session of the United Nations General Assembly is devoted to major aspects of such politics.

Naturally, what we would like to do first of all in this connection is to try and see for ourselves what the idea of a **comprehensive system of international security**—the idea advanced at the 27th CPSU Congress—looks like 18 months after the Congress. This idea has won backing from many states. Our friends—the socialist countries and members of the non-aligned movement—are active co-authors.

This article deals primarily with our approach to the formation of such a system. At the same time it is an invitation for the United Nations member-countries and the world public to exchange views.

I.

The last quarter of the 20th century has brought changes in the material aspect of being—changes revolutionary in their content and significance. For the first time in its history mankind became capable of resolving many problems that had hindered its progress for centuries. From the standpoint of the existing and newly-created resources and technologies, there are no impediments to feeding a population of many billions, to educating it, providing it with housing and keeping it healthy. Despite the obvious differences and potentialities of the various peoples and countries, a prospect has arisen of befitting standards of living for the inhabitants of the Earth.

At the same time dangers have emerged which put into question the very immortality of the human race. This is why new rules of coexistence on our unique planet are badly needed, rules which conform to the new requirements and the changed conditions.

Alas, many influential forces continue adhering to outdated notions concerning ways for ensuring national security. As a result the world is in an absurd situation whereby persistent efforts are being made to convince it that the road to the abyss is the most correct one. It would be difficult to appraise in any other way the point of view that nuclear weapons make it possible to avert a world war. It is not simple to refute it precisely because it is totally unfounded. One has to dispute something which is being passed off as an axiom—because no world war has broken out since the emergence of nuclear weapons, those weapons have averted it. It would seem more correct to say that a world war has been averted despite the existence of nuclear weapons.

Some time back the sides had several scores of atomic bombs apiece, then each came to possess a hundred nuclear missiles, and finally, the arsenals grew to several thousand nuclear warheads. Not long ago Soviet and American scientists made a special study of the relationship between strategic stability and the size of nuclear arsenals. They arrived at the unanimous conclusion that 95 per cent of all US and Soviet nuclear arms can be eliminated without stability being disrupted. This is a killing argument against the "nuclear deterrence" strategy that gives birth to mad logic. We believe that the five per cent should not be retained either. And then the stability will be qualitatively different.

Not laying claims to instructing anyone and having come to realize that mere statements about the dangerous situation in the world are unproductive, we began seeking an answer to the question of the possibility today of a model for ensuring national security which would not be fraught with the threat of a world-wide catastrophe.

Such an approach was in the mainstream of the concepts formed during the evolution of a new mode of political thinking which is permeated with a realistic view of what is surrounding us and happening around us and of ourselves; this view is characterized by an unbiassed attitude to others and awareness of our own responsibility and security.

The new thinking is bridging the gap between word and deed. And we have embarked on practical action. Sure that nuclear weapons are the greatest evil and pose the most horrible threat, we announced a unilateral moratorium on nuclear tests which we observed, let me put it straight, longer than we might have done. ... Then came the January 15, 1986 Statement putting forth a concrete programme for the stage-by-stage elimination of nuclear weapons. At the meeting with President Reagan in Reykjavik we came close to understanding the desirability and possibility of complete nuclear disarmament. And then we took steps making it easier to approach an agreement on the elimination of two classes of nuclear arms—medium- and shorter-range missiles.

We believe this to be possible and realistic. In this connection I would like to note that the Government of Federal Germany has assumed a stand conducive to this to a certain extent. The Soviet Union is proceeding from the premise that a relevant treaty could be worked out before the end of the current year. Much has been said about its potential advantages. I will not repeat them. I would only like to note that it would deal a tangible blow at concepts of the limited use of nuclear weapons and the so-called "controllable escalation" of a nuclear conflict. There are no illusory intermediate options. The situation is becoming more stable.

This treaty on medium- and shorter-range missiles would be a fine prelude to a breakthrough at the talks on large-scale—50 per cent—reductions in **strategic offensive arms under strict observance of the ABM Treaty.** I believe that, given the mutual striving, an accord on that matter could become a reality as early as the first half of next year.

While thinking of advancing toward a nuclear weapon-free world it is essential to see to it even now that security be ensured in the process of disarmament, at each of its stages, and to think not only about that, but also to agree on mechanisms for maintaining peace at drastically reduced levels of **non-nuclear armaments.**

All these questions were included in proposals set forth jointly by the USSR and other socialist countries at the United Nations—proposals for the establishment of a system of international peace and security.

How do we see this system?

The security plan we proposed provides, above all, for continuity and concord with the existing institutions of the maintenance of peace. The system could function on the basis of the UN Charter and the framework of the United Nations. As we see it, its ability to function will be ensured by the strict observance of the Charter's demands, additional unilateral obligations of states, as well as confidence measures and international cooperation in all spheres—politico-military, economic, ecological, humanitarian and others.

I do not venture to foretell how the system of all-embracing security will appear in its final form. It is only clear that it can become a reality only if all means of mass annihilation are destroyed. We propose that all this be pondered by an independent commission of experts and specialists, which would submit its conclusions to the United Nations Organization.

Personally, I have no doubt about the capability of sovereign states to assume obligations even now in the field of international security. Many states are already doing this. The Soviet Union and the People's Republic of China have stated that they will not be the first to use nuclear arms. The Soviet-American agreements on nuclear armaments are another example. They contain a conscious choice of restraint and self-limitation in the most sensitive sphere of relations between the USSR and the United States. Or take the Treaty on the Non-Proliferation of Nuclear Weapons. What is it? It is a unique example of the high sense of responsibility of states.

In reality "bricks" which can be used to start building the future system of security already exist today.

The sphere of the reasonable, responsible and rational organization of international affairs is expanding before our very eyes, though timidly. Previously unknown standards of openness, of scope and depth for mutual monitoring and verification of compliance with adopted obligations, are being established. An American inspection team visits an area where exercises of Soviet troops were held; a group of United States Congressmen inspects the Krasnoyarsk radar station; American scientists install and adjust their instruments in the area of the Soviet nuclear testing range. Soviet and American observers are present at each other's military exercises. Annual plans of military activities are published under the accords within the framework of the Helsinki process.

I do not know a weightier and more impressive argument in support of the fact that the situation is changing than the stated readiness of a nuclear power to renounce nuclear weapons voluntarily. References to an aspiration to replace them with conventional armaments in which there supposedly exists a disbalance between NATO and the Warsaw Treaty in the latter's favour are unjustified. If a disbalance and disproportions exist, let us remove them. We do not tire of saying this all the time and we have proposed concrete ways of solving this problem.

In all these issues the Soviet Union is a pioneer and shows that its words are matched by deeds.

The question of comparing defence spending? Here we will have to put in more work. I think that, given proper effort, within the next two or three years we will be able to compare the figures that are of interest to us and our partners and which would symmetrically reflect the expenditures of the sides.

The Soviet-American talks on nuclear and space arms, and the convention on the prohibition of chemical weapons which is close to being concluded will intensify, I am sure, the advance to detente and disarmament.

An accord on "defence strategy" and "military sufficiency" could impart a powerful impulse in this direction. These notions presuppose a structure for a state's armed forces in which forces would be sufficient for repulsing any possible aggression but inadequate for conducting offensive actions. The first step towards this could be a controlled withdrawal of nuclear and other offensive weapons from borders with the subsequent creation along borders of strips of sparse armaments and demilitarized zones between potential, let us put it this way, adversaries. And in principle we should work for the dissolution of military blocs, the elimination of bases on foreign territory and the return home of all troops stationed abroad.

The question of a possible mechanism to prevent the outbreak of a nuclear conflict is more complex. Here I approach the most sensitive point of the idea of all-embracing security: much will have to be thought over further and improved. In any case, the international community should work out agreed-upon measures for the event of a violation of the all-embracing agreement on the non-use and elimination of nuclear arms or of an attempt to violate this agreement. As for potential nuclear piracy, it appears possible and necessary to consider in advance and prepare collective measures to prevent it.

If the system is sufficiently effective, then it will provide even more effective guarantees of averting and curbing non-nuclear aggression.

The system proposed by us presupposes precisely definite measures which would enable the United Nations Organization, the main universal security body, to ensure its maintenance at a level of reliability.

II.

The division of the world's countries into those possessing nuclear weapons and those not possessing them has split also the very concept of security. But for human life security is indivisible. In this sense it is not only a political, military, and juridical category, but also a moral one. And contentions that there has been no war for already half a century do not withstand any test on the touchstone of ethics. Who said there is no war? There are dozens of regional wars raging in the world!

It is immoral to treat this as something of secondary importance. But the heart of the matter lies in more than just impermissible nuclear haughtiness. The elimination of nuclear weapons would also be a major step towards a genuine democratization of relations between states, towards establishing their equality and their equal responsibility.

Unconditional observance of the United Nations Charter and the right of peoples to choose themselves the roads and forms of their development, revolutionary or evolutionary, is an imperative condition for universal security. This applies also to the right to a social status quo which is exclusively an internal matter. Any attempts, direct or indirect, to influence the development of other than one's own country, to interfere in such development, should be ruled out. Just as inadmissible are attempts to destabilize existing governments from outside.

At the same time the world community cannot remain an outsider to inter-state conflicts. Here it could be possible to begin by fulfilling the proposal made by the United Nations Secretary-General to set up under the United Nations Organization a multilateral centre for lessening the danger of war. Evidently, it would be feasible to consider the expediency of setting up a direct communication line between the United Nations headquarters and the capitals of the countries that are permanent members of the Security Council, and the location of the Chairman of the non-aligned movement.

It appears to us that, in the interests of greater trust and mutual understanding, a mechanism could be set up under the aegis of the United Nations Organization for extensive international verification of compliance with agreements on lessening international tension and limiting armaments, and of the military situation in conflict areas. The mechanism would use various forms and methods of monitoring to collect information and promptly submit it to the United Nations. This would provide an objective picture of the events taking place and timely detection of preparations for hostilities, impede sneak attacks, make possible measures to avert any armed conflict, and prevent such conflicts from expanding and becoming worse.

We are arriving at the conclusion that wider use should be made of United Nations' military observers and United Nations' peace-keeping forces for disengaging the troops of warring sides and for ensuring that ceasefire and armistice agreements are observed.

And of course at all stages of a conflict extensive use should be made of all means of peaceful settlement of disputes and differences between states and good offices and mediation should be offered with the aim of achieving an armistice. The ideas and initiatives concerning the setting up of non-governmental commissions and groups which would analyze the causes, circumstances and methods of resolving various concrete conflict situations appear to be fruitful.

The Security Council permanent members could become guarantors of regional security. They could, on their part, assume an obligation not to use force or the threat of force and to renounce demonstrative military presence, because such a practice is one of the factors fanning regional conflicts.

A drastic intensification and expansion of cooperation between states in uprooting international terrorism are extremely important. It would be expedient to concentrate this cooperation within the framework of the United Nations. In our opinion, it would be useful to create under its aegis a tribunal to investigate acts of international terrorism.

More coordination in the struggle against apartheid as a destabilizing factor of international magnitude would also be justified.

As we see it, all the above-stated measures could become an organic part of an all-embracing system for peace and security.

III.

The events and tendencies of the past decades have expanded this concept, imparting new and specific features to it. One of them is the problem of economic security. A world in which a whole continent can find itself on the brink of death from starvation and in which huge masses of people are suffering from almost permanent malnutrition is not a safe world. Neither is a world safe in which a multitude of countries and peoples are being strangled in a noose of debt.

The economic interests of individual countries or groups of them are indeed so different and contradictory that consensus with regard to the concept of the New International Economic Order seems hard to achieve. We do hope, however, that the instinct of self-preservation will start working here as well. It is certain to manifest itself if we manage to determine the priorities and realize that there are circumstances that are menacing in their inevitability, and that it is high time to abandon the inert political mentality and views of the outside world inherited from the past. This world has ceased to be a sphere which the big and strong divide into domains and zones of "vital interests".

The imperatives of the times compel us to elevate to the rank of politics many common sense notions. It is not philanthropy which prompted our proposal for reduction in interest payments on bank credits and the elaboration of extra benefits for the least developed nations. This holds benefit for all, namely—for a secure future. If the debt burden of the developing world is alleviated, the chances for such a future will grow. It is also possible to limit debt payments by each developing country to the share of its annual export earnings without detriment to development; to accept export commodities in payment for the debt; to remove protectionist barriers on the borders of creditor-nations; and to stop adding extra interest when payments on debts are deferred.

There may be different attitudes to these proposals. There is no doubt, however, that the majority of international community members realize the need for immediate actions to ease the developing world's debt burden. If this is so, through concerted effort it would be possible to start working out a programme.

The words "through concerted effort" are very important for today's world. The interconnection between disarmament and development, confirmed at the recent international conference in New York, can be used in practice if none of the strong and the rich keep themselves aloof. I have already expressed the view that the Security Council member-states, represented by their top officials, could jointly discuss this problem and work out a coordinated approach. I confirm this proposal.

Ecological security. It is dangerous in the direct meaning of the word when currents of poison flow along river channels, when poisonous rains pour down from the sky, when an atmosphere polluted with industrial and transport waste chokes cities and whole regions, when the development of atomic engineering involves unacceptable risks.

Many have suddenly begun to perceive all that not as something abstract, but as quite a real part of their own experience. The confidence that "this won't affect us", characteristic of the past outlook, has disappeared. They say that one thorn of experience is worth more than a whole forest of instructions. For us, Chernobyl became such a thorn. . .

The relationship between man and the environment has become menacing. Problems of ecological security affect all—the rich and the poor alike. What is required is a global strategy for nature conservation and the rational use of resources. We suggest starting its elaboration within the framework of the UN special programme.

States are already exchanging relevant information and notifying international organizations of the state of affairs. We believe that this practice should be turned into a law by introducing the principle of annual reports by governments about their nature conservation activity and about ecological incidents, both those that have already occurred and those that were prevented on the territory of their countries.

To realize the need for opening a common front of economic and ecological security and to start its formation mean defusing a delayed-action bomb planted deep inside mankind's existence by history, by people themselves.

IV.

Human rights. One can name all the top statesmen of our times who threatened to use nuclear weapons. Some may object: it is one thing to threaten and another to use. Indeed, they haven't used them. But campaigning for human rights is in no way compatible with threatening to use weapons of mass destruction. We hold it unacceptable to talk about human rights and freedoms while intending to hang up "chandeliers" of exotic weapons in outer space. The only ordinary element in that "exoticism" is the potential possibility of mankind's annihilation. The rest is in dazzling wrapping.

I agree: the world cannot be considered secure if human rights are being violated. I will only add: it cannot be considered secure if a large part of this world lacks elementary conditions for a life worthy of man, if millions of people have a full "right" to go hungry, to have no roof over their heads and to be jobless and sick indefinitely, since treatment is something they cannot afford, if, finally, the most basic human right, the right to life, is disregarded.

First of all, it is necessary that national legislation and administrative rules in the humanitarian sphere be brought into accordance with international obligations and standards everywhere.

Simultaneously, it would be possible to start coordinating a broad range of practical steps, for instance, to start working out a world information programme under UN auspices to familiarize peoples with the life of others, life as it is and not as someone would like to present it. That is precisely why such a project should envisage ridding the flow of information of "enemy image" stereotypes, of bias, prejudices and absurd concoctions, of deliberate distortion and unscrupulous violation of the truth.

There is much promise in the task of coordinating unified international legal criteria for handling in a humanitarian spirit issues of the reunion of families, marriages, contacts between people and organizations, visa regulations and so on. What has been achieved on this account within the framework of the all-European process should be accepted as a starting point.

We favour the establishment of a special fund of humanitarian cooperation of the United Nations formed from voluntary state contributions through reductions in military spending and private donations.

It is advisable that all states join the UNESCO conventions in the sphere of culture, including the conventions on the protection of the world cultural heritage and on the prohibition and prevention of the illicit import, export and transfer of ownership of cultural property.

Alarming signals of recent times have pushed to the top of the agenda the idea of creating a world-wide network of medical cooperation in treating the most dangerous diseases, including AIDS, and combatting drug addiction and alcoholism. The existing structures of the World Health Organization make it possible to establish such a network relatively quickly. The leaders of the world movement of physicians have valuable ideas on this account.

Dialogue on humanitarian problems could be conducted on a bilateral basis, within the forms of negotiations that have already been established. Furthermore, we propose holding such dialogue within the framework of an international conference in Moscow: we made that proposal at the Vienna meeting in November last year.

Pooling efforts in the sphere of culture, medicine and humanitarian rights is yet another integral part of the system of comprehensive security.

V.

The proposed system of comprehensive security will be effective to the extent to which the United Nations, its Security Council and other international institutes and mechanisms effectively function. It will be necessary resolutely to enhance the authority and role of the UN and the International Atomic Energy Agency. There is a strong need for a world space organization. In the future it could work in close contact with the UN as an autonomous part of its system. UN specialized agencies should also become regulators of international processes. The Geneva Conference on Disarmament should become a forum that would internationalize the efforts for a transition to a nuclear-free, non-violent world.

One should not forget the possibilities of the International Court of Justice either. The General Assembly and the Security Council could approach it more often for consultative conclusions on controversial international legal issues. Its mandatory jurisdiction should be recognized by all on mutually agreed upon conditions. The permanent members of the Security Council, taking into account their special responsibility, should make the first step in that direction.

We are convinced that a comprehensive system of security is at the same time a system of universal law and order which ensures the primacy of international law in politics.

The UN Charter gives extensive powers to the Security Council. Joint efforts are required to ensure that it could use them effectively. For this purpose, it would be expedient to hold meetings of the Security Council at Foreign Ministers' level when opening a regular session of the General Assembly to review the international situation and jointly search for effective ways towards its improvement.

It would be useful to hold meetings of the Security Council not only at the headquarters of the UN in New York, but also in regions of friction and tension as well as to alternate among the capitals of the Security Council permanent member-states.

Special missions of the Council to regions of actual and potential conflicts would also help consolidate its authority and enhance the effectiveness of the decisions adopted.

We are convinced that cooperation between the UN and regional organizations could be considerably expanded. The aim is to search for a political settlement to crisis situations.

In our view, it is important to hold special sessions of the General Assembly on the more urgent political problems and individual disarmament issues more often so as to improve the efficiency of the latter's work.

We emphatically stress the need for making the status of important political documents passed at the United Nations by consensus more binding morally and politically. Let me recall that they include, among others, the final document of the 1st Special Session of the UN General Assembly on Disarmament, and the Charter of Economic Rights and Duties of States.

In our opinion, we should have long ago set up a world consultative council under the UN auspices to bring together the world's intellectual elite. Prominent scientists, political and public figures, representatives of international public organizations, cultural workers, people in literature and the arts, including winners of the Nobel Prize and other international prizes of world-wide significance, and eminent representatives of the churches could greatly enrich the spiritual and ethical potential of contemporary world politics.

To ensure that the United Nations and its specialized agencies operate at full capacity it should be realized that using financial levers to pressure it is inadmissible. The Soviet Union will continue to cooperate actively in overcoming budget difficulties arising at the United Nations.

And, finally, about the United Nations' Secretary-General. The international community elects an authoritative figure enjoying everybody's trust to that high post. Since the Secretary-General is functioning as a representative of every member-country of the organization, all states should give him the maximum of support and help him in fulfilling his responsible mission. The international community should encourage the United Nations' Secretary-General in his missions of good offices, mediation and reconciliation.

*   *   *

Why are we so persistent in raising the question of a comprehensive system of international peace and security?

Simply because it is impossible to put up with the situation in which the world has found itself as the third millennium draws nearer—facing the threat of annihilation, in a state of constant tension, in an atmosphere of suspicion and strife, spending huge funds and the labour and talent of millions of people to increase mutual distrust and fears.

We could speak indefinitely about the need for terminating the arms race and uprooting militarism, and about cooperation. Nothing will change unless we start acting.

The political and moral core of the problem is the trust of states and peoples in one another, respect for international agreements and institutions. And we are prepared to switch from confidence measures in individual spheres to a large-scale policy of trust which would gradually shape a system of comprehensive security. But such a policy should be based on oneness of political statements and real stands.

The idea of a comprehensive system of security is the first project of a possible new organization of life in our common planetary home. In other words, it is a pass into a future where the security of all is a token of the security of each. We hope that the current session of the UN General Assembly will jointly develop and elaborate on this idea.

14. Prospects for a New Era of World Peace

Ronald Reagan

Half a world away from this place of peace, the firing, the killing, the bloodshed in two merciless conflicts have, for the first time in recent memory, diminished. After adding terrible new names to the roll call of human horror—names such as Halabjah, Maydan Shahr, and Spin Buldak—there is, today, hope of peace in the Persian Gulf and Afghanistan.

So, too, in the highlands and coastal cities of southern Africa—places of civil war, places of occupation by foreign troops—talk of peace is heard, peace for the tortured nation of Angola. Sixty-five hundred miles east, in the Southeast Asian country of Cambodia, there is hope now of a settlement—the removal of Vietnam's occupying forces. And, finally, in this hemisphere, where only 12 years ago one-third of the people of Latin America lived under democratic rule, some 90% do so today. And, especially in Central America, nations such as El Salvador, once threatened by the anarchy of the death squad and the specter of totalitarian rule, now know the hope of self-government and the prospect of economic growth.

And another change—a change that, if it endures, may go down as one of the signal accomplishments of our history; a change that is a cause for shaking of the head in wonder is also upon us; a change going to the source of postwar tensions and to the once seemingly impossible dream of ending the twin threats of our time: totalitarianism and thermonuclear world war. For the first time, the differences between East and West—fundamental differences over important moral questions dealing with the worth of the individual and whether governments shall control people or people control governments—for the first time, these differences have shown signs of easing; easing to the point where there are not just troop withdrawals from places like Afghanistan but also talk in the East of reform and greater freedom of press, of assembly, and of religion. Yes, fundamental differences remain. But, should talk of reform become more than that—should it become reality—there is the prospect of not only a new era in Soviet-American relations but a new age of world peace. For such reform can bring peace, history teaches, and my country has always believed that where the rights of the individual and the people are enshrined, war is a distant prospect, for it is not people who make war—only governments do that.

A MOMENT OF HOPE

I stand at this podium, then, in a moment of hope—hope, not just for the peoples of the United States or the Soviet Union but for all the peoples of the world; and hope, too, for the dream of peace among nations, the dream that began the United Nations.

Precisely because of these changes, today the United Nations has the opportunity to live and breathe and work as never before. Already, you, Mr. Secretary General [Javier Pérez de Cuéllar], through your persistence, patience, and unyielding will, have shown, in working toward peace in Afghanistan and the Persian Gulf, how valuable the United Nations can be. And we salute you for these accomplishments.

In Geneva at this very hour, there are numerous negotiations underway—multilateral negotiations at the Conference on Disarmament as well as bilateral negotiations on a range of issues between the Soviets and ourselves. And these negotiations, some of them under UN auspices, involve a broad arms control agenda—strategic offensive weapons and space, nuclear testing and chemical warfare—whose urgency we have witnessed anew in recent days.

And the negotiators are busy, and over the last few years, they've been engaged in more than an academic exercise. There is movement. The logjam is broken. Only recently, when the United States and the Soviet Union signed the INF [intermediate-range nuclear forces] agreement, an entire class of U.S. and Soviet nuclear missiles was eliminated for the first time in history. Progress continues on negotiations to reduce, in massive number, strategic weapons with effective verification. And talks will begin soon on conventional reductions in Europe.

Much of the reason for all of this goes back, I believe, to Geneva itself, to the small chateau along the lake where the General Secretary of the Soviet Union and I had the first of several fireside chats—exchanges characterized by frankness, but friendliness, too. I said at the first meeting in Geneva that this was a unique encounter between two people who had the power to start world war III or to begin a new age of peace among nations. And I also said peace conferences, arms negotiations, proposals for treaties could make sense only if they were part of a wider context—a context that sought to explore and resolve the deeper, underlying differences between us. I said to Mr. Gorbachev then, as I've said to you before, nations do not mistrust each other because they're armed; they're armed because they mistrust each other.

And in that place, by that peaceful lake in neutral Switzerland, Mr. Gorbachev and I did begin a new relationship, based not just on engagement over the single issue of arms control but on a broader agenda about our deeper differences—an agenda of human rights, regional conflicts, and bilateral exchanges between our peoples. Even on the arms control issue itself, we agreed to go beyond the past—to seek not just treaties that permit building weapons to higher levels but revolutionary agreements that actually reduced, and even eliminated, a whole class of nuclear weapons.

What was begun that morning in Geneva has shown results: in the INF Treaty; in my recent visit to Moscow; in my opportunity to meet there with Soviet citizens and dissidents and speak of human rights and to speak, too, in the Lenin Hills of Moscow to the young people of the Soviet Union about the wonder and splendor of human freedom. The results of that morning in Geneva are seen in peace conferences now underway around the world on regional conflicts and in the work of the United Nations here in New York as well as in Geneva.

But history teaches caution. Indeed, that very building in Geneva where important negotiations have taken place—the Geneva accords on Afghanistan, the Iran-Iraq negotiations, for example—we see it today as stone-like testimony to a failed dream of peace in another time. The Palais des Nations was the headquarters of the League of Nations—an institution that was to symbolize an end to all war. And yet, that institution and its noble purpose ended with the Second World War— ended because the chance for peace was not seized in the 1930s by the nations of the world; ended because humanity didn't find the courage to isolate the aggressors, to reject schemes of government that serve the state, not the people.

We are here today, determined that no such fate shall befall the United Nations. We are determined that the United Nations should succeed and serve the cause of peace for humankind.

So we realize that, even in this time of hope, the chance of failure is real. But this knowledge does not discourage us. It spurs us on, for the stakes are high. Do we falter and fail now and bring down upon ourselves the just anger of future generations? Or do we continue the work of the founders of this institution and see to it that, at last, freedom is enshrined and humanity knows war no longer and that this place, this floor, shall be truly "the world's last battlefield."

THE AGENDA OF PEACE

We are determined it shall be so. So we turn to the agenda of peace. Let us begin by addressing a concern that was much on my mind when I met with Mr. Gorbachev in the Kremlin as well as on the minds of Soviet citizens that I met in Moscow. It is also an issue that I know is of immediate importance to the delegates of this assembly who, this fall, commemorate the 40th anniversary of the Universal Declaration of Human Rights.

That declaration says plainly what those who seek peace can forget only at the greatest peril: that peace rests on one foundation—observing "the inalienable rights of all members of the human family." In a century where human rights have been denied by totalitarian governments on a scale never before seen in history, with so many millions deliberately starved or eliminated as a matter of state policy—a history, it has been said, of blood, stupidity, and barbed wire—few can wonder why peace has proved so elusive.

Now let us understand. If we would have peace, we must acknowledge the elementary rights of our fellow human beings. In our own land, and in other lands, if we would have peace, the trampling of the human spirit must cease. Human rights is not for some, some of the time. Human rights, as the Universal Declaration of this assembly, adopted in 1948, proclaims, is "for all people and all nations"— and for all time.

This regard for human rights as the foundation of peace is at the heart of the United Nations. Those who starve in Ethiopia, those who die among the Kurds, those who face racial injustice in South Africa, those who still cannot write or speak freely in the Soviet Union, those who cannot worship in the Ukraine, those who struggle for life and freedom on boats in the South China Sea, those who cannot publish or assemble in Managua—all of this is more than just an agenda item on your calendar. It must be a first concern—an issue above others. For when human rights concerns are not paramount at the United Nations—when the

Universal Declaration of Human Rights is not honored in these halls and meeting rooms—then the very credibility of this organization is at stake, the very purpose of its existence in question.

That is why, when human rights progress is made, the United Nations grows stronger, and the United States is glad of it. Following a 2-year effort led by the United States, for example, the UN Human Rights Commission took a major step toward ending the double standards and cynicism that had characterized too much of its past. For years, Cuba, a blatant violator of its citizens' human rights, has escaped UN censure or even scrutiny. This year, Cuba has responded to pressure generated by the Human Rights Commission by accepting an investigation into its human rights abuses. Fidel Castro has already begun to free some political prisoners, improve prison conditions, and tolerate the existence of a small, independent national human rights group.

More must be done. The United Nations must be relentless and unyielding in seeking change, in Cuba and elsewhere. And we must also see to it that the Universal Declaration itself should not be debased with episodes like the "Zionism is racism" resolution. Respect for human rights is the first and fundamental mission of this body, the most elementary obligation of its members. Indeed, wherever one turns in the world today, there is new awareness, a growing passion for human rights: the people of the world grow united; new groups, new coalitions form— coalitions that monitor government; that work against discrimination; that fight religious or political repression, unlawful imprisonment, torture, or execution. As those I spoke to at Spaso House said to me last June, such movements make a difference.

REGIONAL CONFLICTS

Turning now to regional conflicts, we feel again the uplift of hope. In the gulf war between Iran and Iraq—one of the bloodiest conflicts since World War II— we have a cease-fire. The resolution and the firmness of the allied nations in keeping the Persian Gulf open to international shipping not only upheld the rule of law, it helped prevent further spread of the conflict and laid the basis for peace. So, too, the Security Council's decisive resolution in July a year ago has become a blueprint for a peaceful gulf. Let this war—a war in which there has been no victor or vanquished, only victims—let this war end now. Let both Iran and Iraq cooperate with the Secretary General and the Security Council in implementing Resolution 598. Let peace come.

Moving on to a second region: When I first addressed the UN General Assembly in 1983, world attention was focused on the brutal invasion and illegal occupation of Afghanistan. After nearly 9 long years of war, the courage and determination of the Afghan people and the Afghan freedom fighters have held sway, and today an end to the occupation is in sight. On April 14, the U.S.S.R. signed the Geneva accords, which were negotiated under UN auspices by Pakistan and the Kabul regime. We encourage the Soviet Union to complete its troop withdrawal at the earliest possible date so that the Afghan people can freely determine their future without further outside interference.

In southern Africa, too, years of patient diplomacy and support for those in Angola who seek self-determination are having their effect. We look forward to an accord between the Governments of Angola, Cuba, and South Africa that will bring about a complete withdrawal of all foreign troops—primarily Cuban—from Angola. We look forward as well to full implementation of UN Security Council Resolution 435 and our longstanding goal of independence for Namibia. We continue to support a growing consensus among African leaders who also believe there can be no end to conflict in the region until there is national reconciliation within Angola.

There are new hopes for Cambodia, a nation whose freedom and independence we seek just as avidly as we sought the freedom and independence of Afghanistan. We urge the rapid removal of all Vietnamese troops and a settlement that will prevent the return of the Khmer Rouge to power, permitting, instead, the establishment of a genuinely representative government—a government that will, at last, respect fully the rights of the people of Cambodia and end the hideous suffering they have so bravely and needlessly borne.

In other critical areas, we applaud the Secretary General's efforts to structure a referendum on the Western Sahara. And in the Mediterranean, direct talks between Greek and Turkish Cypriot communities hold much promise for accord in that divided island nation. And finally, we look to a peaceful solution to the Arab-Israeli conflict. So, too, the unnatural division of Europe remains a critical obstacle to Soviet-American relations.

In most of these areas, then, we see progress, and, again, we're glad of it. Only a few years ago, all of these and other conflicts were burning dangerously out of control. Indeed, the invasion of Afghanistan and the apparent will among democratic and peace-loving nations to deter such events seemed to cause a climate where aggression by nations large and small was epidemic, a climate the world has not seen since the 1930s. Only this time, larger war was avoided—avoided because the free and peaceful nations of the world recovered their strength of purpose and will. And now the United Nations is providing valuable assistance in helping this epidemic to recede.

And because we're resolved to keep it so, I would be remiss in my duty if I did not now take note here of the one exception to progress in regional conflicts. I refer here to the continuing deterioration of human rights in Nicaragua and the refusal of the tiny elite now ruling that nation to honor promises of democracy made to their own people and to the international community. This elite, in calling itself revolutionary, seeks no real revolution; the use of the term is subterfuge, deception for hiding the oldest, most corrupt vice of all—man's age-old will to power, his lust to control the lives and steal the freedom of others.

And that's why, as President, I will continue to urge the Congress and the American public to stand behind those who resist this attempt to impose a totalitarian regime on the people of Nicaragua; that the United States will continue to stand with those who are threatened by this regime's aggression against its neighbors in Central America.

Today I also call on the Soviet Union to show in Central America the same spirit of constructive realism it has shown in other regional conflicts—to assist in bringing conflict in Central America to a close by halting the flow of billions of dollars worth of arms and ammunition to the Sandinista regime, a regime whose goals of regional domination—while ultimately doomed—can continue to cause great suffering to the people of that area and risk to Soviet-American relations, unless action is taken now.

ARMS CONTROL NEGOTIATIONS

Moving now to the arms reduction agenda, I have mentioned already the importance of the INF Treaty and the momentum developed in the START [strategic arms reduction talks] negotiations. The draft START treaty is a lengthy document, filled with bracketed language designating sections of disagreement between the two sides. But through this summer in Geneva, those brackets have diminished; there is every reason to believe this process can continue. I can tell this assembly that it is highly doubtful such a treaty can be accomplished in a few months, but I can tell you, a year from now is a possibility—more than a possibility. But we have no deadline. No agreement is better than a bad agreement. The United States remains hopeful, and we acknowledge the spirit of cooperation shown by the Soviet Union in these negotiations. We also look for that spirit to be applied to our concerns about compliance with existing agreements.

So, too, our discussion on nuclear testing and defense and space have been useful. But let me here stress to this General Assembly that much of the momentum in nuclear arms control negotiations is due to technological progress itself, especially in the potential for space-based defensive systems. I believe that the U.S. determination to research and develop and, when ready, deploy such defensive systems— systems targeted to destroy missiles, not people—accounts for a large share of the progress made in recent years in Geneva. With such systems, for the first time, in case of accidental launch or the act of a madman somewhere, major powers will not be faced with the single option of massive retaliation but will, instead, have the chance of a saner choice—to shield against an attack instead of avenging it. So, too, as defensive systems grow in effectiveness, they reduce the threat and the value of greater and greater offensive arsenals. Only recently, briefings I have received in the Oval Office indicate that progress toward such systems may be even more rapid and less costly than we had, at first, thought. Today the United States reaffirms its commitment to its Strategic Defense Initiative and our offer to share the benefits of strategic defenses with others.

And yet, even as diplomatic and technological progress holds out the hope of at last diminishing the awful cloud of nuclear terror we've lived under in the postwar era, even at this moment, another ominous terror is loose once again in the world; a terror we thought the world had put behind; a terror that looms at us now from the long, buried past; from ghostly, scarring trenches and the haunting, wan faces of millions dead in one of the most inhumane conflicts of all time: poison gas, chemical warfare—the terror of it; the horror of it. We condemn it.

The use of chemical weapons in the Iran-Iraq war—beyond its tragic human toll—jeopardizes the moral and legal strictures that have held these weapons in check since World War I. Let this tragedy spark reaffirmation of the Geneva protocol outlawing the use of chemical weapons. I call upon the signatories to that protocol, as well as other concerned states, to convene a conference to consider actions that we can take together to reverse the serious erosion of this treaty. And we urge all nations to cooperate in negotiating a verifiable, truly global ban on chemical weapons at the Conference on Disarmament in Geneva. It is incumbent upon all civilized nations to ban, once and for all—and on a verifiable and global basis—the use of chemical and gas warfare.

Finally, we must redouble our efforts to stop further proliferation of nuclear weapons in the world. Likewise, proliferation in other high-technology weapons such as ballistic missiles is reaching global proportions, exacerbating regional rivalries in ways that can have global implications. The number of potential suppliers is growing at an alarming rate, and more must be done to halt the spread of these weapons. This was a matter of discussion last week between Secretary Shultz and [Soviet] Foreign Minister Shevardnadze. Talks between American and Soviet experts begin on this today. And we hope to see a multilateral effort to avoid having areas of tension like the Middle East become even more deadly battlegrounds than they already are.

PROGRESS AND REFORM IN THE UNITED NATIONS

But in most of these areas, we see not only progress but also the potential for an increasingly vital role for multilateral efforts and institutions like this United Nations. That is why, now more than ever, the United Nations must continue to increase its effectiveness through budget and program reform. The United Nations already is enacting sweeping measures affecting personnel reductions, budgeting by consensus, and the establishment of program priorities. These actions are extremely important. The progress on reforms has allowed me to release funds withheld under congressional restrictions. I expect the reform program will continue and that further funds will be released in our new fiscal year.

And, let me say here, we congratulate the United Nations on the work it has done in three areas of special concern.

- First, our struggle against the scourge of terrorism and state-sponsored terrorism must continue. And we must also end the scourge of hostage-taking.
- Second, the work of the World Health Organization in coordinating and advancing research on AIDS [acquired immune deficiency syndrome] is vital. All international efforts in this area must be redoubled. The AIDS crisis is a grave one; we must move as one to meet it.
- And so, too, is the drug crisis. We're moving now toward a new anti-drug-trafficking convention. This important treaty will be completed in December. I am confident other strong UN drug control programs will also follow. The American people are profoundly concerned and deeply angered. We will not tolerate the drug traffickers. We mean to make war on them, and we believe this is one war the United Nations can endorse and participate in.

Yes, the United Nations is a better place than it was 8 years ago—and so, too, is the world. But the real issue of reform in the United Nations is not limited just to fiscal and administrative improvements but also to a higher sort of reform—an intellectual and philosophical reform, a reform of old views about the relationship between the individual and the state.

FREEDOM AND ECONOMIC DEVELOPMENT

Few developments, for example, have been more encouraging to the United States than the special session this body held on Africa 2½ years ago—a session in which the United Nations joined as one in a call for free market incentives and a lessening of state controls to spur economic development.

At one of the first international assemblies of my presidency, in Cancun, Mexico, I said that history demonstrates that, time and again, in place after place, economic growth and human progress make their greatest strides in countries that encourage economic freedom; that individual farmers, laborers, owners, traders, and managers are the heart and soul of development. Trust them, because where they're allowed to create and build, where they're given a personal stake in deciding economic policies and benefiting from their success, then societies became more dynamic, prosperous, progressive, and free. We believe in freedom. We know it works.

And this is the immutable lesson of the postwar era: that freedom works; even more, that freedom and peace work together. Every year that passes, everywhere in the world, this lesson is taking hold, from the People's Republic of China to Cameroon; from Bolivia to Botswana, and, yes, in the citadel of Marxism-Leninism itself. No, my country did not invent freedom, but, believe me, we impose no restrictions on the free export of our more than two centuries of experience with it. Free people blessed by economic opportunity and protected by laws that respect the dignity of the individual are not driven toward war or the domination of others. Here, then, is the way to world peace.

CLOSING REFLECTIONS

And yet, we Americans champion freedom not only because it's practical and beneficial but because it is also just, morally right. And here, I hope you'll permit me to note that I have addressed this assemblage more than any of my predecessors and that this will be the last occasion I do so. So, I hope, too, I may be permitted now some closing reflections.

The world is currently witnessing another celebration of international cooperation; at the Olympics, we see nations joining together in the competition of sports, and we see young people, who know precious little of the resentments of their elders, coming together as one.

One of our young athletes, from a home of modest means, said that she drew the strength for her achievement from another source of wealth. "We were rich as a family," she said, about the love she was given and the values she was taught.

I dare to hope that, in the sentiment of that young athlete, we see a sign of the rediscovery of old and tested values, values such as family—the first and most important unit of society, where all values and learning begin; an institution to be cherished and protected. Values, too, such as work, community, freedom, and faith—for it's here we find the deeper rationale for the cause of human rights and world peace.

And our own experience on this continent—the American experience—though brief, has had one unmistakable encounter, an insistence on the preservation of one sacred truth. It is a truth that our first President, our Founding Father, passed on in the first farewell address made to the American people. It is a truth that I hope now you'll permit me to mention in these remarks of farewell; a truth embodied in our Declaration of Independence: that the case for inalienable rights, that the idea of human dignity, that the notion of conscience above compulsion, can be made only in the context of what one of the founders of this organization, Secretary General Dag Hammarskjöld, has called "devotion to something which is greater and higher than we are ourselves."

This is the endless cycle, the final truth to which humankind seems always to return: that religion and morality, that faith in something higher, are prerequisites for freedom and that justice and peace within ourselves is the first step toward justice and peace in the world and for the ages.

Yes, this is a place of great debate and grave discussions, and yet, I cannot help but note here that one of our Founding Fathers—the most worldly of men, an internationalist—Benjamin Franklin, interrupted the proceedings of our own Constitutional Convention to make much the same point. And I cannot help but think this morning of other beginnings. Of where and when I first read those words, "and they shall beat their swords into plowshares" and "your young men shall see visions and your old men shall dream dreams." This morning, my thoughts go to her who gave me many things in life but whose most important gift was the knowledge of happiness and solace to be gained in prayer. It's the greatest help I've had in my presidency, and I recall here Lincoln's words when he said only the most foolish of men would think he could confront the duties of the office I now hold without turning to someone stronger, a power above all others.

I think then of her and others like her in that small town in Illinois—gentle people who possessed something that those who hold positions of power sometimes forget to prize. No one of them could ever have imagined the boy from the banks of the Rock River would come to this moment and have this opportunity. But had they been told it would happen, I think they would have been a bit disappointed if I'd not spoken here for what they knew so well: that when we grow weary of the world and its troubles, when our faith in humanity falters, it is then we must seek comfort and refreshment of spirit in a deeper source of wisdom, one greater than ourselves.

And so, if future generations do say of us, that, in our time, peace came closer, that we did bring about new seasons of truth and justice, it will be cause for pride. But it shall be a cause of greater pride still if it is also said that we were wise enough to know the deliberations of great leaders and great bodies are but overture, that the truly majestic music—the music of freedom, of justice and peace—is the music made in forgetting self and seeking in silence the will of Him who made us.

Thank you for your hospitality over the years. I bid you now farewell, and God bless you.

PART TWO

THE UNITED NATIONS AND WORLD ORDER VALUES

General Introduction

"From out there," the astronaut Frank Borman reminded us on seeing earth from Apollo 8, "it really is 'one world.' " With the instant worldwide communications and fast mobilization of national expectations and capabilities, the science and technology of the twentieth century have finally ushered in a global system. We need to leap backward from time to time to see the extent of this transformation in our mental map of the world. In the Middle Ages, there were a half billion people on the earth, and perhaps one-tenth of one percent of them knew that the world was round and that there were people on the other side of the globe. Now five hundred years later—a very short period in the evolution of human species— there are eight times as many people, and only one-tenth of one percent do not know that there are people on the other side of the globe. Peoples of the world now share an Apollo vision and almost instinctively feel that their ultimate fates are inexplicably intertwined. The fact that the overwhelming majority of humankind understands for the first time that human society encompasses the entire planet is a transformation comparable in magnitude to the understanding that the world is round rather than flat.

A normative transformation has been part of the emergence of a global system. The gradual shift of values from monarchical to popular sovereignty has led to the delegitimation and demise of human slavery and slave trade in the nineteenth century and colonialism in the twentieth century. While most individuals in the newly independent states do not yet lead decent lives, the pursuit of decency for all is no longer dismissed as utopian. The Nuremberg principles, too, although marred by the problem of victor's justice and subsequent failures of implementation, represented a normative milestone in the progressive development of an international code of conduct. And because of the expanding networks of interconnection among state and nonstate actors, it is common nowadays to speak of a global political system as a fact of contemporary international life. These sociological, technological, and normative changes are reshaping our images and attitudes with regard to authority structures of an evolving global community. By the turn of the next century, we believe, the world will see a new structure of global governance taking shape. An unresolved crucial question concerns *how* it will come about—by cataclysm, drift, or rational reform and restructuring—and *whether* a new global order will be hegemonic, benignly elitist and technocratic, or democratic. To date, every world historical transformation of any magnitude has come about through cataclysmic global war, but this experience can be discounted as pre-nuclear. We proceed from the premise that we can—and must—intervene individually and collectively in time to shift this ongoing world historical process in nonviolent and nonapocalyptical directions. There is no assurance that this effort will be successful, but the effort itself improves its prospects.

By "world order transformation" we mean a fundamental change in the normative and structural variables of the existing international order to such an extent that a new configuration of political actors with new orientations toward power, well-being, and governance emerges. The emergence of a sense of global human identity and the concern about humane governance necessitate the incorporation of value issues into analytical schemes and into the thinking of critical social movements. The world order approach we adopt in this series of volumes on world order is anchored in the centrality of common core values as a point of departure in the study of global politics. As a frame of reference for all human behavior except a narrow band of the most rigidly instinctive motor behavior, values provide standards for evaluating desirable and preferable human behavior at all levels of social organization. In the political process of both domestic and international society, the important function of values is to lay a moral foundation of shared beliefs and standards as well as to lend or withdraw legitimacy from particular political arrangements. In our time, the UN General Assembly has become the most visible arena for such authoritative definition and allocation of values through its politics of collective legitimation and delegitimation. A vivid instance of delegitimation is the anti-apartheid campaign against the present racist governing structure of South Africa. In this volume, the UN's promise and performance as the world organization are analyzed and assessed in terms of how and to what extent the United Nations shapes and enhances the following world order values: (1) peace; (2) economic well-being; (3) human dignity, justice, and rights; and (4) ecological integrity.

By stressing these world order values as integral components of a preferred future, rather than merely describing them as problems to be placed on the UN agenda, we are consciously striving toward capturing the most dynamic forces of the ongoing transformation of world society. We do not expect that the international system can somehow muddle through to achieve a stable peace. Rather, these world order values are presented as standards for assessing social processes and as goals for guiding global social actors and movements. Thus, the world order values are not terminal points for a brave new world; instead, they serve as a road map for "inventing" a preferred future world order and, as well, for acting in the present.

Although the world order values are specified under four separate categories for analytical convenience, they are organically interrelated. The impact of action or inaction in one value domain upon the other three value domains must be constantly weighed. The synergy of the world order values can be formulated in several ways. First, failure to make progress in relation to one value may result in the deterioration of another. For instance, a low level of economic well-being due to a population explosion and food shortages in a country such as India could make domestic violence and nuclear diplomacy more cathartic and tempting. Second, value-related opportunity costs are always involved in public policy decisions. If resources are devoted to military expenditures, that much less is available for health, education, and welfare. Third, a solution to any given problem may have side effects that are detrimental to the resolution of other problems. The mindless pursuit of economic growth as a means of improving national economic well-being or the single-minded development of nuclear energy and weapons for national "security" may cause a serious ecocidal threat to health and safety.

Since its inception, UN politics, conceptualized as the authoritative value-shaping and value-enhancing processes in the global community, has demonstrated its dialectical twists and turns and unpredictable temper, surging forward, suddenly halting or even receding, and then shifting its course again under the pressure of a new configuration of dominant forces in the changing world. The four world order values suggest a broad range of principal global challenges and problems confronting the world organization. To be sure, different member states have different priorities regarding the relative importance of the issues involved, and they will certainly continue to vary in prioritization in response to shifts in perception of the global systemic environment. Despite these fluctuations, the United Nations, within statist parameters, does generally contribute, with varying degrees of effec-tiveness in different value domains, to the realization of world order values through the norms its sets, the programs it sponsors, and the institutions it establishes by way of its multilateral quasilegislative process.

The world order approach entails three distinct steps: analysis of the current state of the world, including the assessment of global trends; previsioning of a preferred world order; and prescriptive formulation of transition strategies. This approach differs from traditional or mainstream modes of analysis. It embraces a global perspective rather than a national interest or statist view as the point of departure. It also adopts a holistic, integrated mode of analysis to the human condition by conceptualizing the global problematique as a set of interlocking processes and relationships between and among the seemingly discreet national and regional problems. In this way, it seeks to develop a normative global paradigm for the study of value-shaping and value-enhancing processes in a world that is becoming, at one and the same time, increasingly interconnected and fragmented.

The first step is an analysis of the present state of the world in relation to the four values. This endeavor draws upon empirical investigation of the contemporary international system as it has evolved, as it is today, and relies upon the full range of social science research methods. Once a big picture of the world is developed, the trends are projected to give some prognosis about the likely future extrapolated from the continuation of recent developments. Although our general assessment is that the present world is not satisfactorily maximizing world order values, it is essential to have a more dialectical two-eyed view of the potential and constraint of the world organization in proposing the changes needed and the means necessary for achieving them before talking about a preferred future world order.

The second step in the world order approach involves designing alternative world futures. Various models are developed to provide alternative structures of authority that might better enhance the world order values. The construction of models for preferred and plausible futures is a way of establishing a realistic baseline for evaluating competing proposals for global reform (see Part Three). The design that is ultimately selected from the competing alternatives should serve as one's road map for a "from here to there" journey.

Our value judgment and prescriptive choice can be made among alternatives based on the following three dimensions: (1) *desirability*—Would the system achieve the values specified? (2) *workability*—How good are the chances that the system would function as conceptualized and designed? and (3) *feasibility*—Is it reasonable to suppose that this system can be attained, and is there a plausible strategy for effecting the necessary change? Although different actors will probably prefer different future worlds, the very process of "blueprinting" alternative future worlds can be an educational and empowering experience that extends both our horizons of aspiration and our sense of what is possible.

Devising strategies for shifting the existing international order into a preferred one is the third key task. The designing of future worlds can be dismissed as an exercise in wish fulfillment in the absence of credible transition strategies to chart the paths along which such worlds can emerge from present reality. If the arms race is deemed unacceptable in terms of costs and probability of species extinction and a disarmed world is postulated as preferred, the analyst needs to suggest a transition strategy for achieving an alternative global security system. The transition steps involve the identification of existing trends and actors who could be activated through global consciousness-raising and mobilization to invent and bring into being a preferred future. The preferred world is then an image of a reformed world system expressed with some specificity, including a behavioral description of transition politics. Since it is possible to depict a range of preferred systems and transition scenarios, a preferred world is a relevant utopia selected by a social activist because it is more likely to realize his or her value goals. The specification of detail is meant to be illustrative of ways to achieve transition but not to exhaust creative possibilities. The future cannot be preordained, and there are many transition scenarios that would satisfy our value-realizing goals.

Because the world order approach is concerned with the existing and future structures of authority on a global scale, the emphasis is placed on a wide range of actors and institutions. The range of potential actors goes far beyond the nation-states to include universal international organizations such as the United Nations, transnational actors (including multinational corporations), "international regimes," regional organizations, subnational groups, social movements, local communities, and individuals. The term "world order" is also used as a shorthand way of referring to this broad constellation of social actors and the patterns of their relationship in any given international system at a given time in the world historical process. The analysis of the United Nations in this part of the book gives special attention to the institutions and norms that might have an impact—whether positive, negative, or mixed—on the creation of a peaceful, just, and ecologically stable world.

The UN's performance cannot be adequately evaluated unless the world order values are described concretely to provide more specific criteria for assessment. And yet, a value indicator is more easily suggested than accepted. A value indicator's usefulness is related to the degree of its general acceptance. Diverse groups must feel that it does indeed reflect with accuracy those very things it purports to measure. Hence, when new measures for global processes are being designed, the need to convince the public of their validity must also be kept in mind. For example, the number of war deaths or the duration and frequency of war are only beginning to be accepted as valid reflections of the status of peace in the international system. The full utility of such indicators will not be realized until there is widespread agreement on their appropriateness. However, due to the immediate need for some rough measures of the status of the values, it seems useful to suggest two ways of assessing the status of the world order values—global value indicators and parameters.

First, we need global value indicators to describe and evaluate the current status of each world order value. Most value indicators currently in use are still geared to phenomena on the national level. Since the problems are no longer confined to the national domain, the indicators we require should have a corresponding global dimension. Because such global indicators aggregate data about individuals in very diverse social and cultural settings, however, there is also a need to avoid allowing a global average from masking gross disparities and significant suffering on the part of the bottom 33 percent of the world's people. The practice of calculating per capita income by dividing the GNP by the population tells us little about how these resources are actually distributed within the society. Such figures can therefore be grossly misleading, whether they are used to hide inequalities within individual countries or to mask global poverty belts with impressive aggregate numbers about global wealth. At the same time, these indicators can have very important consequential impacts in a policy review and feedback process. The prominence of the GNP as an indicator's national economic health, for instance, encourages political decisions that emphasize production and expansion, while discouraging alternative policy options that stress conservation and the quality of life. With the hidden environmental time bombs suddenly exposed at nuclear weapons facilities in the United States in 1988, we now realize the inadequacy of traditional indicators for measuring the costs of national "security." Since the selection of indicators has important impacts on government decisions, the formulation of new indicators must be undertaken with a clear understanding of their implications for public policy and for the realization of world order values.

Second, it is important to establish parameters for each value that seem acceptable at this point in human history. These parameters of acceptability are introduced to provide as universally acceptable a threshold as possible in each value area. Previous discussions have concentrated on the entire gross global product, even though the bulk of these goods and services were available only to the world's elites. By including a minimal level of acceptable performance for each value, we are consciously attempting to shift the focus of analysis to the human needs of the voiceless bottom third of global society. The measure of "success" in the value-shaping and value-realizing processes in the global political economy, for example, should become the standard of living for those who are least well-off, rather than the progress of the society at large or an average level of per capita income for the world as a whole. Thus, the inclusion of parameters is designed to implement the normative imperative that all individuals are entitled to a minimal level of decency and well-being.

This revised measure of success can be implemented by defining a minimum cut-off level for each value and then determining the number of individuals who live below that standard. Governments could achieve such a standard in a variety of ways, but the parameter itself would help critical social movements to hold policymakers accountable for maldistributions of goods and benefits in a society. The present emphasis is on a floor, but the concept of a ceiling on development or income may become increasingly desirable and necessary in an age of resource scarcity and ecological instability. It is worth noting in this connection that certain societies are already referred to as overdeveloped (and maldeveloped).

The search for the global value indicators and parameters represents preliminary attempts to depict the global problems in a way that both enables the measurement of progress in terms of values and provides a value-specific guide for public policy. The indicators should be consciously global, and a minimum standard of well-being is suggested as a normatively desirable and politically feasible goal against which the politics of the United Nations can also be evaluated. Much of the authoritative allocation of values in UN politics can be understood in terms of two main types of activities in the resolution of concrete issues and problems: the value-shaping process and the value-realizing process. The value-shaping process involves collective legitimation of certain moral claims that reflect collective national and global needs. Specifically, this legitimating process entails the first-stage translation of moral claims into general principles, usually in the form of declarations, and the second-stage translation of these declaratory principles into legal norms defining specific rights and obligations in the form of multilateral conventions. The value-realizing process is more elusive in the sovereignty-centered international system, but it involves collective decisions relating to the establishment of institutional machinery and procedures to "implement" through monitoring and supervising what have been agreed upon as international norms and values. The basic normative and structural constraints within which the UN-sponsored value-shaping and value-realizing processes take place should be kept in mind when assessing the possibilities and limitations of the UN's world order performance.

The United Nations is committed by its Charter to realizing the world order values of peace, economic well-being, and social justice, while ecological balance has been more recently incorporated into the organization's programmatic objectives. In Part Two, each section evaluates the past endeavors of the United Nations in relation to each of the four world order values. In the context of the world order framework, we are also interested in assessing the contribution of the United Nations to the shaping of alternative world orders and the extent to which the UN provides political space for nonstate social actors and movements to act effectively on behalf of securing a more peaceful, just, and ecologically sound world.

The United Nations and International Peace and Security

INTRODUCTION

From its inception, the United Nations considered peace as its overriding objective. The world organization was founded in the aftermath of World War II "to save succeeding generations from the scourge of war." To this end, all member states were prohibited from the threat or use of force. Chapters VI and VII of the Charter empowered the Security Council with various ways and means of settling international disputes and enforcing international peace. Even the economic and social functions (Chapter IX of the Charter) were conceptualized on the premise that such international cooperation would contribute to the cause of peace.

In retrospect, the collective security system as envisioned and embodied in the UN Charter by its founding architects is more notable for its worm's-eye view of immediate reality than for a visionary blueprint for a future world order. The Charter clearly favored the preservation of the status quo over peaceful change. The causes of war and the conditions of peace were conceptualized in terms of empowering the great powers (the victors of World War II) to respond in concert to traditional well-defined cases of international aggression in the manner of World War II, involving the use of overt military force across recognized international boundaries. The deep underlying structural causes of war were beyond the purview of the Security Council. The General Assembly received a vague mandate that it may "consider the general principles of co-operation in the maintenance of international peace and security, including the principles governing disarmament and the regulation of armaments" (Article 11). The Charter also failed to anticipate the rise of subnational and transnational conflicts and terrorism and counterterrorism in the shape of international life to come. In many ways, then, the Charter was designed to perpetuate a traditional condominial world order.

In practice, the United Nations had to adapt itself to the changing systemic conditions such as the emergence of the Soviet-U.S. rivalry (and the collapse of the great-power concert), the nuclear arms race, the rise of the Third World (and the North-South conflict), and the general shift in international structure from unipolarity (U.S. hegemony) to bipolarity and, more recently, to multipolarity. The UN's activities in the international peace and security realm in response to these systemic factors fall under three broad categories: management of international conflicts and disputes through peacekeeping operations; global arms control and disarmament; and conceptual and normative activities to generate a global consensus on the meaning of war and peace in a changing world. Over the years, a rough division of labor and specialization has developed between the Security Council and the General Assembly, with the former playing a dominant, if not an exclusive role in peacekeeping with the exception of the 1956–1963 period, and the latter in global arms control and disarmament (ACD) and conceptual and normative activities. The secretary-general has intermittently played an influential role in good offices and mediation and exerted varying degrees of influence on the activities of the General Assembly and the Security Council. The personal qualities of the secretary-general seem as important to the extent of influence as the formal attributes of the office on the level of international tensions.

The UN's performance in the maintenance of international peace and security has generally fallen far short of the UN's promise. Yet, the track record in this realm has been mixed and evolving. The two cases of UN peacemaking and peace-enforcing activities—Korea and the Congo (both of which occurred at the height of the Cold War)—proved to be so controversial as to foreclose this option indefinitely. The inability of the Security Council to fulfill its intended enforcement role, coupled with the widely shared belief that the United Nations must manifest a minimal demonstration of authority for the maintenance of international peace and security if it is not to suffer the fate of its League predecessor, brought about a politically more feasible and militarily more modest alternative to collective security, or what came to be known as "peacekeeping." Peacekeeping, falling in the gray zone between the pacific settlement provisions of Chapter VI and the enforcement provisions of Chapter VII, has been characterized as a "Chapter VI½" innovation. With the exception of the Korean and Congo cases—and even the Congo case shifted from a peacekeeping to a peace-enforcing direction in the course of its implementation—all UN involvement in the management of international conflicts and disputes can be subsumed under peacekeeping.

Empirical studies of the UN's management of international conflict during its first forty-five years show fluctuations from period to period with the success curve beginning to drop to its lowest levels in the 1970s, followed by a still sharper drop during the first half of the 1980s. Neglect begets neglect, and neglect begets decay in the UN peacekeeping regime. The success curve generally follows the curve for referrals—the more disputes that are referred to the UN, the higher the rate of success in UN management of international conflicts. To be sure, much of the decline in UN effectiveness in this realm after 1970 can be explained in terms of the growing indifference to multilateral conflict management by the permanent members, especially the shift in the U.S. attitude in the wake of its controversial intervention in the Vietnam War.

The Third World became the major culprit and loser in the 1970s and beyond, as it failed to respond to the initiative of the West European countries for a revival of the General Assembly's role in peacekeeping. Even in such an "easy" case as the 1982 Falklands-Malvinas affair and the resulting British-Argentinian war, the Third World refused to revive the Uniting for Peace Resolution by pressing for a transfer of the dispute from the Security Council, where any further action was foreclosed by the British and U.S. veto, to the General Assembly. The regime decay is a story of big power discord in the Security Council; it is also a story of deficient leadership on the part of the Third World in the General Assembly.

However, the new turns of events in 1987–1988 served as a reminder that it was premature to write off the United Nations in the war-peace area. With the muting of East-West tensions, and an effective secretary-general, the UN reestablished its reputation as a useful, even indispensable, instrument, especially for settling intractable regional conflicts in deeply troubled and wounded areas of the world. The first breakthrough occurred on July 20, 1987, when the Security Council passed Resolution 598, literally demanding an end to the fighting in the Persian Gulf and other correlate measures. The resolution was the first to receive unanimous support from the Big Five, leading to the establishment of the United Nations Iran-Iraq Military Observer Group (UNIMOG) in 1988, the first UN maritime peacekeeping mission of its kind. Another breakthrough, painstakingly negotiated by UN Under-Secretary-General Diego Cordovez and signed in Geneva on April 14, 1988, was the agreement to end the nine-year Soviet intervention in Afghanistan and the resultant establishment of the United Nations Good Offices Mission for Afghanistan and Pakistan (UNGOMAP), the first instance of the superpowers becoming co-guarantors of an agreement over a regional conflict involving a superpower as a party to that conflict. Historically, a conflict of this nature was beyond the reach of UN management, as the Big Five had refused to abide by the rule that they should at least abstain from voting in a dispute in which they were directly involved.

After much behind-the-scenes wrangling in the Security Council between the Big Five and the Third World over the size of a new UN peacekeeping force for Namibia, the Security Council finally agreed on the establishment of a smaller peacekeeping force of 4,650 soldiers (instead of 7,500 as foreseen in the original UN plan for Namibian independence and as demanded by African countries). Other regional conflicts in Western Sahara, Indochina, and Central America are now on the UN's active agenda; thus the spurt of UN activity has caused some financial strain. The United Nations was already in serious financial trouble in early 1988 when its peacekeeping bill stood at about $300 million a year, and it is now faced with a rapidly rising peacekeeping bill (projected to rise between $1 billion and $2 billion). Somehow, it is assumed that the funds will become available, especially in light of the positive Soviet attitude and the UN's enhanced reputation.

In a fundamental sense, the real danger is not that UN peacekeeping will decay or die but that it will continue as a paper tiger, distracting UN concerns from the underlying causes of conflict throughout the world. In mid-1982, Israel's invading forces simply rolled through the zone of the United Nations Interim Force in Lebanon (UNIFIL) as if it were an invasion corridor. In August 1982, the U.S.-led Multinational Force (MNF) operating outside the UN aegis was sent to Beirut to oversee the withdrawal of the PLO. Yet the Security Council has continued to extend the tenure of its misbegotten offspring—in the midst of the UN's financial crisis—while UNIFIL persists, despite a rising number of casualties and continuing hostilities between Israel and various elements in Lebanon.

Why? The answer seems rather simple. To borrow from Winston Churchill's well-known comment about democracy, the secretary-general, the Big Five of the Security Council, and the Lebanese all agree that UNIFIL is the worst form of the peacekeeping operation, but there is nothing better to replace it. While the present situation is far from desirable, the withdrawal of UNIFIL could be catastrophic. UNIFIL has even acquired a new humanitarian role as a sort of welfare state, dispensing life's necessities to the area's inhabitants. The disintegration of the MNF should make us more appreciative of the performance of UN peacekeeping operations under near-impossible conditions.

The UN's efforts in global arms control and disarmament have been less impressive. As mentioned earlier, the founding fathers were more concerned about beefing up the UN collective security system militarily than about global disarmament. With the growth of enormous nuclear arsenals altering the threat of war into one of the risk of human extinction, the General Assembly has gradually begun to address arms control and disarmament (ACD) issues that are multilateral in scope and of general concern to the international community. The United Nations has played an important role in catalyzing and codifying broad, if not universal, acceptance of nine of the eleven existing multilateral arms control treaties, including treaties on the Antarctic, outer space, the Latin American nuclear-free zone, nuclear non-proliferation, the sea bed, biological weapons, environmental modification, inhumane weapons, and the South Pacific nuclear-free zone. Most of these treaties were negotiated in the 1960s and early 1970s. One measure of the global disarmament predicament is suggested by a close relationship between world military expenditures and the annual output of UN disarmament resolutions in recent years. For example, the 1982 session of the General Assembly passed a record number of fifty-seven disarmament resolutions, as if to paper over the fact that its Second Special Session on Disarmament (SSOD-II), held in mid-1982, was a complete failure.

It is ironic, but perhaps not surprising, that the UN's normative activities on the use of force have been the most urgent but the least successful. The discord and malaise have been reflected since 1965 in the seemingly futile annual efforts of the thirty-three-member (thirty-four-member since December 1988, with the entry of China) Special Committee on Peace-Keeping Operations and the intersystemic dissension in the Special Committee on the Charter of the United Nations and the Strengthening of the Role of the Organization. It has been exceedingly difficult to reach a global consensus on legal norms and rules concerning the maintenance of world peace and security. This difficulty is illustrated by the irresolvable inter-systemic disagreements on a multilateral treaty on the non-use of force in the Special Committee on Enhancing the Effectiveness of the Principle of Non-Use of Force in International Relations. In four-and-a-half decades of feverish UN lawmaking, no multilateral convention on this issue has ever been concluded under the auspices of the United Nations.

There are three silver linings if one looks hard enough at the clouds looming on the horizon of UN normative activities. First, the United Nations can be credited with a substantial contribution to the international humanitarian law of war through the successful completion of two additional protocols to the 1949 Geneva Conventions and a convention and three protocols on "inhumane weapons." Second, although the UN's response to terrorism has been inadequate, especially its failure to address wholesale state terrorism (nuclear terrorism), such inadequacy has been somewhat compensated for by its legal prescriptions against individual and group terrorist actions affecting international commerce and travel. Finally, after three years of intensive behind-the-scenes negotiations, in 1982 the General Assembly adopted by consensus the Manila Declaration on the Peaceful Settlement of International Disputes. The declaration breaks no new ground, to be sure, but it does reinforce the 1970 Friendly Relations Declaration, reminding member states of their existing Charter obligations and encouraging them to make full use of all UN machinery, including the World Court, for the peaceful settlement of disputes. The Manila Declaration reaffirms the principle of the non-use of force in international relations as a peremptory legal principle (*jus cogens*) of contemporary international law.

We begin this section with the Nuremberg Principles, the most authoritative summary of what was decided at the Nuremberg Tribunal held to address the criminal liability of surviving Nazi leaders. Subsequently, the International Law Commission (ILC) was entrusted by the General Assembly to give its authoritative formulation of the Nuremberg Principles. Thus, the Nuremberg Principles received the UN stamp of approval in June–July 1950. The Nuremberg Principles represent a milestone in the development of international criminal law. They serve as a normative yardstick for assessing the subsequent development of UN lawmaking in the international peace and security domain. Principle III challenges traditional statism in international law, as it blocks any escape route for individuals, including a head of state, from their responsibility for violating the laws of war or for genocidal mistreatment even as directed against one's own citizens.

As early as 1947, the General Assembly directed the ILC to formulate the principles of international law recognized in the Charter and Judgment of the Nuremberg Tribunal and to prepare a draft Code of Offenses against the Peace and Security of Mankind. Forty years later, the ILC still could not agree on a number of fundamental issues such as the *ratione materiae* (Which crimes would the Code cover?), the *ratione personae* (Will the Code apply to individuals or states?), or the methods of enforcing the code. The latest revised schedule indicates that the ILC will complete the first reading of the draft articles by 1991.

We present this selection as an aspirational global norm, not as global reality, and as a reminder to the reader of the gap between UN promise embodied in its declaratory principles and UN performance as made manifest in the codification of legally binding norms and rules. The UN has failed to date to translate the Nuremberg Principles into a code of conduct and to extend them to the postwar perpetrators of "crimes against humanity." Each of the postwar genocides in the hinterlands of the Third World has managed to escape collective sanctions. In the case of the genocidal Khmer Rouge, the "government" even received a subsequent UN stamp of approval and legitimation in the Credentials Committee.

In the second selection in this section, Raimo Väyrynen, a prominent Finnish scholar in peace research, explores the extent to which the external systemic environment in international politics shapes the outer parameters of the UN's performance in the resolution of international conflicts. Transformations in the international systemic environment have also changed the types of conflicts the UN is called upon to resolve as well as altered the UN's own institutional capabilities. Here is a paradox that explains the general crisis of multilateral cooperation: the number and complexity of "peripheral conflicts" referred to the UN have increased at a time when the UN's institutional capabilities have begun to decline. Moreover, the pattern of alignments between the parties to the conflict, rather than the nature of the issues and the participation of great powers, better explains the UN's performance. Strengthening the role of the United Nations in the maintenance of collective security, Varynen concludes, requires greater independent latitude of action for the secretary-general as well as the establishment of standby peacekeeping forces. Rather than being a mere extension, collective security should be developed into a complement to national security.

Our third selection in this section is a report prepared by the Preparatory Committee for the International Conference on the Relationship Between Disarmament and Development. Drawing upon UN sources, it provides an overview of UN normative activities in the formulation of the relationship between disarmament and development in the shape of a background paper for the 1986 International Conference on the Relationship Between Disarmament and Development. The United Nations has gradually come to understand that peace is interrelated with the pursuit of other values and that a stable and long-lasting peace may only be attainable if a sufficient level of economic equity and well-being is ensured. However, the output of UN involvement here has been limited to a great number of hortatory resolutions that are being honored more in their breach than in their observance.

The fourth selection in the section is an essay by Robert Johansen on an alternative global security system. Johansen shows that there are seven security policy models ranging from the U.S. national security model of a nuclear war-fighting capability to one that aims at achieving global security. He favors the global common security model based on the assumption that in a nuclear-ecological age, the distinction between "our" government and "their" governments is less central. "Whether we like it or not," he argues, "in the nuclear-ecologically fragile age, all governments become 'my' government." Johansen specifies four sets of criteria and factors—military factors; political, economic, and ecological factors; social and psychological factors; and institutional factors—in the evaluation of security policies to improve the capacity of the common global security system. In the end, he challenges us to stretch the limits of the possible toward an alternative global security system.

As our final selection in this section, we present Nigel Young's "two-eyed" commentary on the challenges to building "a permanent movement for peace and human survival." From peace movements' past failures and present tensions, Young draws certain normative and strategic lessons that can enlighten and energize a new global peace movement toward achieving a "visionary synthesis, a new model and strategy that is appropriate to a changing global society." Although previous peace movements have been discontinuous and fragmented due to state centricism, limited pressure group concepts of politics, alignment, and lack of social alternatives and a strong communal base, the present peace movement still holds the potential for harnessing and linking localism and globalism, and communalism and cosmopolitanism, as groups such as the Quakers have done over a period of several centuries. Pressures for building a permanent and global peace movement have to be *external* to statism and the state-system, Young contends, for no state of any size in the twentieth century has shown any serious interest in demilitarization. The threat of a global nuclear war gives humanity one last chance for the present peace movement to sustain those essential elements of species survival such as our ability to control the use of violence and to think, feel, and act as "species-beings rather than territorial or national animals."

Taken together, these five selections suggest that the prospect of a more peaceful world depends not only on *how* but also on *where* we look. They also raise twin questions in our reading and assessment of UN performance in the international peace and security domain: What should we *fear*? What can we *hope*? These questions should take account of the changing global setting at this stage, the apparent smoothing of superpower relations, and the new Soviet enthusiasm for a strengthened UN as creating an unprecedented opportunity to increase the prestige and performance of the organization in this central area of war-peace issues.

15. The Nuremberg Principles

Principles of International Law Recognized in the
Charter of the Nuremberg Tribunal and in the
Judgment of the Tribunal
As formulated by the International Law Commission, June–July 1950.

Principle I

Any person who commits an act which constitutes a crime under international law is responsible therefor and liable to punishment.

Principle II

The fact that international law does not impose a penalty for an act which constitutes a crime under international law does not relieve the person who committed the act from responsibility under international law.

Principle III

The fact that a person who committed an act which constitutes a crime under international law acted as Head of State or responsible government official does not relieve him from responsibility under international law.

Principle IV

The fact that a person acted pursuant to order of his Government or of a superior does not relieve him from responsibility under international law, provided a moral choice was in fact possible to him.

Principle V

Any person charged with a crime under international law has the right to a fair trial on the facts and law.

Principle VI

The crimes hereinafter set out are punishable as crimes under international law:
a. Crimes against peace:
(i) Planning, preparation, initiation or waging of a war of aggression or a war in violation of international treaties, agreements or assurances;
(ii) Participation in a common plan or conspiracy for the accomplishment of any of the acts mentioned under (i).
b. War crimes:
Violations of the laws or customs of war which include, but are not limited to, murder, ill-treatment or deportation to slave-labour or for any other purpose of civilian population of or in occupied territory, murder or ill-treatment of prisoners of war or persons on the seas, killing of hostages, plunder of public or private property, wanton destruction of cities, towns, or villages, or devastation not justified by military necessity.
c. Crimes against humanity:

Murder, extermination, enslavement, deportation and other inhuman acts done against any civilian population, or persecutions on political, racial or religious grounds, when such acts are done or such persecutions are carried on in execution of or in connection with any crime against peace or any war crime.

Principle VII

Complicity in the commission of a crime against peace, a war crime, or a crime against humanity as set forth in Principle VI is a crime under international law.

16. The United Nations and the Resolution of International Conflicts

Raimo Väyrynen

I. INTRODUCTION

The work of international organizations and its results are dependent on the prevailing structure and political climate of international relations. Every organization has been established on the basis of a certain distribution of economic and military power, as its institutional manifestation. The organizational objectives, internal structures, and decision-making rules reflect, in other words, the prevailing power relations. They do, however, change over time, and hence the tasks and operational practices of international organizations are from time to time bound to face the challenge of the new external environment. In such a situation the *adjustment capacity* of an organization is of crucial importance; either it is able to transform its objectives and decision-making rules to correspond to the external requirements, or it must stagnate, become gradually irrelevant, and finally wither away.

According to such a perspective, external reality determines the internal functioning of international organizations. A related observation stresses the constraints imposed by the semi-anarchic nature of international relations and in particular by the dominant governments. The ability of international organizations to remove global inequities or threats to collective security are thus dependent on the good will of major powers and on their mutual cooperation. In such a situation international organizations easily become paralysed and powerless (Ohnmacht), though they may also be used as instruments of power by one or more major powers to the detriment of small powers (Übermacht).

Though these alternatives differ from each other in the extent to which major powers prefer to use international organizations as instruments of their foreign policy, they have a common feature as well. In both cases international organizations are perceived as *arenas* in which different forces and powers of inter-state relations meet each other. In such an image, which is characteristic of the bulk of political realism, the autonomy and identity of international organizations is small or non-existent. The influence between the nation states and their common organizations flows in one direction only: from the major powers to the international organizations.

The opposite image of international organizations portrays them as *actors* that enjoy a measure of autonomy, add a new element to international relations, and are able, up to a certain limit, to steer their course. This view derives part of its substance from *functionalism*, according to which international organizations can perform functions such as nation states cannot accomplish. This concerns in particular the organization of international collective action—i.e. aggregating resources and viewpoints, developing options, and implementing them—in fields where unilateral national measures are insufficient. To state this point more succinctly,

222

international organizations are a potential means of resolving the dilemma of individual vs collective rationality in inter-state relations.

A survey of research has inched to a conclusion that 'the prevailing image portrays the United Nations as an arena mirroring the exogenous forces of international politics'. This image is 'wrong only in the sense that it is incomplete'. The United Nations and most other international organizations, for that matter, do indeed add a new category of actors to international relations and have some causal influence of their own. Major powers and other exogenous forces naturally shape the arena and its events. The arena is, however, active rather than passive, modifies the issues relegated to it, and feeds both new issues and old issues in new forms back to national decision-makers, engendering also bilateral consultations between them.

[*   *   *]

After World War I there were several fairly equal powers in Europe. They were not able, however, to establish any stable pattern of cooperation between themselves. The Versailles treaty system discriminated against Germany, Soviet Russia adjusted herself painfully to the role of a revolutionary power, the United States refrained from shouldering the political responsibilities ensuing from her economic predominance, and hence France and England, though the latter only halfheartedly, were left alone to contain the rising Germany. In these circumstances the League was unable to keep a 'specific peace—to legitimize and stabilize a particular settlement based upon victory'. This task fell primarily upon France and England, who used the League as their international instrument to promote the stability of the new postwar order. They were alone too weak to underwrite and implement the legal and material guarantees embodied in the Covenant of the League. Furthermore, the major powers did not live up to the ideal that 'democratic rationalism', which was not even accepted by all of them, can be transplanted from the domestic society to the international order, but rather played the game of power politics for which the League was ill equipped.

After World War II the system of collective security had to be organized in quite different circumstances. There were, to begin with, much fewer states to shape the postwar international order. The United States was in both economic and military terms the leading power, with the necessary qualifications for launching and building up the United Nations. The Soviet Union and England naturally influenced the nature and structure of the new global organization, and left their imprints on the Charter, but were not able to reshape to their own liking the plan promoted by the Roosevelt Administration. Yet, the United Nations was the creation of the Big Five, and for this reason an organization established by the victorious powers. A difference from the League of Nations experience was that after World War II there were no revolutionary powers among the defeated nations, and hence the future of the United Nations came to depend more on the evolution of cooperation among the Big Five and in particular between the United States and the Soviet Union. The new global organization was, in other words, affected by the fact that the world had switched from multipolar instability to bipolar, but strained, stability.

The origins of the United Nations are rooted in the combination of *universal aspirations* and the *US search for leadership* in the world. Universalism was most strongly advocated by the Secretary of State, Cordell Hull, as an antidote to the closed economic and military blocs of the 1930s, which according to his philosophy had been a central cause of war. Cordell Hull strongly advocated free, multilaterally organized trade based on convertible currencies. Hull stated the principle of free trade as the basis of postwar international economic organization in his speech of 23 July 1941. In that same speech he stressed the necessity of establishing an international security organization which 'can—by force, if necessary—keep peace among nations in the future. There must be international cooperative action to set up the mechanisms which can thus ensure peace'.

In the Hullian philosophy free trade and an international security organization complemented each other; the latter had to settle peacefully that residue of conflicts which were not eliminated by the free international operation of market forces. The Hullian universalism embodied in concrete terms the preference for a global organization that would include all the major powers, in the longer run even the defeated ones, and would operate in social and cultural fields in addition to handling economic and security issues. The United Nations had to be comprehensive both in its scope and domain.

Cordell Hull's vision of the postwar international organization was based on the economic and military predominance of the United States, though this was not explicitly stated by him. It has been argued by a number of historians that the image of the United States at the apex of the global hierarchy of power was much more deeply anchored in the mind of Franklin D. *Roosevelt*. For him the United Nations was also unequivocally an instrument of the US policy to build up a preferred world order. Obviously Hull and Roosevelt differed in that the former favoured the reliance on the power of US corporations to reshape the international order, while the latter was more loyal to his New Deal philosophy and hence more ready to resort to the state machinery.

Universal solutions suit the interests of the predominant power. That is why it is no wonder that both Churchill and Stalin were opposed to the Hullian vision. For them the emphasis on the rights enjoyed by sovereign nations was important, since they were able in this manner to resist the US national ambitions embodied in its universalism. Churchill spoke strongly in favour of *regionalism*, which was expected to be the most effective way of preserving as much of the British influence as possible in the postwar international order. Churchill originally envisaged a world council of the United States, Great Britain, and the Soviet Union to which three regional councils for Europe, the Orient, and the Western hemisphere would be subordinated. Roosevelt basically accepted Churchill's plan, though he wanted to add China to the world council, while Hull was strongly against the proposal, since it contradicted his preference for a universal security organization complemented by separate functional agencies. Hull was in the end afraid that regional councils might develop into a balance-of-power system, which was an anathema to him.

Subsequently the problems of regionalism and decision-making structure became the biggest stumbling blocks in the preparation of the United Nations. The question of how the United Nations should be organized was further affected by the disagreement between great powers on the functional scope of the endeavour. The Soviet Union regarded political and security issues as the central ingredient of the UN agenda, while the United States wanted to include economic and social issues as well.

Finally, both of these issue groups could be included into the organization by attributing different decision-making rules for them. In April 1944 the United States agreed upon the division between an Executive Council, composed of four permanent and four rotating members, and the General Assembly. Security issues were to be dealt with primarily in the Council and socio-economic questions in the Assembly. The US position still advocated, however, the principle of majority rule, which was unacceptable to the Soviet Union. In the UN Charter the Soviet insistence on a veto has been taken into account to the extent that in all matters other than the procedural ones, in which majority rule prevails, the majority view must be concurred in by the permanent members of the Security Council (Art. 27).

This concession to the Soviet Union was necessary, since strict adherence to the principle of majority rule could have divided the wartime alliance and jeopardized the ambitious plan for the new international security organization. Yet, too extensive concessions to the Soviet Union in the direction of national sovereignty and veto power would have weakened the domestic political support for the United Nations, in particular among the internationalists and universalists.

[*   *   *]

[II.] THE UNITED NATIONS
AND ITS INTERNATIONAL ENVIRONMENT

Because of the conflicting interests and views of major powers, illuminated by its prehistory, the United Nations has never possessed a unified image. In the social and economic issues it has been more of an actor that has been able to inject its philosophy and action programmes into international relations. Without any doubt the international situation in, for instance, human rights and development issues would have evolved in a different manner without the United Nations. From this perspective the UN is primarily a functional organization on which the Cold War and the resurgence of power politics in the postwar world have left, however, a strong imprint. In security issues the world organization has, with few exceptions, been an arena that has not been capable of contributing to the peaceful settlement of disputes as effectively as its intellectual fathers envisaged.

[*   *   *]

A crucial question relates to the *distribution of power resources*, which refers not only to economic and military capacities but also to the ability of major powers to attract deference and support from smaller members of an organization. Power resources may be either *concentrated* to one or few major powers or *dispersed* more equally among other states of the international system as well (it is reasonable to recognize the fact that power resources are always concentrated to some extent).

Hence there is always at least some inequity in the distribution, and it is relevant to ask whether resources are distributed *symmetrically* or *asymmetrically* between major powers.

Relying on these distinctions it is possible to develop four alternatives for the external environment of an international organization. . . . The hegemonic system is the least complex case, in that it is run by one predominant power. Hegemony in international relations is an *imposed order*, in that the 'true' consent of subordinated states or classes has not been obtained. The imposition can, of course, happen in several different ways, ranging from coercion to the skilful manipulation of incentives to support institutional arrangements favourable to the hegemon. A hegemonistic system may be either exploitative or paternalistic depending on the time span in which interests are satisfied.

A precondition for the hegemonic system to prevail is that the predominant power simultaneously exercises both economic and political leadership within the environment and extends this leadership into international organizations as well. In such a situation other members of the system may either regard the global organization as irrelevant or as an arena for *conflict manifestation*. They may, in other words, express their grievances about the unequal structure of the system, but are hardly able to change it to any significant degree through the organization.

[*   *   *]

In a cooperative bipolar or multipolar system the global organization most probably develops into an actor, in contradistinction to an arena, which may also have legitimizing functions vis-à-vis less powerful members of the system. In effect there is a certain pressure also in the fragmented system to allocate certain political tasks to the global organization in order to inject a modicum of order into the system. In the symmetric case, major powers may use the global organization as their joint instrument to assert their influence in the increasingly volatile and complex international system. In the asymmetric case the leading power may try to build up a 'winning coalition', to which it is able to attract allies from the periphery and hence obtain support to its faltering position. It is in fact possible that in a fragmented international system the role of a global organization may be stronger than in a more hierarchical system, where it is recruited to serve the interests of the few.

The evolution of the United Nations may be approximated by the following sequence: from the concert run by the winners of World War II through the US hegemony towards a gradual fragmentation. This development reflects changes in international power relations, though there is no one-to-one relationship between them. When one is investigating the interaction of external environment and intra-organizational development, the complexities of influence mechanisms and time-lags involved must be taken into consideration.

The impact of changes in international power resources on the activities of an international organization varies, furthermore, from one issue area to another. Within the United Nations the Security Council is, according to the Charter provisions, an oligopolist organ which directly brings the power structure prevailing in the environment into the organization, though for the moment in a somewhat antiquated manner. Thus in the security area the correspondence between environment and intra-organizational practices is greater than in economic and social issues in which the numerical majority of nations is responsible for decisions. Such a majority may be either a tool for a great power circumventing the veto that has stalemated the Security Council or for a coalition of states, such as non-aligned countries, which utilizes the General Assembly for the purposes of conflict manifestation.

[*   *   *]

[III.] UN AS THE COALITION
OF VICTORIOUS POWERS, 1945–7

The alliance relationship established between the great powers during World War II continued, though with frictions, until 1947. In that year both the United States and the Soviet Union issued their own versions on the division of the world into two camps and on the containment of the expansion by the other side (the Truman doctrine and the speech of Zhdanov in the meeting to establish Cominform in September 1947).

In fact some of the conflicts in which permanent members of the Security Council were involved were treated there before the formal outbreak of the Cold War. In 1946–7 both the Iranian issue and the Greek civil war, which became the catalyst of the Truman doctrine, were debated in the Council. The United Nations was thus a relevant organization during this period, and could in fact act successfully in crises connected with the early process of decolonization (in particular Indonesia and Levant). [. . .]

The emerging duopoly of great powers constrained, however, the possibilities of the United Nations to promote collective security in all the issues. Some of the constraints are indicated by the frequent Soviet use of the veto—totally 12 vetoes pertaining to the peaceful settlement of disputes, especially those concerning the Spanish and Greek questions. [. . .] The Western predominance in the United Nations is illuminated by the fact that with the exceptions of the United Kingdom and France defending their colonial interests, this group did not have any need to resort to the veto until 1970, when the Rhodesian issue was taken up in the Security Council. Furthermore, it may be observed that the Soviet vetoes had obviously only minor influence on the outcomes of processes which they tried to block.

The signs of polarization in world politics did not, however, ruin the world organization. This is partly due to the strong support given to the collective security system by small and neutral countries, many of which attached great hopes to the United Nations as a guarantor of international peace and security. Another reason for the survival of the United Nations was probably that the differences between great powers on the future of Eastern Europe were not effectively brought to the Security Council by the Western powers. Hence the confrontation between great powers did not impinge on the Security Council with full force.

[*   *   *]

[IV.] US HEGEMONY, 1948–63

The hegemony of the United States in the economic, military and political spheres coincided with the upturn of the long economic cycle after World War II. Robert O. Keohane has suggested that the period from 1948 to 1963 was a 'long American decade' when the norms and institutions imposed by the United States provided a sort of hegemonic stability for international relations. [. . .]

An important development in the United Nations was sparked by the Korean War, to which the Security Council, in the absence of the Soviet Union, decided on 25 June 1950 to send UN forces. This decision deviated from the provisions of the UN Charter in two significant ways. First, the peace-keeping operation in Korea, or any other operation since then, was not carried out by the national units permanently assigned to the United Nations. An even more serious problem was that the Korean operation was not, as stipulated in Art. 42 and Art. 43, under the control of the Security Council, but the forces were integrated into the US command structure.

The return of the Soviet Union to the Security Council in August 1950 removed the possibility of using the Security Council for political and military operations contradicting Soviet interests. This problem was resolved by the *Uniting for Peace* resolution, which was passed by the General Assembly in November 1950 by 52 affirmative votes, with the five socialist countries opposing and India and Argentina abstaining. According to this resolution, questions pertaining to international peace and security could be transferred by a procedural vote to the General Assembly if the Security Council was stalemated by a veto. The resolution was initiated by the US Secretary of State, Dean Acheson, who obviously aimed at creating a legal basis for further activities of the United States in Korea. In reality the resolution was applied also in other crises in which the United Nations became involved.

The Uniting for Peace resolution was applied on four occasions altogether: in the Suez crisis in 1956, in the Hungarian crisis in the same year, in the Middle East crisis of 1958, and for the last time in the Congo in 1960. It is pertinent to observe that only parts of the resolution were in reality observed, i.e. those concerning the transfer of a security issue to the General Assembly and the capacity to convene it for emergency sessions. The parts neglected in later applications mandated the establishment of the Collective Measures Committee, created the Peace Observation Commission, and recommended the maintenance of UN-designated units in national armed forces. In response to a request from the Collective Measures Committee, only four governments (Thailand, Denmark, Greece, and Norway) expressed their willingness to earmark contingents for UN use.

In fact the legality of the Uniting for Peace resolution and hence the mandate of the General Assembly to establish UN peace-keeping forces has been questioned. The transfer and emergency session devices that survived in the Uniting for Peace resolution served, together with the simultaneous neglect of those parts promoting a more genuine collective security, certain political ends, however. The resolution was a political and legal device by which the United States was able to assure that the United Nations could be used for the maintenance of hegemonic stability.

In the Suez crisis of 1956 the dispute was transferred from the Security Council to the General Assembly, which, against the resistance of France and Great Britain, authorized the establishment of the United Nations Emergency Force (UNEF I) for operations in Sinai. The Soviet Union, in turn, resisted the inclusion of the Hungarian item in the agenda of the Security Council and its subsequent transfer to the General Assembly. The Soviet Union was also criticial towards the UN involvement in the Congo crisis following the decision of the General Assembly to send peace-keeping forces (ONUC) to that area. The Middle East crisis of 1958 was somewhat different in that the Security Council had in June established a military observation group (UNOGIL) for Lebanon. Thereafter the great powers even agreed that the stalemate in the Council on further measures of conflict settlement warranted the transferring of the matter to the General Assembly. Only after great difficulties could the permanent members of the Council agree upon how the resolution mandating this transfer should be formulated.

[*   *   *]

A hegemonic power may try to maintain the stability of international relations by both diplomatic, economic and limited military means. Until the 1960s the United States indeed enjoyed a limited hegemony based on her economic predominance and nuclear superiority. The order and stability of international relations were maintained by unilateral interventions (Lebanon, Cuba, the Dominican Republic, and Vietnam) and by various types of covert operations. Not infrequently the dominant power also resorted to the United Nations, which provided a multilateral channel for cooperation with other major powers and could also legitimize collectively the politics of order. In predominantly bilateral conflicts between the United States and the Soviet Union—such as the Cuban missile crisis and the Berlin crises—the United Nations was used only for subsidiary purposes.

The US hegemony in international relations was limited by the gradual economic and military rise of the Soviet Union, which had a relatively independent base of material power upon which to build political and military influence. With the exception of the period immediately following World War II, the Soviet Union was not directly involved in military confrontations outside the bloc boundary until the 1970s. In the 1950s and 1960s her policy of keeping order was limited to Eastern Europe. This may partly explain why the United States did resort to the use or show of force rather seldom during the Eisenhower Administration. The rate of her military involvement started to increase rapidly from the late 1950s onwards and culminated in the outbreak of the Vietnam War. The national trauma of the Vietnam debacle was among the factors decelerating the use of force in the 1970s.

The functions of the UN peace-keeping efforts in this context can be further clarified by observing that they were never extended to the immediate Soviet sphere of interest. In this way the limits of US hegemony were recognized. On the other hand, multilateral and neutral peace-keeping forces were never sent to numerous conflict theatres in East and Southeast Asia, which were usually assigned to the US sphere. UN peace-keeping was most frequent in the Middle East, where the positions of great powers have been more ambiguous and where the impact of local catalysts for conflict have probably been stronger than elsewhere. In such circumstances UN peace-keeping may have been a substitute for great-power intervention. In the cases of Suez and the Congo at least it was, however, a means for the United States to secure her interests even against her formal allies.

The one-sided character of many UN involvements in international crises may partly account for its low degree of success during the period of US hegemony. [. . .] There are, however, indications that the period 1948–63 was not entirely uniform. The impact of non-aligned and socialist countries started to increase both numerically and politically as early as in the late 1950s (the year 1958 is perhaps a convenient dividing line here). Ernst B. Haas has suggested that the security regime provided by the United Nations went through a change in 1955 when 'permissive enforcement with balancing' developed into 'permissive engagement'. According to his empirical analysis, the period from 1956 to 1965 saw 'some of the United Nations' more dramatic successes' which can be accounted for by the growth of the non-aligned movement, by the decline in the cohesion of the Cold War alliances, and by the crisis diplomacy of the Secretary-General.

To check the validity of these assertions the period of US hegemony was divided into two parts, viz. 1948–58 and 1959–63. During the latter period there were more crises (7.7 vs 4.6 per year), which may indicate that the US world-order policy was eroding. This did not, however, lead to the growth in the UN role, but it became involved in relatively fewer crises in 1959–63 than in 1948–58 (48 per cent vs 59 per cent of the total). Finally, there was no appreciable difference in the rate of success between these two periods (16 per cent vs 17 per cent). The increase in the conflict activity during the latter period provides perhaps an explanation for the more frequent Soviet resort to the veto (2.4 vs 1.6 vetos per year) and implies that in spite of some growth Soviet influence within the United Nations was still rather modest.

The United States' hegemony influenced without any doubt the nature and activities of the United Nations. The world organization was naturally composed of sovereign states, of which socialist countries strongly defended the principle of national sovereignty, and colonies, in turn, wanted to acquire self-determination. The US policy weakened, on the other hand, a strict interpretation of national sovereignty and the principle of non-interference in internal affairs of states. This tendency was reflected, among other things, in the inclusion of human rights issues and civil wars, provided that they were a threat to international peace and security, in the agenda of this world organization. [. . .]

In security issues the United Nations did not develop into an effective instrument of the world-order policy of the United States. It was not used in 1948–64 more frequently or effectively for conflict settlement than during the other periods under investigation. This means that even during its hegemony the United States resorted primarily to national means of safeguarding her political and security interests in the world. Especially in 1949–54 the United Nations was ineffective in producing positive results in the settlement of international conflicts. On the other hand, one has to understand the critical role of the United Nations in promoting US interests in the areas where spheres of influence were not settled (Korea in 1950, Suez in 1956, and the Congo in 1960). This would seem to justify a conclusion that the United Nations played a major complementary but not a primary role in comparison to the bilateral and multilateral treaty arrangements by which the United States safeguarded her security interests in the postwar world.

[V.] SIGNS OF DUOPOLY
AND FRAGMENTATION IN 1964–74

During the 1960s developing nations gradually acquired a two-thirds majority among the members of the United Nations. This group of nations started to seek for closer cooperation in order to be able to influence *en bloc* the work of the world organization. For the first meeting of UNCTAD in 1964, Group 77, to which altogether 126 members now belong, was established. In the beginning Group 77 focused on the promotion of common economic interests of the Third World but since the early 1970s its activities have expanded to other issue areas as well. Still the cooperation between developing countries is, however, most effective within such economic organizations as UNCTAD, UNIDO, IBRD and IMF in the context of which they organize regular ministerial meetings.

As a consequence of the emergence of the Third World, the United Nations has started to go through a process of *deconcentration* or *fragmentation* which reflects a similar development in the entire international system. This means that the centre and peripheries are moving apart from each other, which tends to give rise to problems of management in international relations. This process mirrors a number of interrelated processes; decolonization, the multiplication of states in the Third World, and the selective dispersion of economic and military power from the traditional industrial centres to the semi-peripheries of the world.

The diffusion and pulverization of power is obviously a long-term tendency which cannot be easily reversed. The great powers are facing a dual and hence a contradictory challenge. On the one hand, the diffusion of power to semi-autonomous regional subsystems in the Third World increases the need for cooperation between great powers and, as a consequence, some sort of duopoly in the management of international conflicts. On the other hand, the very same conflicts, which are often products of local conditions, tend to lock them into a global competition. Great powers have to strike a balance between their competitive and cooperative interests in a situation where the transformation of the international situation tends to foster rivalry and instability.

The tendency from hegemony and, to some extent, duopoly, towards deconcentration surfaced in the middle of the 1960s and became even stronger during the 1970s. George Modelski has suggested that a duopolistic/oligopolistic organization may handle its process of deconcentration in three different ways. *De-emphasis* means that the relative, but not necessarily the absolute, weight of dominant powers and the modes of operations favoured by them decline at the expense of other actors. *Disaggregation* leads to the establishment of new lines of activity, which assume a measure of autonomy from the old power structure of the organization. Finally, *diversification* gives rise to alternative structures that replace or, at least, supplement the existing arrangements.

In the United States there have been visible signs of disaggregation, especially in the field of economic development and cooperation, ever since 1964, when UNCTAD was established (other signs include UNIDO, UNDP and TCDC).

Their relative significance has, however, been dwarfed so far in comparison with economic organizations rooted in the era of US hegemony (in particular GATT, IBRD and IMF). Rare efforts at diversification (NIEO and collective self-reliance) through the United Nations have faced even stronger resistance from industrialized countries. All in all, de-emphasis has been the dominant strategy of transformation within the United Nations, as is illustrated by the gradually expanding role of semi-peripheral countries in the 'original' economic organizations (GATT, IBRD and IMF).

The impact of deconcentration and fragmentation in international relations has been even more modest in security issues, where development towards disaggregation and diversification has been almost non-existent. Developing countries have not tried, in other words, to create new lines of activity within the United Nations or alternative structures outside in order to handle their security problems. There are, it is true, regional organizations (such as the OAS, OAU, the Arab League, and the Gulf Cooperation Council) but many of them are not present creations. Empirical evidence indicates that regional bodies may be more effective in handling localized, low-intensity conflicts. Yet there has been no consistent division of labour between the United Nations and regional security organizations, and both seem to have entered a period of decay in their ability to manage inter-state crises.

Dangers embodied in the present international situation appear to have made smaller countries, both from the developed and underdeveloped parts of the world, more conscious of the need to maintain a regime of collective security under the auspices of the United Nations. For a long time these countries did not really care about this regime, and even regarded it as a device of great powers to control the world peripheries. Gradually, the majority of UN members seem to have realized that the provisions of collective security are pertinent to managing the escalation of local crises in the Third World. They may even be utilized in steering the course of great powers, which can block the actions of a united Third World group in the Security Council only by resorting to the veto.

[*   *   *]

In the development of the United Nations the period from 1964 to 1974 was an era of transition. The veto in the Security Council was still used by the Soviet Union, but to an increasing degree also by the United States, Great Britain, and France. The world organization became involved in more conflicts than in any other period, but its rate of success remained low. One reason for this was that the Third World countries were not prepared to resort to collective measures to deter, manage or settle their mutual confrontations. Non-aligned countries rather directed their criticism to the great powers, especially to the United States, and in general to challenges coming from outside their movement. This movement has been more capable of forming a united approach to outside issues than of developing mechanisms to settle its internal problems.

As a consequence of the shifts in the distribution of voting power and in political 'balance points', the significance of the General Assembly increased. The new majority wanted to show its influence by passing a number of radical resolutions: South Africa was expelled from the United Nations in 1974, an observer status was given to the PLO, Yasser Arafat was invited to address the General Assembly, Zionism was condemned as a form of racism, and the reorganization of international economic relations was demanded. Though these conflict manifestations were largely acceptable to the Soviet Union, both superpowers became worried about the tendency to emphasize the role of the General Assembly within the UN system. A counter-reaction to this tendency surfaced on various occasions during the period 1964–75 in the form of great-power cooperation in the Security Council. The signs of duopoly have indeed to be read in the context of the deconcentration and fragmentation of international relations. It has to be recalled, furthermore, that this decennium was characterized by *detente*, which facilitated communication and coordination of policies between great powers. [. . .]

Preconditions for UN peace-keeping operations also changed. The decision to send UN forces (UNICYP) to Cyprus in 1964 was not based any more on the mandate from the General Assembly, but on a consensus reached in the Security Council. Since then it has become obvious to all the parties that the United Nations can work effectively for the implementation of the principle of collective security only when the permanent members of the Security Council can agree upon joint measures. Peace-keeping is now probably more dependent than before on the coincidence of interests among major powers for launching such an operation in a serious international dispute. As pointed out above, such coincidence did not exist until the middle of the 1970s. The establishments of UNEF II after the Middle East war in 1973 and of the United Nations Disengagement Observer Force (UNDOF) on the Golan Heights were endorsed both by the United States and the Soviet Union. The limits of consensus and the change in atmosphere became evident in 1978, when the Soviet Union did not want to legitimize the establishment of the United Nations Interim Force in Lebanon (UNIFIL).

The period of detente signified an effort on the part of the great powers to come to terms with each other in various bilateral and multilateral fora, including the United Nations. In the Western definition detente was primarily a mode of *management of international relations*. Great powers were expected to prevent the outbreak of crises in their own spheres of influence as well as in their mutual relations. Conflicts in the world peripheries, outside the immediate spheres of influence by the great powers or in ambiguous areas, were to be managed in the Security Council.

[*   *   *]

It is not far-fetched to conclude that the rise of the new bilateral, collaborative-competitive relationship between the United States and the Soviet Union provided in certain issues a functional equivalent to the United Nations in the field of collective security. The practice of summit meetings between the US and the Soviet leaders became institutionalized, new fora for arms-control negotiations were opened, and a new multilateral framework for political consultation known as CSCE was established. It may indeed be that in the conditions of detente a universal organization is less needed for conflict resolution than during the periods of more strained international atmosphere when bilateral channels become easily closed or filled with 'noise'. This conclusion pertains, however, only to direct relations between the great powers. As hinted above, the conflict management in volatile areas of the world peripheries may still have to be entrusted to a universal organization where the multitude of global and local interests in such conflicts can be more easily aggregated to a solution.

[VI.] FRAGMENTATION AND DISAGREEMENT, 1975–84

Fragmentation and deconcentration in international relations continued and in fact became increasingly visible throughout the 1970s and the 1980s. The rise of the vocal Third World majority made the United States and some other leading Western powers more and more annoyed with the United Nations. Smaller capitalist countries tried in some UN fora to establish intermediary groups (such as like-minded countries) to accommodate the relations between North and South, but as a rule their impact has been small.

The first signs of the US frustration with the new character and role of the United Nations became visible in the early 1970s. In 1971 the United States, together with France and Great Britain, left the Special Committee on Colonialism, in 1972 she was able to trim her obligatory share of the UN budget by 15 per cent, and in general she objected to expansion of the UN organs and their agendas. The Third World policy of de-emphasis on and diversification from traditional UN institutions and the establishment of new ones, such as UNCTAD and UNIDO, led the United States increasingly to think that her interests can be better promoted outside international institutions.

The Nixon-Kissinger Administration pursued a policy that rested on bilateral cooperation between great powers, on balance of power as well as on regional political and military pacts. In such a scheme there was little room for the United Nations, with the exception of the Security Council, though even it was used less frequently and efficiently after 1974. The straw that broke the camel's back was the 29th session of the General Assembly, which in addition to expelling South Africa and extending an invitation to the PLO, adopted the Charter of Economic Rights and Duties of States, which the United States and other leading Western powers especially disliked. [. . .]

This change in the American attitude towards the United Nations did not come out of the blue, but reflected a long-term decline in the US commitment to the world organization. Both in the elite and popular opinion as well as in official publications and presidential speeches the UN was regarded as less important and effective than in the 1950s in particular. Since the period 1961–5 the majority of the General Assembly had been more often in agreement with the Soviet Union than with the United States, and in 1971–4 the latter prevailed only in one-third of the votes in comparison with the Soviet Union. The duality of the US attitude towards the United Nations was indicated by its continued support to the Security Council 'which continues to be a very useful instrument in a highly charged situation'. [. . .]

The critical attitude of the United States toward the world organization originated, in other words, in the Nixon-Kissinger Administration, from which a direct line can be drawn to the Reagan Administration. Their policy has been coloured by the resort to ideological rhetoric, breeding confrontation with the non-aligned countries and placing emphasis on bilateral and multilateral arrangements outside the United Nations. The Reagan Administration, in particular, has stressed the need to deprive the United Nations of its economic and political functions, which have been 'misused' by the Third World.

The Carter Administration deviated from the policy orientation outlined above. It had a vision of world order, emphasizing human rights and peaceful settlement of disputes, which was to be implemented partly through the United Nations. The Administration, and especially its permanent representative to the world organization, Andrew Young, aimed at accommodating relations between the United States and non-aligned countries in Africa and elsewhere.

The erosion of US power in international relations and their associated fragmentation has brought about a change in the general objectives of her foreign policy. Until the early 1970s the United Nations was a means of American *world-order policy*, which has aimed at assuring international stability and unhindered commerce. According to Stanley Hoffmann, this order has been based on three main pillars: rules of behaviour between the two superpowers, the United Nations, and the liberal order of the world economy. Since 1968, with the advent of Nixon and Kissinger to the helm, the search for world order was replaced by a policy that stresses the *primacy* of the United States in the world. The striving for primacy fosters unilateral national measures instead of collective solutions, redefinition and differentiation of interests to correspond to the available capabilities and, above all, the management of international relations by manipulating the relations between major powers.

[*   *   *]

The erosion of the US support to the United Nations has given rise to demands to strengthen the world organization and to establish a new world order. These demands have not come, however, primarily from the Soviet Union as a polarized view of the world might lead one to expect. The General Assembly has become a forum for articulation and aggregating demands from the Third World and a forum for ideological battle between opposing states or groups of states. The Soviet Union can only marginally steer the opinion formation in the Assembly, and in fact she has experienced difficulties there because of her involvement in a number of regional conflicts. The Soviet policy in the United Nations obviously aims at avoiding the use of the organization for purposes detrimental to Soviet interests. The USSR does not seem to have any positive programme for the development of the United Nations or for accentuating her own influence there.

In the Security Council non-aligned countries have achieved a kind of *collective veto* as they have the majority of nine by which any resolution can be rejected. On the other hand, this majority cannot, even it if is united, push through a resolution if any of the permanent members opposes it. It is, in other words, impossible to impose any decisions on the Security Council; they have to be based on a consensus between all its members. This makes the process of consultation a central ingredient in the work of the Security Council. The 'power vs equality' dilemma in the United Nations has now to be reconciled within the Council.

In this situation it is understandable that the United Nations has not been able to settle international conflicts effectively since the early 1970s. As a matter of fact the regime of collective security and its coherence has decayed. Ernst B. Haas concludes that the decay has been associated with the the decline in the American hegemony, but this explains only a part of this change. The American decline has been associated with another tendency, which has previously been termed fragmentation. Haas in fact corroborates its significance by observing that an increase in the number of voting blocs, i.e. regionalization, and the instability of alignments between states account for the decay: 'the diplomatic and military texture of the world has perhaps grown too complex for effective collective security practices'. Haas also suggests that the small number of metaissues around which consensus could be built, efforts of regional organizations to settle their internal conflicts, and the growing tolerance of unresolved conflicts have also contributed to the decay.

A lesson to be drawn from these observations is that the number of metaissues around which the member states could gather should be increased; laws and rules to regulate warfare could for instance be developed further. New power centres of the world should be incorporated more effectively into the work of the United Nations, and the great powers should tolerate the articulation of their interests. In fact there are signs that such countries as Japan, India, and Brazil are prepared to play a more active role in the world organization, and have even hinted at their interest in becoming permanent members of the Security Council. The stability of alignments could also be improved by making the process of consultation more effective.

[*   *   *]

[VII.] THE UN AND RESOLUTION
OF PERIPHERAL CONFLICTS

The gradual dissemination of power from centres to peripheries, assisted by transnational corporations, will continue to foster collective violence in international relations. The process of deconcentration probably provides an opportunity for local conflicts to materialize more easily. Their destructiveness and complexity is enhanced by the involvement of great powers in these conflicts, by providing political support, sending economic aid, supplying arms and becoming sometimes directly parties to the combats. Global economic crisis and the stagnation of Third World economies is a further contextual factor that fosters violence. As already pointed out, conflicts are also growing more complex; their domestic roots, inter-state confrontations and global linkages become even more intertwined. Consequently, the intractability of conflicts hinders their effective settlement. What is then the role of the United Nations in such a future?

It is normally imagined that the United Nations is not active in Cold-War disputes in which at least one of the permanent members of the Security Council is involved. Empirical studies tend to show, on the contrary, that the UN involvement in conflict settlement has not been dependent on the nature of the issues and on the participation of great powers. Also Cold-War issues have been referred to the

United Nations for treatment. Similarly, confrontations in which great powers were involved have been brought to the world organization, which may, under certain circumstances, be relatively effective in contributing to their solution. The United Nations has, in other words, also intervened in conflicts in which a permanent member of the Security Council has taken part.

More important as an explanatory factor seems to be the pattern of alignments between the parties to the conflict. Three out of ten *intra-bloc conflicts* have been referred to the United Nations; the remaining seven conflicts were either handled by a regional organization, which is probably closely integrated to the bloc structure, or they continued or possibly abated without any cure. More than a half of the *inter-bloc conflicts* have not been referred to any international organization, and about one-third have been brought to the United Nations. Regional organizations have, naturally enough, had only scarce opportunities to resolve such conflicts.
[. . .]

It has been empirically shown that *ad hoc* managers of international conflicts have been more effective than regional or global security organizations (such as the OAU, OAS, UN or ICJ). From this one should not conclude, however, that these organizations are unnecessary. They add a considerable amount of permanence and continuity to conflict management which *ad hoc* actors cannot provide. The relative effectiveness of these actors is, furthermore, partly due to the fact that they do not become involved in conflicts which are particularly intractable. Ad hoc managers contribute rather to the resolution of 'easy' conflicts.

The United Nations may contribute to the resolution of international conflicts in three principal ways. The General Assembly and the Security Council may pass *resolutions* that provide guidelines for conflict resolution. The Secretary-General or his representative may function as a *mediator* in the conflict or provide *fact-finding* services. Finally, the Security Council may dispatch *peace-keeping forces* to the conflict area. It is impossible to say anything definite on the relative effectiveness of these three modes of operation as they are usually used in combination and crises in which they are applied differ widely.

A tentative conclusion may be offered, however, that resolutions and peace-keeping forces are more useful methods than the appointment of mediators. According to the conventional wisdom, UN resolutions are mere expressions of opinions and do not carry much weight in hardnosed international politics. This may be true of some General Assembly resolutions, but in particular in the cases of the Middle East and Namibia, resolutions of the Security Council have provided essential guidelines to which any effort at settlement must comply. These resolutions express the broad consensus that prevails in the international community on the desirable content and form of the settlement of the Middle East and Namibian conflicts. It is true that some parties to these conflicts rebel against the provisions of resolutions, but even they cannot totally ignore their contents.

[*   *   *]

In any future peace-keeping operations the United Nations should have a central role. Various types of multilateral forces serve often too directly the unilateral political and strategic interests of major powers. That is why the resort to their troops should be avoided. Instead, in many regional conflicts the use of local peace-keeping forces, collected by a regional organization such as the OAU, would be useful because they alleviate fears of domination by major powers. The regional peace-keeping forces could be financed at least in part through the United Nations, where collective responsibility for financing peace-keeping should replace the present disproportional distribution of the costs.

The analysis carried out above shows that the Security Council has developed into the organ of the United Nations where decisions pertaining to collective security have to be made and where consensus needed to implement these decisions has to be attained. This means that the capacity of the Security Council should be enhanced. This was realized by the Secretary-General when he observed that 'the Council itself could devise more swift and responsive procedures for sending good offices missions, military or civilian observers or a United Nations presence to areas of potential conflict'. As far as peace-keeping is concerned, the Secretary-General concluded that it 'can function properly only with the co-operation of the parties on a clearly defined mandate from the Security Council'. This means in reality that the *political functions* of peace-keeping operations must be recognized; these operations cannot be reduced to mere military activities. Peace-keeping is a feasible option only when the parties to conflict and the permanent members of the Security Council prefer it to alternative courses of action. [. . .]

Any serious effort to strengthen the role of the United Nations in the maintenance of collective security seems to require some *independent latitude of action for the Secretary-General* within the limits defined by the Security Council. He should, for instance, be allowed to send fact-finding missions to conflict areas by changing procedural provisions pertaining to this issue. This would be a part of the effort to collect, process and store more effectively information on international conflicts and in that way facilitate the work of the Security Council in the pacific settlement of disputes.

In such an effort modern communication and information-retrieval technologies should be utilized more effectively, though this might be interpreted by some member states as an intrusion into their internal affairs. Such fears are, however, exaggerated. If the member states of the United Nations are serious about the need to promote collective security through practical steps, they have to accept such limitations, engendered by the collective action, on their sovereignty as can be imposed upon them at any moment by any major power. Technical solutions to conflict settlement may facilitate the work of the organization. They have to be supported and utilized, however, by political decisions, because otherwise they would only become a monument of technological optimism which erroneously believes that more information and new technologies can solve international problems.

An example of the combination of political and technical solutions to promote collective security is the establishment of *stand-by forces* which can be readily moved to a crisis area if the Security Council so decides. Such forces, maintained today by Nordic countries, are parts of the regular military establishments, but their role could be gradually redefined to serve even more effectively the interests of collective security. Collective security could, in other words, be developed into a complement to national security, while it is today a mere extention of it to which nation states only occasionally resort. The changing nature of statehood and the declining utility and legitimacy of military force, even though still frequently used, presupposes that the unilateral functions of national military forces are complemented by also giving them tasks related to the maintenance of collective security.

Peace-keeping operations have undisputed value in assuring collective security. They cannot, however, in any circumstances replace diplomatic activities by the Security Council, the Secretary-General, and, above all, parties to a dispute, to dissipate the conflict at an early stage and hence to prevent its escalation to large-scale hostilities. Even though peace-keeping operations may complement such diplomatic activities, their use amounts to admitting the failure of the diplomatic machinery. It should be also recalled that the 'tool kit' of the Security Council also contains intermediary instruments, specified in Chapter VII of the Charter, such as political and economic sanctions.

In extreme cases a member state could be removed temporarily from the work of the United Nations or, more preferably, the Security Council should agree on the imposition of sanctions because of serious non-compliance with the Charter and the decisions of the Security Council.

17. Relationship Between Disarmament and Development: An Overview of United Nations Involvement

Preparatory Committee for the International Conference on the Relationship Between Disarmament and Development

To provide a general overview of the subject on the relationship between disarmament and development, this paper attempts to briefly describe the extent and nature of United Nations involvement, conceptual and empirical issues raised and various approaches adopted.

The Preamble to the Charter of the United Nations expresses the determination "to save succeeding generations from the scourge of war" and "to promote social progress and better standards of life in larger freedom". Further, the preamble declares the intention "to employ international machinery for the promotion of the economic and social advancement of all peoples". Article 26 of the Charter refers to the "establishment and maintenance of international peace and security with the least diversion for armaments of the world's human and economic resources". In Article 55 reference is made, *inter alia*, to promoting "higher standards of living, full employment, and conditions of economic and social progress and development" with a view to "the creation of conditions of stability and well-being".

Thus, from the inception of the United Nations, there has been a recognition of the existence of disarmament and development as two vital issues before the international community. In its efforts to achieve its separate goals in the fields of disarmament and development, the United Nations has also progressively become involved with the relationship between these issues. This involvement has grown along with an increasing recognition that a curtailment of the military consumption of resources could be a factor in the resolution of pressing international problems, whether these pertain to matters of peace and security, to international economic co-operation or to a wide range of other social and economic issues.

In the earlier stage of United Nations involvement, the contrast between continuing military expenditures and the unmet socio-economic needs of large sections of humanity also provided a moral dimension to the issue. In the very first decade of the existence of the United Nations, this concern found expression in a number of resolutions. In 1950, the General Assembly adopted resolution 380 (V) determining, *inter alia*, to "reduce to a minimum the diversion for armaments of its human and economic resources and to strive towards the development of such resources for the general welfare, with due regard to the needs of the underdeveloped areas of the world". Since then, the General Assembly has returned to the subject year after year in one form or another. Expressions of concern over the continuing military expenditures, calls for diverting resources released through disarmament for socio-economic development, and interest in examining the various issues raised by the relationship between disarmament and development have all contributed towards a growing United Nations involvement.

The subject has received mounting international attention in the past 15 years. In part, this may be attributed to increased knowledge about the nature and volume of human and economic resources devoted to military purposes and their immediate and long-term consequences. A part of the explanation may also be that in the 1970s the world economy moved towards a more cautious assessment of its limits and possibilities. Increasingly questions were raised as to whether the patterns of production and consumption of resources established during the 1950s and the 1960s could be easily sustained for an indefinite period in the future. There were recurrent inquiries into the use of global resources, including those consumed for military purposes. The subject received more frequent attention after the economic case for disarmament was increasingly argued through a growing realization that resources, howsoever they are defined, are far from infinite and their global military consumption is a factor in national and international economic prospects. Resource-related concerns, for example, were among those considered by the United Nations Conference on the Human Environment held in 1972. The same decade of the 1970s which saw major advances in communications, space exploration, computers and other fields, in a dramatic display of the power of technology, also witnessed the helplessness of humanity to overcome poverty, disease, malnutrition and the effects of natural calamities in many parts of the world.

As a consequence, within and outside the United Nations, suggestions were made for possible alternative uses of the financial, human and technological resources devoted to military purposes. Also, interest was expressed in an examination of the possible effects of military expenditures on national and international economies. In a number of resolutions, adopted without a vote, the United Nations General Assembly expressed its concern for reducing and restraining military expenditures and for creating increased possibilities for reallocating released resources towards those of socio-economic development, particularly for the benefit of developing countries. Through a number of studies carried out with the assistance of governmental and non-governmental experts, the Secretary-General of the United Nations in response to decisions taken by the General Assembly, submitted a series of reports analysing the national and international consequences of the arms race and military expenditures. The conclusions and findings of these expert studies provide information and analyses both about the possible positive effects of disarmament on national and global economic prospects and about the negative impact of arms race and military expenditures on national and international economies. United Nations involvement with the subject of a relationship between disarmament and development has, thus, been a process of identifying issues covered by such a relationship, providing information and analyses required for understanding its various aspects and dimensions, and considering ways and means of releasing additional resources through disarmament measures for purposes of socio-economic development.

In sum, the international context in which the United Nations became involved in the relationship between disarmament and development has been, and continues to be, one of complex interaction between various global issues which have been added to the international agenda, due also to economic and social concerns other than those directly related to military consumption of resources. While there have been differences of view on the nature and extent of such a relationship, and on the courses of action which might be adopted, there has been no disagreement that the two goals—general and complete disarmament under effective international control and the promotion of the economic and social advancement of all peoples—continue to be two major objectives of the United Nations. As pointed out in the first report of the Secretary-General on the Relationship between Disarmament and Development in 1972:

"Disarmament and development are of the greatest importance to the world community. But fundamentally they stand separately from one another. The United Nations has agreed to seek each one vigorously in its own right, regardless of the pace of progress in approaching the other. Sepcifically, nations have agreed that national and international efforts to promote development should be neither postponed nor allowed to lag merely because progress in disarmament is slow."

The members of the United Nations have also jointly recognized a relationship between expenditure on armaments on the one hand and the pursuit of economic and social development on the other. Paragraph 16 of the Final Document of the Tenth Special Session of the General Assembly, held in 1978, the first special session devoted to disarmament stated:

"In a world of finite resources there is a close relationship between expenditure on armaments and economic and social development. Military expenditures are reaching ever higher levels, the highest percentage of which can be attributed to the nuclear-weapon States and most of their allies, with prospects of further expansion and the danger of further increases in the expenditures of other countries. The hundreds of billions of dollars spent annually on the manufacture or improvement of weapons are in sombre and dramatic contrast to the want and poverty in which two-thirds of the world's population live. This colossal waste of resources is even more serious in that it diverts to military purposes not only material but also technical and human resources which are urgently needed for development in all countries, particularly in the developing countries. . . ."

In the Secretary-General's report on the Relationship between Disarmament and Development, a study carried out by a group of governmental experts between 1978 and 1981, the experts stated:

"This investigation suggests very strongly that the world can either continue to pursue the arms race with characteristic vigour or move consciously and with deliberate speed toward a more stable and balanced social and economic development within a more sustainable international economic and political order. It cannot do both. It must be acknowledged that the arms race and development are in a competitive relationship, particularly in terms of resources but also in the vital dimension of attitudes and perceptions. The main conclusion of this report is that an effective relationship between disarmament and development can and must be established."

Subsequently, there have been two further reports of the Secretary-General, to the 38th and 40th sessions of the General Assembly, which, in following up on the report cited above, indicate that within the United Nations there is a continuing system-wide interest in the subject of a relationship between disarmament and development. These reports were prepared in pursuance of resolution 37/84 which requested, *inter alia*, that the Secretary-General should take appropriate action to promote an inter-related perspective on the issues of disarmament and development within the United Nations as a follow-up to the 1981 Report of the Secretary-General on the Relationship between Disarmament and Development.

A widely shared recognition of a relationship between disarmament and development, repeated calls for diverting a part of resources released through disarmament for socio-economic development, and a system-wide interest in the subject within the United Nations indicate the extent of its involvement. However, to understand the evolving nature of the subject, it needs to be pointed out that neither disarmament nor development are static concepts. As the international situation has changed, so too has the United Nations involvement with the relationship between the two issues. The nature of this involvement has also become tied to considerations which affect the problems and prospects of disarmament and development as separate items on the United Nations agenda. Viewed as independent issues, United Nations debates on disarmament are largely influenced by political and military considerations whereas those on development concentrate on socio-economic arguments. Viewed together, both these issues have been considered in the same global context of growing international interdependence. Two aspects of this consideration are equally relevant in affecting the outcome of United Nations deliberations in both the areas of disarmament, and development: one pertains to differing perceptions about threats to national and international security, the other to growing concern about the current uses and future availability of resources on the planet.

In United Nations efforts to achieve measures of disarmament, the pursuit of security is a primary goal. Stemming from the importance accorded in the Charter of the United Nations to the establishment and maintenance of international peace and security, and acknowledging the right of each State to security, the General Assembly has repeatedly recognized that measures of disarmament must lead to undiminished, or improved, security if they are to be accepted. In emphasizing that security should be sought through disarmament, in the Final Document of the Tenth Special Session, the General Assembly states:

"The attainment of the objective of security, which is an inseparable element of peace, has always been one of the most profound aspirations of humanity. States have for a long time sought to maintain their security through the possession of arms. Admittedly, their survival has, in certain cases, effectively depended on whether they could count on appropriate means of defence. Yet the accumulation of weapons, particularly nuclear weapons, today constitutes much more a threat than a protection for the future of mankind. The time has therefore come to put an end to this situation, to abandon the use of force in international relations and to seek security in disarmament, that is to say, through a gradual but effective process beginning with a reduction in the present level of armaments. . . ."

The Final Document also drew attention to the existence of a link between disarmament, security and development in stating:

"The Members of the United Nations are fully aware of the conviction of their peoples that the question of general and complete disarmament is of utmost importance and that peace, security and economic and social development are indivisible, and they have therefore recognized that the corresponding obligations and responsibilities are universal."

Such a triangular interaction was subsequently underlined in the Secretary-General's report on the Relationship between Disarmament and Development.

Notwithstanding the obligations undertaken by the Member Sates of the United Nations, in Article 2, paragraph 4 of the Charter to refrain in the international relations from the threat or use of force, the past 40 years have witnessed numerous conflicts involving the use of force to the detriment of international peace and security. At the same time, the United Nations has increasingly dealt with an array of problems arising from non-military factors like those pertaining to underdevelopment, maldevelopment or absence of development which either create or aggravate tensions of social upheaval and political instability.

The United Nations consideration of problems arising from military and non-military factors has been carried out in a multilateral framework with the result that the interaction between them has been increasingly recognized. United Nations forums dealing with issues of development, for example, have been hearing strategic arguments for considering the issues of resource transfers and economic growth. Similarly, in United Nations debates on disarmament, recurring emphasis has been placed on the economic case for halting and reversing the arms race and on the social and economic benefits that could be gained from better use of the resources thereby released.

With regard to the use of the world's resources, the interaction between politico-military and socio-economic considerations has been even more evident. When the General Assembly, in resolution 1378 (XIV), called the question of disarmament "the most important one facing the international world today", the sense of urgency reflected not only a recognition of a threat to humanity but also, in part, a "consciousness that the resources that make this threat possible, and many more resources devoted to less spectacularly destructive military uses, are being diverted from the task of lightening the burdens and enriching the lives of individuals and of society".

In discussing the general consequences of continuing military consumption of resources, the 1982 Report of the Secretary-General on the Economic and Social Consequences of the Arms Race and of Military Expenditures pointed out:

"Resources used for military purposes compete for resources which could have been otherwise available for socio-economic development. They also affect priorities in the allocation of resources not claimed directly. They aggravate the conflict situations related to resource constraints. And they carry the non-negligible risk of creating conflict situtions which by themselves may become a factor in further escalations of the arms race, aiming additional claims on resources. In all these respects, purely financial outlays do not provide an adequate picture of the magnitude of the human and material resources consumed by the arms race. Nor do they sufficiently indicate the range of options which would be available if only a part of the resources claimed by the arms race were diverted to non-military purposes."

Resource-related issues have generally been a significant factor in determining the pace of socio-economic development, the nature of tensions among nations and the forms of response to conflict situations. But as pointed out in the above-mentioned Report, "Never before has humanity confronted so many resource-related tensions, manifesting themselves in such varied forms, in so many places, at the same time". In the 40 years since the Second World War, historically unprecedented changes have occurred in the nature and volumes of resources consumed for military purposes and in the costs of their utilization. There are those who see no immediate physical constraints on global resources and those who argue that the world is eroding its resource base. But in both cases there is the recognition that human and natural resources are unevenly distributed among States and that States vary widely in their technological capabilities to overcome physical constraints on resources. It is also admitted that an absence of physical limits on global reserves does not preclude conditions of economic scarcity and steeply rising costs for some parts of the world due to geographical circumstance and to the fact that patterns of consumption do not correspond to the geographic location of reserves. Whether considered in the context of disarmament or development, resource-related concerns have been expressed at the possibility of a severe economic dislocation which might occur in the event of a major military conflict, serious political rifts between the centres of consumption and geographic reserves and social upheavals and civil unrest in societies engaged in the task of nation-building amid conditions of resource-scarcity.

In drawing attention to non-military threats to national and international security and in placing development as an issue on the international agenda, developing countries have taken major initiatives at the United Nations. However, the nature and extent of United Nations involvement with the subject of the relationship between disarmament and development arise not ony from the initiatives by developing countries. Industrialized countries, too, have either taken initiatives or associated themselves with the attempts to promote an interrelated perspective on the separate issues of disarmament and development and to find an institutional and operational framework for doing do. Over the years many Member States belonging to East, West, North or South have served on various expert groups appointed by the Secretary-General and contributed through their knowledge, expertise and experience towards evolving a comprehensive approach to the complex interaction between two of the most pressing issues on the United Nations agenda. Among the subjects that have been addressed are the concepts and theories relevant to the relationship between disarmament and development, national and international opportunity costs of the continuing arms race, technological and economic feasibility of converting resources from military to civilian use and consequences of the military use of technology on the process of arms limitation and disarmament.

In providing information and analyses required for understanding the subject in its various aspects and dimensions, the United Nations has carried out several studies with the assistance of qualified governmental and/or consultant experts to examine such issues as the impact of military spending on national economies and of the arms race on international economic relations. Particularly relevant, for example, are a series of studies on the economic and social consequences of the arms race and of military expenditures and the two studies on disarmament and development. The empirical and historical evidence collected in several of these expert studies, as well as the information and analyses available in the periodic reports in the United Nations forums dealing with economic and social issues, were examined in the 1981 Report of the Secretary-General on the Relationship between Disarmament and Development in which extensive use was also made of open literature and specific research papers commissioned worldwide by acknowledged scholars and experts. The unanimous conclusions of the governmental experts from 27 countries who assisted the Secretary-General in the preparation of this Report provide a conceptual framework for understanding the complex relationship between disarmament and development which involves more than a mathematical transfer of a part of disarmament-released resources into channels for socio-economic development in developing countries.

Acknowledging that the arms race and development are in competitive relationship, not only in terms of resources, but also in the vital dimension of attitudes and perceptions, the experts placed the disarmament-development relationship in the context of a triangular interaction between disarmament, development and security. To demonstrate that threats to security may arise both from military and non-military challenges, they argued on the one hand that the arms race itself has grown into a threat to the security of nations and that general and complete disarmament under effective international control, particularly nuclear disarmament, would directly enhance security. On the other hand, it was also argued that there is an array of intensifying non-military factors aggravating the security problems of States in the form of (a) a widespread reduction in prospects for economic growth, (b) impending physical constraints—notably in the field of energy and selected non-renewable raw materials, but also severe stress on the environment and a growing world population—and (c) the morally unacceptable and politically hazardous polarization of wealth and poverty and insufficient development in the developing countries.

As with the concept of security, the experts assisting in the preparation of the Secretary-General's report on Disarmament and Development also unanimously adopted a broad definition of development which was projected as a global requirement in the context of economic interdependence. Relying upon recent experiences to demonstrate that the economic fortunes—and thus the security—of all nations are interdependent and destined to become more so, it was argued that failure to bring the arms race under control is likely to be associated with a vicious circle of confrontation and mutual denial, with declining prospects for mutually advantageous economic co-operation and shrinking options for all nations.

Along with taking a broader view of the concept of disarmament and development, the Secretary-General's 1981 report on the Relationship between Disarmament and Development, prepared by a Group of Governmental Experts, made another point of departure. It noted the fact that some earlier studies on the interaction between issues of disarmament and development reflected a note of caution in projecting too close an association between them, mostly on the grounds that making two intensely desirable but, as yet, unattained goals contingent upon each other could somehow be seen as detracting from the urgency of achieving fast progress in each separately. Consequently, there had been a tendency to remain content with projecting the enormous contrasts between the magnitude of resources claimed by the world-wide military activities and the outlays required to provide for the basic unmet needs of the poorer sections of society, particularly in the developing countries. The relationship between disarmament and development had, thus, acquired a strong normative content on the basis of its desirability. According to the unanimous conclusions of the 1981 Report on the Relationship between Disarmament and Development such an approach did not take full account of the most current economic realities: the developing countries were still in urgent need of greater allocations to meet the expanding demands of their growing populations. The Report stated that the developed world was also beginning to confront the cumulative results of its past patterns of resource-utilization and that the market economies were facing serious socio-economic problems, such as unemployment and inflation. The Report further noted that the centrally planned economies were also under considerable strain to make faster progress in achieving better consumer satisfaction and greater modernization in view of a slow-down in growth rates. The Group took the position that for the world as a whole, the allocation of 5 to 6 per cent of global output for military purposes was becoming a questionable proposition in a climate of sluggish economic growth projections for the 1980s, as compared to the more favourable economic performance in earlier decades. The Group was of the view that the normative appeal to direct some of the armament-related resources into the developmental field acquired an element of self-interest if it could be established that the need for such a reallocation was shared by all social systems irrespective of their current levels of development.

The empirical and historical evidence accumulated in the United Nations studies dealing with the subject point to the post–World War II armament phenomenon as a factor in national and international economic prospects. As stated in the Secretary-General's 1982 report on the Economic and Social Consequences of the Arms Race and of Military Expenditures:

The dynamics of the arms race involve more than a sum total of military expenditures and an updated list of its major and minor participants. The forces driving it, the purposes it serves and its various forms of manifestation have transformed the arms race into a political phenomenon adversely affecting global socio-economic options. By rendering the international politico-economic environment more rigid and more resistant to change, the arms race is fostering concerns for the political and social options chosen by other countries, in particular by those that are deemed to have strategic importance, and it is promoting a pattern of alliances and alignments which reinforce attitudes of confrontation in a situation demanding co-operation, both in international political and economic relations. During the period under review, a prominent feature of contemporary international relations was growing interdependence which has manifested itself in several areas. The world has become increasingly interdependent as it is confronted with problems which either cannot be resolved in any other way than by joint efforts (for example, radioactive pollution by atomic tests, sharing of meteorological information) or because these problems can be resolved on national or regional levels only at higher costs, for example, the development of new sources of energy. The global nature of many problems arising out of physical and economic constraints on human and material resources, makes their solution within regional and political boundaries especially difficult. The arms race, therefore, amounts to a counterproductive choice since it presupposes the existence of conflict in a situation demanding co-operation. . . .

An earlier United Nations report on the same subject, in 1978, stated that the arms race had complicated the process of stabilizing the international monetary system, aggravated the balance-of-payment problems and distorted the desired evolution of international exchange in a period of growing economic interdependence. With regard to the impact of military spending on national economies, the Group of Experts carrying out the 1981 Study on the Relationship between Disarmament and Development, having considered national case studies, took the position that military outlays, by definition, fell into the category of consumption and not investment. Consequently, the Group concluded that steadily high or increasing military outlays were likely to have a depressing effect on economic growth, directly through displacement of investment and indirectly through constraints on productivity which itself depends to a considerable degree on the research and development effort currently biased in favour of military technology.

In calculating the opportunity costs of current military outlays, the Group of Experts, preparing the 1981 Report on the Relationship between Disarmament and Development, found it relatively simpler to assess the sacrifices entailed by national military expenditures than to project the direct and catalytic effects of reversing the global arms race. Recognizing (a) that all military expenditures are essentially government expenditures and, hence, a part of the budget or planning mechanism of Governments; and (b) that socio-economic functions basically reflect a welfare commitment on behalf of the States, it was argued in the same report that any additional resources released through military spending reductions could enable the State to expand its social welfare commitment both directly and indirectly. Direct reallocations could contribute towards improvement in social goals such as education, nutrition, medical care, housing and transport and policies of tax reduction could contribute indirectly to civilian consumption and investment.

Not all the findings and conclusions of United Nations reports and studies relevant to the relationship between disarmament and development have been equally acceptable to all Member States. In some cases, reservations were expressed on the grounds of the methodology used and inadequate analysis: some held the view that absence of reliable, accurate and adequate information from all parts of the world affected the soundness of the findings and conclusions; others took the position that such information should be made available only in the context of specific negotiations dealing with measures of arms limitation and disarmament. There have also been instances when the findings and conclusions themselves have been questioned; either because the underlying political assumptions were not equally shared by all or due to a lack of agreement over the policy recommendations related to the analytical contents. The need to inform, educate and promote further understanding of this subject, however, has been widely recognized. Relevant also in this context is the launching of the World Disarmament Campaign in 1982 by the General Assembly at its Twelfth Special Session, the second special session devoted to disarmament. Aimed at informing, educating, and generating public understanding and support for the United Nations objectives in the field of arms limitation and disarmament, the mandate of the campaign makes specific mention of the relationship between disarmament and international security and disarmament and development recognizing the benefits that could be derived from the reduction of military outlays and the reallocation of released resources for socio-economic development.

As an issue for political decision-making, United Nations involvement with the relationship between disarmament and development has resulted in various recommendations by the General Assembly which broadly fall into three categories: those defining ultimate goals and objectives; those addressed to intermediate measures and those articulating immediate concerns.

Statements of ultimate goals and objectives are found, for example, in proposals such as those for: release of resources for purposes of socio-economic development through general and complete disarmament under effective international supervision and control; resolution of security-related conflicts and conflict situations with a view to removing the underlying causes for the escalating arms race and military expenditures; and conclusion of specific measures of arms limitation and disarmament in accordance with well-defined priorities contained in a comprehensive disarmament strategy. Such proposals may give the impression that of the two issues involved in it, development is at the receiving end of the relationship between disarmament and development.

Recommendations for intermediate measures include proposals such as those aimed at reducing military budgets; making requisite preparations to facilitate the conversion of resources freed by disarmament measures to civilian purposes, especially to meet urgent and social economic needs, in particular in developing countries; and seeking greater understanding and awareness of the complex issues covered by the subject of the relationship between disarmament and development through more accurate and reliable information and analyses. Such proposals tend to view the processes of disarmament and of development as running parallel to, rather than being contingent upon, each other and suggest that an interrelated perspective will contribute towards a faster pace of progress in both areas.

Recommendations articulating immediate concerns focus on measures seeking ways and means to address the urgency of developmental issues and include proposals such as those for the establishment of a disarmament fund for development financed from budgetary savings related to the implementation of disarmament measures as well as from a levy on armaments or voluntary contributions. Such proposals argue that the challenge of developmental issues is of such global nature that it can be satisfactorily met only by exploring all available avenues including the possibility of rechannelling even a fraction of the resources devoted to military purposes to the tasks of socio-economic development.

In this last mentioned respect, United Nations debates over the last three decades have reflected some familiar arguments. The positions taken by Member States on this issue in 1984, when the Disarmament Commission considered the subject in response to General Assembly resolution 38/71 B, were rather similar to those stated during the debates in the Economic and Social Council in 1953 before the establishment of a Special United Nations Fund for Economic Development through resolution 482 A (VIII). The Disarmament Commission agreed that world-wide military spending had acquired a staggering magnitude and that the global trend continued to be towards a faster rate of annual increase in those expenditures. That stood in dramatic contrast to the sombre state of the global economy and had serious implications for the economic prospects of the world, in particular those of the developing countries. Throughout the history of United Nations involvement, there has been a wide readiness to consider devoting a part of disarmament-released resources for purposes of socio-economic development, particularly to the benefit of developing countries. However, there have been reservations both with regard to the timing and the method. Some Member States have declared that they are not in a position to make additional contributions to another development fund; others believe that raising the levels of official development assistance is not an accurate indicator of additional resources available for developmental aid; and still others have pointed out that it would be unwise to create a new funding activity without sufficient funds for its effective operation. There are also those who have insisted that any decisions to reallocate a part of military spending for non-military purposes must be preceded by a reliable and accurate picture of the levels and magnitude of military expenditures, particularly on the part of major military spenders, and those who believe that the creation of such a fund should only be viewed as symbolic of an international willingness to promote military restraint.

During its annual session in 1985, which marked the 40th anniversary of the establishment of the United Nations, the General Assembly decided to convene in 1986 an International Conference on the Relationship between Disarmament and Development, which would be the first under United Nations auspices. At the initiative of France and co-sponsored by 52 Member States from both industrialized and developing regions and belonging to different political groupings, the draft resolution was adopted without a vote by the General Assembly on 16 December 1985 as resolution 40/155. By that resolution the General Assembly endorsed, *inter alia*, the report of the Preparatory Committee for the International Conference on the Relationship between Disarmament and Development.

The General Assembly's decision to convene an International Conference on the Relationship between Disarmament and Development was taken at a time of great significance in the discussion of disarmament issues. It was also a period of deep development crisis and sombre assessments of the world economy prepared by the various United Nations forums dealing with economic and developmental issues. Relating these concerns to the issue of global resources, the 1985 Report on the World Social Situation, *inter alia*, states:

. . . the material foundations for achieving widely-shared social objectives exist on a global level, and that failure and pessimism derive not as much from limitations of the productive capacity of the world economy as from the misdirection of resources and efforts which lead it to perform below potential most of the time and disastrously below capacity periodically.

The General Assembly's decision to convene an International Conference on the Relationship between Disarmament and Development, represents both a recognition of a complex interaction between two vital issues and a willingness to address it at a high political level. Briefly, the main elements covered by this decision to which different degrees of political emphasis have been attached during the various phases of United Nations involvement, are reflected in the three substantive items on the agenda of the International Conference. As stated in paragraph 2 of resolution 40/155, the International Conference to be held in Paris from 15 July to 2 August 1986, would undertake:

(a) Consideration of the relationship between disarmament and development in all its aspects and dimensions with a view to reaching appropriate conclusions;
(b) Consideration of the implications of the level and magnitude of the military expenditures, in particular those of the nuclear-weapon States and other militarily important States, for the world economy and the international economic and social situation, particularly for the developing countries, and formulation of appropriate recommendations for remedial measures;
(c) Consideration of ways and means of releasing additional resources through disarmament measures, for development purposes, in particular for the benefit of developing countries.

In agreeing to identify these various elements for appropriate international consideration, the General Assembly has expressed a mutuality of interests in addressing issues of common concern through concerted global action in an increasingly interdependent world.

18. Toward an Alternative Security System

Robert Johansen

[*   *   *]

[I.] CONTENDING APPROACHES TO NATIONAL SECURITY POLICY

Seven policy models illustrate the range of options relevant to establishing a more secure global system.

1. Current U.S. national security policy illustrates the first policy model: *a nuclear war-fighting capability*. This posture calls for an enormous, continuously expanding arsenal. More firepower of a more advanced nature is required for a war-fighting strategy than is necessary for simple deterrence of war. Tens of thousands of warheads with precise targeting accuracy imply a strategy to destroy selected military targets, such as opposing missile silos, not a plan simply to threaten general destruction for deterrence purposes. Such a strategy assumes that nuclear war can be controlled, limited, and therefore fought without bringing unacceptable destruction. The purpose, to move toward a capability that could disarm one's opponent in a first strike, makes this an unstable policy. Even though a completely disarming first strike remains impossible, the drive to approach it stimulates the arms race and produces enormous anxiety during crises. Fearing that its adversaries may quickly destroy a large part of its nuclear arsenal, a nation is encouraged to adopt a launch-on-warning policy and thus place its weapons on a hair-trigger. Because weapons must be launched before incoming missiles have arrived, such a policy increases the risk of deliberate or accidental nuclear war.

This posture indicates a willingness to use nuclear weapons first. Military planners designed the M-X missile, for example, as an anti-silo weapon. But no one wants to destroy a silo after the missile it houses has left, so the M-X makes most sense for use in a surprise nuclear attack. The antithesis of a defensive weapon, the M-X design increases U.S. invulnerability less than it increases Soviet vulnerability. When the United States increases the other side's vulnerability, the United States also increases its own insecurity.

Because a war-fighting capability has become official U.S. policy, it deserves more elaboration than do other policy models. Many high officials in past administrations, both Republican and Democratic, have favored a nuclear war-fighting capability, including James Schlesinger and Henry Kissinger, Secretaries of Defense and State in the Ford administration, former Secretary of Defense Harold Brown and National Security Advisor Zbigniew Brzezinski in the Carter administration, and Secretary of Defense Caspar Weinberger and Secretaries of State Alexander Haig and George Schultz in the Reagan administration. In a basic study of strategy by the National Security Council, which has become the foundation of the overall U.S. security posture, the United States has outlined a strategy for fighting a protracted nuclear war against the Soviet Union. This guidance statement declares that "United States nuclear capabilities must prevail even under the conditions of a prolonged war." U.S. offensive nuclear forces "must prevail and be able to force the Soviet Union to seek earliest termination of hostilities on terms favorable to the United States."

U.S. policy incorporates ideas more fully elaborated by other national security analysts, perhaps most explicitly by Colin S. Gray and Keith Payne at the Hudson Institute. In an article entitled "Victory Is Possible," they appeal for an increased offensive nuclear capability because "the United States must possess the ability to wage nuclear war rationally." To be rational means to recognize that "war *at any level* can be won or lost. . . ." The U.S. president "must have the ability not merely to end a war, but to end it favorably."

This policy should "enable a president to initiate strategic nuclear use. . . ." Architects of a nuclear war-fighting capability consider the first use of nuclear weapons in an offensive nuclear strategy as a defensive act. Gray and Payne say that "once the defeat of the Soviet state is established as a war aim," the United States "should identify nuclear targeting options that could help restore deterrence, yet would destroy the Soviet state. . . ." A major goal is to kill Soviet leaders. "Striking the USSR should entail targeting the relocation bunkers of the top political and bureaucratic leadership, including those of the KGB; key communication centers of the Communist Party, the military, and government; and many of the economic, political, and military records." In this view, "even limited destruction of some of these targets and substantial isolation of many of the key personnel who survive could have revolutionary consequences for the country."

Many billions of dollars should also be spent, they argue, on anti-missile missiles and on civil defense, because "it would not be in the interest of the United States actually to implement an offensive nuclear strategy no matter how frightening in Soviet perspective, if the U.S. homeland were totally naked to Soviet retaliation."

A war-fighting nuclear policy further stimulates the arms race because the Soviet Union can be expected to imitate new U.S. deployments. Additional Soviet weapons will become the justification for further U.S. increments, just as Soviet deployment of multiple, independently-targetable, re-entry vehicles (MIRVs), which Washington deployed first under the guise of inducing the Soviet Union to negotiate seriously for arms control, later became the rationale for more U.S. weapons.

A war-fighting strategy also increases the risks of deliberate and accidental war. The warning time during which the Soviet leadership must respond will be so short that a launch decision will almost certainly rely heavily on programmed decisions by computers. The Pershing II ballistic missiles scheduled for deployment in West Germany in early 1984 will be capable of destroying Soviet command, control, and communications systems after a six-minute flight. At the least, the Soviet leadership will feel forced to respond when their warning systems first show signs of an attack, rather than to wait for confirmation and risk having their command centers hit.

As Fred Charles Iklé explained in 1980, "The more we rely on launch on warning (or for that matter, the more the Soviets do) the greater the risk of accidental nuclear war. . . . The crux of the matter is that the more important it becomes to launch on warning, the more dangerous it will be. The tightening noose around our neck is the requirement for speed." Yet, the necessary condition for a war-fighting capability is speed to destroy the opponents' missiles before they can lift from their launching sites.

The logic of this approach can only be described as breathtaking. More accurately, the distinction between logic and illogic has been obliterated. According to advocates of this school, bringing nuclear war closer pushes it farther away. They claim that an offensive strategy, even if articulated before war begins, demonstrates defensive purpose. To attack military targets in a first strike, rather than cities in a second strike, allegedly makes war less terrifying. However, since the nature of the attack will more deeply threaten the hold of Soviet leaders on their country the leadership will be more peaceful. In this view, the Kremlin will exercise more caution if the United States exercises less. The United States, to be a more effective peacemaker, must show more willingness to launch a first nuclear strike. "An intelligent U.S. offensive strategy, wedded to homeland defenses, should reduce U.S. casualties to approximately 20 million, which should render U.S. strategic threats more credible."

Advocates of an offensive nuclear strategy represent the more recent manifestation of being ensnared on the dilemmas of dogmatic realism. On the one hand, Weinberger explains that the United States can "prevail" in nuclear war, and Gray and Payne believe that nuclear war can be winnable "at any level." On the other hand, however, even they find their own claims hard to believe. Almost as an afterthought, they reluctantly acknowledge that at some point the costs of war exceed the gains. "No matter how grave the Soviet offense, a U.S. president cannot credibly threaten and should not launch a strategic nuclear strike if expected U.S. casualties are likely to involve 100 million or more American citizens." Ironically, with this acknowledgment the entire, elaborate strategic doctrine falls apart. No U.S. threat, no offensive nuclear strategy can succeed if it carries the risk of 100 million deaths. Yet the Soviet Union can at any moment inflict such destruction. Presumably it will be able to maintain such a capacity regardless of new U.S. deployments. How then, using these very standards, can a major war *ever* be won? It cannot.

The desire for a nuclear war-fighting capability represents a quest to find a new functional equivalent to the old nuclear superiority that the United States enjoyed over the Soviet Union during the 1960s. This effort is not a quest for peace. The striving for predominance—a familiar and, for many, an irresistible pursuit in a balance of power system—confirms the need to move toward a more dependable security system.

2. *Mutual assured destruction* was a policy designed more to deter war than to carry out nuclear battles. This policy requires simply that each side be able to destroy its opponent even after suffering a first strike. Former Secretary of Defense Robert S. McNamara and most officials and academic experts during the 1960s and early 1970s strongly endorsed this strategy. No precision guidance systems or additional warheads and missiles would have been required if the United States and Soviet Union had pursued this policy. Indeed, this strategy fell out of fashion in part because it provided no security rationale for the more sophisticated, more expensive, new generation of weapons that officials, aerospace industries, and the

nuclear establishment wanted to build for reasons of vested interests unrelated to security.

For other reasons as well, many advocates of mutual assured destruction during the 1960s became advocates of a war-fighting capability in the 1980s. They abandoned mutual assured destruction as soon as the prospect of destruction became genuinely mutual. Throughout the 1950s and 1960s the United States was able to inflict massive retaliation upon the Soviet Union for a relatively slight provocation; the Soviet Union, in turn, had no similar capability to devastate the United States.

As this advantage disappeared, "flexible response" gradually came into vogue. Advocates of this doctrine sought to respond to threats or attack with weapons somewhat more proportionate to the threshold of violence that an adversary threatened. This approach emphasized the importance of responses short of all-out nuclear war. On the one hand, a limited conventional attack might be met with a conventional response. Still, the United States always specified that it would not restrict itself from using nuclear weapons just because its adversary did. Tactical nuclear weapons for "limited" nuclear war took on a prominent role in diplomatic bargaining and in preparation for combat. Rather than decrease the reliance on nuclear weapons, flexible response meant that nuclear weapons entered the diplomatic equation at lower thresholds of conflict than ever before. In addition, pinpointing military and industrial targets, rather than exploding large warheads over cities, became a part of U.S. targeting policy for limited nuclear war. Officials developed this posture in part to convince the Soviet Union that an attack on Europe that did not include the United States would be met with tactical nuclear weapons in Europe, since a more massive U.S. nuclear response, which would jeopardize the United States itself, seemed less credible after the Soviet Union developed an intercontinental capacity to destroy the United States. Clearly, this policy opened the way for a nuclear war-fighting strategy.

Seeking to maintain its military superiority over the Soviet Union in the early 1970s, the United States made a major effort to offset the then recently acquired Soviet capacity to destroy the United States. U.S. officials sought to augment at least a psychological advantage that, they believed, would accompany the deployment of additional weapons, even though more warheads were clearly redundant for purposes of deterring an attack itself. The fateful decision to deploy multiple warheads (MIRVs) on a single missile sparked this drive more than five years before the Soviet Union developed a similar capability. By 1971, for example, the United States had already deployed twice as many strategic warheads and bombs as the Soviet Union. The United States also possessed a vastly larger arsenal of tactical nuclear weapons. Even so, U.S. officials launched a major expansion. Within six years, by 1976, the United States more than *doubled* its already superior strategic arsenal. During the same period the Soviet Union had not yet expanded its arsenal to match what the United States had attained in 1970. These massive new deployments, in themselves equal to ten times the number of warheads required for one minimum deterrent force, did not strengthen deterrence; but they did strengthen U.S. faith in the importance of redundant weapons to produce a psychological edge.

Once the Soviet Union achieved an intercontinental nuclear force, a U.S. nuclear threat could no longer easily exert leverage over Soviet behavior in areas unrelated to U.S. vital interests, even though the threat to retaliate against a direct Soviet attack on the United States still remained credible. To regain its eroding influence over Soviet behavior—behavior that U.S. officials opposed yet which did not directly compromise U.S. security—Washington developed new strategic doctrine and weapons. In addition, to increase the number of conflicts where the U.S. nuclear arsenal could be brought credibly to bear, the United States broadened its definition of conflicts in which U.S. vital security interests were at stake. Any dispute that threatened U.S. security presumably could be used to justify a resort to nuclear weapons. The alleged right to use force to secure access to Middle Eastern oil illustrates this geographic expansion of interests. The enhanced radiation (neutron) warhead, the land-based cruise missile, the Pershing II, and nuclear artillery all integrated nuclear firepower into U.S. military responses at levels which previously had been reserved for conventional weapons. These new weapons and doctrine enabled the United States to rely even further on nuclear weapons in order to counter the growing Soviet ability to ignore some of the influence that the U.S. had possessed during its period of nuclear superiority. Overall, the evolution of U.S. and Soviet nuclear strategies from massive retaliation through mutual assured destruction and flexible response to a war-fighting capability demonstrates how the present international system generates pressures for a buildup of arms and an erosion of security.

3. A *minimum deterrent* posture differs from mutual assured destruction in that it would deliberately stop the nuclear arms race by resisting political and economic pressures for overkill and by claiming the need for no more than the minimum number of weapons required to destroy one's opponent. According to this doctrine, four hundred survivable warheads would be sufficient to provide a minimum deterrent for the United States, given the size of the Soviet Union and the existence of only 240 Soviet cities of 100,000 or more in population. In contrast, advocates of mutual assured destruction never placed a ceiling on the nuclear arsenal. Thus U.S. deployment of strategic bombs and warheads, which already numbered more than 850 in 1961, rose to 8,500 by 1975, even though the Soviet Union possessed only a few warheads in 1961, 1,000 in 1967, and 2,500 by 1975. In combining figures for tactical as well as strategic weapons, the U.S. Arms Control and Disarmament Agency reported that the United States already possessed 40,000 warheads by 1972.

Contemporary exponents of a minimum deterrent posture favor such policies as a drastic reduction in nuclear warheads and delivery vehicles, a no-first-use pledge, and efforts to avoid increased military threats against the Soviet Union. In this view, increasing U.S. invulnerability makes sense; increasing Soviet vulnerability does not. At the present stage of technological development, several hundred nuclear missiles in submarines offer the most secure deterrent. Submarines provide advantages over the M-X, because the size and precision of the M-X will increase the threat to the Soviet Union and encourage the Kremlin to expand its arsenal and to adopt a launch-on-warning policy. In any case, further Soviet deployments could make the M-X quite vulnerable soon after its deployment.

The Trident II, although sea-based, would not be needed in a minimum deterrent posture because its precision guidance enables it to threaten the Soviet land-based nuclear force. Submarines that can evade a Soviet attack yet remain far enough from Soviet borders to give the Kremlin sufficient warning time provide the most assurance that accidental and preemptive war will not occur. At the same time they still confront the Soviet leadership with retaliation if they attack the United States. According to these criteria, land-based cruise missiles, which can easily be hidden and moved close to Soviet territory, and Pershing II missiles, which can break Soviet control over their own nuclear forces, would be counterproductive. A minimum deterrent policy would assuage the concern of some Europeans that current plans to modernize NATO nuclear forces reflect a U.S. plan to keep a nuclear war limited to Europe.

As the preceding discussion indicates, mutual assured destruction and a minimum deterrent lead to enormous differences in weaponry. The psychological and political differences are no less significant. Exponents of a minimum deterrent seek to avoid threatening the Soviet Union unless it has made severe, overtly aggressive moves. The goal of this posture is to prevent nuclear war, not to prepare to wage it. Advocates of a no-first-use pledge argue that it would reduce even the risk of a conventional attack by the Soviet Union, because a NATO prepared for a conventional response to a conventional attack poses a more credible deterrent to war than does a nuclear response opposed by many Western Europeans themselves.

Advocates of a minimum deterrent deliberately avoid an arms race by refusing to move beyond minimal levels even though other nations might exceed the minimum. Exponents conclude that the people of the world and even the people of one superpower are safer with only one nuclear war-fighting capability in existence than they are with two—even though the preferred outcome, of course, would be to have none. If one nuclear war-fighting capability is not countered by a second, the odds for escalating tensions and for war by accident or miscalculation diminish considerably.

4. A *defensive weapons system*, based on conventional arms, has received surprisingly little attention, especially given its special relevance to Europe. This approach assumes that genuine security and arms restraint can best be achieved through military power which is ample for defense but which cannot be used for offensive purposes. Those weapons that threaten one's opponents should be eliminated, without negotiations, while other weapons should be designed and deployed to mount a strong defense.

According to this view, the idea that offense provides the best defense "should be a rule of tactics and not of strategy." Advocates argue that a sharp distinction should be made between offensive and defensive uses of all weapons. Although the distinction is always subject to argument, Freeman Dyson states that its main implications are clear: "Bombers are bad. Fighter airplanes and antiaircraft missiles are good. Tanks are bad. Antitank missiles are good. Submarines are bad. Antisubmarine technology is good. Nuclear weapons are bad. Antiballistic missile systems are good." Dyson acknowledges, "This list of moral preferences goes flatly against the strategic thinking which has dominated our policies for the last forty years." Because it goes against "accepted dogmas," it may offer hope for escaping the policy agenda which entraps us.

Unlike the first three models, a defensive posture can succeed in the presence of an inequality of military power as long as it is an excess of defensive capability over offensive capability. Each country can enjoy its own superiority of defensive power without making other states insecure. No government should be unhappy with defensive inequalities because they threaten no one.

For this reason, a defensive system, unlike nuclear deterrence, encourages stability. As discussed earlier, deterrence bears the fatal destabilizing flaw of threatening an opponent, even to the point of committing national suicide. Nuclear deterrence relies on vindictiveness. It has no credibility without willingness to retaliate after being destroyed oneself, even though retaliation can no longer save one's society or do more than further crush civilization and the environment. A continuously credible deterrent functions with confrontation, brinksmanship, and arms buildups.

Ironically, a stable, secure diplomatic climate diminishes the credibility of nuclear threats. For that reason an irrational commander-in-chief can deter an opponent from acts that a more sane, stable leader with the same arsenal could not. Reckless willingness to launch nuclear weapons intimidates. In contrast, a reasoned consideration of the costs and benefits of firing the deterrent makes an opponent less cautious and timid. In times of crisis, mobilization—not calm restraint—enhances the power of deterrence.

I am not arguing that confrontation and instability lead to peace, but that they contribute to a credible threat to use nuclear weapons. Peace admittedly flourishes in a stable international climate. Yet such a peace comes from the stability of international relationships, not from the deterring function of nuclear arsenals themselves. Compared to a nuclear war-fighting capacity, a minimum deterrent posture increases stability and the likelihood of peace, not because the deterring threat is immediate, but precisely because the threat is pushed far into the background and its use limited to a single narrow purpose—to prevent the first explosion of nuclear weapons.

Deterrence, if strictly defined, refers to the coercive influence that results from threats to destroy a potential attacker's assets. The threatened destruction deliberately and vastly outweighs any possible benefits to be derived from attack. Deterrence is not posed directly against the attacking forces. In contrast, defense mounts force to repel an attack and to make the attack fail. Discussion on European security today obscures the line between these two concepts. Nuclear weapons, which have been used mainly as instruments of deterrence, are now being increasingly discussed as if they could be employed in a defensive role. This not only intensifies the arms competition but also causes greater public anxiety over the prospect of nuclear confrontation.

Exponents of a defensive weapons system confront a central security problem: Can one nation be secure without threatening the security of another? Dietrich Fischer points out that "strength" has two different meanings which often are not distinguished. Strength can mean the ability to harm others or the ability to resist harm intended by others. The United States possesses more strength in the first sense than in the second. People who believe that to protect themselves they must threaten others confuse the projection of threats with the immunization against threats. On the other hand, those who believe that to avoid threatening others they must be weak fail to distinguish between withholding threats and making themselves vulnerable. "Purely defensive arms," such as fixed anti-aircraft weapons, increase one's security without threatening the security of others. "Purely offensive arms," such as a vulnerable M-X missile, reduce the security of opponents, without adding to one's own security. Of course, most arms fall between these two extreme categories. They can serve both offensive and defensive purposes. Yet the difference in the degree of defensiveness is important. The security policies of Switzerland and Yugoslavia, countries fiercely determined to maintain their national independence without threatening others, illustrate this approach.

It can be argued that this approach cannot provide defense against nuclear attack without dismantling nuclear arsenals worldwide. This in a fundamental sense is true, but it should be noted that *all* approaches share the inability to avert determined nuclear attack, including the most forbidding variety of a nuclear war-fighting capability. Furthermore, those nations possessing no nuclear weapons are usually not targeted for nuclear attack by countries with nuclear weapons. If, in addition, defensive emphasis reduces arsenals more successfully than do other policies, then it produces a superior security yield. Potentially offensive arms carry the disadvantage of stimulating arms races, threatening opponents, and ultimately leading to greater insecurity for all.

5. A policy to establish a *peacekeeping federation* seeks to strengthen regional and global international organizations so they can verify and eventually enforce multilateral arms reductions. Advocates of this approach believe that a decentralized balance of power system can never provide lasting peace and, therefore, should be replaced. No mystery surrounds the type of system that can keep peace. After all, most disputes inside national societies are resolved without violence. Domestic conflicts often involve millions of people with different languages, religious traditions, races, and lifestyles. If such numbers can co-exist peacefully, then the appropriate conditions and political institutions, if established, could also provide peace for all of the planet's citizens.

According to this view, peace requires a worldwide political organization which includes all societies. In *World Peace Through World Law,* Grenville Clark and Louis Sohn provide the classic expression of this approach. They describe in detail a reformed United Nations system with the purpose of creating "an effective system of enforceable world law in the limited field of war prevention." Strengthening the rule of law and achieving comprehensive disarmament are two central goals. To help accomplish the first, a central authority would replace the existing system of relative international anarchy. The second, once accomplished, would eliminate the capacity of states to overrule that authority's enforcement of peace. The armed forces of all nations would be gradually, simultaneously reduced as international institutions matured. A global agency would retain a limited police capability to patrol contested borders and prevent efforts by any nation to rearm. Each state would diminish its sovereign authority to make war, in return for the consent of other states to assign new legal authority to organs acting on behalf of the community's common interest in peace. The emphasis on federalism signals that the new global governance should be limited, although critics question whether a central organ could possess sufficient power and authority to keep peace without having so much power that it would drastically transform national sovereignty in other areas.

The importance of this policy approach lies more in its theoretical insight than its immediate political appeal. A surprisingly large number of scholars accept the contention that peace requires some system of effective global governance. Yet because they consider it unattainable few work toward creating the conditions to bring a world federation into being.

Since the most serious political liability of this approach remains widespread disbelief in its attainability, advocates might at first encourage the economic, political, and attitudinal conditions needed for the adoption of more modest forms of policy coordination at the global level. The most promising efforts in the immediate future are likely to aim at somewhat narrower purposes, such as establishing an international regime for the use of the high seas. Yet such steps may contribute substantially to the goals of world federation. The effectiveness—though far from unqualified—of various U.N. peacekeeping forces illustrates another feasible step toward the creation of global institutions that eventually could play an enforcement role. Proposals for creating a permanent, individually recruited global police force could advance this precedent one step further.

Feasibility aside, no one should consider the achievement of world federation equivalent to the maintenance of peace. Wars *do* sometimes occur within a single government entity. And peace sometimes reigns between countries that are politically separate. Nonetheless, a dependable peace without more global governance seems a more remote possibility than the growth of global governance itself.

6. A security policy based on *civilian resistance* for national defense is rooted in an understanding, common to all five preceding policies, that the use of power is necessary to defend one's country against external attack. But, unlike the advocates of other approaches, advocates of civilian resistance limit the instruments of power or coercion to nonviolent means. This strategy is rooted in a careful—even if controversial—appraisal of political and military power. The accumulated evidence shows that the power of nonviolent action is usually underestimated, that the unity and applicability of modern military power is often overestimated, and that the costs to one's own society of waging violent conflict are seldom weighed accurately before sending armed forces into action. The leading U.S. exponent of this approach, Gene Sharp, contends that the power of nonviolent action, including strikes, boycotts, obstruction, and total noncooperation, often can resist an aggressor and eventually defeat an occupation force more effectively than can violent resistance.

In addition, advocates stress that protecting a society's democratic values and institutions is more important, strictly speaking, than maintaining control over territory at extreme cost to basic values. Civilian resistance, according to this view, can protect preferred values and institutions more effectively than a military posture that risks the complete unraveling of the social fabric if deterrence fails or the subordination of democratic values to the demands of a garrison state if deterrence "succeeds."

A carefully planned civilian resistance campaign against an external invader has never really been tested. Yet even without advance training or well-defined leadership utilizing a comprehensive strategy, nonviolent action has succeeded in a surprising number of historical cases. The effectiveness of the Norwegian resistance in neutralizing many policies of the German occupation forces in World War II is instructive.

This policy approach is unlikely to receive widespread support until it has been adopted as a security policy in one or two national contexts. The governments of Sweden and the Netherlands have conducted preliminary studies of this strategy but without impact on their security policies. The indifference to civilian resistance, even by small states, reveals the psychological and intellectual inertia of contemporary leadership, as well as the familiar tendency of generals and civilian experts to prepare for the last war. Danish, Norwegian, and Belgian societies, for example, presumably are aware that they cannot defend themselves militarily against outside attacks by any major power. They also know that if they totally renounced the use of force they would be less likely to be targets for nuclear or conventional attack. Furthermore, with advance planning and training, their populations, firmly committed to national independence, could conduct a civilian resistance campaign of indefinite duration with sufficient courage and determination to make it at least as effective as military defense and probably less costly. If countries such as these would adopt civilian resistance or nonmilitary defense policies, they could, by experience and example, probably contribute far more to their own and to human security than they now do by membership in NATO.

7. We can imagine yet another policy, one that aims at achieving *global security*. For reasons of prudence and ethics, its purpose is to provide security equally for all people. In practice, security for one is connected with security for all. In ethics, it is not right that security for one nation should be purchased at the price of insecurity for another. This worldview is informed by an appreciation of diplomatic history and scientific studies of war. It is realism without dogma. Given humanity's unlosable knowledge of the technology of destruction and willingness to use it, this approach finds lasting security possible only with effective efforts to abolish war itself. According to this view, the current international system is, at its base, a war system. Although this system persists with such resilience that it *seems* to be a part of nature, in fact human beings created it. Human beings can transform it.

Such thinking is not new. Yet previous generations have dismissed it as utopian, or at best before its time. But no longer. Eminent realists, if they have avoided dogmatism, now ask how, not whether, to transform the international system. George Kennan, for example, concludes that even "the earliest possible elimination of nuclear weaponry . . . would not be enough, in itself, to give Western civilization . . . an adequate chance of survival. War itself, as a means of settling differences . . . will have to be in some way ruled out. . . ."

Toward that end, a global security policy includes five distinguishing features. First, it tries to prevent the desire for short-range advantages from dominating decisions at the expense of long-run interests. Simply taking a longer view often would yield far-reaching security dividends. Consider, for example, the Soviet and U.S. proposals in 1982 for curtailing the arms race in Europe. On the one hand, the Soviet Union has offered to halt further deployment of SS-20 missiles and has promised to dismantle "hundreds" of intermediate range missiles (SS-4s, SS-5s, and SS-20s) targeted on Europe if in return the United States would not deploy its Pershing II and cruise missiles as planned. On the other hand, President Reagan has offered to forego deploying those same missiles if in return the Soviet Union would dismantle all of its intermediate range missiles targeted on Europe. Both sides categorically rejected the other's proposals as one-sided and totally unrealistic.

Yet any reasonably detached analyst would conclude that either side would be better off in the long run if it simply accepted the other's proposal outright. If by dismantling SS-20s the Soviet leaders could halt the arms buildup before NATO deploys the extremely destabilizing, next generation of nuclear weapons in Europe, they would increase the security of the Soviet people. Similarly, if by cancelling the deployment of the Pershing II and cruise missiles NATO countries could halt the further buildup of Soviet nuclear arms targeted on Europe, they would benefit enormously. U.S. and Soviet rejection of one another's proposals suggests that the two governments do not want to end the arms race so much as to shape its continuation.

Second, the global security approach emphasizes the importance of providing greatly expanded positive incentives rather than relying largely on negative military threats as the means to influence other nations' security policies and to establish a dependable security order. To initiate arms reductions, for example, a state might independently announce that it was halting the testing and deployment of all new nuclear weapons for six months, and that it would extend that period indefinitely if the other side would reciprocate. Contrast this approach with the more common U.S. strategy of building new weapons for bargaining chips in order to threaten the Soviet Union into negotiating seriously for arms reductions. Positive incentives— whether an easing of the arms race, an increase of equitable political representation in international organizations, an extension of favorable trading status, or an offer of other economic benefits—are essential to building a norm against the use of force. On the other hand, military incentives, such as a threat to use national military force to resolve an issue, reinforces the idea that force may be used as a legitimate instrument of foreign policy. This reinforcement occurs even if the use of force is for defensive purposes, because defense is typically self-defined, rather than specified by central institutions representing the world community.

We can prevent any potentially aggressive government from precipitating a war if we can insure that, in the eyes of its governing officials, the benefits of peace outweigh the anticipated benefits of war. Thus policymakers face two broad alternatives in designing policies to deter aggression: they may decrease the benefits of war or increase the benefits of peace. The benefits of war to the Soviet Union or the United States can hardly be decreased further since each has the ability to destroy the other completely. Therefore, the only remaining rational strategy is to increase the benefits of peace.

The emphasis on nonmilitary incentives to channel governments' behavior naturally suggests an expanded role for international organizations or regimes to facilitate cooperation and to regulate intergroup conflict. Transnational public organizations, such as permanent, individually recruited international police force and an international satellite monitoring agency, might be established. These organizations could lay the basis for later establishing a global authority to enforce arms reduction and prohibit the use of force. In these areas a global security policy draws upon its insights from the preceding policy models. Like a peacekeeping federation, regional and global institutions would be established to help resolve conflict peacefully. However, in this instance representation in such institutions would be more complex and would include functional and private organizations as well as national governments. Learning from the advocates of civilian resistance, governments and private organizations might initiate efforts to organize nonviolent measures to help pacify the international system or to restrain dictators.

Third, a global security policy emphasizes a positive image of peace which includes much more than war prevention. At the most general level, the values preferred in a global security policy may be expressed as human rights: (1) the right to peace and to freedom from the threat of genocide and ecocide; (2) the right to security of person against arbitrary arrest, torture, or execution; (3) the right to traditional civil and political liberties; and (4) the right to fulfill all basic needs essential to life. More concretely, to secure the rights and basic needs of all people becomes as important a guideline in decision-making as to secure the institutions of the state. Eliminating the causes of violence, such as poverty and economic inequity, and building the institutions of enforceable peace, such as an effective global monitoring agency for *all* nuclear reactors and fuel processing centers in the world, receive high priority. These more fundamental security goals have in the past been subordinated to a maneuvering for short-term geopolitical advantage.

As indicated at the outset and of most immediate relevance to the field of military affairs, this approach seeks not only to prevent war but eventually also to abolish it as a legitimate institution. Toward that goal, policies aim to reduce arms and to curtail the influence of the military outlook on decision-making. Progress toward the demilitarization of all societies is an important goal of global policy because nothing less can fulfill the human need for security. Moreover, demilitarization facilitates the realization of other preferred values, such as a fair distribution of world resources, a lifting of military repression, and a respect for the environment.

This approach does not assume that a quick abolition of national military forces is possible. But, unlike existing military and arms control policies which tolerate unending reliance on arms, this policy seeks to diminish the importance of arms as points of political leverage, wherever possible, without inviting other actors to engage in aggression. The goal is gradually to increase reliance on nonmilitary defenses, both national and global, while decreasing reliance on military power. This policy moves toward non-nuclear weapons that are specifically designed for defense; places the monitoring of world military deployments and the patrolling of some borders under international auspices; and insures that representation in regional and global institutions becomes more equitable.

Fourth, this approach moves beyond the familiar, singular focus on security for one nation-state. All people of the human race, not one national segment of it, consciously become the beneficiaries of security policies. A sense of species solidarity and global citizenship begins to coexist with more traditional national identity. Similarly, within a society, security should be for all classes of people, not just primarily for the ruling elite.

With a concern for the security of the whole nation and the whole human race, rather than merely for part of either, a new attitude toward "foreign" societies develops. The distinction between "our" government and "their" government begins to fade. Once the nuclear and environmental policies of "foreign" governments directly affect each of us, the actions of other governments become almost as important to us as the actions of our own. In this sense, those governments become "my" governments as well, not because I have elected their officials or sanctioned their politics, but because their decisions affect my life. Similarly, the U.S. government remains "my" government even when it does what I deplore and when I have voted against its elected officials. Whether we like it or not, in the nuclear-ecologically fragile age, all governments become "my" government.

This new way of viewing governments spawns a new way of viewing their interactions. Diplomatic confrontation between two societies, especially when filled with hostility and hatred, loses the virtue it had in the past. For one's government nearby to be militarily number one in the world does not radiate the same glory. One's more distant governments must bear the burdens of military inferiority. Even worse, in the struggle for a military edge, the social and human costs are insufferable: because my various governments compete militarily, they unconscionably squander scarce resources, render many industrious people jobless, and deprive even the employed of means to secure a decent life for their families.

Fifth, in this worldview normative boundaries are at least as important as territorial boundaries. This diplomatic emphasis stems from a grasp of the profound significance of nuclear technology. As Michael Mandelbaum concludes after lengthy study of the consequences produced by the invention of nuclear weapons, "so drastic are these changes that they call into question the very purpose for which all weapons have been used in the past—the conduct of war." In this era the prevention of major war can be no less important than the prevention of territorial conquest. Of course, the diplomatic alternatives are not often so starkly set before us; usually more than two alternatives exist; and the historical outcomes of the threat to conquer or the threat to respond with nuclear weapons are seldom clear.

Mandelbaum's point bears a special urgency for Europeans. Horrifying as war may have been in the pre-nuclear age, most people preferred to risk its consequences rather than allow one European power to dominate the rest. But a growing number of Europeans now believe that the consequences of nuclear war in Europe would be more catastrophic than one nation's domination of the continent, deplorable though this would be. Because such an idea shatters traditional security calculations, a new diplomatic direction, such as suggested in a global security policy, is called for. A global security system provides a rational way to avoid the unacceptable military risks of escalating nuclear arms, on the one hand, and the unacceptable political costs of acquiescing in nuclear blackmail, on the other.

Even from the perspective of a continental power like the United States, security is probably advanced more by promoting a standard against *all* uses of nuclear weapons than by engaging in nuclear threats over any issue. Every threat to use nuclear weapons undercuts the obligation against use. Given this reality, the most vital front line of defense becomes not a new generation of nuclear weapons but a new code of international conduct to restrict the use of military power. This requires moving in a non-nuclear direction—toward conventional defense, world federation, civilian resistance, or global security.

The central means for establishing the new code of conduct is not a politically ineffective outlawry of war in a new Kellogg-Briand Pact, but an amassing of the nonmilitary incentives, mentioned above, to influence even reluctant nations to rely more on transnational processes for their security and less on national military power and self-help. In addition to the informal influences created by a new diplomacy, there also should be formal intergovernmental agreements and monitoring agencies as well. Together, these could eventually constrain the war-making function of national sovereignty. But the purpose is not to abolish the nation-state, it is to enable the nation-state to exercise its sovereignty more safely in other areas.

A global security policy acknowledges that in the nuclear age nations cannot be secure and still be fully sovereign. This is a dramatic reversal of the time-honored truth, now an untruth, that to be secure a nation must be sovereign. For U.S. citizens to be secure requires some limits on the sovereignty of other nations and some control over what other nations can do to the United States. For the United States to reject a degree of control by other nations over U.S. actions means in turn that the United States cannot obtain control over the behavior of others— except through imperial domination, which is no longer a reasonable possibility. In short, to gain limits on the military behavior of others requires willingness to accept limits on oneself. To achieve fair and dependable restraints on the use of force should be the overriding purpose of diplomacy. To achieve such limits is worth paying a price at least as high as now is paid to continue the arms buildup, which decreases our security over time and speeds the decay of human civilization.

The normative boundaries that are to be progressively adjusted and firmly maintained against erosion should differentiate between policies that lead toward justice and injustice, as well as toward peace and war. In practice, the defense of fundamental humanitarian values should begin to assume an influential role in policymaking, a role formerly reserved almost exclusively for the defense of national territory and the assertion of geopolitical advantage. Before U.S. cruise missiles were placed in Europe, for example, people would ask: how does the pending deployment realize the values of peace and security for all people? The old diplomatic approach would have asked: how do the new missiles add to the military strength of the U.S. government?

Because the significance of territorial boundaries recedes in this worldview, the global security approach attenuates the traditional prohibition against intervention in the internal affairs of another state. This change, however, would be limited to authorized intervention aimed at implementing norms established by the world community. Unilateral intervention, which sometimes now occurs in violation of traditional international law, would continue to be prohibited. Humanitarian intervention by an authorized international organization might be used to feed starving Kampucheans, to establish a demilitarized corridor for refugees during war in Lebanon, and at some point even to provide a trusteeship government to dismantle *apartheid* and elect a majority government.

Of course, national boundaries and the importance of territory do not disappear. By its nature, human security always occurs in a particular place. But, according to this view, if the security of all people is to increase, then the importance of territorial boundaries must diminish and that of political, legal, and ethical boundaries for human behavior must increase. This rationale deems it better to strengthen a norm against all use of nuclear weapons than to bolster through nuclear deterrence one's defense of disputed territory. Which side of a national boundary one lives on, important though this may be, can hardly be more important than averting nuclear war which will create enormous loss of life on both sides of the border. Although this thought is unpleasant, denying its truth makes no one more secure.

The motivating force for emphasizing the "human interest" more and a narrow national interest less stems not from sentimental globalism, but from prudent calculations of security needs. As Herz explains, "the new realism of universalism puts . . . the common interest in survival before the traditional interest in seeing one's opponent commit mistakes." The security of one society cannot be achieved without at the same time securing other societies. For example, if either superpower develops new weapons, such as SS-20s or Pershing IIs, in pursuit of increased security for itself, the other will attempt to acquire similar or superior weapons, thus leaving both sides less secure as a result. The most effective way to increase the willingness of all societies to move toward a less militarized global security system is to increase their stake in such a system. Happily, these pragmatic security considerations dovetail with the humanitarian values esteemed by morally sensitive persons in every corner of the globe.

This discussion of global security policy completes our examination of alternative policy models. The next step is to identify criteria for selecting the most useful concrete policies.

[II.] EVALUATING POLICIES

Whenever policymakers choose one policy over another, they employ criteria for judging which will best serve their preferred values. Because these criteria are usually implicit rather than explicit, they often amount to little more than assumptions inherited from a bygone age. The result, then, is the unquestioned application of nineteenth-century balance of power dictates to the technological conditions of the twentieth century.

Just as generals prepare new strategies for fighting the most recent war rather than the next one, so diplomats also prepare to resolve conflict using policies and institutions appropriate for an age that has disappeared. That is why conservatives and liberals alike have been unable to shape an effective U.S. diplomacy in recent years. To illustrate, the use of implicit, unexamined criteria encourages policymakers to select new weapons based on the assumption—which was perhaps correct in an earlier age—that more arms equals more security. Today new arms usually stimulate counter armaments that pose new threats to oneself. Therefore, unless the criteria are changed for selecting policies, misguided choices will result.

By making criteria explicit, policymakers can more easily detect which criteria are outmoded and which policies advance preferred values like peace and security. Explicit criteria for assessing alternative directions—for example, to produce the M-X missile or to freeze the nuclear arms buildup—also help ferret out the policymaker who in fact seeks national power under the guise of seeking world peace. Until there is a clear, well-known basis for judging whether a given policy leads to war or peace, to global equity or to national hegemony, the public cannot easily identify those people who pursue hidden goals which violate the public interest. Only when the criteria for evaluating policies have been made explicit will policymakers be able to select appropriate means to achieve preferred ends, or the public be able to identify the officials who genuinely seek professed ends.

What criteria can we use? Diverse studies of the causes of war and the conditions of peace suggest at least four tests to determine whether policies increase the prospects for peace. Although these guidelines may be insufficiently precise to reflect short-term shifts in the likelihood of war, they do indicate the policy direction that will make the international system less conducive to war.

A synthesis of earlier research suggests that the prospects for peace and security increase as societies demilitarize, depolarize, denationalize, and transnationalize the global political system. These four qualities may be stated as *goals* for nation-states or as *processes* for domesticating the international system. Table [18.1] provides a summary of the trends which make the global system more peaceful or more war prone. Columns 1 and 3 describe national security policies that characterize the ends of the four continua. The central column contains illustrative questions for evaluating the degree to which policies encourage system change on the four continua.

The militarization-demilitarization continuum reflects the following components: (1) the ratios of national military expenditures to the quality of life within the society, to gross national product, and to world military expenditures; (2) the extent to which weapons are restricted to defensive purposes or instead threaten other countries; (3) the nature and scale of arms sales; (4) the number of overseas military installations; (5) the military assistance given to other governments; (6) the prominence of military influence in policymaking; and (7) overall reliance on military instruments in diplomacy. Data for one country should be compared over time and viewed, of course, in comparison both to the parallel activity of rival states and to worldwide totals.

The other criteria are perhaps more difficult to specify. Whereas demilitarization pertains to military affairs, depolarization applies to political and economic conditions, denationalization to social, cultural, and psychological factors, and transnationalization to institutions. More specifically, depolarization reflects political and economic efforts to soften rigid bloc and alliance boundaries, to diminish East-West and North-South conflicts, and to reduce antagonism between adversaries wherever possible. Hegemonic states, for example, should tailor their political and economic policies to achieve greater equity for all societies. Reciprocity in economic and political relations, regardless of a state's ideology, is the touchstone of depolarization.

To illustrate, an industrialized country like the United States would be advancing depolarization if it met the UN's goal of contributing .7 percent of its GNP annually to the economic development of poor nations, if it ratified the Law of the Sea Treaty obligating the world community to reserve some benefits of the common heritage for the world's poor, if it agreed with the Soviet Union to prohibit all nuclear weapons tests as most nonnuclear states have requested, and if it withdrew all its nuclear weapons to points at least 500 kilometers from the line separating NATO and Warsaw Pact nations in Central Europe.

TABLE [18.1]
The evaluation of policies to improve the capacity of the global system to maintain peace

HIGH LIKELIHOOD OF WAR 1	Illustrative Questions for Policy Evaluation 2	HIGH LIKELIHOOD OF PEACE 3
MILITARIZATION →	(military factors) To what extent does a policy reduce preparation for war, reduce the costliness of war if it occurs, increase the prospects for arms reductions, reduce militarily coercive relations between and within nation-states, and increase the capacity of the global system for war prevention?	← DEMILITARIZATION
Security policy pursues traditional diplomacy backed by increasing military power.		Security policy expands the use of non-military power while constricting the use of military power.
POLARIZATION →	(political, economic, and ecological factors) To what extent does policy serve broad global constituencies, rather than a limited national, regional or bloc constituency?	← DEPOLARIZATION
Despite rhetoric to the contrary, policy in practice aims to maintain or accumulate more national power and wealth in the short run.		Policy aims to fulfill all human needs in the short- and long-range future.
NATIONALIZATION →	(social and psychological factors)	← DENATIONALIZATION

To what extent does policy build human solidarity (identification across national boundaries)? Does policy encourage people to acknowledge their commonalities?

Security policy educates the public to be nationally exclusive in identity.

Security policy educates the public to feel a sense of species solidarity.

Policy emphasizes the need for alliance tightness or for unilateral acts of military self-help.

Policy emphasizes the need for multilateral cooperation with all nations to achieve mutual benefit.

Security policy assumes that the national government is all that matters in international relations. Individuals are treated as means to the ends of state power and wealth.

Security policy deliberately attempts to establish the individual as an important subject in international law; human rights covenants are ratified and enforced within a government's own society and elsewhere insofar as possible.

STATE CENTRICITY   TRANSNATIONALIZATION

(institutional factors)

To what extent does policy develop more effective (representative, equitable, functionally useful, non-territorial) world organizations?

Intergovernmental organizations without national veto power and transnational institutions are feared, shunned, or nominally accepted, but without enthusiasm for institutional innovation to encourage the four processes associated here with peace.

Participation in intergovernmental and transnational organizations aims to increase their capacity to help demilitarize, depolarize, denationalize, and and transnationalize world society.

Private organizations and religious groups are encouraged to leave security policy to the government.

Private organizations, religious groups, and individuals participate in efforts to make peace through transnational linkages. Individuals relate directly to people of other countries without channeling contacts always through their national capital.

Denationalization extends the lines of personal and group identity beyond the nation. It seeks to nurture universal respect for human dignity and to promote a political culture of human solidarity. It actively develops political and moral support for the measures required to make progress in demilitarization, depolarization, and transnationalization. A society contributes to denationalization if it actively educates its population about the need for reducing the role of military influence in domestic and international life and for building representative institutions for management of international conflicts. This education should occur through its public schools, in statements by public officials, in its legislative programs and use of public revenues, and in its diplomacy.

Because nationalism contributes to unfair discrimination against other groups, similar to that which accompanies racism, denationalization is analogous to anti-racist education and action. It cleanses nationalism of its most harmful qualities. One test of denationalization is the extent to which a government avoids stirring up chauvinism through frequent military threats or shows of force and resists the temptation to mislead the public through slanted use of classified information and propaganda based on national stereotyping. Applying universal human rights standards as opposed to national security considerations to determine the eligibility of other governments for development aid is another example of denationalization, as is the building of public support for the submission of international disputes to impartial international judicial settlement.

Transnationalization describes the process by which individuals, private organizations, and governments institutionalize the means for peaceful resolution of conflict and a dependable protection of security. The growth of equitable organizations that transcend national boundaries can both shape the content and strengthen the obligatory quality of a new code of international conduct. Without the growth of private and public transnational organizations to help bridle national excesses, state behavior would too easily relapse into the pursuit of national vested interests at excessive cost to the global commonweal.

Measures might include efforts to strengthen multilateral regimes, rather than to rely on bilateral diplomacy, for peacekeeping, for monitoring arms control agreements, for curtailing intervention in nonaligned states, for promoting economic development, and for settling disputes. A country contributes to transnationalization if it actively seeks to create formal organizations or informal arrangements for the preceding activities, if it accepts without reservation the compulsory jurisdiction of world and regional courts, and if it generally fulfills its duties as a good global citizen in existing international organizations like the United Nations.

Each of these four interrelated processes of moving toward global security suggests three foci for examining any country's foreign policy options: (1) a national government's relationship to its major rival(s); (2) a national governments's relationships to other states of substantially different power and position in the global hierarchy; and (3) a national government's relationship with its own people. For example, steps toward demilitarization include these dimensions: reducing the likelihood of war between rivals, reducing the residue of imperialism, and reducing military influence or repression within societies. For NATO and Warsaw Pact countries, these three areas correspond respectively to the tensions between East and West, between North and South, and between rulers and ruled. For states not part of the conflicts between NATO and Warsaw Pact nations, the first area of conflict might be with a regional rival (e.g., Iran and Iraq). These foci also suggest three points of entry into the process of change.

The prospects for peace improve to the extent that governments pursue the policies described in column 3. On the other hand, some or all of the following conditions, reflecting column 1 of the four continua, usually precede war: (1) arms buildups and heavy military influence in decision-making; (2) intense international polarization, inflexible alliance structures, and economic exploitation; (3) exclusive national identification (often buttressed with ideological rigidity and laced with racial overtones) achieved at the expense of external scapegoats; and (4) uninfluential or unfair transnational interactions.

During periods of war, policies most fully incorporate the attributes of column 1. How can the conditions of war in column 1 sometimes produce a period of peace which often reigns after a war ends? As illustrated in World War II, the chain of social forces suddenly snaps at the conclusion of wars, with one side forced to capitulate to the other. Surrender, in which one side's military forces are immobilized and totally exposed to the demands of the other, is a radical act of demilitarization. So profoundly does demilitarization contribute to peace that even coerced demilitarization produces peace if it is accompanied by depolarization between former belligerents.

In such instances, after surrender the previous degree of polarization falls sharply, alliance patterns once again become flexible, prejudicial national stereotyping tapers off, and more positive forms of transnational collaboration flourish. Military capitulation opens the way for the victorious power to act magnanimously, as the United States did in helping to reconstruct Germany and Japan after 1945. The immediate postwar years are usually the most fertile period of each long cycle in international politics. The demilitarization of the capitulating government does more to bring future peace than does the military prowess of any victor, although the victor's nonmilitary diplomacy following the war plays a decisive role. In sum, demilitarization and the attendant qualities noted in column 3 produce peace; peace does not grow out of the conditions of war itself.

Lasting peace did not follow World War I because the conditions of column 3 were never very fully developed. There was no period of magnanimity. Depolarization never occurred. In a sense, World War II was a continuation of World War I. The period following the Second World War held more promise, especially because of transformed roles for Germany and Japan, but opportunities for institutionalizing a less militarized system of international relations were not imaginatively seized. Instead, a nineteenth-century diplomatic orientation stimulated the Cold War between the United States and the Soviet Union.

We can now apply the four criteria to the policies previously discussed and listed here in Table [18.2]. These criteria call sharply into question the utility of present U.S. and Soviet policies, for they are the antithesis of *demilitarization*. The development of more advanced intercontinental and intermediate-range ballistic missiles, more accurate guidance systems, new cruise missiles, larger nuclear submarines, new strategic bombers, satellite targeting systems and anti-satellite warfare

TABLE [18.2]
Approaches to security policy

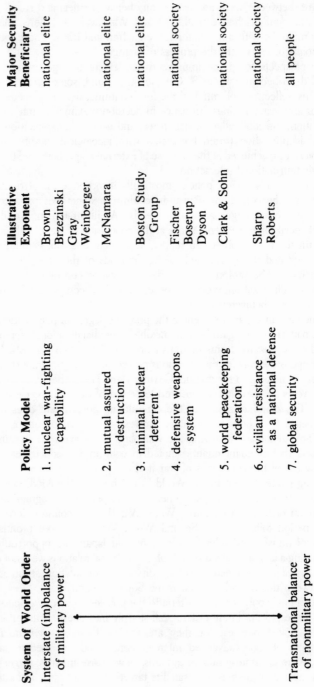

System of World Order	Policy Model	Illustrative Exponent	Major Security Beneficiary
Interstate (im)balance of military power	1. nuclear war-fighting capability	Brown Brzezinski Gray Weinberger	national elite
	2. mutual assured destruction	McNamara	national elite
	3. minimal nuclear deterrent	Boston Study Group	national elite
	4. defensive weapons system	Fischer Boserup Dyson	national society
	5. world peacekeeping federation	Clark & Sohn	national society
	6. civilian resistance as a national defense	Sharp Roberts	national society
Transnational balance of nonmilitary power	7. global security		all people

capability, thousands of additional warheads, more battleships and aircraft carriers—all stimulate reciprocal action by a rival nation. New deployments also whet the military appetites of less militarized, smaller states and encourage them to conclude that a key to being taken more seriously in the diplomatic world is to possess additional weapons, perhaps including nuclear arms. Stimulated by the example of the world's leading military powers, a majority of the world's societies now face increasing military influence in their political processes.

Policies at the top of Table [18.2], especially those relying on nuclear weapons, *polarize* world affairs to an unprecedented extreme. They violate the common interests of a global constituency. The priorities of military competition exacerbate poverty and economic uncertainty. They lead one society openly to prepare to destroy the people of another for the misdeeds of their government over which they frequently have little direct control. As the possibility of war perseveres and resources become more scarce, the militarily strong will increasingly compete for allies and for political influence in the governments of nonaligned countries, intending to gain access to bases and resources and to deny them to their military rivals. No land stands outside superpower rivalry. Global polarization inflames regional sub-polarizations. Together, they make nonviolent resolution of conflict far more difficult.

The policies at the top of Table [18.2] also inhibit the *denationalization* of human affairs and discourage the growth of human solidarity across national boundaries. Indeed national jingoism, not a sense of worldmindedness, helps raise the massive taxes required to pay the enormous costs of a nuclear war-fighting capability. Democratic societies bent on high military expenditures and the projection of power globally *need* a national enemy to help divert money from social programs to military production. Wasting scarce resources hurts almost everyone globally, but the burden falls most heavily on the poor. To justify inequity, a rich nation will frequently discriminate unfairly against other nationalities through its trade, aid, and immigration policies. In addition, expensive preparation for war usually deepens potential class conflicts. It benefits the governing elite, their supporters, and those connected with military production, while the rest of the society pays war taxes and reluctantly raises conscripts. Leaders often stimulate nationalistic fervor to turn attention away from government's failures. In general, advocates of nuclear deterrence implicitly deny respect for human life, especially for people of other nationalities, and for nature. The threat to use nuclear weapons, which is essential to maintaining the deterrent's credibility, is in fact a threat to commit genocide and crimes against other nations.

Finally, policies 1 and 2 impede the effort to develop more effective *transnational* institutions. Superpower nuclear rivalry and the subordination of pressing human needs to the pursuit of geopolitical advantage stifle the growth of equitable and humane world organizations. Even the arms control efforts of the superpowers seldom encourage the development of international organizations for peacekeeping. Rather than working seriously in a multilateral framework, Moscow and Washington prefer bilateral negotiations in order to minimize the influence of views from less militarized societies; the superpowers oppose international monitoring and verification of existing bilateral arms agreements; and they prefer accords, if at all, that

TABLE [18.3]
The contribution of various policies to peace and security: a tentative estimate

Policy Model	Demilitarization	Depolarization	Denationalization	Transnationalization	Total
		(5 point scale of approximation)			
1. war-fighting capability	0	0	0	0	0
2. mutual assured destruction	1	1	0	0	2
3. minimal deterrent	2	2	0	1	5
4. defensive-weapons system	3	4	2	2	11
5. peacekeeping federation	4	4	4	4	16
6. civilian resistance	5	4	3	4	16
7. global security	5	5	5	5	20

slow development of new weapons in other, uncontrolled areas. This maintains their military superiority over weaker countries.

The policies in Table [18.2] are ranked according to how much they demilitarize, depolarize, denationalize, and transnationalize the global political system. Table 18.3 contains the basis for the rankings. Although crude, such explicit approximations are preferable to hidden assumptions without any clear calculus at all. Future research certainly can improve the quality of the estimates. At the least, these rankings can help to focus debate on whether a nuclear war-fighting capability, for example, in any way helps to demilitarize or depolarize international relations.

Applying the criteria of demilitarization, depolarization, denationalization, and transnationalization to the policies that dominate the agendas in Washington and Moscow forces one to reach a painful conclusion: current U.S. policy leads toward war. By pursuing its present course the United States marches toward national suicide, and perhaps toward the death of civilization. U.S. policy undermines, rather than increases, the capacity of the global system to prevent violence. Similar criticisms could be made of the Soviet Union, but neither side's current failures justify the other's reckless military deployments.

Existing policies at the top of Tables [18.2] and [18.3] may seem sensible for those operating under the assumed conditions of the nineteenth-century balance of military power. But those conditions no longer exist. And the policies which have been derived from them now contribute more to the causes of war than they do to the conditions of peace. Nuclear weapons may make political leaders somewhat more cautious, but they do not increase the capacity of an antiquated international system to provide security or abolish war. Indeed, they further strain an international structure already extended far beyond the limits of reliability.

Certainly it would be simplistic to think that the United States might quickly jump from a nuclear war-fighting strategy to the abolition of war or even to a strictly defensive posture based on conventional weapons. Yet it is not unreasonable to think that the United States should now commit itself to steps in that direction. Policy changes obviously need to be planned carefully, with ample safeguards to avoid diminution of security at any point along the way. Yet the most frightening prospect is not the risks involved with change. It is the absence of any effort to devise policies that at the very least would move us away from a war-fighting capability and toward a minimum deterrent, to say nothing of efforts to establish a warless world.

Our remaining task is to identify several achievable steps in that direction.

[*   *   *]

19. Building a Permanent and Globalist Peace Movement

Nigel Young

[*   *   *]

In the contemporary peace movements of Europe, East and West, and of Canada, the United States, Australia, Japan, India and beyond, many old problems have survived along with the sectarian traditions which have helped sustain divisions and ideological obstacles to building a permanent movement for peace and human survival. In particular, the tension between the broad social programme of a New Left or the Greens, and the single issue politics (or single *weapon* politics) of an "MX", "BI", cruise, or neutron or Trident campaign is growing. The clash between blind activism and pure theory, between the aligned and the non-aligned, the programmatic and the single issue, the parliamentarist and extra-parliamentarist, especially over issues of alliances, alignment and direct action may yet again tear the peace movement apart.

If one was to be pessimistic, one could argue from this that in peace politics, people have learnt (and can learn) little from the past, that there is no sense of history. For once again we see a broad social movement with multiple issues but too narrow a social base, lacking strategy and direction, obsessed with negative propaganda and conspiratorial threats of war. If there are major setbacks, fatigue and feelings of powerlessness, defeat and despair will predominate in the coming years.

On the other hand, there are dimensions of the movement which are profoundly empowering; there are signs that the very character of the new peace movement makes it different from the past, that its transnational linkages are more real; that its non-alignment is more firmly understood and articulated; that its grass roots are more firmly planted. In 1982, many abandoned, after SSD II, their last illusions about interstate charades of disarmament dialogues. Its communal dimensions and transnational linkages make the movement ready for a systematic programme of alternative defence rooted in localized civilian resistance. Civil disobedience is now accepted by much of the peace movement and can be linked to the non-co-operation at the heart of the war resistance tradition and Gandhian ideas. Moreover, since the 1960s, the acceptance of a just social programme (for example, socially useful production, not an arms export economy) has become more widespread and is now part of the larger programme (for example, of the Greens and of the New Left). In other words, the dominant tendency is beyond both the single issue and the national framework, beyond state and parties, beyond old alignments and sectarian traditions, whilst building an autonomous and new tradition and a model of action that draws from all of them.

Attempts to be realistic about the discontinuous and fragmented character of the historic peace movements need not lead to an entirely pessimistic prognosis in the present. If one is to deny the very possibility of success of such human endeavor, further study or action might have little justification. But because as a species we cannot afford the luxury of a peoples' peace initiative which ebbs again in the coming years, it is essential that the peace movement uses its collective intellect to forge an analysis of present strengths and past weaknesses that can enlighten strategic and programmatic debates and help de-emphasize certain actions, policies and linkages as against others.

This does *not* mean evolving some monolithic, unitary or reductionist strategy or ideology, as sectarians would hold—the peace movement is as plural as it is international. Pluralism is a source of unity as well as fragmentation: the very diversity of the peace movement described here may be an expression of an inner strength, of a containment of potentially open dialectic, not the clash of blinkered orthodoxies, each contemptuous or dismissive of the historical role and contributions of the next. Within the new peace movement, there is growing understanding of both national and cultural peculiarities and transnational solidarity and symmetry; of the potential complementarity of local and global, of a mass autonomous movement *and* focused pressure within specific structures and institutions; the single issue campaign and the programmatic long-term direction. Peace, women, environment, participation, economic well-being, the secular and the spiritual—the synthesis in peoples' movements is from the communal base.

Research on the history and social character of war resistance reveals that ordinary people are able to oppose and resist war, militarism and war mobilization on a sustained basis most typically when they have both a strong local communal base of organization *and* an identity, as well as certain social factors or orientations (ideology, religion, ethnic linkage) which *transcend* national boundaries and the sovereign edicts of the state.

Within the peace movements themselves, as this paper has tried to illustrate, such vision and strategy linking localism and globalism, cosmopolitanism and communalism, has sometimes descended into a narrow parochialism or become a form of rootlessness. But in groups such as the Quakers (or later, War Resisters' International), an idea of linking the local and the global has often given vision and practical support to peace groups over a period of more than three centuries.

Certain factors (the opposite of "transnational and communal" ones), have been specifically noted in the foregoing analysis as contributing to the failure of the peace movements. The following two sets of ideal type forces are by no means exhaustive but constitute the main dimensions.

1. State centricism (chauvinistic nationalism, ethnocentricism).
2. Limited pressure-group concepts of politics (reformist, secular).
3. Alignment (to parties, states, or state centred ideologies or blocs) for example, co-optation by the social democratic left.
4. Reactive and short-term character (lack of social programme resulting in despair).
5. Lack of social alternatives (no strategy for political change); disempowerment.
6. Gap between (intellectual/political) leadership and grass roots base (élitism); this may be a generation gap.
7. Lack of strong communal base (amorphous superficial coalition character).

The above are the negative features of the peace movement. But as the new peace movement, or parts of it, especially the new women's peace movement, illustrate, these are exactly the problems that are now met by giving greater prominence to such alternative mediums as the following:

1. Localism and communalism (networks of human relationships).
2. Transnationalism/globalism, networking, linkages (peace as a species issue).
3. Autonomism and spontaneity (initiative from below).
4. Direct action and affinity groups (non-violence).
5. Unilateral initiatives (action first).
6. Activation of affinities (bonding across borders).
7. Non-alignment (the peace movement as an independent force).

Although they clearly overlap significantly in terms of empowerment and species identity, these seven elements expressed in diverse activities such as international marches and camps, twinning and nuclear free zones, indicate that a growing disempowerment has taken place and the evolution of violent structures come about. For feminists this may be explicitly linked to seeing the origins of war and the monopoly of violence particularly in patriarchal conquests. It also suggests a potential understanding of the history of resistance to that disempowering process; both old peace groups and the new constituencies are drawn together by affinity and potential, by the growth of a sense of history in the long human struggle for peace, in developing a synthesis that is analysed and understood in a creative way.

In the historic clash between state and civil society, it was those entities under attack such as smaller communities, the churches, smaller political units, intellectual subcultures and autonomous cultural and economic entities, which became the vessels of anti-militarist activity and perspective. These are now regaining their salience as a base for a popular world view. Indeed they are much more than ideas. They have been actualized in specific public events and peoples' movements which are no longer obsessed with altered national policies alone, but grasp the necessity of activating the affinities across military borders, not least the East/West divide: mobilizing groups on the basis of such personal exchange and grass root reciprocity; linkages of activists as well as leaders: twinning communities, municipalities and nuclear free zones; and diplomacy between cities.

The East European strategy, for all its setbacks, is not by any means a lost cause. The swords and ploughshares groups, the trust groups and groups for dialogue, the conscientious objectors, women's groups (sisters across the iron curtain), the youth culture, and the entrenched churches remain a base for future growth. Despite the repression of the Moscow Trust Group, the human rights issue has created space and the end of European division is crucial in relation to the East European state. The ecologically oriented groups can also organize in a way that is less obviously a threat than military issues. All these are platforms for further take-off. There are limits to the co-optation of the peace issue by the state.

This can be seen as part of a globalization of what is a species problem; of breaking with both state-centric and inter-state centred approaches to disarmament. It offers not symmetrical patterned interactions which move up and down the political pyramids of state power, but a slow draining away of legitimacy and attention from state-centred solutions and national frames of reference. Of course, it does not exclude unilateral, national or governmental reciprocity, but "unilateralism" need not be a monopoly of national governments. The new peace movements have shown that from the smallest community to multi-nation, regional zones and proposals, unilateralism as a popular initiative gives a certain power that many peace movements have lacked in the past. It does not forgo pressure on governments, but puts pressure on them from the outside, from the portents of a peace politics that begins to move outside the state system—the dominant features of legitimation—like some radical movements of the past by building non-governmental, cross frontier linkages and strategies.

Such a reality, based on the "true worlds" disguised by 400 or more years of territorial state-growth, offers new insights both to activists and researchers and a fruitful interchange of both. They can empower and give continuity to a sequence of peace movements which has a series of heroic experiences as well as a history of tragic defeats. However inchoate, the present movement holds within it the potential for such a strategy which could bring both continuity, growth and effectiveness.

This survey has indicated how more and more peace traditions have accumulated over the past 200 years—in that sense there has been continual growth. But it has also shown that the mass support of organized public opinion has regularly and dramatically declined: in most countries in the periods after mobilization for war, such as 1914 and 1940. The relation between this public involvement and the small peace groups or sects is itself a problematic one, but in general one can state that as a ratio of population there has been no clear quantitative growth in peace movements since the late nineteenth century. In addition, there is, in any case, no clear correlation between the numbers mobilized, and impact on society or the state.

Clearly the multiple stranded peace traditions described here have so far patently failed to do more than marginally affect the arms spiral. If they follow the patterns of the past, they are likely to fail again. State policies and public attitudes have been significantly shifted on such issues as certain wars (for example, Vietnam) and types of weapons (for example, nuclear), or specific actions (bomb-testing) or conscription. But no twentieth century state of any size has shown any serious inclination to substantially demilitarize itself, and it is clear that increased pressure will have to be largely external to the state apparatus and the system of states.

The peace movement has been divided over aims, methods, analysis and strategy, but has occasionally been forced into a strong coalition by particularly atrocious wars (such as Vietnam) or weapons (nuclear). But its failure has been the central one of failing to achieve a visionary synthesis, a new model and strategy that is appropriate to a changing global society. It has not been able to harness effectively even those emerging social tendencies such as communal and transcendental growth which favour it.

The threat of the breakdown of nuclear deterrence into a global nuclear war gives humanity one last chance to sustain a movement for our global species survival that will emphasize those aspects of society which can save us: the ability to live co-operatively in relatively small human societies; our ability to diffuse and limit political power and control the use of violence; and our ability to act as species-beings rather than territorial or national animals. The peace movement contains within its present character these elements and the potential for such a "permanent and global peace movement". The question remains whether it has the time, the will, the imagination to realize that potential.

The United Nations
and the World Economy

INTRODUCTION

Over the past fifteen years, the multiple crises of a spiraling arms race, resource scarcity, massive poverty, social and political oppression, and environmental deterioration have testified to the increasing importance of and interdependence among world order values. "Thirty years after the Charter was signed at San Francisco," the 1975 Report of Experts entitled "A New United Nations Structure for Global Economic Co-operation" observed, "the ultimate relationship between peace and security issues and economic and social issues is clearer than ever." Yet, it was the escalating Third World debt crisis in 1987–1988 that seemed to become the visible tip of the iceberg, allowing almost everyone to see the advanced system crisis. The global war system and the global poverty system have become two sides of the same system pathology. In 1987, the total outstanding external debt of the Third World exceeded $1,000 billion for the first time, followed closely by the annual world military expenditures of $930 billion.

Of course, Third World debt has troubled policymakers and policy-advisors for years, but now we see more clearly its spreading impact on war and peace, social and political justice, and the environment. In 1987, an international independent panel—the World Commission on Environment and Development—headed by Norway's Prime Minister Gro Harlem Brundtland, released a report establishing the linkages among the environment, development, and conflict. However, the commission went beyond a linkage analysis by accusing the IMF and the World Bank of treating Third World countries harshly and of damaging their natural environments. Many developing countries are pursuing environmentally destructive policies because they are being forced to increase their export earnings in order to repay foreign debts. The multilateral lending agencies and their main stockholders (Western governments) should do more to safeguard the Third World's environment by lightening its debt burden.

In 1988, the Brundtland Commission report was followed by Pope John Paul II's encyclical letter, "The Social Concerns of the Church," the harshest attack he has ever made on the superpowers, accusing them of playing out their imperialistic rivalry in the Third World and thus reducing developing countries to "parts of a machine, cogs on a gigantic wheel." The division of the world into two rival ideological blocs, the encyclical says, "is a direct obstacle to the real transformation of the conditions of underdevelopment," and "each of the two blocs harbors in its own way a tendency toward imperialism."

In late 1988, the World Bank and UNICEF joined the global chorus by releasing their most pessimistic reports ever on the state of social and economic conditions in the Third World. Despite crushing debt loads and deteriorating living standards, according to the World Bank report, interest payments forced a net outflow of $43 billion from debtor countries in 1988 alone. The seventeen highly indebted developing countries gave rich countries and multinational lending institutions $31.1 billion more than they received, triple the amount in 1983, a phenomenon characterized by the Council on Foreign Relations as "a massive, perverse redistribution of income" from the poor to the rich. When the global debt crisis erupted in 1982, developing countries were taking in $18.2 billion more than they paid. Thanks to the debt rescheduling strategy, interest payments today are 33 percent higher than they were in 1982, and the outstanding Third World debt has doubled in that same time period to $1.32 trillion.

Add to the World Bank report the latest UNICEF annual report showing where the greatest impact has really been felt—among the children of the world's poor. Because of this exploding debt bomb, governments in Asia, Africa, and Latin America are reducing spending on services in health, education, and social welfare programs, most needed by the poor, in order to pay off foreign debts. Half a million children died in 1987 because of this sliding back into severe poverty after forty years of progress. While it is too simplistic to blame the International Monetary Fund (IMF) or any other lending institution for this regression in social conditions, the failure of these institutions to alleviate the debt crisis at this time of genuine urgency is a notable failure of the international financial system.

The Latin American debt crisis represents a clear and continuing threat to the continent's new democracies. "As governments lose credibility and authority," according to the report issued in January 1989 by the Inter-American Dialogue, a group of experts from the United States, Canada, Latin America, and the Caribbean, "the appeal of extremist solutions is rising and it becomes harder to institute the economic measures needed for recovery and growth. Latin America may be condemned to a long period of economic hardship and political turbulence, which may force civilian authorities to yield to military rule in some places."

Ironically, the debt crisis may also serve as a teacher of peace learning. As noted in Section 4, peace was breaking out all over the world in 1988, stretching the UN's financial and peacekeeping capabilities to the breaking point. Combat fatigue and economic overextension have become two ways of describing the outbreak of peace-begging in regional hot spots of the world. War may be cheap and easy to initiate, but it is too expensive to sustain for long, much less to win in our times. Peace learning of this kind seemed to spread like a new epidemic in 1988. This latest round of the global debt crisis seems finally to be driving home the linkages among world order values.

The postwar world economic order, resting on the tripod of the World Bank, the IMF, and the General Agreement on Tariffs and Trade (GATT), was designed mainly to deal with economic problems facing Western capitalist countries. In its first two-and-a-half decades, this capitalist world system served the rich and powerful nations well, while providing only first-aid measures for the Third World. The surge of Third World membership in the United Nations in the 1960s began to change the UN agenda and to reshape its institutional landscape in the social and economic fields. Originally, the Economic and Social Council (ECOSOC) was envisioned as the principal organ that would be responsible for generating and coordinating programs in this area. The specialized agencies, though autonomous and only loosely connected to ECOSOC, would in reality carry out many of the specific projects in the field in the implementation of the UN development strategy. By the end of the first development decade (the 1960s), however, the UN development system, according to the United Nations Development Programme (UNDP)-sponsored Jackson report, had "become the equivalent of principalities, free from any centralized control." The report then noted:

This "Machine" now has a marked identity of its own and its power is so great that the question must be asked "Who controls this 'Machine'?" So far, the evidence suggests that governments do not, and also that the machine is incapable of intelligently controlling itself. This is not because it lacks intelligent and capable officials, but because it is so organized that managerial direction is impossible. In other words, the machine as a whole has become unmanageable in the strictest sense of the word. As a result, it is becoming slower and more unwieldy, like some prehistoric monster.

In the 1970s, special programs and their institutional offspring multiplied. When member states agree that some action on a new global issue is necessary, the recent pattern of response has been to hold an international conference on the subject. Each of these UN-sponsored global conferences has usually, in turn, generated some new institutional arrangement, resulting in a multiplication and fragmentation of new programs within the UN system and national governments. In the process, the United Nations has increasingly made economic and social development the primary focus of its work. It has also become mainly an economic and social organization. At least 80 percent of the total resources of the UN system is devoted to the economic and social fields.

Reaching a climax of influence in the aftermath of the successful OPEC oil embargo in 1973, the Group of 77, which operates as the Third World caucus within the UN, had its origin in the first meeting of the United Nations Conference on Trade and Development (UNCTAD) in 1964, and today consists of 126 developing countries, in 1974 convened the Sixth Special Session of the UN General Assembly on Raw Materials and Development. This dramatic session ended with a call for the establishment of a new international economic order (NIEO). In retrospect, NIEO had a rather short life cycle of less than a decade, evolving from the Third World's revolutionary call for transforming the rules of world finance and trade toward a new and more equitable international economic order, to stiff opposition from the North, to momentary reconciliation, to stalemate, and to final neglect and decay. Reacting to the collapse of the Eleventh Special Session of the UN General Assembly, convened in September 1980 to rejuvenate global negotiations for NIEO, Mahbub ul Haq characterized NIEO politics as "this strange environment of formal motions without actual movement."

Although the UN consumed an enormous amount of resources for over a decade, virtually none of NIEO's package was negotiated to fruition. Despite the plethora of global pseudobargainings and hundreds of hortatory resolutions, declarations, and programs of action, the grip of global poverty upon the human condition grows unchecked, and the gaps between the developed and developing countries, with the exception of the four East Asian newly industrialized countries (NICs)—South Korea, Taiwan, Hong Kong, and Singapore—continue to widen. A list of reasons for the demise of NIEO-inspired North-South dialogue is almost as long as that of Third World claims and demands incorporation in the NIEO package. The UN proper has had nothing to do with the so-called "economic miracles" of the East Asian NICs—three of them are not even members of the United Nations.

While the member states were mired in NIEO politics of endless resolution-making, the same governments during the largely overlapping period (1973–1982) were involved in global negotiations, producing an impressive global charter for the oceans—the United Nations Convention on the Law of the Sea (UNCLOS-III). Given the multitude of competing principles and the diversity of conflicting interests to reconcile, this is an accomplishment of a high order. Still, this end product largely embodied the triumph of dominant (coastal) statist interests. Although UNCLOS-III was launched in response to normative pressures to manage the global commons on the basis of shared community interests, the common-heritage-of-mankind concept has been squeezed from all sides by the two hundred-mile exclusive economic zones, covering one-third of the oceans' waters and bed and preempting over 90 percent of their fish and oil. What little area was left under the treaty for the International Seabed Authority under global auspices has been attacked as a great rip-off of the rich nations by the poor, and corporations call it a giveaway. The prospects for a global deep seabed regime coming into operation soon are bleak, given the continued opposition of the United States (joined by the United Kingdom and West Germany) to the Convention; the gap between signatures (159) and ratifications (only 36 of the 60 required for entry into force of the Convention as of late 1988); the current depressed prices for copper, nickel, cobalt, and manganese; and unsettled legal and financial issues. The United Nations has become, it seems, an arena for rectifying certain distortions within the state system and for reconciling conflicting statist interests, but certainly not of transcending them.

The importance of transnational corporations (TNCs) in the globalization of national economies is underscored by the fact that the total value of foreign direct investment in 1985 was some $650 billion, accounted for by approximately 20,000 TNCs with more than 100,000 affiliates throughout the world. In 1974 the forty-eight-member Commission on Transnational Corporations was established as an intergovernmental subsidiary body of ECOSOC. Its main functions are to discuss and keep under review all issues related to TNCs, to draft a UN Code of Conduct on Transnational Corporations, and to advise ECOSOC on all matters relating to TNCs. From the beginning, the formulation of a Code of Conduct embodying the most comprehensive provisions governing various aspects of the relationship between host countries and TNCs with the status and authority of a definitive international legal instrument has been the commission's highest priority. After more than a decade of negotiations, an intergovernmental working group has finally succeeded in producing a draft Code of Conduct in which about 80 percent of the provisions were agreed upon by the members of that group. However, there is as yet no consensus on some key provisions relating to the treatment of TNCs, such as the standards applicable to nationalization, the entitlement of TNCs to "national treatment," and the precise formulation of the applicability of international law to foreign direct investment.

We begin this section with the text of the NIEO Declaration, adopted by consensus as General Assembly Resolution 3201 (S-VI) on May 1, 1974, at the Sixth Special Session of the General Assembly on Raw Materials and Development. As a collective consensual document, the Declaration defies easy generalization. Nonetheless, it does express all the main Third World grievances and demands as a point of departure for the establishment of a new international economic order. It also stands as a strange but perhaps unavoidable mixture of the Third World's *dependencia* theory and the First World's theory of international liberalism, invoking at one and the same time statist, international, and global principles (e.g., sovereignty, interdependence, and common global interest). The Declaration conceptualizes a new international economic order exclusively in terms of interstate redistributive justice by paying a high world order price. That price involves the subordination of domestic reforms for human justice to the primacy of state-to-state arrangements. Lack of progress on international reform serves as an alibi for delaying domestic reforms for human justice. In purely normative terms, then, the Declaration leaves the political and moral problem of disjuncture between interstate and human justice unresolved.

In our second selection in this section, Johan Galtung presents a comparative and structural analysis of NIEO. Galtung sees NIEO as the Third World's attempt to bring about certain specific changes in the world structure. Galtung conceptualizes the NIEO and the basic needs (BN) approaches as two "grand designs" in contemporary development theory and practice as a way of exploring the extent to which the two approaches are mutually compatible, contradictory, or conflicting in terms of the issues and the parties involved. As an intergovernmental organization, the UN is prone to inter- rather than intranational transformation. Likewise, most Third World elites favor a "shallow" interpretation of NIEO, just as the First World elites generally favor a shallow BN interpretation. Galtung advocates the reorientation of the debate by insisting upon symmetry. Both North and South "must see the broad interpretations of NIEO and of BN as applicable to *all parts of the world*" (emphasis in original). According to Galtung, one strategy that may help transcend the present contradiction between the two grand designs is that of self-reliance. Yet, we face a paradox in the global political economy of the 1980s. The export-oriented development strategy does not work for most Third World countries, but the autocentric self-reliant development strategy has not worked any better.

Cheryl Payer, in the section's third selection, offers a trenchant analysis of the impact of the Third World debt crisis in reshaping the roles of the IMF and the World Bank. The IMF is dead, she pronounces, and the World Bank has come to fill the void by moving in the direction of more program lending, more policy conditionality, and more emphasis on encouraging private investors. Yet, Payer is far from sanguine about the World Bank's new role as the central manager of the debt crisis. Though written in 1986, her generally skeptical assessment of the management of the debt crisis has been amply borne out by the developments of the past four years. The main U.S. initiative, known as the Baker Plan, never got off first base. By July 1988, eight borrowers were more than six months overdue on loans to the World Bank, compared with none in 1984. The World Bank's leverage as the global credit rating agency no longer works as effectively as it used to, as more and more Third World countries find less and less incentive in keeping up payments to the bank because what they owe on interest and principal from earlier loans exceeds what they can expect to receive in new loan disbursements. Faced with rising delinquencies on its loans for the first time in its history, the World Bank had to raise provisions for loan losses to $500 million in mid-1988, while offering the same tired and overgeneralized advice of becoming an NIC as the only way for the indebted Third World countries to escape from their debt traps.

The next selection brings our attention to the establishment of the South Commission in 1987—an important event completely ignored in the U.S. press— and its purpose, orientation, and terms of reference. The commission is an independent organ whose members are drawn exclusively from the South, acting in their individual capacities to bring their individual and collective knowledge and experience to bear on issues of "sustainable, people-centered, self-reliant development." In a sense, the commission is a belated response to disappointments with UNCTAD and NIEO. Unlike NIEO, the South Commission stresses "the need for purposeful domestic reform" as an integral component in its task of devising "a new global system of collective economic security." The commission sees its role as a catalyst for a new process of consciousness-raising and mass mobilization for a more people-oriented development strategy for the South. As an independent body, the commission may well be able to produce a more coherent set of alternative development policies and strategies. Yet, one doubts whether an entity without formal status can have any real impact upon the policies of governments and upon international organizations in the area of development.

In the section's last selection, Chadwick F. Alger proceeds from the premise that all proposals for change in the present international economic order require more creative thinking about the role of people in the future global order. Alger argues that statism distorts our perception of the changing global order and imposes limits on the possible. World order proposals tend either to move top-down based on expanded global institutions or to rest on greater cooperation among nation-states. Neither is concerned with how subnational communities would be linked to proposed future world orders. Alger's call for "thinking globally but acting locally" leads to a greater emphasis on fulfilling people's needs and self-reliance. In this way, we can really move from here to there, thinking of "local and regional communities as the constituent entities of humankind" and transforming the present international order into "a system of self-reliant communities linked together in the service of the needs of the inhabitants of these communities." Alger challenges us to think about future world order in a manner that is innovative for international relations—as if people's needs and interests really mattered.

Throughout the selections above, a series of questions is raised, all relating to the general issues of what the UN has contributed to economic well-being and what more is necessary to achieve a satisfactory level of this world order value. Among the specific questions raised are: What are valid criteria for judging UN performance in this domain? What strategy should Third World countries pursue in order to ensure both national economic improvements and distribution of benefits more equitably to their people? How can the trade relations be restructured to facilitate a more just and equitable international trade order? What role can the UN play in ensuring both sufficient flows of resources from the rich to the poor and the effective use of funds within the Third World?

20. The Declaration on the Establishment of a New International Economic Order

The General Assembly

Adopts the following Declaration:

DECLARATION ON THE ESTABLISHMENT OF A NEW INTERNATIONAL ECONOMIC ORDER

We, the Members of the United Nations,

Having convened a special session of the General Assembly to study for the first time the problems of raw materials and development devoted to the consideration of the most important economic problems facing the world community,

Bearing in mind the spirit, purposes and principles of the Charter of the United Nations to promote the economic advancement and social progress of all peoples,

Solemnly proclaim our united determination to work urgently for THE ESTABLISHMENT OF A NEW INTERNATIONAL ECONOMIC ORDER based on equity, sovereign equality, interdependence, common interest and co-operation among all States, irrespective of their economic and social systems which shall correct inequalities and redress existing injustices, make it possible to eliminate the widening gap between the developed and the developing countries and ensure steadily accelerating economic and social development and peace and justice for present and future generations, and, to that end, declare:

1. The greatest and most significant achievement during the last decades has been the independence from colonial and alien domination of a large number of peoples and nations which has enabled them to become members of the community of free peoples. Technological progress has also been made in all spheres of economic activities in the last three decades, thus providing a solid potential for improving the well-being of all peoples. However, the remaining vestiges of alien and colonial domination, foreign occupation, racial discrimination, *apartheid* and neo-colonialism in all its forms continue to be among the greatest obstacles to the full emancipation and progress of the developing countries and all the peoples involved. The benefits of technological progress are not shared equitably by all members of the international community. The developing countries, which constitute 70 per cent of the world's population, account for only 30 per cent of the world's income. It has proved impossible to achieve an even and balanced development of the international community under the existing international economic order. The gap between the developed and the developing countries continues to widen in a system which was established at a time when most of the developing countries did not even exist as independent States and which perpetuates inequality.

2. The present international economic order is in direct conflict with current developments in international political and economic relations. Since 1970, the world economy has experienced a series of grave crises which have had severe

288

repercussions, especially on the developing countries because of their generally greater vulnerability to external economic impulses. The developing world has become a powerful factor that makes its influence felt in all fields of international activity. These irreversible changes in the relationship of forces in the world necessitate the active, full and equal participation of the developing countries in the formulation and application of all decisions that concern the international community.

3. All these changes have thrust into prominence the reality of interdependence of all the members of the world community. Current events have brought into sharp focus the realization that the interests of the developed countries and those of the developing countries can no longer be isolated from each other, that there is a close interrelationship between the prosperity of the developed countries and the growth and development of the developing countries, and that the prosperity of the international community as a whole depends upon the prosperity of its constituent parts. International co-operation for development is the shared goal and common duty of all countries. Thus the political, economic and social well-being of present and future generations depends more than ever on co-operation between all the members of the international community on the basis of sovereign equality and the removal of the disequilibrium that exists between them.

4. The new international economic order should be founded on full respect for the following principles:

(*a*) Sovereign equality of States, self-determination of all peoples, inadmissibility of the acquisition of territories by force, territorial integrity and non-interference in the internal affairs of other States;

(*b*) The broadest co-operation of all the States members of the international community, based on equity, whereby the prevailing disparities in the world may be banished and prosperity secured for all;

(*c*) Full and effective participation on the basis of equality of all countries in the solving of world economic problems in the common interest of all countries, bearing in mind the necessity to ensure the accelerated development of all the developing countries, while devoting particular attention to the adoption of special measures in favour of the least developed, land-locked and island developing countries as well as those developing countries most seriously affected by economic crises and natural calamities, without losing sight of the interests of other developing countries;

(*d*) The right of every country to adopt the economic and social system that it deems the most appropriate for its own development and not to be subjected to discrimination of any kind as a result;

(*e*) Full permanent sovereignty of every State over its natural resources and all economic activities. In order to safeguard these resources, each State is entitled to exercise effective control over them and their exploitation with means suitable to its own situation, including the right to nationalization or transfer of ownership to its nationals, this right being an expression of the full permanent sovereignty of the State. No State may be subjected to economic, political or any other type of coercion to prevent the free and full exercise of this inalienable right;

(*f*) The right of all States, territories and peoples under foreign occupation, alien and colonial domination or *apartheid* to restitution and full compensation for the exploitation and depletion of, and damages to, the natural resources and all other resources of those States, territories and peoples;

(*g*) Regulation and supervision of the activities of transnational corporations by taking measures in the interest of the national economies of the countries where such transnational corporations operate on the basis of the full sovereignty of those countries;

(*h*) The right of the developing countries and the peoples of territories under colonial and racial domination and foreign occupation to achieve their liberation and to regain effective control over their natural resources and economic activities;

(*i*) The extending of assistance to developing countries, peoples and territories which are under colonial and alien domination, foreign occupation, racial discrimination or *apartheid* or are subjected to economic, political or any other type of coercive measures to obtain from them the subordination of the exercise of their sovereign rights and to secure from them advantages of any kind, and to neo-colonialism in all its forms, and which have established or are endeavouring to establish effective control over their natural resources and economic activities that have been or are still under foreign control;

(*j*) Just and equitable relationship between the prices of raw materials, primary commodities, manufactured and semi-manufactured goods exported by developing countries and the prices of raw materials, primary commodities, manufactures, capital goods and equipment imported by them with the aim of bringing about sustained improvement in their unsatisfactory terms of trade and the expansion of the world economy;

(*k*) Extension of active assistance to developing countries by the whole international community, free of any political or military conditions;

(*l*) Ensuring that one of the main aims of the reformed international monetary system shall be the promotion of the development of the developing countries and the adequate flow of real resources to them;

(*m*) Improving the competitiveness of natural materials facing competition from synthetic substitutes;

(*n*) Preferential and non-reciprocal treatment for developing countries, wherever feasible, in all fields of international economic co-operation whenever possible;

(*o*) Securing favourable conditions for the transfer of financial resources to developing countries;

(*p*) Giving to the developing countries access to the achievements of modern science and technology, and promoting the transfer of technology and the creation of indigenous technology for the benefit of the developing countries in forms and in accordance with procedures which are suited to their economies;

(*q*) The need for all States to put an end to the waste of natural resources, including food products;

(*r*) The need for developing countries to concentrate all their resources for the cause of development;

(*s*) The strengthening, through individual and collective actions, of mutual economic, trade, financial and technical co-operation among the developing countries, mainly on a preferential basis;

(*t*) Facilitating the role which producers' associations may play within the framework of international co-operation and, in pursuance of their aims, *inter alia* assisting in the promotion of sustained growth of the world economy and accelerating the development of developing countries.

5. The unanimous adoption of the International Development Strategy for the Second United Nations Development Decade was an important step in the promotion of international economic co-operation on a just and equitable basis. The accelerated implementation of obligations and commitments assumed by the international community within the framework of the Strategy, particularly those concerning imperative development needs of developing countries, would contribute significantly to the fulfilment of the aims and objectives of the present Declaration.

6. The United Nations as a universal organization should be capable of dealing with problems of international economic co-operation in a comprehensive manner and ensuring equally the interests of all countries. It must have an even greater role in the establishment of a new international economic order. The Charter of Economic Rights and Duties of States, for the preparation of which the present Declaration will provide an additional source of inspiration, will constitute a significant contribution in this respect. All the States Members of the United Nations are therefore called upon to exert maximum efforts with a view to securing the implementation of the present Declaration, which is one of the principal guarantees for the creation of better conditions for all peoples to reach a life worthy of human dignity.

7. The present Declaration on the Establishment of a New International Economic Order shall be one of the most important bases of economic relations between all peoples and all nations.

21. The New International Economic Order and the Basic Needs Approach

Johan Galtung

INTRODUCTION: THE UNIVERSE OF DISCOURSE

First, a few words by way of definition. The New International Economic Order (NIEO) stands for a new way of ordering the international economic system so as to bring about, first, improved terms of trade between the present-day centre and periphery countries (in other words, the First World and the Third World countries); secondly, more control by the periphery over the world economic cycles that pass through them (the controls to include nationalization of natural resources, soil, processing facilities, distribution machinery, financial institutions, etc.); and, thirdly, increased and improved trade between the periphery countries themselves.

To be sure, there are other ways of listing the issue areas of NIEO. But the three characteristics listed above are related directly to the world structure, and they bring into sharp focus the specific changes sought to be made in that structure.

Very crucial in the evaluation of NIEO at the international level—which is the level at which it is intended to work—is the relative weight assigned to the first and the remaining two components. If the first predominates, the present structure may get frozen, though possibly at a higher level so far as the income of the periphery countries is concerned. This is already visible in the petroleum-exporting countries, which may be said to be the first to strike out for NIEO (without consensus, it is true, but after years of negotiation and discussion). There is now in these countries more money at the disposal of those who usually dispose; how exactly it is disposed of is instructive (on luxury consumer goods, capital goods for industrialization and sophisticated weapons).

If, however, the other two components predominate, the present world structure might be changed, the industrial capacities of the Third World countries might increase, and the centre-periphery trade might decrease (in relative terms) while that between the Third World countries increases. According to the World Bank, the increase in manufacturing production in 1961–1965 was 8.7% in the developing countries and 6.2% in the industrialized countries; in 1966–1973, the corresponding figures were 9.0% and 6.2%; and in 1974–1975 the increase was 4.5% in developing countries and −4.7% in industrialized countries. In the sphere of trade, however, the expectation that it would increase between the Third World countries has not been borne out; 'the most rapid rate of growth in trade has been between the industrialized countries'.

The NIEO deals essentially with the relations between industrialized and developing countries at the global level (because, among other reasons, it is articulated in the UN between states or blocs of states). It is thus a *macro* approach to the problem of development. The BN approach, on the other hand, is a *micro* approach. It goes down to the level of the individual human being and, therefore, sees development in terms of the fulfilment of basic needs at the individual level. Some, like this author, argue that that is the only level at which basic needs have to be met, if one has in mind basic *human* needs, not such abstractions as, for example, 'urban needs' (for sewage), 'historical needs' (collectivization of the means of production), 'national needs' (for military defence or for a national language)— all of which are, at most, merely the necessary condition for meeting basic *human* needs.

It needs to be emphasized that the BN approach is meaningful only if it is accompanied by a list of needs. The list that comes out of the Programme of Action adopted at the 1976 ILO World Employment Conference, which divided needs into 'minimum requirements of a family for private consumption' (adequate food, shelter, clothing, household equipment, furniture) and 'essential services for the community at large' (safe drinking water, sanitation, public transport and health, educational and cultural facilities), is open to criticism on three counts: that it draws too rigid a line between private and public; that it allocates satisfiers (they are not needs) to these areas; and that it neglects non-material needs.

But however perfect the list, it must have a rider: *the first priority must always be given to those most in need.*

In other words, BN approach would set priorities in production and distribution. It would give the first priority to the production of what is essential to meet human needs, and in such a way that it goes to meet the needs of the most needy. It would give a much lower priority to production of goods for other than human needs, for non-basic needs, and for the needs of those less in need (obvious examples of which are national airlines, cars, food too expensive to be within reach of the masses).

It should be emphasized, though, that 'lower priority' does not mean that these goods will never be produced, but only that they may be produced 'later', even 'much later'. There is nothing in the BN approach that strictly limits the concerns of a society to the satisfaction of basic needs—and certainly not at the lowest level. The BN approach does not call for asceticism or puritanism; all that it insists on is a certain order of priorities: first meet the basic needs of those most in need (assuming that the others have already had their basic needs met), and then, *and only then*, go about satisfying other needs if they are felt. The basic theoretical and empirical question in connection with the BN approach has to do with the ordering of these pursuits in terms of time. The assumption is that the pursuit of non-basic needs will stand in the way of meeting basic needs.

NIEO VERSUS BN APPROACH: THE ISSUES, THE PARTIES

There are at least two aspects of any conflict formation: the *issues* and the *parties*. On the subject of the relation between NIEO and the BN approach, on the level of issues the questions to be asked are: Is it theoretically possible to implement both the NIEO and BN approaches at the same time and at the same place (compatibility)? Or do they in some ways exclude each other simply because one comes in the way of the other (contradiction or conflict)? At the level of the parties, the set of questions is different: What kind of actors (individuals, groups and classes of individuals; states, groups and classes of states) favour one or the other? How do these actors relate to each other on other issues? How will this spill over into the relationship between the NIEO and BN approaches?

In discussing the issues, we shall first present the BN critique of NIEO and then the NIEO critique of BN.

BN *Critique of NIEO*

We shall begin with a relatively abstract analysis detached from the concrete realities of today. It cannot be denied that the two approaches can be compatible, but under certain conditions. In the NIEO there is a *potential* for more economic surplus to accumulate in the Third World countries. But the far more important question is whether it is used to meet the basic needs of those most in need. Economic surplus, it is well known, can be used in several ways, depending on where in the society it is generated, who decides how it will be disposed of, and what kind of decision is made. To take it for granted that it will necessarily be used to meet basic needs is extremely naive. A more realistic understanding is that most people in control of the economy will tend to use it for what *they* see as the pressing needs—be they 'national needs', non-basic needs, or the needs of those less in need.

In the *most optimistic model* imaginable, a society is so organized that much of the economic surplus remains at the level where it was generated. This can occur when, for instance, farmers are in control of land and workers of factories to the point where they can decide what to produce, how to distribute the produce, and how to dispose of the surplus. Under these conditions, it seems reasonable to assume that the hungry masses in the rural areas will prefer to produce food that can be eaten on the spot by themselves and their families. Lappè and Collins rightly observe:

Hungry people can and will feed themselves if they are allowed to do so. If people are not feeding themselves, you can be sure powerful obstacles are in the way . . . the most fundamental constraint to food self-reliance is that the majority of the people are not themselves in control of the production process and, therefore, more and more frequently do not even participate.

Similarly, workers will prefer to produce things that can be used for meeting basic needs, particularly in connection with farming, thus relating their activities to those of the farmers, guaranteeing to both themselves and the farmers at least a minimum in the way of food, clothing and shelter (shelter being a typical item for farmer-worker direct cooperation).

It may be argued that this does not take care of medical services and schooling, so one would add to the model the idea that the surplus generated on, or siphoned into, the top of society will trickle down in the form of free and easily accessible facilities in these two fields.

In contrast to this, the *most pessimistic model* is a society so organized that the surplus generated at the bottom not only 'trickles up' but is pumped upwards through the powerful mechanism of élite ownership (private or state) into the centres of control located in the country's capital or in the world economic centres.

As to the economic surplus entering the top layer, the élites keep it for themselves, using it for purposes different from those of the BN approach. Evidently, whereas in the former case one might envisage a convergence between the living conditions of the élites and the masses, in the latter case a divergence will be unavoidable.

To one who thinks that the pessimistic model gives a more realistic picture of a majority of Third World countries today, the NIEO and BN approaches will appear to be, in fact, contradictory. It may be argued, however, that NIEO has not created this situation in the Third World; indeed, it is to correct this situation that NIEO has been proposed. NIEO is an *inter*-national arrangement, and all that needs to be done is to complement it with corresponding *intra*-national measures to make the picture conform to the 'optimistic' model.

But to proceed with the argument. NIEO cannot but affect the international situation. For one thing, NIEO may stimulate international trade. (We say 'may', not 'will' advisedly; for no one can say what course the total volume of world trade would take.) This will cause an increasing proportion of the economic factors of Third World countries to be steered in the direction of producing exportable goods. This means that a higher priority will be given to the use of, for instance, soil for the production of commodities for export than to its use for the production of food for direct consumption; coffee rather than black beans, to use the oft-quoted Brazilian example. It also means that an increasing production of the economic cycle in the country will pass through a narrow and easily controlled gate: the major import-export facilities (ports, airports, border crossing-points) and banking facilities as well as other financial instruments.

Since these points can be controlled by a small number of people, themselves controlled by private and state leadership, this will result in increasingly centralized control of the entire economic machinery. As a contrast to this, imagine a country based on a high level of local self-reliance, production for consumption mainly on the spot, exchange between these units when there is surplus production, low level of external trade, even low level of monetization of the economic cycle—an economic obviously much more difficult to control centrally. Now, which of the two types of countries would be able to move easily to satisfy the basic needs of those most in need?

Again, the answer will, to a large extent, depend on the kind of decision the élites take. If past experience is any guide, the outlook is not very bright. The élites might decide to convert much of the net earned income into means of control of possible external (and even more so, internal) enemies—in other words, the police and the army. For a very good reason, too; for the gap between expectations raised by NIEO and the continuation of the sad reality concerning basic needs may be intolerable for certain segments of the population, which might then try all means within its power to change the regime.

This is as far as one can carry the argument based on informed doubt about NIEO at present. This argument is perhaps inspired by empirical information about the Third World countries that were the first to benefit from increased income due to the increased prices for their commodities. In short, the conclusion would be something like this: No doubt there are great possibilities of compatibility between the NIEO and BN approaches, but there are possibilities also of contradiction, depending on the international structure. In a brilliant analysis of this structure, Samir Amin observes:

The incredible resistance of the developed world to this reduction [of the inequality of the international division of labour] is evidence that the center, despite so many misleading speeches, cannot do without the pillage of the Third World. If that pillage were to stop, the center would be forced to adjust to a new, less equal international division of labour. Then, and only then, could one begin to speak of a genuine world order, and not merely of new terms of the unequal international division of labour.

The NIEO Critique of BN Approach

The Third World arguments against the BN approach, heard in conferences where the two 'Grand Designs' are discussed, can be summed up in six propositions:

1. *The BN approach is an effort to sidetrack the NIEO issue.* The real issue is international economic justice, and to throw in the BN approach is an effort to widen the agenda—possibly to insinuate into the essentially political discussion a *condition prealable:* No NIEO concessions to be given before BN policies are adopted. Since the First World is sceptical of the Third World ability to implement such policies, this amounts to postponing NIEO concessions or conventions indefinitely.

It is hardly relevant in this connection to argue, for instance, that the BN approach dates back to 1972 while the NIEO cannot claim to go farther back than the Sixth Special Session of the UN in 1974, and that therefore BN approach cannot be said to be an afterthought pregnant with ulterior motives. The reason why this is beside the point is that neither approach can be said to have a definite birth-date. Both are, rather, names of trends that have been operating in the world for a long time. NIEO can be traced back to UNCTAD I (Geneva, 1964), and the genesis of BN approach can be traced to social welfare policies pursued in welfare states and rooted in the compassion for the lowest and the most underprivileged and unfortunate found in many religions. The question is not whether some key points on the socio-political trajectories of these two approaches can be neatly ordered in time; the question is how the two approaches are used politically. NIEO is seen as a codification of a kind of *inter*-national social justice, whereas the BN approach is concerned with *intra*-national social justice (inside Third World countries). If the BN approach had taken within its purview and made it applicable to the whole world, with the focus on non-material needs as sharp as it is on material needs, so that the shortcomings in the First World showed up as clearly as those in the Third World, then NIEO and BN approaches might be seen as two independent issues. The way the BN approach has been launched, and applied predominantly *only* to the Third World, the Third World has every reason to regard it as a ploy for side-tracking the world economic issue raised by NIEO.

2. *The BN approach is a new way of legitimizing external intervention.* Most Third World countries are former colonies; large parts of the Third World still are neo-colonies. Colonialism is gone, and neo-colonialism will also go. So now comes the BN approach to legitimize intervention when military-political formulas will cease to work and direct economic investment will be threatened. Basic needs, like basic rights, attach to *individuals* in Western thinking, which means that it is only

at the individual level that their satisfaction can be monitored. The Third World posits against this the primacy of basic *national* needs and *national* rights as codified in the Charter of Economic Rights and Duties of States. National needs and rights are claimed, satisfied or left unsatisfied in the international context. The Third World insistence that it is up to the Third World countries to decide, severally or collectively, how best to use this basic national right intranationally is clearly an anti-interventionist position. It does not say, 'We shall continue to exploit our masses, and it is none of your business.' It only says, 'Whatever we do inside our countries is none of your business.' In the light of past history, the First World's disavowal of interventionist intentions does not carry conviction, nor does its protestation that the BN approach will not have any unintended consequences. For it is clear that a BN clause added to a NIEO agreement might mean that a number of NIEO components (for example, a decrease in debt burdens, an increase in ODA) would be made conditional on the implementation of BN policies. This implies that implementation (necessarily at the individual level) inside Third World nations would be monitored by some international agency. One can easily imagine an international bureaucracy set up to supervise such agreements. However the agency might be staffed, the cycles of reporting and decision-making would have to pass through the First World centres to make sense of monitoring. On this reasoning, the First World can be suspected of supporting the BN approach precisely because other historically familiar handles of intervention are slipping.

3. *The BN approach is an instrument to enlarge the First World's market in the Third World.* The First World fears that NIEO will increase, perhaps greatly, the Third World competitive capability in the world market. The Third World supply of goods may increasingly be sufficient to meet Third World demand, thereby closing *de facto* the Third World market to First World exports. (The *de facto* closure could be also made *de jure* before or after, or independently of, the *de facto* closure.) Some way will, therefore, have to be found to so relate the growth of Third World supply to the growth of Third World demand that a substantial portion of demand was still left unsatisfied.

This can be done in several ways. For instance, the revolution of rising expectations (increasing the middle-class demand for goods) is one, population control (reducing the number of those with needs but without effective demand) is another, and the BN approach may be a third. Indeed, the BN approach may, in fact, succeed in doing what population control largely failed to do. If one hears less about the population explosion today than one did some years ago, it may be because the First World has realized that the explosion is not all that bad: after all, the teeming millions are *potential* customers! All that need be done to convert them into *actual* customers is to bring them to a certain economic level so that, with their increased purchasing power, they can express their needs in terms of effective demand. And this is where the BN approach comes in. Instead of aiming at raising the expectations of the middle class, why not aim at raising the purchasing power of the vast Third World proletariat—in the countryside and in the city slums, living on the fringe of the money economy (as distinguished from self-supporting farmers, nomads and other groups that live outside this economy), in numbers much more promising than the middle classes ever were.

It is not difficult to visualize the implications of this type of reasoning. The BN approach would provide what is needed for the satisfaction of basic needs from the market. For the rest, schooling provided free; medical services, likewise free; meals, free or highly subsidized (in canteens, maybe). The list could be extended to cover basic clothing and basic housing. From single individuals the gains may be next to nothing, but from a country as a whole they could be something to be satisfied with. It is the First World that would be contracted to build the infrastructure for all these services, presumably to be provided by the state. The payments would be made from out of the increased assets resulting from the NIEO—a neat way of recycling NIEO-dollars via the BN formula.

There is also the possibility of marketing what is needed to meet basic needs; international agribusiness, construction business, textile business and pharmaceuticals are already in the field. (The field of school materials, however, does not seem, as yet, to be so effectively transnationalized, educational video-cassettes being a possible exception.) For all this to become a large-scale business at the level of those more, if not most, in need, two things have to happen: prices have to be lowered and the purchasing power of those at the bottom has to be raised. As the former can be, at least potentially, a function of the latter, a beginning might be made with efforts to raise purchasing power. One way of doing this is through higher guaranteed minimum wages and full employment—in others words, the kind of approach that ILO advocates. And where is the money for this to come from? Why, from the income accruing to the Third World countries from a more just international economic order and from big transnational corporations catering to the people most in need, who will now be knocking at the doors of the market in the language the market understands: coins, later on bills, and then, maybe, cheques.

Whether it is the market device (for some of the basic needs) or the non-market device (for other needs), or a combination of both, that may be used, it will prepare the ground for a *planetary bargain:* 'We give you the NIEO, you give us the right to compete with you in your own market for the satisfaction of basic needs.' Needless to say, this extremely limited perspective on basic needs (confined to material needs) totally disregards the issue of identity; the urge to be master of one's own situation; to be a subject, and not merely an object. As to freedom, the proponents of this new strategy for the First World penetration into the Third World via the BN formula would claim that the monetized approach offers more freedom of choice than is possible when basic needs are satisfied through deliveries in kind. They would further argue that a person should not only be given a choice in consumer goods, several brands of food, several types of clothes, but also enabled to decide his/her own trade-off formula between food and clothes, given a minimum income. One can very well imagine transnational corporations making 'basic-needs packages', containing food, textiles, drugs and some educational material in proportions to be decided by the customer, given the price-range of the package. If that formula, or some other similar formula, works, there might be room for an accelerating population explosion.

4. *The BN approach is intended to slow down the growth of Third World economies.* Generally speaking, there are two approaches to most problems that

concern the Third World today: one aims at strengthening the weaker states/countries, and the other aims at strengthening the weakest individuals in those territorial units. This is very clearly seen in the choice of technologies. On the one hand, there are the capital-intensive, labour-extensive, research-intensive and administration-intensive technologies that might eventually make it possible for Third World countries to play the First World game according to rules made by the First World. On the other hand, there are the capital-extensive, labour-intensive, research-extensive and administration-extensive technologies that are much more relevant for the satisfaction of the basic needs of those most in need. The first approach is, for obvious reasons, the approach of the national élites; the second approach is, for equally obvious reasons, the approach of the less privileged groups, when, that is to say, left to themselves—such as the groups building China's people's communes in the beginning of the life-cycle of that institution.

The first approach, which is highly capital-absorbing, may also be capital-generating. The second approach does not generate capital but other values, human values: restoration/strengthening of nature's ecological balance, autonomy, creativity, participation, etc. The two approaches cannot mix well because the two are mutually inconsonant. The extent to which local self-reliant communities can be incorporated in a national economic structure (i.e. one that uses capital-intensive technology and produces for exchange rather than for use) without being 'perverted' is strictly limited. Conversely, the extent to which self-reliant local communities (i.e. those that use capital-extensive technology and produce for use rather than for exchange) can go their own way without weakening the 'national purpose' (i.e. the capability of participating on an equal footing in the international game as defined by the First World) is strictly limited. The *self-reliant basic needs approach* redefines the national purpose. It involves rearrangement, not in the allocation of capital, but in the allocation of human and social energy, creativity, mobilization, etc.

The case of China is very instructive. A China in which the 70,000 communes, with their production for use rather than for exchange, dominate does not constitute much of a threat to the First World in terms of economic competition in the world market, although it makes it extremely difficult for the First World to penetrate economically into the Chinese market. A China that changes over to an economy dominated by capital- and research-intensive technology—making use of a labour force of about 600 million—may, in the first run, cause some satisfaction in First World capitals (if only because it ceases to be a threat as an alternative model of development), but, in the second run, may cause considerable anxiety (because of its economic power). Such an apprehension has already been expressed: 'Every aspect of world economics and politics will be transformed if these educated new Chinese in the 1990s attain a level of productivity even approximately in accord with their ability, and hell knows if they don't.' There is no doubt that, under certain conditions, a systematically pursued BN approach, whether or not based on local self-reliance as a major ingredient, may make the Third World less of a threat to First World economic hegemony.

The case of Germany and Japan, where the Western 'allied' powers followed different tactics is equally instructive. After some time the 'allies' realized that it was important that both be integrated into the military machine of the West, not only to benefit from their military tradition and experience, but also to reduce their economic competitive strength in the world market by forcing them to divert much more of their production factors in the military direction, including buying military wares from the West. (It should be noted that the military production and marketing system is protectionist; it is not an open world market but a market where one is expected to trade within an alliance, or at least not far outside it, the protection mechanisms being legitimized through concepts of security and secrecy.) This policy, however, failed to put an efficient brake on German and Japanese economic growth in the 1950s; for the integration of a country into a highly capital-intensive and research-intensive military machine tends to push the economic growth of the country along the same line, possibly after a time-lag of some years. If a country chooses the self-reliant path of development, it does not neglect its security, but relies for it, not on capital-intensive conventional army, but on guerrilla (possibly non-military) defence of a highly localized nature.

5. *The BN approach is an effort to reduce technical assistance.* The capital component of BN approach—particularly if it is based on self-reliance, mobilizing local forces and resources, building on local traditions—is relatively minor. External technical assistance is, to a large extent, ruled out as antithetical to self-reliance. Just as the First World might like to push the BN expenses in general on to the Third World leadership, it might also like to rid itself of obligations of technical assistance, thereby improving its own competitive capability. One cannot miss the hint in UK's position:

Since our experience, and that of other donors who are trying to direct more aid towards the poor, suggests that there is a risk that at least initially rates of disbursement may fall, we will need to continue to finance other projects which are economically sound and to which developing countries attach priority if we are to disperse the UK aid programme as fully and effectively as possible.

However this may be, it is clear that a systematic change in the BN direction would raise a number of questions in connection with any kind of project in a Third World country. These questions have, to some extent, been raised by the World Bank recently. But the relationship between the various BN approaches, on the one hand, and the quantum of ODA, on the other, is not yet quite clear.

6. *The BN approach is a weapon of defence against the poor.* The BN approach springs less from compassion for the poor than from fear of the poor. The poor are seen as a vast amorphous mass of people increasingly conscious and envious of what the First World has and desirous of getting it anyhow. It is the image of the 'hordes' knocking on the doors of Western affluence. The more contemporary, political version of the same image—the communist subversion.

Together with this image comes the hypothesis that the danger is roughly proportionate to the poverty of the 'hordes', implying that a reduction in their number means a reduction of the danger. One way of reducing the number of the poor is through 'nature's regulatory devices' (earthquakes, tidal waves, floods, etc.), another is through genocide, yet another is through population control, and, finally, the more 'positive' approach: reducing the number of the poor by making them less poor through the BN approach.

The point simply is that the BN approach is a mystification of clear global power politics. It aims at reducing the political power of the Third World through the elimination of a major power element used, sometimes discriminately and sometimes indiscriminately, during the last generation or so: the threat of communist subversion ('if more aid is not given, it cannot be ensured that the forces of subversion will be contained').

It may be noted parenthetically that the proposition that subversive 'aggression is proportionate to poverty' has not been proven. The historical experience is that very poor people tend to be apathetic because, among other reasons, of lack of resources, and that it is only when they manage, in one way or another, to move out of poverty that they can begin to think of revolution. Nonetheless, it is generally believed that the proposition cannot be dismissed as one out of touch with reality. From the beginning, First World technical assistance has been urged and justified on the ground that it prevents conflicts from escalating and eventually becoming a threat to First World countries themselves. Hesitant parliaments have used this argument in defence of technical assistance. This idiom has been found to be more convincing and effective than the humanitarian idiom—or even the development idiom for that matter. Technical assistance without doubt plays a part in foreign commercial policy, as a way (through tied aid) of steering the flow of orders from the periphery to the centre and as a way of creating goodwill in the wake of which general trade treaties might be more easily forged. Technical assistance is also used as an instrument in foreign-power policy, for shaping alliances to cope with present and future conflicts. The BN approach is a variation on this—only more refined, more directly aimed at the exact point inside societies from which a conflict is likely to emanate. Whether the assumption is right or wrong is not important. What is important is that it is *believed* to be correct by a sufficient number of decision-makers in the First World.

Having examined the issues in the debate between the NIEO and BN advocates, we may now look at the *parties* involved in the debate.

NIEO-BN Debate: The Parties

It is clear that the polarization is between the First World and the Third World, with the Second (Socialist) World sitting, generally speaking, on the fence. To put it differently, there is a contradiction between the centre (the capitalist world) and the periphery (the developing part of the world). This contradiction was brought about by historical circumstances but is still being built into the world structure. The Third World—or, to be more precise, the Third World élites—calls for NIEO; the First World (both élites and masses) is far from enthusiastic and tends to say, with a former US secretary of state, that 'the present world system has served us well' (us may also be written US). It looks for arguments against a redistribution of the world income. One such argument is the BN approach: 'What is the good of NIEO? It will only enrich the Third World élites. Look at the way they treat their own people.' This type of argument is most articulated in the Protestant northern fringe of the First World, perhaps by upper middle class intellectuals with an oversensitive conscience, who show far more concern for economic development oriented to the needs of those most in need (unlike their hardened compeers far less worried about the plight of the masses) than for their own disproportionate share of the world income. Naturally, they seize upon any argument they can find against NIEO. This process has already started, the World Bank having been among the first to articulate some kind of BN approach.

That the Third World would hit back was only to be expected. But one hopes that this would make for an honest searching debate on the fundamental issues involved. The quality and validity of an argument lie in the eye of the beholder. To the Third World, the need for NIEO (in sum, a fairer distribution of the global wealth) is, not only conceptually but also in terms of basic norms of social justice, too obvious to need pleading. Similarly, to BN advocates nothing can be more sound or more reasonable in human terms than the uplift of those most in need. They would concede, of course, that the criteria and methods were open to discussion, but not the fundamental goal of the elimination of poverty. Both parties tend to view the opposition of the other as a subterfuge for pure self-serving. One can predict that the First World would dismiss the Third World argument in favour of NIEO as a disingenuous plea for ensuring privileges to Third World élites; and the Third World would regard the First World argument in favour of BN as a justification, equally disingenuous, of preserving the First World privileges at the international level.

We are now set to examine whether the NIEO and BN approaches are compatible or conflicting and in what sense and to what extent. But before we engage ourselves in that exercise, it may be useful to take stock of what has been said so far.

On the plane of issues, the six arguments brought up against the BN approach all converge to make the point that the BN approach is more than meets the eye, that it is not what it is dressed up to look like, and that there are other things behind and underneath. These are probings into the motivation of the BN approach. Understandably, for NIEO affects the interests in the old international economic order and is used to define parties and actors in a conflict of interests. The arguments against NIEO are directed against NIEO as it has been presented. The arguments against the BN approach seem to have been generated by the arguments against NIEO—in other words, third generation arguments. It is possible that if a consistent BN approach had been presented first (i.e. if the World Employment Conference of 1976 had been held before the Sixth Special Session of the UN General Assembly on 1 May 1974), then the nature and order of arguments would have been different. On the plane of parties, what is noteworthy is that although the issues are *debated* by different political actors, all essentially refer to the same actor—the Third World, the assumption (fallacious, as will become clear later) being that the Third World is debatable but the First World is not.

CONCLUSION: NIEO AND BN CONTRADICTORY OR COMPATIBLE?

The answer depends on whether NIEO is interpreted in a shallow sense (i.e. without involving intranational transformation) or in a deeper sense (i.e. requiring at least some measures of intranational transformation). It depends, too, on whether BN is interpreted in a shallow sense (i.e. with non-material needs kept out) or in a deeper sense (requiring the inclusion of non-material needs). Finer distinctions could admittedly be made, but these are sufficient to summarize the foregoing discussion as under:

	NIEO without intranational transformation	NIEO with intranational transformation
BN without non-material needs	A : Compatibility	C : Compatibility
BN with non-material needs	B : Contradiction	D : Compatibility

To spell out the table:

A : *Compatibility*, in the sense that the satisfaction of basic needs is managerially possible. It depends on the manner of 'recycling NIEO-dollars for basic needs', from the top down, with or without First World participation.

B : *Contradiction*, the most important non-material needs in this connection are autonomy, being subject rather than object, having a major say in one's own situation as opposed to being a client/consumer. This applies also to the rich countries that have been the beneficiaries of the old international economic order.

C : *Compatibility*, in the sense that the surplus generated locally will, to a large extent, remain at the bottom, and the surplus generated at, or entering, the top will trickle down. The combination is a 'soul-less' one; it is economistic, not taking non-material concerns into consideration.

D : *Compatibility*, in an optimal combination. There is a transformation of the intranational order that permits a richer perspective of basic needs to come into play.

This raises the question of where the total world system is heading. As seen from the point of view of the way the United Nations' machinery is processing the two concepts of NIEO and BN, it seems to be heading towards the combination A. The UN being an intergovernmental machinery, it will have a tendency to focus on inter- rather than intra-national transformation (although the situation is not very clear-cut). It would be easy to obtain a majority for *inter*-national transformation when the majority of member-countries are victims of the old international economic order that dominates the world. This can then be combined with a majority against mandatory *intra*-national transformations, except for minor matters, under the general formula of non-intervention in national sovereignty—assuming that there is sufficient solidarity among the victims of the old international economic order.

At the same time, the UN machinery will probably continue to concentrate on the shallow interpretation of basic needs (i.e. without including non-material needs). There could be another possibility, though: the UN concern with human rights may lead to a broadening of the concept, through the basic-needs concern of such organizations as the ILO and the UNICEF. But one must reckon with the pervasive influence of the hierarchy principle: *first*, material needs and *then* non-material needs. It is easier to obtain a consensus on material than on non-material needs. Around this formulation various types of ideologies (liberalism and Marxism, for instance) can be brought together, bridges can be built between East and West, North and South. To achieve a consensus, the temptation to strip the concepts of BN and NIEO of its richness must be great. The deeper interpretation of the concepts are just too painful! This dénouement is bound to disappoint those to whom both NIEO and BN have much richer connotations. The rhetoric to be heard will doubtless be that of D (see table), the reality will be akin to A. But is it possible to move from A towards D to make the reality correspond better to the rhetoric?

One approach is obvious: never to give in to the shallow interpretations of NIEO and BN, always insisting that NIEO is meaningful only with intra-national transformations and BN only with the inclusion of non-material needs. The nature of the transformation and the non-material needs will be open to discussion, of course. It is obvious that the interpretations will vary according to the concrete situation in time and place; but one must guard oneself against being duped by these obvious considerations into facile compromises with the shallow interpretation of either. For the most likely outcome of compromises can only be that even material needs will be left unsatisfied, and even if satisfied they will be satisfied in a managerial, even corporate, fashion.

But neither should one succumb to the polarization that now seems to be crystallizing, with the Third World élites standing for a shallow NIEO interpretation and the First World for a shallow BN interpretation. One way of reorienting this debate would be to insist on symmetry: both parties must see the broad interpretations of NIEO and of BN as applicable to *all parts of the world*. There are some obvious transformations that will have to take place in the First World if NIEO is to be really implemented, such as more emphasis on agriculture again; probably much more emphasis on local energy production; more emphasis on local, national, subregional and regional self-reliance; even self-sufficiency in some fields. There will probably have to be an orientation towards other life-styles, more compatible with the objective situation brought about by NIEO. As for BN, both parties could use the full spectrum of basic human needs—such as security needs, welfare needs, identity needs, freedom needs—and discuss the situation both in their own and in other countries. This would certainly widen the agenda; but care must be taken to keep in check the propensity to score points, as against the adversary in a conflict ('*You* have to undertake basic internal structural reform,' 'What about the mental illness rates in *your* country?'). This, however, puts no bar on self-criticism and criticism by others in an effort to improve the social order everywhere.

Then there is another, much more action-oriented approach. The basic formula that may transcend the present contradiction between the New International Economic Order and the Basic Needs approach is probably *self-reliance*. Self-reliance here is understood to mean a three-pronged approach: regional self-reliance, national self-reliance *and* local self-reliance. Self-reliance would mean raising the level of self-sufficiency and cooperation with others. Thus, regional self-reliance in the Third World, for example (the region being the Third World as a whole, the continental subdivisions, the subcontinental possibilities), would mean not only a much higher level of Third World production for its own consumption, but also a change in the pattern of exchange with the 'developed' parts of the world towards more equity. The old pattern of exporting commodities in return for manufactured goods and services—even with the terms of trade not only stable but also improved— would gradually recede into the background in favour of trade of commodities against commodities, manufactures against manufactures, services against services (intrasector trade). In other words, regional self-reliance at this level would pick up the aspects of NIEO that are more oriented towards South-South trade and increased control by the South of economic structures in general, de-emphasize the terms-of-trade approach in relation to the North, and go in for truly equitable North-South trade.

However, even with all this there would be no guarantee against the stronger countries in the South exploiting the weaker ones. Hence *national* self-reliance as a safeguard against such aggrandizement. The reasoning can be extended: national self-reliance provides no guarantee against national élites exploiting their own masses, hence local self-reliance as a similar protective shield. (This shield is admittedly less strong, since there is much less of institutional protection for local units than for national units. For one thing, they do not have secure and/or defendable borders. For another, they do not have armies—often not even distinct identities that would motivate any kind of defence.) But the character of local self-reliance would be the same: increased local self-sufficiency, combined with horizontal exchange with other units at the same level (in a future world, not necessarily only other units in the same country).

If the local unit is to carry the burden of self-reliance alone, it is doubtful whether it would be able to create a sustainable material base in most parts of the world. The national unit as an equalizer that could level out the sharp differences in economic geography in space and in the annual cycles (not only in agriculture, but also in the distribution of natural calamities) is crucial. But self-reliance at the national level alone, as experience has clearly shown, is not enough to achieve a more just, a more equitable international economic order as envisaged in the NIEO designs. Hence the need for self-reliance at the regional, national and local levels at the same time, the rationale being that the regional level is best suited for the NIEO approach and the local level for the BN approach, on both material and non-material dimensions. The national level entity will have to be reorganized both upwards and downwards; it will have to integrate with other units at the same level for collective solidarity action and restructure itself so that local level units are given a chance to unfold themselves.

Admittedly, this is an abstract formula, and this is not the place to develop all the details to give it flesh. But it should be made clear how apparent contradictions can be resolved. In the present world, short both on strong regional machineries (with the exception of the OPEC cartel action) and on structural transformations that would vest more autonomy at the local level, not only in political but also in economic and socio-cultural affairs, the NIEO and BN approaches may become more contradictory than they would be in a world differently organized. Hence, the task is to understand these relations better, not to feel that one must be against one or the other or both because of the very real issues involved and the equally real conflict polarizations.

For, regardless of the strong arguments that can be raised against these approaches seen in isolation and divorced from the broader political and historical context, there are extremely strong forces behind both. Seen in a UN perspective, it may be said that they both represent a third phase in United Nations development strategies. The first phase was *the import substitution phase* (developing countries have to produce themselves rather than import from developed countries), a phase motivated, among other things, by the perceived deteriorating terms of trade, with the United Nations Economic Commission for Latin America (CEPAL) providing the theoretical underpinnings. The second phase, partly growing out of frustration with the first one (manufactured goods produced in developing countries tended to become even more expensive) can be characterized as *the commodity export phase*, motivated by the 'need' to earn foreign currency. This phase was, of course, more popular with the First World countries as it promoted their interest in exactly this type of trade. But there [were] two basic problems: on the one hand, it became increasingly clear that somehow the developing countries were cheated in the bargain, that world resources were distributed highly asymmetrically in favour of the developed countries by this kind of arrangement (a polite way of saying that there was exploitation at work); and, on the other hand, it became equally clear that the masses in general were the losers. (For reasons mentioned in the introduction the internal gaps widened and misery increased.) The responses to these two problems, in a sense created by the same structure and the same process, were, in our view, the New International Economic Order and the Basic Needs approach. And this heralds the beginning of the third phase.

The two approaches must be recognized for what they are: political movements, created and crystallized by particular historical situations. One can be against them or in favour of them, but one must recognize that they simply *are*, they *exist*, they *unfold* themselves like tidal waves. The political task is to help steer this tremendous political energy in directions that serve true human and social development, to deepen them and to find ways of resolving the contradictions between them.

22. The World Bank: A New Role in the Debt Crisis?

Cheryl Payer

The International Monetary Fund is dead; long live the World Bank! The message brought by US Secretary of the Treasury James Baker to the Annual Meeting of the IMF and World Bank in Seoul, Korea, in October 1985, wasn't quite that explicit, but it could easily be read between the lines.

Three years of experience with the IMF model for containing the debt crisis came to a climax in 1985 with clear evidence of disaster. Mexico, which had been show-cased as the bankers' idea of a model country, fell out of compliance with its IMF agreement after an expensive national election. Instead of displaying humble gratitude to the banks for granting his country the 'reward' of a multi-year debt rescheduling, the Finance Minister, Jesus Silva Herzog, used the formal signing ceremony to deliver a threat: if Mexico did not receive a positive net transfer of money from the banks, it would not pay its interest in the future.

On the South American continent the news was just as bad. The newly-elected governments of Brazil and Peru both announced that they didn't want any IMF programme in the foreseeable future. And Argentina, which made a stunning turn-around in just a few months' time from bankers' nemesis to bankers' favourite, was in compliance with the IMF only because it had designed its own stabilisation programme and sold it to the Fund, rather than vice versa. The Argentine stabilisation programme, although rubber-stamped by the IMF, contains one important element which the Fund has not countenanced elsewhere: a heavy emphasis on price controls.

The bad news for the IMF didn't end there. As an article in the *New York Times* explained in November 1984, the IMF and World Bank have always been the first to be paid back when debtor countries have anything to spend in a debt crisis, because they are what amounts to the international credit rating agency. But even as that article was published, the Fund was struggling with the fact that more than twenty countries (many in Africa) were *not* repaying their borrowings from the Fund. In 1985 newspapers carried the story that the IMF couldn't even collect its own debts. And if this was true, how could it ensure repayments of the much larger debts to commercial banks?

The IMF was designed to provide short-term support to the balance-of-payments of troubled debtors, and is supposed to operate as a revolving fund. Its loans (technically speaking, 'purchases' of hard currency with local currency) are repayable within a three to five year period after they are disbursed. The Fund's net lending in the years the debt crisis broke, 1981–4, amounted to a total of $28 billion, or an average of seven billion each year. Net lending slowed to a trickle in 1985, and in the next three years repayments are scheduled to amount to $21 billion. The IMF will soon become a net recipient rather than supplier of funds to Third World borrowers.

Those borrowers have, through the years, tolerated the imposition of IMF conditionality only because they wanted the money from the Fund itself and from other creditors that pegged their own lending to compliance with an IMF austerity programme. Even before 1985, compliance with Fund-imposed conditions was notable mostly for its absence. If the IMF were a private consulting firm which had to sell its advice, it would have gone out of business long ago.

The bargain has always been money for conditionality. As the money runs out, so will the patience of governments, whether left or right in their political complexion, with conditions which have long been regarded as more in the interest of the creditors than the borrowers.

The IMF's future as a dispenser of funds is now dependent on the willingness of past borrowers to return large sums of money to it even though they are still in crisis. In the words of the Morgan Guaranty Trust newsletter, 'Should Brazil or Mexico wish to enter into a second extended-facility arrangement, they too could find—as Chile discovered several months ago when it requested a three-year facility—that new loans from the Fund roughly match the repayments of principal from prior drawings falling due after 1986.'

The IMF's credibility has also been hurt by the very efforts of the Reagan administration to strengthen its authority. Every major debtor country was required to conclude a high conditionality stand-by or extended facility with the IMF as a condition for a debt re-scheduling agreement. Because such agreements were essential for preserving the stability of the international banking system, it was only a matter of time until even the most conventional and conservative of Latin American technocrats realised that they were in the driver's seat and could write their own ticket, as Argentina has done.

THE WORLD BANK GETS WHEELED OUT

With the collapse of the IMF 'let's pretend it's just temporary' strategy, US officials had to cast about for a new gimmick. Upgrading the role of the World Bank, which has been out of the limelight since the inauguration of Ronald Reagan and the outbreak of the crisis, was an obvious solution, although it is doubtful that it will prove to be the correct one.

Although Treasury Secretary Baker's name is on the plan which puts the bank in a starring role, the original idea may have come from the Federal Reserve Board Chairman, Paul Volcker, who has played a strong supporting role at Baker's side since the initiative was unveiled. In May 1985, Volcker proposed a wider role for the World Bank in a speech presented to the Bankers' Association for Foreign Trade, and he developed the idea in testimony before Congress last summer. 'Where have you guys been?', he challenged World Bank executives as long ago as July 1984.

The Bank executives' full response to that question was probably not printable in a family newspaper. There are solid reasons for the Bank's position on the sidelines of the debt crisis, which Mr Volcker, not a stupid man, should have been aware of. Putting it simply, since 1981 when Ronald Reagan was inaugurated US President and A W Clausen succeeded Robert McNamara as President of the

World Bank, the Bank has been caught between the Scylla of the capital markets and the Charybdis of the Reagan administration's ideological hostility to multilateral banks.

The World Bank depends on borrowing money in the world's capital markets for most of the money onlent by its hard-loan component, the IBRD. It is dependent on the support of the US administration, its largest shareholder, for increases in subscribed capital which would permit an increase in lending by the IBRD, since its charter does not permit it to make loans in excess of its capital. And it is almost totally dependent on government allocations for its soft-loan component, the IDA.

During the more than four and a half years that elapsed between the Reagan inauguration and the Baker initiative, the US administration systematically weakened the Bank by denying it the financial support it needed to expand lending. Clausen's efforts to crank up a new general capital increase for IBRD were received coolly. Commitments from the US to the Sixth Replenishment of IDA that were supposed to be disbursed over three years were stretched out over four.

When the seventh replenishment of IDA was negotiated, the US fell out of step with the other Part I (developed countries) contributors by refusing to contribute its full pro-rated share of the total agreed upon. This so angered the other Part I members that several of them agreed to contribute to a separate pool of funds, and ruled that US-based firms would not be permitted to bid for contracts financed by those funds. (The episode lends support to the theory that the whole foreign aid business is nothing but an export-financing scheme.)

The other side of Clausen's dilemma was the scrutiny of the capital markets from which the Bank borrows most of its funds for lending. Although critics blame lack-lustre executive leadership and bureaucratic red tape for the Bank's failure to come to the rescue with large amounts of debt relief, there were compelling structural reasons to explain why the Bank had evolved in this way.

Several critics suggested, for example, that the Bank should abandon its highly conservative 1:1 ratio of loans to capital. Commercial banks, they suggested, have ratios which are close to 20:1 and the Bank's 'old fogeyism' was preventing a much-needed expansion of lending. Changing the articles of agreement to allow just a 2:1 ratio would instantly double the money it could lend without going through the cumbersome process of a capital increase.

It all seemed so easy. Clausen knew that it wasn't, and rejected the idea. He had come to the World Bank from the presidency of what was then the world's largest commercial bank (Bank of America) and was certainly not unaware of the seriousness of the debt crisis nor unwilling to increase new and untied lending. Although it is hardly possible to 'bail out' the commercial banks (the sums needed are just too big), increased lending by the World Bank could make life easier for them in the short run.

But the IBRD raises the bulk of its funds from large investors, state and private, who see it as a good investment, and the guarantee of the Bank's developed member-countries is what makes it a good investment. Raising the 'gearing ratio' of loans to capital would dilute the guarantee that these lenders depend upon and instantly raise the Bank's cost of capital on new borrowings. It would make the Bank much more dependent on the perception of the market, and in the mid-1980s that perception would not be favourable. If commercial banks no longer consider loans to Latin America (and troubled borrowers elsewhere) as good business, the more conservative bond markets would certainly shun investments in an institution whose main business was bailing those troubled borrowers out of their commercial bank loans.

Unlike the IMF, which was designed to operate in (short-term) crises, the World Bank's method of lending made it a much less suitable tool for emergency bail-outs. The Bank's charter (Article III, section 4(vii)) states that 'Loans made or guaranteed by the Bank shall, except in special circumstances, be for the purpose of specific projects of reconstruction or development.'

In a debt crisis, however, the most urgent need of a borrower is not for projects which will have a pay-off, if any, only in five or ten years' time; the country needs the money now, to pay debt service and this year's import bill. Project loans are actually counter-productive in such an environment if they tie up other complementary resources which might be put to more immediate use elsewhere in the economy. World Bank loans have traditionally done just that: it has been a deliberate policy of the World Bank to require the borrowing government to demonstrate its commitment to projects financed by the Bank by pledging so-called 'counterpart' funds, and making complementary investments of its own.

The World Bank was the first institution to study the problem of debt repayment and debt crises seriously (in the studies by Dragoslav Avramovic published between 1958 and 1965) and is still the major source of statistics on debt as publisher of the annual *World Debt Tables*. Yet, ironically, its own lending operations assumed that the flow of external capital towards its Third World borrowers would always continue, despite the reverse flows of interest payments and amortisation of capital required by the IBRD's 'business-like' loans.

In the occasional national debt crises of the 1960s and 1970s, the World Bank urged other creditors to reschedule repayments, but refused on principle (that is, with a careful eye on the rating of its bonds in the capital markets) to reschedule its own. The only debt-management technique which McNamara used when net transfers from the World Bank became negative in 1970 after he took office was the massive expansion of gross new lending which allowed borrowers to cover their old debt service with little pain. World Bank lending, like commercial bank lending, resembled a Ponzi scheme, with the old debt service paid out of new borrowings.

Clausen was well aware of this fact and prepared to continue the game. Just before he assumed the presidency of the Bank, he told an interviewer, 'If we don't provide this expanded level of support [for the multilateral agencies]—comes the revolution. It's as simple as that. We have to do it or else we will destroy ourselves.' But the 1982 debt crisis could not be patched up according to the old model of the 1960s and 1970s. When Clausen tried to push the same buttons that McNamara pushed, he got no response.

Clausen has been responsible for several innovations in Bank policy and procedures. His first steps upon taking office were to move Bank lending from a fixed-rate to a floating-rate basis, and to institute new commitment fees for IBRD loans and IDA credits. These innovations made the World Bank look more like a commercial bank, and contributed to the fat profits the Bank has declared in recent years.

The commitment fees reduced the net transfer from the Bank to its borrowers, but floating interest rates, contrary to expectations, actually reduced the interest burden to borrowers. When floating rates were introduced in 1982, interest rates on bank loans were at an all-time high of 11.6 per cent. The switch to a floating-rate system permitted the Bank to pass on savings to its floating-rate borrowers as the interest rates on its own borrowing from the capital markets fell. Under the variable rate system, rates on all outstanding loans are reset every six months to reflect the Bank's own cost of borrowing: rates charged to the Bank's borrowers have fallen from 11.43 per cent in 1982 to 8.82 per cent in the last half of 1985.

These interest rates are somewhat deceptive, however, as the Bank tries to borrow at the lowest *nominal* interest rate. That is, it borrows in currencies which have a low interest rate and passes the foreign exchange risk on to its borrowers. During the Clausen years the Bank has been a pioneer in the sophisticated business of currency and interest-rate 'swaps' with other investors. 'Swaps' have allowed the bank to borrow high-interest funds in US dollars and swap them for nominal low-interest funds in Swiss francs, deutschmarks and yen. In this way, the Bank can borrow more funds in those markets than the national authorities allow them to borrow directly.

More immediately important to the borrowers, however, are the innovations on the lending side of World Bank operations. Here the changes have moved in three interrelated directions as a result of the debt crisis: towards more programme lending, more policy conditionality and more emphasis on encouraging private investors. All three are responses to the debt crisis.

Structural adjustment loans, or SALs, were introduced in 1980, as a response to the second 'oil shock'. The Bank perceived, incorrectly as it turned out, that the price of oil would continue to rise in real terms in the 1980s. But it was also, and more prophetically, an anticipation of and an attempt to avert the impending debt crisis, since commercial banks were displaying increasing reluctance to raise their exposure to many Third World countries.

SALs were unlike the usual project lending of the Bank because the funds could be quickly disbursed and used to pay for general imports. Untied financial support in exchange for policy changes in the borrowing country: the basic bargain for World Bank SALs is the same as that of the IMF stand-by arrangements and Extended Fund Facility. This has led to considerable blurring of the distinction between the roles of the two Bretton Woods institutions and to occasional juris-dictional wrangles between them.

A report on the earliest structural adjustment programmes (1 February 1980 to 30 June 1981) revealed the far-reaching range of the Bank's conditionality under these loans: trade and exchange-rate policies, policies in the energy, agriculture, and industry sectors, the review of national investment priorities, the financial performance and efficiency of public sector enterprises, the budget, tax policy, interest rates, and debt management—no important sector of the borrower's eco-nomic life is left untouched.

This obviously raises questions of how World Bank SALs differ from IMF Extended Fund Facilities, and it is a question which the Bank and Fund themselves have not always been able to answer. The official policy pronouncement on the subject was approved in 1967 and revised in 1970. It decreed that the Bank should have primary responsibility for 'the composition and appropriateness of development programs and policy evaluation, including development priorities', while the Fund had primary responsibility for 'exchange and restrictive systems, for adjustment of temporary balance-of-payments equilibrium and for evaluating and assisting members to work out stabilization programs'.

The Bank and the Fund do not disagree fundamentally on the major issues of policy conditionality. The Bank, like the Fund, opposes most forms of trade and payment restrictions and tries to promote the interests of foreign investors. When the two institutions clash, it is more over means than ends.

One significant difference is that the Fund has operated throughout its existence mainly in situations of foreign exchange crisis, since its services were not needed when capital was flowing freely into a country. The Bank, by contrast, evolved during decades when most countries were enjoying foreign capital in-flows and its role was that of channelling the funds from itself and other lenders into what it decreed to be the most important development priorities. Its bureaucratic structure is not accustomed to operating in today's conditions, when the capital in-flows dry up and reverse direction. The Bank's projects run into severe problems when the borrowing government can't afford to allot the necessary 'counterfeit' funds or supply the essential infrastructure, which helps to explain why the Bank failed to meet its own lending targets in the fiscal year 1985.

The Bank's SALs, however, are even more ambitious than IMF programmes because they intend a more lasting effect. IMF austerity measures, such as budget-cutting and credit ceilings, can be, and regularly are, reversed quickly as soon as the desired money is disbursed. Bank SALs clearly intend to make more lasting institutional changes which cannot be so readily reversed.

This more lasting effect can be a promise or a danger, depending on one's opinion of the wisdom of the Bank's development philosophy. Tony Killick, a critic of IMF austerity programmes, believes that World Bank conditionality is significantly different from that of the IMF and represents a hope for the future development of the country he studied, that is, Kenya.

Robin Broad, who studied the implementation of IMF and World Bank programme loans in the Philippines, sees no essential difference between the two. Indeed, she concluded that the World Bank, discreetly coached behind the scenes by the IMF, succeeded in achieving exactly those institutional changes which the IMF had tried, but failed, to implement. She perceived both programmes as aimed primarily at destroying protectionism and forcing the adoption of a strategy of export-led growth.

SALs were not the only vehicle through which the World Bank transferred non-project tied money in exchange for policy changes by the recipient country. Sector policy loans, in which the policy changes were directed at a particular but important sector, also helped to move money. In the fiscal year 1985, more than one billion dollars was committed in sector adjustment loans, compared to only 232 million in SALs.

Another programme with which the Bank tried to meet the new requirements of the post-1982 debt crisis era was its Special Action Programme or SAP. The emphasis in this programme was on speeding up disbursements, which normally lag several years behind commitments, in order to make money available in a hurry to needy borrowers. The programme, which was in effect for only two years, succeeded in raising the percentage of disbursements to commitments from 61 per cent in 1982 and 1983 to 72 per cent in 1984 and 76 per cent in 1985.

But all of these programs together were only a drop in the bucket compared with the annual outflow of capital from Latin America. Of the ten major debtor countries, only the Philippines and Yugoslavia received SALs. Until the Baker initiative, it was agreed that non-project lending should not exceed 10 per cent of the Bank's total lending programme, or 30 per cent of its lending to a specific borrower. And it must be remembered that without a capital increase for the IBRD, and expanded contributions to IDA, all these special programmes were merely pushing money around from some borrowers to others and from future years to the present, not making more of it available.

Brazil illustrates the drawbacks of this programme. It was one of the main beneficiaries of the SAP: its borrowings increased from an average of $299 million per year in 1980–82 to an average of $935 million in 1983 and 1984. But when the disbursements were used up, Brazil still could not afford to supply the counterpart funds needed to complete the projects and now has to begin repaying some loans on projects which are not even completed. Net transfers from the World Bank to Brazil may be negative in 1986.

PROMOTING PRIVATE ENTERPRISE

The World Bank's contributions to managing the debt crisis are not limited to lending its own money. The Bank has always considered its real mission to be the promotion of private loans and investment in the Third World. The conditions attached to its own lending have pushed to improve the climate for private capital (including emphasising changes in the borrower's legal and taxation system which favour foreign investment). And its persistent attempts to encourage commercial banks to consider selected Third World borrowers as excellent credit risks mean that it bears a considerable share of responsibility for the current debt débâcle. It is, even now, encouraging India and China to get ever deeper into debt.

Since the outbreak of the debt crisis, the Bank under Clausen's leadership has redoubled its efforts to entice private capital to the now much less attractive Third World arena. It has three new strategies to promote private capital flows: for the banks, new forms of co-financing; for equity investments, more activity by its International Finance Corporation subsidiary, and a new investment guarantee institution, MIGA.

Clausen's former institution, the Bank of America, was the first commercial bank to co-finance a project with the World Bank (in 1976). 'I liked it then as a commercial banker; I like it now as a development banker', he said in a 1982 interview. In January 1983 the Bank introduced a new type of co-financing with commercial banks, which they called the B-loans, to distinguish them from the Bank's traditional lending.

The new programme permitted a close relationship between the World Bank and the private banks in which the World Bank would either (1) participate directly in the later maturities of the loan, or (2) guarantee the later maturities, or (3) accept a contingent liability if a portion of a loan remained unpaid after expiration of the original maturity. This would happen if a borrower were guaranteed that its annual debt-service payments would remain stable although interest received by the commercial banks would fluctuate according to the market. If interest rates rose, the borrower would pay full interest but reduced amortisation, and the unpaid amount would be payable after the contracted expiration date. It is this unpaid amount that would be guaranteed by the World Bank.

The advantage to the borrower in these cases, the Bank stated, would be the availability of loans for longer periods and at better rates than the borrowers could normally obtain in the market. For some countries, of course, the money would not have been obtainable at all from the market without the Bank's participation. The lenders would receive 'comfort' from their association with the World Bank and the right to 'exchange of information and joint consultation' on the economic condition of the borrowers.

The latest (fiscal year 1985) annual report states that eleven B-loans, utilising all three options (direct participation, guarantee and contingent liability) had been signed in 1984 and 1985. The directors expressed satisfaction with the pilot programme and extended it for another year.

In mid-1985, however, the Bank got into trouble when the US Treasury objected to its plan to guarantee $200 million of commercial bank lending to Chile as part of a total rescue package amounting to more than a billion dollars, including one of the Bank's own SALs. The objections forced the World Bank to rewrite its loan and the guarantees, this time tying the money to a project to co-finance highway construction. Under the new plan the World Bank would supply $140 million and guarantee a further $150 million of bank loans.

This episode suggests that the Bank's guarantee power will be used sparingly, but it also illustrates the critical role that the guarantee function can play. Despite the US Treasury's reluctance, it 'became convinced bankers wouldn't lend Chile the money it needs to cover its international payments deficit this year and next without the World Bank guarantee, and that could push Chile to default on its $20 billion foreign debt.' A senior US Treasury official was quoted as saying that the Treasury didn't want to 'put Chile to the wall and play Russian roulette with the banks.'

The B-loan strategy, like most other components of the official management of the debt crisis, assumes that the capital market for the Third World will get back to normal in the near future. But what if it doesn't, as seems more likely? Guarantees are cheap, as long as they are never used. But if they ever have to be used—if the debt crisis gets worse rather than better—they will be either very costly to the guarantor, or worthless.

The direct investment solution to the debt crisis is popular with the Reagan administration, and the World Bank is trying valiantly to promote it. Private foreign investment has its disadvantages, of course; one reason for the fad for sovereign loans in their heyday was the disillusionment on the part of both investors and host countries with foreign equity investment. Countries were unhappy because vital parts of their economies were under foreign control and profits were shipped out of supposedly capital-short economies; investors were vulnerable to exchange controls and nationalisation, as well as taxation and labour legislation which hobbled their freedom of action.

The Bank's sponsorship of the Multilateral Investment Guarantee Agency (MIGA), which was approved by the Board of Governors at the 1985 annual meeting, attempts to promote a new surge of investment by providing insurance against those fears of investors. MIGA is authorised to cover private investors against these risks:

* Risk of host government restrictions on currency conversion and transfer.
* Risk of loss resulting from legislative actions or administrative actions and omissions of the host government that have the effect of depriving foreign investors of ownership or control of, or substantial benefits from, their investments.
* Risk of repudiation of government contracts where investors have no access to a competent forum, face unreasonable judicial delays, or are unable to enforce rulings issued in their favour.
* Risk of armed conflict or civil unrest.
* Other non-commercial risk.

MIGA will have a capital base of SDR 1 billion, with a complicated voting formula designed to assure rough parity between capital-exporting and capital-importing countries. In fact it seems designed to offend or threaten no one. Since other investment guarantee programmes such as the US's OPIC already exist, MIGA is intended to supplement such schemes through co-insurance and re-insurance, and is for investments that are not eligible for national or private coverage. It will, however, give the World Bank yet one more handle with which to lobby governments to improve the climate for foreign investment.

The International Finance Corporation has come into new prominence in the current climate of acclaim for the private investor as the key to development. Although still much smaller than the IBRD and IDA, the International Finance Corporation, the Bank's subsidiary devoted to direct lending to and co-investment with private, including foreign, investors is in the process of doubling its capital base and operations. It has an ambitious five-year plan for 1985–9, during which it hopes to invest $7.4 billion of its own money in projects and to act as catalyst for over $25 billion from other investors and lenders.

In addition to its traditional function of promoting private direct investment, preferably in the form of joint ventures between local and foreign investors, the IFC has become very active in promoting the flow of foreign portfolio investment to the Third World. In portfolio investment, investors purchase non-controlling shares of Third World corporations, often in the form of stock market mutual funds.

One recent IFC operation was the underwriting of the Korea Fund, under which large institutional investors in industrial countries can purchase shares of South Korean companies. Negotiations are under way for similar funds for Brazil and Thailand, with India a possible future candidate. Another type of fund, the Emerging Markets Growth Fund, will invest funds from Europe, Asia, and the US in stocks listed on stock exchanges of several different Asian and Latin American countries.

This growth in portfolio sales to institutional investors may be the big news of the 1980s. It is estimated that US investors now own $16 billion in foreign stocks, up from $3 billion only five years ago. Although only a fraction of these are in Third World stocks, the IFC is working hard to open up markets such as that in Korea which are otherwise closed to foreign investors.

If the debt crisis persists, however, these investors may find that this is just another way to lose money. Third World stock exchanges are notoriously volatile and scandal-prone. The commercial bankers have long cast hungry eyes on the huge amounts of money owned by US pension funds and insurance companies; now, with the assistance of the World Bank, they are beginning to tap these funds.

The IFC is perfectly conscious that they are helping to bail out the banks. According to an internal document of the corporation obtained by a journalist, 'It may be possible to convert some bank claims on LDCs into obligations in investment trusts which could be traded abroad. If this can be done, foreign banks may be able to encash or liquefy loan positions while the debtor country converts an external debt obligation into a long-term marketable foreign claim.' The paper pointed out that commercial banks represent only 35 per cent of national-savings flows in developed countries, whereas institutional investors absorb a further 30–40 per cent of savings, 'all of which are available for long-term investment.'

As portfolio investment rises, direct foreign investment has declined from an average of $11.6 billion per year in 1979–82 to $9.1 billion in 1984. The IFC itself has suffered from 'deterioration in the condition' of its portfolio in the wake of the debt crisis. As Clausen observed in a speech last year, 'factors inhibiting commercial lending usually inhibit direct investments too'.

THE 'BAKER INITIATIVE'

The 'Baker initiative' of September–October 1985 had two prongs. The first was aimed at the African debt crisis, the second at Latin America.

The African countries that were threatening to default on some $7 billion in repayments to the IMF were not large borrowers from the banks. They had become indebted through borrowing on concessional terms from official creditors, and would have to be rescued by concessional official finance, For these countries Baker proposed a joint World Bank–IMF lending pool totalling $5 billion. The proposal suggested that $2.7 billion worth of repayments due to the IMF's Trust Fund should be channelled to countries in difficulty, and that the Fund and the Bank should cooperate in enforcing conditionality on these countries.

When the IMF interim committee met in Seoul, it endorsed the idea of devoting the Trust Fund money to a special fund for Africa, but refused to agree to joint IMF-Bank operations and conditionality. It is not yet clear where the rest of the money will come from to make up the total of $5 billion, or how this fund will be related to the Africa fund already established by the Bank. The IMF has to help bail *itself* out this time, although it is also not clear how $2.7 or even $5 billion will serve to bail out countries which owe a total of $7 billion to the fund.

The second prong of the Baker strategy is designed for Latin America and five other countries which are heavily indebted to commercial banks. According to the proposal, the private banks are to put up $20 billion in new money over the next three years while the World Bank and the Inter-American Development Bank will accelerate their disbursements and concentrate them in high conditionality pro-gramme lending to the designated countries, for an additional amount of $9 billion in the same period.

The abrupt turn-around in the US attitude toward the World Bank was rich in irony. At the time of the Seoul meeting, the US had not yet voted in favour of the IFC's capital increase, nor had it contributed to the IDA's Special Facility for sub-Saharan Africa which began operations in July 1985 with funds of only $255 million. After years of turning a cold shoulder to Clausen's pleas for more funds and making it clear that he would not be reappointed when his term as president expires in June 1986, the Reagan administration suddenly grabbed most of his blueprints and began to exalt the role of an institution with a lame-duck executive.

Despite assurances that the Baker proposal did not intend to down-grade the role of the IMF, that is exactly what it was doing, for two good reasons. The first is that the Fund itself is running out of money, as explained above. The second reason is that the Fund is inextricably identified with painful 'austerity' programmes that are no longer acceptable, nor even very effective in the few countries (such as Jamaica) where they are sincerely applied.

By comparison with the IMF, the World Bank's overall net transfers are still respectively positive: for the IBRD, disbursements minus repayments minus interest and fees left a net transfer of $2.4 billion in the fiscal year 1985. IDA disbursements, although slightly lower than the two previous years, were nearly $2.5 billion and reverse flows were negligible . . . . With stepped-up disbursements and a general capital increase in the near future, gross disbursements could keep ahead of the repayment and interest flow for several more years. And the Baker plan would lift the previous limits (10 per cent of total lending) for policy-linked quick-disbursing programme loans such as the SALs and the sector policy loans.

But the Bank itself is not immune to the same repayment problems suffered by commercial banks and the IMF, although it likes to pretend it is. This year, for the first time in its history, the Bank admitted it had a non-accruing loan, defined as one on which interest payments were more than six months late. (The IDA had already admitted, that Chad had been in arrears for more than four years on an IDA credit, so this was a 'first' only for the IBRD.)

Political reasons certainly explain why Nicaragua was nearly nine million dollars in arrears on its World Bank repayments—the Reagan administration has made it clear that the Sandinistas will receive no new loans from the Bank—and political hostility probably explains why the loan was placed in non-accrual status, when past arrears have been quietly covered up. Payments from countries other than Nicaragua which were overdue more than three months amounted to $2.46 million at 30 June 1985, a very small amount relative to the total portfolio, but much larger than the $352,000 reported at the end of the previous fiscal year.

In the current debt situation, the Bank's announced policy of never rescheduling a loan seems unrealistic rather than reassuring. Like the commercial banks, the

World Bank keeps payments current by lending new money to errant debtors (except Nicaragua).

The World Bank does have funds to lend, but there is another reason it has been wheeled on stage to replace the IMF. The debtor countries are tired of austerity and want to get back to growth. The Reagan administration is trying to co-opt this bandwagon. 'Growth' has replaced austerity as the new buzzword. George Shultz, the US Secretary of State, told a Brazilian journalist who approached him after a speech at the UN, 'Take this down carefully. We support economic growth.'

Reading between the lines of explanations by US Treasury officials, in which the thought is frequently expressed that countries must have 'hope' and must be able to see 'light at the end of the tunnel', the suspicion grows that the World Bank's traditional association with 'development' is being exploited as a sugar-coating to make present austerity palatable.

This is precisely how the World Bank was used in the economic restructuring of the Philippines economy, according to Robin Broad's analysis. 'The IMF had failed in its attempt to sell a similar package,' she wrote, 'in part because it could not shake its image as purveyor of austerity and social upheaval.' The Bank, on the other hand, 'was aided by its more benevolent image as a bestower of funds for long-term development projects. Clothed in this benevolence, the World Bank was able to act out the short-term stabilization role of the IMF.'

Substantively the Baker plan contains very little that is really new. It proposes that everyone continue doing what they were supposed to have been doing anyway: the countries are to obey conditions laid down by the Fund and the Bank, the commercial banks are to lend more to countries they now *know* are bad risks, and the US government will, maybe, cough up some more funds sometime in the future. If the formula hasn't worked before, why should it work now?

The additional money, if any, which the plan will mobilise will not but much compliance, or growth. The $29 billion envisioned in the Baker plan should be compared with the interest bill of $135 billion which the fifteen selected debtor countries will have to pay over the same three years. The US Congress may be even less willing to approve a capital increase for the World Bank than they were to vote a similar increase for the IMF which barely squeaked through in 1983, but without the capital increase the Bank will soon find itself in the same trouble the IMF is in now.

The Baker plan is an act of desperation, not a viable blueprint for solving the debt crisis. The US government is playing poker with an empty hand, while pressuring the banks to throw good money after bad in a last-ditch attempt to purchase conditionality and prevent independent decision-making in the debtor countries. But things are falling apart fast, and the next few years should be extremely interesting.

23. Towards a Development Strategy and Action Programme for the South

The South Commission

A. THE PURPOSE OF THE SOUTH COMMISSION

1. As the 20th century draws to a close, it is imperative to make a fresh and objective analysis of the formidable economic, social and political challenges confronting the nations of the Third World, and of the ways to meet these.

2. The South Commission is meant to respond to this need. Its purpose is to produce such an analysis and to derive from it a strategy and a set of policy and action-oriented proposals which stem from the South and are based on the needs of the South.

3. The Commission is an independent body. Its members are all from the developing countries. They act in their individual capacities and bring to their assignment a diversity of development experience acquired in their own countries and internationally.

4. This is the first time that a group of thinkers and practitioners exclusively from the South, broadly reflecting interests and conditions of different regions and countries that make up the Third World, will apply their collective mind, over a period of time, to the issues of sustainable, people-centered, self-reliant development. By that is meant development which is socially just, economically efficient and ecologically sound.

5. The Commission will seek to fashion a well-founded, realistic and practical strategy and programme of action for the Third World. It will highlight the immense potential of South-South cooperation as a means of widening development options open to the Third World. And, it will also address itself to the task of equitable management of an increasingly complex and interdependent world economy.

B. THE SETTING—CRISIS AND OPPORTUNITY

6. The drive for development received a massive impetus following post World War II decolonization. The newly sovereign nations recognised that political independence would acquire its true meaning and substance only if they could overcome the state of chronic poverty and underdevelopment which they had inherited.

7. In their quest for development and modernization, developing countries faced formidable obstacles. Their economies were weak and underdeveloped, and were linked in a subordinate manner to the economies of developed nations. Their political structures were fragile, and their social structures were involved in processes of change that were frequently painful for those involved. These conditions often severely limited their absorptive capacity for the productive use of resources and their ability to mobilise additional internal resources for development.

8. Further, they had to contend with the inequities of the post-war international trading and financial system, which had been designed and set up by the developed countries to promote their own interests. The system was not geared to be sufficiently responsive to the needs of development. And the South was seen by and large as a minor appendage to the world economy, a geographic and political periphery that was supposed to continue to play a well-defined role in support of the traditional centres of economic and political power.

9. Despite these handicaps, the overall record of national development in the countries of the South was fairly impressive until the closing years of the 1970s, even though the pace of social and economic change fell short of their aspirations and objective needs.

10. Judging by the trends of growth rates, savings and investment ratios, industrialization and the modernization of traditional agriculture, and such sensitive social indicators as school enrolment and life expectancy at birth, several developing countries amply demonstrated their capacity to make productive use of available physical and human resources. Yet there were a number of unsatisfactory features of the development scene. In particular, fair distribution of the gains of economic development, and the creation of new productive employment opportunities for the growing labour force, had received inadequate attention.

11. The decade of the 1980s, however, has witnessed a severe discontinuity and reversal of the earlier more hopeful trends in growth performance. It has been characterized by a profound development crisis in which both current consumption and productive investments have continued to fall year after year in a large number of developing countries. Financial systems and resource mobilization have experienced an unprecedented strain. Development processes have been shaken to their very foundations in many Third World countries. Many of them are in a state of political, economic and social disarray. Important economic and social goals and programmes have had to be shelved, while a number of basic development indicators show a sharp retrogression.

12. Development is a multidimensional process in which a large number of variables, both internal and external, interact and influence the pace and direction of social and economic change. The current economic crisis had highlighted the deficiencies of development and of the development planning process in Third World countries, including the allocation and utilization of resources and the management of public financial systems and public sector enterprises.

13. However, it is clear that the sharp deterioration in the international economic environment for development in the 1980s has played by far the major role in triggering off the acute development crisis which now afflicts Third World countries. Among the indicators of this unpropitious environment are the unsustainable and crushing burden of external indebtedness, substantial decline in export earnings due to acutely depressed commodity prices and increasing protectionism, steeply declining flows of resource transfers from developed to developing countries, and the chronic instability of international currency markets as well as the prevalence of abnormally high levels of real interest rates.

14. Yet, apart from some rather tentative, ad hoc and often unsuccessful efforts at international crisis management, there has been no attempt to grapple with the

basic task of systemic reform so as to make for the efficient and equitable management of global interdependence in the interest of all countries.

15. Instead, international development cooperation has virtually come to a standstill. North-South negotiations have been stalemated. International actions aimed at promoting development, which had been agreed earlier, remain as distant as ever in terms of implementation. The United Nations and international development institutions have been in retreat.

16. The income and development disparities between developing countries and the industrialized North have widened. New gaps are emerging, mostly based on rapid scientific and technological advances in the industrialized countries. These have significant yet still only dimly perceived implications for economic and power relationships between South and North, and for the shape of the world's political economy in general.

17. In the major developed market countries in the North, shifts in the political balance of forces have led to increased emphasis on the role of market forces and a diminished role for the state in the management of social and economic processes and change. These shifts have had a significant global fall-out. The emphasis on the primacy of market has further weakened the already fragile structure of multilateral cooperation in support of Third World development. There has been a serious questioning of the basic principles of multilateralism and of the appropriateness of cooperative international action, especially that aimed at altering or modifying the outcome of market forces. Moreover, prescriptions for domestic development based on this new orthodoxy have been pressed upon the developing countries through the conditionality criteria of international financial institutions. This was done without regard for their realism or relevance, or for the feelings of these countries and their peoples.

18. Yet, every crisis also carries in itself the opportunity for change. The countries of the North have not been spared from mounting and very serious domestic problems and social tensions, unemployment, and economic stagnation. They have also been experiencing increasing conflicts of interest and problems in mutual relations. With growing frequency, doubts are now being expressed regarding the adequacy of the established models to deal with contemporary problems and demands.

19. In particular, the recent instability of the stock and foreign exchange markets and the repercussions of this on the international economy have highlighted the urgent need for a significant degree of collective management of the world economy. Even those circles and decision-makers in the North most opposed to such cooperation now appear to realize, albeit with continuing reluctance, that present practices cannot continue for much longer, and that it may be in the best interest of their own countries to consider new approaches.

20. Important structural and political changes are also occurring in the North, spearheaded by continuing scientific and technological change. These changes have significant implications for humankind, for international cooperation, for the developing countries and for the shape of things to come in the years ahead. Were they to be used for the common good of the peoples of the world and given appropriate policy guidance, new vistas could be opened up and many challenges overcome.

21. Following many decades of global confrontation and an accelerating arms race, the first promising steps are being taken to defuse tensions and reduce the risk of nuclear war. The improvements in East-West relations and the efforts to reduce the nuclear arms race may increase the possibilities of global cooperation and create a political environment favourable to resolution of the outstanding issues on the international development agenda. An additional factor in this evolving environment arises from changes taking place in the centrally-planned economies, their greater outward orientation and participation in international economic relations.

22. In the South itself, where social tensions and economic crises have become the main feature of the 1980s, there is a new consciousness that the severe deprivation and retrenchment forced on it in the name of adjustment has reached the limits of endurance. The need for purposeful domestic reform is appreciated. There is renewed emphasis on national self-reliance and greater South-South cooperation as a means of coping with the South's continued victimization by a global system in the design and management of which the South has very little to say.

23. In the North also, there is a growing awareness that the destitution to which many Third World countries have been reduced in the wake of the debt crisis has severe disruptive consequences for the world economy as a whole. There is now a somewhat greater, albeit limited, willingness to recognize the contribution that growth in the Third World could make to a more healthy world economy, to a faster growth of international trade and to easing the payments imbalances that exist among major developed countries.

24. The evolving situation thus contains a number of elements which, if harnessed properly, could provide the basis for a fresh start in the task of devising a new global system of collective economic security in which promotion of Third World development would be a key constituent. These positive and more hopeful tendencies are, however, still not strong enough to break the powerful hold of the status quo.

25. But an opportunity now exists for change. This opportunity must be seized. With all interests and countries represented, a global agenda and framework for action needs to be worked out. It should allow for a collective resolution of the existing problems and challenges and also those which will arise in the coming decades. And, it should enlist the promise of scientific and technological change for the good of all peoples and for sustainable development. In the absence of such a new global design of international cooperation for development, the world community will remain mired in mounting contradictions and multiplying crises. These will be a constant threat to peace and lead to a highly unstable world, divided into some countries with the prospect of expanding opportunities and the power to dominate, and the majority locked in poverty, destitution and dependence.

26. The South must take an active part in this process. It must begin by reassessing its own situation and options. New ways must be found to revive and sustain the development process by relying to the maximum extent possible on the South's own capabilities and resources. The creative potential of national self-reliance and South-South cooperation must be fully harnessed. Simultaneously, there must be a careful reassessment of the role of the South as an actor on the global scene, including the role it could play as a new engine for sustaining the

momentum of economic expansion in the world economy. The South's power and influence in ensuring a more equitable management of the world economy will certainly be enhanced thereby. The South Commission has been created to respond to this challenge.

C. TERMS OF REFERENCE OF THE SOUTH COMMISSION

27. Taking this situation as its starting point and in order to assist in the process of positive change and to help mobilize the peoples of the South, the Commission has set for itself the following closely interrelated objectives which constitute its terms of reference:

(a) *Analysis of national development experience in the South and elaboration of an integrated perspective and vision of the future*

The Commission will undertake a critical analysis of post-World War II development experience and the lessons it holds for development planning in the future. Having defined development, it will assess the weaknesses and strengths of the developing countries; their development prospects; the constraints they face; the options open to them; and the scope for improved mobilization and utilization of their physical, financial and human resources.

On the basis of this analysis, the Commission will outline development goals and objectives for the year 2000 and beyond. In doing so, it will take into account the changing demographic, social and economic conditions in the Third World, and the evolving global environment.

The Commission will also make suggestions for reformulating and updating, wherever necessary, the patterns and strategies of growth to achieve the goals of self-reliance, development and equity. In doing so it will take into account both the immense promise and potential offered by modern science and technology and the current human and other resource realities. In all its work the Commission will pay special attention to issues relating to poverty and hunger, the satisfaction of basic human needs, human resource development and industrialization of the Third World.

(b) *Analysis of the global environment*

The Commission will analyse and comment on the evolving global environment as this is influenced by political, economic and technological changes in the North; it will assess the implications of this evolution for the South and for the planning of development in the South.

It will study: the nature of the evolving interdependence of the world; the impact and effects of the transnationalization process; the interrelationship between development and issues relating to world peace and security; the state of the biosphere, with the challenges this poses to humankind and the management of the global commons. On the basis of these studies the Commission will make appropriate proposals for the equitable management of global interdependence and the building of a new world order.

(c) *South-South cooperation for collective self-reliance*

The Commission will carefully assess the role of South-South cooperation in widening the options for development strategies. It will analyse the experience acquired by current and past efforts to achieve such cooperation at every level. It will draw upon this experience to identify weaknesses and obstacles to South-South cooperation, and propose measures that will help to overcome them and to promote a fuller use of the existing potential for collective self-reliance in the South. The Commission will thus seek to foster various modes of South-South cooperation (sub-regional, regional, interregional and global) as an essential support to processes of self-reliant national development.

The Commission will examine the need for and the value of a permanent, institutionalized support mechanism for South-South cooperation. It will thus consider whether there is a need for a Third World secretariat and a forum at the global level which, *inter alia*, would promote greater knowledge of the South among the countries and the peoples of the South, serve as a focus for continuing interaction and mutual consultations among developing countries, carry out research and support their negotiations with the North, and act as a focal point for the exchange of information relevant to development.

(d) *South-North relations*

The Commission will assess the state of South-North relations, and analyse their post-war evolution. On the basis of this assessment, and its analysis of the present and probable future global environment, and the imperatives of development, the Commission will examine: the current position of the South in relation to the North; and see how the voice of the South can be strengthened, and its role enhanced, in the search for and implementation of greater equity in a new world order.

The Commission will seek to rethink, to update and, where necessary, to reformulate the intellectual foundations, the strategy and tactics, and the institutional structures of the South in its dealings with the North. The Commission will highlight the close linkages that exist between the international arrangements for money, finance and trade and their impact on the pace of development in the world economy in general and in the South in particular. It will pay special attention to issues related to a reform of international arrangements for trade, science and technology, money and finance, and intellectual property; the management of transnational actors and processes; the global commons and the human environment; and the future of multilateralism and reform of the United Nations system.

D. THE TASK OF THE SOUTH COMMISSION

28. The task of the South Commission is an exciting and challenging one. It hopes to act as a catalyst that will help set in motion a fresh process of public consciousness-raising and also an intellectual reassessment of policy, of action, and

of institutional initiatives on the part of the developing countries. For, it bears repeating, the mobilization of the polities and peoples of the developing countries is essential if their future is to be shaped by them, and in accordance with their own wishes; if they are to improve their position on the global scene; and they are to meet the domestic challenges of growth, development and equity.

29. The terms of reference that the Commission has set for itself are broad and flexible. They will enable it to deal with the major problems now facing the countries of the South. Further, the Commission is an independent body, made up of people acting in their individual capacities. It will thus be free from the constraints which inevitably inhibit governments or government representatives in commenting on problems or in arriving at common positions.

30. The Commission is primarily speaking to its own constituency in the South. It intends to express its views unequivocally, and to concentrate its efforts and energies in a quest for clarity in defining the problems facing the South, in seeking answers to these problems and in suggesting a concrete action programme to be taken—especially by the South.

31. But the Commission is addressing global problems, and the shared interests of the community of nations. Thus, it will also speak to the world at large. It will aim at enlightening, provoking, and persuading an audience in the North, both among public opinion in the Eastern and Western countries, and among those who decide and shape the political processes in these countries and whose decisions have profound consequences beyond their national and regional boundaries for all peoples in this increasingly interlocked and interdependent world.

32. The Commission will be concerned with the past, present, and future. It will deal with ideas, conceptual frameworks, as well as action-oriented programmes. Indeed, one of its main objectives will be to suggest practical measures to cope with the problems facing the South to which policy- and decision-makers and the peoples in developing countries will give serious consideration.

33. The South Commission's objectives, as outlined above, are ambitious and all-encompassing. It is confident that it will not be alone in its undertaking. It will rely heavily on the support of peoples, government and institutions of Third World countries, and welcome that of friends and well-wishers in the North. Indeed, the extent to which the Commission fulfils its objectives will depend on the degree and quality of the support it received from outside its own membership, and on its ability to mobilize and benefit from such support.

34. By the end of its three-year mandate, the Commission expects that a self-sustaining political and intellectual process will be under way, carrying forward the ideas and actions which emerge from its work.

MEMBERSHIP OF THE SOUTH COMMISSION

Chairperson

Julius K. Nyerere, POB 9151, *Dar-es-Salaam*, Tanzania

Members

Ismail-Sabri Abdalla, POB 43, Orman, Guizeh, *Cairo*, Egypt
Abdellatif Al-Hamad, POB 21923, 13080 *Safat*, Kuwait
Cardinal Paulo Evaristo Arns, Ave Higienopolis 890, 01238 Sao Paulo, SP, Brazil
Solita Collas-Monsod (Ms), National Economic & Development Authority, Amber Avenue, Pasig, Metro Manila, Philippines
Eneas da Conceicao Comiche, Banco de Moçambique, POB 423, Maputo, Mozambique
Gamani Corea, 21 Horton Place, Colombo 7, Sri Lanka
Aboubakar Diaby-Ouattara, BP 2658, Abidjan 01, Côte d'Ivoire
Aldo Ferrer, Ave del Libertador 1750, 1425 Buenos Aires, Argentina
Celso Furtado, Minister of Culture, Esplanada dos Ministerios, Bloco L, 9 Andar, 70047 Brasilia DF, Brazil
Enrique Iglesias, Presidente, Banco interamericano de desarrollo, 808 17th Street NW, Washington DC 20577, USA
Devaki Jain (Ms), DAWN, Milap Vatika 19c/UA, Jawahar Nagar, New Delhi 110 007, India
Simba Makoni, Executive Secretary SADCC, Private Bag 0095, Gaberone, Botswana
Michael Manley, PNP Headquarters, 89 Old Hope Road, Kingston 6, Jamaica
Jorge Eduardo Navarrete, Ambassador of Mexico, 8 Halkin Street, London SW1X 7DW, UK
Pius Okigbo, POB 7907 Victoria Island, Lagos, Nigeria
Augustin Papic, Temisvarska 5a, 11000 Belgrade, Yugoslavia
Carlos Andrés Pérez, Ave Libertador, Torre Las Delicias PH, Caracas, Venezuela
Jiadong Qian, Permanent Representative of the People's Republic of China, Chemin de Surville 11, 1213 Petit-Lancy, Switzerland
Shridath Ramphal, Commonwealth Secretary-General, Marlborough House, Pall Mall, London SW1, UK
Carlos Rafael Rodriguez, Consejo de Estado, Palacio de la Revolución, La Habana, Cuba
Abdus Salam, International Centre for Theoretical Physics, POB 586, 34100 Trieste, Italy
Marie-Angélique Savané (Ms), c/o PNUD, BP 154, Dakar, Sénégal
Tan Sri Ghazali Shafie, 15 Jalan Ampang Hilir, 55000 Kuala Lumpur, Malaysia
Tupuola Efi Tupua Tamasese, Deputy Prime Minister, POB 191, Apia, Western Samoa
Nitisastro Widjojo, Jl. Imama Bonjol 4, Jakarta, Indonesia
Layachi Yaker, BP 01 Bir Mourad Rais-Allende, 16300 El Djezair, Algeria

Secretary-General

Manmohan Singh, South Commission Secretariat, CP 228, 1211 Geneva 19, Switzerland

24. Role of People in the Future Global Order

Chadwick F. Alger

INTRODUCTION

The changing international order suggests the necessity of thinking more intensively about the role *people* might and should play in the future global order. By people we mean, with Webster's, 'persons who form part of the aggregate of human beings'. The subject is far broader than public participation in foreign-policy making by national governments. It is also more than public involvement in international nongovernmental organizations. What we are asking is the role *all* persons who form part of the aggregate of human beings might and should play in the future global order. Three changing aspects of the present international order suggest that it would be a mistake to ask a narrower question which would assume traditional institutional framework for this participation:

The first is the degree to which people everywhere, in their daily lives, are increasingly involved in global processes—food production and consumption, resource production and consumption, manufacture and consumption of consumer goods, environmental pollution, inflation, and employment. This is an *integrative* process of peoples. For the most part, people have not willed this integration. Most are not even aware of it. It has been thrust upon them as large and powerful organizations (in manufacturing, distribution, finance and government) have employed new technology in the pursuit of their objectives.

The second is three kinds of *disintegrative* processes within nation-states: (i) In some cases, decentralization is taking place as national governments, particularly in larger countries faced with a growing agenda of social and economic issues, cannot adequately serve public needs from a single center. (ii) In other cases, ethnic, cultural and economic regions within nation-states desire internal autonomy and sometimes even want direct relations with other countries and their subunits. (iii) In still other cases, new technologies in transportation and communication are permitting and encouraging intensive direct international involvement of cities and regional areas within countries, causing *disintegrative* tendencies within the country but setting in motion *integrative* processes with respect to regions outside the country.

Third is the change taking place in proposals for Third World participation in the future global order. These proposals, mostly under the label of a New International Economic Order, increasingly emphasize self-reliance and fulfillment of needs. These emphases challenge formerly unquestioned assumptions about the role of the nation-state in Third World development. Earlier, there seemed to be an essential difference between opportunities for participation by people in industrialized countries and those in Third World countries. In the older industrialized countries, an increasing number of commentators had considered it necessary to think more creatively about transnational participation of people. In some respects, the old nation-states seemed to have outlived their usefulness. But voices from the

Third World seemed to be saying in unison that national development was required before people in Third World countries could begin to enjoy widespread participation in national affairs, let alone participation in international affairs. As we shall describe more fully later, serious emphasis on self-reliance and fulfillment of needs in the Third World may require opportunities for Third World people to more directly control the international dimension of their lives.

It is not easy to tease out the implications of these three factors for the future, but they do suggest one important implication. The political fragmentation of the colonial empires that were established in Africa, Asia and Latin America seems to be only the first stage in the transformation of the basic organization of humankind. Initial proposals for a New International Economic Order were primarily demands for extending the political independence of nation-states that split off from these empires to include economic independence. But the process does not stop here. Units other than the presently recognized nation-states are demanding direct linkage to the world, and others are being propelled there by new technologies. It is very difficult even to speculate about what kind of global future this will bring about or how one might advocate steering this emerging system into desirable directions. The present nation-states will not be the exclusive building blocks for the future global order. Yet, virtually all future thinking has assumed that this will be the case. Likewise, those who are advocating self-reliance and fulfillment of needs tend to imply that decolonization will stop at existing national borders. The three major trends outlined above suggest that self-reliance and fulfillment of needs will require that people become full participants in the global systems in which they are involved, overcoming traditional deference in foreign policy matters to elites in present national capitals.

This paper will describe the evolution of criteria for a New International Economic Order, examine the implications of these emerging criteria for local communities in the Third World, and the public attitudes in industrialized countries toward the Third World as well as the potential new forms of linkage between local communities, both within the Third World and between communities in the industrialized world and the Third World.

Before these matters are discussed, it will be necessary to consider the analytic and perceptual problems that the nation-state unit of analysis creates in thinking about people in a future global order. This will lead to a hard look at the nation-state as it is today and to a consideration of the integrative aspects of nation-state disintegration.

NATION-STATE AS A PERCEPTUAL AND ANALYTIC PROBLEM

Although the nation-state did not begin to emerge until the late 17th century, it provides the perceptual screen through which scholars, journalists and policy-makers tend to view the past, present and future world. Past history of the various ethnic, cultural and political units is reinterpreted in terms of present nation-state boundaries. The fact that nation-states are heterogeneously composed tends to be lost. Yet, writes Harold R. Isaacs: 'If the homogeneously national nation-state ever did exist anywhere, it does not exist any more, except perhaps in one or two places on earth, as in Japan. Remarkably, Isaac's main point is beautifully confirmed, while his example is refuted, by Kimitada Miwa when he writes how the 'myth and ideology about a unified imperial state' erased the memory that the Japanese are a multi-racial people composed of conquerors and the conquered'.

Increasing interest in transnational relations has been exceedingly useful in extending the traditional nation-state paradigm, although the results produced thus far have two overall deficiencies. First, there is a tendency to overemphasize the recent growth in transnational relations and to overlook the processes that have linked humankind across distances for centuries—in religion, science, education, trade, technology—whatever the form of political and economic organization. Second, even work on transnational relations has not reconceptualized the basic unit of analysis—the nation-state. Any activity originating within the boundaries of a nation-state tends to be given a nation-state label. For example, trade between Fukuoka and Pusan would be viewed as Japanese-Korean trade, thereby preventing the analyst from perceiving and interpreting its relevance to past, present and future regional sentiment in Fukuoka. This is not to say that national trade statistics are not useful for some purposes, but they may obscure important transnational phenomena. Quincy Wright was keenly aware of this issue when he wrote:

It is not only the nations which international relations seeks to relate. Varied types of groups—nations, states, governments, peoples, regions, alliances, confederations, international organizations, even industrial organizations, cultural organizations, religious organizations—must be dealt with in the study of international relations, if the treatment is to be realistic.

Wright recognized that 'the term international relations is too narrow—perhaps *relations between powerful groups* would be technically better'. But he decided to use the term 'international relations' because 'it seems advisable to accept predominant usage'.

THE NATION-STATE OF TODAY

Before proceeding to a discussion of future relations among people across national boundaries, it is useful to examine more closely what the nation-state actually is today. The customary usage of this concept prevents many people from perceiving opportunities and responsibilities of global processes that link them to distant parts of the world in their daily lives—as consumers and producers of commodities and information, as investors and entrepreneurs, and as users of a diversity of global utilities in communication and transportation. The term nation-state actor is often used as a label for an entity for which the label national governmental actor would be more precise. The use of the latter term would help remove part of the mythology built around the activities of national governments in their relationships with other national governments—the mythology that tends to assume that they usually act legally and in the interest of people within their national boundaries. The myth has such a firm hold on the minds of people that even those who challenge national governments on a diversity of domestic issues are unwilling to do so with respect to their relations with other national governments. That is why the so-called democracies have never really applied democratic processes to foreign policy.

Many national governments do not actually represent the people within their national boundaries. In some cases, an urban clique or a tribe, an ethnic group or an interest group, simply use its control of external access as a means for controlling the remainder of the population in the pursuit of its own group interest. National governments vary greatly in wealth, function and influence, from Western Samoa to Singapore to Nepal to Peru to Sweden to France to the Soviet Union. Thus it is important to remember that the term national government covers a great variety of actors who represent a variety of groups—clique, tribe, city, corporation, ethnic group, interest group, military-industrial complex, etc.

INTEGRATIVE ASPECTS OF DISINTEGRATION OF NATION-STATE

Two trends are changing the world, both results of the application of new technologies to a variety of human activities. The first could be called an integrative process. An indicator of this process is the geometric growth in international, both governmental and nongovernmental, manufacturing, extractive, and financial organizations, largely in respone to the impact of technology on transportation and communication. The second process could be called disintegrative. The causes of disintegration may be more complicated, but one of these is the expanding functions of national governments, especially in the area of social services, spawning bureaucracies too large and cumbersome to adequately serve human needs. This has stimulated a move toward decentralization and has created a more fertile environment for within-nation ethnic and nationality groups, and regions, to demand greater autonomy— for example, in Catalonia, Breton, Scotland, Quebec, etc. The Mexican poet Octavio Paz may have had in mind both the demise of international colonial empires in Africa, Asia and Latin America and the growing challenge to internal colonialism when he said, 'Our century is a huge cauldron in which all historical eras are boiling and mingling.'

The cauldron that Paz perceived is vividly exemplified by Western Europe, where integrative processes move national capitals closer together at the same time as provinces and peripheral areas seek greater autonomy from national capitals. The Galway Declaration of the First Convention of the Authorities of European Peripheral Regions declares:

Everything is happening as if the construction of Europe was the concern of some privileged regions situated around the large capitals and large conurbations of North-West Europe, from London to Milan, from Paris to Hambourg, and could not interest to the same extent the peripheral regions, distant provinces, at the edges of Europe . . . Therefore around Europe in antithesis to the polygon of large urban republics where population, political power and financial means are concentrated, a sort of second Europe is tending to emerge.

When attention is focused on the internal processes of nation-states, the increased self-consciousness of provinces and peripheral areas is viewed as disintegrative. In fact, provinces and peripheral areas are not necessarily against all forms of integration, but simply wish integration to serve their interests. This is dramatized by the active part played by representatives from these areas in the European Conference of Local Authorities and by their demand for a new body in the Council of Europe on which they would be directly represented. It is also exemplified by the attention given to foreign policy (with a Scandinavian orientation) by the Scottish Nationalist Party and by the close ties of Quebec with France. Orianne eloquently highlights the integrative thrust of some nation-state disintegration: 'Time and mankind patiently strive to put together again what treaties and systems of law once tore asunder to meet the requirements of a particular type of political organization.'

The impact of technology on transportation and communication is making it possible for regions formerly isolated to establish direct links beyond their national boundaries. For example, before the jet airplane, air travel to Europe and Asia originated from a few cities on the east and west coasts of the United States. Now it originates from Houston, Atlanta, Pittsburgh, Cleveland, St. Louis and Chicago. Soon there will be more. If charter flights were included, the list would comprise at least thirty cities. Were we to add cities linked directly abroad by satellite, telex and other forms of electronic communication, many more cities would be included. In the same way, inland cities in Africa, Asia, Europe and Latin America are being increasingly linked directly to cities in other countries. The negative consequences and potential of new technologies for global linkages have received much attention as nation-states have used them for military purposes and transnational manufacturing and financial organizations have used them to build global conglomerates that outstrip all but a few nation-states in wealth and influence. But little attention has been given to the actual and potential opportunities they offer for direct participation in global systems.

NEW INTERNATIONAL ECONOMIC ORDER

The demand for a New International Economic Order evolved out of the new international political order that was created by the breakup of colonial empires into a number of countries. It should be noted that the so-called decolonialization did not dismantle the political units created by the colonialists for controlling colonial peoples. Instead, the new 'nation-states' were, for the most part, turned over to elites trained by their former colonial masters. The colonial elites thereby acquired a vested interest in the institutions they had inherited. Eventually, those in control of the new 'nation-states' sought to extend political independence to economic matters as well.

To a large degree, the United Nations has been the arena in which the New International Economic Order (NIEO) has been fashioned. While many conferences have been held outside the United Nations, it is unlikely that the pressure for the NIEO would have been built up as rapidly without opportunities for African, Asian and Latin American cooperation on the forums of the United Nations, which led to UNCTAD, the 'Group of 77', and the Sixth (1974) and Seventh (1975) Special Sessions of the General Assembly. Through this collaborative process, the Third World countries have gradually redefined their needs, moving from primary reliance on technical assistance to loans and grants of capital, to basic changes in the international economic system that would give them the ability to earn their own way through stable commodity prices, export of manufactured products, control over their own resources, access to new technology, and new mechanisms for Third

World collaboration. There have also been related demands for a new order with respect to information and communication.

At the same time, the goal of this process, *development*, has been invested with a new meaning. In the late 1950s and early 1960s, development normally meant increase in GNP per capita, primarily through mimicking Western industrialization in the Westernized sectors of Third World countries. The concept of GNP was part of the 'nation-state' mythology that ignored distribution inside national boundaries. GNP is now widely challenged as a measure of development, and Western economic development models are being increasingly rejected. Instead, satisfaction of needs and self-reliance are being proposed as indicators of development.

The 1975 Dag Hammarskjöld Report, 'What Now: Another Development', is illustrative of this approach. It was prepared on the occasion of the Seventh Special Session of the United Nations General Assembly in September 1975 at the initiative of the Dag Hammarskjöld Foundation and the UN Environment Program, with contributions from people in many countries. To distinguish the goal of the effort from earlier approaches, the authors label their goal as 'another development'. Concerned that development, in the sense of national economic growth rates, has usually not reduced mass poverty and alienation, they pose the following as 'elements of a conceptual framework' for their report:

1. Geared to the satisfaction of needs, beginning with the eradication of poverty.
2. Endogenous and self-reliant, that is, relying on the strength of the societies which undertake it.
3. In harmony with the environment.
4. Another development requires structural transformations.
5. Immediate action is necessary and possible.

Satisfaction of human needs and self-reliance are seen as closely intertwined:

Whether in food, habitat, health or education, it is not the absolute scarcity of resources which explains poverty in the Third World, but rather their distribution, traditional mechanisms fostering inequality having been aggravated by an indiscriminate imitation of the patterns of the industrialized societies. . . .

These observations do not imply jettisoning all that has been achieved to date. But what has so far been done should have been incorporated into innovative solutions stemming from the rich cultural diversity of mankind. At the very least, what should have been avoided was the devotion of almost exclusive attention to imported solutions that respond to other problems and interests.

Thus it is emphasized that 'another development' would be based on serving human needs as defined by people in specific cultural situations, rather than on building new institutions patterned after those in other countries and often responsive to needs in other countries.

Ecological considerations of 'another development' are closely linked to self-reliance and fulfillment of needs, preventing ecological issues from becoming a concern of only the industrialized world. The consumption of 68% of nine major minerals (oil excepted) by 18% of the world population in the industrial market economies, and the pressure this creates on the outer limits of the biosphere, is posed as a matter for Third World concern. Unequal economic relations is presented as a source of ecological problems when

peasants deprived of access to fertile soil monopolized by large landowners or by foreign companies have no other resource but the cultivation of marginal zones, contributing to erosion, deforestation and soil exhaustion, while consumption by the rich, modelled on that of the industrialized societies adds the pollution of wealth to that of misery. . . . In another development, on the contrary, the preservation and enhancement of the environment are inseparable from the satisfaction of needs.

Local Third World Communities
in the New International Economic Order

The meaning given to self-reliance is of critical importance. The authors carefully point out that it means neither isolation nor autarchy, but 'the autonomous capacity to develop and to make decisions, including that of entering into relations, on an equal footing, with other countries, which nations are bound to do'.

The structural transformation that will bring self-reliance would require changes in structures within countries as well as structures linking them to other countries, because of the joint exploitation of the Third World by both national governments and transnational corporations. The existing situation is characterized by:

- An international power structure largely based in the market-economy industrialized countries, but organically linked, in part of the Third World, to local structures, sometimes controlling them directly;
- Unequal economic relations, at the international level as well as within the majority of national systems;
- The contradiction between the privileged of both worlds should not conceal the contradiction between the exploiters and the exploited within each society. The latter, and principal, contradiction will often be more difficult to overcome than the former, which is secondary in so far as the exploitation of the poor is essential to the existence of the rich in each society, whereas the centre has much greater autonomy in relation to the periphery.

The authors are of the view that structural transformation must reach down to the local community:

Self-reliance acquires its full meaning only if rooted at the local level, and when local communities are fully able to practice it; thus, it is linked with structural reforms giving the poorest people the means to improve their lot. One could indeed imagine—and there have been cases—the ruling class of a Third World country, whether belonging to OPEC or not, improving its economic relations with the industrialized world by means of national or collective self-reliance and increasing at the same time its domination over its own people.

The change in structures within countries requires 'democratization of power', and 'decentralization', leaving each local community

to manage its own affairs and to enter into relations on an equal footing with others, in order to solve their common problems . . . Public and private bureaucracies would be subject to social control. The opacity of social mechanisms would give way to greater transparency, enabling the individual and the community to take control over their own lives.

Writing two years later, Ponna Wignaraja also emphasized the local role in development in an article provocatively titled 'From the Village to the Global Order: Elements in a Conceptual Framework'. Sharing the basic objectives of 'another development' (see Figure [24.]1) he advocates 'a shift of decision-making power toward the poor by initiating a "bottom-up" process, the village becoming the focal point of development'. He is concerned that the New International Economic Order could 'lock Third World countries into the very system from which they should initially de-link' rather than being an order 'which emerges naturally as the new process of national development is set in motion'. Wignaraja devotes even more attention to local autonomy than 'another development', building explicitly on the village and advocating decentralization of decision-making and participatory democracy.

The arguments of 'another development', a synthesis of the thinking of a group of individuals with global composition, and of Wignaraja, reflect, the concern expressed by many that a New International Economic Order would not improve the condition of people in Third World countries without internal changes in these countries. Among the advocates of local self-reliance are Jimoh Omo-Fadaka, Jan Tinbergen, Nathan M. Shamuyarira, Rajni Kothari, Paul T.K. Lin, and Ali A. Mazrui. Johan Galtung argues that without control over local natural resources 'by the local population through patterns of local self-reliance with mass participation, a New International Order may even make things worse. For example, higher commodity prices could lead to increased use of resources for production of exports rather than satisfying local needs, with profits enabling national elites to exercise even greater control over local populations and intensifying their harmony of interest with elites in other countries. Like others, Galtung argues against drawing a 'dividing line between international and intra-national affairs compartmentalizing the two away from each other in an unrealistic manner'.

The type of analysis that we have summarized is pictured in Figure [24.]2. The NIEO argues for more symmetrical relationships between national elites in developed countries and those in Third World countries, as represented by adding the dotted line linking national elites. Many commentators say that benefits from NIEO would flow primarily to these elites unless local and regional communities became more self-reliant, as represented by the dotted lines linking local and regional communities to national elites.

This line of thinking could lead to fundamental challenges to the basic structure of the nation-state system. In the present situation, national elite's control of subnational groups is greatly enhanced by their control of external political and economic relations. What will the implications of true local self-reliance be for this control? Minimally, it would require greater local and regional participation in foreign-policy making. Most likely, it would create new forms of governmental and nongovernmental organizations reflecting local and regional interests in foreign-policy making and execution. Looked at from another angle, given the present control of international linkages by national elites and the way in which these linkages support local and regional dependence, is local and regional self-reliance

FIGURE [24.]1 The macro framework for "another development." From P. Wignaraja, "From the Village to the Global Order: Elements in a Conceptual Framework," *Development Dialogue* 1 (1977), p. 41. Reprinted by permission of *Development Dialogue.*

OBJECTIVES

Human development
1 Fulfilment of men and women in terms of:
   a Finer values b Economic aspirations
2 Release of creative energies
3 Self-reliance
4 Cooperation
5 De-alienation
6 Participation

PROCESS

Structural transformation and mobilization
1 Shift of decision power:
   a Planning in the small
   b Planning in the large
2 Village as the focal point of development
3 Education:
   a Raising mass consciousness
   b Remoulding of élites
4 Total mobilization*
   a Transforming labour into means of production
   b Use of local resources
   c Development of appropriate technology

---

* Reinforced by participatory democracy, supported at the micro level by new principles of project design and evaluation; a dual approach, R & D and action research; and resulting in a needs-based product mix

---

GLOBAL STRUCTURE

De-linking and re-linking
for the
New global order

FIGURE [24.]2   Within-country and between-country self-reliance

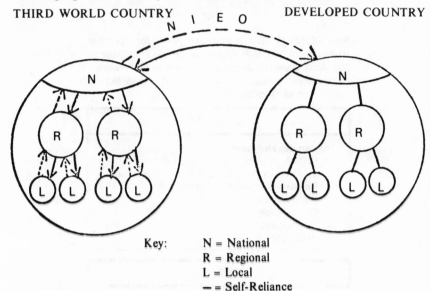

Key: N = National
        R = Regional
        L = Local
        — = Self-Reliance

possible without a change in structures through which national elites control relations with other societies?

Self-reliance advocates are not yet thinking about these issues. There is a general tendency for advocacy to leap from local self-reliance to self-reliant nations, to collective self-reliance among nations within regions, to collective self-reliance among Third World countries. It is important for self-reliance advocates to think more clearly about linkages between self-reliant communities in the light of general agreement that self-reliance does not mean isolation or autarchy. Overall, the question is whether self-reliance can be achieved in the context of a neat hierarchical design— from local to regional to national to international. Can self-reliance work in large, diverse countries such as India, Indonesia and Brazil? Will not local communities and regions with different climates and different resources require qualitatively different external linkages? Does self-reliance imply smaller constituent units for international relations and for the global system? Will not self-reliance require different kinds of external linkages for local communities and regions near national boundaries?

These kinds of questions are exemplified by Figure [24.]3. Does self-reliance imply the possibility and need for direct linkages between regions and local communities in different nations? For the moment, the question will be limited to the Third World. There might be concern that such relationships would fragment the Third World. In fact, much fragmentation is actually caused by the existence of stronger ties between Third World elites and industrialized country elites than between elites in different Third World countries. Could not increased regional and local ties across Third World national boundaries help strengthen Third World unity? Would these possibilities not help local and regional communities to find

FIGURE [24.]3 Implications of within-country self-reliance for regional and local linkage between Third World countries (dotted lines)

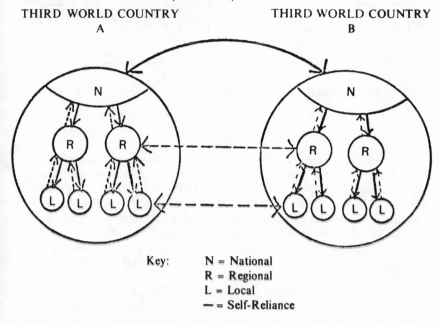

THIRD WORLD COUNTRY
A

THIRD WORLD COUNTRY
B

Key: N = National
R = Regional
L = Local
— = Self-Reliance

alternative markets, technologies, capital and sources of supply that would be more compatible with their objective of self-reliance.

Industrialized Countries
in the New International Economic Order

Thus we see that speculation about the means whereby people in the Third World could satisfy their needs in conditions of self-reliance is leading to a fundamental challenge to the internal organization of nation-states and to the special privileges of national governments with respect to linkages between peoples. What are the implications of 'another development' and similar approaches toward a future world order for people in Europe, Japan and North America? Overall, most people in these areas are getting more rewards from transnational activities than are most people in the Third World. On the other hand, there is a very unequal distribution of the rewards, although somewhat less so than in the Third World. While people in Europe, Japan and North America have more opportunity to participate in national governmental decision-making, this is not so in the case of foreign policy, in which there is a well-established expectation that the public will defer to a small elite which supposedly knows best when it comes to the presumed esoteric and difficult procedures for defining the so-called national interest and putting it into practice through foreign policy. The public has even less opportunity to influence the policies of multinational manufacturing, financial and distribution organizations,

FIGURE [24.4] Moving the public from perception to self-conscious action

even though the headquarters of these conglomerates might be in their own local community.

[*   *   *]

How might more people acquire a deeper sense of participatory involvement in Third World issues that would set in motion a process of participatory learning? In one possible approach, we have been engaged in an experimental action research project in Columbus, Ohio, since 1972. We are trying to help people to develop competence with respect to international issues by a participatory learning process that begins in the context of local links to the world. The first step is to provide people with descriptive information on local links to the world, with respect to agriculture, trade, investment, religion, medicine, education and ethnic groups. This information should heighten *perception* of international linkages which can lead to *self-conscious involvement* in these linkages (Figure [24.4] . . .). At this point it can become possible for people to *evaluate* the international involvements, their own as well as that of other individuals and organizations in their community. Are we shipping our food where it is really needed? Are we using more than our fair share of a specific resource? Are products we sell abroad serving important needs? This could lead to *responsible participation* that is consistent with proclaimed values. This, then, might help to produce a *foreign policy agenda* for individuals and organizations in a local community that is based on the international linkages of the daily lives of people in that community. Were this done in a number of communities, it could also produce a foreign policy agenda for a large society that is responsive to its constituent communities.

Thus far, our experience suggests that individual citizens cannot be moved through a process of participatory learning without two supporting factors. First, there must be sustained organized activity that is deliberately devoted to this objective. Second, participatory learning must take place in an organized context which supports and sustains citizen involvement. Experience also suggests that two kinds of inputs must be made to counteract parochial tendencies in participatory learning rooted in a single community. First, local citizens need information on the perceptions, values, priorities and needs of people in other countries with whom local activity is linked. Second, nonparochial standards are required in planning, implementing and evaluating international activity—e.g. UN declarations, or declarations of international religious institutions.

Other organizations in the United States have also tried to activate public involvement in foreign policy issues through projects in local communities. The Student Advisory Committee on International Affairs has organized South African, and Media and Foreign Policy projects in New York City, a Racism and Latin

American Policy Project in San Francisco, a Politics of Ocean Management Project in Claremont, California, a Pacific Northwest Timber Project in Eugene, Oregon, Defense Industry and Conversion Projects in Boston and St. Louis. Organized by graduate students in each community, projects were developed out of actual international involvement by local individuals and institutions.

Perhaps the widest interest in stimulating local involvement in international issues has been focused on multinational corporations. One organization so involved is an ecumenical coalition of church investors cooperating in the Interfaith Center on Corporate Responsibility. With respect to South Africa alone, they report a resolution by the Sisters of Charity and the Women's Division of the United Methodist Church asking Goodyear to disclose information on its operations in South Africa; a resolution of the United Methodist Church, the Episcopal Church and 12 other religious groups seeking information on IBM relationships with the South African military; and a resolution of the Christian Church, the Capuchins and others requesting the Kennecott Corporation to cease new investment in every community offer a local connection for issues raised by these groups, not only with respect to South Africa, but also with respect to promotion of infant formula in developing countries, type of equipment distributed in developing countries, importation of Rhodesian chrome, etc.

LINKING PEOPLE IN THIRD WORLD AND INDUSTRIALIZED COUNTRIES

There is a largely unchallenged assumption that the interests of people in Third World countries can only be pursued and protected by Third World national governments. Since most of these countries are weak in comparison with the powerful governmental and business institutions in the industrialized world, it is further assumed that the interests of Third World people can only be pursued and protected by a 'trade union' of Third World national governments. From one perspective, this is a very persuasive argument. When the Third World is fragmented in the face of powerful institutions in the industrialized world, it should obviously unify and challenge these institutions. From another perspective, it seems prudent to ask whether people in the Third World are not falling into the same trap as people in the industrialized world, which have turned over direction of external relations to coalitions of national governments. The politico-military institutions which have evolved out of this relinquishment of popular control of external relations are generally not serving human needs in the industrialized world. Is the Third World once again following an alien model that is not suited to the intrinsic needs of Third World people? Is a new model implied by those searching for paths toward fulfillment of human needs and self-reliance in Third World communities?

It is [necessary] that those designing new forms of economic, social and political organization to serve the needs of Third World people examine closely existing institutions for external relations because they are largely patterned after foreign models. There are two issues that require attention: (i) The need for new norms and institutions for local and regional participation in foreign policy-making of national governments and (ii) new norms and institutions enabling local communities and regions to exercise some direct control over powerful governmental and business organizations in industrialized countries which have direct impact on people in local and regional communities in the Third World.

[*   *   *]

People in these communities must be given the competence to personally perceive, evaluate and react to these activities in their own communities. This should be done for two reasons. First, only in this way can people discern their interests with respect to these forces and develop the competence to communicate their interests to local, regional and national governments. Second, there are occasions when national governments do not protect local and regional communities against transnational forces that impinge on local needs (such as preserving the environment, maintaining employment, preserving culture or conserving resources). Direct local action against transnational forces is then required.

As local and regional communities develop competence in their transnational relationships, they will occasionally wish to enlist transnational support from those with common interests in other Third World countries and in industrialized countries for action against undesirable transnational impact upon them. For example, Hazel Henderson urges citizen movements in industrialized countries concerned with consumer and environmental protection, economic and social justice and corporate accountability to make their information available to citizens in the Third World. She fears that citizen movements in industrialized countries may simply force multinationals to move to Third World countries and thereby export the problems they have created in industrialized countries. Through information sharing with Third World counterparts, citizen movements in industrialized countries could enable them to realistically calculate the social costs of specific multinational enterprises.

[Also to be considered are] ways in which extended direct contacts between local communities and regions might permit Third World communities to obtain needed technology, investment and markets from industrialized communities in the context of relationships that would be more symmetrical than the existing ones. This, of course, would have to be done very selectively. After all, local communities and regions in industrialized countries are the home base for very powerful economic institutions. But would not the self-reliance possibilities for Third World local communities and regions make this option worth considering under certain conditions? At present, Third World communities aspiring to self-reliance are sometimes frustrated by collaboration between their own national governments and multinational corporations. Might not Third World local communities and regions be a better match for local and regional organizations in industrialized countries? Could they (i) develop symmetrical working relationships with smaller corporations, avoiding the giant conglomerates, (ii) relate to subnational, less powerful governmental institutions, and (iii) collaborate with more responsive local nongovernmental groups? Might not this approach succeed in usefully fragmenting the powerful country if it is carried out in the context of very explicit criteria for self-reliance? For example, 'another development' urges four major guidelines for selective participation in the international economic system by Third World countries. Such guidelines, requiring much more specificity when applied to individual cases, could equally apply to linkages between local communities or regions:

1. There is a minimum degree of links required to sustain the development process.

2. There is a maximum degree of links beyond which no effective sovereignty can be maintained.

3. There are affirmative links which reinforce self-reliance.

4. There are regressive links which weaken self-reliance.

John E. Fobes has urged more specific rules for assuring 'equal footing' in partnership undertakings, such as:

1. Each party must be allowed to *give* something to the relationship.
2. New ways of evaluating and assessing the impact of linkage must be developed so all significant impacts can be accounted for.
3. Linkage should be tested against criteria such as:
   (a) Does it encourage wider involvement and participation?
   (b) Does it stimulate new initiatives?
   (c) Does it promote communication through new channels?
   (d) Does it insure greater involvement of women?

Fragmentation in industrialized countries would at the same time enhance self-reliance in local communities and regions within industrialized countries themselves. Increasingly, local enterprises are being absorbed into multinational giants, with control over international operations moved to a distant corporate office. Foreign investment of local banks is absorbed into consortia operations, obscuring local perception and understanding of the impact of local investment. Most aid programs are handled by national organizations, with local people simply putting money in envelopes. As a result, local people have little perception and understanding of the aid programs they support. And young people desiring involvement in these programs must emigrate to the national headquarters of aid organizations in order to become involved. In this way local communities lose important competence for international involvement.

If local communities and regions in industrialized countries were more self-reliant in their international involvements, might it not be possible for their intrinsic humanitarian and fairness sentiments to be reflected in their foreign policies? Could it not then be more possible for Third World people and industrialized world people to develop agreed norms for symmetric relationships?

CONCLUSION

The view that has emerged from this inquiry suggests an approach to future world order that is quite different from most world order thinking. World order proposals tend to build either from the top down (i.e. with global institutions) or from existing nation-states up. Neither of these approaches is concerned with how subnational communities would link to proposed global structures. This may be because these future world orders have been primarily the creations of cosmopolitans—scholars and other elites—who do not relate to the world from local communities or regions but as part of a national governmental and nongovernmental elite and perhaps also as part of a cosmopolitan transnational or international elite that is selected from national elites. As these cosmopolitans expound on proposals for future global orders, they ironically believe that most people (i.e. those who inhabit local communities around the world) prevent their implementation because they are inadequately educated in the perspectives of cosmopolitans. Yet we have uncovered very suggestive evidence that the future global orders of most cosmopolitans may simply be irrelevant to the needs of people in local communities.

Of course, the root of the problem is that the public is not consciously linked to present global systems, though they live in a sea of transnational linkages in the form of food, clothing, medicine, information, music, films, and a host of manufactured goods. To those few who receive any international education, it tends to be presented as an activity of foreign ministers, heads of state and the governmental foreign service. If the broader transnational approach is taken, it may also include the activities of corporations and even international nongovernmental organizations. But all of these are presented in the context of academic paradigms that do not link people in local communities. This is largely because scholars have written tons of books that offer agonizing details on how a handful of national elites endeavor to control the world and/or how these elites control the participation of the people in their country in the world. This attention to the powerful is not surprising and not necessarily bad. But the fact that scholars do virtually nothing in helping people in local communities to acquire a deeper understanding of their daily involvements in the world is regrettable. It is reasonable to conclude that it must be done if Third World communities are to experience 'another development' that achieves self-reliance and satisfaction of needs. It is likewise reasonable to conclude that local communities in the industrial world will not be willing to make the sacrifices and adjustments that will be required of them unless they have knowledge through which they acquire confidence that their sacrifices and adjustments are achieving desired goals.

Finally, those readers skeptical of our effort to discern new opportunities for people to participate in the development of global futures should recall our introductory explication of the ways in which the organization of humankind is in a state of flux. We would also remind them that the so-called nation-state model through which most of us look at the world is preventing us from seeing and interpreting this change. Emphasis on fulfillment of needs and self-reliance are forcing those interested in global futures to think of local and regional communities as the constituent entities of humankind. This requires a different approach than that seeking law and order between nation-states. This does not mean that no national government has a useful role to play. But it does liberate us to ask what the appropriate role of a specific national government might be in a specific situation.

There is considerable evidence that the needs of most people, as they are affected by national governments' foreign policies, cannot be served by simply changing the policy-makers. People's needs can only be served by developing new participatory mechanisms for public involvement in foreign policy-making that overcome traditional abdication of responsibility to a small elite in a national capital. As people in many communities and situations gain participatory experience, they will be increasingly able to discern the kinds of links to the world that will serve their needs. The desirable role of present national governments will no doubt vary with different issues and with the size of the country. But it would seem inevitable, particularly in larger countries, that people in self-reliant local and regional communities will require increased capacity to formulate and execute their own policies for relationships across present national boundaries. They might link with one group with respect to marketing a commodity, with another group with respect to a pollution problem, with a still different group with respect to a fisheries problem, and with a variety of functional global organizations. In this way, the world would evolve into a system of self-reliant communities linked together in the service of the needs of the inhabitants of these communities. It is unlikely that aspirations for self-reliance and fulfillment of needs can be achieved any other way.

The United Nations
and Social Justice

INTRODUCTION

Many factors have reflected and affected UN action in the enhancement of the world order value of human rights—what we broadly refer to as social justice. As an extension of the state system, the United Nations has no independent powers. It can only function within the parameters set by its member states. The Charter itself provides an indeterminate and somewhat inconsistent mandate. On the one hand, the principle of state sovereignty and equality (Article 2[1]) and the principle of nonintervention in matters essentially within the domestic jurisdiction (Article 2[7]) suggest an escape clause for the state oppressors. On the other hand, Articles 55–60 establish a broad mandate for the entire UN system for international cooperation in economic, social, cultural, educational, health, and related fields. Inevitably, UN human rights politics has responded to the dialectical play of political forces in relation to these two seemingly conflicting principles.

Systemic changes are clearly more important than the Charter in regard to value prioritization in UN human rights politics. Changes in UN membership and superpower relationship have exerted an important impact on UN action. The linkages between human rights (or social justice) and other world order values have been particularly troublesome. Many from both the left and the right have argued that some governments that deny their citizens social justice have succeeded in mobilizing their societies to achieve respectable economic growth and even economic well-being and equity for their people. Therefore, it seems possible to proceed, at least in the short run, to satisfy economic needs while simultaneously denying minimum social justice and human rights to a population. Others have argued that the cause of global peace, especially among nuclear superpowers, should take priority over the promotion of even the most minimal human rights. Hence, it is viewed as irresponsible to complicate the process of superpower détente politics with the injection of human rights issues as, for instance, in relation to East Europe.

How has the United Nations responded to these conflicting claims and systemic changes? The development of UN human rights politics can be understood in terms of two main types of activities in successive stages: the value-shaping process and the value-realizing process. During the first two decades of its existence, the

345

United Nations was mainly concerned with the value-shaping process involving the first-stage translation of moral claims into general standards and principles, usually in the form of declarations, and the second-stage translation of standards and principles into legal norms defining specific rights and obligations in the form of multilateral treaties. The UN succeeded in producing what has come to be known as the International Bill of Rights, consisting of the Universal Declaration of Human Rights, the International Covenant on Civil and Political Rights and Its Optional Protocol, and the International Covenant on Economic, Social, and Cultural Rights. The International Bill of Rights can be more broadly defined as encompassing the entire corpus of international human rights law, including forty-seven UN-sponsored legal instruments.

Since the mid-1960s, UN activities have expanded beyond the value-shaping process involving collective choice in the establishment of institutional machinery and procedures to monitor the implementation of human rights instruments. In short, the UN shifted from the value-shaping process to the value-realizing process. To be sure, the value-shaping process has continued in the drafting of more human rights instruments relating to more categories of human rights abuse, but the main attention has shifted to "UN action." The membership has been consistently and increasingly concerned since the mid-1960s with various issues involving the denial of human rights, most consistently with those denials occurring in southern Africa. The patterns of UN concern are inconsistent, obviously influenced by political factors more than the severity of the deprivation. Thus, genocidal policies in Burundi, Uganda, Kampuchea, and East Timor were generally overlooked, while South Africa became an easy target for its apartheid. Soviet and Chinese denials of human rights were more easily ignored, while those of Israel and Chile were repeatedly and ritualistically censored. Yet, the double standard is hardly a monopoly of any one country or of a group of aligned countries, as made manifest by the Soviet role in Poland and Afghanistan and the U.S. role in Chile, South Korea, Israel, and El Salvador.

In a sense, the Khmer Rouge genocide offers a textbook case of how the cause of human rights is effectively subordinated in practice to the logic of geopolitics. Owing to the dominance of statist norms over human rights norms in UN politics and the Machiavellian logic of global geopolitics over human rights in U.S. foreign policy, the Khmer Rouge genocide in Kampuchea was uncensored and unsanctioned. Ironically, it took nothing less than an armed invasion of Kampuchea (aided and abetted by the Soviet Union) to put an end to the genocidal bloodbath committed by the Khmer Rouge, aided by China and abetted by the United States. The post-Holocaust genocidal processes in the hinterland of the Third World have defied any clear ideological East-West division. There are many skeletons in virtually every global actor's closet.

Under these muddled conditions, it is not surprising to hear conflicting voices and interpretations. Some detractors of the United Nations emphasize its political shortcomings and seek to discredit it altogether in the area of human rights. Others, in a more positive vein, associate themselves with what the United Nations has already achieved and can still achieve, especially the legitimating role of UN value-shaping and norm-setting activities.

What is often overlooked is the extent to which the nonstate actors have taken the normative initiative in the value-shaping process and the extent to which UN-legitimated human rights norms and instruments produce second-order effects for human rights activists in local and national settings. More than in any other value domain, the UN-sponsored International Bill of Rights has made it easier for the oppressed to think globally but act locally. It is a powerful weapon in the hands of the oppressed. The ratification of two human rights covenants by the Czech government provided Charter 77, the Czech human rights group, with a legitimating instrument in its struggle at home. On the fortieth anniversary of the Universal Declaration of Human Rights in early December 1988, China joined the global chorus of paeans with its own glowing commentaries. On December 5, 1988, timed to coincide with the fortieth anniversary of the Universal Declaration of Human Rights and also with the tenth anniversary of China's Democracy Wall movement, Ren Wanding, a former Democracy Wall movement leader, released a four-page letter addressed to the UN Commission on Human Rights (of which China is a member), Amnesty International, and the Hongkong Commission on Human Rights, asking for inquiries into the condition of Democracy Wall activists and participants in the 1986–1987 student movement who are still in prison.

Even in the context of statist politics in the United Nations, charges of bias and double standards represent one side of the story. In the 1980s, a quiet revolution of sorts occurred, as made evident in a significant decline in bias and double standards in UN human rights politics. In 1987–1988, China, the Soviet Union, and the United States all became more positive in their attitudes toward UN human rights politics. The global appeal of human rights is such that it even penetrated the castle of Chinese sovereignty. Increasingly, the Chinese leadership has found it necessary to give lip service to universal human rights, although in the aftermath of its crackdown on the domestic movement for democratization in June 1989, the Chinese rhetorical endorsement of human rights is problematic. The Soviet turn-about on human rights has been, in contrast, dramatic, substantive, and more likely to be sustained. "Human rights and fundamental freedoms" have become an integral component of Gorbachev's comprehensive global security system. Even President Reagan praised, albeit in a self-serving way, UN performance in human rights in recent years in his farewell address to the United Nations (see Selection 14).

As for the future of UN action in the field of human rights, several issues deserve our attention. First, we must evolve a conception of what it is possible to do within the UN framework. Second, we must be concerned with how this conception relates to other questions of the organization's role in a movement for global reform. Is the UN the best or the only forum for the promotion of social justice, especially if the goals of promotion are viewed as antagonistic to the policies of important member states? What are the links between social justice on a national level and overall progress toward the realization of world order values during the transition process? What should be the specific UN priorities during this process? Third, which organs of the UN can contribute most to the promotion of which human rights at what stage of the world historical process? It may be that the less-noticed actors within the UN system, such as the International Labor Organization

(ILO), are more effective in influencing national human rights performance. Perhaps it is precisely because the ILO is relatively unnoticed that it can be more effective than the General Assembly, at least in some dimensions of human rights.

Finally, in approaching the promotion of human rights, it is important to comprehend the relevance of cultural and ideological differences. The Western liberal emphasis on individual rights is not shared to nearly as great an extent in either non-Western or socialist societies, where greater stress is placed upon collective group rights. Given such diversity, it seems important to seek a shared conception of social justice while preserving diverse social and political systems. Thus, the United Nations, while building a global consensus on universal minimum conditions, should guard against translating such a consensus into rigid dogma.

In this section, the readings are intended to touch upon various aspects of these complex and controversial questions of UN human rights politics. We begin with the Universal Declaration of Human Rights. As a widely recognized common standard of achievement for all peoples and all nations, it has exerted the most significant and sustained global influence in the value-shaping process. The Declaration also served as the main catalyst and inspiration for the international legislative process in the field of human rights and provided guidelines for voluntary human rights organizations. Its provisions, repeatedly cited as the legitimizing authority in the international decisionmaking process, have even found their way into the constitutions of newly independent states. To be sure, many governments are cynical, paying lip service to the Declaration while at the same time withholding the application of its principles and standards from their own citizens. Nonetheless, the Declaration does represent an agreed starting point for discussion of human rights questions in any international forum, and it has achieved such an authoritative status that even repressive governments have never based their policies upon an outright refusal to heed the Declaration's principles and standards. The long-term socializing and educational impact of the Declaration, while difficult to measure, definitely seems constructive.

In the section's second selection, Samuel S. Kim argues that the concept of human rights is a product of its time and is its dominant normative temper. He explores the elements of change and continuity in the evolution of human rights thinking in terms of the "concept of three generations" advanced by the jurist Karel Vasak. Drawing upon, but somewhat altering, the concepts, principles, assumptions, and approaches embodied in the three-generation evolution of human rights thinking, Kim develops a human rights–human needs developmental model that embodies world order assumptions, principles, and values. The reader needs to question: Is the world order hierarchy of human rights in the selection desirable and feasible?

In our third selection in this section, David P. Forsythe examines the UN human rights performance during the first forty years (1945–1985), its institutional and procedural changes as well as the reasons these changes occurred. In the most recent decade, according to Forsythe, doctrinal disputes over the relationship between socioeconomic and civil-political rights—and over which had priority—gave way to an increasing focus on the protection of specific civil and political rights. Without completely denying the validity of the Moynihan-Kirkpatrick thesis, Forsythe presents a counterthesis about the successful side of UN performance in the field of human rights. Forsythe argues that UN performance should not be judged in terms of its immediate impact on state behavior. "The importance of United Nations activity on human rights lies," he concludes, "in this long-term socialization process in which one source of legitimacy is given or withheld according to human rights performance." Forsythe's argument about the Soviet rejectionist stand may strike some readers as dated in the wake of the Gorbachev revolution.

Our next selection is an excerpt from "The Nairobi Forward-Looking Strategies for the Advancement of Women," adopted by the World Conference to Review and Appraise the Achievements of the United Nations Decade for Women, Nairobi, Kenya, 15–26 July 1985, and also adopted without a vote by the General Assembly at its fortieth session in 1985. The selection provides both a retrospect of UN involvement and a prospect of future action for the years 1986–2000. Equality is conceptualized as a goal and a means of participation so as to help women realize their potential to be more fully human. Such equality can best occur in conditions of international peace and security; hence the linkage among equality, development, and peace. Value linkage of this kind is justified on the assumption that women are subject to "compound discrimination." Yet, the linkage is so extensive and indiscriminate—note how it is linked with such a spent movement as NIEO—as to weaken the centrality of women's rights on its own intrinsic merit. Thus the strategies virtually ignore domestic social, cultural, and political factors. To explain and formulate the strategies for the year 2000 almost exclusively in terms of an external invisible hand seems almost an alibi for inaction.

In the section's last selection, we are forced to remember the forgotten genocide of the twentieth century and to reassess the limitations of the UN-based human rights regime. The establishment of the Permanent Peoples' Tribunal is a testimonial to the moral and political failures of the state system—and of the UN as an extension of the state system—as instruments of social justice. The tribunal attempts to overcome such failures through the process of acknowledgment. "Indeed, acknowledging genocide itself" is, as the tribunal's verdict on the Armenian genocide states, "a fundamental means of struggling against genocide. The acknowledgment is itself an affirmation of the right of a people under international law to a safeguarded existence." The tribunal's involvement in forgotten and ignored pre- and post-Holocaust genocidal processes proceeds from the premise that any genocide against any people at any time ultimately works toward the "degradation and perversion of humanity as a whole." Still, the tribunal is not an alternative to the United Nations. Rather, it constitutes a nonstate people's organization relying upon its own normative authority to disseminate information that raises public awareness and that might influence the United Nations to be more active in the politics of acknowledgment as a global instrument of social and human justice. The United Nations is asked not to be complice in the crime of silence.

In reading the selections of this section, the reader should keep in mind the relationship between UN human rights activities and the overall prospects for achieving more humane governance. Given the dominance of statist norms and interests, can the UN formulate—and act upon—an adequate conception of international social and political justice? Why has the UN failed in some dimensions and succeeded in others? What alternative arrangements and actors exist to promote and realize the world order value of human rights? Is the attainment of minimum levels of human rights observance, including democratization, a prerequisite for the pursuit of other world order values?

25. The Universal Declaration of Human Rights

Preamble

Whereas recognition of the inherent dignity and of the equal and inalienable rights of all members of the human family is the foundation of freedom, justice and peace in the world,

Whereas disregard and contempt for human rights have resulted in barbarous acts which have outraged the conscience of mankind, and the advent of a world in which human beings shall enjoy freedom of speech and belief and freedom from fear and want has been proclaimed as the highest aspiration of the common people,

Whereas it is essential, if man is not to be compelled to have recourse, as a last resort, to rebellion against tyranny and oppression, that human rights should be protected by the rule of law,

Whereas it is essential to promote the development of friendly relations between nations,

Whereas the peoples of the United Nations have in the Charter reaffirmed their faith in fundamental human rights, in the dignity and worth of the human person and in the equal rights of men and women and have determined to promote social progress and better standards of life in larger freedom,

Whereas Member States have pledged themselves to achieve, in co-operation with the United Nations, the promotion of universal respect for and observance of human rights and fundamental freedoms,

Whereas a common understanding of these rights and freedoms in of the greatest importance for the full realization of this pledge,

Now, therefore,

The General Assembly

Proclaims this Universal Declaration of Human Rights as a common standard of achievement for all peoples and all nations, to the end that every individual and every organ of society, keeping this Declaration constantly in mind, shall strive by teaching and education to promote respect for these rights and freedoms and by progressive measures, national and international to secure their universal and effective recognition and observance, both among the peoples of Member States themselves and among the peoples of territories under their jurisdiction.

Article 1

All human beings are born free and equal in dignity and rights. They are endowed with reason and conscience and should act towards one another in a spirit of brotherhood.

Article 2

Everyone is entitled to all the rights and freedoms set forth in this Declaration, without distinction of any kind, such as race, colour, sex, language, religion, political or other opinion, national or social origin, property, birth or other status.

Furthermore, no distinction shall be made on the basis of the political, jurisdictional or international status of the country or territory to which a person belongs, whether it be independent, trust, non-self-governing or under any other limitation of sovereignty.

Article 3

Everyone has the right to life, liberty and the security of person.

Article 4

No one shall be held in slavery or servitude; slavery and the slave trade shall be prohibited in all their forms.

Article 5

No one shall be subjected to torture or to cruel, inhuman or degrading treatment or punishment.

Article 6

Everyone has the right to recognition everywhere as a person before the law.

Article 7

All are equal before the law and are entitled without any discrimination to equal protection of the law. All are entitled to equal protection against any discrimination in violation of this Declaration and against any incitement to such discrimination.

Article 8

Everyone has the right to an effective remedy by the competent national tribunals for acts violating the fundamental rights granted him by the constitution or by law.

Article 9

No one shall be subjected to arbitrary arrest, detention or exile.

Article 10

Everyone is entitled in full equality to a fair and public hearing by an independent and impartial tribunal, in the determination of his rights and obligations and of any criminal charge against him.

Article 11

1. Everyone charged with a penal offence has the right to be presumed innocent until proved guilty according to law in a public trial at which he has had all the guarantees necessary for his defence.

2. No one shall be held guilty of any penal offence on account of any act or omission which did not constitute a penal offence, under national or international law, at the time when it was commited. Nor shall a heavier penalty be imposed that the one that was applicable at the time the penal offence was committed.

Article 12

No one shall be subjected to arbitrary interference with his privacy, family, home or correspondence, nor to attacks upon his honour and reputation. Everyone has the right to the protection of the law against such interference or attacks.

Article 13

1. Everyone has the right to freedom of movement and residence within the borders of each State.
2. Everyone has the right to leave any country including his own, and to return to his country.

Article 14

1. Everyone has the right to seek and to enjoy in other countries asylum from persecution.
2. This right may not be invoked in the case of prosecutions genuinely arising from non-political crimes or from acts contrary to the purposes and principles of the United Nations.

Article 15

1. Everyone has the right to a nationality.
2. No one shall be arbitrarily deprived of his nationality nor denied the right to change his nationality.

Article 16

1. Men and women of full age, without any limitation due to race, nationality or religion, have the right to marry and to found a family. They are entitled to equal rights as to marriage, during marriage and at its dissolution.
2. Marriage shall be entered into only with the free and full consent of the intending spouses.
3. The family is the natural and fundamental group unit of society and is entitled to protection by society and the State.

Article 17

1. Everyone has the right to own property alone as well as in association with others.
2. No one shall be artitrarily deprived of his property.

Article 18

Everyone has the right to freedom of thought, conscience and religion; this right includes freedom to change his religion or belief, and freedom, either alone or in community with others and in public or private, to manifest his religion or belief in teaching, practice, worship and observance.

Article 19

Everyone has the right to freedom of opinion and expression; this right includes freedom to hold opinions without interference and to seek, receive and impart information and ideas through any media and regardless of frontiers.

Article 20

1. Everyone has the right to freedom of peaceful assembly and association.
2. No one may be compelled to belong to an association.

Article 21

1. Everyone has the right to take part in the government of his country, directly or through freely chosen representatives.
2. Everyone has the right of equal access to public service in his country.
3. The will of the people shall be the basis of the authority of government; this will shall be expressed in periodic and genuine elections which shall be by universal and equal suffrage and shall be held by secret vote or by equivalent free voting prodedures.

Article 22

Everyone, as a member of society, has the right to social security and is entitled to realization, through national effort and international co-operation and in accordance with the organization and resources of each State, of the economic, social and cultural rights indispensable for his dignity and the free development of his personality.

Article 23

1. Everyone has the right to work, to free choice of employment, to just and favourable conditions of work and to protection against unemployment.
2. Everyone, without any discrimination, has the right to equal pay for equal work.
3. Everyone who works has the right to just and favourable remuneration ensuring for himself and his family an existence worthy of human dignity, and supplemented, if necessary, by other means of social protection.
4. Everyone has the right to form and to join trade unions for the protection of his interests.

Article 24

Everyone has the right to rest and leisure, including reasonable limitation of working hours and periodic holidays with pay.

Article 25

1. Everyone has the right to a standard of living adequate for the health and well-being of himself and of his family, including food, clothing, housing and medical care and necessary social services, and the right to security in the event of unemployment, sickness disability, widowhood, old age or other lack of livelihood in circumstances beyond his control.
2. Motherhood and childhood are entitled to special care and assistance. All children, whether born in or out of wedlock, shall enjoy the same social protection.

Article 26

1. Everyone has the right to education. Education shall be free, at least in the elementary and fundamental stages. Elementary education shall be compulsory.

Technical and professional educational shall be made generally available and higher education shall be equally accessible to all on the basis of merit.

2. Education shall be directed to the full development of the human personality and to the strengthening of respect for human rights and fundamental freedoms. It shall promote understanding, tolerance and friendship among all nations, racial or religious groups, and shall further the activities of the United Nations for the maintenance of peace.

3. Parents have a prior right to choose the kind of education that shall be given to their children.

Article 27

1. Everyone has the right freely to participate in the cultural life of the community, to enjoy the arts and to share in scientific advancement and its benefits.

2. Everyone has the right to the protection of the moral and material interests resulting from any scientific, literary or artistic production of which he is the author.

Article 28

Everyone is entitled to a social and international order in which the rights and freedoms set forth in this Declaration can be fully realized.

Article 29

1. Everyone has duties to the community in which alone the free and full development of his personality is possible.

2. In the exercise of his rights and freedoms, everyone shall be subject only to such limitations as are determined by law solely for the purpose of securing due recognition and respect for the rights and freedoms of others and of meeting the just requirements of morality, public order and the general welfare in a democratic society.

3. These rights and freedoms may in no case be exercised contrary to the purposes and principles of the United Nations.

Article 30

Nothing in this Declaration may be interpreted as implying for any State, group or person any right to engage in any activity or to perform any act aimed at the destruction of any of the rights and freedoms set forth herein.

26. Global Human Rights and World Order

Samuel S. Kim

AN OPPRESSION/LIBERATION DICHOTOMY

"One picture," says an old Chinese proverb, "is worth more than ten thousand words." If we were to search for one model picture that captures all the anomalies, brutalities, and contradictions of international politics, Picasso's great painting *Guernica*—his trenchant condemnation of the dehumanization of Spanish fascism and the terror bombing of the city of Guernica—could be that one picture. *Guernica* sharpens our sensitivity to the sand heap of invisible bodies and bones crushed and buried at the foundations of repressive local and global governance.

There is something very old and very new in contemporary human rights politics. The contemporary pursuit of human rights is part of the age-old struggle for human emancipation, part of the ongoing historical process. This long struggle is marked by a series of revolutions against religious and secular tyranny—the Protestant Reformation, the American, French, Russian, Chinese, Cuban, and Iranian revolutions—that conquered the credo of inevitability. Each revolution has expanded the bounds of moral claims in politics. Each revolution in varying manners and degrees has contributed significantly to the broadening of the concept of human rights. Each revolution progressively raised the threshold of intolerance for inhumane governance. As a result, the human rights movement, which originated in the West in the wake of the Enlightenment, has spread to all parts of the world.

What makes the contemporary struggle for human liberation novel is its elusive and contradictory quality. Ours is the best *and* the worst of times for human rights. From the optimistic side, it can be said that the level of human consciousness has been significantly raised and the tenure of oppressive regimes has become shorter. In a world of increasing interdependence and instant communications, it is becoming more and more difficult for an oppressor to hide oppression, for the oppressed to be resigned to hopelessness, and for the rest of us to remain indifferent. The voices of the oppressed are becoming more and more difficult to silence, for the very act of silencing makes the voices more audible. Both Shariati and Biko were tormented and killed but their voices for the oppressed remain unstilled.

From the pessimistic—and perhaps more "realistic"—side of the situation, ours is indeed the worst of times for human rights. Never before in human history have there been such glaring gaps between rhetoric and reality, between norms and behavior, and between claims and capabilities. The recent revival and rhetorical celebration of human rights cannot obfuscate the extent to which state behavior has been dehumanized in the service of local oligarchies and tyrannies as well as of corporate and geopolitical interests. Hedley Bull captured an important dimension of international reality when he said that "international order is preserved by means which systematically affront the most basic and widely agreed principles of international justice."

However, Bull's observation begs several important questions. To what extent and in what manner can it be said that "the most basic and widely agreed priciples of international justice" merely reflect and codify the voices of the strong, rich, and articulate, ignoring the voices of the weak, poor, and inarticulate? To what extent and in what manner can it be said that the study of global human rights politics proceeds as if people mattered, heeding the voices of those who are either victims of oppression or who speak on behalf of the oppressed, i.e., the weak, poor, and inarticulate? To what extent does human rights politics ignore the structural deficiencies of the world economic and political systems that condition the behavior of state elites? [. . .]

THE EVOLUTION OF HUMAN RIGHTS THINKING

Whether "universal" human rights exist at any given moment is rarely self-evident and always open to debate. What cannot be disputed is that there is no such thing as universal human rights whose validity has been accepted at all times, by all peoples, and in all places. Much like the closely connected concepts of justice, freedom, and equality, the concept of human rights has both evolutionary and revolutionary potential. In an open and democratic milieu, it is a dynamic concept, constantly evolving and expanding, seeking a closer interface between empirical and normative reality. In a closed and oppressive milieu, it is a revolutionary concept legitimizing the call for a new order. In short, the evolution of human rights thinking is a continuing process whose future is always open and unpredictable. It is seldom in a steady state.

The concept of human rights is a product of its time. It invariably reflects an evolutionary or revolutionary change of normative power in social and political processes. In order to have a better understanding of the dynamic process of human rights politics in the development of modern international relations—that is, in the authoritative shaping and sharing of human rights values—it is useful to evaluate the elements of change and continuity in terms of the "concept of three generations" advanced by the prominent French jurist Karel Vasak, Director of UNESCO's Division of Human Rights and Peace from 1976 to 1980.

Throughout the history of modern international relations there have been three generations of human rights emanating from three competing schools of thought: the first generation of civil and political rights; the second generation of social, economic, and cultural rights; and the third generation of solidarity rights. Of course, the three generations of human rights is a simplified abstraction of the complex and confusing picture of human rights politics. It is also a heuristically useful model that shows the dominant school of thought at a given period as well as the changing patterns and trends in the development of human rights politics. Vasak has characterized the three generations of human rights as corresponding to the three normative components of the motto of the French revolution: *liberté*, *égalité*, and *fraternité*.

The First Generation of Civil and Political Rights

The expression "human rights" is of relatively recent origin. It can be traced back to the "rights of man" (*droits de l'homme*) movement of the last quarter of the eighteenth century in Europe. The eighteenth-century social philosophers and political revolutionaries of Europe and America may be regarded as the founding fathers of the first generation of human rights. Although the notion of human dignity is embedded in all non-Western cultures and civilizations, the contemporary sense of human rights as entitlements that inhere in being born as a member of the human race is distinctively Western.

The ideas and principles embodied in the American Declaration of Independence, in the Virginia Bill of Rights of 1776, in the French Declaration of the Rights of Man and of the Citizen, and in the American Bill of Rights—thanks to the dominant position of Western Europe and the United States in the development and codification of international norms—have become the central model of human rights. "The American and French revolutions," writes Louis Henkin, "and the declarations that expressed the principles that inspired them, took 'natural rights' and made them secular, rational, universal, individual, democratic, and radical."

The first generation of human rights is impregnated with the Western political philosophy of liberal individualism. Each human person, by virtue of his/her membership in the human race, is supposedly endowed with, and entitled to, certain natural and inalienable human rights such as "life, liberty, and property" (Locke) or "life, liberty, and the pursuit of happiness" (Jefferson). The essence of the concept of human rights in this Western liberalism was negative "freedom from" rather than positive "rights to." This essentially negative conception of human rights was also meshed with the dominant social and economic doctrine of laissez-faire. In short, human rights in the Western liberal tradition are more or less romanticized as a triumph of Lockean-Hobbesian individualism over Hegelian statism.

The supreme worth of the individual has been the core value of liberal constitutional democracy in the West. The moral and political strength of the Western tradition of liberal democracy is attested to by the frequency with which its key concepts and principles have been invoked to legitimize revolutionary calls against oppressive rule and by the extent to which its key concepts and principles have been constitutionalized as a protective shield of individual citizens from the oppressive hand of political authority. Richard Falk has argued that this represents the "comparative advantage" of the liberal West. Louis Henkin has observed on the power of the Western liberal model: "What the United States (borrowing from its English mother) and France planted and disseminated now decorates almost every constitution of today's 150 states—old or new, conservative or liberal or radical, capitalist or socialist or mixed, developed or less developed, or underdeveloped."

More significantly, the rights of individuals predominate in the International Bill of Rights—the Universal Declaration of Human Rights, the International Covenant on Civil and Political Rights and Its Optional Protocol, and the International Covenant on Economic, Social, and Cultural Rights. The preamble of the declaration states that "recognition of the inherent dignity and of the equal and inalienable rights of all members of the human family is the foundation of freedom, justice and peace in the world," while twenty out of the thirty articles are devoted to the elaboration of individual civil and political rights. The preambles of the two covenants are identical, repeating the above quote from the preamble of the declaration and stating that "the equal and inalienable rights . . . derive from the inherent dignity of the human person."

The first generation of human rights is not without its "comparative disadvantage." The expression "all Men are created equal" embodied in the American Declaration of Independence—and "all men are equal by nature and before law" embodied in the French Declaration of the Rights of Man and of the Citizen— was misleading in theory and practice. It was only a half-truth that tended to obscure rather than clarify the relentless "pursuit of happiness" by some men against other men (and women). Until recently, the Western liberal individualistic conception of human rights provided little remedy against abuses of civil and political rights committed by social agents other than the government. Under the banner of liberal individualism, it is only state action of specific character that is proscribed. Individual or corporate invasion of individual civil and political rights, much less social, economic, and cultural rights, has generally remained beyond the purview of legal protection.

It is easy to see why and how liberal individualism can be used as a legitimizing instrument of structural violence in domestic and international politics. Freedom became the most powerful weapon to justify inequality. Freedom was not like a commons that became available to all in equal quantity. Much like money, the rich, the powerful, and the articulate had more know-how, more access, and more influence in the shaping and sharing of the first generation rights. As Marx once argued: "None of the so-called rights of man goes beyond the *egoistic* man. . . . Far from viewing man here in his *species-being*, his *species-life* rather appears to be an external framework limiting his original independence." Kenneth Boulding revealed the embedded norm of Western liberal individualism—and in a sense confirmed the veracity of Ali Shariati's argument—when he said: "Without sharp inequalities, we would not have had the Parthenon or the cathedrals . . . or the great cultural achievements of any of the past civilizations."

The sanctity of private property so deeply embedded in Western individual-corporate liberalism is uniquely inhospitable to the human rights of present *and* future generations, as it justifies the freedom to limitless material acquisition. Once the right to private property (the pursuit of happiness) is elevated to an alienable status, it unavoidably accelerates the process of selective humanization (and selective dehumanization) in the wealth-accumulating process. This process, as Christian Bay has argued, extends "our traditional rights and liberties to corporations as if they were human beings." On the other hand, private property rights and markets, having being placed on the same pedestal as human rights and freedoms, can easily become a threat to democracy. The persistent "elitist" bias and insensitivity to the problematique of private property rights among the liberal advocates of human rights in the West have allowed this dehumanization to continue unexamined and unchecked.

In a legal sense, the inalienable rights of all men meant no more than the rights of citizens, and the correlative civil and political rights of citizens have been denied to many because of their "race, colour, sex, language, religion, political or other opinion, national or social origin, property, birth or other status" (Article 2 of the

Universal Declaration of Human Rights). "We think [the people of the negro race] . . . are not included, and were not intended to be included," declared the majority of the U.S. Supreme Court in *Dred Scott* v. *Sanford* in 1857, "under the words 'citizens' in the Constitution, and can therefore claim none of the rights and privileges which that instrument provides for and secures to citizens of the United States."

That Alexis de Tocqueville, James Bryce, Harold Laski, and other European writers were so impressed by the strength of egalitarian thought and practice in American society sheds more light on the reality of the Old World than of the New World. Notice, for example, the recent British refusal to admit entry of certain East African Asians, even though they "were British passport holders, they were severely harassed by the anti-Asian policies of General Amin and they had members of their families resident in Britain." If England was the cradle of parliamentary democracy, it has also been the chief propagator of white racism, which spread and germinated in a new, and in some cases a more virulent, form in the white settlement colonies of the United States, Canada, South Africa, Southern Rhodesia, New Zealand, and Australia. The immigration and naturalization laws and practices of these countries are full of racist norms and implications. That Western imperialism was legitimized under such "human rights" slogans as Manifest Destiny, the White Man's Burden, and Mission Civilisatrice requires no further elaboration. In a broader sense, "if the West has been the fountainhead of liberal constitutional democracy, it has also been the breeding ground of Facism and Nazism."

The moral credibility of Western liberal individualism has been greatly compromised by its self-styled champion, the United States. Unlike the other Western powers, the United States has been endemically prone to delude itself and others by disguising its imperial geopolitics in benign and altruistic slogans of human rights. While condemning the gunboat diplomacy of the other imperial powers in China in the nineteenth century, the United States seldom lost time claiming its share of victors' spoils through the most-favored-nation clause. At the turn of the century this Janus-faced policy was epitomized in the Open Door, a "me-too colonialism" legitimized as the protection of China's political and territorial integrity. President Wilson's championship for human rights as expressed in his call at Versailles for the right to national self-determination was no more credible than President Carter's revival of human rights as the centerpiece of U.S. foreign policy.

The long-standing, self-serving championship of universal human rights has significantly diluted the "comparative advantage" of liberal America. The liberal delimmas and contradictions were brought to the fore in President John F. Kennedy's mixture of statist and globalist metaphors in his crusade for "freedom": "Ask not what your country can do for you, ask what you can do for your country" (statism at home); "Let every nation know, whether it wishes us well or ill, that we shall pay any price, bear any burden, meet any hardship, support any friend, oppose any foe to assure the survival and success of liberty. This much we pledge—and more" (globalism abroad). Some twenty years later prominent political scientist Samuel Huntington echoes the same theme: "The expansion of American power is not synonymous with the expansion of liberty, but a significant correlation exists between the rise and fall of American power in the world and the rise and fall of liberty and democracy in the world."

Ironically, then, "liberty" is not only an instrument of liberation on the part of the oppressed but it can also become a legitimating instrument in the service of an unjust social order in domestic and international politics. In the course of heated and prolonged clash between Western and Third World delegates on the issue of individual human rights versus collective rights (or the rights of peoples) at a special UNESCO conference in December 1982, Amadou-Mahtar M'Bow, UNESCO's Director General, nicely captured both sides of this dialectic about the New World Information Order when he said: "If the [Western] media has the liberty to say what they like, then others [the Third World] have the right to judge what they say. What becomes of freedom when people claim to inform according to their own view and then refuse or seek to refuse to allow others to judge what they say? When this is the case, there is no liberty but the monopoly."

Generally, the individual rights of the first generation were more formal than real, more procedural than substantive, more political than economic, and more civil than social. From a just and humane world order perspective, then, the most problematic feature of the first generation of human rights lies in its persistent abstraction of human rights in a manner irrelevant to the basic needs of humankind. Just as liberty often served as an ideological weapon to maintain an inegalitarian social order at home, liberty has also been turned into a propaganda weapon in the ongoing hegemonic rivalry between the two superpowers. In the domain of North-South relations, "liberty becomes an answer," as Fouad Ajami put it, "to the Third World's demand for global equity."

Within the home turf, paradoxically enough, there is a crisis of faith and confidence in the Western model of democracy. Far from believing and acting as if democracy represents the "comparative advantage" of the West, the Trilateral Commission, representing the more liberal elements of ruling elites in the industrial democracies, has questioned the very governability of Western democracy in the face of the twin challenges from the Soviet Union and the Third World. The West in general and the United States in particular has taken freedom too far, we are told, and we must therefore limit the rights and liberties of citizens if "democracy" (liberal-guided democracy?) is to survive.

The Second Generation of Economic, Social, and Cultural Rights

The human predicament arising out of the abuses and misuses of capitalist development provided a point of departure for the Marxist/socialist antithesis formulation of human rights in the nineteenth century. With the Russian Revolution of 1917, this philosophy found a home base. Out of this philosophical and political background emerged the second generation of economic, social, and cultural rights. Given the "minority" and "opposition" status of the Soviet Union in the normative domain of international politics, the internationalization of these rights was rather slow in coming. The economic, social and cultural rights of the second generation received a secondary status in the Universal Declaration of Human Rights (Articles 22–29). With the massive entry of newly independent countries into the United Nations and the gradual ascendancy of the Third World as a dominant actor in UN politics, second generation rights have come of age. After nearly two decades of struggle, the economic, social, and cultural rights were legitimized when the General Assembly adopted (and opened for ratification) the International Covenant on Economic, Social, and Cultural Rights on December 16, 1966.

The defining characteristics of the second generation rights may be summarized briefly. First, they are *collective* rights, i.e., the rights of human beings in their various group and social roles and capacities. Second, they are *positive* rights, which to be achieved had to be demanded of the state. Third, they are social rights to *basic human needs*—the right to work, the right to education, etc. Fourth, they are rights to social *equality*, demanding an equitable participation in the authoritive shaping and sharing of human rights values. And finally, they are not human rights in the first generation sense of those inalienable rights that inhere in the nature of being a human person but human rights formulated and presented as affirmative *aspirations* of humanity, calling for state intervention in the allocation of resources. In comparison with the rights of the first generation, then, the rights of the second generation are more collective than individual, more social and economic than civil and political, more concrete than abstract, more positive than negative, more equality-oriented than liberty-oriented, and more substantive than procedural.

The establishment of a closer human rights/human needs interface is the most significant contribution of the second generation. For the masses of humanity, civil and political rights are practically meaningless in the absence of basic economic, social, and cultural rights and the minimum satisfaction of basic human needs. President Roosevelt's Four Freedoms—freedom from *want* and *fear* as well as freedom of speech and religion—nicely summed up the basic spirit of the second generation of human rights. By broadening people's social and economic rights and by linking them to civil and political rights, the Four Freedoms represented a revolution of sorts—a second Bill of Rights—in U.S. human rights thinking. Unfortunately, however, this new human rights thinking seems to have been cut off at the water's edge.

The human rights of the second generation are not without some theoretical and practical difficulties. The heroic assumption that the state can be trusted as a progressive agent of human welfare stands on shaky theoretical and empirical grounds. This assumption draws upon the most problematic feature of contemporary Marxist polity—the contradiction between the traditional conceptualization of the state as an instrument of class exploitation (hence the idealized theory of the withering away of the state) and the actual development of a bureaucratic, centralized, and militarized superstate. In his *The State and Revolution* (1917), Lenin argued forcefully that "The State is the product and the manifestation of the *irreconcilability* of class antagonisms. The State arises when, where, and to the extent that the class antagonisms *cannot* be objectively reconciled. And, conversely, the existence of the State proves that the class antagonisms *are* irreconcilable."

In the contemporary international system still imbued with neo-Darwinian ethos, the state acquires its own "security" interests and myths. Once trapped in this competitive drive for security, power, and status, human interests are not abandoned; they are merely given low priority or shelved as long-term ends. The response-to-frustration school of thought in psychology has even suggested that the state serves as an instrument of the ruling class to prevent "the frustrated from expressing their aggression against their frustrators."

Closely connected to the problem of the superstate is a means-end dichotomy implied in the second generation concept of human rights. More often than not the inconsistent and selective application of internationally legitimized human rights principles is rationalized as a necessary or unavoidable means in the long-run pursuit of human well-being. Although first and second generation rights are often claimed to be indivisible and interdependent, in practice it is often otherwise, as many Third World rulers justify their short-term suppression of civil and political rights in the name of long-term developmental imperatives. "Developmental fascism," argues Eqbal Ahmad, is one of the common characteristics of the neofascist state in the Third World.

There is no empirical support for incompatibility between the two types of human rights. The world order approach rejects this means-end dichotomy. [. . .] [T]he world order approach to transition politics rests upon the centrality of values, values that cannot be placed in abeyance pending the completion of the transition process. On the contrary, these values apply to the means as well as to the ends of transition politics. Both the Marxist and Machiavellian traditions have been insensitive to the procedural and substantive indivisibility of means and ends. We can never justify dysutopian means in the pursuit of utopian ends. In his trenchant critique of the utopian element in socialism, religious and social philosopher Martin Buber argued that the utopian socialist "refuses to believe that in our reliance on the future 'leap' we have to do now the direct opposite of what we are striving for; he believes rather that we must create here and now the space *now* possible for the thing for which we are striving, so that it may come to fulfillment *then*." In short, there is—or ought to be—a transtemporal indivisibility of the first and second generation human rights.

Indeed, the insensitivity to the mutually enhancing or corrupting effects of the relationship between means and ends so evident in the actual practice of many Third World and socialist politics weakens the moral credibility of this contemporary approach. This is not to deny or minimize the enduring contributions of the Marxist theory and polity in the field of human rights: its revolutionary identification with, and struggle for, the oppressed and the exploited; its probing of the root causes of human rights abuses (structural violence); the admirable accomplishment in meeting the basic human needs of its own population as made evident in the PQLI performance of China, Cuba, and the Soviet Union; and the enlargement of the global human rights agenda in a manner more congenial to the struggling masses of humanity. Still, the Marxist approach as embodied in the second generation of human rights suffers from the problems of overcompensation—overreliance on economic rights; overreliance on collective rights; and overreliance on the "benign hand" of the state.

This presents a perplexing practical question in the Third World. How can we balance the greater economic and social equity of socialist polities with the greater cultural and intellectual openness of capitalist nations? In a comparative analysis of the deep structural pressures toward oppressive governance in both socialist and capitalist Third World countries, Richard Falk concluded that "the costs of the transition to socialism seem higher in practice than those of the persistence of a capitalist social order, thereby offsetting to a significant extent the humanitarian structure advantage of socialism." Yet capitalism as a whole is seen as inappropriate for the Third World because in failing to deal with mass poverty it creates a structural tendency for repressive rule. Given economic, social, demographic, ecological, and other structural constraints, a socialist human rights model is preferable, he argues, though not a sufficient precondition for the realization of human rights values.

The Third Generation of Solidarity Rights

Almost every problem of global magnitude and concern has attracted a UN-sponsored global conference in the 1970s. The subject of human rights has the dubious distinction of being the only exception. The third generation of solidarity rights filled this gap by restructuring the debate on human rights in more holistic, planetary terms. Clearly, the Third World's successful decolonization revolution provides the background from which the third generation of human rights is struggling to be born. At this point, however, solidarity rights are still at a preliminary, norm-formulating stage.

The solidarity rights of the third generation include the right to peace, the right to development, the right to healthy and ecologically balanced environment, and the right to share the common heritage of mankind. In a fundamental sense, this is an attempt to update, expand, and reformulate human rights in terms more compatible with the changing requirements of human solidarity in a contradictory world marked by increasing interdependence and fragmentation. In his inaugural lecture to the Tenth Study Session of the International Institute of Human Rights in July 1979, Karel Vasak presented the defining characteristics of the solidarity rights of the third generation in the following terms:

[the solidarity rights] are new in the aspirations they express, are new from the point of view of human rights in that they seek to infuse the human dimension into areas where it has all too often been missing, having been left to the State, or States. . . . [T]hey are new in that they may both be *invoked against* the State and *demanded* of it; but above all (and herein lies their essential characteristics) they can be realized only through the concerted efforts of all the actors on the social scene; the individual, the State, public and private bodies and the international community.

The concept of the solidarity rights may be new, but its normative components are not. Hence, it may be more accurate to characterize the rights of the third generation as synthetic and synergetic ones, drawing upon, and interconnecting, various existing "rights" in a holistic framework of aspiring human solidarity. The most salient feature of solidarity rights lies in the expansion of human rights to embrace the whole planet. Solidarity rights can justly claim to be *universal* human rights, for they require the concerted efforts of all social forces and actors for their implementation. Each of the major components making up the solidarity rights deserves a brief mention.

The right to peace is not difficult to infer from various international norms, including the UN Charter. In the latter half of the 1970s the right to peace gained increasing support from various international organizations, NGOs, and human rights scholars. In its Resolution 5 (XXXII) in 1976, the UN Human Rights

Commission declared: "Everyone has the right to live in conditions of international peace and security and fully to enjoy economic, social and cultural rights, and civil and political rights." The final report of the UNESCO Expert Meeting on Human Rights, Human Needs, and the Establishment of a New International Economic Order, held in June 1978, states: "By virtue of the proclamation contained in the United Nations Charter to the effect that human rights and freedoms shall be respected and the use of force prohibited, one of the basic rights of each individual is embodied in international law, namely, the right to peace."

In its Declaration on the Preparation of Societies for Life in Peace, the General Assembly reaffirmed "the right of individuals, States and all mankind to life in peace" (in the preamble) and "Every nation and every human being, regardless of race, conscience, language or sex, has the inherent right to life in peace" (para. 1). This declaration was passed by a recorded vote of 138-0-2 as Resolution 33/73 on December 15, 1978, with only Israel and the United States dissenting. The Polish human rights scholar Adam Lopatka asserts that the right to peace embodied in the declaration "legalizes what had merely been a political and moral aspiration" and "constitutes a binding norm for UN organs and for organizations belonging to the UN family."

The concept of "the right to development" was first formulated in 1972 by Keba M'Baye, who served as first President of the Supreme Court of Senegal, Vice-President of the International Institute of Human Rights, President of the International Commission of Jurists, and member of the UN Commission on Human Rights. M'Baye is currently serving a nine-year (1983–1991) term as a judge on the International Court of Justice. On February 21, 1977, the Commission on Human Rights adopted a resolution—Resolution 4 (XXXIII), which M'Baye had sponsored—inviting the UN Secretary-General, in cooperation with UNESCO and the other competent specialized agencies, to undertake a study of "the international dimensions of the right to development as a human right in relations with other human rights based on international co-operation, including the right to peace, taking into account the requirements of the New International Economic Order and the fundamental human needs." What emerged two years later is a comprehensive (161-pages-long) report of the Secretary-General on the right to development as a human right.

The right to development as a human right is a holistic idea which seeks to establish a closer interface between human rights and human development. The novelty lies not only in the linking of the two but also in the placement of individual and collective rights and needs in a mutually complementary framework. The right to development as a human right also acknowledges the individual and collective right to participate in the authoritative shaping and sharing of human rights and development values.

Although the right to a healthy and balanced environment and the right to the common heritage of mankind are also included in the category of solidarity rights, their conceptual and operational linkage to human rights has not received full definition and elaboration. Suffice it here to say that the Declaration of the United Nations Conference of the Human Environment proclaims in its preamble that "Both aspects of man's environment, the natural and the man-made, are essential to his well-being and to the enjoyment of *basic human rights*—even the right to life itself." The right to the common heritage of mankind—or the right to own, and benefit from, the common heritage of mankind—was first suggested in 1967 by Arvid Pardo in his capacity as the Maltese Ambassador to the United Nations, and was almost unanimously endorsed by the General Assembly in its "Common Heritage of Mankind" Declaration in 1970. This vague but revolutionary declaration afffirmed, *inter alia*, that the area "between the limits of national jurisdiction, as well as the resources of the area, are the common heritage of mankind" and was embodied in the 1982 UN Convention on the Law of the Sea.

The right to a healthy and balanced environment and the right to the common heritage of mankind as new human rights embody both individual and collective dimensions. The collective dimension of the right to the common heritage of mankind, argues Hector Gros-Espiell, establishes the international community itself as a subject, i.e., a bearer of rights and obligations, of international law. The individual dimension of the right to the common heritage of mankind, argues Stephen Marks, gives new meaning to individual rights "freely to participate in the cultural life of the community, to enjoy the arts and to share in scientific advancement and its benefits" (Article 27 of the Universal Declaration of Human Rights) by extending them to the international community as well.

As will be shown in the next section, the solidarity rights of the third generation are more congenial that the first and second generation rights to our world order approach to human rights. The solidarity rights have embraced all four world order values in a synthetic and synergetic framework of human unity. They have embodied the participatory efforts of all social forces and actors in the authoritative shaping and sharing of human rights values. They strike a balance between the first and second generation rights in calling for state abstention as well as state action in different domains of human rights. The solidarity rights also imply the quest for a relevant utopia by projecting the notion of universal human community interests.

In spite of these strengths, solidarity rights represent no more than aspiring norms. At this point they enjoy the rather ambiguous status of international human rights norms. Even among strong advocates of global human rights, there is a kind of ideological fatigue in the unceasing elaboration and reformulation of new human rights at a time when the existing norms are systematically ignored and violated. There is also a sense in which normative exercise can serve as an easy escape from deeper structural realities of the state system. In short, the necessary conditions of universal hospitality needed to give full expression and implementation of the solidarity rights are still largely lacking in the prevailing system of world order.

A WORLD ORDER/HUMAN RIGHTS INTERFACE

It is possible to establish a world order/human rights interface based on the foregoing discussion. This is not to introduce a fourth generation of human rights but, for analytical and prescriptive purposes, to develop a human rights/human developmental model that is sensitive to world order assumptions, principles, and values. In doing so, I draw upon, but somewhat alter, the concepts, principles, assumptions, and approaches embodied in the three-generation evolution of human rights thinking. The establishment of a world order/human rights interface calls for the following tasks: (1) clarifying core assumptions and principles; (2) redefining "human rights"; (3) formulating the human rights/human needs nexus; and (4) establishing a world order hierarchy of human rights.

The Core Assumptions and Principles

The starting point for establishing a world order/human rights interface is a holistic and humanistic affirmation of the supreme value of human life and development. No matter how one defines "world order," it is a man-made order. The quality of world order and the quality of "human rights" are mutually enhancing or corrupting. Human rights when properly defined and effectively implemented become living norms of a just world order. In a negative sense, the deterioration of the existing world order means a corresponding increase in life-destroying, life-diminishing, life-devaluing, and life-degrading effects, and vice versa. In a positive sense, the protection and promotion of human life and its potential to becoming more fully human means a corresponding enhancement of a just and humane world order. The most basic task of a world order approach to global human rights politics is to define and reduce the large discrepancies between what *is* and what *ought to be* in the human condition.

Our image of human nature always influences how we define the outer limits and possibilities of resolving the discrepancies between empirical and normative human realities. What can then be said of a world order conception of human nature? Briefly summarized, it acknowledges the dual and plastic inner nature of human beings, a delicate and changing balance between human cruelty and human kindness, between the limits imposed by the necessity of basic biological needs and the possibilities of spiritual transcendance, and between deprivation-induced aggressive impulses and deeply embedded yearnings for the ultimate truth and unity of humanity.

More specifically, a world order/human rights interface is based on the following core assumptions and principles:

- Every human life, regardless of its location in social, territorial, and ethnic space, is of equal value and therefore entitled to equal protection;
- Each human life is an end itself and as such it cannot be devalued as a means to the rights of others;
- Each human person or group is entitled to democratic participation in the shaping and reshaping of human rights values;
- Each human person or group is entitled to equal benefit in the sharing of human rights values;
- Human rights are mutually interdependent and indivisible, but some rights are more basic and essential than others in human development;
- The affirmation of the supreme value of human life and dignity is the only way to reconcile the conflicts between cultural relativism and universal human rights norms.

The Meaning of "Human Rights"

As noted earlier, the postwar witnessed a socialist and Third World revisionist challenge to the dominant Western liberal conception of human rights. Still, the Western concept of human rights, defined largely in legal procedural terms, enjoys a dominant status in the human rights debate. Even in the domain of international human rights politics the dominant modes and orientations of the 1950s and 1960s, as best exemplified in the West European human rights system with its elaborate adjudicative mechanisms, emphasized the establishment of international legal procedures to enhance respect for human dignity.

However, a legalistic conceptualization of human rights has some serious theoretical and practical difficulties. As the U.S. civil rights movement and the Soviet (Stalin) Constitution of 1936 have clearly shown, *having* human rights in a legal sense is not the same as *enjoying* human rights in an empirical sense. Most legal analyses do not go beyond standard-setting and norm-making activities, leaving the deep structure of the existing social order unexamined and unchallenged. In other words, legal protection is only one way, and certainly not the most effective way, of enhancing human dignity.

A legalistic approach tends to encumber *universal* human rights with Western, middle-class, conservative norms and biases. It has been shown that a concern for human dignity is central to all non-Western cultural traditions, yet human rights in the Western legal sense are alien to Islamic, African, Chinese, and Indian approaches to human dignity. Even in Western countries with well-established court systems, the status of law as an instrument of human rights and human dignity is problematic. Law is a powerful instrument in the hands of those who have money, power, influence, and knowledge, but it is a remote abstraction for the poor, the powerless, and the inarticulate. In a world torn by cultural relativism, fragmentation, and massive deprivation of basic human needs, to define universal human rights in terms of civil and political rights and duties is to make human rights irrelevant to the quest for a just and humane world order.

More seriously, a legalistic approach incurs the danger, willingly or unwillingly, of becoming an instrument of ideological manipulation in cold-war politics. Procedural violence to the human rights of a few prominent intellectuals in the Soviet Union receives wide condemnation and publicity in the United States, whereas substantive violence to the human rights of a hundred of thousands of people in "friendly regimes" can barely manage to receive token rebuke and publicity. Freedom House, a New York-based neoconservative organization, issues every January its annual "comparative study of freedom" report and map ranking of all the nation-states of the world on a descending scale from 1 (the "most free") to 7 (the "least free"). Looking at the world as through Alice's Looking-Glass, this survey almost invariably comes up with a Humpty Dumpty definiation of "freedom." "That South Africa can be deemed more 'free' than Tanzania," writes Fouad Ajami, "is testimony to the intellectual tyranny of form over substance."

What should be the just world order conception of human rights? Based on the core assumptions and principles clarified earlier, we define "human rights" as follows: *Human rights are those claims and demands essential to the protection of human life and the enhancement of human dignity, which should therefore enjoy full social and political sanctions.* Substance is given more weight than form in this definition, since there is growing consensus on the substantive value of human life and dignity. The legitimacy of each human right is based on its indispensability first to the protection of human life and then to the realization of our being and becoming progressively more fully human, whatever form this may take in each cultural and political space. This definition therefore implies a hierarchy of human rights values linked with human growth and development.

A Human Needs/Human Rights Nexus

How can we implement the above definition in a manner appropriate to the quest for a just world order? My contention is that this can be done by establishing a closer nexus between human needs and human rights. A human needs/human rights nexus does not mean that the two categories are the same concepts. It is merely designed to seek a closer relationship between indispensable needs and actual rights. As Johan Galtung and Anders Wirak have suggested, human needs are located *inside* individual human beings, whereas human rights are located *between* them.

The needs/rights nexus is a complicated and dynamic one, as some needs evolve into the status of socially sanctioned rights while other needs remain individual. On the other hand, some rights have no basis, or only a tenuous basis, in needs. One legal scholar has argued that the notion of need as a basis for entitlement is evolving into the central feature of the contemporary international law of development. To conceptualize human rights in terms of human needs—and this is what the human needs/human rights nexus is all about—is to place the human rights debate more firmly at the center of the ongoing struggle of the oppressed and exploited for human emancipation.

There are several specific advantages in taking a needs-based approach to human rights. First of all, it has now been demonstrated in "health psychology" that the human being has basic specieswide needs that must be met in order to avoid "sickness and subjective ill-being." Health psychologist Abraham Maslow has observed that the deprivation of basic needs makes the human person yearn persistently for their gratification. Left ungratified, the deprived person sickens and withers. Maslow therefore used "basic needs" and "basic values" interchangeably.

Second, there is growing empirical evidence in support of the concept of basic human needs. Findings from two separate global surveys provide examples. The picture that emerges from sociophychologist Hadley Cantril's global survey of the patterning of human concerns is that the demands human beings everywhere impose on their society or political culture have a biologically built-in design that sooner or later must be accommodated. The universalized pattern of human concerns, Cantril concludes, entails first and foremost the satisfaction of survival needs and such other needs as physical and psychological security, the search to create new hopes and visions and to enlarge the range and quality of satisfactions, and the desire to experience one's own identity, integrity, and worthwhileness. In more recent surveys sampling two-thirds of the world's population to measure their human needs and satisfactions, the Gallup International Research Institutes found that the main needs of the inhabitants of the major regions of the world "center about their economic welfare, their health, and family life." "One of our principle conclusions" says the report, "is that economic privation seems to affect the spirit as well as the body. Poverty adversely colors attitudes and perceptions. Although one probably could find isolated places in the world where the inhabitants are very poor but happy, this study failed to discover any area that met this test."

In short, a human needs/human rights nexus overcomes to a significant extent the problem of formulating universal human rights norms against the background of prevalent cultural fragmentation. Third, this nexus avoids the legal and theoretical abstraction associated with the first-generation conception of human rights. Violations of civil and political rights are more difficult to monitor without imposing a culture-specific criterion. On the other hand, human rights as reformulated in terms of specieswide human needs are more specific and concrete, hence easier to measure and monitor as universally acceptable norms (life, health, well-being, etc.).

Finally, a human needs/human rights nexus minimizes the elitist (class) biases so prevalent in the human rights discourse and politics. "Until we endeavor to bring human need priorities into the picture, I submit," argues Christian Bay, "the natural preferences of jurists and philosophers for the wellbeing of members of their own class will tend to determine the prevailing views of the relative importance of rights—or even the difference between 'human rights' and 'so-called human rights.'" A human needs/human rights nexus decisively shifts its main focus from the intellectual deprivation of middle-class elites in communist regimes to the basic human needs deprivation of the poor, weak, and inarticulate of the two-thirds of humanity concentrated in the Third World.

A World Order Hierarchy of Human Rights

To say that different categories of human rights are mutually interdependent and indivisible, as commonly and conveniently asserted in the UN debate, is not to say that they are or can be equal. Some human rights are inherently more essential than others to the enhancement of human dignity. The human rights essential to meeting *basic* needs cannot be placed on an equal footing with those rights essential to meeting *meta* needs. If we accept the proposition that human needs (both basic and meta) "are related to each other in a hierarchical and developmental way, in an order of strength and of priority," it is possible to construct a normative model of the typology and priority of human rights.

Christian Bay's analogy of reputable hospitals—that they do not treat all patients equally and that emergency wards and intensive care units give priority treatment to those who are most gravely injured or most seriously ill—is most instructive in establishing a world order hierarchy of human rights values. A just world order approach to human rights therefore contends that the claims of the oppressed—those in the global poverty belt who are powerless to cry out—deserve preferred treatment as most seriously injured victims in the global system. Since women are so widely discriminated against and have such low and marginalized status in the development process of most communities throughout the world, they too deserve special treatment.

The Right to Human Life. This is an absolute, irrevocable, and nonderogable right that should enjoy the most preferred position in the hierarchy of human rights values. The loss of life cancels all other human rights. Violence . . . is a pathological force that destroys or diminishes life-sustaining and life-enhancing processes. The normative significance of the right to peace (the absence of war) and positive peace (the absence of structural violence) are the greatest lifesavers in human affairs. The catchy slogan, "Better Dead Than Red"—there seems to be no counterpart slogan in the communist world—is symptomatic of pathology among the "freedom crusaders." The right to human life is essential to meeting survival needs that are transtemporal, transcultural, and transnational. The Biblical commandment "Thou Shalt Not Kill" should be the first and foremost principle of universal human rights.

The status of the right to human life in world politics is problematic. In one formulation or another, this right has received international legitimization in various parts of the International Bill of Rights as well as in the resolutions of the UN Commission on Human Rights and of the General Assembly. Yet the practical (behavioral) significance of this legitimation seems marginal for several reasons. The concept of the right to peace as a human right is relatively new and not without controversy. By repeatedly invoking the principle of interdependence and indivisibility between all human rights, the United Nations has failed to endow this right with the preferred position it deserves. In addition, the term "peace" has been subject to so many self-serving qualifications and reservations that it has become almost meaningless. Worse yet, it seems to serve as a symbolic instrument in the global politics of competitive legitimation and delegitimation devoid of any discernible impact on the actual strategic behavior of key global actors. As long as the deep structure of the war system remains untransformed, the right to peace or life, even when fully legitimized, can merely serve as a reminder of the discrepancies between normative claims and structural constraints.

The Right to Human Health. The right to human life really means the right to a healthy human life, and positive peace (the absence of structural violence) as distinct from the right to exist. Put differently, this right means an equal right *against* disease or an equal freedom *from* disease. Next to physical survival, therefore, health is the most basic human need throughout the world. Without it the human person loses much of the quintessential quality of being human. Without it the human person cannot develop toward being and becoming more fully human. Without health life loses its meaning and value, and other human rights become academic. In mapping out its global strategy for health, WHO noted: "Most deaths in most developing countries result from infectious and parasitic diseases. These are closely related to prevailing social and economic conditions, and impede social and economic development." The right to human health should be placed just below the right to human life in the hierarchy of human rights values.

The Right to Human Development. This right is a multidimensional one. It covers the largest domain of human needs/human rights, straddling both material basic needs and nonmaterial meta needs, individual and collective needs, and, in the parlance of UN human rights debates, economic, social, and cultural rights and civil and political rights. Recognizing a measure of complementarity between the two categories of rights forming the right to development, I still contend that the satisfaction of basic human needs deserves a prior claim since this constitutes the necessary, if not sufficient, condition for the realization of the nonmaterial meta needs (individual freedom needs and social identity needs).

The basic human needs—which, translated into entitlements, would include the right to adequate food, the right to safe water, the right to decent shelter, the right to education, and the right to work—are precisely the basic guarantees for human life and health. Their value and indispensability are so widely shared and so deeply felt in the inner nature of human beings everywhere that they have a legitimate claim to being a universal human right. Although there is no clear and concise definition of "right to development," it has been contended that "almost all of the elements that constitute the right to development are the subject of existing declarations, resolutions, conventions or covenants."

At the same time, the widespread phenomenon of "developmental fascism" warns of the danger of the prior claim of material needs being twisted into an excuse for oppressive rule. Unless or until the human factor reenters the development process as the main subject, not an object, unless or until the satisfaction of human material and nonmaterial needs are embodied as the primary purpose of the development process, and unless or until national development and human development are redefined in mutually complementary terms, however, developmental fascism will acquire its own self-sustaining momentum, claiming a heavy toll on human freedom.

The right to human development as a universal human right is then designed to seek a more humane interface between individual and national development so as to bring about the realization of the potentialities of the human person in harmony with the social process of his/her community. This redefines development in terms of a hierarchical expansion of human and social potentialities in a mutually complementary way. In short, development becomes a dynamic process of creating conditions conducive to the material, moral, and spiritual advancement of the whole human being in both individual and social capacities. Nonmaterial human needs such as individual freedom needs and social identity needs are part of this human development process. In order to ensure greater equality and social justice in the shaping and sharing of human rights values, the notion of popular participation has to be incorporated as an integral part of the right to human development. People must be allowed to participate in inscribing their own needs and dreams in shaping their own destiny. This is the meaning of the right to self-determination in the context of the human rights debate.

The Right to Human Environment. The right to a healthy and ecologically balanced environment is correlative to the rights to human life, human health, and human development. It is of vital concern to all human beings because of its organic linkage to the satisfaction of basic human needs. Even in a nonmaterial sense, the quality of human life is a function of the human environment. The right to a healthy environment is a solidarity right in so far as its implementation calls for the collective sharing of efforts and responsibilities of all human beings in their varying individual and social capacities. It is also a solidarity right in the sense of uniting the needs of present and future generations. The right to human environment is a holistic and normative answer to the clear and continuing danger of ecocide. As human dependence on environment quality becomes increasingly evident, the status of the right to human environment as a human right will find a more secure place in the evolving international law of development.

[*   *   *]

THE HUMAN RIGHTS PROBLEMATIQUE

The human rights problematique is caught in the abiding discrepancies and disjunctures between great hopes and great despondency, between universal human rights norms and omnipresent oppressive structures, and between growing popular demands for a share in shaping human dignity values and the ideological misappropriation of such values by a minority of dominant elites. The gap between what is and what ought to be is greater in the field of human rights than in any other domain of global politics.

Oppression is a function of governing structures and processes in domestic and international societies. Yet mush of the prevailing approach has been preoccupied with surface symptoms rather than with structural causes. UNHCR's relief and resettlement operations, although essential for the immediate alleviation of human suffering, conveniently ignore the root causes of rule by violence. No doubt this "humanitarian" and apolitical approach assuages the moral conscience of the international community and assures its necessary financial and political support. Likewise, the regime's "promotional" activities, functioning in isolation from the struggle of the oppressed, create only the illusion of movement.

The human rights problematique cannot be overcome to any significant degree without transforming the existing world order system. The inner logic of the global human rights regime follows the interests of the dominant state actors. As the official report of the Fifth Assembly of the World Council of Churches states, "it is far more likely that the will and strength to end oppression come from those who bear the brunt of it in their own lives rather than from the privileged persons, groups, and nations."

With the phenomenal growth and proliferation of our technological and military capabilities has come a steady, if silent, extension of oppressive forms of social reality. When human rights are understood as consisting of the right to human life, the right to human health, the right to human development, and the right to a balanced and stable environment, the zone of oppressive social reality expands far and wide. Deeply rooted conceptual, normative, and structural problems obstruct the quest for a more humane governance.

Conceptions of human rights reflect the prevailing intellectual and political currents of society at a given time. Despite considerable variance in different cultural and temporal zones, however, one imperative seems to spread like a global epidemic of our time—the imperative of "national security." Whether defined in terms of economic development, military buildup, or status drive, it always sides with abstract state interests over empirical human needs. "National security" is a blind spot, disguising the brutal, dehumanizing forms of social oppression and legitimizing the selective destruction of humanity.

At the core of this problematique lies the acceptance of dehumanization as a necessary evil for societal "progress." Dehumanization may be defined as the isolation of certain individuals or groups in society, defined as having unequal (subhuman) status, outside the prevailing moral and legal restraints of society. Racism is the most ubiquitous and virulent form of dehumanization. It is hardly surprising that the era of "race relations" and the era of European overseas colonialism developed hand in hand from the fifteenth century onward.

Dehumanization comes in many forms. The narrow definition of human identity in terms of a common race, a common culture, or a common language contributes to the tenacity of national chauvinism—the "our country or people right or wrong" syndrome. In social psychology this syndrome is termed the "mote-beam phenomenon," a cognitive process of overestimating in-group's virtues and out-group's vices. Ali Mazrui has argued that this dichotomy—expressed as native versus foreigner, friend versus foe, familiar versus strange, Orient versus Occident, East versus West, North versus South, developed versus developing countries—has become "an iron law of dualism, a persistent conceptualization of the world in terms of 'us' and 'them.' "

Ironically, however, the heightened sense of ethocentric security or solidarity engendered by this dualism has a self-destructive quality. Whatever measure of solidarity achieved in a given territorial space is more than offset by the intensification of intercultural, interracial, and international conflict. Until they are anchored more firmly in an inclusive sense of human brotherhood and human species solidarity, universal human rights will remain adrift in the vortex of global geopolitics. Given the intensification of transnational interactions, Charles Beitz has argued, it is no longer tenable to approach international relations as a Hobbesian state of nature with it prevailing beliefs about the confinement of moral obligations within the cocoon of each sovereign state. The solidarity rights of the third generation, though still in a preliminary phase, are aimed at arresting this drift of international human rights norms.

Another conceptual problem stems from our willingness to accept structural violence as an integral part of domestic and foreign policy. The crimes of Hitler, Stalin, Pol Pot, and Amin are universally recognized and condemned because these tyrants were unwilling or unable to institutionalize their oppressive rule. Contrast the treatment of President McKinley and President Truman in U.S. diplomatic and military historiography. The former is derided for his moral agony and vacillation over extending the Manifest Destiny doctrine to the Philippines, but the latter is praised for showing courage (that is, for having no moral qualms) in his "genocidal" decision to destroy Hiroshima and Nagasaki. Dehumanization has developed to the point where we cannot recognize such obvious symptoms of social and leadership pathology.

In an age marked by slow economic growth, resource depletion, demographic explosion, and global stagflation, the value of natural resources is rising and the value of human life is declining. The neo-Darwinian perception of nasty and brutish social reality inexorably works its way toward the "triage" solution, a new form of dehumanization parading in the sheep's clothing of ecological sanity and survival. As increasing numbers of the world's population are perceived as irrelevant to the global production of goods and services, they also become marginalized (dehumanized) in the politics of global human rights.

Despite great advances in the progressive development and codification of international human rights legislation, some serious normative problems persist. First and foremost, traditional human rights norms are born and bred in the hard shell of state sovereignty. Note also the hypersensitivity of China, the Soviet Union, and the United States about initiating any institutional reform that would appear to endow the present human rights regime with a supranational authority. Human rights norms are relegated to the status of "soft" norms enjoying poor compliance and weak enforcement, which in turns strengthens the self-fulfilling cynicism that global human rights are utopian blueprints made only to be ignored. In the field of human rights, contempt begets contempt.

The old "realist" bifurcation of morality into private and public, domestic and international, also lingers. In a classical exposition of this argument, Reinhold Niebuhr argued elegantly, if somewhat unconvincingly, that, given the fundamental difference between the morality of individuals and the morality of collectives, group relations, including international relations, "must therefore always be predominantly political rather than ethical." In a similar vein, contemporary liberal statists—Hedley Bull, Ernst Haas, and R. J. Vincent, to cite three notable examples—argue that the quest for international order is inherently at odds with the quest for universal human rights and that therefore the former should have a prior claim over the latter. This system-maintaining approach is based on the arbitrary but traditional separation of politics and morality. It runs counter to the empirically more tenable, normatively more congenial notion of politics as an authoritative value-shaping and value-realizing process. At any rate, this "realist" posture, given its firm grips on both policymaking and mainstream international relations discourse, must be recognized as a serious normative constraint.

The main normative problem, then, lies in the persisting dominance of statist norms over humanist norms. As Immanuel Kant argued in the third article of *Perpetual Peace*, the parameters of universal human rights norms (the cosmopolitan or world law in the Kantian term) are severely limited by the conditions of a "universal hospitality." Bounded universal hospitality may be seen as a function of the oppressive structures of governance in both domestic and international societies. As long as norm-making takes places within the setting of oppressive and unjust social structures, the protection of human rights is more likely to occur as a successful outcome (regime transformation) of struggle between opposed social forces in domestic society.

Given the global dominance/dependence system, however, domestic regime transformation always encounters external constraints, as exemplified by the Soviet role in Poland and Afghanistan and the U.S. role in Chile, South Korea, and El Salvador. Gernot Kohler has advanced the concept of "global apartheid," the macrostructure of extreme global inequality "in cultural, racial, social, political, economic, military and legal terms, as is South African apartheid." The South African apartheid regime is continuously sustained by the support it receives from the outside world, principally the Western powers and Israel, precisely because it is part of the global nexus between the war system and the poverty system.

Theoretically, the state is a double-edged sword that can cut either way on human rights—it can be a protector or a perpetrator. More often than not, however, state power is seized and abused by a dominant class minority, divorced from the general will of the people. When state power is brought into the struggle for power and prestige in the international scene, it rapidly loses its "humanity." Even in interstate cooperation, the domino principle encourages the solidarity of all Hegelian statists, for the failure of one state to uphold the sanctity and inviolability of its national and territorial integrity and unity becomes a threat to all. State interests are the basis for a lowest-common-denominator approach to global human rights politics.

The growth of superstatism in the United States and the Soviet Union suggests that the state, once locked in international rivalry, feels compelled to expand its domain of power and freedom. This expansion invariably comes about at the expense of human rights. Human rights, instead of limiting state power, are constantly being limited by state power. Yet a reversal of the *raison d'être* of the state intensifies violent social conflict, which it turns justifies further brutalization of political culture with its wholesale trampling of human rights.

In the foreseeable future, we are likely to witness the rise and fall of many repressive regimes, with a rather volatile impact on the status of human rights in national societies. The prospects of global transformation are less promising. The forces that generated global apartheid are so omnipotent and omnipresent that any struggle for human emancipation at the global level seems doomed. Steve Biko has reminded us, however, of the danger of allowing the oppressor—and the oppressive reality—to control and manipulate our world view into a self-immobilizing and self-fulfilling defeatism. Without being sentimental or utopian, a just world order approach rejects the credo of inevitability, seeking the voices of the oppressed as a way of articulating a praxis for human emancipation.

27. The United Nations and Human Rights, 1945-1985

David P. Forsythe

Between 1945 and 1985 there has been a marked change in the treatment of human rights at the United Nations. On the foundation of a few vague references to human rights in the UN Charter there has evolved an International Bill of Rights indicating numerous obligations of increasing salience. This core of global rules has been supplemented by a series of particular human rights instruments, some with special control mechanisms. Once the subject of human rights seemed idealistic and abstract, but by the 1980s there was growing attention through an increasing array of UN organs to specific countries and patterns of behavior such as torture and people who have disappeared. The subject of humans rights has not faded away like that of military coordination under the Security Council nor has it remained on the back burner like the Trusteeship Council. Rather it has emerged more and more as one of the subjects to which member states give great attention, if not always for the same reasons.

Considerable debate exists at the United Nations over the significance of this change in the treatment of human rights. Clearly, the institutional and procedural changes in the field of human rights have been striking. It also seems clear that there is some legal significance to these changes. At least it now can be said that states have accepted a number of new legal obligations and that numerous "cases" exist which can be used as "precedent" should actors choose to do so in pursuit of human rights values. Ambivalence begins to set in when one tackles the subject of the practical significance of these changes for the condition of human rights beyond UN meeting rooms. There is considerable disagreement about what constitutes progress in human rights and how to discern it. Debate also exists over whether events at the United Nations constitute a global regime on human rights.

Attention will be given first to the more striking institutional and procedural changes at the United Nations concerning human rights to be followed by a discussion of some of the reasons why these changes have occurred. In these first two sections evidence will be presented which should help correct a widespread misunderstanding about the UN and human rights. The third section will tackle the difficult subject of the significance of the changes. What can one realistically expect from the United Nations on human rights issues? What has the UN achieved measured against this standard of expectation? If the conclusion is ambivalent, both optimistic and pessimistic, perhaps this will prove understandable in a complex and uncertain world.

AN OVERVIEW

There are a variety of views on the historical evolution of the United Nations and human rights. Most observers agree on three early stages, each lasting about a

377

decade. From 1945 or 1947 to 1954 human rights diplomacy at the UN focused on the drafting of norms—the elaboration of the Charter provisions on human rights. From about 1954 to around 1967 optimists say human rights diplomacy turned to indirect protection or promotion effects through seminars and publications of various studies on human rights problems in general, without naming countries or specific patterns of behavior. Pessimists see this period as one of inaction despite a supposed UN action plan on human rights. This view has some merit, although numerous persons at the UN were active on several human rights matters. The Eisenhower administration, however, traded away much activity on human rights at the UN in return for the demise of the movement in the U.S. Congress for a "Bricker amendment" to the Constitution which would have limited executive authority in foreign affairs. A third stage clearly starts around 1967 when activity at the United Nations began to target selective protection of rights in specific countries like South Africa and Israel. Shortly after, this concern for specifics was broadened to other targets. At one point these efforts at protection became almost global, especially after the two major Covenants—or treaties—on human rights came into legal force. Most countries were not guaranteed freedom from some type of "UN" supervision of their rights record. Whether there will be a fourth stage beyond these three is a matter of debate.

Because the definition of most historical eras is partly arbitrary, I will speak simply of before and after the mid-1960s. Before the 1960s there was a certain "timidity" on the part of member states in approaching the human rights issue, and almost all expectations were low about utilizing the United Nations to act on human rights questions. The superpowers had not been terribly interested in international human rights at the start of the San Francisco Conference in 1945, although the U.S. responded to nongovernmental organization (NGO) pressures enough to get Article 55 placed in the Charter to give a legal basis to human rights activity. This climate of opinion controlled events at the United Nations during its first years. This climate of opinion controlled events at the United Nations during its first years. The UN Human Rights Commission, an instructed body reporting to the Economic and Social Council (ECOSOC), issued a self-denying ordinance in 1947 holding that it had no authority to hear specific complaints about human rights violations. The commission functioned basically as a research and drafting organ. As part of its action (or inaction) plan of the 1950s, states were asked to voluntarily report on their rights policies. Reports were generally self-serving and not subjected to careful review. When the commission's Subcommission on the Prevention of Discrimination and the Protection of Minorities, composed of experts uninstructed by their states' governments, had a rapporteur who became assertive and tried to push an analytic summary drawn from state reports, the subcommission buried the project. Western states sought the termination of the commission's subgroups and ironically succeeded in stopping the one on freedom of information. The one on discrimination and minorities was barely saved by other coalitions. The one on women continued as a separate commission. Sporadic resolutions on particular subjects like forced labor did not change the dominant pattern of this early period which was marked more by lip service to human rights than by specific protection efforts.

The Universal Declaration of Human Rights was adopted in 1948. The two major Covenants were negotiated (one on civil and political rights, the other on economic, social, and cultural rights). These instruments came to have considerable salience legally and politically. However necessary this drafting was, in this first period it was accompanied by considerable foot-dragging. Even Eleanor Roosevelt, the U.S. representative to the Human Rights Commission, argued repeatedly that the Declaration was not intended to be legally binding. The Covenants, while substantially completed by 1954, were not approved by the General Assembly and opened for signature until 1966, and did not reach the number of required adherences for entry into legal force until 1976. Most states seemed anxious about accepting specific and binding obligations and did not want the UN Human Rights Commission or other organs of the UN to be assertive in the cause of human rights.

Prior to the mid-1960s, however, a number of human rights instruments were developed. Concern with labor rights and slavery carried over from the time of the League of Nations. New legal instruments were created concerning refugees, genocide, women's political rights, and the rights of the child. Toward the end of this first period treaties were drafted on prevention of racial discrimination and discrimination in education. It was as if states could not help themselves from drafting documents proclaiming high-minded goals, even if their specific policies fell short of the standards they were approving. Many states failed to submit required reports to the Committee on the Elimination of Racial Discrimination (CERD) after adhering to the treaty.

In the second twenty years of the United Nations the situation changed markedly. Efforts increasingly moved from the general and the abstract to the specific and the concrete. Some drafting efforts continued—for example, on a special instrument concerning torture. The UN accepted the principle of the permissibility of individual petitions and created several mechanisms to deal with them. Increasingly UN bodies used publicity to pressure specific states. Targets were not limited to South Africa and Israel, or even Chile. Increasingly across the UN system there was a fragile but persistent movement toward improved supervision of states' policies on human rights. More and more human rights treaties came into legal force and various agencies tried to see that they were implemented.

The Human Rights Committee. The UN Covenant on Civil and Political Rights came into legal force for adhering states in 1976. Since then the number of states that are bound under the treaty has grown to about seventy-five. These elect an eighteen member committee of uninstructed persons to review state reports and to hear individual petitions from persons whose state has accepted an optional protocol permitting such action (about thirty at the time of this writing). The committee does not take instructions from UN bodies, but it reports to the General Assembly and interacts with the UN Secretariat. By most accounts since 1978 the committee has been energetic and assertive, seeking to make the review process as rigorous as possible, but staying within the bounds of a generally cooperative attitude toward states.

In 1980 an important discussion arose about the authority of the committee in the light of Article 40, paragraph 4 in the Civil-Political Covenant. This reads: "The Committee shall study the reports submitted by the States Parties to the present Covenant. It shall transmit its reports, and such general comments as it may consider appropriate, to the States Parties. The Committee may also transmit to the Economic and Social Council these comments along with the copies of the reports it has received from States Parties to the present Covenant."

A majority of the thirteen members participating in the debate wanted to give considerable scope to the world "study" and not be deterred from vigorous action by the word "general." This majority was made up of Third World as well as western members. Clear support for an active a committee came from Ecuador, Jordan, Tunisia, and Senegal, as well as West Germany and Norway. The members from Eastern Europe—especially from the USSR, East Germany, and Romania— were a distinct minority. Eventually a compromise statement was reached: "general comments" would be addressed to state parties; the committee could comment on the implementation of the Covenant; protection of human rights was a proper subject for the committee, not just promotion; the committee could take up the subject of "the implementation of the obligation to guarantee the rights set forth in the Covenant . . . ;" the committee might later consider further what duties it would undertake; the Secretariat would be asked to make an "analysis" of states' reports and the pattern of questions by members. Subsequently other comments by members indicated that many would continue to push for a serious review process and that an attempt would be made to be systematic in order to establish patterns over time. If this compromise seemed in the short run a concession to the East Europeans, it contained ample language to legitimize expansive and assertive action by the western and Third World members. Since 1980, "general comments" has been used to interpret the Covenant in a specific way.

In 1981 the committee publicly criticized Uruguay for its treatment of certain individuals. The committee in effect rejected a report from Chile and criticized the inadequacies of several other reports. The committee also requested the Secretariat to put pressure on Zaire for its failure to file a report on time. Many states have been questioned closely about their reports and policies; frequently additional information is requested and provided. Aside from the Soviet Union and its close allies, the nature of questioning does not usually follow ideological alignments. At one point in 1983 the member from Yugoslavia seemed very tough on the subject of Nicaragua's treatment of the Miskito Indians. At another point the member from West Germany was exceedingly tough in addressing the presenter of the report from France. The member from Tunisia led the effort to put pressure on Zaire.

The Human Rights Committee has not functioned for very long. Its authority, procedures, and impact are still in flux. It seems clear thus far that the majority on the committee, irrespective of turnover, intend to have as much impact as the committee can generate. National laws in Sweden and Senegal have been changed apparently as a result of committee questioning.

The Human Rights Subcommission. The United Nations Subcommission on Prevention of Discrimination and Protection of Minorities has become over time an uninstructed body on human rights in general, functioning under the Charter under whatever mandates might be received from its parent commission, ECOSOC, or the General Assembly, and under whatever initiatives it might seize for itself.

On the one hand its membership has not been that different from its instructed parent which elects its twenty-six members. In 1982, according to the index of Freedom House, ten members came from "Free" nations, seven from "Partly Free," and nine from "Not Free." Many individuals have served as instructed representatives of a state and at another time as supposed uninstructed members of the subcommission. This is a prevalent personnel pattern not limited to Eastern European delegations and one that reappears in the Human Rights Committee as well. On the other hand the members of the subcommission have been so assertive at times that superior bodies have found it necesary to suppress the subcommission's activity, ignore its projects, change its mandates, or change its membership. The subcommission has been more willing to use public pressure on states than its superiors and has also sought to do as much as possible on a number of specific problems like detained or disappeared persons. It has tried a variety of procedures to improve its efficacy, such as instituting working groups on particular problems which meet before regular sessions. The working group on slavery has been notable in this regard. It is the U.N. body of first recourse for private communiques under important resolutions, and it has performed that review with seriousness of purpose since 1972. At times the subcommission has attempted direct, public, and specific protection; for example, it sent a telegram to the government of Malawi concerning a violation of human rights.

Once, there was some fear that the expansion of the subcommission's membership and thus an increase in Third World members would dilute or slant its activity. This does not appear to have happened. In the 1980s members from Eastern Europe, joined by the one from Pakistan, tried to establish the principle that the subcommission would act only by consensus. This would have given a blocking role to a minority which might wish to curtail the persistently assertive subcommission. This move was rejected, with a number of Third World members lining up with western members. The subjects taken up by the subcommission, the states criticized, and the resolutions passed do not show a simple East-West or North-South bias. At the time of this writing the subcommission seemed as serious and assertive as in the past, and as seriously circumscribed.

The Human Rights Commission. The United Nations Human Rights Commission is an instructed body elected by ECOSOC and now comprised of forty-three states. Using the rating system of Freedom House, one finds that in 1982 the commission was made up of seventeen states classified as "Not Free," ten as "Partly Free," and sixteen as "Free." If 63 percent of the states making up a human rights body show major deficiencies in their own records concerning civil and political rights, one might reasonably expect that body to be less enthusiastic in its activiity. This assumption, however, is not completely substantiated by the facts.

If one looks at the last decade of the commission, after the drafting of the Covenants and later after two expansions of its membership, it can be said that doctrinal disputes over the relationship of socio-economic and civil-political rights— and over which had priority—gave way to an increasing focus on the protection of specific civil and political rights. During the 1980s the West has become increasingly successful at enlisting majority support for new implementation measures to protect civil and political rights. In 1980 the Commission for the first time indirectly condemned an Eastern bloc ally by passing a resolution calling for withdrawal of foreign forces from Kampuchea. In the following two sessions, the Commission denounced foreign intervention in Afghanistan. The West also narrowly succeeded in getting Commission action on Poland and Iran in 1982. [There were also] several important Western-sponsored resolutions adopted by consensus—involving the appointment of special rapporteurs on mass exoduses and summary or arbitrary executions and studies on the role of the individual in international law.

The key to these and other developments within the commission has been the role of Third World states which are truly nonaligned. They have voted their concern for self-determination in Kampuchea and Afghanistan, and they have also voted for economic rights and against racial discrimination. Some Third World states like Senegal have been vigorous and balanced in their attention to human rights violations. Evidently a number of Third World states are genuinely interested in human rights, even civil and political rights. Daniel Patrick Moynihan, the former U.S. Ambassador to the United Nations, noted that one of the merits in framing issues in terms of human rights, rather than democracy pure and simple, was that a state did not have to be a democracy to pursue the subject with some real interest. Of course some Third World states of various ideological stripe have sought to limit the activity of the commission. For example, Pakistan, India, and Ethiopia have all taken restrictive positions in commission debates at one time or another. And any Third World state will seek to block attention to its own transgressions.

Yet in the final analysis Third World support for western positions, and vice versa, has allowed the commission to do as much as it has. Since 1978 the commission has been publishing a "Black List" of states which have been the subject of private complaints as noted confidentially by the subcommission. Over time this list has shown considerable balance. To be sure, it is correct to observe that this "Black List" is a very weak form of pressure; specifics about the subject of the complaint are not provided. A working group of the commission has been focusing in a balanced way on states in which persons "disappear" by forceful action. A summary statement about the commission seems accurate:

Representatives continue to assert the principle of non-intervention when it suits their national interest, but in practice most members of the Commission have supported some initiatives to protect the human rights of citizens against violation by their own governments . . . the Commission has systematically reviewed confidential communications alleging violations by members . . . the Commission has expanded its concern for violations far beyond the early narrow focus on South Africa and Israel and has reviewed allegations involving over thirty states. Members and NGOs now disregard the former taboo against attacking states by name in public debate and make sweeping public indictments. After thirty years, the Commission has become the world's first intergovernmental body that regularly challenges sovereign nations to explain abusive treatment of their own citizens.

The Economic and Social Council (ECOSOC) receives the reports of the Human Rights Commission as well as state reports under the U.N. Covenant on

Economic, Social, and Cultural Rights—a treaty now in legal force in about eighty states. In this part of the United Nations system there does not at first glance seem to be striking change in the treatment of human rights. The conventional wisdom has been that on human rights ECOSOC functions as a "post office," carrying mandates from one body to another. A recent analysis by an insider argued that ECOSOC was still giving "very superficial scrutiny" to state reports on socio-economic rights and had failed to develop or borrow standards by which to observe violations. Yet within ECOSOC several further points can be noted, even if ECOSOC votes reflect decisions made in the commission or subcommission.

In the late 1960s Third World states pushed for specific attention to human rights violations by South Africa and Israel in many parts of the United Nations system. Stimulated by reports not only from the Human Rights Commission but also from the U.N. Special Committee on Decolonization, ECOSOC passed E/RES/1235 in 1967. This resolution—originally intended only for situations of racism, colonialism, and alien domination but amended by the West to include other human rights violations—authorized ECOSOC's suborgans to deal with specifics revealing a pattern of gross violations of human rights. The following year an effort to close the barn door failed; ECOSOC again refused to limit the scope of 1235 to only some violations of human rights, and thus the Human Rights Commission and its subcommission were authorized to take up specific patterns with full publicity.

Three years after the passage of 1235, ECOSOC adopted E/RES/1503 which permitted its suborgans to deal with private communications alleging violations of human rights. This resolution permitted NGOs as well as individuals—anyone with direct and reliable knowledge—to lodge an allegation confidentially with the Secretariat, which then passed a sanitized version to the subcommission for possible future action.

The result of these two resolutions in ECOSOC was to make possible the expanded activity of the Human Rights Commission and Subcommission. Specifics could be pursued and private information could be formally utilized. There was both a public and confidential process, although the two did not always remain distinct. The point worth stressing is that certain Third World and western states succeeded in authorizing more serious attention to human rights. An effort by the Eastern Europeans and other Third World states to keep the process limited to the international pariahs was not successful. The margin of success for the majority was very small on both resolutions. The key to the majority, in addition to western states, was certain Third World states which sought a balanced approach to human rights protection.

General Assembly. Much has already been written about the General Assembly and its standing committees regarding human rights. A widespread impression, supported by a number of facts, is that the Assembly has "politicized" human rights by employing double, unfair, or unacceptable standards. Israel is publicly and harshly criticized by a special committee made up of three states that do not even have formal diplomatic relations with the Jewish state. Yet the Soviet Union's gulag is never formally condemned by the UN bodies discussed in this article. The litany about the tyranny of the majority in the General Assembly is too well known to require restatement. Considerable attention has also been given to the view that the majority has tried to erase serious attention to civil and political rights by elevating social and economic rights to a place of exclusive priority.

I will suggest a counter thesis and give just one example as evidence. Much is wrong with the General Assembly's treatment of human rights. Politics controls; equity suffers. Increasingly, however, one sees in the Third Committee on Social and Humanitarian Affairs the same alignment on votes that one finds in other UN bodies—namely, ECOSOC and the Human Rights Commission. The result is improved balance in the treatment of human rights produced by the western and Third World coalition noted earlier. Take the following example.

In 1982 in the Third Committee there was another doctrinal debate about the priority of rights. As the representatives of both New Zealand and Senegal noted, the debate was about the balance between individual and collective socio-economic rights. An Irish resolution emphasized the former, a Cuban the latter. The crux of the matter came down to whether each resolution could be adopted without distorting amendments, thus signifying that each type of right had importance. The Cuban resolution was voted upon first and adopted by 104–1 (U.S.) with 24 abstentions (mostly western). The Irish resolution was finally adopted 75–30–22. Voting with the West in the majority was forty-six nonaligned states. A similar alignment carried the day on paragraph 12 of the Irish resolution which authorized a study of the mandate for a possible High Commissioner for Human Rights.

As on any vote in any political body, no one simple reason explains a coalition. The list of those voting for the Irish resolution does not reflect a club of the pure on civil and political rights. Paraguay, for example, voted for it. Despite the fact that the Cuban resolution was assured passage and the Irish was not, the end result was that individual civil and political rights received equal formal endorsement. This was made possible by the number of Third World states that were not prepared to endorse in principle a one-sided approach to human rights.

Security Council. The Security Council has not been generally linked to the protection of human rights. But, on the two occasions when the Council reached a "decision" in relation to the Charter's Chapter VII concerning enforcement action, the real issue at stake was human rights. The decision in the 1960s to consider Ian Smith's Unilateral Declaration of Independence in Rhodesia as a threat to peace meriting mandatory economic sanctions was a decision designed to implement the right to self-determination for the majority in what was to become Zimbabwe. That right is the first right listed in each of the two general UN Covenants on Human Rights. The decision in the 1970s to consider arms traffic with South Africa as a threat to the peace requiring a mandatory ban on such traffic was an indirect approach to the subject of apartheid as a gross violation of internationally recognized human rights, and perhaps as a violation of self-determination as well. Especially with regard to South Africa and Namibia, the Council has called upon states to implement the principles contained in the Universal Declaration of Human Rights. As a member of the Secretariat has observed, in these actions the Council "treated respect for the basic provisions of the Declaration as a legal obligation of States as well as of their nationals."

THE REASONS

It can be seen from the preceding incomplete synopsis that the United Nations has changed with respect to human rights. What are the underlying reasons for this change? At least five sets of factors contributed to this modification.

States' Foreign Policies. A view with some popularity in the 1980s is that events unfold at the United Nations according to a struggle between the United States and the rest of the world. Therefore, any progress on human rights questions results from the quality of the diplomacy of the U.S.-led West. This view is overstated, although it is correct in a certain sense.

The Soviet bloc, joined by some Third World states, has been consistently hostile to international civil political rights and to any meaningful UN review process. The Soviet interpretation of human rights under Marxism, one that is inhospitable to the prima facie meaning of UN instruments, is stated openly.

The political freedoms—freedom of the press, of expression, of assembly—are interpreted from class positions as conditions of the consolidation of the working people and the spread of socialist ideology which rules out the 'freedom' of anti-socialist propaganda, the freedom to organize counter-revolutionary forces against the fundamentals of socialism.

Thus the individual has the right to say and do only what the party-state decrees is progressive for socialism. The Soviet-led socialist bloc will try to avoid real supervision of its rights policies by a nonsocialist review body. The Soviet Union has maintained this dual position from 1947 when it opposed having the UN Human Rights Commission made up of uninstructed individuals, and 1948 when it first tried to postpone and then finally abstained on the vote on the Universal Declaration, to the 1980s when it argued that the UN Human Rights Committee should have no real control over states' interpretation of the Civil-Political Covenant. The member of that committee from East Germany even argued that the committee had no right to take any action whatsoever when a state failed to submit a required report. On issue after issue during the first forty years of the United Nations, the Soviet Union and its allies, joined occasionally by such non-Marxist authoritarian states as Pakistan and the Philippines, tried to suppress attention to international civil-political rights and to vitiate real UN supervision of rights policies.

The Soviets and their shifting bedfellows on human rights have not always, or even fundamentally, triumphed at the United Nations because of two factors. First, other states have displayed an equally persistent interest in a different interpretation of civil and political rights (as well as a real interest in socio-economic rights) and have fought for a genuine review process at the UN. One thinks primarily of the Scandinavian states, but also at times the United States, the rest of the western coalition, and some Third World states.

Second, a self-serving interpretation equal to that of the Soviets by some U.S. administrations has offset the Soviet position and in a dialectical process caused a number of states to seek a compromise leading to a certain type of progress. If the Soviet Union consistently displayed a double standard in favor of socialist states, so the United States at times manifested a double standard in favor of authoritarian and capitalist states aligned with it. When a rapporteur for the subcommission wrote a report criticizing economic relations which supported the governing junta in Chile after 1973, the United States helped suppress it. When resolutions were introduced in various UN organs criticizing gross violations of human rights in El Salvador and Guatemala, the United States voted against them. At one point the U.S. voted against a commission study on the right to food, and the U.S. was the only government to vote against World Health Organization voluntary guidelines designed to protect mothers and infants from questionable marketing practices by the Nestlé Corporation. The Reagan administration likes to publicly castigate leftist governments such as Cuba's while remaining silent about mass political murder by governments of the right such as Argentina's. U.S. Ambassador Jeane Kirkpatrick had written approvingly of such double standards. Thus an American double standard, an American self-serving bias could be and was observed at the United Nations. This provided a counterpoint to the Soviet position.

Because some states were genuinely interested in a cosmopolitan human rights program and sought a compromise between the self-serving positions of the superpowers, states' foreign policies greatly contributed to the alteration of the United Nations' record on human rights. State hypocrisy, narrow self-interest, and blatant double standards, along with more cosmopolitan forces, combined to produce a certain progress over time.

Nongovernmental Organizations (NGO). One of the main reasons why the United Nations record on human rights is different in the 1980s from the earlier days is because of the activity of nongovernmental international organizations. Groups such as Amnesty International, the International Commission of Jurists, the International League for Human Rights, and others have been creative and energetic in keeping the pressure on states to acknowledge and then implement international human rights standards.

NGO information started various UN organs down the path of a slow but eventually interesting treatment of human rights violations in Equatorial Guinea in the 1970s. Confidential NGO information was provided to the subcommission, and eventually the commission sent a rapporteur for an in-country visit which led to a public report critical not only of the fallen regime but of the current one as well. NGO pressure after the passage of E/RES/1235 quickly broadened the subcommission's focus beyond Israel and South Africa; information was submitted on Greece then under military rule and also on Haiti. NGOs successfully pushed for passage of E/RES/1503 permitting confidential communiques of broad scope. They kept the pressure on states to do something about the growing problem of torture, and pushed successfully for a special group on disappeared persons. NGO reports are used openly by the Committee of Experts under the Racial Discrimination Convention. In the Human Rights Commission their information is referred to formally by Secretariat reports. In the Human Rights Committee it is now acknowledged that members can informally use NGO reports as a basis for questioning the accuracy of state reports.

Nongovernmental organizations have been so active on human rights at the United Nations that various states have threatened to curtail their activity, sometimes succeeding, but more often failing. The Soviet Union, for example, tried unsuccessfully to exclude NGO reports from ECOSOC and its suborgans. Other threats have been made (by Argentina and Iran, for example) to deny a NGO group consultative status, but these have not been carried out. The very fact that NGOs are attacked suggests that these groups are taken seriously by states. Several observers believe that NGO activity is essential for continued efforts at protecting human rights.

Secretariat. Members of the Secretariat have contributed to the changing United Nations record on human rights, from the Secretary-General down through the Directors (now Assistant Secretaries-General) for Human Rights to the Secretariat officials who service the various human rights working groups. The five Secretaries-General to date have been supportive of human rights to varying degrees. On a number of occasions the Secretary-General has used his good offices for quiet diplomacy designed to correct some human rights problem. Publicly they have endorsed the cause, as when Javier Pérez de Cuéllar said in his 1983 Annual Report, "In the common quest to realize the ideals and objectives of the Charter, we must never lose sight of the quality of the world we are seeking to build and of the ultimate raison d'etre for all our objectivities: the individual human being. . . ."

The head of the human rights division (now centre) in the Secretariat has always been a westerner: John P. Humphrey of Canada, Marc Schreiber of Belgium, Theo van Boven of the Netherlands, and Kurt Herndl of Austria. Van Boven was perhaps the most assertive, so much so that he was dismissed by de Cuéllar after conflicts with certain states like the Soviet Union and militarily-ruled Argentina which was diplomatically supported by the U.S. Humphrey was highly active in a somewhat more diplomatic way, playing a key role in the drafting of the Universal Declaration, suggesting ideas to states who then pursued them through the United Nations system, and strongly defending civil and political rights as traditionally understood by the West. Schreiber was perhaps less dynamic than van Boven or Humphrey, although these things are difficult to prove given the possibility of extensive quiet diplomacy. Herndl has held his position for only a short duration at the time of writing.

Uninstructed Individuals. Individuals, especially those on the subcommission and the Human Rights Committee must be given credit for contributing to increased efforts at specific protections. There are other uninstructed bodies not given adequate attention in this article because of lack of space: the Committee of Experts under the Racial Discrimination Convention, the Commission on Women, the Commission on Discrimination Against Women, the Committee of Experts, the Freedom of Association Commission of the International Labor Organization, and the office of the High Commissioner for Refugees (HCR). The HCR is perhaps the UN uninstructed agency given the highest marks for its human rights work and it merits extended analysis. On all these bodies there have been individuals keenly interested in the protection of human rights. They have generated some influence, impossible to measure in the aggregate. A number of these persons have come from the Third World.

World Public Opinion. One can certainly overstate the importance of the hoary idea of world public opinion. Even so, I think it prudent to note what other scholars have observed. "National political leaders have to reckon with the possibility, and on occasion the reality, that powerful voices in their own societies will echo the words of the General Assembly, as they have done on issues of colonialism, human rights . . . and humanitarian assistance." If this is what is meant by world public opinion, then there is probably a process at work that bears noting and merits more research attention in the future.

It seems highly probable, but not proven in all cases, that various public groups draw some of the inspiration and legitimacy for their human rights activity from United Nations resolutions, declarations, and conventions. Various groups in Eastern Europe refer to these documents, as well as to others such as the Helsinki Accord. Human rights groups in Argentina did the same in addition to relying on human rights instruments under the Organization of American States. Obviously there is some overlap between what is called world public opinion and the impact of nongovernmental organizations. Yet there exist some groups and private citizens who do not act directly through the United Nations system but who are active at home in demanding that their governments abide by global, United Nations standards on human rights. In that sense there is something which passes for world public opinion, weak and uneven in distribution, but extant and possibly even growing. There is fragmentary evidence that even in closed societies governments are asked by some of their citizens to observe the human rights standards endorsed at the United Nations.

THE SIGNIFICANCE

The significance of United Nations activity on human rights can be discussed according to immediate and long-term effects. The immediate impact is usually slight, for the United Nations does not primarily bring about direct protection, although such efforts exist from time to time: telegrams to Malawi; public reports about specific individuals in Uruguay; public debates about specific policies, states, and persons; special reports about Equatorial Guinea. These efforts of direct protection will continue; states, individuals, and groups will pressure the United Nations to take short-term action on particular problems.

There is not much evidence, however, that such human rights protection activity by the UN bodies discussed in this article has had much impact on target states, at least in the short run. In some cases negative and public approaches have backfired, as when Augusto Pinochet's Chile in the 1970s used United Nations pressure about human rights violations to produce a national plebiscite endorsing his military regime. While one can chart some cosmetic change in South Africa in terms of abandonment of petty apartheid, it is difficult, if not impossible, to find decisive change in the states targeted by the United Nations for human rights abuses, much less information which would allow one to attribute any change directly to the United Nations. Furthermore, when a ruling group is determined to consciously violate human rights, it is doubtful that any international arrangement short of armed intervention will bring an end to these violations. Witness Greece under the colonels, Argentina under the junta, the USSR since 1917.

The bulk of United Nations activity on human rights is not designed to produce a short-term change. The Human Rights Committee's main activity is to produce a record of *patterns* over time drawn from states' reports and members' questions. Under E/RES/1503, confidential communications and the subcommission's analysis are supposed to deal with patterns of gross violations of human rights. The commission's publication of a "Black List" devoid of specifics is designed to focus on certain states *over time*. What would be required for successful direct protection? The authority to command violating parties to do otherwise? The ability to enforce such a command? Overwhelming political pressure directed to human rights violations to the exclusion of other interests? No United Nations human rights body has such authority and power. Only the Security Council comes close, and even its power to enforce is tenuous as seen in the history of economic sanctions on Rhodesia.

Those most familiar with the United Nations and human rights understand that the organization does not normally utilize its authority and power for direct protection. As a general rule, only states and a few international agencies have the capacity to attempt direct protection: the European Court and Commission on Human Rights, the Inter-American Commission on Human Rights, the International Committee of the Red Cross, and the United Nations High Commissioner for Refugees. The United Nations' primary raison d'etre in the human rights field is long-term and can be viewed in two ways. One can say that the sum total of UN activity is supposed to socialize or educate actors into changing their views and policies on human rights over time toward a cosmopolitan human rights standard as defined by United Nations instruments. Or one can say that the sum total of UN activity is to dispense or withhold a stamp of legitimacy on member states according to their human rights record.

A version of the latter view has gained some currency in American circles in the 1970s and 1980s. Ambassadors Moynihan and Kirkpatrick, among others, have charged that the United Nations is a dangerous place where a majority attempts to delegitimize the western democracies while legitimizing their own violations of civil and political rights in the name of economic development. This article demonstrates that the Moynihan-Kirkpatrick thesis is essentially correct when applied to Soviet bloc and some Third World states, but that it is not accurate as a description of the over-all United Nations record on human rights.

It does seem correct to highlight the socialization process and the dispensing of legitimacy, which are two sides of the same coin, as the main activity of the United Nations in the human rights area. It can be persuasively argued that in some cases—for example, Anastasio Somoza's Nicaragua, the Shah's Iran, perhaps Ferdinand Marcos's Philippines—the ruling regime lost its legitimacy in the eyes of important actors because of human rights violations. The United Nations' definition of human rights, along with other international standards and actors, probably contributed to the process.

The examples above might suggest that primarily non-Marxist authoritarian states have the most to fear from attention to international standards of human rights. Certainly the major democratic states have shown periodic discomfort about their close alignments with human rights violators. Yet it also seems true that Marxist states have problems of legitimacy and do not fare well when international sources of legitimacy are denied. Surely those who rule Poland have not been helped by persistent condemnation by the International Labor Organization (ILO), not to mention sporadic censure by the UN Human Rights Commission. There are a number of Soviet specialists who believe that achieveing international legitimacy is still a pressing problem and priority for the Soviet Union itself, not to mention Nicaragua under the Sandinistas.

The importance of United Nations activity on human rights lies in this long-term socialization process in which one source of legitimacy is given or withheld according to human rights performance. Any number of states are in need of the United Nations' stamp of approval, or in need of avoiding its disapproval, although all have other sources of legitimacy such as their own traditions, performance, and internal procedures. A feature which weakens United Nations impact is the disorganized state of its human rights endeavors. The various rights agencies are not well coordinated *inter se* or with the General Assembly.

At some point the long-term effects of the UN must become short-term if the organization is to show real impact on states and individuals. Socialization and manipulation of legitimacy must change specific behavior and must lead to direct protection by some actor if the United Nations is to manifest real significance for human rights. In a few situations this linkage can be demonstrated. In the case of *Filartiga v. Peña Irala* in the United States, a federal court held torture to be prohibited by customary international law, using United Nations instruments and actions as part of its legal reasoning. This case opened the possibility of specific prosecution for torturers of any nationality who appear in the jurisdiction of the United States. Other courts in the U.S. have also used United Nations instruments and activity on human rights as part of their decisions. Other states beyond the U.S. show some influence from UN instruments in their legal and administrative decisions. Politically it is clear that various groups and individuals refer to events at the United Nations to justify their existence and activity, and it is highly likely that in areas like the Southern Cone of South America in the 1980s the United Nations—along with other bodies—had a real if indirect impact on human rights and even the structure of national politics.

A smattering of evidence suggests that United Nations activity on human rights can have some real impact over time in changing behavior by contributing to direct protection by national authorities. Other evidence suggests that in other situations United Nations activity has very little, if any, impact.

CONCLUSION

We do lack for criticism of the United Nations when it comes to human rights. Already noted was the Kirkpatrick-Moynihan thesis, as well as the argument that socio-economic matters are being used to exclude attention to civil and political rights. Ernst Haas writes that UN efforts to implement human rights standards "do not work." Richard Ullman concludes that "the UN human rights machinery has become so politicized as to be almost completely ineffective for either monitoring or for enforcement." Moses Moskowitz reminds us that the United Nations' standards on human rights remain vague and their supervision weak.

Facts support these views, some of which have not been emphasized here either for lack of space or because this conventional wisdom is widely known. The United

Nations review system is neither so streamlined nor so authoritative as that under the European Convention on Human Rights. United Nations core procedures are less developed and less effective than those used by the ILO. Some UN bodies have been less dynamic than the Inter American Commission on Human Rights. Information from nongovernmental organizations is more formally employed in some international regimes such as the European Social Charter and the European Convention on Human Rights. After all, even the League of Nations permitted individual petitions and accorded nongovernmental organizations a good deal of formal status on human rights.

And yet there is a second view. Antonio Cassese remarked that much criticism of the United Nations is "largely unfounded." In the same vein, Louis Henkin argued that "disappointment may reflect unwarranted expectations." Both of these authors speak to the point stressed by John Gerard Ruggie: United Nations activity and "international human rights instruments are designed not to provide human rights or to enforce human rights provisions, but to nudge states into permitting their vindication." Or, in Henkin's words, "For the most part, human rights can only be promoted indirectly" by the United Nations.

This article has shown in some detail that the second view can be supported by a number of facts, even if the first view remains correct in its own way. Even if there has been inequitable treatment of human rights in the General Assembly and even if there has been a lack of sustained success in direct protection efforts, there has been a marked and improved record of treating human rights in the other organs of the United Nations system, even at times in ECOSOC and the Third Committee. This improved record holds the promise of a more equitable dispensation of legitimacy from the United Nations. The process of socialization in pursuit of a cosmopolitan understanding of human rights, however, could be undone by concerted attack by member states.

There is a formal human rights regime associated with the United Nations, despite the fact that expectations of important parties are dissimilar. The Soviet Union does not accept and international standard on civil and political rights, and the Reagan administration does not accept the existence of socio-economic rights. Yet a core coalition of states drawn from the industrialized democracies and from the truly nonaligned Third World have repeatedly acted together to maintain the United Nations human rights regime and to try to embarrass states that violate its rules. The various mechanisms of the regime remain somewhat chaotic, since not all supervising bodies or decision-making organs act in concert. Warts and all, in the last analysis a "tutelary regime" associated with the United Nations seeks to improve human rights policies by states. The Peña case, *inter alia*, shows clearly that this indirect protection can eventually have discernible effect.

28. The Nairobi Forward-Looking Strategies for the Advancement of Women, Adopted by the World Conference to Review and Appraise the Achievements of the United Nations Decade for Women

A. HISTORICAL BACKGROUND

The founding of the United Nations after the victory in the Second World War and the emergence of independent States following decolonization were some of the important events in the political, economic and social liberation of women. The International Women's Year, the World Conferences held at Mexico City in 1975 and Copenhagen in 1980, and the United Nations Decade for Women: Equality, Development and Peace contributed greatly to the process of eliminating obstacles to the improvement of the status of women at the national, regional and international levels. In the early 1970s, efforts to end discrimination against women and to ensure their equal participation in society provided the impetus for most initiatives taken at all of those levels. Those efforts were also inspired by the awareness that women's reproductive and productive roles were closely linked to the political, economic, social, cultural, legal, educational and religious conditions that constrained the advancement of women and that factors intensifying the economic exploitation, marginalization and oppression of women stemmed from chronic inequalities, injustices and exploitative conditions at the family, community, national, subregional, regional and international levels.

In 1972, the General Assembly, in its resolution 3010 (XXVII), proclaimed 1975 International Women's Year, to be devoted to intensified action to promote equality between men and women, to ensure the full integration of women in the total development effort and to increase women's contribution to the strengthening of world peace. The World Plan of Action for the Implementation of the Objectives of the International Women's Year, adopted by the World Conference of the International Women's Year at Mexico City in 1975, was endorsed by the General Assembly in its resolution 3520 (XXX). The General Assembly, in that resolution, proclaimed 1976–1985 the United Nations Decade for Women: Equality, Development and Peace. In its resolution 33/185, the General Assembly decided upon the sub-theme "Employment, Health and Education" for the World Conference of the United Nations Decade for Women: Equality, Development and Peace, to be held at Copenhagen to review and evaluate the progress made in the first half of the Decade.

In 1980, at the mid-point of the Decade, the Copenhagen World Conference adopted the Programme of Action for the Second Half of the United Nations Decade for Women: Equality, Development and Peace, which further elaborated on the existing obstacles and on the existing international consensus on measures

392

to be taken for the advancement of women. The Programme of Action was endorsed by the General Assembly that year in its resolution 35/136.

Also in 1980, the General Assembly, in its resolution 35/56, adopted the International Development Strategy for the Third United Nations Development Decade and reaffirmed the recommendations of the Copenhagen World Conference (General Assembly resolution 35/56, annex, para. 51). In the Strategy, the importance of the participation of women in the development process, as both agents and beneficiaries, was stressed. Also, the Strategy called for appropriate measures to be taken in order to bring about profound social and economic changes and to eliminate the structural imbalances that compounded and perpetuated women's disadvantages in society.

The strategies contained in the World Plan of Action and in the Programme of Action were important contributions towards enlarging the perspective for the future of women. In most areas, however, further action is required. In this connection the General Assembly confirmed the goals and objectives of the Decade—equality, development and peace—stressed their validity for the future and indicated the need for concrete measures to overcome the obstacles to their achievement during the period 1986–2000.

The Forward-looking Strategies for the Advancement of Women during the Period from 1986 to the Year 2000 set forth in the present document present concrete measures to overcome the obstacles to the Decade's goals and objectives for the advancement of women. Building on principles of equality also espoused in the Charter of the United Nations, the Universal Declaration of Human Rights, the International Covenant on Civil and Political Rights, the International Covenant on Economic, Social and Cultural Rights, the Convention on the Elimination of All Forms of Discrimination against Women, and the Declaration on the Participation of Women in Promoting International Peace and Co-operation, the Forward-looking Strategies reaffirm the international concern regarding the status of women and provide a framework for renewed commitment by the international community to the advancement of women and the elimination of gender-based discrimination. The efforts for the integration of women in the development process should be strengthened and should take into account the objectives of a new international economic order and the International Development Strategy for the Third United Nations Development Decade.

The Nairobi World Conference is taking place at a critical moment for the developing countries. Ten years ago, when the Decade was launched, there was hope that accelerated economic growth, sustained by growing international trade, financial flows and technological developments, would allow the increased participation of women in the economic and social development of those countries. These hopes have been belied owing to the persistence and, in some cases, the aggravation of an economic crisis in the developing countries, which has been an important obstacle that endangers not only the pursuance of new programmes in support of women but also the maintenance of those that were already under way.

The critical international economic situation since the end of the 1970s has particularly adversely affected developing countries and, most acutely, the women of those countries. The overall picture for the developing countries, particularly the least developed countries, the drought-stricken and famine-stricken areas of Africa, the debt-ridden countries and the low-income countries, has reached a critical point as a result of structural imbalances and the continuing critical international economic situation. The situation calls for an increased commitment to improving and promoting national policies and multilateral co-operation for development in support of national programmes, bearing in mind that each country is responsible for its own development policy. The gap between the developed and developing countries, particularly the least developed among them, instead of narrowing, is widening further. In order to stem such negative trends and mitigate the current difficulties of the developing countries, which affect women the most, one of the primary tasks of the international community is to pursue with all vigour the efforts directed towards the establishment of a New International Economic Order founded on equity, sovereign equality, interdependence and common interest.

B. SUBSTANTIVE BACKGROUND
OF THE FORWARD-LOOKING STRATEGIES

The three objectives of the Decade—equality, development and peace—are broad, interrelated and mutually reinforcing, so that the achievement of one contributes to the achievement of another.

The Copenhagen World Conference interpreted equality as meaning not only legal equality, the elimination of *de jure* discrimination, but also equality of rights, responsibilities and opportunities for the participation of women in development, both as beneficiaries and as active agents.

Equality is both a goal and a means whereby individuals are accorded equal treatment under the law and equal opportunities to enjoy their rights and to develop their potential talents and skills so that they can participate in national political, economic, social and cultural development and can benefit from its results. For women in particular, equality means the realization of rights that have been denied as a result of cultural, institutional, behavioural and attitudinal discrimination. Equality is important for development and peace because national and global inequities perpetuate themselves and increase tensions of all types.

The role of women in development is directly related to the goal of comprehensive social and economic development and is fundamental to the development of all societies. Development means total development, including development in the political, economic, social, cultural and other dimensions of human life, as well as the development of the economic and other material resources and the physical, moral, intellectual and cultural growth of human beings. It should be conducive to providing women, particularly those who are poor or destitute, with the necessary means for increasingly claiming, achieving, enjoying and utilizing equality of opportunity. More directly, the increasingly successful participation of each woman in societal activities as a legally independent agent will contribute to further recognition in practice of her right to equality. Development also requires a moral dimension to ensure that it is just and responsive to the needs and rights of the individual and that science and technology are applied within a social and economic framework that ensures environmental safety for all life forms on our planet.

The full and effective promotion of women's rights can best occur in conditions of international peace and security where relations among States are based on the respect for the legitimate rights of all nations, great and small, and peoples to self-determination, independence, sovereignty, territorial integrity and the right to live in peace within their national borders.

Peace depends on the prevention of the use or threat of the use of force, aggression, military occupation, interference in the internal affairs of others, the elimination of domination, discrimination, oppression and exploitation, as well as of gross and mass violation of human rights and fundamental freedoms.

Peace includes not only the absence of war, violence and hostilities at the national and international levels but also the enjoyment of economic and social justice, equality and the entire range of human rights and fundamental freedoms within society. It depends upon respect for the Charter of the United Nations and the Universal Declaration of Human Rights, as well as international covenants and the other relevant international instruments on human rights, upon mutual co-operation and understanding among all States irrespective of their social political and economic systems and upon the effective implementation by States of the fundamental human rights standards to which their citizens are entitled.

It also embraces the whole range of actions reflected in concerns for security and implicit assumptions of trust between nations, social groups and individuals. It represents goodwill toward others and promotes respect for life while protecting freedom, human rights and the dignity of peoples and of individuals. Peace cannot be realized under conditions of economic and sexual inequality, denial of basic human rights and fundamental freedoms, deliberate exploitation of large sectors of the population, unequal development of countries, and exploitative economic relations. Without peace and stability there can be no development. Peace and development are interrelated and mutually reinforcing.

In this respect special attention is drawn to the final document of the tenth special session of the General Assembly, the first special session devoted to disarmament encompassing all measures thought to be advisable in order to ensure that the goal of general and complete disarmament under effective international control is realized. This document describes a comprehensive programme of disarmament, including nuclear disarmament, which is important not only for peace but also for the promotion of the economic and social development of all, particularly in the developing countries, through the constructive use of the enormous amount of material and human resources otherwise expended on the arms race.

Peace is promoted by equality of the sexes, economic equality and the universal enjoyment of basic human rights and fundamental freedoms. Its enjoyment by all requires that women be enabled to exercise their right to participate on an equal footing with men in all spheres of the political, economic and social life of their respective countries, particularly in the decision-making process, while exercising their right to freedom of opinion, expression, information and association in the promotion of international peace and co-operation.

The effective participation of women in development and in the strengthening of peace, as well as the promotion of the equality of women and men, require concerted multi-dimensional strategies and measures that should be people-oriented.

Such strategies and measures will require continual upgrading and the productive utilization of human resources with a view to promoting equality and producing sustained, endogenous development of societies and groups of individuals.

The three goals of the Decade—equality, development and peace—are inextricably linked to the three sub-themes—employment, health and education. They constitute the concrete basis on which equality, development and peace rest. The enhancement of women's equal participation in development and peace requires the development of human resources, recognition by society of the need to improve women's status, and the participation of all in the restructuring of society. It involves, in particular, building a participatory human infrastructure to permit the mobilization of women at all levels, within different spheres and sectors. To achieve optimum development of human and material resources, women's strengths and capabilities, including their great contribution to the welfare of families and to the development of society, must be fully acknowledged and valued. The attainment of the goals and objectives of the Decade requires a sharing of this responsibility by men and women and by society as a whole and requires that women play a central role as intellectuals, policy-makers, decision-makers, planners, and contributors and beneficiaries of development.

The need for women's perspective on human development is critical since it is in the interest of human enrichment and progress to introduce and weave into the social fabric women's concept of equality, their choices between alternative development strategies and their approach to peace, in accordance with their aspirations, interests and talents. These things are not only desirable in themselves but are also essential for the attainment of the goals and objectives of the Decade.

The review and appraisal of progress achieved and obstacles encountered at the national level in the realization of the goals and objectives of the United Nations Decade for Women: Equality, Development and Peace . . . identifies various levels of experience. Despite the considerable progress achieved and the increasing participation of women in society, the Decade has only partially attained its goals and objectives. Although the earlier years of the Decade were characterized by relatively favourable economic conditions in both the developed and developing countries, deteriorating economic conditions have slowed efforts directed towards promoting the equal participation of women in society and have given rise to new problems. With regard to development, there are indications that in some cases, although the participation of women is increasing, their benefits are not increasing proportionately.

Many of the obstacles discussed in the Forward-looking Strategies were identified in the review and appraisal. . . . The overwhelming obstacles to the advancement of women are in practice caused by varying combinations of political and economic as well as social and cultural factors. Furthermore, the social and cultural obstacles are sometimes aggravated by political and economic factors such as the critical international economic situation and the consequent adjustment programmes, which in general entail a high social cost. In this context, the economic constraints due in part to the prevailing macro-economic factors have contributed to the aggravation of economic conditions at the national level. Moreover, the devaluation of women's productive and reproductive roles, as a result of which the status of women continued to be regarded as secondary to that of men, and the low priority assigned to promoting the participation of women in development are historical factors that limit women's access to employment, health and education, as well as to other sectoral resources, and to the effective integration of women in the decision-making process. Regardless of gains, the structural constraints imposed by a socio-economic framework in which women are second-class persons still limit progress. Despite changes in some countries to promote equity in all spheres of life, the "double burden" for women of having the major responsibility for domestic tasks and of participating in the labour force remains. For example, several countries in both the developed and developing world identify as a major obstacle the lack of adequate supportive services for working women.

According to responses from the developing countries, particularly the least developed, to the United Nations questionnaire to Governments . . . , poverty is on the increase in some countries and constitutes another major obstacle to the advancement of women. The exigencies created by problems of mass poverty, compounded by scarce national resources, have compelled Governments to concentrate on alleviating the poverty of both women and men rather than on equality issues for women. At the same time, because women's secondary position increases their vulnerability to marginalization, those belonging to the lowest socio-economic strata are likely to be the poorest of the poor and should be given priority. Women are an essential productive force in all economies; therefore it is particularly important in times of economic recession that programmes and measures designed to raise the status of women should not be relaxed but rather intensified.

To economic problems, with their attendant social and cultural implications, must be added the threat to international peace and security resulting from violations of the principles of the United Nations Charter. This situation, affecting *inter alia* the lives of women, constitutes a most serious obstacle to development and thus hinders the fulfilment of the Forward-looking Strategies.

What is now needed is the political will to promote development in such a way that the strategy for the advancement of women seeks first and foremost to alter the current unequal conditions and structures that continue to define women as secondary persons and give women's issues a low priority. Development should now move to another plane in which women's pivotal role in society is recognized and given its true value. That will allow women to assume their legitimate and core positions in the strategies for effecting the changes necessary to promote and sustain development.

C. CURRENT TRENDS AND PERSPECTIVES TO THE YEAR 2000

In the absence of major structural changes or technological breakthroughs, it can be predicted that up to the year 2000 recent trends will, for the most part, be extended and adjusted. The situation of women, as it evolves during the period 1986–2000, will also cause other changes, establishing a process of cause and effect of great complexity. Changes in women's material conditions, consciousness and aspirations, as well as societal attitudes towards women, are themselves social and cultural processes having major implications and a profound influence on institutions such as the family. Women's advancement has achieved a certain momentum that will be affected by the social and economic changes of the next 15 years, but it will also continue to exist as a force to be reckoned with. Internal processes will exercise a major influence in the economic sphere, but the state of the global economic system and of the political, social, cultural, demographic and communication processes directly affected by it will invariably have a more profound impact on the advancement of women.

At the beginning of the Decade there was an optimistic outlook for development, but during the early 1980s the world economy experienced a widespread recession due, *inter alia*, to sharp inflationary pressures that affected regions and some groups of countries, irrespective of their level of development or economic structure. During the same period, however, the countries with centrally planned economies as a group experienced stable economic growth. The developed market economy countries also experienced growth after the recession.

Despite the recovery in the developed market economy countries which is being felt in the world economy, the immediate outlook for recovery in developing countries, especially in the low-income and the least developed countries, remains bleak, particularly in view of their enormous public and private external debts and the cost of servicing that debt, which are an evident manifestation of this critical situation. This heavy burden has serious political, economic and social consequences for them. No lasting recovery can be achieved without rectifying the structural imbalances in the context of the critical international economic situation and without continued efforts towards the establishment of a new international economic order. The present situation clearly has serious repercussions for the status of women, particularly underprivileged women, and for human resource development.

Women, subject to compound discrimination on the basis of race, colour, ethnicity and national origin, in addition to sex, could be even more adversely affected by deteriorating economic conditions.

If current trends continue, the prospects for the developing world, particularly the low-income and least developed countries, will be sombre. The overall growth in the developing countries as currently projected will be lower in the period 1980–2000 than that experienced in the period 1960–1980. In order to redress this outlook and thereby promote the advancement of women, policies should be reoriented and reinforced to promote world trade, in particular so as to promote market access for the exports of developing countries. Similarly, policies should be pursued in other areas which would also promote growth and development in developing countries, for example, in respect of further lowering interest rates and pursuit of non-inflationary growth policies.

It is feared that, if there is slow growth in the world economy, there will inevitably be negative implications for women since, as a result of diminished resources, action to combat women's low position, in particular, their high rates of illiteracy, low levels of education, discrimination in employment, their unrecognized contribution to the economy and their special health needs, may be postponed. A pattern of development promoting just and equitable growth on the basis of justice and equality in international economic relations could make possible the attainment of the goals and objectives of the International Development Strategy, which could make a significant improvement in the status of women while enhancing women's effective contribution to development and peace. Such a pattern of development has its own internal dynamics that would facilitate an equitable distribution of resources and is conducive to promoting sustained, endogenous development, which will reduce dependence.

It is very important that the efforts to promote the economic and social status of women should rely in particular on the development strategies that stem from the goals and objectives of the International Development Strategy and the principles of a new international economic order. These principles include, *inter alia*, self-reliance, collective self-reliance, the activation of indigenous human and material resources. The restructuring of the world economy, viewed on a long-term basis, is to the benefit of all people—women and men of all countries.

According to estimates and projections of the International Labour Office, women constitute 35 per cent of the world's labour force, and this figure is likely to increase steadily to the year 2000. Unless profound and extensive changes are made, the type of work available to the majority of women, as well as the rewards, will continue to be low. Women's employment is likely to be concentrated in areas requiring lower skills and lower wages and minimum job security. While women's total input of labour in the formal and informal sector will surpass that of men by the year 2000, they will receive an unequal share of the world's assets and income. According to recent estimates, it seems that women have sole responsibility for the economic support of a large number of the world's children, approximately one third and higher in some countries, and the numbers seem to be rising. Forward-looking strategies must be progressive, equitable and designed to support effectively women's roles and responsibilities as they evolve up to the year 2000. It will continue to be necessary to take specific measures to prevent discrimination and exploitation of their economic contribution at national and international levels.

During the period from 1986 to the year 2000, changes in the natural environment will be critical for women. One area of change is that of the role of women as intermediaries between the natural environment and society with respect to agro-ecosystems, as well as the provision of safe water and fuel supplies and the closely associated question of sanitation. The problem will continue to be greatest where water resources are limited—in arid and semi-arid areas—and in areas experiencing increasing demographic pressure. In a general manner, an improvement in the situation of women could bring about a reduction in mortality and morbidity as well as better regulation of fertility and hence of population growth, which would be beneficial for the environment and, ultimately, for women, children and men.

The issues of fertility rates and population growth should be treated in a context that permits women to exercise effectively their rights in matters pertaining to population concerns, including the basic right to control their own fertility which forms an important basis for the enjoyment of other rights, as stated in the report of the International Population Conference held at Mexico City in 1984.

It is expected that the ever-expanding communications network will be better attuned than before to the concerns of women and that planners in this field will provide increasing information on the objectives of the Decade—equality, development and peace—on the Forward-looking Strategies, and on the issues included in the subtheme—employment, health and education. All channels, including computers, formal and non-formal education and the media, as well as traditional mechanisms of communication involving the cultural media of ritual, drama, dialogue, oral literature and music, should be used.

Political and governmental factors that are likely to affect prospects for the achievement of progress by women during the period 1986–2000 will depend in large measure upon the existence or absence of peace. If widespread international tensions continue, with threats not only of nuclear catastrophe but also of localized conventional warfare, then the attention of policy-makers will be diverted from tasks directly and indirectly relevant to the advancement of women and men, and vast resources will be further applied to military and related activities. This should be avoided and these resources should be directed to the improvement of humanity.

To promote their interests effectively, women must be able to enjoy their right to take part in national and international decision-making processes, including the right to dissent publicly and peacefully from their Government's policies, and to mobilize to increase their participation in the promotion of peace within and between nations.

There is no doubt that, unless major measures are taken, numerous obstacles will continue to exist which retard the participation of women in political life, in the formulation of policies that affect them and in the formulation of national women's policies. Success will depend in large measure upon whether or not women can unite to help each other to change their poor material circumstances and secondary status and to obtain the time, energy and experience required to participate in political life. At the same time, improvements in health and educational status, legal and constitutional provisions and networking will increase the effectiveness of the political action taken by women so that they can obtain a much greater share in political decision-making than before.

In some countries and in some areas, women have made significant advances, but overall progress has been modest during the Decade, as is evident from the review and appraisal. During this period, women's consciousness and expectations have been raised, and it is important that this momentum should not be lost, regardless of the poor performance of the world economy. The changes occurring in the family, in women's roles and in relationships between women and men may present new challenges requiring new perspectives, strategies and measures. At the same time, it will be necessary to build alliances and solidarity groups across sexual lines in an attempt to overcome structural obstacles to the advancement of women.

The World Plan of Action for the Implementation of the objectives of the International Women's Year, the Declaration of Mexico on the Equality of Women and their Contribution to Development and Peace, 1975, regional plans of action, the Programme of Action for the Second Half of the United Nations Decade for Women: Equality, Development and Peace, and the sub-theme—employment, health and education—the Declaration on the Participation of Women in Promoting International Peace and Co-operation and the Convention on the Elimination of All Forms of Discrimination against Women remain valid and therefore constitute the basis for the strategies and concrete measures to be pursued up to the year 2000. The continuing relevance of the goals of the United Nations Decade for Women: Equality, Development and Peace—and of its sub-theme—health, education and employment—should be stressed, as should the implementation of the relevant recommendations of the 1975 Plan of Action and the 1980 Programme of Action, so as to ensure the complete integration of women in the development process and the effective realization of the objectives of the Decade. The challenge now is for the international community to ensure that the achievements of the Decade become strong building blocks for development and to promote equality and peace, especially for the sake of future generations of women. The obstacles of the next 15 years must be met through concerted global, regional and national efforts. By the year 2000 illiteracy should have been eliminated, life expectancy for all women increased to at least 65 years of good quality life and opportunities for self-supporting employment made available. Above all, laws guaranteeing equality for women in all spheres of life must by then be fully and comprehensively implemented to ensure a truly equitable socio-economic framework within which real development can take place. Forward-looking Strategies for the advancement of women at the regional level should be based on a clear assessment of demographic trends and development forecasts that provide a realistic context for their implementation.

The Forward-looking Strategies and multidimensional measures must be pursued within the framework of a just international society in which equitable economic relations will allow the closing of the gap that separates the industrialized countries from the developing countries. In this regard, all countries are called upon to show their commitment as was decided in General Assembly resolution 34/138 and, therefore, to continue informal consultations on the launching of global negotiations, as decided by the General Assembly in decision 39/454.

D. BASIC APPROACH TO THE FORMULATION OF THE FORWARD-LOOKING STRATEGIES

It is necessary to reiterate the unity, inseparability and interdependence of the objectives of the Decade—equality, development and peace—as regards the advancement of women and their full integration in economic, political, social and cultural development, for which purpose the objectives should remain in effect in the operational strategies for the advancement of women to the year 2000.

The Forward-looking Strategies are intended to provide a practical and effective guide for global action on a long-term basis and within the context of the broader goals and objectives of a new international economic order. Measures are designed for immediate action, with monitoring and evaluation occurring every five years, depending on the decision of the General Assembly. Since countries are at various stages of development, they should have the option to set their own priorities based on their own development policies and resource capabilities. What may be possible for immediate action in one country may require more long-range planning in another, and even more so in respect of countries which are still under colonialism, domination and foreign occupation. The exact methods and procedures of implementing measures will depend upon the nature of the political process and the administrative capabilities of each country.

Some measures are intended to affect women and others directly and are designed to make the societal context less obstructive and more supportive of their progress.

These measures would include the elimination of sex-based stereotyping, which is at the root of continuing discrimination. Measures to improve the situation of women are bound to have a ripple effect in society, since the advancement of women is without doubt a pre-condition for the establishment of a humane and progressive society.

The feasibility of policies, programmes and projects concerning women will be affected not only by their numbers and socio-economic heterogeneity but also by the different life-styles of women and by the constant changes in their life cycle.

The Forward-looking Strategies not only suggest measures for overcoming obstacles that are fundamental and operational, but also identify those that are emerging. Thus, the strategies and measures presented are intended to serve as guidelines for a process of continuous adaptation to diverse and changing national situations at speeds and modes determined by overall national priorities, within which the integration of women in development should rank high. The Forward-looking Strategies, acknowledging existing and potential obstacles, include separate basic strategies for the achievement of equality, development and peace. In line with the recommendations of the Commission on the Status of Women, acting as the Preparatory Body for the Conference at its second session, particular attention is given to "especially vulnerable and underprivileged groups of women, such as rural and urban poor women; women in areas affected by armed conflicts, foreign intervention and international threats to peace; elderly women; young women; abused women; destitute women; women victims of trafficking and women in involuntary prostitution; women deprived of their traditional means of livelihood; women who are sole supporters of families; physically and mentally disabled women; women in detention; refugee and displaced women; migrant women; minority women; and indigenous women".

Although addressed primarily to Governments, international and regional organizations, and non-governmental organizations, an appeal is made to all women and men in a spirit of solidarity. In particular, it is addressed to those women and men who now enjoy certain improvements in their material circumstances and who have achieved positions where they may influence policy-making, development priorities and public opinion to change the current inferior and exploited condition of the majority of women in order to serve the goals of equality for all women, their full participation in development, and the achievement and strengthening of peace.

29. A Crime of Silence:
The Armenian Genocide

Permanent Peoples' Tribunal

PREAMBLE

The most fundamental of all assaults on the right of peoples is the crime of genocide. Nothing is graver in a criminal sense than a deliberate state policy of systematic extermination of a people based on their particular ethnic identity. This centrality of genocide to the works of the Permanent Peoples' Tribunal is embodied in its basic framework of law set forth in the Universal Declaration of the Rights of Peoples (Algiers, 4 July 1976).

Article 1 of the Algiers Declaration asserts: 'Every people has the right to existence.' Article 2: 'Every people has the right to respect of its national and cultural identity.' Article 3: 'Every people has the right to retain peaceful possession of its territory and to return to it if it is expelled.'

And finally, Article 4 confronts directly the reality of genocide: 'None shall be subjected, because of his national or cultural identity, to massacre, torture, persecution, deportation, expulsion or living conditions such as may compromise the identity of integrity of the people to which he belongs.'

Yet, it may still be asked, why so many years after the alleged genocide, should the Tribunal devote its energies to an inquiry into the allegations of the Armenian people. After all, the basic grievance of massacre and extermination is fixed in time sixty-nine years ago in 1915. The Tribunal is convinced that its duties include the validation of historic grievances if these have never been properly brought before the bar of justice and acknowledged in an appropriate form by the government involved.

In this instance, the basis for an examination and evaluation of these Armenian allegations is especially compelling. Every government of the Turkish state since 1915 has refused to come to grips with the accusation of responsibility for the genocide events.

In recent international forums and academic meetings, the Turkish government had made a concerted effort to block inquiry of acknowledgement of the Armenian genocide.

Furthermore, the current Turkish government has not taken cognizance of these most serious charges of responsibility for exterminating the Armenian people. On the contrary, additional charges implicate the present Turkish government in continuing these exterminist policies.

Particularly relevant in this regard are the charges of deliberate destruction, desecration, and neglect of Armenian cultural monuments and religious buildings. The Tribunal adopts the view that charge of the crime of genocide remains a present reality to be examined and, if established, to be appropriately and openly acknowledged by leaders of the responsible state. The victims of a crime of genocide are entitled to legal relief even after this great lapse of time, although this relief must necessarily reflect present circumstances.

Here, also, the attitudes of the Armenian survivors and their descendants are also relevant. Any people rightfully insist and seek a formal recognition by legal authorities of crimes and injustices found to have been committed at their expense. The more extreme the injustice and the longer it is covered up, the more profound is this longing for recognition. The Tribunal notes with regret that the frustration arising from this denial of acknowledgement has seemingly contributed to the recourse to terroristic acts against Turkish diplomats and others. The hope of the Tribunal is to facilitate a constructive process of coming to terms with the Armenian reality, which may lead to a resolution or moderation of the conflict that may arise from it.

Genocide is the worst conceivable crime of state. Often, the state responsible is protected from accountability by other states and by the international framework of the organizations, including the United Nations, composed exclusively of states. One striking feature of the Armenian experience is the responsibility of other states who, for reasons of geopolitics, join with the Turkish government in efforts to prevent, even at this late date, a thorough inquiry and award of legal relief.

The Permanent Peoples' Tribunal was brought into existence partly to overcome the moral and political failures of states as instruments of justice. The Tribunal has inquired into the Armenian grievances precisely because of the long silence of the organized international society and, especially, of the complicity of leading Western states (with the recent exception of France) who have various economic, political, and military ties with the Turkish state.

The Tribunal also acts because it is deeply concerned with the prevalence of genocide and genocidal attitudes in our world. As members of the Tribunal we believe that the uncovering and objective documentation of allegations of genocide contributes to the process of acknowledgement. To uncover and expose the genocidal reality makes is somewhat harder for those with motives of cover up to maintain their position. By validating the grievances of the victims, the Tribunal contributes to the dignity of their suffering and lends support to their continuing struggle. Indeed, acknowledging genocide itself is a fundamental means of struggling against genocide. The acknowledgement is itself an affirmation of the right of a people under international law to a safeguarded existence.

THE FACTS

I. Historical Introduction

The presence of the Armenian people in Eastern Anatolia and the Caucasus is attested from the sixth century B.C. onward. For two millennia the Armenian people alternated between periods of independence and vassaldom. A succession of royal dynasties came to an end with the collapse of the last Armenian kingdom in the fourteenth century. Having adopted Christianity as their state religion in the early part of the fourth century as well as their own alphabet, both of which gave them a national identity from this period, the Armenians were often persecuted because of their faith by various invaders and suzerains. Though they occupied a geographical position which, as a strategic crossroads, was particularly vulnerable, the Armenians were able until the First World War to create and preserve on their historic territory—which the Turks themselves called Ermenistan—a language, a culture, and a religion: in short, an identity.

Following the disappearance of the last Armenian kingdom, the greater part of Armenia fell under Turkish domination, while the Eastern regions were under the control first of Persia, then of the Russians, who annexed them in the nineteenth century.

Like other religious minorities, the Armenian community (or 'millet') enjoyed religious and cultural autonomy within the Ottoman Empire and, indeed, was left more or less in peace during the classical period of the Empire's history, in spite of the Armenians' status as second-class citizens ('rayahs').

But with the decline of the Empire in the nineteenth century, conditions grew steadily worse and the climate became one of oppression. The growth in population and the arrival or successive waves of Turkish refugees from Russia and the Balkans as well as the sedentarization of nomads (Kurds, Circassians, etc.) upset the balance of populations and increased the pressure of competition for land, creating numerous problems of tenure in the agrarian sector. The result was a deterioration in the fortunes of the Armenian population, who were mostly peasants and farmers. Modernization and reform were made difficult by the fossilized structure of the Empire. The few attempts at reform (formation of a modern army, taxation in coin) merely impoverished the peasantry further. At the same time, the emergence of national feelings in the Balkans was leading increasingly to the independence of peoples who had hitherto been under Ottoman rule. The Empire was being steadily weakened, not least due to its foreign debt.

From 1878, following the Russian-Turkish war the Armenian question became a factor in the question of the Orient. Article 16 of the Treaty of San Stefano (1878) provided that a series of reforms would be carried out in Armenian areas under Russian guarantee. However, following a reversal of alliances, the Treaty of Berlin (1878) relieved Turkey of part of its obligations and charged Great Britain to supervise the reforms: but they were never implemented.

A revolutionary movement began to develop within the Armenian community (Dashnak and Hunchak parties). Following the Sasun insurrection in 1894, approximately 300,000 Armenians were massacred in the Eastern provinces and in Constantinople on the orders of Sultan Abdul Hamid. Protests by the Powers led to more promises of reforms which, again, were never kept; the guerilla ('fedayis') struggle continued. From the turn of the century onward, Armenian revolutionaries also began to cooperate with the Young Turk party in the definition of a federalist plan for the Empire. Following the hopes generated by the constitutional revolution of 1908 Young Turk ideology, under pressure of the exercise of power and external events as well as from the radical wing of the movement, began to develop toward a form of exclusive nationalism which found expression in Pan-Turkism and Turanism.

The Armenians' situation in the Eastern provinces had not changed either as the result of the revolution or of the overthrow of Abdul Hamid in 1909 (massacres of Adana), and demands for reforms were again made by the Entente Powers. These demands were eventually heard in February 1914, and two inspectors were appointed to supervise their implementation. These appointments were considered by the Ottoman government as unacceptable interference.

At the outbreak of the First World War, the Ottoman Empire was uncertain as to which side to join. At the beginning of November 1914, under German pressure, it sided with the Central Powers. This placed the Armenians in a difficult position. They occupied a territory which Turkey considered as vital to the realization of its Turanist imperialistic ambitions with regard to the peoples of Transcaucasia and Central Asia. Furthermore, the division of the Armenian people between the Ottoman Empire (2,000,000 Armenians) and Russia (1,700,000) inevitably meant that the two sections of the population found themselves on opposing sides. At the Eighth Congress of the Armenian Revolutionary Federation at Erzerum in August 1914, the Dashnak party rejected Young Turk requests to engage in subversive action among the Russian Armenians. From the beginning of the war, the Turkish Armenians behaved in general as loyal subjects, signing up with the Turkish army. The Russian Armenians, on their side, were routinely conscripted into the Russian army and sent to fight on the European fronts. In the first months of the war, Russian Armenians enrolled with volunteer corps which acted as scouts for the Tsarist army—the Russian answer to the plan Turks had submitted to Armenians in Erzerum some months earlier. The Erzerum refusal and the formation of these volunteer battalions were used as arguments by the Young Turks to allege Armenian treachery. Enver, who had been appointed Supreme Commander of the Turkish forces, achieved a breakthrough into Transcaucasia in the middle of winter, but was defeated at Sarikamish as much by the weather conditions as by the Russian army. Of the Turkish Third Army's 90,000 men, only 15,000 remained. In the depressed aftermath of the defeat in the Caucasus, the anti-Armenian measures began.

II. The Genocide

Beginning in January 1915, Armenian soldiers and gendarmes were disarmed, regrouped in work brigades of 500 to 1,000 men, put to work on road maintenance or as porters, then taken by stages to remote areas and executed. It was not until April that the implementation of a plan began, with successive phases carried out in a disciplined sequence. The signal was first given for deportation to begin in Zeytun in early April, in an area of no immediate strategic importance. It was not until later that deportation measures were extended to the border provinces.

The pretext used to make the deportation a general measure was supplied by the resistance of the Armenians of Van. The vali of Van, Jevdet, sacked outlying Armenian villages and the Van Armenians organized the self-defence of the city. They were saved by a Russian breakthrough spearheaded by the Armenian volunteers from the Caucasus. After taking Van on May 18th, the Russians continued to press forward but were halted in late June by a Turkish counteroffensive. The Armenians of the vilayet of Van were thus able to retreat and escape extermination.

When the news of the Van revolt reached Constantinople, the Union and Progress (Ittihad) Committee seized the opportunity. Some 650 personalities, writers, poets, lawyers, doctors, priests, and politicians were imprisoned on April

24th and 25th, 1915, then deported and murdered in the succeeding months. Thus was carried out what was practically the thorough and deliberate elimination of almost the entire Armenian intelligentsia of the time.

From April 24 onwards, and following a precise timetable, the government issued orders to deport the Armenians from the eastern vilayets. Since Van was occupied by the Russian army, the measures applied only to the six vilayets of Trebizond (Trabzon), Erzerum, Bitlis, Diarbekir, Kharput, and Sivas. The execution of the plan was entrusted to a 'special organization' (SO), made up of common criminals and convicts trained and equipped by the Union and Progress Committee. This semi-official organization, led by Behaeddin Shakir, was under the sole authority of the Ittihad Central Committee. Constantinople issued directives to the valis, kaymakans, as well as local SO men, who had discretionary powers to have moved or dismissed any uncooperative gendarme or official. The methods used, the order in which towns were evacuated, and the routes chosen for the columns of deportees all confirm the existence of a centralized point of command controlling the unflooding of the program. Deportation orders were announced publicly or posted in each city and township. Families were allowed two days to collect a few personal belongings; their property was confiscated or quickly sold off. The first move was generally the arrest of notables, members of Armenian political parties, priests, and young men, who were forced to sign fabricated confessions then discreetly eliminated in small groups. The convoys of deportees were made up of old people, women, and children. In the more remote villages, families were slaughtered and their homes burned or occupied. On the Black Sea coast and along the Tigris near Diarbekir boats were heaped with victims and sunk. From May to July 1915, the Eastern provinces were sacked and looted by Turkish soldiers and gendarmes, SO gangs ('chetes'), etc. This robbery, looting, torture, and murder were tolerated or encouraged while any offer of protection to the Armenians was severely punished by the Turkish authorities.

It was not possible to keep the operation secret. Alerted by missionaries and consuls, the Entente Powers enjoined the Turkish government, from May 24, to put an end to the massacres, for which they held members of the government personally responsible. Turkey made the deportation official by issuing a decree, claiming treason, sabotage, and terrorist acts on the part of the Armenians as a pretext.

Deportation was in fact only a disguised form of extermination. The strongest were eliminated before departure. Hunger, thirst, and slaughter decimated the convoys' numbers. Thousands of bodies piled up along the roads. Corpses hung from trees and telegraph poles; mutilated bodies floated down rivers or were washed up on the banks. Of the seven eastern vilayets' original population of 1,200,000 Armenians, approximately 300,000 were able to take advantage of the Russian occupation to reach the Caucasus; the remainder were murdered where they were or deported, the women and children (about 200,000 in number) kidnapped. Not more than 50,000 survivors reached the point of convergence of the convoys of deportees in Aleppo.

At the end of July 1915, the government began to deport the Armenians of Anatolia and Cilicia, transferring the population from regions which were far distant from the front and where the presence of Armenians could not be regarded as a threat to the Turkish army. The deportees were driven south in columns which were decimated en route. From Aleppo, survivors were sent on toward the deserts of Syria in the south and of Mesopotamia in the southeast. In Syria, reassembly camps were set up at Hama, Homs, and near Damascus. These camps accommodated about 120,000 refugees, the majority of whom survived the war and were repatriated to Cilicia in 1919. Along the Euphrates, on the other hand, the Armenians were driven ever onward toward Deir-el-Zor, approximately 200,000 reached their destination. Between March and August 1916, orders came from Constantinople to liquidate the last survivors remaining in the camps along the railway and the banks of the Euphrates.

There were nevertheless still some Armenians remaining in Turkey. A few Armenian families in the provinces, Protestants and Catholics for the most part, had been saved from death by the American missions and the Apostolic Nuncio. In some cases, Armenians had been spared as a result of resolute intervention by Turkish officials, or had been hidden by Kurdish or Turkish friends. The Armenians of Constantinople and Smyrna also escaped deportation. Lastly, there were cases of resistance (Urfa, Shabin-Karahisar, Musa-Dagh). In all, including those who took refuge in Russia, the number of survivors at the end of 1916 can be estimated at 600,000 out of an estimated total population in 1914 of 1,800,000 according to A. Toynbee.

In Eastern Anatolia, the entire Armenian population had disappeared. A few survivors of the slaughter took refuge in Syria and Lebanon, while others reached Russian Armenia. In April 1918, in order to circumvent provisions of the Treaty of Brest-Litovsk stipulating that Bolshevik Russia cede Batum, Kars, and Ardahan to Turkey. Transcaucasia declared independence, forming a shortlived Federation which was to break up into three republics in May 1918: Georgia, Armenia, and Azerbaijan.

At its defeat in November 1918, Turkey recognized the Armenian state and even ceded to it in the following year the vilayets of Kars and Ardahan.

All the allied governments had solemnly promised on several occasions, in statements by their representatives Lloyd George, Clemenceau, Wilson, etc., to ensure that justice was done by the 'martyred Armenian people'.

In April 1920, the San Remo Conference proposed that the United States accept an Armenian mandate, and that, whatever the United States decision, President Wilson should define the frontiers of the Armenian state and that the peace treaty with Turkey should designate him as referee in the question of the Turkish-Armenian frontiers.

The Treaty of Sèvres (August 10, 1920), which recognized the Armenian state and ratified the frontiers drawn by President Wilson, did not, however, settle the issue. This Treaty, which was signed by the government in Constantinople and which shared out large sections of Anatolia to the Italians, the British, and the French as well as favoured the Greeks in the Aegean Sea, was unacceptable to Mustafa Kemal, who rejected it. The Republic of Armenia under the leadership of the socialist Armenian Revolutionary Federation (Dashnak) was soon caught in a vice between the Kemalist offensive and Bolshevik Russia. When, on November

20, 1920, President Wilson officially set forth the territorial limits of the new state, the collapse of the Republic was only a few days off. The vilayets of Kars and Ardahan were retaken by Turkey (Treaty of Alexandropol) and what remained of Armenia (approximately 30,000 sq. km.) became Soviet on December 2, 1920.

On July 24, 1923, the Treaty of Lausanne was signed by the Great Powers and the new Republic of Turkey with no mention of Armenia or the rights of Armenians. The Armenian question was closed.

III. The Evidence

The Tribunal is invited to pronounce judgement on the charge of genocide brought on the basis of the events of 1915–1916.

The Tribunal considers that the facts presented above are established on the basis of substantial and concordant evidence. This evidence has been produced and analyzed in the various reports heard by the Tribunal, to which numerous documents have been submitted.

A near-exhaustive bibliography of these sources has been drawn up by Professor R.G. Hovannisian, *The Armenian Holocaust*, Cambridge, Massachusetts, 1981.

Not counting the Ottoman archives—which are inaccessible—the main documents are as follows:

- The German archives, which in view of the status of Germany as ally of the Ottoman Empire, are of prime significance. Especially worthy of note are the reports and eyewitness observations of Johannes Lepsius, of Dr. Armin Wegner, of the charitable organization 'Deutscher Hilfsbund', of Dr. Jacob Kunzler, of the journalist Stuermer, of Dr. Martin Niepage, of the missionary Ernst Christoffel, and of General Liman von Sanders; the latter related how the Armenian populations of Smyrna and Adrianopolis were spared as a result of his resolute personal intervention.
- The reports of German diplomatic and consular personnel who were the eyewitnesses of the conditions of the dispersion of the Armenians at Erzerum, Aleppo, Samsun, etc.
- The American archives, which also contained very ample material in confirmation of the above (reports by missionaries, consuls, and charities) and 'Internal Affairs of Turkey, 1910–1919, Race Problems,' State Department, and the memoirs of the American Ambassador in Constantinople, Henry Morgenthau.
- The British authorities' Blue Book on these events, published in 1916 by Viscount Bryce.
- The minutes of the Trial of the Unionists (Ittihadists) on charges brought by the Turkish government following the defeat of the Ottoman Empire.

  At the time of this trial, which took place between April and July 1919, the Turkish government collected evidence of the deportation and massacres and tried those responsible—the majority in their absence—by a court martial. The court convicted most of the defendants, including Talaat, Enver, and Jemal, who were sentenced to death in absentia.
- The reports submitted to the Tribunal by four survivors of the massacres who lived through the events as children.

IV. The Turkish Arguments

The Tribunal has examined the Turkish arguments as set forth in the documents submitted to it.

The refusal of the Turkish government to recognize the genocide of the Armenians is based essentially on the following arguments: lower estimate of death toll; responsibility of Armenian revolutionaries; counter-accusations; denial of premeditation.

- The number of Armenians living in the Ottoman Empire in 1914 has been variously estimated at 2,100,000 by the Armenian Patriarchate; 1,800,000 by A. Toynbee; and about 1,300,000 by the Turks. In spite of different estimates of the number of victims, the Armenians and almost all the Western experts agree on the proportion; approximately two thirds of the population. The Turks claim that the consequences of the 'transfer' were on a much smaller scale, resulting in the disappearance of 20–25 percent of the population due to generally poor wartime conditions. The Turkish state also points out that losses were heavy on the Muslim side. This argument appears to overlook the fact that Armenians have almost entirely disappeared from Anatolia. The population of Turkey is currently about 45 million, of whom less than 100,000 are Armenians.
- In order to shift responsibility away from itself, the Turkish government alleges that Armenians committed acts of sedition and indeed of treason in time of war. However, the Tribunal has found that the only armed actions undertaken within the Ottoman Empire were the Sasun revolt and the resistance of Van in April 1915.
- A further argument advanced by the Turkish state is the accusation that it was the Armenians who supposedly committed genocide against the Turks. It is true that in 1917 (i.e. more than a year after the deportation and extermination of the Armenians was completed) a number of Turkish villages were annihilated by Armenian troops. The Tribunal considers that these acts, however blameworthy, cannot be considered as genocide. Furthermore, the Tribunal notes that these acts were committed some considerable time after the mass slaughter suffered by the Armenians.
- Lastly, the Turkish state rejects the charge of premeditation, impugning the authenticity of the five telegrams sent by the Minister of the Interior, Talaat, which were certified as authentic by experts appointed by the Court at the trial of Soghomon Tehlirian at Berlin-Charlottenburg in 1921. Tehlirian was acquitted of the murder of Talaat in view of the crimes against humanity perpetrated by the Young Turk government. The German Ambassador, Wangenheim, for his part, left no doubt, as early as July 7, 1915, as to the premeditation of the events: 'these circumstances and the manner in which the deportation is being carried out are demonstration of the fact that the government is indeed pursuing its goal of exterminating the Armenian race in the Ottoman Empire.' (Letter concerning the extension of the deportation measures to provinces not under threat of invasion by the enemy [No. 106 in the collection *Deutschland und Armenien*, 1914–1918] in the Wilhelmstrasse archives and published by the Rev. Lepsius.)

In 1971, the United Nations Commission on Human Rights asked its Sub-Committee on the fight against discriminatory measures and the protection of minorities, comprising independent experts, to undertake a 'study of the question of the prevention and punishment of the crime of genocide'.

In 1973 and 1975, the two interim reports which were submitted to the Sub-Committee by the special rapporteur contained a paragraph 30 which read as follows: 'In modern times, attention should be drawn to the existence of fairly abundant documentation relating to the massacre of the Armenians, considered as the first genocide of the twentieth century.'

In the final report submitted to the Commission in 1979, the aforementioned paragraph 30 was omitted.

The Commission's Chairman observed that the omission had given rise to such a wave of protest that its effects were assuming proportions which had possibly not been anticipated by the author. He therefore invited the rapporteur, when putting the finishing touches to his report, to bear in mind this reaction and statements made by Commission delegates following the omission.

The special rapporteur never reported back to complete his mission and the Sub-Committee, in pursuance of Economic and Social Council Resolution 1983/33, appointed another special rapporteur with instructions to fully revise and update the study on the question of the prevention and punishment of the crime of genocide.

The Tribunal has found that the Turkish delegation, in opposing the adoption of the above-mentioned paragraph 30, essentially advanced the following arguments:

- that the facts alleged were a distortion of historical truth.
- that the term genocide did not apply since the events concerned were not massacres but acts of war.
- and lastly, that harking back to events which took place as long ago as the beginning of the century would merely serve to stir up ill feeling.

On the first two points, concerning the facts and the law, the Tribunal has examined the arguments submitted in the case before it and trusts that in so doing it has contributed to meeting the wish of the Commission for Human Rights that efforts should be made to enable the Sub-Committee to complete its task taking into consideration all the material which has been submitted to it.

On the third point, the Tribunal can only observe that the refusal to adopt paragraph 30, quoted above, far from allaying concern, has given rise to passionate reaction.

IN LAW

I. On the Rights of the Armenian People

The Tribunal notes that the Armenian population groups which were the victims of the massacres and other atrocities which have been reported to it constitute a people within the meaning of the law of nations.

Today, this people has the right of self determination in accordance with Article 1,S2 of the United Nations Charter and the provisions of the Universal Declaration of the Rights of Peoples adopted in Algiers on July 4, 1976. It is incumbent upon the international community, and primarily, on the United Nations Organization, to take all necessary measures to ensure the observance of this fundamental right, including measures the prime object of which shall be to enable the effective exercise of that right.

The Tribunal wishes to stress the special obligations which are placed upon the Turkish state in this regard arising from the general rule of the law of nations as well as from individual treaties to which it has been party and which date back approximately one hundred years. In this connection, the Tribunal draws special attention to the fact that by virtue of Article 61 of the Treaty of Berlin, the aforementioned state entered into an obligation as early as 1878 to assign to the Armenian people within the Ottoman Empire a regime guaranteeing its right to flourish in a climate of security under the supervision of the international community. The Tribunal also notes that promises of self determination which were made to the Armenian people at the time of the First World War were not kept, since the international community unduly permitted the disappearance of an Armenian state which in principle had been clearly recognized both by the Allied and associated Powers and by Turkey itself in the Treaty of Batum.

The fact that the right of this state to peaceful existence within recognized borders as a member of the international community has not been observed, no more than was the right of the Armenian population to exist peacefully within the Ottoman Empire, cannot however be considered as effectively extinguishing the rights of the Armenian people, or of relieving the international community of its responsibility toward that people.

The Tribunal records that the fate of a people can never be considered as a purely internal affair, entirely subject to the whims, however well intentioned, of sovereign states. The fundamental rights of this people are of direct concern to the international community, which is entitled and duty bound to ensure that these rights are respected, particularly when they are openly denied by one of its member states.

In this particular case, this conclusion is still further corroborated by the fact that, even before the right of peoples to self determination was explicitly affirmed by the United Nations Charter, the rights of the Armenian people had already been recognized by the states concerned under the supervision of representatives of the international community.

II. On the Charge of Genocide

a) General Rules Applicable to Charges of Genocide. According to the Convention on the Prevention and Punishment of the Crime of Genocide, which was adopted by the United Nations General Assembly on December 9, 1948, genocide is 'a crime under international law', 'whether committed in time of peace or in time of war' (Article I).

Genocide means any of the following acts committed with intent to destroy, in whole or part, a national, ethical, racial or religious group, as such:

(a) Killing members of the group;
(b) Causing serious bodily or mental harm to members of the group;
(c) Deliberately inflicting on the group conditions of life calculated to bring about its physical destruction in whole or in part;
(d) Imposing measures intended to prevent births within the group;
(e) Forcibly transferring children of the group to another group. (Article II).

According to Article III:

The following acts shall be punishable:
(a) Genocide;
(b) Conspiracy to commit genocide;
(c) Direct and public incitement to commit genocide;
(d) Attempt to commit genocide;
(e) Complicity in genocide.

Lastly, Article IV stipulates that persons guilty of one of the aforementioned acts shall be punished: 'whether they are constitutionally responsible rulers, public officials or private individuals.'

The Tribunal considers that these provisions must be accepted as defining circumstances in which genocide is to be punished in accordance with the law of nations, in spite of the fact that certain broader definitions exist.

This convention formally came into force on January 12, 1951 and was ratified by Turkey on July 31, 1950. It should not be inferred from this, however, that acts of genocide cannot be the object of an indictment in law if such acts were committed either before the convention came into force or within the territory of a state which had not ratified the Convention. While it is true that the Convention places upon signatory states obligations to prevent or punish a crime which is not defined in any other instrument, it must nevertheless be judged to be declaratory of law inasmuch as it condemns genocide itself.

This declaratory force of the instrument arises from the wording of the Convention itself. In the preamble, the contracting parties 'recognize that throughout history, genocide has inflicted severe losses on humanity' and 'conform' in Article I that genocide constitutes a crime in the law of nations. This confirmation necessarily implies that this crime existed before December 9, 1948. It is, moreover, generally acknowledged by international legal doctrine, which reflects the undeniable reality of a collective conscience of states. It is of little consequence that the term 'genocide' itself was only recently coined. The only point of relevance is that the acts which it describes have long been condemned.

Once such declaratory force is accepted, the Tribunal is not required to determine the precise date of origin of the rule proscribing genocide codified by the Convention. It is sufficient for the purposes of the Tribunal to establish that this rule was indisputedly in force at the time when the massacres described to it were committed. Indeed, it emerges clearly from the deeds that have been done and the statements that have been made arising from the Armenian question, however justifiable these may or may not be or have been for various reasons, that the 'laws of humanity' condemned the policy of systematic extermination pursued by the Ottoman government. The Tribunal wishes to stress in this regard that such laws, however pressing the need for their formalization at the present time, do not merely reflect imperative moral or ethical rules; they also express positive legal obligations which cannot be ignored by states on the pretext that they have not been expressed formally in treaties, as is confirmed by the example of the Martens clause in the area of the law of warfare. Moreover, the condemnation of crimes committed during the First World War bears out the belief of states that such crimes could not be tolerated legally even though no written rules explicitly forbade them. The Tribunal recalls in this connection that such condemnation was pronounced on crimes against humanity as well as war crimes; it should furthermore be emphasized that Article 230 of the Treaty of Sèvres expressly invoked the responsibility of Turkey in massacres perpetuated on Turkish territory. Certainly this treaty has not been ratified, and the obligation of punishment which it stipulated has therefore never operated; however, this fact does not detract from the clear manifestation afforded to us today by the content of that treaty that the states of that time were indeed conscious of the illegality of the crime which we now call genocide.

For these reasons, the Tribunal considers that genocide was already prohibited in law from the time of the first massacres of the Armenian population, since the 1948 convention served only to give formal expression, and indeed in a qualified formulation, to a rule of law which is applicable to the facts which formed the basis of the charge brought before this tribunal.

b) The Charge of Genocide of the Armenian People. The following observations would seem to be necessary on examination of the evidence which has been submitted to the Tribunal, the substance of which is reported below.

There can be no doubt that the Armenians constitute a national group within the definition of the rule outlawing genocide. This conclusion is all the more evident since they constitute a people protected by the right to self determination which necessarily implies that they also constitute a group, the destruction of which is outlawed by virtue of the rule pertaining to genocide.

There is no doubt regarding the reality of the physical acts constituting the genocide. The fact of the murder of members of a group, of grave attacks on their physical or mental integrity, and of the subjection of this group to conditions leading necessarily to their deaths, are clearly proven by the full and unequivocal evidence submitted to the Tribunal. In its examination of the case the Tribunal has focussed primarily on the massacres perpetrated between 1915 and 1917, which were the most extreme example of a policy which was clearly heralded by the events of 1894–1896.

The specific intent to destroy the group as such, which is the special characteristic of the crime of genocide, is also established. The reports and documentary evidence supplied point clearly to a policy of methodical extermination of the Armenian people, revealing the specific intent referred to in Article II of the Convention of December 9, 1948.

The policy took effect in actions which were attributable beyond dispute to the Turkish or Ottoman authorities, particularly during the massacres of 1915–1917. The Tribunal notes on the one hand, however, that in addition to the atrocities committed by the official authorities, the latter also used malicious propaganda and other means to encourage civilian populations to commit acts of genocide against the Armenians. It is further observed that the authorities generally refrained from intervening to prevent the slaughter, although they had the power to do so, or from punishing the culprits, with the exception of the trial of the Unionists. This attitude amounts to incitement to crime and to criminal negligence, and must be judged as severely as the crimes actively committed and specifically covered by the law against genocide.

On the evidence submitted, the Tribunal considers that the various allegations (rebellion, treason, etc.) made by the Turkish government to justify the massacres are without foundation. It is stressed, in any event, that even were such allegations substantiated, they could in no way justify the massacres committed. Genocide is a crime which admits of no grounds for excuse or justification.

For these reasons, the Tribunal finds that the charge of genocide of the Armenian people brought against the Turkish authorities is established as to its foundation in fact.

c) The Consequences of the Genocide. The Tribunal recalls that, as is the case with all other crimes against humanity, genocide is by definition a crime to which no statute of limitations can apply by virtue of general international law, as confirmed by the Convention on the Non-Applicability of Statutes of Limitations to War Crimes and Crimes against Humanity, which was adopted by the United Nations General Assembly on November 26, 1968.

All those responsible for the massacres, whether 'they are constitutionally responsible rulers, public officials or private individuals' are thus subject to penalties, which states are under an obligation to apply in order to observe the guarantees attached to the exercise of the enforcement of justice.

Apart from the question of penalties, genocide is furthermore a violation of the law of nations for which the Turkish state must assume responsibility. Its first duty arising from this position lies in a basic obligation incumbent upon it to admit the facts without seeking to dissemble and to deplore the commission of this act. This in itself would constitute minimal redress for the incalculable moral injury suffered by the Armenian nation.

The Tribunal wishes to draw special attention to the fact that international practice as applied to the Turkish state since the time of these events affords sufficient legal basis to establish that the identity and continuity of this state have not been affected by the upheavals in the country's history since the dissolution of the Ottoman Empire. Neither its territorial losses nor the reorganization of its political system have been such as to detract from its continued identity as a subject of the law of nations. Consequently, it cannot be considered that successive Turkish governments since the constitution of a Kemalist republic are justified in refusing to assume a responsibility which remains with the state they represent in the international community.

The Tribunal further notes that nothing in the statements or conduct of the Armenian people or of the states sharing the responsibility of safeguarding its rights can be interpreted as implying their waiver of the blame attaching to those guilty of the genocide. Like its predecessors, the present Turkish government is therefore bound to assume this responsibility.

A crime of this nature violates obligations which are so essential to the international community that the authors of a recent draft Article on the responsibility of states have rightly described it as an 'international crime of state' within the meaning of the law on the responsibility of states, in other words, no longer within the purview of ordinary criminal law. As a result, and as is indeed confirmed by the special obligations of the international community toward the Armenian people, any member of this community has the right to call the Turkish state to account regarding its obligations, and in particular, to elicit official recognition of the genocide should this state persist in denying it, and is furthermore authorized to take any measure of aid and assistance on behalf of the Armenian people as provided by the law of nations and the Declaration of Algiers, without being accused in so doing of illicit interference in the affairs of another state.

Finally, it is incumbent upon the international community as a whole, and more especially through the United Nations Organization, to recognize the genocide and to assist the Armenian people to this end. Indeed, it cannot be considered entirely justified, neither in allowing a crime to be committed against one of its peoples which it is obligated to protect in the same way as any one of its states, nor in tolerating the wrongful denial of such a crime until today.

The Armenian genocide which took place during the First World War was the first act of its kind in a century during which genocide and the horror associated with it have, alas, become widespread.

The perpetration of such atrocities has not been confined to societies which certain people might describe as underdeveloped. On the contrary, in some cases they have been committed by nations generally considered to be the most developed and the most scientifically advanced. In fact, the most significant example in the whole of the twentieth century involved the application of advanced technology and sophisticated organization in the genocide of the European Jews by the Nazis, a genocide which caused human suffering to a degree barely conceivable and which ultimately led to the extermination of approximately six million people.

In previous sessions, the Tribunal had had occasion to condemn genocides committed against the people of El Salvador (decision of February 11, 1981), the Maubere people of Eastern Timor (decision of June 21, 1981), and the Indian people of Guatemala (decision of January 31, 1983).

The Tribunal notes that one of the most serious consequences and one of the most disturbing effects of genocide—above and beyond the irreparable wrongs inflicted upon its immediate victims—is the degradation and perversion of humanity as a whole.

FOR THESE REASONS

In answer to the questions which were put to it, the Tribunal hereby finds that:

- the Armenian population did and do constitute a people whose fundamental rights, both individual and collective, should have been and shall be respected in accordance with international law;
- the extermination of the Armenian population groups through deportation and massacre constitutes a crime of genocide not subject to statutory limitations within

the definition of the Convention on the Prevention and Punishment of the Crime of Genocide of December 9, 1948. With respect to the condemnation of this crime, the aforesaid Convention is declaratory of existing law in that it takes note of rules which were already in force at the time of the incriminated acts;

- the Young Turk government is guilty of this genocide, with regard to the acts perpetrated between 1915 and 1917;
- the Armenian genocide is also an 'international crime' for which the Turkish state must assume responsibility, without using the pretext of any discontinuity in the existence of the state to elude that responsibility;
- this responsibility implies first and foremost the obligation to recognize officially the reality of this genocide and the consequent damages suffered by the Armenian people;
- the United Nations Organization and each of its members have the right to demand this recognition and to assist the Armenian people to that end.

The United Nations
and Ecological Balance

INTRODUCTION

For centuries, an awareness of human dependence on nature has always been present, at times even dominant. Only "recently" in the long span of human evolution has a notion that man's perpetual progress is exempt from the laws of ecology emerged, fostering the illusion of independence—an exemptionalist mentality—in human development. Modern thinking, rooted in the ideas of Francis Bacon and Thomas Hobbes, holds the anti-ecological assumption that nature is God's bounty to be exploited for "the relief of the inconveniences of man's estate." Progress has come to mean nothing less than the capacity to conquer nature in the service of corporate and national material wealth, power, and expansion. Of course, some preindustrial societies floundered or disappeared through the decay and destruction of their habitat brought about by ecological carelessness or ignorance, involving soil exhaustion, deforestation, overgrazing, and overhunting.

What is new about the contemporary ecological crisis are its planetary scale, magnitude, intensity, and complexity. Earlier environmental concerns had been perceived as mainly local, transnational (as with contamination on one side of the border being carried by air or water to the other side), and occasionally multinational (as when sewage is put into an international river or lake or when a fishing ground or species is being overexploited). Now there is a growing realization that many environmental issues affect the well-being not only of a nation or two but of the global community as a whole. The planet's life-support ecosystems, which also support the world economy, are deteriorating at an alarming pace—the world's forests are shrinking, its deserts expanding, its soils eroding, its plant and animal species dwindling, its ozone layer thinning, and its temperature rising, all of which pose clear and continuing dangers of unprecedented but still unknown magnitude to virtually all of the planet's ecosystems. The annual budget required to reverse the world's most pressing environmental crises and place the developed and developing nations on the path to sustainable development was given as $150 billion in 1988.

"Ecological balance" refers to the proper ordering of the relationship between human society and the environment. This value is composed of two distinct but closely intertwined categories of issues: issues relating to the quality of life and issues concerning the use of global resources. The quality of life issues include both the deterioration of the environment resulting from industrialization and the deprivation of individuals caused by limited development. In the developed countries, the vulnerability of the human habitat is illustrated by such problems as air pollution; dumping in lakes, rivers, and oceans; the breakup of oil tankers; and contamination by hazardous materials such as nuclear and chemical wastes. Throughout much of the developing world, people suffer from underdevelopment that subjects them to famine, disease, deforestation, and desertification. These concerns are closely connected with the other values of economic well-being and social justice. By considering the human relationship to the environment in terms of the quality of life, the world order value of ecological balance forces examination of both the *natural* environment and the *social* environment.

The second set of problems relating to ecological balance concerns the use of resources. While the debate of the 1970s over growth versus the limits to growth has generated heated discussion about the capacity of the market system to prevent total depletion and the capability of science and technology to rescue humankind from scarcity, the fact remains that in recent years, most people, governments, and international organizations have come to appreciate the importance of conserving scarce resource stocks for a sustainable ecodevelopment as well as for the benefit of future generations.

Directly linked with the issue of resource depletion is the question of the equitable sharing of existing resources. However, redistribution as an important part of the value of economic well-being and improved living standards may be easier to accomplish in the context of a constantly expanding resource base and world economic growth. Once some concept of potential limits to these resources is introduced, difficult questions arise as to the proper allocation and use of existing resources. Should scarce resources be husbanded for the future generations of developed societies, or should they be shared today to lift the living standards of those struggling in poverty and disease? A greater sharing of resources among peoples is necessary to raise present living standards to an acceptable minimum while continuing to bear in mind the approaching limits and the impact of resources use on future generations. The beneficial use of resources is an important element of the value of ecological balance, relating both to the efforts to protect reasonably priced supplies from approaching limits and to a more equitable sharing of resources among the peoples of the world.

In relation to either facts or policy, it is important to achieve a common understanding, reflective of both world public opinion and governmental outlook, that can underpin global policy. It is obvious that the United Nations is the natural forum through which such a global understanding can and should emerge. It is also revealing that the Charter, despite its generality, never anticipated an ecological role for the organization. Indeed, the environmental issue area discloses a UN potential for responding to unanticipated global problems (and opportunities) to enhance the quality of world order. Whether or to what extent the UN's potential in this issue area is realized is a matter of interpretation. National governments do not fully agree on the character and hierarchy of environmental threats and what to do about them. Controversy persists about who is mainly responsible and who should bear the major financial burden for action to overcome these threats, and about the extent to which a commitment to environmental quality should burden the everyday struggle in the Third World to promote economic expansion and to alleviate mass poverty. As noted in Section 6, the Third World debt crisis has already begun to exact a heavy environmental toll.

We need new methods of social accounting to assess the environmental and social impacts and costs of various human activities. The cost of a factory or a housing project needs to include some calculation of the environmental costs to the community as a whole. Conventional economics does not count the environmental and social costs of development, let alone assign them to the polluting individual manufacturers. A new accounting system is now in order. Can we still say, after the Three Mile Island and Chernobyl ecodisasters, that nuclear power is more cost-effective than other forms of commercial energy? How are we to assign costs for the anxiety and psychological suffering of those potentially exposed to harmful doses of radioactivity? After nearly thirty-eight years of secrecy and cover-up, the U.S. public finally discovered in 1988 that its nuclear weapons production facilities were being operated unsafely and the evidence of danger suppressed. These facilities had become ticking environmental time bombs. Can we still calculate national defense expenditures without factoring in the ecological and public health costs? Even the gross national product is an inappropriate measure of our output because it does not include the ecological perspective essential to our spaceship earth. Shifts in perception of what constitutes useful indicators are essential to evaluating social activities in the ecological context. Likewise, some choices must also be made about the impact of allocating further resources to already developed nations, as against using these resources to raise the poverty floor in developing countries. New methods of evaluation are needed to consider the environmental impact and alternative sharing of resources.

Concern over the ecological balance value leads individuals and national governments to take a global and futurist approach. The need to maintain the unity of the biosphere requires solutions on a global basis, and the time span must be lengthened to include future generations rather than simply the next year or even the next five years. Ecological balance can be attained only if planning perspectives are expanded from the state to the globe and from the immediate future to the long run.

This is not to minimize the important contributions that individual and local groups can make today to enhance ecological balance. Indeed, considerably opportunity exists to contribute to this particular world order value through a wide variety of personal and social choices: political involvement, social movement, personal investment strategy, life-style changes, and family planning. Through ethical investing we can individually and as a group use our money to support our values, setting in motion a "virtuous circle" and shifting the flow of local and national economies toward a new economic order. Consumer groups and NGOs have in many instances taken the lead in insisting on higher-quality environments and protection from environmental dangers.

In the 1980s, the environmental movement finally came to regard the war system as the greatest environmental predator and polluter of the earth. In 1981, environmental groups constituted one of the core groups in the antinuclear movement that swept through Western Europe. In the United States, 6,000 local groups are concerned with the interrelated issues of peace, the environment, and social justice, all thinking globally but mainly acting locally. Concrete and empowering manifestations of the linkage politics employed by these local groups are efforts to have their communities or regions declared peace zones or nuclear-free zones, which involves a symbolic commitment to a different set of priorities. According to a recent estimate, there are 2,840 nuclear-free cities, counties, and towns in seventeen countries, with many Third World countries involved in getting their regions declared nuclear-free. The concept of a nuclear-free zone, embodied in a series of multilateral arms control treaties, was inspired by, developed, and lobbied through the global networks of international nongovernmental organizations (INGOs). Elise Boulding reminds us that such "nonmilitary innovations in the world security arena are INGO innovations. They do not come from national governments." In mid-1982, Friends of the Earth, a U.S.-based conservation group, issued a public manifesto, linking ecological balance and antinuclearism: "Until recently we were content to work for our usual constituency: life in its miraculous diversity of forms. We have spoken for the trees and plants, the animals, the air and water, and for the land itself. . . . But the nuclear war contemplated by the U.S. and Russia would kill life of *all* kinds, indiscriminately, on a scale and for a length of time into the future that is so great that it qualifies as the major ecological issue of our time" (emphasis in original).

What are the implications of the ecological crisis for the governing arrangements of international life, especially the degree to which ecological prudence could be reconciled with the type and extent of laissez-faire associated with the present state system? The United Nations Conference on the Human Environment at Stockholm in June 1972 marked the emergence of ecological issues as topics for worldwide concern and signaled the beginning of a major effort within the UN system to enhance environmental quality. Given the constraints of the international system, Stockholm can be viewed as a remarkable accomplishment. Some 1,200 governmental delegates from 113 countries, surrounded by 27,000 planetary citizens from all over the world, assembled to inaugurate global ecopolitics. In the first UN-sponsored global conference of its kind, the world organization took the initiative in formulating general principles and a 109-point action plan. In January 1973, the General Assembly, implementing recommendations of the Stockholm Conference, established a new global regime of coordination on environmental affairs, the United Nations Environmental Programme (UNEP), in Nairobi, Kenya.

Since 1973, UNEP has served as the global environmental conscience, catalyst, and coordinator of the UN system in shaping and sharing this fourth world order value. Its multiple activities and roles also mirror the outer limits and possibilities of UN performance in this issue area. With a small professional staff of 180 personnel and a modest annual budget of about $45 million, UNEP's main mission is to provide and prod others (national governments and specialized agencies) into thinking and doing. As a catalyst, UNEP has been effective in influencing such specialized agencies of the UN system as the World Health Organization (WHO), the World Meteorological Organization (WMO), the United Nations Educational,

Scientific, and Cultural Organization (UNESCO), the Food and Agricultural Organizations of the United Nations (FAO), the International Maritime Organization (IMO), the International Fund for Agricultural Development (IFAD), and the International Labour Organization (ILO) to incorporate environmental concern into their respective sectoral programs and activities. Even the World Bank, particularly its president Barber Conable, has recognized the failure of ecologically irresponsible development strategies. "We must reshape not just the Bank's outlook and activities," Conable said in May 1987, "but also the customs and ingrained attitudes of hundreds of millions of individuals and of their leaders." In 1987, the World Bank took some preliminary steps, including the establishment of an Environment Department to undertake an urgent assessment of environmental threats to the thirty most vulnerable developing nations and a continent-wide initiative against desertification and destruction of forests in Africa. Whether such attitudinal, conceptual, and organizational changes can be fully translated into an ecologically sound and sustainable development strategy for the bank's lending program is far from assured. UNEP has also helped twenty-two Third World countries in setting up and enforcing environmental legislation.

UNEP also works as the chief monitor of the state of the world environment through its Earth Watch, keeping its eyes and ears open to all corners of the planet day and night. UNEP's Earth Watch does its monitoring and assessing by pulling together into a single global system—the Global Environment Monitoring System (GEMS)—the monitoring systems of as many as 142 nations, employing some 30,000 scientists and technicians. UNEP's monitoring activities fall into five closely linked programs, each containing various monitoring networks with built-in provisions for training, technical assistance, and evaluation and review: (1) resource monitoring, (2) climate-related monitoring, (3) ocean monitoring, (4) health-related monitoring, and (5) long-range transport of pollutants monitoring. UNEP's monitoring and assessing process is an integral part of its knowledge-expanding process. UNEP issues an annual state of the world environment report.

Finally, but no less important, UNEP has acted as a crucial political broker in the international environmental treaty-making process. The Montreal Protocol on Substances that Deplete the Ozone Layer—endorsed by forty-five nations in late 1987 and entered into force on December 16, 1988—is the most recent and widely noted accomplishment, the outcome of ten years of sustained scientific and diplomatic effort by UNEP. Yet, the treaty dramatizes the widening lag time between UN performance and world environmental deterioration. Less than six months after the treaty was signed, celebration gave way to bad news—ozone depletion was found to be three times greater than assumed by the treaty. This finding is particularly troubling in light of the longevity of ozone-damaging chlorofluorocarbons (CFCs). UNEP prepared a diplomatic lawmaking conference in Switzerland in 1989 for the purpose of adopting a Global Convention on the Control of Transboundary Movements of Hazardous Wastes.

The Stockholm Declaration of the UN Conference on the Human Environment, the first selection in this section, seems a logical point of departure for assessing post-Stockholm developments. The compromise necessary to produce this twenty-six principle Declaration was achieved by reasserting the acceptance of statism and by separating global pollution, poverty, population, and politics from their underlying social, political, economic, and cultural causes. The Declaration has never achieved the status and authority of the Universal Declaration of Human Rights, but it remains of historical interest and some policy significance. In May 1982, the second UN conference on the global environment—officially called the Session of a Special Character of the Governing Council of the United Nations Environment Programme—was held in Nairobi, Kenya, to commemorate the tenth anniversary of the Stockholm Conference and to assess the measures taken to implement the Declaration and action plan adopted at Stockholm. The Nairobi Declaration reaffirmed *pro forma* the principles of the Stockholm Declaration as providing "a basic code of environmental conduct for the years to come." In fact, however, the Stockholm Declaration was more or less relegated to the UN bureaucratic back burner in the 1980s. Instead, the "Environmental Perspective to the Year 2000 and Beyond"—the result of the four years' work of a special Intergovernmental Intersessional Preparatory Committee of the UNEP, drawing concepts, ideas, and recommendations from the report of the World (Brundtland) Commission on Environment and Development, "Our Common Future"—has been adopted by the General Assembly as a broad framework and blueprint for action on the local, regional, and international levels aimed at achieving environmentally sound and sustainable development.

In our second selection in the section, F. H. Knelman presents a trenchant critique of what went wrong at Stockholm. Knelman is an independent Canadian academic observer who was a delegate to the Dai Dong Independent Conference, an INGO counterconference held on June 1–6, 1972, at the Graninge Stifsgard, a small retreat center situated on the beautiful but polluted Baltic a dozen miles from Stockholm, which ended with the adoption of the Dai Dong Declaration: Independent Declaration on the Environment. He forcefully argues that the style of ecopolitics within individual states is also evident in efforts by states at the international level: "Tokenism, co-option, jurisdictional juggling, expiation by legislation, and the trade-off of unmentionables were all quite common." The Dai Dong Declaration calls for basic changes in our political, economic, and social structures but also insists upon the need for changes in our individual life-styles to ensure human survival in a way that facilitates human fulfillment. In contrast, the Stockholm Declaration avoided mentioning such behavioral adjustments. Despite a critical stance, Knelman concedes that Stockholm was "a small but clear step toward the great global revolutionary change that is beginning."

In the section's third selection, John G. Ruggie gives a working definition of the concept of the "global problematique" as a complex interplay of ecological, technological, social, economic, and political factors within the world system that is generated by the increasing scale of human activity in the context of planetary life-support ecosystems. He then applies the concept by examining the pattern of activities of international organizations in the environmental issue area in response to the global problematique. International organizations play significant roles, Ruggie argues, in developing holistic perspectives of the global problematique, institutionalizing new areas of global concern and new constituencies, defining the issues to be placed on the global policy agenda, and expanding the collective knowledge base to facilitate appropriate governmental decisions. Yet, the existing structure of the global system conditions the involvement of international organizations in such a way as to make it impossible to bring about system transformation. International organizations can merely provide access, Ruggie contends, to counterhegemonic ideas and groups to develop and seek to operationalize an alternative world order.

Our next selection in the section is the World Charter for Nature adopted by the General Assembly on October 28, 1982, by a recorded vote of 111:1 with the United States casting the sole dissenting vote. In response to a suggestion made by President Mobutu Sese Seko of Zaire, in 1975 a multinational task force began to draft the World Charter for Nature, which was finally sponsored and submitted by thirty-four Third World countries as an annex to a draft resolution at the 37th Session of the General Assembly. Despite the peremptory language, the charter was intended to exert political and moral, not legal, pressure on member states. Still, it is a notable expression of a Third World normative initiative in global ecopolitics. Conceptually, the charter is a testimonial that the Third World as a whole has come of age on this issue. Many developing countries have learned bitter ecological lessons the hard way. The charter also marks a conceptual shift from a concentration on wildlife preservation toward a concern for the wider pressures affecting the natural environment and a growing recognition that the integration of both conservation and development is the only way to a sustainable society.

The section's final selection gives highlights of the World (Brundtland) Commission report. The report presents massive evidence that "sustainable development"—growth that respects environmental limits and constraints—is the only answer to the development problematique. The report shuns technocratic functionalism by advocating that environmental concerns must be integrated into political and economic decisionmaking. In the real world, evironmental and political issues are linked, as are environmental stresses (i.e., deforestation causes soil erosion, air pollution kills forests, etc.). The report goes beyond general recommendations for change by making three specific proposals for: (1) the establishment of an independent body, made up mostly of NGOs, scientific organs, and industry groups, to assess global environmental dangers; (2) the adoption of a universal declaration on environmental protection and sustainable development, followed by a convention under UN auspices; and (3) a call to the General Assembly to transform the report into a UN Programme on Sustainable Development.

As noted earlier, the third proposal has been partially adopted. The "Environmental Perspective" was prepared by the UN in tandem with the Brundtland Commission report as part of a dual process to bring into play both governmental and nongovernmental ideas. It is encouraging that the Brundtland Commission report served as a major input in the final formulation and adoption of the "Environmental Perspective" by the General Assembly in December 1987 (nine months after the release of *Our Common Future*). This experience contrasts with the governmental assault on the nongovernmental Cocoyac Declaration a dozen years earlier. This dynamic of a ground-breaking governmental document *following* a ground-breaking nongovernmental report is itself indicative of a new kind of transnational populism. In the end, both documents converged on the concept of sustainable development.

The year 1988 may be said to have been the worst of ecological times—and the best of ecological times. Multiple symptoms of advanced ecological pathology became more and more evident for more and more people—the bad news about ozone depletion; global warming and the greenhouse effect; Brazil's burning of the Amazon rain forests and the cold-blooded murder of Chico Mendez, a trade unionist who dared to challenge slash-and-burn developers; acid rain identified for the first time as a major peril to marine life in Atlantic coastal waters; Japan's dispatching its whaling fleet to the Antarctic for a hunting trip in defiance of an international ban; an exposé of the U.S. cover-up of ecological hazards in its aging nuclear weapons plants; a new kind of international traffic in toxic wastes (now called "underworld pollution"); chilling news from Beijing that some 20 million Chinese may starve and another 80 million will endure severe food shortages brought on by "man-made" floods and droughts (the consequences of indiscriminate deforestation over the years to obtain firewood, timber, and agricultural clearance); and the appearance of "environmentsl refugees" on the social landscape of the world.

Thanks to the advanced ecological pathology that cuts across North-South and East-West divides—and to global warming—1988 also witnessed the first signs of a greening of superpower politics. At last, environmental security shifted from low to high politics, from the bureaucratic backwaters to the center stage of a new kind of geopolitics. Chernobyl, perestroika, glasnost, and Gorbachev were all part of the birth process of a new ecological thinking in the Soviet Union. At the 1988 annual session of the General Assembly, the Soviet Union called for the creation of "an international regime of environmental security." In his celebrated UN speech of December 7, 1988, Mikhail Gorbachev announced his plans for partial unilateral disarmament but also mentioned the environment more than twenty times. Environmental security is an integral part of Gorbachev's comprehensive global security system.

Less dramatically but no less surprisingly, George Bush projected himself as an environmentalist during his electoral campaign, promising *inter alia* a convocation of a world environmental conference that would involve the Soviet Union and China. In December 1988, the week after Gorbachev's UN speech, the science academies of the United States and the Soviet Union formed a joint committee on global environmental issues. The appointment of William K. Reilly, a conservationist with excellent credentials in global environmental issues, as head of the U.S. Environmental Protection Agency and a more positive approach to the acid rain problem are early signs of a Bush breakaway from the anti-environmentalism of the Reagan era. Of course, as we write, the jury is still out as to the success and sufficiency of the Bush-Gorbachev approach to global environmental politics, but there is basis for hope.

30. The Stockholm Declaration

The United Nations Conference on the Human Environment,
Having met at Stockholm from 5 to 16 June 1972,
Having considered the need for a common outlook and for common principles
to inspire and guide the peoples of the world in the preservation and enhancement
of the human environment,

I

Proclaims that:
1. Man is both creature and moulder of his environment, which gives him
physical sustenance and affords him the opportunity for intellectual, moral, social
and spiritual growth. In the long and tortuous evolution of the human race on this
planet a stage has been reached when, through the rapid acceleration of science
and technology, man has acquired the power to transform his environment in
countless ways and on an unprecedented scale. Both aspects of man's environment,
the natural and the man-made, are essential to his well-being and to the enjoyment
of basic human rights—even the right to life itself.
2. The protection and improvement of the human environment is a major issue
which affects the well-being of peoples and economic development throughout the
world; it is the urgent desire of the peoples of the whole world and the duty of all
Governments.
3. Man has constantly to sum up experience and go on discovering, inventing,
creating and advancing. In our time, man's capability to transform his surroundings,
if used wisely, can bring to all peoples the benefits of development and the
opportunity to enhance the quality of life. Wrongly or heedlessly applied, the same
power can do incalculable harm to human beings and the human environment.
We see around us growing evidence of man-made harm in many regions of the
earth: dangerous levels of pollution in water, air, earth and living beings; major and
undesirable disturbances to the ecological balance of the biosphere; destruction and
depletion of irreplaceable resources; and gross deficiences, harmful to the physical,
mental and social health of man, in the man-made environment, particularly in
the living and working environment.
4. In the developing countries most of the environmental problems are caused
by under-development. Millions continue to live far below the minimum levels
required for a decent human existence, deprived of adequate food and clothing,
shelter and education, health and sanitation. Therefore, the developing countries
must direct their efforts to development, bearing in mind their priorities and the
need to safeguard and improve the environment. For the same purpose, the
industrialized countries should make efforts to reduce the gap themselves and the
developing countries. In the industrialized countries, environmental problems are
generally related to industrialization and technological development.

5. The natural growth of population continuously presents problems for the preservation of the environment, and adequate policies and measures should be adopted, as appropriate, to face these problems. Of all things in the world, people are the most precious. It is the people that propel social progress, create social wealth, develop science and technology and, through their hard work, continuously transform the human environment. Along with social progress and the advance of production, science and technology, the capability of man to improve the environment increases with each passing day.

6. A point has been reached in history when we must shape our actions throughout the world with a more prudent care for their environmental consequences. Through ignorance or indifference we can do massive and irreversible harm to the earthly environment on which our life and well-being depend. Conversely, through fuller knowledge and wiser action, we can achieve for ourselves and our posterity a better life in an environment more in keeping with human needs and hopes. There are broad vistas for the enhancement of environmental quality and the creation of a good life. What is needed is an enthusiastic but calm state of mind and intense but orderly work. For the purpose of attaining freedom in the world of nature, man must use knowledge to build, in collaboration with nature, a better environment. To defend and improve the human environment for present and future generations has become an imperative goal for mankind—a goal to be pursued together with, and in harmony with, the established and fundamental goals of peace and of world-wide economic and social development.

7. To achieve this environmental goal will demand the acceptance of responsibility by citizens and communities and by enterprises and institutions at every level, all sharing equitably in common efforts. Individuals in all walks of life as well as organizations in many fields, by their values and the sum of their actions, will shape the world environment of the future. Local and national governments will bear the greatest burden for large-scale environmental policy and action within their jurisdictions. International co-operation is also needed in order to raise resources to support the developing countries in carrying out their responsibilities in this field. A growing class of environmental problems, because they are regional or global in extent or because they affect the common international realm, will require extensive co-operation among nations and action by international organizations in the common interest. The Conference calls upon Governments and peoples to exert common efforts for the preservation and improvement of the human environment, for the benefit of all the people and for their posterity.

II

Principles

States the common conviction that:

Principle 1

Man has the fundamental right to freedom, equality and adequate conditions of life, in an environment of a quality that permits a life of dignity and well-being, and he bears a solemn responsibility to protect and improve the environment for present and future generations. In this respect, policies promoting or perpetuating *apartheid*, racial segregation, discrimination, colonial and other forms of oppression and foreign domination stand condemned and must be eliminated.

Principle 2

The natural resources of the earth, including the air, water, land, flora and fauna and especially representative samples of natural ecosystems, must be safeguarded for the benefit of present and future generations through careful planning or management, as appropriate.

Principle 3

The capacity of the earth to produce vital renewable resources must be maintained and, wherever practicable, restored or improved.

Principle 4

Man has a special responsibility to safeguard and wisely manage the heritage of wildlife and its habitat, which are now gravely imperilled by a combination of adverse factors. Nature conservation, including wildlife, must therefore receive importance in planning for economic development.

Principle 5

The non-renewable resources of the earth must be employed in such a way as to guard against the danger of their future exhaustion and to ensure that benefits from such employment are shared by all mankind.

Principle 6

The discharge of toxic substances or of other substances and the release of heat, in such quantities or concentrations as to exceed the capacity of the environment to render them harmless, must be halted in order to ensure that serious or irreversible damage is not inflicted upon ecosystems. The just struggle of the peoples of all countries against pollution should be supported.

Principle 7

States shall take all possible steps to prevent pollution of the seas by substances that are liable to create hazards to human health, to harm living resources and marine life, to damage amenities or to interfere with other legitimate uses of the sea.

Principle 8

Economic and social development is essential for ensuring a favourable living and working environment for man and for creating conditions on earth that are necessary for the improvement of the quality of life.

Principle 9

Environmental deficiencies generated by the conditions of under-development and natural disasters pose grave problems and can best be remedied by accelerated development through the transfer of substantial quantities of financial and technological assistance as a supplement to the domestic effort of the developing countries and such timely assistance as may be required.

Principle 10

For the developing countries, stability of prices and adequate earnings for primary commodities and raw materials are essential to environmental management since economic factors as well as ecological processes must be taken into account.

Principle 11

The environmental policies of all States should enhance and not adversely affect the present or future development potential of developing countries, nor should they hamper the attainment of better living conditions for all, and appropriate steps should be taken by States and international organizations with a view to reaching agreement on meeting the possible national and international economic consequences resulting from the application of environmental measures.

Principle 12

Resources should be made available to preserve and improve the environment, taking into account the circumstances and particular requirements of developing countries and any costs which may emanate from their incorporating environmental safeguards into their development planning and the need for making available to them, upon their request, additional international technical and financial assistance for this purpose.

Principle 13

In order to achieve a more rational management of resources and thus to improve the environment, States should adopt an integrated and co-ordinated approach to their development planning so as to ensure that development is compatible with the need to protect and improve environment for the benefit of their population.

Principle 14

Rational planning constitutes an essential tool for reconciling any conflict between the needs of development and the need to protect and improve the environment.

Principle 15

Planning must be applied to human settlements and urbanization with a view to avoiding adverse effects on the environment and obtaining maximum social, economic and environmental benefits for all. In this respect, projects which are designed for colonialist and racist domination must be abandoned.

Principle 16

Demographic policies which are without prejudice to basic human rights and which are deemed appropriate by Governments concerned should be applied in those regions where the rate of population growth or excessive population concentrations are likely to have adverse effects on the environment of the human environment and impede development.

Principle 17

Appropriate national institutions must be entrusted with the task of planning, managing or controlling the environmental resources of States with a view to enhancing environmental quality.

Principle 18

Science and technology, as part of their contribution to economic and social development, must be applied to the identification, avoidance and control of environmental risks and the solution of environmental problems and for the common good of mankind.

Principle 19

Education in environmental matters, for the younger generation as well as adults, giving due consideration to the underprivileged, is essential in order to broaden the basis for an enlightened opinion and responsible conduct by individuals, enterprises and communities in protecting and improving the environment in its full human dimension. It is also essential that mass media of communications avoid contributing to the deterioration of the environment, but, on the contrary, disseminate information of an educational nature on the need to protect and improve the environment in order to enable man to develop in every respect.

Principle 20

Scientific research and development in the context of environmental problems, both national and multi-national, must be promoted in all countries, especially the developing countries. In this connexion, the free flow of up-to-date scientific information and transfer of experience must be supported and assisted, to facilitate the solution of environmental problems; environmental technologies should be made available to developing countries on terms which would encourage their wide dissemination without constituting an economic burden on the developing countries.

Principle 21

States have, in accordance with the Charter of the United Nations and the principles of international law, the sovereign right to exploit their own resources pursuant to their own environmental policies, and the responsibility to ensure that activities within their jurisdiction or control do not cause damage to the environment of other States or of areas beyond the limits of national jurisdiction.

Principle 22

States shall co-operate to develop further the international law regarding liability and compensation for the victims of pollution and other environmental damage caused by activities within the jurisdiction or control of such States to areas beyond their jurisdiction.

Principle 23

Without prejudice to such criteria as may be agreed upon by the international community, or to standards which will have to be determined nationally, it will be essential in all cases to consider the systems of values prevailing in each country, and the extent of the applicability of standards which are valid for the most advanced countries but which may be inappropriate and of unwarranted social cost for the developing countries.

Principle 24

International matters concerning the protection and improvement of the environment should be handled in a co-operative spirit by all countries, big and small, on an equal footing. Co-operation through multilateral or bilateral arrangements or other appropriate means is essential to effectively control, prevent, reduce and eliminate adverse environmental effects resulting from activities conducted in all spheres, in such a way that due account is taken of the sovereignty and interests of all States.

Principle 25

States shall ensure that international organizations play a co-ordinated, efficient and dynamic role for the protection and improvement of the environment.

Principle 26

Man and his environment must be spared the effects of nuclear weapons and all other means of mass destruction. States must strive to reach prompt agreement, in the relevant international organs, on the elimination and complete destruction of such weapons.

21st plenary meeting
16 June 1972

31. What Happened at Stockholm

F. H. Knelman

June 1972 may well turn out to be a prophetic period in the history of humankind. Between 1 June and 17 June, three separate conferences on the human environment took place in Stockholm, Sweden. From 1 to 6 June the Dai Dong Independent Conference met; and from 5 to 17 June the official United Nations Conference on the Human Environment (1200 delegates from 113 countries) and its unofficial parallel meeting, the Environment Forum, organized by various citizen groups, both took place. Nothing profound, in the sense of substantive developments, occurred at any of these events. The official conference was largely an exercise in futility, the Dai Dong conference had its own frustrations, and the Environment Forum was a kind of ecological circus. The historical significance of these activities arises more from a sense that they represent a turning point, the beginning of a great and profound change, global in extent and impact, than from any of their specific achievements, which were less than modest.

We may be experiencing the end of the Scientific Revolution—the greatest intellectual and social upheaval the world has witnessed. Unfortunately science was born with a tragic flaw and quickly became adapted to the imperatives of power of nation-states. Its dual traditions, the Faustian and the Baconian, still contend today. At the same time we may be witnessing the beginning of a new intellectual and social revolution dedicated to human survival and fulfilment. This will not mean the renunciation of science and technology but their control and direction for human fulfilment. The signs are present and profound. The British Blueprint for Survival, the Menton Message circulated by the International Fellowship of Reconciliation, and the growth around the world of concerned scientist and citizen groups were all indications of a growing identification of the global problem and a convergence of those seeking its solution. And, finally, there came the official United Nations Conference on the Human Environment.

Some years ago, before the environment issue had become fashionable, I proposed the development of world environmental control systems as a functional approach to peace. Functionalism as a method of achieving higher levels of international organization has such an obvious application to the world environmental crisis that I had considered it as a basis for re-examining the theory linking authority to a specific international activity and thus decreasing the historically intimate relationship between authority and territory. The Security Council of the United Nations was to have been entrusted with this specific function of becoming the common government of world law and order. So far it has failed as a supra-sovereign agency, largely because of the constant lag in its function of keeping nations peacefully apart. The task of bringing nations peacefully together has been accomplished, in part, through some of the United Nations agencies, particularly UNESCO, but their powers are too limited for successful functioning.

History and technology have had different effects on national sovereignty. The historical process has accentuated and perpetuated the autonomy of sovereign states. When a state surrenders its sovereignty, through conquest or revolution, it is really only a transfer. Modern technology, however, has rendered national sovereignty obsolete. In particular the revolutions in communications and in power have created a world in which the sharing of sovereignty is essential for the survival of the human species. As long as the level of operational integration remains less than the area encompassing the problem, we cannot find ultimate solutions. We may be able to defer crises but we can never avoid them. The problem involves the planet as a system.

Each day the evidence accumulates that pollution knows no boundaries, national or regional, and this principle of indivisibility, central to ecology, creates the need for national interdependencies. David Mitrany has written prophetically that 'sovereignty cannot in fact be transferred effectively through a formula, only through a function.' I believe that new functions exist which transcend all possible reasons for resisting the transfer of sovereignty. The most important of these is the need for world control of pollution to avert a breakdown of the environment and the ensuing catastrophic effects. The nature of the global threat transcends ideological and political boundaries. Its analysis and control therefore require international cooperation. Functionalism has had mixed success in the past, but the novel situation prevailing in the second half of the twentieth century offers a new basis for using this approach.

The road to Stockholm may be viewed as 300 years old or 2 years old. Both time spans have a certain historical significance. Some 300 years ago the Scientific Revolution flowered, setting nation-states on a course of material development that has led to the modern urban and industrial nation. Two years ago Sweden recommended that the United Nations call a conference on the human environment. It was no accident that Sweden initiated this call. More consciously than any other nation, the Swedish people had become aware of the profound contradiction between the ecological imperative and the economic imperative, between the preservation of the quality of life and a dedication to an exponential increase in the quantity of life. Sweden witnessed the growth of *dis*benefits and *dis*economies from environmental degradation which began to rival in scope the great benefits and economies of the technological society. Recognizing this contradiction between economic growth and the preservation of a quality environment, between the demands of the present and a concern for the future, Sweden stood at the crossroads of a prophetic decision: Gross National Product or Grand National Purpose?

Nineteen-seventy was also the twenty-fifth anniversary of the United Nations. Early that summer, Secretary-General U Thant called together some twenty-five wise persons to assess the effectiveness of the United Nations during its first quarter-century and to recommend a course for the future. The conclusions of this unofficial conference were not happy ones. The record of the United Nations was one of failure and frustration. Its effectiveness in maintaining international law and order had been largely negative: the Middle East, the Congo, Korea, Nigeria, Pakistan— a long history of failures, with Indochina the crowning futility. The consensus of this meeting was that only one issue in the world held the promise of transcending political and geographical boundaries and discovering unity in a consensus of concern. This issue was environmental degradation and U Thant was advised to steer the United Nations in the direction of uniting and directing this concern. War and poverty had not succeeded in providing the basis for mutual aid, benefit and security. Maxim Litvinov, the Soviet representative in the League of Nations, had long before stated a profound ecological principle: 'Peace is indivisible.' Now, perhaps having witnessed the global impact of pollution, the time was ripe for the world to resurrect its faith in the capacity for human co-operation—in the interests of human survival. The result was to call the Conference on the Human Environment for June 1972 in Stockholm. A Canadian, Maurice Strong, was named secretary-general of the conference. Chosen to organize the conference more for his zeal, energy, and administrative ability than his knowledge of environmental matters, he was given the power, prestige, and rank to organize this great undertaking.

I had been encouraged to believe in the relative integrity of Sweden's motives and had written and spoken often in this vein. There were positive social indicators to support this. Yet when I expressed this view at conferences, the loudest laughs usually came from Swedish delegates, who then assured me that while they were flattered, I was somewhat misinformed. Confidential discussions with relatively senior members of the Swedish economic ministry have tended to support this view and to disabuse me to some degree of my idealism. The government of Sweden apparently was motivated more by the need to stabilize the status quo of the hierarchy of international economic power than by a pure moral concern for environmental quality. Sweden had learned the bitter lesson that the costs of domestic anti-pollution measures lowers profits and decreases one's competitive position in world trade. Uniform global environmental standards might freeze the status quo and with it Sweden's GNP per capita, the second highest in the world (excluding Kuwait). Sweden is still relatively moral as nations go, but no nation can be that moral. For a while it had tried to compete in the global anti-pollution market but quickly discovered the United States and Japan were more competitive. Now Sweden is seriously considering entering the world trade in conventional arms, where it has technological and economic advantages. National moralities are after all fragile in the face of economic imperatives.

It was the recognition that the official conference on the environment would be torn with conflicts that prompted the International Fellowship of Reconciliation (IFRC) to call an independent conference in Stockholm just before the United Nations meeting. Taking off from the message of a group of seven scientists (including two Nobel laureates) who had met in Menton in 1970, the IFRC raised the necessary funds to sponsor the Dai Dong Independent Conference on the Environment. The Menton Message focussed on resource depletion, population, overcrowding and hunger, and war. It called for a moratorium on unassessed technological innovations, increased pollution control and recycling, the curbing of population growth, and a search for the means to abolish war and to disarm, particularly in the nuclear and CBW areas. The Menton Message, presented to U Thant in May 1971 and published in the UNESCO *Courrier* of July 1971, was thus read in thirteen languages by millions of people. The message had been circulated earlier among environmentalists around the world and over 2200 had subscribed to its views. This statement became the basis of the Dai Dong conference and was officially presented to a plenary session of the United Nations conference.

Dai Dong differed in several fundamental ways from the official conference. Its major feature was its supranational approach and its emphasis on world peace. (The name itself is derived from an ancient Chinese concept: 'For a world in which not only a man's family is his family, not only his children are his children, but all the world is his family and all children are his.') The conference linked social, political, economic, and cultural structures with the urgent problems confronting the world—nuclear war, population growth, environment, and the maldistribution of resources and power. Moreover, it viewed the environmental problem not simply in terms of symptoms such as pollution, but rather as the habitat of all living things and therefore involving the relationships between pollution, poverty, population, politics, and war. It also avoided the error of homocentricity: *all* living things are precious. The focus of Dai Dong was its ecological overview, its search for solutions through the creation of a global consciousness and commitment and the development of a world community. Thirty-one men and women from twenty-four countries, representing a variety of professions, took part in Dai Dong. About half of the delegates were from the Third World, and there were also delegates from Poland and Czechoslovakia who, together with the USSR and Hungary, boycotted the official conference. This boycott had ostensibly arisen because there was no apparent formula for inviting the German Democratic Republic which is among the twenty most industrialized nations in the world. As a consequence most of the countries in the East European communist bloc, whose support is essential if environmental control is to succeed, did not take part in the preparation or activities of the United Nations conference.

Before analyzing the differences and, surprisingly, similarities of the two conferences and assessing their relative successes and failures, it would seem worth while to provide a conceptual model of the global environmental scene, viewing it in terms of geographical, political, economic, cultural, and national structures.

THE ECOLOGICAL IMPERATIVE
AND ITS SOCIAL CONTRADICTIONS

The fundamental conflict, evident at Stockholm, is the innate contradiction between what might be called the ecological imperative on the one hand, and the economic, political, and national (sovereignty) imperatives on the other. The basic principle of ecology is indivisibility. To achieve long-term stability, it is essential that ecological solutions be integrative, holistic, systemic, that they operate at least on the whole of a particular ecosystem if not on the global ecosphere. Any solution that is partial, that operates at some level below the totality of the system, cannot succeed. You cannot clean up Lake Erie simply by restricting the input of municipal sewage, as the recent Great Lakes treaty between the United States and Canada proposes. This effluent is only one of three major polluting inputs, the other two being industrial waste and agricultural run-off. All three must be controlled or the end is ultimate defeat.

The very existence of nation-states, arranged in a hierarchy of political, economic, and military power, each jealously guarding its position in that hierarchy, each struggling to consolidate and improve its position, is in absolute conflict with global environmental control and abatement systems. The problem is exacerbated by the enormous maldistribution of power—economic, political, technological, and exploitive—among the nations of the world. Global environmental control without a radical redistribution of power and resources is unacceptable to the have-not nations since they view this control as an attempt to freeze fundamental inequalities.

This conflict is as evident within nations as it is between nations. Within nations, gross regional disparities make uniform environmental standards unacceptable to the poorer areas since uniformity of control would again freeze inequalities. It is an economic law that capital tends to move to regions where, other things being equal, profits may be maximized. Why should industry move from Ontario to Nova Scotia if the costs of anti-pollution devices are the same in both regions? Why should capital be attracted to Quebec rather than Ontario if the same situation applies? Capital will tend to be attracted to pollution havens whether these be areas of 'soft' legislation or 'soft' enforcement. What is true of the internal competition of national corporations is equally true of multinational corporations and nation-states. Economic power thrives on competition. Ecology is based on mutuality and indivisibility. Power is based on zero-sum games. Ecology is based on non–zero-sum games. The world game (not Fuller's) is a product of the blind power and growth drives, automated, built in to the very nature of the systems themselves.

The politics of pollution transcend the politics of partisanship, inter-personal, intergroup, or international. The threat of planetary pollution with its capacity to destroy all species should offer a new basis for human co-operation and a new unifying principle, creating the possibility of a global morality and a new planetary politics. The combined threat of the hunger crisis, the nuclear hazard, the ecological crisis, and the maldistribution problem transcends all power struggles. There can be no territorial, no political, no psychological victor in any existing or potential human conflict—not in Vietnam, not in Pakistan, not in the Middle East, nowhere! For victor and loser together will perish, if not with a bang then a whimper in a world which can no longer sustain life.

This is not idle imagination, science fiction, or the alarmist propaganda of proponents of blind action or disarming dismay. It is the objective judgment of the majority of independent scientists. The world stands in mortal peril. It is only a matter of time, and tomorrow, if not today, may be too late to reverse the course towards global disaster. To provide a timetable for this disaster is difficult, but it is not unreasonable to expect a serious collapse of our environment if we do not act soon. Survival demands action and the politics of survival demand that this global action originate with the United Nations.

It is within this theoretical context that the specific details of the problems and achievements of the Stockholm conferences must be assessed. In general, the major conflicts were related, whether through commission or omission, to maldistribution of resources, population, nationalism, sovereignty, ideology, and war. The direct environmental problems were, in one way or another, secondary to these other issues.

The Dai Dong declaration rejected traditional economic growth and development, with its uncontrolled 'hard' technologies and its new imperialism—the multinational corporation—as incompatible with environmental protection, the just distribution of resources, and the protection of differing cultures. The United Nations conference implicitly and explicitly expressed its faith in traditional economic growth and technology, using the time-worn and now historically invalidated argument that this was the only path to the equalization of development. This has proved untrue for both the have and the have-not nations. Nor has increased GNP per capita in countries like Canada and the United States led to a more equitable distribution of resources. War, like the supersonic transport (SST) and nuclear testing, was among the many forbidden subjects at the United Nations conference, although Olof Palme, prime minister of Sweden, had the courage to blast the United States for its programme of ecocide in Indochina and demanded that 'ecological warfare cease immediately.' The war in Vietnam is not only a programme of war by starvation and ecological destruction, but it is also war by cultural genocide. Yet it remained a forbidden subject, except, of course, for the Chinese.

War and violence versus non-violence as a revolutionary means was a major point of discussion at Dai Dong. Complete agreement was not achieved in that some delegates felt wars of liberation were justified and that an unqualified statement of opposition to war could be interpreted as a defence of the open terrorism through which certain régimes resist the just claims of their peoples. Some resolution was achieved, however, in that there was general agreement that the burden of guilt should be placed on the social violence and injustice of the state, not on those who resist it, and that those who seek to end wars and are committed to non-violence must develop alternative means to bring about social change and to end injustice as rapidly as possible. There was a consensus that to avert the major threats to survival revolutionary and not reformist changes were needed. Some of the delegates maintained that violent revolutionary means were imposed by social conditions and not selected on principle.

In general, while Dai Dong experienced some powerful differences of opinion, the spirit and practice of free, open, and unmanipulated dialogue prevailed. The delegates all felt the consensus was almost complete, that only shades of difference remained. It welcomed the confrontations of principle, believing that it is through such dialogues that an operational consensus will ultimately be reached. In contrast, the United Nations conference, like the recent Republican convention in the United States, was almost totally managed, rehearsed, and manipulated. It was reliably reported that some delegations, such as those from Canada and the United States, were completely briefed down to the last detail on every actual or anticipated issue. To a great degree this conference was American in style and content and this was true as well of the ecology circus known as the Environment Forum. In the rush for involvement in the Forum, a host of non-government organizations (NGOS) from campfire girls to manufacturers' associations sought formal invitations or planned to attend informally. Stuart Brand of the Whole Earth Catalogue brought a large and varied group to Stockholm (called the Life Forum), including the Hog Farm Commune (an attempt to set up a 'para-primitive society' with minimal environmental impacts, part Rousseau and part hippie), the poets Gary Snyder and Michael McLure, and the Black Mesa Defence Committee (a North American Indian group). In addition, there was another American group called POWWOW and an international group with rather strong leftist leanings called OY. Finally, there was the Folklets (people's) Forum, a coalition of about thirty environmental political groups from Scandinavia who organized a programme of events focussing on the political and economic roots of the environmental problem. The result was largely a mish-mash of confused non-communication.

NATIONALISM AND SOVEREIGNTY

The inherent tragedy of nationalism could not be exemplified more eloquently than in the sad spectacle of the game of politics played at Stockholm. The disunited nations jealously guarding real or token jurisdictions, all now invalidated by the global peril, indulged in a parody of false pride which could be described as 'divided we stand, divided we fall.' That all those powerful passions should be unleashed in the name of some limited and false jurisdiction of geography, of region, of colour, or of creed, all of which are divisive and therefore anti-ecological, was almost a matter of despair. Neither the lessons of history nor those of biology seem to have been absorbed by the governments of the nations of the world. The politics of experience like the politics of nation-states create the major barrier to discovering solutions to the global threats to survival.

And, somehow, the small and infrequent voices of internationalism tended to sound hollow and academic against the background noise of polemical debate on national advantage and disadvantage. And while these schisms among the nations were most evident at the United Nations conference, it also touched the Dai Dong conference. Even there, the issue of sovereignty split the delegates and while these differences were not as profound or as covert as in the United Nations conference, they were, nevertheless, significant and revealing. On the issue of sovereignty, it mattered little if a delegate were official or unofficial. The reaction was largely from the gut rather than the head. Third Worlders of radically different ideologies reacted more or less uniformly in violent protest against the concept of population as an issue and for absolute sovereignty as an unassailable principle. This view had been expressed earlier by a meeting of seventy-seven Third World countries in Peru and later, in October 1971, the Brazilian ambassador to the United Nations declared that in some aspects of environmental concern he detected in the wealthy countries 'a malicious trend according to which the old patterns of colonial paternalism were being preserved by a pseudo-scientific outlook to justify underdevelopment.'

These reactions are really not unexpected. Sovereignty is what you crave if you lack it in form or content, or if you are in the process of winning it. You cannot share what you do not have and it is valid that the winning of sovereignty must precede the sharing of it. Those most jealously guarding their sovereignty were therefore those who held it most tenuously, had won it most recently, or were still struggling to achieve it by violent or non-violent means. The former colonies of the 'great powers' and the crypto-colonies of the new imperialists struggling for real independence were least prone to discuss the need for supra-sovereign agencies and functions. The giving up of sovereignty became, like population control, an issue virtually exclusive to western representatives, at least at the Dai Dong conference. Nobody at the official conference seriously proposed this drastic but ultimately necessary component of the ecological imperative. Each proposal for some small step in the direction of vesting authority in the interests of the common survival of all was viewed by its opponents as another, more subtle technique for imperialist manipulation and exploitation.

In general the Third World employed the hippie philosophy of 'leave us alone and let us do our thing.' Redistribution of resources and development were highly acceptable as empty, pious promises of a better world. But each attempt to recommend organizational forms for such a redistribution, which would inevitably mean some sacrifice of sovereignty, was vehemently rejected. Statements of principle concerning the common and equal ownership of the world's resources were greeted enthusiastically. Any practical act for achieving this global equality met with suspicion. The facts that neither resources nor exploitive power is uniformly distributed and equally that the power to exploit often resides in the countries without the resources were accepted. But again nationalism stood solidly in the way of revolutionary restructuring for redistribution. This nationalism was explicitly expressed by the Third World and implicit in the positions of the economically developed countries.

Thus the issues which disunited the nations at Stockholm were precisely those that violate the ecological imperative of indivisibility: nationalism, ideological differences, sovereignty, and maldistribution. Each is inherently anti-ecological in that it divides and separates nations by territory, politics, ideology, and profound differences in economic development. Each erodes a united co-operative approach to the global problem of environmental degradation. Each stands in conflict with the common cause and common concern essential to the ecological imperative.

THE POPULATION CONFRONTATION

Related in large part to ideological and economic differences was the question of population growth which split the conferences along both economic and ideological lines, though with some notable exceptions in both cases. Generally, population was viewed as put-on, plot, or problem depending on the speaker: Third Worlder, Maoist or neo-Maoist, or westerner. Thus the split was based both on ideology and on differences in economic development. The ideological split was more clearly derived from the Chinese Marxists than from the Eastern European variety.

To some degree all Third Worlders, with the notable but not sole exception of India, considered population control either as a sinister covert plot or simply as a non-issue that would be automatically solved by the 'proper' socio-economic system. It seems an ecologist is an ecologist is an ecologist unless he is a Maoist, an economist, or a Third Worlder.

The population problem did not receive a thorough airing at the United Nations meeting and the final statement of that conference was weak and ambivalent on the issue. Indeed, at all three conferences, the arguments raged fiercely over a spectrum from complete denial that a problem exists to affirmation that population is the ultimate problem. The former position was often held jointly by strange bedfellows—some but not all traditional Marxists, neo-Maoists, the government of China (although China practises the most effective, efficient, and thorough population control yet witnessed), and the new technocrats who always expand the ultimate carrying capacity of our planet by a variety of technological 'fixes' each with its own unperceived flaw. Those most concerned with the population problem manifested themselves in the first place as neo-Malthusians resurrecting the spectres of overpopulation and, finally, as organizations concentrating their activities around concepts such as zero population growth (ZPG) and attributing most, of not all, ills (including pollution) to this one factor. People are pollution is their dominant theme while the Left screams 'it's an imperialist plot' or 'it's your baby, Rockefeller,' a reference to the view of John D. Rockefeller III that 'no problem is more urgently important to the well-being of mankind than the limitation of population growth,' and to the support provided by him for birth control and family planning mostly directed to the peoples of the Third World.

That there is, for many of its supporters, a racist element involved in the idea that population is the source of all our miseries is undeniable. This attitude is to be found among both the power élite and the man in the street. It is the neo-fascist fear of being overwhelmed by some 'impure' or 'inferior' race whose population growth exceeds that of some 'master' race, however defined.

That population is an ecological factor is undeniable. Barring a change in the quality of production in economically developed countries, an increase in consumption per capita of a stable population or stable consumption per capita with a growing population will lead to further resource depletion and pollution. Resource consumption, population, and pollution are intimately connected and we in the western world are guilty of over-consumption and thus of creating most of the pollution. In the global accounting of environmental degradation, it is thus more incumbent upon the West to control its population. It is equally incumbent on Canada not to sell its resources to countries like the United States, who do not control environmental degradation or population, for in doing so we become accessories to the collapse of the global biosphere.

The Third World is already convinced, partly through suspicion but more often through sound evidence, that the western world views third-world population growth as a threat and its own as a promise. Canada cannot preach what it does not practice. We cannot export population concern and technology unless we also enact population control measures internally. Canada should adopt zero population growth as a policy but with adequate civil rights safeguards.

In his speech at the United Nations conference on 10 June, Tang-ke, the chairman of the delegation of the People's Republic of China, spoke of his government's 'beginning to work in a planned way to prevent and eliminate industrial pollution of the environment.' (He did not pretend that China had eliminated pollution as the neo-Maoists in the West proclaim.) He then made a classical statement of technological optimism, virtually identical to that of western techno-cratic optimists: 'The history of mankind has proved that in the race of development of production, science and technology always surpasses by far the rate of population growth.' 'The possibility of man's exploitation and utilization of natural resources is inexhaustible.' He went on: 'Our government has always advocated family planning and the publicity, education and other measures adopted over the years have begun to produce effects.' Nevertheless he felt obliged to add: 'It is wholly groundless to think that population growth in itself will bring about pollution and damage the environment and give rise to poverty and backwardness.' Except for the unbelievable allusion to the inexhaustibility of natural resources, there is nothing to disagree with in China's statements concerning population. China is practising ZPG and certainly population growth, in itself, is not the cause of environmental degradation. This statement bears little resemblance to the wild, venomous, and ranting slogans of the neo-Maoists. Their views are as invalid factually as their behaviour is psychotic, characterized by an equal lack of humour and of humanity. At the Dai Dong conference, a group led by M. Taghi Farvar, who had worked with Barry Commoner, made varying comments on the population question. All tended to downgrade the problem, admittedly with much less malice and tendenciousness than many neo-Maoists. In general, at the Dai Dong conference, as at the United Nations conference, the split on the population issue separated Third World from other representatives. Farvar began with a denial but finally acknowledged the population problem, although he placed little emphasis on it and adopted a position similar to Commoner's, which downgrades programmes of population control.

Nevertheless the issue of population control continues to polarize opinions, some viewing it as an imperialist plot and others as a global problem. For people of the Third World and the poor of the rest of the world, the former view is an understandable 'gut' reaction. This is a pity and a loss for all those who are concerned with the threat to the future. Every effort should be made to transcend ideological differences and achieve a consensus on this issue. There is much truth on both sides of the argument and it is in this common truth that the consensus should be sought. In part, this consensus must acknowledge the relationship of the population problem to the socio-economic system. It must allow that population, while an ecological factor, is not as significant as other factors. It must admit that famines and poverty are often, though not always, the result of maldistribution and not absolute shortage. But it must also incorporate the ecological understanding of the significance of population in its impact on the total environment, on pollution, poverty, and stress. There can be no valid position that denies the finiteness of the world's life-support resources no matter how many technological 'fixes' we can imagine or ideology can generate.

THE MALDISTRIBUTION DILEMMA

Of all the bases of conflict at Stockholm, none is more significant than the gross maldistribution of consumption, of power, of access to energy and resources, between the economically developing and the economically developed world. The world was so constituted by the processes of history that a minority of people controls the majority of the world's resources from calories to capital. This fact is perhaps the most urgent threat to global survival. It lies at the heart of human conflict within nations and between nations. It divides the world into the have and have-not countries, and in many of the have countries creates a huge gulf between rich and poor. It has many faces, all of them grotesque and inhuman. Moreover, it is not only a maldistribution of wealth but also of health and justice. The poor, the deprived, and the dispossessed, comprising the vast majority of the world's people, are the selective victims of these gross maldistributions.

One of the major areas of maldistribution is in the consumption of the critical resources, materials, and energy that are the basis of economic development. Just two nations, the United States and Japan, with some 9 per cent of the world's population are consuming close to 40 per cent of the world's energy. And their rates of growth indicate a doubling of consumption in 10 to 12 years. This means that by 1985 they will consume almost 80 per cent of the world's energy at present rates of production. By 2000 given no cessation in the growth of their consumption, these two nations will be consuming 160 per cent of present production.

Two additional facts make this arithmetic even more serious. Since energy is ultimately the measure of all goods and services produced, this gross maldistribution in world energy consumption reflects directly not merely on economic maldistribution, but a maldistribution of the other social necessities that sustain and nurture life. The net result of this gross difference in the levels and rates of consumption coupled with no viable schemes for redistribution is that some three-quarters of the world's population is destined to live in perpetual deprivation. To add to this global injustice, energy consumption and production is closely related to environmental degradation. Thus countries like the United States are not only economic imperialists but also pollution imperialists. The proportion of the global burden of pollution that they contribute is roughly equal to the proportion of their consumption. Thus they bear the major responsibility for the stresses on the global ecosphere. It is this double-edged Damoclean sword hanging over the heads of all the people in the world that was the major source of friction at Stockholm. It is the failure to share burden and benefit that divides the have and have-not countries of the world.

The developed world has overdrawn the global bank account of fossil energy by a prolonged system of deficit budgeting. Both oil and natural gas resources will begin to dwindle after 1990. The global maldistribution problem is the ultimate Malthusian dilemma of uncontrolled growth and two-thirds of the world's population face the prospect of an unending future of deprivation and a growing disparity between their lot and that of the affluent. The technocrats would not agree but they are responsible for the problem. It would thus be suicidal to look to them for the solution. The developed world must live within a fixed budget of energy consumption or face global ecological disaster and increasing social violence arising from maldistribution or depletion of present energy sources and critical resources. Much of the problem lies in the human incapacity to deter gratification. Rich and poor are alike in this.

The poor are tied to the immediate return. They live on the edge of existence. They cannot defer gratification beyond the next twenty-four hours. Their perception of threat or hazard is immediate. For them, survival is a day-to-day struggle. The rich and the haves, whether economic or political institutions, are geared to short-term gratification. They cannot defer gratification beyond an acceptable rate of return on their economic or political investment. This tends to be three to five years, whether the period for return on invested capital or a return to political power.

Neither of these views can govern. Both assume postures of short-term returns, not an adequate basis for preserving the future. Ecology is based on long-term gratification, on the ability to defer gratification in order to assure the future. The poor are concerned with immediacy and our economic and political structures are based on only short-term deferments. Thus there is a double bind involved, the conflict between the rich and the poor and between ecology and the inability to defer gratification, whether immediate or short, whether for existence or power. The concomitant of this inability to live for the future is the natural tendency to defer or discount the social costs of environmental degradation.

Of course the new technocrats preach the virtues of energy substitution or other technological 'fixes' and in their technocratic euphoria are unconcerned about maldistribution, satisfied with their technical solutions created in social vacua. That other barriers to the transportation of technology are insurmountable or that the new technology has its own attendant backlash, both environmentally and socially, does not disturb their blind faith in technology.

STOCKHOLM IN PERSPECTIVE

In June 1972, official, semi-official, and unofficial groups, dedicated in small or large part to global concerns but with widely different ideological assumptions about the nature of the environmental problem, assembled in Stockholm. Groups and people came with good and dubious intentions, some to indulge in self-fulfilling prophecies which attempted to reduce environment and population to non-issues, some to manipulate and dominate in the name of the status quo or revolution, and some in good faith to begin the seemingly impossible task of creating a global community to treat global problems at a global level. Judgments of success or failure, like all such judgments, reflect the values, interests and biases of the judge. The official organizers of all the conferences made the predictable judgment that their part of the proceedings was relatively or highly successful. And so it will be for this author, who attended Dai Dong as a formal delegate.

Although it could not be a matter of proof, the reading of the Dai Dong Declaration to a plenary session of the United Nations conference had a salutary, if not critical impact. At that point, 9 June, the conference was hopelessly divided and continued so until virtually the last day, when some of the main differences were superficially patched up in order to present the semblance of a common declaration. The politics of environment which operate within nations were operable on the international level. Tokenism, co-option, jurisdictional juggling, expiation by legislation, and the trade-off of unmentionables were all quite common. The profound global issues—Canada's proposed $30-billion onslaught on the north and the Arctic, the United States' much greater rape of the environment with the Trans-Alaska Pipeline System, the Quebec government's ecocidal and culturally genocidal $10-billion James Bay project, the proposed clearing of the Amazon rain forests by Brazil, continued nuclear testing underground and in the atmosphere, the SST, chemical warfare in Indochina, the new epidemics of 'river blindness,' malaria, and intestinal dysentry along the Nile from Uganda to Egypt, and the outbreak of malaria among the refugees in Cambodia, the broader environmental issues involving the huge burden of poverty, the importance of the genuine liberation struggles of dispossessed and deprived peoples forcibly exposed to a degraded physical and social environment in Angola, Mozambique, and other places, the problem of industrial safety and public health in the economically developed countries, the relationship of environment to socio-economic systems and their supporting 'hard' technologies, and the population issue—all were glossed over, ignored, traded off as mutually unmentionable, or given token treatment. The spirit of Dai Dong was notably absent while all the divisive forces remained unaltered and unabated.

James Branch Cabell, the American novelist, once wrote: 'The optimist proclaims we live in the best of all possible worlds and the pessimist fears this is true.' So judgment is often not perspective. Extreme pessimism and extreme optimism are equally suspicious. Maurice Strong, the able secretary-general of the United Nations conference, stated after the conference that 'what many skeptics thought would be a rhetorical statement has become a highly significant document reflecting a community of interests among nations regardless of politics, ideologies or economic status.' One can accept this as an honest expression, while totally doubting it as a valid assessment. The statement of Jack Davis, Canada's Minister of the Environment, that the success of the conference was 'beyond my wildest dreams,' simply attests to the tameness of his dreams. Canada's development programme and complicity in Arctic development violates the very principle which it brought to the United Nations in its submission that 'baseline surveys to establish a scientific view of the state of various environmental systems should be undertaken at the earliest possible time.' Canada's great Arctic Waters Pollution Prevention Act was passed in 1970 but not proclaimed until August of 1972. Canada's Northern Inland Waters Act has no regulations and, like most of our environmental legislation, is unenforceable or unenforced. The key question—to develop or not to develop—is never the question. And self-laudatory assessments in an election year by politicians is hardly likely to inspire respect. Nor do organizers of conferences often admit failure.

The absence of the USSR and most other countries of the Eastern European communist bloc was a serious gap and severely reduced the necessary unanimity of approach to global environmental controls. One cannot deal with the degradation of the Baltic in the absence of East Germany. Western Europe and Scandinavia cannot solve their environmental problems without Eastern Europe.

On the positive side, total abandonment of nuclear weapons tests was demanded at Stockholm in a joint statement issued by Canada, Ecuador, Fiji, Japan, Malaysia, New Zealand, Peru, and the Philippines. This was ignored by the nuclear powers or powers to be, as were pleas about chemical warfare. Similarly, Scandinavia's strong condemnation of the SST was opposed by none other than Britain's Secretary of State for the Environment, Peter Walker, who defended the multi-billion dollar investment. The net result was a watered-down token concern. While in Washington the Supreme Court has now ruled that the United States government is not liable for damage created by sonic booms from high-flying military supersonic jets, while traditional economic growth remained firmly entrenched on its heavenly pedestal, delegates from Finland and Denmark, for example, made searching comments about these seeming contradictions with environmental protection. But these views were treated with disdain or indifference by the big powers.

By the evening of 16 June 1972, the world (minus a few key countries) had its first Declaration on the Human Environment. As an official spokesman for the Third World said earlier that day: 'We must agree on a Declaration here in Stockholm. If it goes to New York, it will be even worse.' The original declaration had been dismembered to the point of total devitalization. The final declaration was a kind of compromise of irreconcilable positions, often akin to a Picasso painting, in that it faced both ways at the same time, reflecting a total disagreement on how to manage the environment. The gulf between nations, whether on the basis of economic development or ideology, remained as deep and as wide as before, despite Maurice Strong's brave words.

In the end, however, perspective demands we view Stockholm as a small but clear step toward the great global revolutionary change that is beginning. Stockholm was at once the hope and despair of the world. Stockholm was the United Nations at its worst and its best. The cynics cannot dismiss it simply as one small step forward for the United Nations and one giant step backward for humanity. Certainly Stockholm displayed international tokenism and national protectionism, but the conferences were also extremely meaningful dialogues among adversaries. Those dialogues tended to transcend the crystallized postures of almost every delegate to the official and unofficial conferences. The revealed differences were painful but the revelation was positive in that most participants must have been affected in some degree by enhanced insights into the mental sets of others as well as their own. The three worlds came their way, spoke their way, and went their way. A few small voices spoke for one world and these voices, like the Dai Dong concept, are on the side of history and will help create a future that is viable. Dai Dong will go on with its message of transnationalism and it is to be hoped that a new world constituency will develop to deliver it.

32. On the Problem of "The Global Problematique": What Roles for International Organizations?

John G. Ruggie

I. INTRODUCTION

In the summer of 1980, the United Nations is to commence what is being called a set of 'global negotiations'. These are to address, separately but simultaneously and comprehensively, matters related to energy, raw materials, trade, development, money and finance. The agenda for these negotiations is premised on two conceptions that go beyond any previous basis for North-South talks: (i) that the world economy is not simply a collection of separate national economies linked to one another by external interactions of varying degrees of intensity, but a single, integrated global system; and (ii) that the concern of these negotiations is not simply North-South transfers, but the effective management of the functional interdependencies that exist among the component parts of the world economy, to be sure with an eye toward more equitable distribution.

It is difficult to anticipate what will be the precise outcome of these negotiations, if indeed one can speak at all of such a thing as an outcome as though it were likely to be a discrete product. In the end, and if the past is any guide to the future, it may well be that what these negotiations signify will be as important as what they accomplish. What they signify is an increasing tendency for international organizations to define the international policy agenda in ever more holistic terms, and to maintain that such holistic perspectives are necessitated by the growing functional interdependencies among global processes and problems. These functional interdependencies, moreover, are taken to reflect fundamental changes in the material world. Both the tendency and the justification have been most clearly articulated in a series of international conferences that international organizations have initiated over the course of the past decade or so on various aspects of global issues. Thus, and not without irony, at a time during which the last remnants of the normative association of international organizations with world government finally disappeared from the scene, international organizations have become actively associated with the concept of global governance. In the words of one recent report, directed to the General Assembly of the United Nations, it sometimes appears that international organizations are being asked, unrealistically, 'to carry the whole burden of the agenda facing humanity'.

The material changes that are invoked as necessitating holistic perspectives and comprehensive policy responses are often described by the term 'the global problematique'. However, it isn't altogether clear just what this comprises. If memory serves correctly, the term was first coined when the limits-to-growth scenario momentarily captured international attention as expressing the essence of what used to be known as the world environmental crisis. It then referred to a complex of problems and processes concerning the planet *itself*. Since then the list of constituent factors has grown apace. Simple inventories typically include the issues of world poverty, underdevelopment, economic dislocation, population growth, natural resource depletion, nuclear proliferation and world militarization, as well as alienation, disaffection and cultural malaise. In other words, the list now includes most everything that is problematical *on* the planet. And among the many criteria employed in considering these problematical things as being global in character is that they occur in many places, affect many people, take place in areas beyond or across national jurisdiction, pose the danger of future world conflict, offend universal moral standards, threaten the physical survival of humankind, emanate from the same underlying structure, and require action at the global level. If the meaning of the term has become unclear, it is even less clear what international organizations, which have been intimately involved in generating the term and in expanding its meaning, may be expected to do about the phenomena it comprises.

This article is a preliminary sorting exercise. In Part II, I try to construct a working definition of 'the global problematique', one that captures more than tactical or rhetorical issue-linkage, attempts to universalize particularistic concerns, or any type of functional interdependencies in and of themselves. Accordingly, by the term 'problematique' I mean an indivisibly related complex of processes and problems. By the term 'global' I mean universal within the world system. And by using the definite article 'the' I mean to connote a singularity, a phenomenon that is one-of-a-kind historically and that is of a one-of-a-kind variety. In sum, from the many and diverse uses of 'the global problematique' I sort out the one that meets these specifications. It has to do with the increasing scale of human activity, viewed within the context of planetary life-support systems. The increasing scale of human activity so conceived, together with its causes and consequences, I take to circumscribe 'the global problematique'. In Part III, I survey some of the activities of international organizations that may be said to constitute responses to 'the global problematique', in the attempt to see what has been the impact of these material changes. I show that there has been an expansive effect on what international organizations do and get involved in, but that the patterns exhibited by their behavior and involvement cannot be explained by the fact of the material changes. In Part IV, I propose the outlines of a model of change that does account for the patterns of international organizational activity, and which offers some insight into what this signifies for broader patterns of global governance.

II. THE 'PROBLEMATIQUE'

My point of departure is the increasing scale of human activity in the context of the productive and regenerative capacities of the biophysical resource bases and ecosystems within which human life exists. This increasing scale, together with its causes and effects, triggers a complex interplay of ecological, technological, social, economic and political factors, to which I shall refer as 'the global problematique'. It goes without saying that no precise or universally accepted specification of it is possible at this time. Yet enough is known for us to be able to construct an extended working definition and overview of its major manifestations and the core of its cause-effect complex.

Some of its manifestations are coming to be universal in character. They include the mounting world demand for food, energy, materials, and social services of all kinds; growing shortages and even depletion of easily recoverable minerals, fossil fuels and other natural resources, of fresh water, and of favorable soils and suitable climate for agriculture; more general signs of ecological disequilibria especially visible in and around large urban areas, reflecting a growing disjuncture between spatial development patterns throughout the world system and the infrastructure available to serve the world's population, such as housing, health and educational facilities, networks of production, exchange and disposal; attending high rates of inflation together with recessionary tendencies, other forms of social disarticulation and political instability. In the industrialized areas of the world, more particularistic manifestations of the 'problematique' include pollution and contamination of the various media, such as air, water and soils, and associated health effects, as well as a growing sense of vulnerability to the second-order consequences of some high-technology responses to pressing problems, of which nuclear power production is the most topical and perhaps the most critical case. Particularistic manifestations in the poorer developing regions of the world include soil erosion and depletion, especially of marginal lands, massive deforestation in the tropical and semitropical areas, desertification in the semiarid zones, the reappearance of diseases, such as malaria, that had been contained and even eliminated years ago, and the near-epidemic eruption of others, of which schistosomiasis is most commonly associated with ecological factors. [. . .]

In sum, what distinguishes the processes and problems that go to make up the so-called global problematique from a simple inventory of disparate pressing concerns is that they are systematically related to one another at both ends of the cause-effect chain; their commonality of cause has to do with the fact that they are in some considerable measure the products of a relatively small number of deeply rooted social forces; and their commonality of effect has to do with sustainability and limits, and the functional interdependencies and potential for mutual vulnerability that these produce. And they are distinguished as being global in character in the dual sense that they are shaped and conditioned by social forces that themselves constitute a world-system of relations, and their effects increasingly make the productive and regenerative capacities of planetary life-support systems a variable element within this world-system.

III. INTERNATIONAL RESPONSES

It helps very little to jump, as some have been inclined to do, from the emergence of a complex of interrelated global problems, no matter how pressing they may be, to prescribed behavior that 'the international community' must undertake or court disaster. For the international community is not an agency that can act in its own behalf, for its own good. 'Those who write as if it were find policymakers slow to act upon their advice.' The international community is governed by political, social and economic structures over which it exercises little control. And its agenda is set by the 'tyranny of small decisions' by virtue of which no actor views itself as contributing to global problems, either because the immediate impact of its actions may be limited in scope or intensity or because, from its vantage point, its actions appear to be the most rational or profitable to adopt and pursue. Thus, while problems may cry out for global solution, effective measures continue to depend on the willingness and ability of public and private actors at other levels of social organization in the world system to change their behavior.

What can international organizations do to help bring about such changes? One possible answer is that international organizations can do a great deal, but that it has become necessary at this particular point in history to strengthen them and to increase national commitment to them. This may or may not be so, it matters little. As Kenneth Waltz has put it, 'Necessities do not create possibilities. Wishing that final causes were efficient ones does not make them so.' Another possible answer is that international organizations can do little if anything. If the scope of their activities in general is constrained by factors beyond their reach, this is likely to be all the more so when it comes to altering the behavior of those same factors. This answer is indisputable. But to say that the scope of activities of international organizations is *constrained* is not to say that there are no activities at all. And if there are activities then the *possibility* exists that they may have consequences that are unintended and perhaps not even recognized by the actors themselves.

In any case, I propose to deal with the question indirectly, by briefly describing, assessing and accounting for some of the things that international organizations are attempting to do. Keep in mind that the range of my survey is highly circumscribed by my concern. I am *not* interested in everything international organizations seek to do about all the sectoral components of the complex of interrelated global processes and problems which I described above. It is the *complex* itself that concerns me: what are international organizations attempting to do about comprehending it, and about coping with the functional interdependencies and mutual vulnerabilities that it produces?

So circumscribed, we can summarize the roles of international organizations under two headings: (i) expanding the collective knowledge base, and (ii) enhancing the institutional capacity for collective policy. Some illustrations follow:

(i) Knowledge Base

Sheer ignorance about the precise structure, dynamics and consequences of the so-called global problematique is a major constraint on formulating effective responses to it. This is not to imply that knowledge is a sufficient condition for action, but it is certainly a necessary one. International organizations have been associated with three types of activities to expand the collective knowledge base in this domain.

Research. Knowledge is required of phenomena at several levels of complexity. The first, simply, is the actual state of affairs with respect to the key component parts of the 'problematique'—in other words, inventories and analyses yielding current assessments, long-term trends, and projections of future needs and availabilities. A good deal of this information is being collected already, including on natural resources use and reserves, demographic changes, patterns of urbanization, agricultural production, energy production and consumption, and of course various national accounts statistics. However, some of it is scattered among specialized governmental, intergovernmental and nongovernmental agencies, it is not always compatible, and it often exists in forms of aggregation that are not immediately useful from a policy-making perspective. Other types of information that are highly pertinent are not generally available. These include data about the mechanisms shaping the level and pattern of economic activity in different societies, including the effects of changes in market and price structures, external and internal terms of trade, consumption patterns for different types of goods by different social groups, and so on. Graciela Chichilnisky has noted the self-reinforcing circle in econometrics that is generated by this data deficiency: statistics are designed with certain theoretical frameworks in mind, therefore what is observed is largely determined by existing theory; however, what is or is not observed in turn largely determines what new theories can be constructed, for theory that is not validated by observations carries little weight. And so on. In the even softer social realms, virtually nothing exists of a standardized or reliable nature. International organizations over time have managed to contribute to the introduction of new concepts and data and to stimulating new theoretical work. UNCTAD is an obvious case in point. But their degree of freedom to do so in sensitive realms of course is severely delimited. For example, in its basic human needs survey, the ILO is forced to work through governments to obtain disaggregated data on basic needs satisfaction and policies designed to enhance it.

A second level of complexity concerns specific relationships among these component parts. Here the gulf between physical parameters on the one hand, and socioeconomic factors on the other is quite large. Perhaps the most successful case of a global research effort in this area is the Man and the Biosphere program of UNESCO (MAB). In 1968, UNESCO, with the participation of the United Nations, the FAO and WHO, as well as the International Biological Program of the International Council of Scientific Unions (ICSU) and the International Union for the Conservation of Nature and Natural Resources, organized an intergovernmental conference on 'the scientific basis for rational use and conservation of the resources of the biosphere'. MAB, which has been fully operational since 1976, is one of its results.

MAB consists of an intergovernmental and interdisciplinary research program, organized around 14 themes which are pursued through some 500 research projects in more than 50 countries. Roughly speaking, the themes informing these projects fall into four categories: (1) the structure and functioning of different levels of ecosystems (for example, the role of temperate forests in fixing, storing and supplying energy; the functioning of tropical forest ecosystems; dynamic changes in terrestrial ecosystems); (2) deliberate interactions between man and local ecosystems (the impact of irrigation on arid land, the effects of pest management and fertilizer use on terrestrial and acquatic ecosystems, the consequences of tourism and of major engineering works on surrounding environments); (3) more general interactions between human activity and the biosphere (in the form of pollution, demographic changes, human settlements, and similar factors); and (4) the study of perceptions of environmental quality (including, literally, individuals' perceptions, and also the development of policy planning models.)

The key to the execution of the program lies with the National Committees of MAB, each of which assumes responsibility for its country's participation. They provide the material resources as well as the research staff and infrastructure. In addition to the scientific results they produce, participants benefit from on-the-spot training in research and project management. This no doubt is the most significant by-product of MAB. Regional cooperative ventures also have emerged. The role of the international machinery has been to devise and articulate the common research themes, to encourage research projects that are consistent with these themes and to see that they are carried out using compatible methodologies, to facilitate the systematic exchange of information and findings, and to help provide assistance where necessary. MAB has maintained close ties with other UN bodies and with nongovernmental scientific organizations, especially the ICSU Special Committee on Problems of the Environment. The cost of the central machinery is modest.

Other cases exist of efforts to organize international collaborative research on aspects of the structure, dynamics and consequences of the growing scale of human activity. All, however, are largely single-sector in scope, and concern issues in agriculture, public health, meteorology, oceanography and hydrology. Few touch upon socioeconomic factors even to the extent that MAB does. And MAB, not surprisingly in view of its sponsorship, has paid far more attention to the physical consequences side of the equation than to the socioeconomic input side. To the extent that socioeconomic factors are considered, they tend to get addressed in highly aggregate form, like 'population' and 'urbanization', rather than in terms of specific income groups, trade patterns or productive systems interacting with specific resource settings.

The need for more comprehensive research, utilizing forms of data that depict a broad array of discrete social, economic and biophysical factors was acknowledged in General Assembly resolution 3345 (XXIX). It requested the Secretary-General to 'take appropriate measures to provide facilities for co-ordinated multidisciplinary activity aimed at synthesizing, integrating and advancing knowledge' about the interrelationships between population, resources, environment and development. Thus far, the effect of this resolution has been to yield a report by the Secretary-General, describing ongoing and planned research in the UN system in these nine areas: carrying capacity of land and associated ecosystems; soil degradation, desertification and deforestation; resource utilization and disparities in levels of income; integrated rural development; urban concentration of population; industrialization; marine resources and pollution; environmental health problems; and climatic change. While noting how promising this research is in terms of potentially demonstrating concrete forms of interrelationships between population, resources, environment and development, the report concludes that it nevertheless continues to reflect 'specialized concerns' and that it remains 'confined within narrow bounds to specific issues'.

Lastly, at a third level, the entire complex of processes and problems needs to be grasped in holistic terms, as an integrated set of relationships among social, economic, political, technological and ecological processes. Very little is known at this level. There have been numerous attempts to construct global models, beginning with the stagnationist scenarios contained in *The Limits to Growth*, which was published in 1972. By now their shortcomings are well known. Those models that take into consideration resource-bases and ecosystems pay virtually no attention to technological innovation or to socioeconomic and political factors. Those that take social forces as their point of departure tend to be 'soft', and quite naive about physical constraints and dynamics. Only the model developed by the Fundacion Bariloche relates a concrete socioeconomic factor, income distribution, to physical effects, resource depletion and environmental degradation. But it is largely a conceptual model. Recent efforts undertaken as part of UNITAR's Project on the Future, to simulate the effects of markets, income distribution, and technologies of production in various aspects of North-South economic transactions are important, because they tend to undermine some of the assumptions and expectations of existing models while demonstrating that it is possible to conceive and to formulate rigorous models of alternative patterns of development. For example, the simulations show that, depending upon the technologies of production and certain demographic factors, an increase in exports from developing countries even on the basis of more favorable terms of trade can have immiserating consequences for the exporting country. But the formal model includes neither resource factors nor socio-political issues, which are supplemented by means of scenario analyses.

Global modeling of this sort is not likely soon to be comprehensive in scope or to yield definitive results. There are too many limitations and constraints to be overcome, both intellectual and political. At the same time, however, these efforts have had significant heuristic effects. Such effects may be seen generally when we compare our present intuitive understanding of this complex of issues with the formulation contained in *The Limits to Growth*. More concretely, heuristic effects may be seen in the form of long-term policy pronouncements from the United Nations, which if nothing else may come to shape indicative planning exercises by this organization.

Data Storage Retrieval and Exchange. In an ideal world, decision-makers would have ready access to the stock of knowledge about this complex of global processes and problems. They would have at their disposal systems of interdisciplinary information and data storage, retrieval and exchange, in which procedures are standardized and data are compatible. Such systems do not now exist.

A more modest function can be performed by telling decision-makers where—if at all—information that they require does exist, thereby linking sources and users of information by means of a referral service. An illustration of the latter is the INFOTERRA network (formerly, International Referral Service) established by the UN Environment Programme. The idea for such a service grew out of the Stockholm Conference (United Nations Conference on the Human Environment, June 1972), which made numerous references to the need for the exchange of information and endorsed the concept of a referral service. It began to function about four years later, though it became more fully operational only recently.

INFOTERRA collects and disseminates not information but *sources* of information. It does not provide the user with substantive answers, but with names, addresses and telex/telephone numbers of institutions from which answers are available. This it does for over two dozen topics related to the mission of the UN Environment Programme and for environmentally-related planning and decision-making more generally. The topics include aspects of the atmosphere, oceans and climate, energy, renewable and nonrenewable resources, chemical and biological agents and processes, and wild-life, animals and plants; as well as more socially-infused concerns such as population, food and agriculture, health, industry and technology, transportation, human settlements and land use. INFOTERRA is not equipped nor is it intended to handle queries by specialists in their specialized disciplines; it is strictly a service for policy-makers.

The referral network is organized by a Programme Activity Centre (PAC) located in Nairobi, and it works through a system of national, regional and sectoral 'focal points'. The Programme Activity Centre was responsible for constructing the network, which meant to get governments and other agencies interested in participating. And it then designed and devised the computerized switchboard. This function gives it the responsibility to store and update information sources, to devise and distribute the tools of access to the network, such as directories and manuals, to provide training in its use, and to plan and coordinate its expansion. The PAC assumes no responsibility for the quality of the information exchanged. The cost of its activities has ranged between US $600 000 and $800 000 per annum.

The network is built upon and works through focal points, the most important of which are national. In the United States, for example, the Environmental Protection Agency is the national focal point, and it established, for the purposes of working within INFOTERRA, the US International Referral Center. Focal points collect information on sources within their jurisdiction and pass it on to INFOTERRA in standardized form for inclusion in the Directory. In many cases, the need to respond to requests for information via INFOTERRA may trigger the creation of national environmental information services within countries, drawing on both governmental and nongovernmental sources. Regional focal points are to be created within the EEC and CMEA, though financial support for them has been lacking. Sectoral focal points are to be established within UN agencies, though here too progress has been slow. While focal points are the building blocks of the referral service, its actual operation makes possible direct communication between a variety of potential users and sources.

INFOTERRA began to function in 1976, and grew rapidly thereafter. By 1978 there were 87 national focal points, 48 countries had registered sources with it, the number of actual sources registered has reached 6500 (as compared to 200 in 1976), and the system was used about 150 times a month (up from a mere 15 the year before). However, many focal points still are little more than officially designated government offices which are not active in the system, and among those that are active only 20 have at least one full-time staff person.

Apart from the normal difficulties that one expects when attempting to construct anything new that requires collaboration within and among governments and international agencies, INFOTERRA encountered problems which similar systems in the future also are likely to run into. These stemmed from the fact that information does not exist in a socioeconomic vacuum. Information, and information technology even more so, are goods which are owned or controlled by concrete public and private actors. Therefore, the design of a system, the characteristics of the technology to be used, and its subject coverage all have important economic, social and political implications—even if, as is the case with INFOTERRA, the service is provided free of charge. In constructing INFOTERRA, the basic cleavage divided the technologically advanced countries and the developing nations. Some of the early initiators of INFOTERRA from the advanced countries saw it as a centralized, high-technology (on-line, satellite-based, computerized) system concerned largely with physical parameters and problems, especially pollution. Many developing countries viewed this design as locking them into existing patterns of technological dependence *vis-a-vis* the North, as they would be encouraged to acquire sophisticated equipment, machinery and know-how, while the system itself paid little attention to the environmental problems of most serious concern to them such as soil erosion, human settlements, and natural resource depletion. UNEP attempted to resolve these differences by broadening the range of information sources to be included in INFOTERRA, and by opting for the gradual build-up of a decentralized system in which there would be no technological constraints on participation. In the process, however, some of the enthusiasm for INFOTERRA of early supporters in the advanced countries has waned.

At present, INFOTERRA is the only operational international referral service; others are at various stages of trial and error in planning and construction. Thus, internationally available information coverage is spotty and it is highly uneven. The degree of harmonization among these emerging systems is virtually nonexistent. And information that its owners construe in [proprietary] terms is not freely available, while information related to national security concerns of course is not included at all. The definitions of these terms rest with the sources of the information.

Monitoring and Early Warning. One of the characteristics of both the causes and the effects of the so-called global problematique is their irreversibility at least in the short run. As a result, timely warning becomes an essential ingredient of effective responses. A fully fledged 'early warning system' would consist of three component parts: (1) the continuous observation and measurement of selected parameters, in accordance with a fixed time schedule and spatial plan, using comparable methodologies and standardized procedures for collecting the data; (2) the capacity for assessing the significance of parametric changes, which implies not only the possession of certain kinds of scientific knowledge but also the ability to perform risk analyses; and (3) the surveillance of compliance with accepted standards. No such system exists anywhere, either domestically or internationally, though fragments may be found at both levels.

Internationally, the activity of monitoring physical parameters has been undertaken for many years. For example, the International Council for the Exploration of the Seas established a data center on physical aspects of oceanography as far back as 1902. Systematic weather observations go back to the middle of the last century, and an integrated World Weather Watch has existed for a decade. In recent years monitoring systems have sprung up in a number of fields. All of these, however, have been sectoral and single-medium oriented, and most cover but a small number of the possible range of parameters within any given sector. With the exception of monitoring radionuclides from atomic weapons tests, none of these has self-consciously concerned itself with man-induced phenomena. And attempts to extend coverage to socioeconomic parameters have been successfully resisted to date.

The most comprehensive monitoring system now in existence is in the field of the human environment. Launched by the UN Conference on the Human

Environment, the Global Environmental Monitoring System (GEMS) includes climate-related monitoring, monitoring of long-range transport of pollutants, health-related monitoring, monitoring of terrestrial renewable resources, and ocean monitoring.

GEMS in essence is a label that covers two different sets of activities in each of the above categories: (i) monitoring undertaken by UN Agencies and related bodies, some of which the UN Environment Programme (UNEP) seeks to coordinate; and (ii) attempts to elaborate existing systems, to fill gaps and to initiate new activities altogether which are also carried out through the UN system but which UNEP supports financially.

Among the first set of activities are the monitoring of living resources in the [aquatic] environment, conducted by UNESCO and FAO; the FAO Fisheries Data Centre; oceanographic monitoring undertaken jointly by the International Oceanographic Commission (IOC) and the World Meteorological Organization (WMO), in the framework of the Integrated Global Ocean Stations System (IGOSS); the World Weather Watch (WWW) of the WMO; and health-related monitoring of the World Health Organization (WHO). The degree of coordination actually provided by UNEP is problematical.

Since 1975, the activities in which UNEP has taken a direct interest and has contributed to with its own financial resources and organizational support have grown considerably. In the area of climate-related monitoring, the major program consists of some 100 stations that have been established by the WMO to determine trends in background atmospheric pollution. With respect to the long-range transport of pollutants, a network of 42 stations has been established in 12 European countries in which samples of air, rain and airborne particulates are collected and analyzed; this program is carried out by the ECE. In the area of health-related monitoring, organized by the WHO, the aim is to develop greater unity among programs concerning the health effects of air pollution, water quality and food contamination, and to gain greater understanding of the transfer of pollutants between media. Some 180 air monitoring stations have been established in 60 cities, the water-quality monitoring program eventually will comprise 300 to 400 sampling stations, and 19 countries now contribute data on food contamination. When it came to terrestrial renewable resources, the immediate need was to develop methodologies for assessing such processes as soil erosion. Samplings have also been undertaken in arid and semiarid ecosystems. Lastly, in the area of ocean monitoring, the most fully developed program is the Mediterranean Pollution Monitoring and Research Programme, in which 83 marine science institutions from 16 Mediterranean countries and the EEC participate, and which is being implemented with assistance from the FAO, IAEA, IOC, WHO and WMO.

As is the case with UNEP's INFOTERRA, the activities UNEP supports directly in the field of monitoring come under the guidance of a Programme Activity Centre, which is located in Nairobi. It was established in 1975, the period between the Stockholm Conference in 1972 and that date having been taken up by intergovernmental negotiations concerning what should be monitored and by whom. The advanced industrial countries were interested primarily in certain pollutants. Developing countries were more interested in health and resource-related parameters. A compromise ultimately was struck, which broadened the scope of the monitoring program-to-be, but also diluted its progress, especially since, at the urgings of the developing countries, financial allocations for monitoring as a whole were reduced simultaneously. But by the time of the fifth session of UNEP's Governing Council, held in 1977, the developing countries had become the most ardent supporters of GEMS, stressing its potential contribution to national development planning. On the organization of the system there was never any disagreement among countries, though there was a good deal of it between UNEP and UN Agencies. In the end, they and governments agreed that GEMS would consist to the maximum extent possible of existing systems. The GEMS-PAC spends approximately $2 million per annum.

Gradually, then, a more comprehensive environmental monitoring system is coming into existence. In relation to the totality of global processes and problems sketched out earlier in this paper, however, its range still is narrow. Nor is it likely soon to acquire the other functions of an early warning system.

Conclusion. In sum, data collected and relationships analyzed, information exchanged and parameters monitored, research activities prescribed and proscribed, all exhibit the influence of many factors other than the simple need to know. They exhibit the collective interest of governments in limiting external intrusions into domestic jurisdictional space, as well as particularistic interests of specific countries, social groups and transnational actors. They exhibit concern with military security and with intellectual property. They exhibit the consequences of intellectual fragmentation among scientific disciplines as well as the institutional fragmentation of the United Nations system and of national governments.

And yet, while each of these conditions what can be done, things are done, and some of the things that are done today could not have been done previously. As we have seen, international organizations sometimes initiate. Governments sometimes change their minds. Transnational actors sometimes acquiesce. Above all, intersectoral issues, of which the human environment was a prototype, have had integrative and expansive effects on the collective knowledge base that is available to the international community. What determines the *patterns* of integration and expansion I take up briefly in the final part of this paper.

(ii) Institutional Capacity

An expanding knowledge base presumably has *some* effect on policy. The nature of this effect, however, is indeterminate and at best is likely to be indirect. For the past decade or so, international organizations have participated in more direct attempts to enhance the collective institutional capacity to cope with such functional interdependencies and mutual vulnerabilities that are deemed to exist in the domain of concern to us here, and to influence the forces that give rise to them in the first place. Again we can identify three distinct types of activities.

Institutionalization. The major instrument that is available to international organizations for prodding the development of this sort of institutional capacity is conference diplomacy. During the 1970s, there was a series of international conferences on themes and problems related to the global 'problematique': the human environment (Stockholm, 1972), population (Bucharest, 1974), food (Rome, 1974), industrialization (Lima, 1975), employment (Geneva, 1976), human settlements (Vancouver, 1976), water (Mardel-Plata, 1977), desertification (Nairobi, 1977), primary health care (Alma Ata, 1978), climate (Geneva, 1979), and science and technology for development (Vienna, 1979). To these ought to be added selected aspects of the Third United Nations Conference on the Law of the Seas, the Special Sessions of the General Assembly on the New International Economic Order (1974, 1975), the invocation of the so-called global negotiations (1980), and preparations for the international development strategy for the 1980s (1979–1980).

These conferences vary widely in terms of their manifest accomplishments. The 'actions' flowing from their 'action plans' sometimes seem to be a poor return on investment. Indeed, one observer has gone so far as to argue that the conferences detract from rather than contribute to progress on the issues they address. And it is unlikely in any case that governments would agree to a similar round of *ad hoc* conferences in the foreseeable future, though special sessions of the General Assembly are likely to continue and to become more frequent. However, it is a mistake to view conference diplomacy solely in terms of legislative outcomes. The Mertonian distinction between manifest and latent functions is a meaningful one to make here. The activities may be as important as their products. If the *activities* succeed, they will have three consequences apart from their substantive accomplishments: to trigger the creation of constituencies where none exist, within the institutional system comprised of governments, international agencies and nongovernmental organizations; to establish permanent networks among such constituencies; and to articulate, support and sustain a continuing policy role for these constituencies *vis-a-vis* competing bureaucratic actors. In other words, they potentially contribute to processes of institutionalization and thereby affect policy formation. This perhaps is most effectively illustrated by reference to one of the more successful instances of conference diplomacy and institutional follow-up, the Stockholm Conference on the Human Environment.

The preparatory process for Stockholm was so designed that it could 'succeed' even if the conference itself were never to be held—which, at one point, was a very real possibility. Success here assumed a novel meaning in the lexicon of international organizations: it was defined as stimulating an interest in environmental matters within countries in which none had existed previously, breaking down the sectoral divisions that existed within national governments no less than in international agencies, and helping to construct a permanent domestic bureaucratic constituency for whatever international environmental activities the UN might undertake in the future. In the pursuit of the first objective, the Secretary-General of the conference, Maurice Strong, visited some 90 UN member-states. Heads of state and government were alerted to global environmental trends and were queried about their own particular environmental situations. To stimulate greater coordination among domestic ministries, the mechanism of requesting a variety of reports from governments was utilized. Some of these were called 'basic' reports, and described particular national environmental problems and experiences. These typically required coordination among several technical ministries, such as agriculture, transport, public health, mines and resources, and the like. At one point, 15 such reports were being prepared within the US government alone. Others were called 'national' reports, and they provided an overall description of national environmental problems and activities, as well as a statement of objectives for the conference. These required a greater degree of central coordination and some discussion of national priorities. Governments which lacked interest were prodded. Governments which could not afford the exercise were aided by special grants that Strong had arranged for from Scandinavia and Canada. Those who needed administrative help got it from the conference secretariat. It was not the product that counted but the activity. The activity, it was hoped, would lead to the creation of national environmental policies and ministries. The hope was not misplaced, as departments of the environment were created where none had existed before and even where none had ever been contemplated. At a minimum, therefore, the preparatory process could claim success in having helped to implant environmental concerns within the institutions of national governments. The conference itself, if held and if successful, would add to the stature of these new ministries in the domestic bureaucratic game, because its success and the attention paid to it would reflect well on them. And, having helped to create permanent agencies domestically, it was thought that whatever international organization the conference established would have a permanent domestic bureaucratic constituency. In sum, the preparatory process was not simply a means to define an agenda, to collect background information and to formulate specific measures. It was also a means to effect permanent change in the domestic bureaucracies of governments, and to establish a basis for subsequent international action. An analogous strategy was attempted *vis-a-vis* international agencies, nongovernmental organizations and, once the UN Environment Programme came into existence, industry groups as well. The UNEP in turn was envisaged as a forum and, especially through the use of its Environment Fund, a stimulus for the continuing elaboration of the collective environmental policy of these various actors.

To say that the Stockholm Conference and its institutional followup is illustrative of the latent functions of conference diplomacy is not to say that collective environmental policy is uniformly effective, or that it reflects some transcendent ecological interest. Neither is the case. But it is to say that in some measure the human environment has become institutionalized as a 'vested interest' within the system, and that international policy processes and outcomes to some extent differ as a result from what they would be otherwise.

No doubt there have been more failures than successes. And it has not proved possible simply to duplicate the Stockholm model on subsequent occasions. Nevertheless, similar effects can be attributed to other instances on conference diplomacy. The most notable of course is UNCTAD, whose consequences for institutionalization extend to the organization of permanent international negotiating groups, which, if nothing else, has enhanced the collective institutional capacity of the developing countries. Thus, apart from whatever may be its substantive accomplishments, a significant long-term contribution of conference diplomacy resides in its potential impact on the processes of institutionalization that shape the context of collective policy formation.

Generating Alternative Patterns. To have succeeded in institutionalizing a constituency and in constructing and implementing plans and programs of action is to have altered the institutional framework of collective policy-making and to have produced additional capabilities by means of which to respond incrementally to collective problems. However, to have so succeeded does not mean that the factors and forces giving rise to such problems are affected as a result or that the incremental responses will be adequate to the tasks at hand. Growing recognition of this fact in certain international organization circles has led to a growing concern with the idea of stimulating 'alternative patterns of development'.

On the whole, there is little that international organizations can do or be used for to directly influence the course of national development patterns. Some influence is exercised over developing countries, however. And this is where the concern with alternative patterns has most clearly materialized. The two chief instruments of this influence are the funds and technical assistance provided for specific projects by development banks and agencies, and the legitimation that is dispensed in support of more general development models both by these actors and by broader processes like the negotiations on the Development Decades. With the very limited exception of IMF stabilization packages, no analogous source of influence exists over the industrialized countries.

Until recently, development banks and assistance agencies gave virtually exclusive support to the kinds of development efforts that promised to replicate and comport with capital- and energy-intensive patterns of the industrialized countries. For example, at one time loans for large-scale infrastructure projects that typically are designed for urban-based and export-oriented industry consumed nearly half of total World Bank loans. Historically, almost all energy aid has been for high-grade and large-scale electrical energy production whose output was aimed at urban industrial facilities and amenities. Agricultural aid has been much smaller and has favored projects modeled on the high-input systems of the industrialized countries and products destined for export. Support for water supply and waste disposal projects has been meager and similarly has overwhelmingly favored large-scale urban projects. In comparison, rural development has received miniscule support. And some vital areas, like forestry management, received no support at all until the past decade.

To some extent this is changing. For example, current World Bank plans call for increasing the proportion of loans going to rural development and agriculture from 28% to 35% of total; for health, education, family planning and water supply to rise to 26%; and for support for infrastructure projects to decrease to 40% of all loans granted. Moreover, the IBRD has increased its allocations for oil and gas exploration in small and medium-sized fields in developing countries. Even the fuel-wood shortage has attracted some concern. Signs of similar shifts in emphasis may be seen in technical assistance agencies and the UNDP, where projects concerning self-provisioning farming, sites and services upgrading in urban slums, alternative methods of energy production, and alternative technologies and basic needs provision in general now receive somewhat greater support than they did in the past. These changes reflect a variety of motives. Industrialized countries have been inclined to support them as long as their focus is on the alleviation of absolute poverty in the developing countries. The latter have been inclined to lend their support as long as reduced dependency on the North is held out as a promise. To a lesser degree, and largely on the part of international officials and nongovernmental organizations active in the field of development assistance, these changes also reflect a growing sensitivity to the problem of the long-term sustainability of these patterns. The shifts are significant, but in no case have they reversed the prior emphasis of funding or technical assistance programs.

As for the legitimation of general development models by official bodies, it appears that the past consensus has eroded without any new approach enjoying universal support. The preparations for the Third United Nations Development Decade, for example, reveal at least three differing contenders, which are advanced by three different institutional actors. In the intergovernmental committee that is preparing the development strategy, the only significant change from the previous development decades concerns the 'restructuring' of international economic relations, in keeping with the principles of the New International Economic Order. Whereas the two prior strategies focused on aggregate growth rates and country-to-country transfers, both of which were abstracted from any real international economic context, the world economy proper will be a component of the third strategy. But on no other issue are governments likely to adopt a position that differs substantially from the past. The World Bank, which may be presumed to be strongly influenced by the major donor countries in this regard, has advanced a direct antipoverty strategy, especially for the poorest countries. It includes an acceleration in but a different composition of economic growth, redistributive policies and social services to ensure that the benefits of such growth actually reach the poor, and the reduction of high fertility rates so that population growth does not consume whatever are the benefits of economic growth. Lastly, participants in this process who have a quasi-autonomous institutional base, such as the Committee for Development Planning and the Task Force on Long-Term Development Objectives of the Administrative Committee on Co-Ordination, have voiced the greatest concern with alternative patterns of sustainable development in a global perspective.

Perhaps the most significant consequence of these partial shifts toward 'alternative patterns' is to undermine the unchallenged hegemony that traditional models of economic growth have enjoyed in the past within the official international development community. But for the developing countries as a whole, the only effect of this is likely to be indirect and long-term, via whatever changes it may produce in the theory and ideology of development economics. In countries that depend extensively on official external assistance, more concrete effects may result from the conditionality of loans and grants or from the impact of specific development projects. In other cases, governments simply may choose to follow 'alternatives' paths. It is doubtful whether these changes will have any direct effect on the so-called newly industrializing countries, in which 'indebted industrialization' financed in private international capital markets is beginning to outpace even the 'transnational industrialization' of direct foreign investment. There, as in the industrialized countries, such 'alternative patterns' as may emerge are likely to result from factors related specifically to price, quantity and the pressure of increased social costs, and not from the lending policies or the indicative plans of international organizations.

Legitimizing Counter-Hegemonic Forces. If the international community is governed by structures over which it exercises little control, the degree of involvement by international organizations in reshaping deeply rooted social forces within the world system of course will be minimal. And it is. But to an extent it does exist. It exists on the fringes of the intergovernmental system, in the form of symposia and seminars, where officials attending in their private capacity mingle with representatives of concerned nongovernmental organizations and individual experts in one thing or another. Some of these occasions are quite modest in purpose, and seek merely to stimulate the exchange of experiences and ideas. Others also strive to articulate a consensus view on desirable courses of action. At their most ambitious, however, these occasions have been part of a broader thrust to delegitimate the dominant modes of production, consumption, exchange and distribution in the world system (*i.e.* the capitalist world economy), and to sketch out and seek to act upon an alternative normative vision. The dimension of ecological holism frames most of these endeavors and forms the one common basis of envisioned alternatives, but whether the specificity of the critique of capitalist institutions is social democratic or Marxist in inspiration, or whether it reflects ethical or even esthetic opposition, is largely determined by who attends and what the particular issues under consideration are. The only consistent support from governments has come from a small number of nonaligned countries, often including Algeria, Tanzania, Yugoslavia, sometimes Mexico, sometimes Venezuela, and from the so-called like-minded countries of Scandinavia and (depending on shifting governmental coalitions) the Netherlands.

Again I proceed by way of illustration. The case described below is not of any great intrinsic importance. Moreover, as an attempt at collective delegitimation and at giving form to an alternative normative vision, it is not an exemplar of intellectual or even tactical sophistication. However, I cite it because it is both interesting and significant in what it reveals.

In October 1974, UNEP and UNCTAD held a symposium on 'Patterns of Resource Use, Environment and Development Strategies' in Cocoyoc, Mexico. The meeting comprised experts serving in their individual capacities. It was presided over by Barbara Ward and hosted by President Echeverria. It issued a document, which was called 'The Cocoyoc Declaration'.

The symposium concluded that 'mankind's predicament is rooted primarily in economic and social structures and behavior within and between countries.' The ultimate source of the problematique is the structure of the world economy: the market mechanism reflects effective demand, not ecological or human needs; the distribution of wealth favors an over-consumptive minority, while it further marginalizes the majority; and the rate and price of resource extraction, which determine the future development potential of all, reflect what dominant interests want and not what human beings need. The Symposium urged a series of domestic and international structural changes that would help bring about new patterns of global development, making economic relations more responsive to ecological needs on the one hand, and to basic human needs on the other.

Following the Cocoyoc Symposium, UNEP began complementary work on a conceptual overview of the environment/development nexus, on an analytical exploration of 'irrationality' and 'wastefulness' in natural resource use, and on an elaboration of the idea of 'ecodevelopment', the alternative model of development favored by the Symposium. In each case, reports prepared by the UNEP secretariat were to be presented to groups of governmental experts, who would pass judgement on them and forward them to an intergovernmental forum for ultimate adoption as morally binding statements of principle. In sum, the Cocoyoc exercise was one ingredient in a broader design on the part of UNEP, the purpose of which was to reframe the conceptual and normative bases of environmental planning and decision-making, by linking the global environmental situation to the structure of the world economy, and by proposing certain principles of economic behavior in order to produce desirable ecological outcomes.

Proving Weber's dictum that ideas are interests too, UNEP's design was vehemently opposed by governments. The major Western industrialized countries uniformly responded by noting pointedly that UNEP was not in business to concern itself with international economic relations, let alone to restructure them. They were joined by the Soviets in criticizing what they perceived to be faulty logical premises, inconsistencies as well as empirical inadequacies in the Cocoyoc Declaration and the subsequent documentation on the set of issues Cocoyoc raised. The United States also affected UNEP's frame of mind much more profoundly.

American expressions of displeasure apparently involved no less a figure than the then Secretary of State, Henry Kissinger. The US criticized the Symposium for castigating the market mechanism, and for blaming world poverty and environmental degradation on it. This is simplistic economics, the US maintained, because it ignores the role of that mechanism in the creation of wealth—which the Symposium was so keen to redistribute. Moreover, it is simplistic politics because it frees the developing countries from any responsibility for their own contribution to world environment and development problems, and because it ignores the impact of the socialist countries as well. The US was also unhappy with what it took to be a generally hostile tone of the Symposium, and with the imbalance of obligations between developing and industrialized countries that the Declaration appeared to enunciate. The US concluded by reminding UNEP that activities carried out under UN auspices, which are supported by all UN members, should be more representative of diverse views. Not long thereafter, a meeting is said to have taken place between the Secretary of State and the Executive Director of UNEP, in which these issues were further "discussed." Subsequently, although not directly related to Cocoyoc but serving to attract UNEP's attention just the same, the United States announced that its pledged contributions to the UNEP Fund would be withheld while reviewed.

For their part, the developing countries were no less unhappy. Their representatives had talked from the time of the Stockholm Conference about socioeconomic structures and about the need to alter economic relations as one means of protecting and enhancing the human environment. But what they meant by this was international financial support for their environmental problems, and the manipulation of international economic relations for the same end. They sought to have more and different subject areas added to the list of UNEP's priorities, and to have compensatory measures introduced into their external economic relations with the industrialized countries for any loss of trade or other economic opportunity that was due to environmental restraints, as an additional means whereby the international community would support environmental protection activities in the Third World. But the Cocoyoc Declaration was something else altogether. It was as much a critique of domestic socioeconomic arrangements in developing countries as it was of international economic relations—albeit in more muted language. The Symposium objected to what it saw as domestic exploitation as it had to international, and called for domestic economic decentralization, full participation and civil rights, land reform, the use of intermediate technologies, and generally for 'justice in the distribution of benefits' which it found lacking. Still more important, although the Symposium appeared to want to resist it in its public Declaration, the link between the character of international economic relations and the domestic constituencies in developing countries which benefit from them and help to sustain them was inescapable. Thus, a critique of the international economic order became, *ipso facto*, a critique of domestic elites in the Third World. One could not criticize the first without also criticizing the second, and one could not criticize the two on different grounds, for in the framework of the Symposium they were part and parcel of the same global 'structure'.

The response of the developing countries was predictable: this is not what they had had in mind at all. Worse still, the Symposium came at a time when Third World governments were exposed to increasing pressure from international development agencies and bilateral aid donors for not doing enough for the poorest 40% or so of their populations. Now UNEP was joining in this chorus. As a result, in subsequent deliberations in UNEP concerning the concepts of environment and development, the developing countries were every bit as destructive of Cocoyoc-infused proposals as were the industrialized countries. Brazil put the finishing touches on this entire sequence of events. Having succeeded in emasculating the documentation on these three subjects in the context of an intergovernmental expert group, Brazil, at the 5th Governing Council of UNEP in 1977, expressed broad agreement with the results. And they urged that no further efforts be undertaken to develop definitions and indicators of 'irrationality', 'wastefulness', and so on, because additional conceptualization only would lead to diminishing returns.

In the end, an implicit quid pro quo was reached among governments that had disagreed on this very issue for several years. It was a quid pro quo of mutual abstinence in the face of an alternative that was threatening to all. The environment-development nexus accordingly was defined in terms of identifying and seeking to internalize negative effects of development projects, and in terms of supporting efforts to devise technical alternatives that are environmentally sound to begin with. This UNEP was asked to help with. It does so on its own and in conjunction with other organizations in the UN system. It advocates the environmental dimension in North-South economic negotiations. And it continues to seek to raise consciousness and to pose important issues, as it did recently in a series of intergovernmental seminars on the topic of 'Alternative Patterns of Development and Life Styles'. As a result, the intergovernmental system is exposed to a variety of issues, reflections and experiences, and it may even develop a shared vocabulary by means of which to describe them. This may enhance its collective adaptive capacity. But on the programmatic front, these activities remain well within what Robert Cox describes as the hegemonic consensus.

Thus, if only intellectually and in the hope of engendering new norms and expectations, international organizations have been used in attempts to affect the domestic and international structures and forces that shape world-wide modes of production, consumption, exchange and distribution. These attempts have taken the form largely of seeking a measure of intergovernmental legitimation for counter-hegemonic challenges and ideas. That this goes on at the fringes of the intergovernmental system, and that it has met with little direct success of course causes no surprise. However, as is illustrated by the case described above, governments do not take such efforts lightly. They react vehemently to protect particularistic interests. But they also react with equal vehemence to protect their collective interest in the basic structure of international jurisdictional rights. And when this latter is threatened, as it is by definition by attempts to act upon a genuinely holistic global ideology, the effect is to [facilitate] the crystallization of a revived hegemonic consensus.

Conclusion. The past decade or so has witnessed continuous attempts by international organizations to prod the development of greater collective institutional capacity for responding to aspects of the global 'problematique'. These attempts have been most successful and their effects most widespread when their objective has been to expand existing institutional frameworks of collective policy formation, by institutionalizing the participation of new functional and political constituencies. Conference diplomacy has been a major instrument of this process. Less success has been achieved in attempts to redirect the policy process toward producing alternative patterns of development. The lending policies, technical assistance programs and indicative plans of international agencies have been the major instruments of this endeavor. While changes in development thinking ultimately may have indirect effects throughout the world system, direct effects for the moment are partial in kind and limited to certain of the developing countries. Lastly, the involvement of international organizations in reshaping the very structures and forces of the world political economy has been marginal and has taken the form of attempts to [delegitimate] existing norms and institutions and, by providing access to counter-hegemonic ideas and groups, to develop and seek to operationalize an alternative normative order. To some extent, these attempts are succeeding within the international secretariats. Among governments, however, their effects appear to be to expand the existing range of consensus in an assimilative rather than a transforming adaptation.

IV. WHAT KIND OF CHANGE?

This survey of the responses of international organizations to the emerging global 'problematique' affords an opportunity to summarize briefly changes in patterns of global governance that are exhibited therein.

In this domain of activity, international organizations are playing an increasing role in global governance. The role is not that of actor but of catalyst of intergovernmental processes. International organizations have played an increasing role in developing holistic perspectives of the complex of global processes and problems, and in expanding the collective knowledge base concerning it. They have become increasingly active in initiating the expansion of policy processes to incorporate new areas of concern. And they are increasingly effective in defining the issues that come to constitute the collective policy agenda. In this measure, the 'problematique' has had expansive and integrative effects on international policy.

But international organizations are emanations of social, political and economic structures over which they have little control. They serve the forces that generate them. If the scope of their activities in general is conditioned by factors beyond their reach, this is likely to be all the more so when attempts are entertained to alter some of these factors. Hence, the attempts by international organizations to affect the collective institutional capacity is more constrained than attempts to expand the collective knowledge base. And the precise patterns of organizational involvement in both reflect the general and the particular interests of dominant actors, public and private, national and transnational.

Is the global 'problematique' likely to produce a *transformation*, not simply of the physical setting of world politics but of global governance as well? The discussions above suggest that the 'problematique' is producing *change* but that this change is *rule-governed*. It is analogous to the change produced by state intervention in market economies. Any such intervention violates specific instances and expressions of private property rights. But the fundamental structure of private property rights conditions, shapes, and constrains the character of such intervention. Indeed, such intervention strengthens the long-term viability of the capitalist system of economic organization. Thus change occurs but it is ruled-governed change. And so it is with "intervention" by international organizations in the world system. Change occurs—sometimes substantial change—according to a certain logic which, however, does not itself change. Accordingly, I conclude that there is nothing inherent in the emergence of a material basis for planetary politics that would suggest at this point a transformation of the intergovernmental system beyond the patterns depicted above.

33. The World Charter for Nature

The General Assembly,

Reaffirming the fundamental purposes of the United Nations, in particular the maintenance of international peace and security, the development of friendly relations among nations and the achievement of international co-operation in solving international problems of an economic, social, cultural, technical, intellectual or humanitarian character,

Aware that:

(*a*) Mankind is a part of nature and life depends on the uninterrupted functioning of natural systems which ensure the supply of energy and nutrients,

(*b*) Civilization is rooted in nature, which has shaped human culture and influenced all artistic and scientific achievement, and living in harmony with nature gives man the best opportunities for the development of his creativity, and for rest and recreation,

Convinced that:

(*a*) Every form of life is unique, warranting respect regardless of its worth to man, and, to accord other organisms such recognition, man must be guided by a moral code of action,

(*b*) Man can alter nature and exhaust natural resources by his action or its consequences and, therefore, must fully recognize the urgency of maintaining the stability and quality of nature and of conserving natural resources,

Persuaded that:

(*a*) Lasting benefits from nature depend upon the maintenance of essential ecological processes and life support systems, and upon the diversity of life forms, which are jeopardized through excessive exploitation and habitat destruction by man,

(*b*) The degradation of natural systems owing to excessive consumption and misuse of natural resources, as well as to failure to establish an appropriate economic order among peoples and among States, leads to the breakdown of the economic, social and political framework of civilization,

(*c*) Competition for scarce resources creates conflicts, whereas the conservation of nature and natural resources contributes to justice and the maintenance of peace and cannot be achieved until mankind learns to live in peace and to forsake war and armaments,

Reaffirming that man must acquire the knowledge to maintain and enhance his ability to use natural resources in a manner which ensures the preservation of the species and ecosystems for the benefit of present and future generations,

Firmly convinced of the need for appropriate measures, at the national and international, individual and collective, and private and public levels, to protect nature and promote international co-operation in this field,

Adopts, to these ends, the present World Charter for Nature, which proclaims the following principles of conservation by which all human conduct affecting nature is to be guided and judged.

I. GENERAL PRINCIPLES

1. Nature shall be respected and its essential processes shall not be impaired.

2. The genetic viability on the earth shall not be compromised; the population levels of all life forms, wild and domesticated, must be at least sufficient for their survival, and to this end necessary habitats shall be safeguarded.

3. All areas of the earth, both land and sea, shall be subject to these principles of conservation; special protection shall be given to unique areas, to representative samples of all the different types of ecosystems and to the habitats of rare or endangered species.

4. Ecosystems and organisms, as well as the land, marine and atmospheric resources that are utilized by man, shall be managed to achieve and maintain optimum sustainable productivity, but not in such a way as to endanger the integrity of those other ecosystems or species with which they coexist.

5. Nature shall be secured against degradation caused by warfare or other hostile activities.

II. FUNCTIONS

6. In the decision-making process it shall be recognized that man's needs can be met only by ensuring the proper functioning of natural systems and by respecting the principles set forth in the present Charter.

7. In the planning and implementation of social and economic development activities, due account shall be taken of the fact that the conservation of nature is an integral part of those activities.

8. In formulating long-term plans for economic development, population growth and the improvement of standards of living, due account shall be taken of the long-term capacity of natural systems to ensure the subsistence and settlement of the populations concerned, recognizing that this capacity may be enhanced through science and technology.

9. The allocation of areas of the earth to various uses shall be planned, and due account shall be taken of the physical constraints, the biological productivity and diversity and the natural beauty of the areas concerned.

10. Natural resources shall not be wasted, but used with a restraint appropriate to the principles set forth in the present Charter, in accordance with the following rules:

(*a*) Living resources shall not be utilized in excess of their natural capacity for regeneration;

(*b*) The productivity of soils shall be maintained or enhanced through measures which safeguard their long-term fertility and the process of organic decomposition, and prevent erosion and all other forms of degradation;

(*c*) Resources, including water, which are not consumed as they are used shall be reused or recycled;

(*d*) Non-renewable resources which are consumed as they are used shall be exploited with restraint, taking into account their abundance, the rational possibilities of converting them for consumption, and the compatibility of their exploitation with the functioning of natural systems.

11. Activities which might have an impact on nature shall be controlled, and the best available technologies that minimize significant risks to nature or other adverse effects shall be used; in particular:

(*a*) Activities which are likely to cause irreversible damage to nature shall be avoided;

(*b*) Activities which are likely to pose a significant risk to nature shall be preceded by an exhaustive examination; their proponents shall demonstrate that expected benefits outweigh potential damage to nature, and where potential adverse effects are not fully understood, the activities should not proceed;

(*c*) Activities which may disturb nature shall be preceded by assessment of their consequences, and environmental impact studies of development projects shall be conducted sufficiently in advance, and if they are to be undertaken, such activities shall be planned and carried out so as to minimize potential adverse effects;

(*d*) Agriculture, grazing, forestry and fisheries practices shall be adapted to the natural characteristics and constraints of given areas;

(*e*) Areas degraded by human activities shall be rehabilitated for purposes in accord with their natural potential and compatible with the well-being of affected populations.

12. Discharge of pollutants into natural systems shall be avoided and:

(*a*) Where this is not feasible, such pollutants shall be treated at the source, using the best practicable means available;

(*b*) Special precautions shall be taken to prevent discharge of radioactive or toxic wastes.

13. Measures intended to prevent, control or limit natural disasters, infestations and diseases shall be specifically directed to the causes of these scourges and shall avoid adverse side-effects on nature.

III. IMPLEMENTATION

14. The principles set forth in the present Charter shall be reflected in the law and practice of each State, as well as at the international level.

15. Knowledge of nature shall be broadly disseminated by all possible means, particularly by ecological education as an integral part of general education.

16. All planning shall include, among its essential elements, the formulation of strategies for the conservation of nature, the establishment of ecosystems and assessments of the effects on nature of proposed policies and activities; all of these elements shall be disclosed to the public by appropriate means in time to permit effective consultation and participation.

17. Funds, programmes and administrative structures necessary to achieve the objective of the conservation of nature shall be provided.

18. Constant efforts shall be made to increase knowledge of nature by scientific research and to disseminate such knowledge unimpeded by restrictions of any kind.

19. The status of natural processes, ecosystems and species shall be closely monitored to enable early detection of degradation or threat, ensure timely intervention and facilitate the evaluation of conservation policies and methods.

20. Military activities damaging to nature shall be avoided.

21. States and, to the extent they are able, other public authorities, international organizations, individuals; groups and corporations shall:

(*a*) Co-operate in the task of conserving nature through common activities and other relevant actions, including information exchange and consultations;

(*b*) Establish standards for products and manufacturing processes that may have adverse effects on nature, as well as agreed methodologies for assessing these effects;

(*c*) Implement the applicable international legal provisions for the conservation of nature and the protection of the environment;

(*d*) Ensure that activities within their jurisdictions or control do not cause damage to the natural systems located within other States or in the areas beyond the limits of national jurisdiction;

(*e*) Safeguard and conserve nature in areas beyond national jurisdiction.

22. Taking fully into account the sovereignty of States over their natural resources, each State shall give effect to the provisions of the present Charter through its competent organs and in co-operation with other States.

23. All persons, in accordance with their national legislation, shall have the opportunity to participate, individually or with others, in the formulation of decisions of direct concern to their environment, and shall have access to means of redress when their environment has suffered damage or degradation.

24. Each person has a duty to act in accordance with the provisions of the present Charter; acting individually, in association with others or through participation in the political process, each person shall strive to ensure that the objectives and requirements of the present Charter are met.

34. Towards Common Action: Proposals for Institutional and Legal Change

The World Commission on Environment and Development

In the middle of the 20th century, we saw our planet from space for the first time. Historians may eventually find that this vision had a greater impact on thought than did the Copernican revolution of the 16th century, which upset humans' self-image by revealing that the earth is not the centre of the universe. From space, we see a small and fragile ball dominated not by human activity and edifice but by a pattern of clouds, oceans, greenery, and soils. Humanity's inability to fit its activities into that pattern is changing planetary systems fundamentally. Many such changes are accompanied by life-threatening hazards, from environmental degradation to nuclear destruction. These new realities, from which there is now no escape, must be recognized—and managed.

The issues we have raised in this report are inevitably of far-reaching importance to the quality of life on earth—indeed, to life itself. We have tried to show how human survival and well-being could depend on success in elevating sustainable development to a global ethic. In doing so, we have called for such major efforts as greater willingness and co-operation to combat international poverty, to maintain peace and enhance security world-wide, and to manage the global commons. We have called for national and international action in respect of population, food, plant and animal species, energy, industry, and urban settlements. The previous chapters have described the policy directions required.

The onus for action lies with no one group of nations. Developing countries face the challenges of desertification, deforestation, and pollution, and endure most of the poverty associated with environmental degradation. The entire human family of nations would suffer from the disappearance of rain forests in the tropics, the loss of plant and animal species, and changes in rainfall patterns. Industrial nations face the challenges of toxic chemicals, toxic wastes, and acidification. All nations may suffer from the releases by industrialized countries of carbon dioxide and of gases that react with the ozone layer, and from any future war fought with the nuclear arsenals controlled by those nations. All nations will also have a role to play in securing peace, in changing trends, and in righting an international economic system that increases rather than decreases inequality, that increases rather than decreases numbers of poor and hungry.

The time has come to break out of past patterns. Attempts to maintain social and ecological stability through old approaches to development and environmental protection will increase instability. Security must be sought through change. The Commission has noted a number of actions that must be taken to reduce risks to survival and to put future development on paths that are sustainable.

Without such reorientation of attitudes and emphasis, little can be achieved. We have no illusions about 'quick-fix' solutions. We have tried to point out some pathways to the future. But there is no substitute for the journey itself, and there is no alternative to the process by which we retain a capacity to respond to the experience it provides. We believe this to hold true in all the areas covered in this report. But the policy changes we have suggested have institutional implications, and it is to these we now turn—emphasizing that they are a complement to, not a substitute for, the wider policy changes for which we call. Nor do they represent definitive solutions, but rather first steps in what will be a continuing process.

In what follows we put forward, in the first place, what are essentially conceptual guidelines for institutions at the national level. We recognize that there are large differences among countries in respect of population size, resources, income level, management capacity, and institutional traditions; only governments themselves can formulate the changes they should take. Moreover, the tools for monitoring and evaluating sustainable development are rudimentary and require further refinement.

We also address, in more specific terms, the question of international institutions. The preceding chapters have major implications for international co-operation and reforms, both economic and legal. The international agencies clearly have an important role in making these changes effective, and we endeavour to set out the institutional implications, especially as regards the United Nations system.

I. THE CHALLENGE FOR INSTITUTIONAL AND LEGAL CHANGE

Shifting the Focus to the Policy Sources

The next few decades are crucial for the future of humanity. Pressures on the planet are now unprecedented and are accelerating at rates and scales new to human experience: a doubling of global population in a few decades, with most of the growth in cities; a five- to tenfold increase in economic activity in less than half a century; and the resulting pressures for growth and changes in agricultural, energy, and industrial systems. Opportunities for more sustainable forms of growth and development are also growing. New technologies and potentially unlimited access to information offer great promise.

Each area of change represents a formidable challenge in its own right, but the fundamental challenge stems from their systemic character. They lock together environment and development, once thought separate; they lock together 'sectors', such as industry and agriculture; and they lock countries together as the effects of national policies and actions spill over national borders. Separate policies and institutions can no longer cope effectively with these interlocked issues. Nor can nations, acting unilaterally.

The integrated and interdependent nature of the new challenges and issues contrasts sharply with the nature of the institutions that exist today. These institutions tend to be independent, fragmented, and working to relatively narrow mandates with closed decision processes. Those responsible for managing natural resources and protecting the environment are institutionally separated from those responsible for managing the economy. The real world of interlocked economic and ecological systems will not change; the policies and institutions concerned must.

This new awareness requires major shifts in the way governments and individuals approach issues of environment, development, and international co-operation. Approaches to environment policy can be broadly characterized in two ways. One, characterized as the 'standard agenda', reflects an approach to environmental policy, laws, and institutions that focuses on environmental effects. The second reflects an approach concentrating on the policies that are the sources of those effects. These two approaches represent distinctively different ways of looking both at the issues and at the institutions to manage them.

The effects-oriented 'standard agenda' has tended to predominate as a result of growing concerns about the dramatic decline in environmental quality that the industrialized world suffered during the 1950s and 1960s. New environmental protection and resources management agencies were added on to the existing institutional structures, and given mainly scientific staffs.

These environment agencies have registered some notable successes in improving environmental quality during the past two decades. They have secured significant gains in monitoring and research and in defining and understanding the issues in scientific and technical terms. They have raised public awareness, nationally and internationally. Environmental laws have induced innovation and the development of new control technologies, processes, and products in most industries, reducing the resource content of growth.

However, most of these agencies have been confined by their own mandates to focusing almost exclusively on the effects. Today, the sources of these effects must be tackled. While these existing environmental protection policies and agencies must be maintained and even strengthened, governments now need to take a much broader view of environmental problems and policies.

Central agencies and major sectoral ministries play key roles in national decision making. These agencies have the greatest influence on the form, character, and distribution of the impacts of economic activity on the environmental resource base. It is these agencies, through their policies and budgets, that determine whether the environmental resources base is enhanced or degraded and whether the planet will be able to support human and economic growth and change into the next century.

The manadated goals of these agencies include increasing investment, employment, food, energy, and other economic and social goods. Most have no mandate to concern themselves with sustaining the environmental resource capital on which these goals depend. Those with such mandates are usually grouped in separate environment agencies or, sometimes, in minor units within sectoral agencies. In either case, they usually learn of new initiatives in economic and trade policy, or in energy and agricultural policy, or of new tax measures that will have a severe impact on resources, long after the effective decisions have been taken. Even if they were to learn earlier, most lack the authority to ensure that a given policy is implemented.

Environmental protection and sustainable development must be an integral part of the mandates of all agencies of governments, of international organizations, and of major private-sector institutions. These must be made responsible and accountable for ensuring that their policies, programmes, and budgets encourage and support activities that are economically and ecologically sustainable both in the short and longer terms. They must be given a mandate to pursue their traditional goals in such a way that those goals are reinforced by a steady enhancement of the environmental resource base of their own national community and of the small planet we all share.

New Imperatives for International Co-operation

National boundaries have become so porous that traditional distinctions between local, national, and international issues have become blurred. Policies formerly considered to be exclusively matters of 'national concern' now have an impact on the ecological bases of other nations' development and survival. Conversely, the growing reach of some nations' policies—economic, trade, monetary, and most sectoral policies—into the 'sovereign' territory of other nations limits the affected nations' options in devising national solutions to their 'own' problems. This fast-changing context for national action has introduced new imperatives and new opportunities for international co-operation.

The international legal framework must also be significantly strengthened in support of sustainable development. Although international law related to environment has evolved rapidly since the 1972 Stockholm Conference, major gaps and deficiencies must still be overcome as part of the transition to sustainable development. Much of the evidence and conclusions presented in earlier chapters of this report calls into question not just the desirability but even the feasibility of maintaining an international system that cannot prevent one or several states from damaging the ecological basis for development and even the prospects for survival of any other or even all other states.

However, just at the time when nations need increased international co-operation, the will to co-operate has sharply declined. By the mid-1980s, multilateral institutions were under siege for many, and often contradictory, reasons. The UN system has come under increasing attack for either proposing to do too much, or more frequently, for apparently doing too little. Conflicting national interests have blocked significant institutional reforms and have increased the need for fundamental change. By the mid-1980s, funds for many international organizations had levelled off or declined in both relative and absolute terms.

Bilateral development assistance has declined as a percentage of gross national product (GNP) in many industrial countries, falling even further below the targets proposed in the early 1970s. The benefits and effectiveness of aid have come under serious question, in part because of criticism based on environmental considerations. Yet, sustainable development creates the need for even greater international aid and co-operation.

Nations must now confront a growing number, frequency, and scale of crises. A major reorientation is needed in many policies and institutional arrangements at the international as well as national level. The time has come to break away. Dismal scenarios of mounting destruction of national and global potential for development—indeed, of the Earth's capacity to support life—are not inescapable destiny. One of the most hopeful characteristics of the changes the world is racing through is that invariably they reflect great opportunities for sustainable development, providing that institutional arrangements permit sustainable policy options to be elaborated, considered, and implemented.

II. PROPOSALS FOR INSTITUTIONAL AND LEGAL CHANGE

The ability to choose policy paths that are sustainable requires that the ecological dimensions of policy be considered at the same time as the economic, trade, energy, agricultural, industrial, and other dimensions—on the same agendas and in the same national and international institutions. That is the chief institutional challenge of the 1990s.

There are significant proposals for institutional and legal change in previous chapters of our report. The Commission's proposals for institutional and legal change at the national, regional, and international levels are embodied in six priority areas:

• getting at the sources,
• dealing with the effects,
• assessing global risks,
• making informed choices,
• providing the legal means, and
• investing in our future.

Together, these priorities represent the main directions for institutional and legal change needed to make the transition to sustainable development. Concerted action is needed under all six.

Getting at the Sources

National Policies and Institutions. The way countries achieve sustainable development will vary among the many different political and economic systems around the world. Governments differ greatly in their capacity to monitor and evaluate sustainable development, and many will need assistance. Several features should be common to most countries.

Sustainable development objectives should be incorporated in the terms of reference of those cabinet and legislative committees dealing with national economic policy and planning as well as those dealing with key sectoral and international policies. As an extension of this, the major central economic and sectoral agencies of governments should now be made directly responsible and fully accountable for ensuring that their policies, programmes, and budgets support development that is ecologically as well as economically sustainable.

Where resouces and data permit, an annual report and an audit on changes in environmental quality and in the stock of the nation's environmental resource assets are needed to complement the traditional annual fiscal budget and economic development plans. These are essential to obtain an accurate picture of the true health and wealth of the national economy, and to assess progress towards sustainable development.

Governments that have not done so should consider developing a 'foreign policy for the environment'. A nation's foreign policy needs to reflect the fact that its policies have a growing impact on the environmental resource base of other nations and the commons, just as the policies of other nations have an impact on its own. This is true of certain energy, agricultural, and other sectoral policies discussed in this report, as well as certain foreign investment, trade, and development assistance policies and those concerning the import or export of hazardous chemicals, wastes, and technology.

Regional and Interregional Action. The existing regional and subregional organizations within and outside the UN system need to be strengthened and made responsible and accountable for ensuring that their programmes and budgets encourage and support sustainable development policies and practices. In some areas, however, especially among developing countries, new regional and subregional arrangements will be needed to deal with transboundary environmental resource issues.

Some countries already enjoy comparatively well developed bilateral and regional structures, although many of them lack the mandate and support required to carry out the greatly expanded role they must assume in the future. These include many specialized bilateral organizations such as the Canada/USA International Joint Commission; subregional agencies in Europe such as the different Commissions for the Rhine River, the Danube River, and the Baltic Sea; and organizations such as the Council of Mutual Economic Assistance (CMEA), the Organization for Economic Co-operation and Development (OECD), and the European Economic Community. These bodies provide member countries with a strong foundation on which to build. Although most of them have effective programmes for international co-operation on environmental protection and natural resources management, these programmes will need to be strengthened and adapted to new priorities. The regional organizations in particular need to do more to integrate environment fully in their macroeconomic, trade, energy, and other sectoral programmes.

Similar organizations among developing countries should be strengthened, particularly at bilateral and subregional levels. Organizations such as the Organization of African Unity, the Southern Africa Development Coordination Conference, the Gulf Cooperation Council, the Arab League, the Organization of American States, the Association of South East Asian Nations, and the South Asian Association for Regional Cooperation could work together to develop contingency plans and the capacity to respond quickly to critical economic and environmental statistics, baseline quantity and quality surveys of shared resources, and early-warning capabilities to reduce environment and development hazards. They could develop and apply in concert basic common principles and guidelines concerning environmental protection and resource use, particularly with respect to foreign trade and investment. In this respect, developing countries have much to gain through sharing their common experiences and taking common action.

A new focus on the sustainable use and management of transboundary ecological zones, systems, and resources is also needed. There are, for example, over 200 distinct biogeographic zones in the world. Moreover, most non-island countries in the world share at least one international river basin. The entire national territories of nearly one-quarter of those countries is part of an international river basin. Yet over one-third of the 200 major international river basins in the world are not covered by any international agreement, and fewer than 30 have any co-operative institutional arrangements. These gaps are particularly acute in Africa, Asia, and Latin America, which together have 144 international river basins.

Governments, directly and through the UN Environment Programme (UNEP) and the International Union for the Conservation of Nature and Natural Resources (IUCN), should support the development of regional and subregional co-operative arrangements for the protection and sustained use of transboundary ecological systems with joint action programmes to combat common problems such as desertification and acidification.

Global Institutions and Programmes. At the global level, an extensive institutional capacity exists that could be redirected towards sustainable development. The United Nations, as the only intergovernmental organization with universal membership, should clearly be the locus for new institutional initiatives of a global character.

Although the funds flowing to developing countries through UN programmes represent a relatively small portion of total official development assistance (ODA) flows, the UN can and should be a source of significant leadership in the transition to sustainable development and in support of developing countries in effecting this transition. Under existing conditions the UN system's influence is often fragmented and less effective than it might be because of the independent character of the specialized agencies and endemic weaknesses of co-ordination. However, recent moves towards organizational reform and greater economy and efficiency could improve the capacity of the UN to provide this leadership, and should include sustainable development as an important criterion.

All major international bodies and agencies of the UN system should be made responsible and accountable for ensuring that their programmes and budgets encourage and support development policies and practices that are sustainable. Governments, through parallel resolutions in the respective governing bodies, should now begin to reorient and refocus the mandates, programmes, and budgets of key agencies to support sustainable development. They should also insist on much greater coordination and co-operation among them.

Each agency will need to redeploy some staff and financial resources to establish a small but high-level centre of leadership and expertise. That centre should be linked to the programme planning and budget processes.

Each agency should be directly responsible for ensuring that the environmental and resource aspects of programmes and projects are properly taken into account when they are being planned, and that the financial resources needed are provided directly from its own budget. In line with these new responsibilities, the following bodies should also assume full financial responsibility within their own budgets for certain programmes presently supported by the Environment Fund of UNEP: the World Health Organisation on 'Environmental Health', the Food and Agriculture Organization (FAO) on 'Agricultural Chemicals and Residues', the UN Disaster Relief Office on 'Natural Disasters', the UN Industrial Development Organisation on 'Industry and Transport', the International Labour Organisation on 'Working Environment', the UN Department for Disarmament Affairs on 'Arms Race and the Environment', the Department for International Economic and Social Affairs on 'Environmental Aspects of Development Planning and Cooperation', the UN Educational, Scientific, and Cultural Organisation (UNESCO) on 'Education', and the UN Development Programme (UNDP) on 'Technical Cooperation'. UNEP (discussed extensively in the next section) should continue to co-operate closely with these agencies and help identify new programme needs and monitor performance.

As in each agency, there is also a need for a high-level centre of leadership for the UN system as a whole with the capacity to assess, advise, assist, and report on progress made and needed for sustainable development. That leadership should be provided by the Secretary-General of the United Nations Organisation.

Governments at the UN General Assembly should therefore take the necessary measures to reinforce the system-side responsibility and authority of the UN Secretary-General concerning interagency co-ordination and co-operation generally, and for achieving sustainable development specifically. This will require that the representatives of those same governments in the governing bodies of all major UN organizations and specialized agencies take complementary measures. This could be done as an integral part of the parallel resolutions just proposed on building sustainable development objectives and criteria into the mandates, programmes, and budget of each agency.

To help launch and guide the interagency co-ordination and co-operation that will be needed, the UN Secretary-General should constitute under his chairmanship a special UN Board for Sustainable Development. The principal function of the Board would be to agree on combined tasks to be undertaken by the agencies to deal effectively with the many critical issues of sustainable development that cut across agency and national boundaries.

Dealing with the Effects

Governments should also strengthen the role and capacity of existing environmental protection and resource management agencies.

National Environmental Protection and Natural Resources Management Agencies. Strengthening of environmental agencies is needed most urgently in developing countries. Those that have not established such agencies should do so as a matter of priority. In both cases, bilateral and multilateral organizations must be prepared to provide increased assistance for institutional development. Some of this increased financial support should go to community groups and non-governmental organizations (NGOs), which are rapidly emerging as important and cost-effective partners in work to protect and improve the environment locally and nationally, and in developing and implementing national conservation strategies.

Industrialized countries also need greatly strengthened environmental protection and resource management agencies. Most face a continuing backlog of pollution problems and a growing range of environment and resource management problems too. In addition, these agencies will be called upon to advise and assist central economic and sectoral agencies as they take up their new responsibilities for sustainable development. Many now provide institutional support, technical advice and assistance to their counterpart agencies in developing countries, and this need will grow. And, almost inevitably, they will play a larger and more direct role in international co-operation, working with other countries and international agencies trying to cope with regional and global environmental problems.

Strengthen the United Nations Environment Programme. When UNEP was established in 1972, the UN General Assembly gave it a broad and challenging mandate to stimulate, coordinate, and provide policy guidance for environmental action throughout the UN system. That mandate was to be carried out by a Governing Council of 58 member states, a high-level UN interagency Environment Co-ordination Board (ECB), a relatively small secretariat located in Nairobi, and a voluntary fund set initially at a level of $100 million for the first five years. UNEP's principal task was to exercise leadership and a catalytic influence on the programmes and projects of other international organizations, primarily in but also outside the UN system. Over the past 10 years, the Environment Fund has levelled off at around $30 million annually, while its range of tasks and activities have increased substantially.

This Commission has recommended a major reorientation and refocusing of programmes and budgets on sustainable development in and among all UN organizations. Within such a new system-wide commitment to and priority effort on sustainable development, UNEP should be the principal advocate and agent for change and co-operation on critical environment and natural resource protection issues. The major priorities and functions of UNEP should be:

- to provide leadership, advice, and guidance in the UN system on restoring, protecting, and improving the ecological basis for sustainable development;
- to monitor, assess, and report regularly on changes in the state of the environment and natural resources (through its Earthwatch programme);
- to support priority scientific and technological research on critical environmental and natural resource protection issues;
- to develop criteria and indicators for environmental quality standards and guidelines for the sustainable use and management of natural resources;
- to support and facilitate the development of action plans for key ecosystems and issues to be implemented and financed by the governments directly concerned;
- to encourage and promote international agreements on critical issues identified by Earthwatch and to support and facilitate the development of international law, conventions, and co-operative arrangements for environmental and natural resource conservation and protection;
- to support the development of the institutional and professional capacity of developing countries in all of these areas and help them develop specific programmes to deal with their problems and advise and assist development assistance agencies in this respect; and
- to provide advice and assistance to the United Nations Development Programme, the World Bank, and other UN organizations and agencies regarding the environmental dimensions of their programmes and technical assistance projects, including training activities

Focus on Environmental Protection Issues. UNEP has been a key agent in focusing the attention of governments on critical environmental problems (such as deforestation and marine pollution), in helping develop many global and regional action plans and strategies (as on desertification), in contributing to the negotiation and implementation of international conventions (on Protection of the Ozone Layer, for example), and in preparing global guidelines and principles for action by governments (such as on marine pollution from land-based sources). UNEP's Regional Seas Programme has been particularly successful, and could serve as a model for some other areas of special concern, especially international river basins.

UNEP's catalytic and co-ordinating role in the UN system can and should be reinforced and extended. In its future work on critical environmental protection issues, UNEP should focus particularly on:

- developing, testing, and helping to apply practical and simple methodologies for environmental assessment at project and national levels;
- extending international agreements (such as on chemicals and hazardous wastes) more widely;
- extending the Regional Seas Programme;
- developing a similar programme for international river basins; and
- identifying the need for and advising other UN organizations and agencies in establishing and carrying out technical assistance and training courses for environmental protection and management.

Priority to Global Environmental Assessment and Reporting. Although more is known about the state of the global environment now than a decade ago, there are still major gaps and a limited international capability for monitoring, collecting, and combining basic and comparable data needed for authoritative overviews of key environmental issues and trends. Without such, the information needed to help set priorities and develop effective policies will remain limited.

UNEP, as the main UN source for environmental data, assessment, and reporting, should guide the global agenda for scientific research and technological development for environmental protection. To this end, the data collection, assessment, and state of the environment reporting functions (Earthwatch) of UNEP need to be significantly strengthened as a major priority. The Global Environment Monitoring System should be expanded as rapidly as possible, and the development of the Global Resource Information Database should be accelerated to bridge the gap between environmental assessment and management. Special priority should be accorded to providing support to developing countries to enable them to participate fully in and derive maximum benefits from these programmes.

Strengthen International Environmental Co-operation. The UNEP Governing Council cannot fulfill its primary role of providing leadership and policy guidance in the UN system nor have a significant influence on national policies unless governments increase their participation and the level of representation. National delegations to future meetings should preferably be led by Ministers, with their senior policy and scientific advisers. Special provisions should be made for expanded and more meaningful participation by major non-governmental organizations at future sessions.

Increase the Revenue and Focus of the Environment Fund. The UNEP voluntary funding base of $30 million annually is too limited and vulnerable for an international fund dedicated to serving and protecting the common interests, security, and future of humanity. Six countries alone provided over 75 per cent of the 1985 contributions to the Environment Fund (the United States, Japan, USSR, Sweden, the Federal Republic of Germany, and the United Kingdom). Considering the critical importance of renewed efforts on environmental protection and improvement, the Commission appeals to all governments to substantially enlarge the Environment Fund both through direct contributions by all members of the UN and through some of the sources cited later in this chapter in the section 'Investing in Our Future'.

A substantial enlargement of the Environment Fund seems unlikely in the current climate of financial austerity. Any additional funds made available by states for UN development programmes and activities will likely be channelled largely through UNDP and the development programmes of other UN agencies. Moreover, as recommended earlier, the budgets of all of those agencies should be deployed so that environmental considerations are built into the planning and implementation of all programmes and projects.

The Environment Fund can be made more effective by refocusing the programme on fewer activities. As other UN agencies assume full responsibility for certain activities now provided through the Environment Fund and finance them entirely from their own budgets, some resources will be released for other purposes. These should be concentrated on the principal functions and priority areas identified earlier.

Expanding support and co-operation with NGOs capable of carrying out elements of UNEP's programme will also increase the effectiveness of the Environment Fund. Over the last decade, non-governmental organizations and networks have become increasingly important in work to improve environmental protection locally, nationally, and internationally. However, financial support from the Environment Fund for co-operative projects with NGOs declined in both absolute and relative terms in the last 10 years, from $4.5 million (23 per cent of the Fund) in 1976 to $3.6 million (13 per cent) in 1985. The amount and proportion of Environment Fund resources for co-operation and projects with NGOs should be significantly increased by using the capacities of those NGOs that can contribute to UNEP's programmes on a cost-effective basis.

Assessing Global Risks

The future—even a sustainable future—will be marked by increasing risk. The risks associated with new technologies are growing. The numbers, scale, frequency, and impact of natural and human-caused disasters are mounting. The risks of irreversible damage to natural systems regionally (for example through acidification, desertification, or deforestation) and globally (through ozone layer depletion or climate change) are becoming significant.

Fortunately, the capacity to monitor and map Earth change and to assess risk is also growing rapidly. Data from remote sensing platforms in space can now be merged with data from conventional land-based sources. Augmented by digital communications and advanced information analysis, photos, mapping, and other techniques, these data can provide up-to-date information on a wide variety of resource, climatic, pollution, and other variables. High-speed data communications technologies, including the personal computer, enable this information to be shared by individuals as well as corporate and governmental users at costs that are steadily falling. Concerted efforts should be made to ensure that all nations gain access to them and the information they provide either directly or through the UNEP Earthwatch and other special programmes.

Governments, individually and collectively, have the principal responsibility to collect this information systematically and use it to assess risks, but to date only a few have developed a capacity to do so. Some intergovernmental agencies have a capacity to collect and assess information required for risk assessment, such as FAO on soil and forest cover and on fisheries; the World Meteorological Organization on climate; UNEP on deserts, pollutants, and regional seas. Quasi-governmental organizations like IUCN have a similar capacity. These are only a few examples from a long list. But no intergovernmental agency has been recognized as the centre of leadership to stimulate work on risk assessment and to provide an authoritative source of reports and advice on evolving risks. This gap needs to be filled both within and among governments. Beyond our proposal that the global environment assessment and reporting functions of UNEP should be significantly strengthened, the Commission would now propose that UNEP's Earthwatch be recognized as the centre of leadership on risk assessment in the UN system.

But neither UNEP nor other intergovernmental organizations can be expected to carry out these important functions alone. To be effective, given the politically sensitive nature of many of the most critical risks, intergovernmental risk assessment needs to be supported by independent capacities outside of government. Several national science academies and international scientific groups—such as the International Council of Scientific Unions and its Scientific Committee on Problems of the Environment, with special programmes such as the newly inaugurated International Geosphere-Biosphere Programme [. . .] the Man and the Biosphere Programme of UNESCO; quasi-governmental bodies such as IUCN; and certain industry groups and NGOs—are active in this field. But, again, there is no recognized international non-governmental centre of leadership through which the efforts of these groups can be focused and co-ordinated.

During the 1970s, the growing capacity of computers led various governments, institutes, and international bodies to develop models for integrated policy analysis. They have provided significant insights and offer great promise as a means of anticipating the consequences of interdependent trends and of establishing the policy options to address them. Without suggesting any relationship between them, early attempts were all limited by serious inconsistencies in the methods and assumptions employed by the various sources on which they depended for data and information. Although significant improvements have been made in the capability of models and other techniques, the data base remains weak.

There is an urgent need to strengthen and focus the capacities of these and other bodies to complement and support UNEP's monitoring and assessment functions by providing timely, objective, and authoritative assessments and public reports on critical threats and risks to the world community. To meet this need, we recommend the establishment of a Global Risks Assessment Programme:

- to identify critical threats to the survival, security, or well-being of all or a majority of people, globally or regionally;
- to assess the causes and likely human, economic, and ecological consequences of those threats, and to report regularly and publicly on their findings;
- to provide authoritative advice and proposals on what should or must be done to avoid, reduce, or, if possible, adapt to those threats; and
- to provide an additional source of advice and support to governments and intergovernmental organizations for the implementation of programmes and policies designed to address such threats.

The Global Risk Assessment Programme would not require the creation of a new international institution as such, as it should function primarily as a mechanism for co-operation among largely non-governmental national and international organizations, scientific bodies, and industry groups. To provide intellectual leadership and guide the programme, there should be a steering group composed of eminent individuals who together would reflect a broad cross-section of the major areas of knowledge, vocations, and regions of the world, as well as the major bodies active in the field.

The steering group would serve as the focal point for identifying the risks to be addressed by the programme, agreeing on the research needed to assess those risks, and co-ordinating the work among the various participating bodies. It could form special consortia and task forces made up of experts from these bodies and it would also establish special expert and advisory groups consisting of world-known authorities in specialized areas of science, economics, and law. The steering group would be responsible for the overall evaluation of results, for their wide dissemination, and for follow-up activities.

The steering group would also be charged with helping mobilize funds for implementing the programme through contributions by the Environment Fund of UNEP, states, foundations, and other private sources. Funding would principally be for the purpose of financing the various activities that would be carried out by other organizations as part of the programme, with only a small portion required to meet the costs of the steering group.

Making Informed Choices

As is evident from this report, the transition to sustainable development will require a range of public policy choices that are inherently complex and politically difficult. Reversing unsustainable development policies at the national and international level will require immense efforts to inform the public and secure its support. The scientific community, private and community groups, and NGOs, can play a central role in this.

Increase the Role of the Scientific Community and Non-Governmental Organizations. Scientific groups and NGOs have played—with the help of young people—a major part in the environmental movement from its earliest beginnings.

Scientists were the first to point out evidence of significant environmental risks and changes resulting from the growing intensity of human activities. Other non-governmental organizations and citizens' groups pioneered in the creation of public awareness and political pressures that stimulated governments to act. Scientific and non-governmental communities played a vital role in the United Nations Conference on the Human Environment in Stockholm.

These groups have also played an indispensable role since the Stockholm Conference in identifying risks, in assessing environmental impacts and designing and implementing measures to deal with them, and in maintaining the high degree of public and political interest required as a basis for action. Today, major national 'State of the Environment' reports are being published by some NGOs (in Malaysia, India, and the United States, for instance). Several international NGOs have produced significant reports on the status of and prospects for the global environment and natural resource base.

The vast majority of these bodies are national or local in nature, and a successful transition to sustainable development will require substantial strengthening of their capacities. To an increasing extent, national NGOs draw strength from association with their counterparts in other countries and from participation in international programmes and consultations. NGOs in developing countries are particularly in need of international support—professional and moral as well as financial—to carry out their roles effectively.

Many international bodies and coalitions of NGOs are now in place and active. They play an important part in ensuring that national NGOs and scientific bodies have access to the support they require. These include regional groups providing networks linking together environment and development NGOs in Asia, Africa, Eastern and Western Europe, and North and South America. They also include a number of regional and global coalitions on critical issues such as pesticides, chemicals, rain, seeds, genetic resources, and development assistance. A global network for information exchange and joint action is provided through the Environment Liaison Centre (ELC) in Nairobi. ELC has over 230 NGO member groups, with the majority from developing countries, and is in contact with 7,000 others.

Only a few international NGOs deal on a broad basis with both environment and development issues, but this is changing rapidly. One of them, the International Institute for Environment and Development, has long specialized in these issues and pioneered the conceptual basis for the environment/development relationship. Most of them work with and support related organizations in the developing world. They facilitate their participation in international activities and their links with counterparts in the international community. They provide instruments for leadership and co-operation among a wide variety of organizations in their respective constituencies. These capabilities will be ever more important in the future. An increasing number of environment and development issues could not be tackled without them.

NGOs should give a high priority to the continuation of their present networking on development co-operation projects and programmes, directed at the improvement of the performance of NGO bilateral and multilateral development programmes.

They could increase their efforts to share resources, exchange skills, and strengthen each other's capacities through greater international co-operation in this area. In setting their own house in order, 'environment' NGOs should assist 'development' NGOs in reorienting projects that degrade the environment and in formulating projects that contribute to sustainable development. The experience gained would provide a useful basis for continuing discussion with bilateral and multilateral agencies as to steps that these agencies might take to improve their performance.

In many countries, governments need to recognize and extend NGOs' right to know and have access to information on the environment and natural resources; their right to be consulted and to participate in decision making on activities likely to have a significant effect on their environment; and their right to legal remedies and redress when their health or environment has been or may be seriously affected.

NGOs and private and community groups can often provide an efficient and effective alternative to public agencies in the delivery of programmes and projects. Moreover, they can sometimes reach target groups that public agencies cannot. Bilateral and multilateral development assistance agencies, especially UNDP and the World Bank, should draw upon NGOs in executing programmes and projects. At the national level, governments, foundations, and industry should also greatly extend their co-operation with NGOs in planning, monitoring, and evaluating as well as in carrying out projects when they can provide the necessary capabilities on a cost-effective basis. To this end, governments should establish or strengthen procedures for official consultation and more meaningful participation by NGOs in all relevant intergovernmental organizations.

International NGOs need substantially increased financial support to expand their special roles and functions on behalf of the world community and in support of national NGOs. In the Commission's view, the increased support that will allow these organizations to expand their services represents an indispensable and cost-effective investment. The Commission recommends that these organizations be accorded high priority by governments, foundations, and other private and public sources of funding.

Increase Co-operation with Industry. Industry is on the leading edge of the interface between people and the environment. It is perhaps the main instrument of change that affects the environmental resource bases of development, both positively and negatively. [. . .] Both industry and government, therefore, stand to benefit from working together more closely.

World industry has taken some significant steps through voluntary guidelines concerning industry practices on environment, natural resources, science, and technology. Although few of these guidelines have been extended to or applied regionally in Africa, Asia, or Latin America, industry continues to address these issues through various international associations.

These efforts were advanced significantly by the 1984 World Industry Conference on Environmental Management (WICEM). Recently, as a follow-up to WICEM, several major corporations from a number of developed countries formed the International Environment Bureau to assist developing countries with their environment/development needs. Such initiatives are promising and should be encouraged. Co-operation between governments and industry would be further facilitated if they established joint advisory councils for sustainable development—for mutual advice, assistance, and co-operation in helping to shape and implement policy, laws, and regulations for more sustainable forms of development. Internationally, governments in co-operation with industry and NGOs should work through appropriate regional organizations to develop basic codes of conduct for sustainable development, drawing on and extending relevant existing voluntary codes, especially in Africa, Asia, and Latin America.

The private sector also has a major impact on development through commercial bank loans from within and outside countries. In 1983, for example, the proportion of the total net receipts of developing countries from private sources, mostly in the form of commercial bank loans, was greater than all ODA that year. Since 1983, as indebtedness worsened, commercial bank lending to developing countries has declined.

Efforts are being made to stimulate private investment. These efforts should be geared to supporting sustainable development. The industrial and financial corporations making such investments, and the export credit, investment insurance, and other programmes that facilitate them, should incorporate sustainable development criteria into their policies.

Providing the Legal Means

National and international law has traditionally lagged behind events. Today, legal regimes are being rapidly outdistanced by the accelerating pace and expanding scale of impacts on the environmental base of development. Human laws must be reformulated to keep human activities in harmony with the unchanging and universal laws of nature. There is an urgent need:

- to recognize and respect the reciprocal rights and responsibilities of individuals and states regarding sustainable development,
- to establish and apply new norms for state and interstate behaviour to achieve sustainable development,
- to strengthen and extend the application of existing laws and international agreements in support of sustainable development, and
- to reinforce existing methods and develop new procedures for avoiding and resolving environmental disputes.

Recognizing Rights and Responsibilities. Principle 1 of the 1972 Stockholm Declaration said that 'Man has the fundamental right to freedom, equality and adequate conditions of life, in an environment of a quality that permits a life of dignity and well-being. It further proclaimed the solemn responsibility of governments to protect and improve the environment for both present and future generations. After the Stockholm Conference, several states recognized in their Constitutions or laws the right to an adequate environment and the obligation of the state to protect that environment.

Recognition by states of their responsibility to ensure an adequate environment for present as well as future generations is an important step towards sustainable development. However, progress will also be facilitated by recognition of, for example, the right of individuals to know and have access to current information on the state of the environment and natural resources, the right to be consulted and to participate in decision making on activities likely to have a significant effect on the environment, and the right to legal remedies and redress for those whose health or environment has been or may be seriously affected.

The enjoyment of any right requires respect for the similar rights of others, and recognition of reciprocal and even joint responsibilities. States have a responsibility towards their own citizens and other states:

- to maintain ecosystems and related ecological processes essential for the functioning of the biosphere;
- to maintain biological diversity by ensuring the survival and promoting the conservation in their natural habitats of all species of flora and fauna;
- to observe the principle of optimum sustainable yield in the exploitation of living natural resources and ecosystems;
- to prevent or abate significant environmental pollution or harm;
- to establish adequate environmental protection standards;
- to undertake or require prior assessments to ensure that major new policies, projects, and technologies contribute to sustainable development; and
- to make all relevant information public without delay in all cases of harmful or potentially harmful releases of pollutants, especially radioactive releases.

It is recommended that governments take appropriate steps to recognize these reciprocal rights and responsibilities. However, the wide variation in national legal systems and practices makes it impossible to propose an approach that would be valid everywhere. Some countries have amended their basic laws or constitution; others are considering the adoption of a special national law or charter setting out the rights and responsibilities of citizens and the state regarding environmental protection and sustainable development. Others may wish to consider the designation of a national council or public representative or 'ombudsman' to represent the interests and rights of present and future generations and act as an environmental watchdog, alerting governments and citizens to any emerging threats.

A Universal Declaration and a Convention on Environmental Protection and Sustainable Development. Building on the 1972 Stockholm Declaration, the 1982 Nairobi Declaration, and many existing international conventions and General Assembly resolutions, there is now a need to consolidate and extend relevant legal principles in a new charter to guide state behaviour in the transition to sustainable development. It would provide the basis for, and be subsequently expanded into, a Convention, setting out the sovereign rights and reciprocal responsibilities of all states on environmental protection and sustainable development. The charter should prescribe new norms for state and interstate behaviour needed to maintain livelihoods and life on our shared planet, including basic norms for prior notification, consultation, and assessment of activities likely to have an impact on neighbouring states or global commons. These could include the obligation to alert and inform neighbouring states in the event of an accident likely to have a harmful impact on their environment. Although a few such norms have evolved in some bilateral and regional arrangements, the lack of wider agreement on such basic rules for interstate behaviour undermines both the sovereignty and economic development potential of each and all states.

We recommend that the General Assembly commit itself to preparing a universal Declaration and later a Convention on environmental protection and sustainable development. A special negotiating group could be established to draft a Declaration text for adoption in 1988. Once it is approved, that group could then proceed to prepare a Convention, based on and extending the principles in the Declaration, with the aim of having an agreed Convention text ready for signature by states within three to five years. To facilitate the early launching of that process the Commission has submitted for consideration by the General Assembly, and as a starting point for the deliberations of the special negotiating group, a number of proposed legal principles embodied in 22 Articles that were prepared by its group of international legal experts. These proposed principles are submitted to assist the General Assembly in its deliberations and have not been approved or considered in detail by the Commission. A summary of the principles and Articles appears as Annexe 1 of this report.

Strengthen and Extend Existing International Conventions and Agreements. In parallel, governments should accelerate their efforts to strengthen and extend existing and more specific international conventions and co-operative arrangements by:

- acceding to or ratifying existing global and regional conventions dealing with environment and development, and applying them with more vigour and rigour;
- reviewing and revising those relevant conventions that need to be brought in line with the latest available technical and scientific information; and
- negotiating new global and regional conventions or arrangements aimed at promoting co-operation and co-ordination in the field of environment and development (including, for example, new conventions and agreements on climate change, on hazardous chemicals and wastes, and on preserving biological diversity).

It is recommended that the UNEP secretariat, in close co-operation with the IUCN Environmental Law Centre, should help in these efforts.

Avoiding and Settling Environmental Disputes. Many disputes can be avoided or more readily resolved if the principles, rights, and responsibilities cited earlier are built into national and international legal frameworks and are fully respected and implemented by many states. Individuals and states are more reluctant to act in a way that might lead to a dispute when, as in many national legal systems, there is an established and effective capacity as well as ultimately binding procedures for settling disputes. Such a capacity and procedures are largely lacking at the international level, particularly on environmental and natural resource management issues.

It is recommended that public and private organizations and NGOs help in this area by establishing special panels or rosters of experts with experience in various forms of dispute settlement and special competence on the legal and substantive aspects of environmental protection, natural resources management, and sustainable development. In addition, a consolidated inventory and referral system or network for responding to requests for advice and assistance in avoiding or resolving such disputes should be established.

To promote the peaceful and early settlement of international disputes on environmental and resource management problems, it is recommended that the following procedure be adopted. States should be given up to 18 months to reach mutual agreement on a solution or on a common dispute settlement arrangement. If agreement is not reached, then the dispute can be submitted to conciliation at the request of any one of the concerned states and, if still unresolved, thereafter to arbitration or judicial settlement.

This proposed new procedure raises the possibility of invoking a binding process of dispute settlement at the request of any state. Binding settlement is not the preferred method of settling international disputes. But such a provision is now needed not only as a last resort to avoid prolonged disputes and possible serious environmental damage, but also to encourage and provide an incentive for all parties to reach agreement within a reasonable time on either a solution or a mutually agreed means, such as mediation.

The capabilities of the Permanent Court of Arbitration and the International Court of Justice to deal with environmental and resource management problems also should be strengthened. States should make greater use of the World Court's capacity under Article 26 of its Statute to form special chambers for dealing with particular cases or categories of cases, including environmental protection or resource management cases. The Court has declared its willingness and readiness to deal with such cases fully and promptly.

Investing in Our Future

We have endeavoured to show that it makes long-term economic sense to pursue environmentally sound policies. But potentially very large financial outlays will be needed in the short term in such fields as renewable energy development, pollution control equipment, and integrated rural development. Developing countries will need massive assistance for this purpose, and more generally to reduce poverty. Responding to this financial need will be a collective investment in the future.

National Action. Past experience teaches us that these outlays would be good investments. By the late 1960s, when some industrial countries began to mount significant environmental protection programmes, they had already incurred heavy economic costs in the form of damage to human health, property, natural resources, and the environment. After 1970, in order to roll back some of this damage, they saw expenditures on environmental pollution measures alone rise from about 0.3 per cent of GNP in 1970 to somewhere between 1.5 per cent and, in some countries, 2.0 per cent around the end of the decade. Assuming low levels of economic growth in the future, these same countries will probably have to increase expenditures on environmental protection somewhere between 20 to 100 per cent just to maintain current levels of environmental quality.

These figures relate only to expenditures to control environmental pollution. Unfortunately, similar figures are not available on the level of expenditures made to rehabilitate lands and natural habitats, re-establish soil fertility, reforest areas, and undertake other measures to restore the resource base. But they would be substantial.

Nations, industrial and developing, that did not make these investments have paid much more in terms of damage costs to human health, property, natural resources, and the environment. And these costs continue to rise at an accelerating pace. Indeed, countries that have not yet instituted strong programmes now face the need for very large investments. Not only do they need to roll back the first generation of environmental damage, they also need to begin to catch up with the rising incidence of future damage. If they do not, their fundamental capital assets, their environmental resources, will continue to decline.

In strictly economic terms, the benefits of these expenditures have been generally greater than the costs in those countries that have made them. Beyond that, however, many of these countries found that economic, regulatory, and other environmental measures could be applied in ways that would result in innovation by industry. And those companies that did respond innovatively are today often in the forefront of their industry. They have developed new products, new processes, and entire plants that use less water, energy, and other resources per unit of output and are hence more economic and competitive.

Nations that begin to reorient major economic and sectoral policies along the lines proposed in this report can avoid much higher future levels of spending on environmental restoration and curative measures and also enhance their future economic prospects. By making central and sectoral agencies directly responsible for maintaining and enhancing environmental and resource stocks, expenditures for environmental protection and resource management would gradually be built into the budgets of those agencies for measures to prevent damage. The unavoidable costs of environmental and resource management would thus be paid only once.

International Action. Developing countries, as stated earlier, need a significant increase in financial support from international sources for environmental restoration, protection, and improvement and to help them through the necessary transition to sustainable development.

At the global level, there is an extensive institutional capacity to channel this support. This consists of the United Nations and its specialized agencies; the multilateral development banks, notably the World Bank; other multilateral development co-operation organizations, such as those of the European Economic Community; national development assistance agencies, most of whom co-operate within the framework of the Development Assistance Committee of OECD or of the Organization of Petroleum-Exporting Countries; and other international groups, such as the Consultative Group on International Agricultural Research, that play an important role and influence on the quality and nature of development assistance. Together, the development organizations and agencies are responsible for the transfer of about $35 billion of ODA annually to developing countries. In addition, they are the source of most technical assistance and policy advice and support to developing countries.

These organizations and agencies are the principal instruments through which the development partnership between industrial and developing countries operates and, collectively, their influence is substantial and pervasive. It is imperative that they play a leading role in helping developing countries make the transition to sustainable development. Indeed, it is difficult to envisage developing countries making this transition in an effective and timely manner without their full commitment and support.

Reorienting Multilateral Financial Institutions. The World Bank, International Monetary Fund (IMF), and regional Development Banks warrant special attention because of their major influence on economic development throughout the world. [. . . T]here is an urgent need for much larger flows of concessional and non-concessional finance through the multilateral agencies. The role of the World Bank is especially important in this respect, both as the largest single source of development lending and for its policy leadership, which exerts a significant influence on both developing countries and donors. The World Bank has taken a significant lead in reorienting its lending programmes to a much higher sensitivity to environmental concerns and to support for sustainable development. This is a promising beginning. But it will not be enough unless and until it is accompanied by a fundamental commitment to sustainable development by the World Bank, and by the transformation of its internal structure and processes so as to ensure its capacity to carry this out. The same is true of other multilateral development banks and agencies.

The IMF also exerts a major influence on the development policies of developing countries and [. . .] there is deep concern in many countries that the conditions accompany its lending are undermining sustainable development. It is therefore essential that the IMF, too, incorporate sustainable development objectives and criteria into its policies and programmes.

Several countries have already formally instructed their representatives on the Board of the World Bank to ensure that the environmental impacts of projects proposed for approval have been assessed and adequately taken into account. We recommend that other governments take similar action, not only with regard to the World Bank but also in the Regional Banks and the other institutions. In this way they can support the ongoing efforts within the Banks and other institutions to reorient and refocus their mandates, programmes, and budgets to support sustainable development. The transition to sustainable development by the development assistance agencies and the IMF would be facilitated by the establishment of a high-level office in each agency with the authority and resources to ensure that all policies, projects, and loan conditions support sustainable development, and to prepare and publish annual assessments and reports on progress made and needed. A first step is to develop simple methodologies for such assessments, recognizing that they are at present experimental and need further work.

In making these changes, the multilateral financial institutions fortunately have some base on which to build. In 1980, they endorsed a Declaration of Environmental Policies and Procedures Relating to Economic Development. Since then they have been meeting and consulting through the Committee of International Development Institutions on the Environment (CIDIE). Some have articulated clear policies and project guidelines for incorporating environmental concerns and assessments into their planning and decision making, but only a few have assigned staff and resources to implement them, notably the World Bank, which is now considering even further institutional changes to strengthen this work. Overall, as pointed out by the UNEP Executive Director in his statement reviewing the first five years of work, 'CIDIE has not yet truly succeeded in getting environmental considerations firmly ingrained in development policies. There has been a distinct lack of action by several multilaterals.' CIDIE members have 'gone along with the Declaration in principle more than in major shifts in action.'

In order to marshal and support investments in conservation projects and national conservation strategies that enhance the resource base for development, serious consideration should be given to the development of a special international banking programme or facility linked to the World Bank. Such a special conservation banking programme or facility could provide loans and facilitate joint financial arrangements for the development and protection of critical habitats and ecosystems, including those of international significance, supplementing efforts by bilateral aid agencies, multilateral financial institutions, and commercial banks.

In the framework of the Council of Mutual Economic Assistance, there has been since the early 1970s a Committee for Environmental Protection with the participation of the heads of appropriate organizations in the member states. This Committee coordinates the relevant research and development programmes and, in some cases, organizes technical assistance for the interested member states, involving the Investment Bank of CMEA.

Reorienting Bilateral Aid Agencies. Bilateral aid agencies presently provide nearly four times as much total ODA as is provided by international organizations. [. . . A] new priority and focus in bilateral aid agencies is needed in three main areas:

- new measures to ensure that all projects support sustainable development;
- special programmes to help restore, protect, and improve the ecological basis for development in many developing countries; and
- special programmes for strengthening the institutional and professional capacities needed for sustainable development.

Proposals for special bilateral aid programmes in the areas of agriculture, forestry, energy, industry, human settlements, and genetic resources are made in earlier chapters of this report. The first two priority areas in this chapter also contain proposals for strengthening the institutional and professional capacities in developing countries. The focus here is therefore on the first area: new measures to ensure that all bilateral aid projects support sustainable development.

Over the past decade, bilateral aid agencies have gradually given more attention to the environmental dimensions of their programmes and projects. A 1980 survey of the environmental procedures and practices of six major bilateral aid agencies indicated that only one, the US Agency for International Development, had systematic and enforceable procedures backed by the staff resources necessary to carry them out. Since then, others have made some progress on the policy level, increased funds for environmental projects, and produced guidelines or checklists to guide their programmes. However, a 1983 study of those guidelines concluded that there was little evidence of their systematic application.

An important step towards concerted action was taken in 1986 with the adoption by OECD of a recommendation to member governments to include an environmental assessment policy and effective procedures for applying it in their bilateral aid programmes. It is based on a detailed analysis and studies carried out by a joint group of governmental experts from both the Development Assistance Committee and the Environmental Committee. The recommendation includes proposals for adequate staff and financial resources to undertake environmental assessments and a central office in each agency to supervise implementation and to assist developing countries wishing to improve their capacities for conducting environmental assessments. We urge all bilateral aid agencies to implement this recommendation as quickly as possible. It is essential, of course, that this should not reduce aid flows in the aggregate or slow disbursements or represent a new form of aid conditionality.

New Sources of Revenue and Automatic Financing. We have made a series of proposals for institutional change within and among the organizations and specialized agencies of the UN system in sections on 'Getting at the Sources' and 'Dealing with the Effects'. Most of those changes will not require additional financial resources but can be achieved through a reorientation of existing mandates, programmes, and budgets and a redeployment of present staff. Once implemented, those measures will make a major difference in the effective use of existing resources in making the transition to sustainable development.

Nevertheless, there is also a need to increase the financial resources for new multilateral efforts and programmes of action for environmental protection and sustainable development. These new funds will not be easy to come by if the international organizations through which they flow have to continue to rely solely on traditional sources of financing: assessed contributions from governments, voluntary contributions by governments, and funds borrowed in capital markets by the World Bank and other international financial institutions.

Assessed contributions from governments have traditionally been used largely for the administrative and operating costs of international organizations; they are not intended for multilateral assistance. The total assessed contributions from governments are much smaller than the amount provided through voluntary contributions and the prospects of raising significant additional funds through assessed contributions are limited.

Voluntary contributions by governments give the overall revenue system some flexibility, but they cannot be adjusted readily to meet new or increased requirements. Being voluntary, the flow of these funds is entirely discretionary and unpredictable. The commitments are also extremely short-term, as pledges are normally made only one or two years in advance. Consequently, they provide little security or basis for effective planning and management of international actions requiring sustained, longer-term efforts. Most of the limited funds provided so far for international environmental action have come through voluntary contributions, channelled principally through UNEP and NGOs.

Given the current constraints on major sources and modes of funding, it is necessary to consider new approaches as well as new sources of revenue for financing international action in support of sustainable development. The Commission recognizes that such proposals may not appear politically realistic at this point in time. It believes, however, that—given the trends discussed in this report—the need to support sustainable development will become so imperative that political realism will come to require it.

The search for other, and especially more automatic, sources and means for financing international action goes almost as far back as the UN itself. It was not until 1977, however, when the Plan of Action to Combat Desertification was approved by the UN General Assembly that governments officially accepted, but never implemented, the principle of automatic transfers. That Plan called for the establishment of a special account that could draw resources not only from traditional sources but also from additional measures of financing, 'including fiscal measures entailing automaticity'.

Since then, a series of studies and reports have identified and examined a growing list of new sources of potential revenue, including:

- revenue from the use of international commons (from ocean fishing and transportation, from sea-bed mining, from Antarctic resources, or from parking charges for geostationary communications satellites, for example);
- taxes on international trade (such as a general trade tax; taxes on special traded commodities, on invisible exports, or on surpluses in balance of trade; or a consumption tax on luxury goods); and
- international financial measures (a link between special drawing rights and development finance, for example, or IMF gold reserves and sales).

In its 1980 report, the Brandt Commission called for raising additional funds from more automatic sources such as those cited above. In its follow-up report in 1983, the Brandt Commission strongly urged that these most 'futuristic' of all the Report's proposals not be lost completely from view. Nevertheless, they again sank below the short-term horizon of the international agenda.

The World Commission on Environment and Development was specifically given the mandate by the UN General Assembly to look once again beyond that limited horizon. We have done so and, given the compelling nature, pace, and scope of the different transitions affecting our economic and ecological systems as described in this report, we consider that at least some of those proposals for additional and more automatic sources of revenue are fast becoming less futuristic and more necessary. This Commission particularly considers that the proposals regarding revenue from the use of international commons and natural resources now warrant and should receive serious consideration by governments and the General Assembly.

III. A CALL FOR ACTION

Over the course of this century, the relationship between the human world and the planet that sustains it has undergone a profound change. When the century began, neither human numbers nor technology had the power to radically alter planetary systems. As the century closes, not only do vastly increased human numbers and their activities have that power, but major, unintended changes are occurring in the atmosphere, in soils, in waters, among plants and animals, and in the relationships among all of these. The rate of change is outstripping the ability of scientific disciplines and our current capabilities to assess and advise. It is frustrating the attempts of political and economic institutions, which evolved in a different, more fragmented world, to adapt and cope. It deeply worries many people who are seeking ways to place those concerns on the political agendas.

We have been careful to base our recommendations on the realities of present institutions, on what can and must be accomplished today. But to keep options open for future generations, the present generation must begin now, and begin together, nationally and internationally.

To achieve the needed change in attitude and reorientation of policies and institutions, the Commission believes that an active follow-up of this report is imperative. It is with this in mind that we call for the UN General Assembly, upon due consideration, to transform this report into a UN Programme of Action on Sustainable Development. Special follow-up conferences could be initiated at the regional level. Within an appropriate period after the presentation of the report to the General Assembly, an International Conference could be convened to review progress made and promote follow-up arrangements that will be needed over time to set benchmarks and to maintain human progress within the guidelines of human needs and natural laws.

The Commissioners came from 21 very different nations. In our discussions, we disagreed often on details and priorities. But despite our widely differing backgrounds and varying national and international responsibilities, we were able to agree to the lines along which the institutional change must be drawn.

We are unanimous in our conviction that the security, well-being, and very survival of the planet depend on such changes, now.

PART THREE

THE UNITED NATIONS AND THE FUTURE

General Introduction

As we have stressed throughout this volume the world system is growing more integrated, more fragile, and more vulnerable to catastrophic rupture. Breakdowns of economic, ecological, and political arrangements have become increasingly difficult to contain. There is growing evidence that rates of pollution, population growth, and urbanization are overwhelming existing global capacities.

In such a setting, the United Nations by now is generally appreciated as being indispensable, but it is also in danger of being overwhelmed by pressures to perform beyond its means or of being distracted by the politics of the hour. The UN is held on a short leash by the principal donor governments. These governments zig and zag with respect to their degree of UN commitment. Most governments remain overwhelmingly concerned with the inner realities of their countries. They are rarely willing to devote resources or even serious attention to the United Nations. Their acknowledgment of a global agenda remains largely rhetorical. No shifts in fundamental behavioral patterns are discernible.

In our judgment, for many reasons, the world would benefit from a stronger, more autonomous United Nations. The strength of the organization can be assessed by its rate of budgetary growth, degrees of media attention, its capacity to bring effective capabilities to bear on major world issues, and the willingness of leading states to uphold UN decisions, especially when they run counter to national policy. The organization's autonomy has to do with greater independence as to funding sources (e.g., an ocean or space use tax administered by the UN), more security from great-power criticism for principal international servants working for the United Nations, and a greater ability to reach decisions impartially—even in the face of superpower opposition.

Other dimensions of evolution seem important, but none more so than widening the circle of formal participation beyond that tightly held by sovereign states. It would be particularly appropriate to allow nongovernmental organizations (NGOs) to play a more formal role in debate (and even voting) on matters within their sphere of competence. As well, it would be desirable to give representatives of social movements a forum within the United Nations and even a procedure by which to mount grievances. The UN Commission on Human Rights has been moving, although cautiously, in this direction. Finally, it may be time to propose seriously the possibility of "a second assembly"—a peoples' assembly of the UN—in which representatives from different regions are selected by direct popular vote.

As we have stressed, the history of the United Nations can be read as a cyclical pattern of hopes raised and hopes dashed or as a linear spiral of either an ascending or a descending character. In effect, we can perceive the United Nations as an arena of repetition and continuity, exhibiting mainly small variations in mood and role but essentially keeping its character as a subordinate set of actors in the form of international institutions, acting at the disposal of the states. We can also perceive the United Nations as poised in this last decade of the millennium to receive a massive input of resources as the last best hope of human survival and even betterment. The positive attitude of the Soviet Union, if it persists and elicits reciprocal responses, is a hopeful and, from the perspective of only a few years earlier, totally unexpected development.

There is no doubt that the world political system is far more difficult to manage from the level of the soverign state than it appeared to be in 1945. This is generally understood, despite an offsetting complacency that reflects the avoidance of any truly catastrophic breakdown during these several decades. Somehow, the avoidance of a nuclear war or the outbreak of World War III over the last four-and-a-half decades fosters an illusion of stability and permanence. The political will does not yet seem to exist to make any dramatic changes in the role of the United Nations with respect to contested behavior by sovereign states. Leading governments reserve their option to defy UN decisions and expect few serious adverse consequences to follow from such defiance.

Perhaps, without too much wishful thinking, the coming of the year 2000 will inspire grander visions of the future and stimulate a penchant for innovation. Bold and imaginative statespersons from a caucus of states, perhaps drawing notable thinkers and moral authority figures into their circle, might even be ready to propose a constitutional convocation for the year 1997 under UN auspices with the objective of planning the structure of a more ambitious sequel to the existing organization as the institutional basis for world order in the next century.

Millennial consciousness may also be encouraged by a gathering storm of ominous ecological warnings. The dangers associated with acid rain, ozone depletion, deforestation, ocean pollution, and global warming are likely to grow worse. It is also probable that catastrophic accidents like those at Chernobyl and Bhopal will deepen, sharpen, and widen the inchoate vision of a shared planetary destiny. Dark conjurings of the future will undoubtedly abound in the next decade, but it is also likely that political leaders of states will be more receptive to globalist, long-range thinking. In this regard, Gorbachev may be a precursor of a new world outlook, as well as a startlingly innovative influence on the world stage. The very unexpectedness of Gorbachev's shift in the Soviet approach to international relations suggests that we should not foreclose even seemingly improbable changes in the world. We also need to appreciate that Gorbachev may fall from power and his outlook be supplanted and that other unanticipated advances and setbacks in the world order prospects are likely to occur in the decade ahead.

Against the background of such expectations, students and intellectuals must let their imaginations run ahead of current expectations. It is important not to be fenced in by the prevailing consensus as to what is possible. This imperative to let the political imagination flourish applies to all domains of human endeavor, but we focus here on institutional arrangements of global scope that proceed from the base reality of the United Nations in 1990. The purpose of this last section of the volume is to generate a dialogue on what kinds of changes initiated by what social forces and political actors can improve the UN's capacity to contribute to the realization of world order values. The related purpose is to return to the question posed at the outset—How can the United Nations be developed as an actor and arena (or as a group of distinct actors and arenas) that helps fulfill the normative potential of a world order constituted primarily of sovereign states? Is the United Nations itself a catalyst for the emergence of a new world order that is likely to ensure human survival and the satisfaction of basic human needs?

The United Nations
at a Crossroads

INTRODUCTION

In thinking about the future of the United Nations, we would do well to acknowledge an indeterminacy of prospect, a circumstance expressed by the section title. This indeterminacy is also expressed by a mixture of an increasing number of roles for the organization, especially in the peace and security area, and a persisting financial crisis that itself is part of a wider challenge mounted by some states and social forces against the legitimacy of the United Nations as it has evolved.

There is an irony in the reversal of attitudes on the part of the superpowers over the life cycle of the organization. Of course, these attitudes are in constant flux, and there are strong reasons to believe that in the years ahead, the United States will resume its generally supportive relationship with the United Nations. There are several reasons for such optimism: (1) the Bush presidency seems to be more disposed toward an internationalist stance than was the Reagan presidency; (2) the constructive Soviet participation challenges the United States to act in the same manner if it is to retain its diplomatic stature in the world; (3) the organization has accommodated some of the earlier U.S. criticisms and enjoys more congenial leadership; and (4) the organization has proved its utility in a number of regional trouble spots and is likely to be less controversial, especially if the United States becomes part of the consensus on Palestinian self-determination and the anti-apartheid campaign.

As we have argued throughout, the prospects are confusing because of these mixed signals and conflicting trends. In this section, we sample some images of a stronger, more significant United Nations (as assessed either by reference to world order values or by the normative potential implicity in the Charter conception of UN goals and principles). We seek mainly to show some promising directions of development. We do not investigate scenarios for breakdowns that could unfold if the organization finds itself consistently underfinanced or overwhelmed by problems of a world economy in disarray or by ecological challenges that impact upon the basic health and well-being of the peoples of the world.

The opening selection in this section is a substantial excerpt from the 1988 report of Secretary-General Javier Pérez de Cuéllar. This report illustrates, to a degree, a renewed sense of confidence about the important roles of the United Nations with regard to conflict resolution and peacekeeping at a regional level. The expansion of the UN agenda is also evident. The secretary-general's report also suggests the financial uncertainties that plague the work of the organization. Two directions of reform suggest themselves for consideration: more reliable and autonomous financing arrangements that are removed from the political whims of member states, and peacekeeping forces that can be trained and kept available for a variety of missions, possibly including disaster relief and natural emergencies.

The section's second offering is by Marc Nerfin, a respected veteran UN observer from Switzerland, who tries to set forth some ideas for a coherent pattern of reform, or strengthening, in light of the world situation. As with other reappraisals, it is written beneath the shadow of controversy that endangers the United Nations as an actor, yet it is also mindful of the pull of survival-oriented global problems in inducing a more powerful and representative world organization. Nerfin's proposal of "a third chamber" for citizens is worthy of our most careful reflection. Could such an innovation help lead us into the next century in a positive spirit?

The third item in this section is an executive summary of a United Nations Association (UNA) report on the future of the organization. The UNA is made up of prominent citizens who support the United Nations, but generally in the context of regarding it to be a useful instrument for promoting national interests. This kind of "realism" has been especially characteristic of the U.S. chapter of the UNA. Thus, one can read UNA publications as an expression of the level and character of mainstream support for the United Nations. UNA in its reports carefully avoids giving any impression of idealistic concern about the future of the United Nations—its approach is informational, practical, and modest.

The section's fourth selection is an example of Soviet "new thinking" on international policy issues. This offical document, associated with Vladimir Petrovsky, one of the most articulate Soviet expositors of its globalist posture, proposes using the United Nations as an arena for dialogue about how a transition to "comprehensive security" (from national security) should be facilitated by the organization. This Soviet initiative took the form of an aide-memoire to the UN secretary-general. It puts forward for discussion a series of specific steps that could enhance the UN's role and capacity in the area of peace and security. It suggests a stronger UN role and an understanding that security for the peoples of the world requires a general framework administered on behalf of the community of states. The notion of "comprehensive" is relevant in two dimensions: (1) security is about more than weapons—it is about economic, political, and cultural circumstances as well; and (2) security is not a matter of meeting military strength with military strength but of creating procedures and approaches at the global level that prevent war. The aide-memoire reiterates Soviet support for an increased use of international law to deal with disputes between states, especially increased reliance on the World Court at The Hague.

The fifth selection in this section is by Silviu Brucan, a Romanian academician who has written widely on international relations and prides himself on being a realist. It is a notable piece because of its sense that a world of states is being pushed toward transformation by fundamental tendencies toward integration in

The United Nations at a Crossroads 503

social, political, and economic spheres. Brucan, a voice from Bucharest who preceded the new thinking in Moscow but who sounds similar, regards the objective situation as requiring control mechanisms on a global scale. He moves far in the direction of advocating and predicting a development that seems close to world government and that is needed if a global collapse is to be avoided.

The section's sixth selection is by Richard A. Falk. Although not explicitly concerned with the United Nations, it reasserts the focus on transformative politics and the primacy of world order values. The essay treats new social movements as vehicles for value realization and seeks to discover whether their emergence in the contexts of resistance politics within states and transnationally has or might have global implications. Thinking about peace movements and movements for human rights and democracy, ecological defense, and feminism suggests a series of popularly based claims on (and visions of) the future. These social forces as actors take a positive attitude toward the United Nations and the Rule of Law in world affairs. Can such attitudes have political weight, or will these movements lose momentum or be coopted or repressed? Should the United Nations reach out to incorporate these forces as paths to its own reorientation and renewal?

The final selection, by Saul H. Mendlovitz, involves an application of world order thinking to the domains of action and policy. It proceeds on the assumption that populist initiatives are necessary at this stage to supplement the actions of governments and international institutions; at the same time, it envisages the activist project to be centered around the promotion of a global constitutional order capable of promoting peace and justice.

No doubt, more questions and issues need to enter the necessary dialogue on how to build a more just and humane world order as we approach the next millennium.

35. Secretary-General Pérez de Cuéllar's 1988 Report on the Work of the Organization

I

Last year, in my report on the work of the Organization, I said that the sails of the small boat in which all the people of the Earth were gathered seemed to have caught a light but favourable wind. At the time, with the clouds of controversy still dark, a less cautious metaphor would have appeared unwarranted. A succession of developments has, however, justified my reasoned hope. With careful and patient navigation, the vessel has come within sight of large sections of the shore.

The developments of the past months have not been fortuitous. They are the result of diplomatic activity sustained over the years by the United Nations and intensified recently. On matters of international peace and security, the principal organs of the United Nations have increasingly functioned in the manner envisaged in the Charter. The working relationship of the Security Council and the Secretary-General has rarely if ever been closer. I am thankful for this as also for the recent improvement in international relations at the global level that has opened new possibilities for successful action by the world body. Multilateralism has proved itself far more capable of inspiring confidence and achieving results than any of its alternatives. Millions around the world have had a gratifying demonstration of the potential of the Organization and the validity of the hopes they place in it.

The international situation is still, of course, marked by points of strain and danger, visible or lurking. Complacency about the resolution of complex problems that still face us is impermissible. However, the possibilities of bringing peace to troubled regions through the efforts of the United Nations have plainly come into view.

II

The conclusion of the Geneva Accords in April represented a major stride in the effort to secure a peaceful solution of the situation relating to Afghanistan and provide a basis for the exercise by all Afghans of their right to self-determination. It is the first instance of the world's two most powerful States becoming co-guarantors of an agreement negotiated under the auspices of the Secretary-General. The full implementation of the Accords in good faith by all the signatories will significantly serve the goal of peace in the region and the world. Immediately after the Accords came into effect, the United Nations Good Offices Mission for Afghanistan and Pakistan (UNGOMAP) began monitoring their implementation, including the withdrawal of foreign troops from Afghanistan. Moreover, within weeks thereafter, the United Nations initiated a humanitarian and economic assistance programme, with a Co-ordinator specially appointed by me, to help the people of Afghanistan in meeting their serious economic and humanitarian needs at this critical moment in their history.

On 20 August, a cease-fire was secured in the eight-year long Iran-Iraq war in the context of the full implementation of Security Council resolution 598 (1987). A United Nations Iran-Iraq Military Observer Group (UNIIMOG) was deployed as at the time and date of the cease-fire. Simultaneously, invitations were extended to the two Governments to send their representatives for direct talks at a high level under my auspices. The talks started on schedule on 25 August. The entire process has exemplified the efficacy of a mandate entrusted to the Secretary-General when actively supported by the Security Council and backed by the complementary efforts of other Member States. For success in the complex task of implementing Security Council resolution 598 (1987), it is essential that both Iran and Iraq continue to act on the conviction that genuine peace will provide to each of them opportunities for reconstruction and progress that a fragile situation cannot. On my part, I will do my utmost to help achieve the just and lasting solution envisaged by the Security Council.

There has been an improvement in prospects for the independence of Namibia. Recent diplomatic activity has made a significant contribution to the peace process in southern Africa, which should facilitate a settlement in Namibia without further delay. The date of 1 November 1988 has been recommended for beginning the implementation of Security Council resolution 435 (1978). In the light of these developments, the Secretariat has undertaken a review of its contingency plans in order to hold itself in readiness for the timely emplacement of the United Nations Transition Assistance Group in Namibia. It is my hope that current efforts will finally succeed in bringing independence to the people of Namibia.

For many years, the question of Cyprus has involved the continuous exercise of the good offices of the Secretary-General on the basis of a mandate entrusted to him by the Security Council. My latest initiative has evoked greater receptivity from both sides. At the discussion the leaders of the two sides had in my presence on 24 August, they expressed their willingness to meet without any preconditions and to attempt to achieve by 1 June 1989 a negotiated settlement of all aspects of the Cyprus problem. Confirming their desire to co-operate with me in my mission, they agreed to start talks on 15 September and to review with me the progress achieved at the initial stage.

During the past year, the prospects for peace in South-East Asia have also improved, through the initiation of a dialogue between the Kampuchean parties and other concerned countries. This is an encouraging trend as it confirms the interest on all sides in achieving a political solution to the problem. I sincerely hope that concrete progress will soon be achieved on the main substantive issues. I have presented to the parties a number of specific ideas intended to facilitate the elaboration of a framework for a comprehensive political settlement. I remain at their disposal to help bring this process to fruition.

After long effort, an appropriate climate has been established for a just and durable solution of the problem of Western Sahara. Along with the head of the Organization of African Unity, I submitted a peace plan to which the parties concerned conveyed their acceptance with some remarks and comments on 30 August. This will entail a significant operation in the area for the United Nations, with both civilian and military components. I hope that, with the necessary goodwill on all sides, we will soon witness a final settlement of the problem, which will undoubtedly help consolidate the present favourable trend in the region.

All these problems in their different contexts, have been moved towards solutions in consonance with the principles of the Charter of the United Nations, with diplomatic activity at multilateral and other levels proceeding in convergent directions. For itself, the United Nations does not seek, and was never meant to seek, any kind of diplomatic autarky; what it requires is that diplomacy among Governments, especially those which are concerned with a particular issue, situation or region, should help realize the aims that it has defined. With the United Nations indicating the principles and the direction for efforts to settle a dispute, all relevant points of diplomatic contact and influence in the network of multilateral relationships can be coherently drawn upon to achieve the objectives of peace. Recently we have had encouraging evidence of the practicality of this process.

There are other regional problems that continue to cause international concern. The situation in the Middle East, a critically important region of the globe, has repercussions on relationships in a far wider sphere. The members of the Security Council have recently expressed their grave concern over the continued deterioration of the situation in the Palestinian territories occupied by Israel since 1967, including Jerusalem. The uprising since December 1987 has vividly demonstrated the dangers of stalemate resulting from inability to agree on a negotiating process. Even the urgently required measures to enhance the safety and protection of the Palestinian people of the territories, through the application of the Fourth Geneva Convention relative to the Protection of Civilian Persons in Time of War of 12 August 1949 will neither remove the causes of the events that prompted Security Council resolution 605 (1987) nor bring peace to the region. As the underlying problems can only be resolved through a comprehensive, just and lasting settlement based on Security Council resolutions 242 (1967) and 338 (1973), and taking fully into account the legitimate rights of the Palestinian people, including self-determination, what is needed is an urgent effort by the international community, led by the Security Council, to promote an effective negotiating process towards a solution that will secure the interests of both the Israeli and the Palestinian peoples and enable them to live in peace with each other. The next few months may provide opportunities to accelerate this endeavour.

The situation in Central America is the result of convulsions within societies originating in underdevelopment and unjust socio-economic structures. The signing of the Guatemala Procedure in August 1987 signalled the determination of the five Central American Presidents to find solutions to the region's problems free from outside interference and the pressure of geo-political conflicts. I agreed to participate in the impartial international verification of the process of pacification. Furthermore, at the request of the General Assembly, I formulated a special plan for economic co-operation for Central America, which was considered by the Assembly in May. However, a year after the signing of the Guatemala Procedure, the momentum for peace appears to be faltering and the considerable progress made to date seems to be seriously threatened. The principal merit of the Agreement lay in its requirement for simultaneous progress on two broad fronts: democratization and the cessation of armed hostilities. Its success depends on full compliance and a concerted effort by the signatories as well as the co-operation of all the Governments and parties involved.

The situation in Korea is a legacy of the Second World War and its aftermath. Sustained dialogue between North and South Korea could lead to real progress towards resolving the outstanding issues. It is necessary for all those who are in a position to do so to help foster an atmosphere conducive to an amicable solution of differences between the two sides. Both Governments are aware of my readiness to assist them whenever and in whatever manner they desire.

The region of southern Africa is suffering from a conflict with three dimensions: the question of Namibia, the acts of destabilization against the neighbouring States of South Africa and the system of *apartheid* in South Africa itself. I have already referred to the progress made on the question of Namibia. Acts of destabilization have threatened peace in the whole region. Developments in, or relating to, the continuance of a situation of racial discrimination, which is so repugnant to the spirit of our age, lend further force to the repeated—and hitherto unheeded—urgings of the international community that *apartheid* be dismantled. These urgings provide a renewed opportunity to the Government of South Africa to signal an acceptance of what is just as well as inevitable—the end of *apartheid*. I would appeal to that Government to respond to them in that spirit. Postponing or evading this change of course is fraught with dangers which all the people of the country and its neighbours would certainly wish to avoid.

III

The present juncture of efforts and potentialities opens fresh perspectives for our common political endeavour. This seems to have prompted the observation increasingly heard in recent months that we may be entering a new phase of world affairs. I take the observation as neither a politician's promise nor a scientist's conclusion. A vast range of actions and policies is required to prove it right. If opportunities for breakthroughs on a variety of issues are to be seized, it seems to be important that we keep in mind the implications of our experience, whether of success or of stalemate, in the efforts to resolve the major political questions on our agenda. In this report, I shall deal with these implications and the emerging outlook for the United Nations. As the resurgence in public interest in the Organization has been rather sudden, it is appropriate to recall the long background of efforts, accomplishments and setbacks behind our current experience.

We are all aware of the reasons why, during the first four decades of its existence, the United Nations has been unable to put in place the reliable system of collective security that its Charter envisaged. This system was based on the assumption that the grand alliance of the victors of the Second World War would continue and develop into their joint custodianship of world peace. Furthermore, in the words of one of the principal architects of the world Organization, the late President Roosevelt, the system implied "the end of the system of unilateral actions, exclusive alliances and spheres of influence and balances of power and all the other expedients which have been tried for centuries and have always failed". The chastening experience of the most extensive war fought on this planet was expected to transform the older patterns of power relations.

However, developments during the early years of the Organization went contrary to expectations. The assumed radical change was hindered by a variety of factors as far as relationships at the highest plane of global power were concerned. A whole set of circumstances created a continuing climate of mutual suspicion and fear. In such a climate, the great Powers often looked at the United Nations from different angles, with the result that issues that could have been resolved through their joint endeavour became instead added subjects of controversy between them. An almost insuperable obstacle was thus placed in the way of the United Nations to give world peace a durable foundation.

In the difficult phase that naturally ensued—and that has lasted for decades— many who believed in the essentiality of the United Nations were thrown on the defensive. They were driven to enumerate the political achievements of the United Nations in specific cases, but these appeared slim in comparison with the great unresolved issues of our time. I believe that the accomplishments of the world Organization, at any stage of its career, were far larger than what appeared from the case usually made in its defence. Along with the undeniable central fact that the United Nations was often brought to an impasse, in the field of maintaining international peace and security, by the inability of the permanent members of the Security Council to develop a common approach, there was also the fact, equally central, that the United Nations did not allow this factor to block its endeavours; with ingenuity and realism, it found other ways of at least defusing conflicts. If, in one vital respect, it fell short of the Charter, in other respects it kept pace with, and often served as, a catalyst of the process of rapid and peaceful change.

The United Nations played a decisive role in the process of decolonization, which has changed the political complexion of the globe and given vast populations control over their destiny. It gave authoritative definition to human rights and devised monitoring and other mechanisms for encouraging greater respect for them. It codified international law. In partnership with its specialized agencies, it established guidelines to deal with new problems and emerging concerns ranging from the environment, population, the law of the sea, the safeguarding of the rights of the hitherto disadvantaged segments of society like women, children, the aging and the handicapped to terrorism, drug abuse and the incidence of AIDS. It has responded to situations of disaster and dire human need; it has provided protection to refugees. It has had notable successes in the campaign for conquest of avoidable disease in the poorer parts of the world; it has taken measures towards food security and child survival. It has raised consciousness of global economic imperatives; through its development programmes and the specialized agencies, it has represented a vital source of economic and technical assistance to developing countries.

In the political field, even when disabled by differences among the permanent members of the Security Council, the United Nations has displayed a capacity for innovation and played a role that on no reckoning can be considered peripheral. It has repeatedly acted to limit and control armed conflicts; without the peace-keeping operations launched by it, the theatres of conflict would have undoubtedly repre- sented far greater danger to the wider peace. On major international disputes, it has suggested terms of just settlement. The formulation of such terms is the first requirement for bringing a dispute within a manageable scope and weeding out its implacable elements: this requirement the United Nations has repeatedly sought to fulfil. Above all, the Organization has maintained emphasis on the great objectives of arms limitation and disarmament, the self-determination of peoples and the promotion of human rights, which are essential for the strengthening of universal peace.

These achievements have been made against the backdrop of the most massive transition in the history of the human race. The emergence of new States has taken place at the same time that there has been a proliferation of global concerns, stemming partly from the emerging problems I mentioned above, partly from the impact of advancing technologies and partly from a new mass consciousness of rights leading to the non-acceptance of old inequities within or between societies. The United Nations has not only given shape and expression to the sense of world community but established a basis for nations to develop a concerted response to their common problems.

IV

Our experience has thus shown that co-operative management of a variety of global problems, reflecting a community of interest among Member States, is an entirely workable idea. We have now come to, or are nearing, a stage where the extension of this approach to solving some of the major political issues on our agenda is within our reach.

Changes in perceptions and attitudes, of which we have had pronounced signs since the last session of the General Assembly, suggest that we may be witnessing a transition, however slow or occasionally uncertain, towards a new pattern of relationships at the global level. The transition has the logic of necessity behind it. It is certainly justified by the insupportable cost and the incalculable dangers of a self-perpetuating arms race. It could derive support from the realization that security cannot be viewed in military terms alone nor does the application of military power resolve situations in traditionally expected ways. It is, or can be, propelled by the need for greater attention to the problems of economic modernization or to the social problems that economic growth has left untouched. It is evidenced by trends towards horizontal co-operation between States adhering to different social systems without prejudice to their political alignments. It would seem to respond to the multi-polarity of the world's economic power. All these factors, combined with the technological revolution and the sense of global interdependence, seem to call for radical adjustments of outlook on the part of the world's leadership. There is, of course, no guarantee against temporary reverses or setbacks in the process, nor can ambivalence in the relationships of power blocs be excluded. However, the direction appears to be better set and helped by weightier factors now than at any time in recent years. How this transition will affect the United Nations and how it has been affected by the United Nations are questions of practical import that merit the most serious reflection on our part.

The world community has rightly acclaimed the statesmanship displayed by the leaders of the Union of Soviet Socialist Republics and the United States of America in jointly expressing their shared perception that a nuclear war cannot be won and must never be fought, in initiating a constructive dialogue between their Governments and in concluding the Treaty on the Elimination of Their Intermediate-Range and Shorter-Range Missiles, in December 1987. I believe that the international community, articulating its political consciousness through the United Nations, is more than a witness to agreements that narrow the division between the world's most powerful States. It is deeply affected by, and concerned with, the issues at stake. The sustained emphasis by the United Nations on the goals of arms limitation and disarmament, especially in the nuclear field, and the declared non-alignment of the majority of its Member States, with its implied negation of the concept of expanding spheres of rival influence, have helped to provide the political and mental environment for the ongoing process of mutual accommodation between the great Powers. Not only the mathematics of the arms equation and its economic cost, but also the attitudes of the world beyond have been factors behind this process.

V

There is a school of thought that holds that the great Powers do not need the world Organization except as a symbol of the world community and that its meetings merely provide a convenient opportunity for periodic bilateral exchanges. The view seems to derive support from the dissatisfaction with the working of the United Nations expressed by one or another of these Powers at different times. However, it fails to recognize their interest in maintaining their positions of respect and influence in a changing world situation. There can hardly be a better place than the United Nations for any Power, large or small, to enhance its influence in the best sense of the term. The United Nations offers every country a forum where, with its resources of knowledge and experience, it can take a lead in framing the universal agenda, draw attention to new concerns and new ways of solving problems and contribute to the process of peaceful change. For a country, large or small, to turn its back, to whatever extent, on the United Nations would be to surrender a good part of its actual or potential influence. To follow a two-track policy—at one level, to owe allegiance to the Charter and, at the other, to seek to marginalize the United Nations—would be to act contrary to the goal of harmonizing the actions of nations in the attainment of their common ends.

Moreover, while, in the normal course, the great Powers, like others, resolve or reduce their differences through negotiations outside the United Nations, they need the United Nations to come to grips with issues that concern other nations and that, in one way or another, impinge on their own relationships as well. In this respect, the great Powers need to show a sensitivity to the expressed wishes of the majority of Member States. I have not the slightest doubt that these wishes are based on genuine concerns and not on any primordial opposition, far less hostility, to the policies of one or another major Power. All this argues for greater, not less, support of the United Nations, for engagement and not grudging participation in its work.

I welcome the efforts being made to control rhetorical inflation in the debates of the General Assembly, to promote civility in dialogue and indeed to develop, even if gradually, a balance between debate and negotiation, the parliamentary and the diplomatic approaches, which are equally part and parcel of the United Nations. Continuing public debate is meant to exert pressure towards negotiations; when it can no longer do so, it defeats the aims of its own sponsors. Resolutions are meant to keep alive the goals to be achieved and to ensure that these goals are not lost sight of in a multitude of other concerns. In that perspective, they can become an indispensable factor for the successful outcome of negotiations and can be perceived as resolutions in the full sense of the term, not as incantations or mere formulations of theory. But they become ineffective when they look like stock resolutions. There needs to be an adjustment of political attitudes on all sides to the double requirement of making resolutions more purposeful and of paying respect to them as genuine expressions or reminders of widely shared concerns.

VI

A primary fact of the present world situation is that, while the power to destroy the Earth is concentrated in a few hands, the power to make and strengthen peace is widely dispersed.

This makes the engagement of the United Nations—the only instrumentality that can ensure the full representation of all concerned parties and relevant viewpoints—central to the great task of resolving regional conflicts. The Organization's long experience of handling these conflicts has certain implications that, I feel, need to be taken into account for sound and workable policies in future.

Some of these implications flow so directly from the Charter that to restate them can look like emphasizing the obvious. Yet, at the hopeful stage we have reached now, they have gained fresh pertinence from a practical point of view. The Charter obligation of settling international disputes by peaceful means and in conformity with the principles of justice and international law, for instance, would imply that these disputes should be kept under constant review by the Security Council. This, in turn, would preclude an attitude of passivity towards a conflict when it is in a phase of relative quiescence. It would certainly not justify tacit acceptance of an inherently brittle *status quo* in the context of any conflict.

Another implication of our current and recent experience is that when an armed conflict erupts and as long as it persists the utmost care needs to be taken by other Powers, global or regional, not to add to its size or intensity. This does not exclude sympathy with the side perceived to be the victim. As I said in my annual report five years ago, regional conflicts have been viewed as wars by proxy among more powerful nations. The improved bilateral relations between the major Powers could arrest this dangerous trend. But not only they are involved. When the tensions or differences between the major or middle-sized Powers are grafted onto a conflict that could otherwise be confined to those immediately involved, the conflict is not only widened: it becomes intractable as one or the other party feels encouraged in its obduracy and neither feels any incentive to explore the possibilities of compromise. Moreover, the Charter obligation of activating or supporting the United Nations in resolving a conflict is inconsistent with what may be called permissive neutrality.

The whole Charter system of collective security rests on the permanent members of the Security Council applying a sense of common purpose to addressing a conflict as soon as it erupts. As long as they view regional problems in the framework of their own rivalries solutions will be blocked. Once this dark shadow is removed from the diplomatic landscape these problems can be addressed in the right perspective. This would result in a more judicious and principled use of the veto. A principle underlying the Charter is that membership of the Security Council, both permanent and non-permanent, is to be regarded as service to the cause of peace rather than as a function of unilateral positions or interests. With the adoption of resolution 598 (1987) by the Security Council, there has been a reassuring and unanimous interest in restoring the Council's peace-making capacity. I believe that fresh avenues have been opened for a consideration again of some of the ideas I submitted in my annual reports in 1982 and 1983 about making the Security Council more effective.

The effectiveness of the Security Council, however, requires that once it has made a determination on a dispute all Member States give it full support in the sense not only of accepting an agreed text, but of providing strong diplomatic backing for it. The Charter certainly calls for the application of the collective influence of Member States to lend irresistible weight to a just solution. Furthermore, in carrying out its duties under the responsibility of maintaining international peace and security, the Security Council acts on behalf of all Member States.

Peace-keeping operations have proved to be an inescapable necessity in the context of many conflicts. Their success, however, depends not only on the consent of the parties, but also on the consistent support of the Security Council, on a clear and practicable mandate, on the readiness of Member States to volunteer troops and on adequate financial arrangements. These considerations become more important in view of the evolving world situation, which could well assign a broader role to the peace-keeping operations of the United Nations. They might possibly have to be extended to the maritime environment and adapted to new types of situations that have international implications. I believe that attention should be paid to the need for the United Nations to be better prepared for launching peace-keeping operations, sometimes at short notice. In the broad context of these operations, it is gratifying that all permanent members of the Security Council are now in favour of the peace-keeping aspect of the Organization's work. The valour, heroism and sacrifice of the soldiers of peace who man these operations evoke the most heart-felt tribute from all of us.

Peace-keeping, of course, can only be a palliative if it is not made to serve as a prelude to, or to accompany, negotiations towards a comprehensive settlement. A situation of stalemate or worse about the resolution of the dispute underlying a conflict can cause frustration and despair, which, in the long run, may jeopardize the usefulness of the peace-keeping operation itself, regardless of how well it has managed to moderate or control the conflict.

Moreover, I feel that better possibilities for peace-making can be realized by the employment of a more forthright kind of diplomacy. Let us not forget that peace is secured by agreements, not by the illusion of agreements. When negotiations are envisaged, the adoption of a resolution by the Security Council lays the ground for—but does not necessarily conclude—the diplomatic process required. Negotiations on the basis of the resolution are rendered more difficult if different interpretations are put on its provisions by its framers. The adoption of an agreed text on a controversial issue has certainly the merit of defining the terms of its settlement; in this sense, a vague definition (providing a certain latitude for negotiations) is preferable to no definition at all. However, what is required for solutions to emerge is not merely the endorsement of an agreed text by the members of the Council but also their shared understanding of that text and co-ordinated policy on its basis. A cohesive approach in the spirit of the Charter, regardless of differences of perception, interest or ideology, is indispensable for resolving conflicts. [. . .]

[VII]

Resolving conflicts is a prime responsibility of the United Nations but avoiding them is equally necessary for the maintenance of peace.

The continents of Asia, Africa and Latin America have been the scene of a large number of armed conflicts during the existence of the United Nations. It is one of the most disquieting features of our age that inter-State conflicts should occur when Governments could easily avail themselves of the machinery of the United Nations or of other multilateral organizations to help resolve their disputes. The number of those killed in hostilities between Iran and Iraq provides a massive—and, I hope, conclusive—testimony to the human cost of war.

Fortunately, there are also glimmerings of hope in diverse areas of Asia, Africa and Latin America. Some signs of developing common regional perspectives are visible at several points of the globe. Moreover, encouraging examples have been set of States resorting to judicial settlement of their disputes. I would appeal to Governments to make it a practice, as far as possible, to refer justiciable cases to the International Court of Justice. A tradition will thus be established of having recourse to law, which can avert many possible conflicts, with their incalculable waste. Moreover, the hopes we derive from a change of perception and attitude at the global level will be considerably fortified if similar changes dispel fears and suspicions at the regional level. [. . .]

Global society has been lately much afflicted by disregard for international law. It is obvious that international confidence would rest on quicksand if the domestic necessities felt by Governments were allowed to override the international obligations they have solemnly undertaken. Without international law respected by all States there can be no stable framework for multilateral co-operation in our highly complex world of sovereign States and conflicting interests. It sounds axiomatic yet it needs to be stressed that States or other international persons are bound by treaties that have been properly concluded and that have entered into force. The principle that treaties must be complied with and carried out in good faith, commonly expressed in the maxim *pacta sunt servanda*, is basic to the Charter. Respect for international agreements is not only one of the fundamental principles of international law; it is the foundation of the organized international community. If this principle were abandoned, the whole superstructure of contemporary international law and orga-nization, including the functioning of the United Nations, the effectiveness of the decisions of its competent organs and resort to international arbitration or judicial settlement of justiciable disputes, would collapse. It is in the equal interest of all

States, large or small, to work towards a world where nations will operate within a complete, coherent and viable system of law. Any movement away from this goal holds equal danger for all.

[VIII]

Disarmament and the regulation of armaments, with the least diversion for armaments of the world's human and economic resources, to use the language of the Charter, will remain a decisive test of the improvement of international relations and the strengthening of peace. The Charter envisaged a system for regulating armaments when the arms race had nowhere reached its present scale and when it did not threaten to be, as it is now, both a cause and an effect of tensions between States at the regional as well as the global levels.

Over the years, considerable work has been done in formulating the principles that should govern disarmament and defining the issues involved in it. However, the translation of these principles into actual plans has remained an elusive goal. In a global climate of distrust, at times exaggerated, the arms race acquired an air of inevitability and discussions about halting and reversing it appeared futile. However, the refreshing change signified by the signing of the Treaty on the Elimination of Their Intermediate-Range and Shorter-Range Missiles by the USSR and the United States as well as the prospect of a reduction in strategic nuclear weapons seemed to furnish a propitious background to the special session of the General Assembly devoted to disarmament, which was held from 31 May to 25 June this year. The impressive number of national leaders that attended the session was an indication of the level of concern—and hope—felt all over the world on this issue. The proceedings had a largely non-polemical tone and the bulk of the text proposed for adoption was generally agreed upon.

[*   *   *]

[IX]

A most deplorable feature of the present international scene is the frequency and magnitude of violations of fundamental human rights in different countries and regions. Summary arrests and executions, disappearances of individuals, the systematic practice of torture and killings of unarmed demonstrators continue to impose a heavy burden on the world's conscience. There have been reports of the forced exodus and even massacres of large groups of human beings. Timely demonstration of serious concern by Member States is essential if such appalling situations are to be checked now and prevented in future.

The Organization's work in the field of human rights, beginning with the Declaration, joined later by the two International Covenants on Human Rights and the Optional Protocol to the International Covenant on Civil and Political Rights to form the International Bill of Human Rights, has set universally accepted standards for the observance of human rights. The work continues as we approach, for example, the adoption of conventions protecting the rights of two especially vulnerable groups: children and migrant workers. A basis has been laid for constructive dialogue between Governments and the relevant expert committees. This year witnessed the first session of the newest such body, the Committee against Torture. Yet the struggle remains to give living reality to the provisions that have been made for promoting respect for human rights. Unless a consciousness of these rights becomes a vital element in the political ethos of a society, they are likely to be denied or truncated. [. . .]

[X]

In the economic sphere, the international community needs to act urgently in three areas: debt, trade and commodities, and human resources development.

For many developing countries, the crushing burden of external debt is crippling the development effort. Some progress has been made in dealing with debt problems of the poorest countries, especially those in Africa. I am happy to note the contribution to that end made by the report of the Advisory Group on Financial Flows for Africa, which I constituted last year. But the problems of the middle-income countries are no less pressing. The co-responsibility of debtor and creditor countries for the debt crisis has been increasingly recognized as has the mutual interest in breaking the current deadlock. There is a need promptly to fulfil the commitments made as well as to intensify the search for innovative solutions. Pursuant to a resolution of the General Assembly at the forty-second session, I have personally met with a group of eminent personalities to explore ways and means of finding durable, equitable and mutually agreed solutions to the debt problems of developing countries. I shall make a report to the Assembly separately on this subject.

[*   *   *]

The international community responds generously to emergency requirements and to calls for immediate alleviation of dire needs. Unfortunately, international assistance programmes do not attract the same measure of support when long-term development is at stake. As is demonstrated in Africa, such programmes are necessary if the affected groups are to resume productive lives. Failing this, millions continue to languish in poverty, depending on external assistance for their survival. Remedial action needs to be taken so that they can again become self-reliant and contribute to national development.

[*   *   *]

When global problems call for global solutions, the value of the United Nations to Member States is apparent to all. Successful global initiatives, whether in the political field (which I mentioned earlier) or in the economic, social or humanitarian sphere, mean operational activities at country or subregional level. Two examples may suffice here.

The global AIDS initiative launched under the leadership of the World Health Organization is already being reflected in country-level activities supported by the United Nations Development Programme, which has been designated the operational arm in this important venture, together with the United Nations Population Fund and the United Nations Children's Fund for whom maternal and child health are primary concerns.

The International Conference on Drug Abuse and Illicit Trafficking, held at Vienna in 1987, assigned a greatly increased role and responsibility to the United Nations, which it is fully committed to meet. Here again, at the country level, the United Nations Fund for Drug Abuse Control and the United Nations Development Programme have joined forces to assist in the development and implementation of specific actions.

[*   *   *]

[XI]

The state of the Earth's environment is pre-eminently a problem that should evoke a solidarity of response from all nations. It has, however, reached a stage where, without a global ethic and the necessary law, it can give rise to divisive issues with political implications.

The problem is linked with those of poverty, the growth in the world's population to 5 billion and the prospects for sustainable development. It also involves issues of international responsibility. As such, it has too many aspects for any single country or even a group of countries to be able to deal with effectively. A coherent and well-co-ordinated approach can be developed only at the multilateral level.

This year, with the apprehension that the greenhouse effect has begun to affect our planet, public anxiety around the world has increased about the deterioration of the environment. The United Nations Environment Programme has proceeded, together with the World Meteorological Organization and the International Council for Scientific Unions, to develop internationally accepted assessments of the reality as well as the causes and impact of climatic change. The aim is to co-ordinate government policies to prevent, limit, delay or adapt to this change. With the help of a dialogue between scientists and policy makers, an international agreement needs to be evolved and, if necessary, one or more legal instruments adopted in order to address the effects of this ominous phenomenon in planetary experience.

A constructive precedent has been established in this context with the adoption of the Montreal Protocol on Substances that Deplete the Ozone Layer at a conference convened by UNEP in September 1987. This as well as the 1985 Vienna Convention for the Protection of the Ozone Layer constitute a major step in the development of international environmental law and set an example of managing a world problem before it leads to irreversible damage to human health and the environment.

These reassuring signs of progress notwithstanding, the crisis deepens as a growing population finds itself driven to use irreplaceable natural resources. Desertification, soil erosion, deforestation, swollen cities becoming gigantic sources of pollution, on the one side, and the emission of pollutants into the air by industry, on the other, can have a cumulative and well-nigh unmanageable effect. The unprecedented drought in certain agricultural areas, the acid rain and the more recent phenomenon of trafficking in, and dumping of, toxic wastes are examples of the vexatious issues that need to be forestalled by timely action. Here again, guidelines have been formulated preparatory to a global convention governing the environmentally sound management of hazardous wastes and their movement across frontiers. The issue will require exchange of information, technical assistance in monitoring and control and emergency response in case of accident.

As the Conference on Sustainable Development convened by the Prime Minister of Norway at Oslo in June so lucidly brought out, all issues in the field of environment call for a genuine working partnership among nations in the interest of keeping their common home in good condition.

[XII]

Considering the vast sweep and scope of the possibilities now opening for constructive multilateral action through the United Nations, the financial health of the Organization needs to be immediately restored. The United Nations cannot function without money. It is still seriously short of funds. This situation includes both an immediate shortage of cash, which threatens insolvency in the next few months, and the virtual depletion of reserves. Lack of reserves means that the Organization will not be able to mount new operations.

The impact of the crisis is heightened by the increasing responsibilities of peace-making and peace-keeping which the Organization has had to assume. Taking into account the new operations which the United Nations is likely to undertake in the next 12 months, its total annual expenses will rise very significantly.

[* * *]

[XIII]

Reform and renewal in the United Nations has been one of my main preoccupations. As Secretary-General, I have shared the feeling that the accretions of four decades and a certain inflation of activity had encouraged a bureaucratic resistance to self-review and that we needed a leaner and more effective apparatus. As I have submitted two progress reports on this subject to the General Assembly, the second in April this year, it is not necessary to go into the details of the implementation of Assembly resolution 41/213.

[* * *]

Reform is not an end in itself but a means of improving the services the Organization renders to Member States. The emerging world situation, with major conflicts on the way to solution, is bound to impose additional responsibilities on the Organization—political, economic and humanitarian. It would be paradoxical and discordant if the Organization should face financial difficulties precisely when it has to meet the demands of a more constructive phase of international affairs.

[XIV]

The advent of a new year, decade or century, or even a new millennium does not necessarily open a new page in the calendar of human experience. There seems to be a growing consciousness, however, that, while humanity has made phenomenal progress in the twentieth century, it has also reaped a harvest of wars and upheavals which, with better wisdom, could have been avoided. The current and preceding decades have witnessed much dangerous confusion. It is not a fanciful supposition that Governments will adjust better to a qualitatively changed and changing world environment. If the expectation is right, the United Nations will be used more purposefully than it has been before. I have in mind the use made of it by all Powers—the great, the medium and the small. [. . .]

36. The Future of the United Nations System: Some Questions on the Occasion of an Anniversary

Marc Nerfin

INTRODUCTION: THE CONTEXT

This paper is being written on the occasion of the 40th anniversary of the United Nations, when the very age of the organization invites one to take into account the *time perspective*, both backward and forward. Looking beyond the trees of recent seasons, one should observe the forest of the last 40 years—twice the lifetime of the League of Nations—and, similarly, look ahead to future years. Showing perhaps more ingenuity than the founding fathers, one should endeavour to imagine the year 2000, or even the next 40 years, and how to get there. Such an awareness of the time dimension should inform our thinking about each and every question to be addressed.

One should first attempt to assess what has really changed since 1945, and what has not changed. The most striking factor is the geo-political transformation of a largely colonized world into a polity of 159 sovereign member states of the United Nations, that is the emergence of the Third World, both in numbers (now 127 countries) and in organization (the Non-aligned movement, founded 30 years ago in Bandung; the Group of 77, founded 20 years ago at UNCTAD I; and a number of regional and other South-South groups). One should also ponder over the rise of Japan and Western Europe, and the challenge they pose to the hegemony of the two superpowers which grew out of the 1939–1945 war. And one should attempt to gauge the real significance of the demographic explosion (two out of three of our fellow human beings today were not yet born when the UN was created). What has also changed is the perception that humankind has of itself. The world as seen in 1945 from San Francisco or Lake Success was essentially white, western and christian; its basic paradigms were newtonian. The global projection of such a limited vision did not make it any less limited. Today, largely as a result of the 'great awakening' of the South, but also because we can now view our planet from outer space, humankind is recapturing its wholeness. No one can any longer ignore the existence of the *cultures*, in the widest sense, of Africa, pre-columbian Americas, Arabia, Asia and the Pacific.

What has *not* changed, on the other hand, is the unequal exchange, whatever the innovations in its mechanisms, the hegemony of the North over the South and underdevelopment.

We are at the same time confronted with the immediate holocaust of starvation in Africa, which threatens 30 million human beings, many of whom are likely to die this year, with the possible holocaust of the nuclear winter, with the persisting crisis of underdevelopment and maldevelopment and with the current crisis in the world economy and in international relations (USA-USSR, Afghanistan, Central

America, Kampuchea, Iraq-Iran). Under such circumstances, how can we possibly, so as to be able to act, understand better the nature of this general crisis, its multiple aspects, causes and consequences—positive and negative—and their systemic interrelatedness. These include:

1. *the economic and financial crisis:* the inadequate and extrovert nature of most growth processes and its links with the persisting unequal exchange, both within and between countries, and the resulting poverty; the origins and consequences of the debt, its relative importance for the world system and for the debtor countries, its servicing as reverse transfer both from South to North and from poor to rich, the use of the borrowed resources (outward-oriented production capacity, arms purchase, elite consumption, speculation, private investment abroad, corruption *versus* need-satisfaction-oriented investments, import substitution), the evolution of the rate of interest, the US responsibility (dollar value and real debt burden), the role of the capital market (autonomy from both national interests and productive processes), the rate of profit of the banking system; protectionism and Third World deteriorating terms of trade;

2. *the environmental crisis:* the implications of the withering away of the resource base (deforestation, desertification); the externalization of costs to neighbours (e.g. the acid rains originating from UK or Czechoslovakia); urban decay; new risks as exemplified by the Mexico explosion or Bhopal; the outer limits of the biosphere (ozone layer, climatic changes, etc); the hegemony of short-term rentability; the social causes (the combination of poverty and affluence, that is injustice) of ecological deterioration;

3. *the social crisis:* the growth and irreversibility of unemployment; the challenges to the welfare state; the marginalization of the urban poor in the South; the 'new poor' in the North; the small farmer as an endangered species all over the globe; the migrations from South to North; the tide of xenophobia and racism; persisting gender oppression; growing feelings of powerlessness and alienation among people and societies;

4. *the cultural crisis:* the homogeneization of societies; the role of the mass media (propaganda, malinformation, advertisement, standard consumption values and patterns); westernization of the elites of the South; ethnocentrism and lack of recognition of the Other's values; the identity crisis; the loss of both roots and a *raison d'être*; the poor understanding of the ethnic resurgence;

5. *the ideological crisis:* fundamentalism and integrism—be they capitalist, marxist or religious—their roots and utilization; the shaking Western modernization paradigms—that is, to use different terms, the moral crisis and the spiritual crisis;

6. *the political crisis:* the rise of the authoritarian state in the Third World, and the fragility of the re-born democracies of South America; the risks of 'friendly fascism' in the US; the failure of the Soviet system (which did not 'catch up', except, perhaps, in weaponry) and the lack of success of the internal reform movements; the pervasiveness of bureaucracies (public and private) everywhere; the negation of human rights;

7. *the security crisis:* the impact of bi-polarization and hegemonic policies; East-West rather than South-North approaches; invasions (Afghanistan or Grenada);

destabilization; terrorism, private and statist; militarization of economies and societies; the scramble for resources and the diversion of resources from the satisfaction of human needs; the ever-open questions of Palestine and Southern Africa; the local wars made possible by arms exports; and, above all, the nuclear risk;

8. *the Third World differentiation crisis:* the 1973/74 missed historical chance for genuine South-South cooperation; relations between oil exporting, NICs and poorest countries; the contradictions within the Non-aligned movement, and the lack of leadership after the death of Nehru, Nasser, Tito, Boumedienne; the inability to establish permanent secretariats in either the Non-aligned movement or the Group of 77;

9. *the theoretical crisis:* the wave of neo-conservatism as an acid test for past development theories; state/market relations in both East and West; the relevance of international discussions for national development strategies and practices; the limited impact of alternative models;

10. *the development cooperation crisis:* the reasons for dwindling expectations and resources; the cooperation 'fatigue'; the shift from aid to Third World development to aid to Northern exports; the role of food aid; the crisis of multilateral channels.

This list is not exhaustive, but it is long enough to suggest that we are light-years away from a mere 'cyclical' economic crisis. As a matter of fact, and without any doomsday suicidal complacency, we are probably in the midst of a *mutation* crisis. What is at stake is indeed survival, and, should we survive, the conditions of a new age on this planet, that is, the deepest implications of *Another Development*. Another Development is rooted in the local spaces where people live, but it has national, regional and global dimensions. In the global space, the only available instrument is the United Nations system. This is both the essential challenge that it has to face, and the source of all its contradictions. Its crucial importance, when seen in this light, explains the focus of this paper on the UN system as an *instrument*.

THE INSTITUTIONAL CRISIS

For the crisis is also institutional, and the United Nations system is not immune. Different actors, however, have different perceptions of what constitutes the crisis of the UN. The actors are many: the International Organizations unit in the US State Department and committed Third World representatives or former representatives; Western journalists and the opinions they inform and influence one way or another; UN desk staff and senior civil servants in Western capitals and conventional ministries in Third World countries; Non-aligned countries and client countries; countries withdrawing (USA from Unesco or Poland from ILO) and countries sometimes threatened with exclusion; UN civil servants of all grades and citizens who 'in UN believe'. . . . There are probably as many perceptions of the crisis as there are actors. The crisis is thus ill-defined, and it would be prudent, for anyone entering this debate, to recognize that his/her views are likely to be partial in both senses of the word.

It may be helpful, at least in a first stage of the discussion, to distinguish between the 'external' and the 'internal' elements of the crisis. There is of course a tendency, among those who criticize the system, to focus on the internal determinants, and among those who defend it, to see only the external ones. Both categories are real, but if they are not tackled as related parts of a whole, any discussion is likely to end in deadlock.

External Determinants

Since the lead in the criticism levelled against the UN is being assumed by the Reagan administration and some of its supporters (for instance the Heritage Foundation) as well as by some of the US media, it is worthwhile to try to elucidate the motivations behind the anti-UN campaign. In this connection, the following elements may be considered:

1. *the declining hegemony:* the US used to control the deliberative organs of the system, but its capacity to influence the votes of governments as such or of individual delegates has decreased as Third World solidarity, including its expression through group voting, has increased. Furthermore, its control over the execution of decisions (through key staff and the power of the purse), whilst still very much part of daily reality, appears to be somewhat receding;

2. *resistance to attempts at regulating or restructuring world economic relations:* Third World efforts towards restructuring world economic relations (the New International Economic Order, the Charter of Economic Rights and Duties of States) or their embryonic regulation (the Convention on the Law of the Sea, the codes of conduct on transfers of technologies, activities of transnational corporations, marketing of drugs or baby food) and the concomitant emergence of the idea of development *accountability* all somewhat reduce the omnipotence of free enterprise. US companies, which are subject to some control at home, however, oppose its introduction in the other spaces where they operate;

3. *the role of ideology:* the new self-assertiveness of the US, the desire to overcome the moral crisis linked with the Vietnam war, its strategic superiority, the general feeling of being the leader of the world, all these—not to mention obscure but terrifying Armageddon analogies—are translated into ideological postures such as those of the Heritage Foundation, which believes the US no longer needs the UN since 'it no longer serves US national interests'.

Another external determinant seems to be the weakness of the other founders of the UN in the North, the Europeans, in facing the crisis. Setting aside the most conservative governments, even those who where known as 'like-minded' seem to have accepted the US case without much discussion, even if their national interests, as smaller powers, would have required a more positive, more autonomous approach. It is as if the economic crisis, rather than imperial postures, had fostered shortsighted unilateralism in Western Europe and provoked a decline in the interest in multilateralism.

True enough, the frustrations over the incapacity of the UN to solve major pending problems—be they political (Palestine or South Africa) or economic (the restructuring of world economic relations)—are often transformed into rhetorical statements and symbolic votes, all the more frequent as they have no impact on either problems or solutions. This image, being one which is created by the media, may affect the credibility of the institution in the North. But what is not usually reported is the fact that the masters of the old order do not recognize the claims of the South and are simply not prepared to negotiate with its representatives.

It is indeed impossible not to note the lopsided nature of the media discussion of the UN crisis: there is much talk, for instance, about the 'crisis of UNCTAD', which reflects better the aspirations of the South, and none about the IMF, which acts as the sheriff of the Western banking system. There is much noise about the crisis of Unesco, but none about, for example, IAEA, ICAO, ITU, WIPO or WMO, which are necessary to the North. Seen from this angle, the 'UN crisis' is largely a Northern expression of a felt challenge to the old order and a reflection of the North's unwillingness to accept that change is necessary.

Internal Determinants

This does not imply that there are no internal problems. On the contrary, there are many, reflecting the aging of the institution as well as the difficulties in adapting to new situations. Among the internal factors of the crisis, the following call for particular scrutiny:

1. *the proliferation of agencies, programmes, funds, etc:* the need to restructure the system as a whole was advocated as far back as 1969 by the Jackson Report and 1975 by the Dag Hammarskjöld Report, *What Now: Another Development* and by the Ad hoc Committee on Restructuring. Instead, attempts were made to address new problems through the establishment of new agencies, thus making even more difficult a system-wide and systemic approach to development cooperation;
2. *the proliferation of diplomatic meetings:* if anything, these are draining the limited resources of Third World and small industrialized countries rather than helping them. This may explain at least some of the problems in the quality of representation and the style of deliberation (lengthy, repetitive speeches, lack of real discussion);
3. *the proliferation of bureaucratic reports:* their volume has reached proportions, which exceed the managing or decision-making capacity of any government or delegation; the general decline in UN studies is more serious still, since they are intended for wider audiences;
4. *the whole problematique of the Secretariat and its staffing:* the problem is not one of sheer numbers since the UN bureaucracy, which deals—and rightly so— with almost every aspect of the peace and development problematique, remains rather modest compared to, for instance, that of the European Communities or to most national administrations and many local ones. The real questions are about the methods of recruitment and election (including the highest positions), duration of tenure, working conditions, efficiency, competence, integrity and independence of the Secretariat. There is, however, no evidence that the Third

World is more responsible for the present unsatisfactory state of affairs than, say the permanent members of the Security Council;

5. *the question of the costs:* this is a result of the previous deficiencies and, again, the question is not that of the total cost, which is very small in global terms, whatever yardstick one uses, but rather that of the effectiveness of the operation, the deployment of resources, and, perhaps above all, its financing.

All these problems (and many others, such as the system's relations with the media and other opinion-formers and with the scientific community) are not only real ones, but they affect principally those countries, which have a stake in a better performance of the organization, e.g. the Third World and those smaller powers in the North which have no pretence at world leadership and need a strong international organization. To limit the discussion at this point to the realm of the governments, one may hope that the 40th anniversary could be used as an opportunity to launch a serious drive towards streamlining and strengthening the UN system.

BUT, WHAT IS THE UN?

The crisis of the UN, at this point, would appear to be (i) *a reflection of the crisis of multilateralism*, itself prompted partly by the current politcial, economic and ideological crisis, and partly by the fact that some of the founding fathers no longer recognize their creature, which seems to be escaping them; and (ii) *an image crisis*, rooted in the difficulties of adapting the system to new realities, but resulting also from real shortcoming, however deliberately magnified they have been, and wherever the responsibility lies.

But there is also *an identity crisis*, and any serious discussion should endeavour to clarify what the UN really is, and what it can and cannot do, or, or put it differently, understand better *the distance between the United Nations as an aspiration and the United Nations as a reflection of realities* (geo-political, cultural, and others) and explore the margin of liberty that such a distance may offer.

Being *le fait du Prince*, the UN is primarily an instrument of governments, and this may be seen not only as its original sin but also as its major shortcoming. It can function properly only when there is a measure of agreement among governments, and anyhow it has only the political power they delegate to it. Thus, the UN is in many respects more a mirror of the contradictions of the world than anything else; and, as folk wisdom always knew, breaking the mirror does not improve the image and refusing to see reality brings bad luck.

As a mirror, the UN cannot be held responsible for the failure of the super powers to live up to the commitments to *peace* they accepted when signing the Charter; it cannot be held responsible for their lack of willingness to limit armaments, for their military interventions or for the arms exports, without which the 'local wars' which have never stopped in the Third World since 1945 could not have taken place to such an extent.

Similarly, the UN cannot be held responsible for the failure to set up a proper *development cooperation* mechanism or even a coherent approach to genuine development, since it could not and still cannot go much beyond what governments (so-called 'donors' and 'recipients' alike) want or will tolerate.

The question of *human rights* is perhaps more ambiguous, or, rather, it may be seen to throw some light on the ambiguities of the system as such. On the one hand, one would expect the UN and its member governments to duly perform the task of policing those which violate the adopted conventions. In this sense, the Commission on human rights has an unescapable mandate. On the other hand, governments' usual lack of action in this field (even if there have been exceptions, notably during the presidency of Jimmy Carter) reflects the realities of the 'raison d'Etat' and exemplifies again the unwillingess of many governments to take seriously their own commitments. At the same time, the UN has, for instance, provided a tribune to the victims of torture and sent emissaries to visit prisons. Some of its senior staff have shown an exemplary conduct in this respect. Still the question needs to be posed: is the UN as such responsible for the deficiencies, or is it rather that it was naive to expect governments to do more, and that instruments of the civil society, such as Amnesty International, the Permanent People's Tribunal or the Red Cross are better suited to the task?

Third World *decolonization* is by and large completed, and it would be useful to analyse to what extent, and why, the UN seems to have performed rather well in this respect. Is it only because the two super powers did not have the same interests as their British and French colleagues occupying permanent seats on the Security Council, because Italy had been defeated, and because Belgium and Portugal were only minor powers and the latter reproved as a mere vestige of the pre-war undemocratic regimes?

Still, even in their own space, governments are not everything, and there is something which could be called a *UN entity*, which always had a measure of autonomy, and may thus be seen as constituting 'the UN'. This entity is made up of three distinct but interrelated layers: (i) *governments in their capitals* (that is, when there is a UN policy, which is not the normal case, the small group of policy makers and senior civil servants who define the government position in the UN assemblies); (ii) *the permanent delegations* (only a study based on insights would reveal the relative autonomy of delegations, but it is well known, for instance, that except for major or well organized powers, influence, in New York or elsewhere, depends more on the quality of the delegation than on the weight of the country); and (iii) *the Secretariat*, which, whatever its essential collective and individual dependence on its governmental masters, enjoys a certain freedom of initiative. These three constituents of the 'UN entity' are living in a kind of symbiosis through contacts between delegates and Secretariat (quasi-permanent with resident missions, less frequent but no less regular with visiting delegations) as well as through personnel movements among them: what proportion of new staff members, especially at the decision-making levels, come from the UN desk in the capitals and from permanent delegations?

The relative margin of autonomy of this UN entity appears rather limited in the political sphere of UN acitivities, and somewhat wider in the development cooperation sphere. In either case, it is probably this margin which caused rising expectations of the UN. However, since it does exist, it may be just as well to try to assess the UN performance from this perspective. After all, the very idea of an international organization implies that there is something which cannot be reduced to the sum of governmental decisions; there has always been a cadre of truly international civil servants, supported by enlightened national ones, who place a global vision above narrow national interests, competition and rivalries, and act at the service of the world at large. The capacity of such forerunners of a world to be to influence the course of events is obviously determined by their imagination and independence.

This is to say that 'the UN' has also a *moral role:* even in its 'operational activities', the UN is no substitute for governmental action, but the extent to which it has influenced, positively or negatively, peace and development, and in the latter field, theory and practice, should be assessed, as well as its role as the vehicle of the first sense of global awareness ever to occur on this planet.

An agenda for evaluation may, in this light, cover such topics as:

1. the avoidance of war (eg. the role of Secretary-General U Thant in the 1962 'missile crisis' in Cuba); the peace-keeping operations in West Asia and elsewhere; the experience of the 'blue helmets'; the Congo operation; education for peace and the promotion of disarmament;
2. the process of Third World decolonization;
3. the limitations, achievements and potential of the Commission on human rights;
4. the role of the UN system in such strictly global affairs as the common heritage of mankind (especially in the Law of the Sea but also with reference to outer space and 'intellectual property'), as well as in expanding knowledge (including statistical) of this planet and its inhabitants;
5. the role of the UN system in postal services (UPU), civil aviation (ICAO), maritime transport (IMO), telecommuniations (ITU), or meteorology (WMO);
6. the development of international law and the place of the International Court of Justice;
7. the role of the Committee for Development Planning, ECOSOC, the Secretariat and others in the elaboration of the three International Development Strategies; the relevance of these strategies to both national development and international cooperation; their usefulness in socializing the development debate and fostering the cooperation movement; their limitations reflecting the prevailing development ideology and the vested interests at stake;
8. the contribution of the sectoral agencies, funds, programmes, etc., to the strengthening of the autonomous capacity of societies to develop, meet their needs and master technologies, for example, FAO and the World Food Council as far as food is concerned, WHO for health, Unesco for education, science and cultural understanding, Habitat for housing and human settlements, ILO for labour protection, UNIDO for industry, UNEP for environment, etc.;
9. the role of ECOSOC, UNCTAD, the regional commissions and their institutes, such as ILPES or IDEP, as well as UNITAR, UNRISD, and perhaps UNU, in clarifying and enriching development theory;
10. the role of UNCTAD in facilitating and moralizing North-South trade and in providing a forum for discussion on the restructuring of the world economy;

of the Regional Commissions in support of regional cooperation; and of the Centre on Transnational Corporations in providing information and analysis on global economic power;
11. the results of the 'operational activities' of the system, those of UNDP, UNICEF, IFAD, WFP, UNFPA, HCR, UNDRO, UNWRA, etc. on the one hand, as well as those of the Bretton Woods institutions, the IMF and the IBRD, on the other. This should include an analysis of the relevance of the implicit models of development informing such activities, the nature of the interaction between suppliers and users of resources, the level and quality of transfers, and the proportion of such transfers which have really contributed to the autonomous capacity to develop, as well as, in the case of relief agencies, the quality, relevance and timeliness of their interventions;
12. the influence of the Joint Inspection Unit through monitoring the functioning of the system; were its analyses properly studied and its conclusions acted upon?
13. the influence of the major World Conferences, since Stockholm in 1972 (environment, population, food, human settlements, desertification, water, science and technology, agrarian reform and rural development, new and renewable sources of energy and, as far as actors are concerned, women) in bringing to the fore the emerging themes of the development problematique, in offering new approaches to old themes and generally, because they reached far beyond the space of governments, contributing to a new global awareness; similarly, the role and significance of the many thematic 'days', 'years' or 'decades';
14. finally, but of great relevance for the next century, the use by the United Nations University of its autonomy (somewhat unique in the UN system) to tackle the fundamental questions of the future through linking up with forward-looking scientists, the wise among us, and the new social actors.

Among the general *criteria* against which to evaluate such activities, one should take into account the contribution of the UN system to the exchange of experiences and the generation and dissemination of new ideas, as well as the countless personal contacts it has facilitated among men and women from all regions and many cultures.

In the final analysis, the basic question is simple: *could the world as we know it today be possible without the United Nations?* The answer is equally simple: no.

There has been no world war since the founding of the organization. Third World decolonization has been virtually completed. Small and otherwise powerless countries now have a tribune. Development cooperation, however problematic, has started. The feeling that we belong to this only one earth is spreading.

The UN is the first attempt in history at global organization, that is at establishing rules accepted by all. It is the first tool ever for global dialogue, understanding, conflict resolution and cooperation. They bear a terrible responsibility, those who weaken the United Nations by refusing the rules of the game, outside which there is only the law of the jungle—that is underdevelopment, war and death.

On the contrary, the UN needs *strengthening*. This can be achieved only through re-thinking, re-structuring, and up-grading. Forty years of experience, that is of achievements, mistakes, shortcomings, failures, successes, and new perceptions of the world and humankind, are there to learn from. We are better equipped than in 1945 to make the UN a more effective tool for peace and development.

WHICH UN FOR THE WORLD?

The creation of the United Nations, 40 years ago, was an act of faith, and its *aggiornamento*, starting in this anniversary year, has also to be an act of faith. There is, however, a difference. Today's faith is based on the record of these years.

The next question is: *What UN do we need?* This would be beyond the scope of these notes, meant only to start a discussion, and not to offer details of a blueprint. Enough has been written (and not acted upon) to provide food for thought to institutional designers. But a few questions might be of help in mapping out the territory of a better UN. Some of the following are in fact mere extensions of existing practices, others are newer; some may be answered within the framework of the existing Charter, others would require amendments. This is not important at this stage.

Further, the *aggiornamento* will not come from governments alone. However 'realistic' the proposals, governments as such will not act collectively if not pushed. One cannot be limited by too narrow a concern for what governments may now find 'feasible' since change, if it is to come, will result only from a *movement of opinion*.

Such a movement is possible. For perhaps the most important fact about the United Nations, in this anniversary year, is the result of an opinion survey carried out in May in the US, the UK, Japan, the Federal Republic of Germany and France [. . . T]he message from the five hard-core industrial countries is crystal-clear:

1. whenever people do have an opinion about the United Nations, the majority (except in Japan) considers it is doing a good job;
2. an even larger majority, in all five countries, does not believe, as some American integrists claim, that the world would be better off without the UN; and
3. except in the US (where this is the position of half of those expressing an opinion), at least six out of ten people do not think that the Third World has too much influence on the UN.

In understanding the UN, people are ahead of governments, just as there have always been people and movements ahead of governments for decolonization, for peace, for human rights, for women's liberation, for the environment, and for consumers self-defense.

This offers to the UN a line of action to consider when it ponders its future this autumn: *get closer to the people*. Here are five questions which, one way or another, appear relevant to the future of the United Nations and its *aggiornamento* in that direction.

1. Which Functions?

The UN may not have the power to change the world, but it can certainly do more than record speeches and ineffective resolutions on peace and development whilst *de facto* reflecting the *status quo*. As the only global instrument, that is, strictly speaking, as the only instrument of the human species as such, and if it is to smooth the transition from the old order(s) to the new, more humane, order(s) which survival requires, is not its primary role to be *open*,

- open to *new realities*, notably the multifaceted emergence of the Third World, within and without the nation states;
- open to *new aspirations*, notably the people's expressed need for liberation from the threat of nuclear omnicide, from hunger and other forms of maldevelopment, and for mastering their lives;
- open to *new paradigms*, notably those concerning security, development, relations between societies, human beings and genders, as well as between the species and the environment of which it is part and parcel?

In order to be, in short, open-ended to the future, could the UN do more and better, in a universal, independent and pluralistic manner, to

- monitor both nature and societies, through the collection, analysis and dissemination of all relevant information;
- facilitate the sharing of experiences and ideas;
- promote mutual understanding and education, through dialogue and negotiation among countries, cultures, and societies;
- formulate alternative policy options for the steering of the world society in transition?

2. Can the UN Decision-Making System Be Improved?

The voting system in the UN General Assembly is based on the principle of 'one country, one vote', but the Security Council has a politically-weighted voting system, and the Bretton Woods institutions (and UNDP) an economically-weighted one, and whatever the noises about 'automatic majorities', the UN by and large still operates under the control of the big powers of the North.

Would it be possible to overcome such an outdated pattern without moving from one hegemony (real) to another one (possible)? Could an arbitration or reconciliation system be worked out?

Could the fact that, say, Brazil, India or Nigeria, and the US, the USSR or China, have a larger global responsibility than Vanuatu, Dominica, or the Seychelles, be reconciled with the fundamental right of every polity, whatever its size, to have a proper say in planetary affairs, that is in matters concerning its survival?

Could a new system, reflecting both the general and the different responsibilities of different countries in different matters be imagined? Could, for instance, the voting system of IFAD or that of the International Sea-Bed Authority be a precedent for other operational agencies?

Could the post-war Unesco system be revisited, rehabilitated and perhaps extended to other agencies? Its Executive Board was then composed of competent persons serving in their personal capacity 'on behalf of the Conference as a whole and not as representatives of their government'. Only in 1954 were members of

The United Nations at a Crossroads

the Board made to represent their governments—as a result of a 1952 proposal by the US government, which today complains about 'statism'.

3. Can the UN System Have a Greater Financial Autonomy?

Resourses at the disposal of the UN system are not commensurate with the magnitude of the needs of development cooperation. How could these resources be increased and become more automatic?

What scope is there for reducing administrative expenditure in favour of development cooperation expenditure (but who ever complained about the administrative budget of the World Bank, which is fully automatic, being financed by the difference between the interests paid to lenders on the market and interests paid by borrowers, that is Third World countries)?

Can a levy on the use of the global commons or a tax on military expenditures be collected by the UN and affected to development cooperation?

The US share in the regular budget of most UN agencies is 25 per cent, and more in most voluntary programmes. This is in agreement with the principle of the capacity to pay embodied in most national tax systems. This also gives the US an excessive leverage on UN activities, either indirectly through staffing or directly through the power of the purse. Can the scale of assessment be modified and the share of any one country be limited to, say, 10 per cent of the total, without decreasing the total income?

Are there effective ways to delink the payment of dues from influence on the actual functioning of the organization?

4. How Can the Secretariat Become Truly Independent?

Article 100 of the Charter provides that the Secretariat 'shall not seek or receive instructions from any government' and that 'each Member of the United Nations undertakes to respect the exclusively international character of the responsibilities of the Secretary-General and the staff and not seek to influence them'.

Possibly no other article of the Charter has been more widely ignored than this crucial one. The super powers have been and remain particularly guilty in this respect, from the dismissal of staff members during the McCarthy era in the US to the exploitation of USSR (or USA) staff positions by the KGB (or the CIA). More generally, this provision has been virtually nullified by the routine submission of appointments to governmental clearance, probably the major weakness of the Secretariat.

True enough, Article 100 expresses the liberal naivety of the founding fathers, who sought to fashion the institution in their image. Even without 'instructions', members of the Secretariat, belonging as they do to different cultures (political, ideological, etc.), cannot but reflect them 'in the discharge of their responsibilities'.

Yet, could the independence of the Secretariat be improved?

How could a Secretariat, of largely American-British-French parentage (as recently as 10 years ago, members were still primarily drawn from these three countries), become a truly pluralistic image of the diversity of world societies and polities?

Could the best traditions of its servants, both past and present, become the model rather than the exception? Could the example of a Dag Hammarskjöld inspire all Secretariat members, from the most modest to the top?

Do the answers, or at least some of them, reside in different selection procedures; in the enforcement of criteria based exclusively on efficiency, competence, integrity and commitment; and in the delegation of appointment decisions to independent committees of people who themselves have strictly and consistently and over a long time met such criteria? Would the limitation of the terms of tenure restrict bureaucratization? Would the institution of a staff college help? Could the experience of religious orders or revolutionary parties in the selection, apprenticeship and development of their cadre, be of relevance? What mechanisms of social account-ability for Secretariat members could be set up?

How could member states be made to respect their commitment to respect the independence of the Secretariat?

In sum, how could the margin of autonomy of the Secretariat component of 'the UN entity' be widened? How could the Secretariat become the melting pot of a new cadre of men and women exclusively devoted to the world community at large and to its emancipation? There is perhaps no more important question for the future of the UN.

5. Can the UN Give a Voice to All Social Actors?

States and governments, important as they are and will continue to be, do not reflect the richness of societies. Even when democratically elected, governments represent at best the majority of a society, not the whole of it, and UN continuity suffers from shifting majorities, as exemplified by the fate of the Convention on the Law of the Sea. There are other social actors. Some represent the economic powers, such as, in the global space, the transnational corporations or the inter-national banking system. They are part of the problem, and they must also be part of the solution. People in their diversity (and contradictions) express themselves through other actors: religious movements, peace movements, consumer movements, ethnic movements, trade unions . . . Can the UN accommodate these actors?

This would require a radical alternative to past and current thinking and practices.

The question is not to 'mobilize the opinion' (a catch phrase which one will hear in almost every anniversary speech, including those of the Secretary-General): the people are quite able to 'mobilize' themselves, if necessary. The question is not whether to tinker with the bureaucratic arrangements for the so-called 'non-governmental organizations' in 'consultative status' with the UN and its specialized agencies. The question is whether the UN will be able to perceive that its real constituency lies beyond governments, and is the peoples and the people. The challenge is to seize the opportunity of the 40th anniversary and of the crisis to re-think and re-establish the UN's relations with the people and their associations.

Can one think of a three-Chamber UN, one representing the governments, or first system (which we may call *The Prince Chamber*), another the economic powers, or second system (*The Merchant Chamber*), and another the people and their associations, or third system (*The Citizen Chamber*).

Can one think, perhaps along the lines of the European Parliament or through some arrangement with the Inter Parliamentary Union, of giving a space in the UN assemblies to the current political minorities, since they may well be tomorrow's majorities?

Are there more immediate ways to open up the UN system to the people? What could the third system itself do? What mechanisms can be devised and established which would make the UN, as it is now and as it may unfold, at least *accountable* to the people?

CONCLUSION: HOPE AND RESPONSIBILITY

Whatever the depth of the crisis and the predicament looming upon us, there is no excuse for despondency. On the contrary. If 'crisis' means moment of decision, which it did in Greek, our ability to make the right decisions depends on our capacity not to lose sight of the underlying hopes.

Through these first 40 years of the United Nations, scientific, technological, conceptual, practical and, *lato sensu*, political advances have been many and significant. There have been many positive changes in our understanding of nature and society, and the experiences accumulated offer a prodigious capital to choose from and build on. Our task is now to sketch a vision of a more humane world and to explore ways to approach it.

Democracy has had its setbacks. They continue. But dictatorships have not been able to resist people's pressure, in Greece, Portugal or Spain or, more recently, in Argentina, Brazil or Uruguay. In Western Europe and in North America, the people's response to and sense of solidarity with those starving in Africa has been overwhelming. Everywhere, over the last 40 years, people have been ahead of governments.

Finally, perhaps, one major reason for hope and confidence is the very youth of humankind. More than half of those living today are less than 25 years old, and the children of today are going to be in charge tomorrow.

At the same time, this places an unavoidable responsibility upon the adults of today, the artisans of the present world order, *to keep the option of life open* and to manage the transition to a world in which people can truly live. In this anniversary year, the first responsibility in this respect is to invent and explore new institutional paths to make the UN the instrument we need. For the UN is much more than 159 member states: it is a *project* which, as the only embryo of a planetary organization, belongs to all of us, members of the human species living on this *only one earth*.

A THREE-CHAMBER UN?

1985 is the year of the 40th anniversary of the United Nations. Occurring as it does in the midst of a crisis of multilateralism—some not recognizing their creature, others rejecting the very idea of international organization—this anniversary may offer an opportunity to think about possible ways to rejuvenate and strengthen the Organization.

Not only were the majority of the current 159 member states not independent 40 years ago, but most of the four billion human beings now living on this planet were not yet born. Rather than looking back, can't we see this as an invitation to try and imagine the UN of the next 40 years?

It may be too early to discuss the role of the UN in a world which, assuming we avoid the nuclear and the famine holocaust, our stuttering imaginations find it difficult to figure out. The challenge is rather to invent and explore an institutional path enabling the real social actors, all of them, to tackle the problems facing humankind.

In the global sphere where the UN evolve, the Prince (or governmental power) and the Merchant (or economic power), which control most decisions, have proven unable to offer effective approaches to peace and development. The voices of the third power, that of the people and of the peoples—in whose name the UN Charter was promulgated—remain largely unheard. Could not the people and their associations, which we call the third system—or the Citizen—have a say in the Organization?

Utopian as it may appear today—as did so many ideas, now part of the conventional wisdom, before someone took the first step towards implementing them—couldn't we sketch out a possible UN of 2025? Redeeming its original sin of having been conceived, brought into being and grown up as an organization of governments, the UN of our children and grandchildren will probably reflect better the societies of the world and the actors who make them alive.

This could for instance be achieved through a three-chamber General Assembly of the United Nations. The *Prince Chamber* would represent the governments of the states (not likely to wither away). The *Merchant Chamber* would represent the economic powers, be they transnational, multinational, national or local, belonging to the private, state or social sectors, since at the same time we need them and need to regulate their activities—which is better done with them. The *Citizen Chamber*, where there should be as many women as men, would, through some mechanism ensuring adequate representativity, speak for the people and their associations. At the very least, this would make it possible for citizens to hold Princes and Merchants *accountable* for the consequences of the exercise of their power.

This is a far cry from present arrangements under which, with one or two limited exceptions in ILO (presence of Trade Unions) and UNESCO (some national commissions), bureaucracies, on behalf of governments and on their own, run the place while maintaining the fiction of non-governmental organizations or 'NGOs'.

The concept of 'NGOs' is politically unacceptable because it implies that governments are the centre of society and people its periphery. Further, the hundreds of 'NGOs' in 'consultative status' with the UN Economic and Social Council (ECOSOC) do not 'consult' on anything, and it may be just as well, constituting as they do a very mixed bag of groups ranging from, say, the International Association of the Soap and Detergent Industry to the Christian Peace Conference. . . . Worse, however, is perhaps the situation of the 'NGOs' used by the Department of Public Information which, again with some exceptions, still considers them as conveyor belts of intergovernmental or bureaucratic wisdom distilled from above to a 'public opinion' seen as a passive receptacle.

Perhaps some imaginative and innovative institution designers could start working and offer to the world community, as a 40th anniverary present, some ideas on how to move from the present state of affairs to something more apt to enable people to participate in the management of the planet.

It would be futile, at this stage, to direct the exercise at governments. Like most past re-structuring efforts (by far more modest), this one will, in the short term at least, strike the shelves of politico-bureaucratic lack of vision and vested interests. The exercise should on the contrary, not only be directed at, but carried out with, the social actors themselves, the women and the young, the peasants and the city dwellers, the producers and the consumers, the peace marchers and the ecological sit-in people, all those who are vitally interested in Another Development inter-weaving peace, justice and a better life for all.

The first result of such an endeavour may well be to give us a new sense of hope and confidence in the United Nations, a sense without which there may not be any United Nations or, for that matter, any nations in 2025.

37. A Successor Vision:
The United Nations of Tomorrow

UN Association of the USA

Crises in the lives of organizations often spark a rethinking of basic purposes, strategies and agendas. The purpose of this report is to help ensure that the current situation of the United Nations, which is one of deep crisis, leads to a sharper definition of goals, a more effective deployment of means, and a revitalized mandate.

A paradoxical situation confronts the U.N. and other international organizations today. On one hand the gap between the legal and political sovereignty of nation states and their ability to give sovereignty concrete shape—whether in air quality, energy security, jobs, surety against nuclear warfare, etc.—has never been larger. Yet while this "sovereignty gap" seems to cry out for international solutions, it has actually produced very little innovation to equip our existing international machinery to do the job. In parts of the international system some cautious modernizing is taking place. At the center of the system, however, there is deep skepticism about the present capacity of the United Nations to respond usefully to most global problems.

Many factors lie behind this skepticism: frustration with the U.N.'s ineffectiveness in the security field; its frequent failure to contribute usefully to the management of many global problems outside the traditional security area; deficiencies in its management and in its public information programs; the junior level of many of the delegates who sit on its many main intergovernmental committees, especially those in the economic and social area, etc.

In the face of such problems the prevailing skepticism is unsurprising, yet it does not reflect a balanced evaluation either of U.N. performance or of the nature of the factors which affect that performance. The U.N. has rendered many services of incalculable value to its members and to the world community: the fostering of decolonization; peacekeeping and peacemaking efforts; defense of human rights; assistance to refugees; the development and extension of international law; promotion of collective action on such common problems as environment, population, resource strain, et al.

While this is an impressive record, many of the achievements mentioned belong to a time when the U.N. played a more central part in the cooperative management of world problems than it does today. Many diagnoses have been offered to explain this increasing marginalization: management handicaps embedded in the staff structure and institutional culture; lack of intellectual leadership; lack of political will; excessive politicization. The panel considered each of these but found none of them completely satisfactory. Instead, it believes that the U.N.'s current situation derives from two more basic problems: the ambiguity of its specific world role and its failure to change that role as the world has changed.

The panel believes that the role of the U.N. at the close of the 20th century is determined by two factors, each pulling in opposite directions: the causes and the effects of most major challenges facing governments are international, while the authority for dealing with those problems remains vested in nation states. This mix of opportunity and constraint dictates a responsibility to promote international cooperation by connecting an unsentimental assessment of national interests with an uncontestable vision of common goals.

Yet the present system of international organizations, of which the U.N. is theoretically the center, is not organized to carry out this mission due to weaknesses in its structure and flaws in the assumptions that determine how it defines its work. To correct that situation, this report proposes a new vision for the United Nations composed of three essential parts:

RELATING FUNCTIONS TO STRUCTURE

1. the U.N. should identify common interests among its members;
2. it should convert those common interests into common views; and
3. it should strive to convert those common views into cooperative action.

This formula already typifies the United Nations' most successful efforts, but for the generality of U.N. activities it remains the exception rather than the norm. A sharper definition of the functions of the U.N. in relation to the U.N. system, and a new structure, particularly in the economic and social area, are indispensable.

Global Watch

In order to identify the issues on which convergence of interests exists, the U.N. needs: (i) a setting where emerging issues of urgent global significance can be spotlighted and their implications for national and international policy choices and human welfare given prominent international attention by a small senior body; (ii) a capacity at the staff level to monitor, and put into usable form, data on "global watch issues," to systematically examine implications for national and international security and welfare, and to identify overlapping interests and the margins for potential agreement.

Consensus-Building

A more systematic approach to consensus-building at the United Nations is indispensable. It should incorporate the following elements:

- affected parties: Communities of interest are more easily formed and collective action taken when negotiations and decisions include only those countries most directly affected by the issue
- equity-security: Links between economic equity and security (in the broadest sense of *human* security) are increasingly direct, and future consensus-building efforts, particularly as they relate to the crossover between economic, technological, and environmental concerns, must reflect that linkage.
- representational diplomacy: To assure speed of consultation, minimal procedural and parliamentary delay, and participation at senior levels, global watch discussions should not be conducted in universal membership bodies but in a forum which,

while of limited size, would be composed of countries drawn from the entire membership of the U.N. according to a system of rotating representation.

Consensus Conversion: Stimulating Collective Action

As the need for effective management of international issues grows more acute, a more direct U.N. role in defining and proposing specific mechanisms for cooperation—occasionally even in helping to set up the necessary logistical apparatus—will be necessary.

STRENGTHENING STRUCTURE

The panel has given considerable attention to the deficiencies of the present U.N. structure in the economic and social area, these include: a generally low level of representation; overlap between the General Assembly, the Economic and Social Council, and UNCTAD; a lack of intellectual authority; the absence of a system for identifying emerging global issues; and the weakness of coordination and joint planning in the U.N. system. While institutional changes are clearly needed, a balance has to be struck between what may be desirable ultimately, and the kinds of constructive practical steps which member states could undertake immediately. Consequently, the panel has made the following recommendations:

Ministerial Board

To provide a high-level center for the conduct of global watch consultations described above, a small Ministerial Board of not more than 25 governments should be established in affiliation with ECOSOC. The Board would be composed of delegates with the seniority and expertise to consult effectively, issue communiques and initiate or propose ad hoc actions with regard to matters on which there is agreement that enhanced international management is essential.

Functions. GLOBAL WATCH—high-level consultations and exchange of views on any urgent international problems not within the jurisdiction of the Security Council; CONSENSUS-BUILDING—through ad hoc working groups of the most affected countries the Board will forge communities of interest on matters before it; CONVERTING AGREEMENTS INTO ACTION—when appropriate the Board shall propose actions by or under the aegis of the U.N. proper (General Assembly would have to authorize), by other international agencies, by individual U.N. member countries.

Agenda. The Board could address any issues of imminent or clearly foreseeable consequence for human security and welfare not within the jurisdiction of the Security Council, e.g., matters associated with natural disasters, the global biosphere, the special problems of the least developed countries, international debt, disease control, illegal capital flight, international narcotics trafficking, cross border population movements, urban overpopulation, etc.

Composition and Procedures. The 25 members would consist of a core of permanent members made up of the largest developing and developed countries, and a larger number of rotating members (criteria for determining "permanent" and "rotating" might be population and economic size); it is expected that governments would be represented at a high level by ministers or other officials from the ministries which are most directly relevant to the agenda subject; meetings would be held on an as-needed basis, normally 1–3 days in duration; all decisions would be taken by consensus.

Support. The Board would be supported by a Bureau of Global Watch located in the Department of International Economic and Social Affairs (DIESA). Drawing heavily upon electronic and computer-based information networks such as UNEP's Earthwatch, and utilizing the existing resources of DIESA, the Bureau would gather, update, monitor and analyze a global data base on each item which the Board has placed on its "human security" agenda.

Organizational Status. While ultimately the Board should be given an explicit basis in the Charter, for the present it should be attached to ECOSOC but report to the Assembly directly once a year at the same time as the ECOSOC makes its report.

Why a New Body? Existing U.N. machinery is inadequate to address, authoritatively and effectively, urgent issues of human security and welfare. The Second and Third Committees and ECOSOC are too large, too comprehensive in their agendas, and their delegations often too junior to have the authority for so important a task.

A TWO-STEP APPROACH TOWARD
A MORE INTEGRATED U.N. SYSTEM

Why is a more integrated system necessary?: It is essential to create an apparatus for identifying, analyzing and proposing responses to the kinds of issues described above that is integrated intellectually and employs the sectoral expertise of the U.N.'s economic and social agencies in a coordinated manner. Most problems requiring international management overlap the spheres of several agencies and U.N. programs. YET THERE IS NO CENTER AT THE CENTER OF THE U.N. SYSTEM and therefore no means for putting to work the system's rich potential for interdisciplinary analysis to identify the global issues on which national interests converge and where high levels of cooperation are necessary and feasible.

The Two-Step Approach: The panel recommends creation of a single commission, composed of the Directors General of all the main agencies in the economic and social fields, mandated to develop integrated responses to global issues through joint programming, and development of a consolidated U.N. system budget. Such a Commission however is not feasible for immediate implementation due to the scale of the constitutional, structural and budgetary changes involved. The panel therefore adopted the Commission as a medium-term goal toward which the U.N. system should evolve. As an immediate step in the direction of the U.N. Commission it calls for a commission with advisory powers only.

Step 1—The U.N. Advisory Commission:

COMPOSITION: the Advisory Commission would consist of 5 persons, selected by the Secretary-General, with outstanding international reputations in the economic and social field.

FUNCTION: It would identify emerging issues of a global or regional scale that cross over several agencies fields of concern. Following consultations with agency heads, it would propose joint approaches to these problems. It would also present proposals to the new Ministerial Board suggesting actions by member states or international institutions regarding these "crossover" issues. It would conduct regular reviews of the major program emphases in the economic and social area in light of global trends. Finally, it would prepare the agendas and follow-up on the decisions of the annual U.N. system summits (a proposal of the Group of 18 adopted last December), and participate in the summits on a co-equal basis with the specialized agency heads.

SUPPORT: The Advisory Commission would be served by a small inter-agency staff seconded from the U.N.'s main economic and social agencies.

Step 2—The U.N. Commission:

COMPOSITION: The Commission would be composed 15 to 18 Commissioners, including Directors General of the principal specialized agencies and the Bretton Woods organizations. Commission would be nominated by the Ministerial Board and confirmed by the General Assembly, except for the heads of the IMF, World Bank and GATT whose appointment procedures would not change.

FUNCTION: The Commission would have the same functions as the Advisory Commission except that it would also prepare a consolidated U.N. system program budget from the submissions of every participating agency (except for the IMF, World Bank and GATT) for submission to the General Assembly for its approval.

SUPPORT: The Commission would have its own budget and, like the Ministerial Board, would draw upon DIESA for substantive support.

Development Assistance Board

In order to improve the quality and coherence of U.N. development assistance and to reduce overlap and duplication, the separate executive boards of UNDP, UNFPA, WFP, and UNICEF should be replaced by a single Development Assistance Board. The Board would exercise oversight of all program proposals, conducting reviews before the start of fundraising efforts in order to ensure influence upon the overall scope and content of work programs. The Board would also be responsible for development of a conceptual framework for U.N. development assistance which leads gradually to appropriate specialization.

Elimination of Second and Third Committees;
Expansion of ECOSOC to Plenary Size

To eliminate the nearly complete duplication of agendas and debates between the Economic and Social Council (ECOSOC) and the General Assembly's committees dealing with economic and social matters (Second and Third), and to end the waste of scarce human resources which results from this duplication, the Second and Third Committees of the General Assembly should be discontinued and their duties assumed by ECOSOC, which would be enlarged to plenary size and strengthened by structural and procedural reforms, including addition of a Reports and Agenda Committee.

Merger of the Special Political Committee into the Fourth Committee

In view of the steady decline in the agenda and responsibilities of the Fourth Committee as the global movement toward decolonization nears completion; in view of the overlap in significant parts of the agendas of the Fourth Committee and the Special Political Committee; and in view of the Secretary-General's recent decision to combine the secretariats for special political questions, regional cooperation, decolonization and trusteeship, and the Council on Namibia into a single Department, the Special Political Committee and the Fourth Committee should be merged. The new committee should be called "Committee for Non-Self-Governing Territories and Special Political Questions."

Merger of the Department of International Economic and Social Affairs (DIESA) with the Office of the Director-General for International Economic Cooperation (DIEC)

To improve the identification, study and management of interrelated economic and social issues by the U.N., the main economic and social secretariats (DIESA and DIEC) should be combined into a single department headed by the Director-General. The expanded DIESA should be reorganized along interdisciplinary lines, it should support the work of the Ministerial Board and the Advisory Commission and it should have expertise and data-monitoring capability in every major economic and social area embraced by the U.N. system.

PEACE AND SECURITY

The panel believes that the U.N.'s limitations in the peace and security field are more the product of contemporary international relations than of shortcomings in U.N. management or structure. Unlike social, economic and humanitarian affairs, major structural changes in U.N. peace and security mechanisms appear unpromising. Instead, consensus-building, practical implementation, and selectivity in focusing on tasks where the U.N. has a comparative advantage are critical to improving U.N. performance. This will entail some rethinking of priorities, strategies, goals and directions along lines elaborated in the report. Among the specific proposals recommended are the following:

Strengthening Cooperation With Regional Bodies

The Secretaries-General of the United Nations and of regional organizations and their deputies should meet on a regular basis to exchange information regarding emerging disputes that might threaten international peace and security, to discuss joint measures where appropriate, and to consider common problems of financial, logistical and political support.

Multilateral Inspection Teams

Arms reductions, because they impose higher security risks than traditional arms control steps, demand thorough, reliable and impartial verification, often beyond the capabilities of national technical means based largely on satellites. In cases involving the production or storage of weapons, satellite reconnaissance is clearly not sufficient and on-site inspection by one's adversary is generally unacceptable. There may be instances where the U.N. could provide multilateral inspection teams from a politically balanced mix of countries for third-party inspection and reporting.

Ad Hoc Compliance Review Groups

Ad hoc review groups could be established under the aegis of the Security Council to examine compliance questions related to multilateral agreements and questions arising from the reports of the proposed Multilateral Inspection Teams. After considering reports of questionable practices or apparent violations, review groups could initiate consultations between the parties, and could refer serious breaches to the full Security Council.

THE SECRETARY-GENERAL

1. In choosing an individual to serve as Secretary-General, the most important international civil servant, member states have a responsibility to select someone with the qualities of leadership, integrity, vision and intellect necessary to carry out this enormously demanding job.

2. The Secretary-General should vigorously defend his duties and prerogatives as chief executive and recognize that his responsibilities under the Charter require him to be an initiative-taker rather than a caretaker in the service of efficient management.

3. The Secretary-General should make explicit and binding delegations of authority to capable individuals with executive responsibility for: (i) planning and development of the program budget; (ii) financial and administrative policy with particular emphasis on the personnel area; (iii) and coordination of related activities of the U.N. proper and the U.N. group.

4. To establish a coherent administrative structure of manageable proportions, responsibility for the departmental activities funded by the U.N.'s regular budget should be coordinated in a small cabinet chaired by the Secretary-General and including among its members the Under-Secretary-General for Administration and Management and the Director General.

5. Effective as of the next election, Secretaries General should be elected for a single term not to exceed seven years.

38. Towards Comprehensive Security Through the Enhancement of the Role of the United Nations

Vladimir Petrovsky

The purpose of the discussion within the United Nations of the item "Comprehensive system of international peace and security" is to launch a broad international dialogue, above all within the United Nations, on the ways and means of ensuring comprehensive security in military, political, economic, ecological, humanitarian, including human rights, and other fields on the basis of strict compliance with the Charter of the United Nations and the enhanced role and effectiveness of the United Nations in the maintenance of international peace and in the solution of global problems.

The fundamental position of the Union of Soviet Socialist Republics on this subject is contained in the article by M. S. Gorbachev "Reality and safeguards for a secure world" (see A/42/574-S/19143, annex). On the eve of the forty-third session of the United Nations General Assembly, the Soviet Union is stating its approach to certain specific aspects of ensuring comprehensive security, namely: enhancing the effectiveness of the United Nations and of its main bodies, more extensive use of United Nations peace-keeping operations and the affirmation of the primacy of international law in inter-State relations. At the same time the USSR is also prepared to discuss other aspects of international security as may be proposed by other States.

I

In the opinion of the Soviet Union the search by all States for ways and means to enhance the effectiveness of the United Nations should be aimed at the full and unselective implementation of the provisions of the Charter, active use of its machinery and procedures, and promotion of the ability of the United Nations to take effective preventive measures to avert international crises and conflicts. The USSR proposes that efforts be made to reduce the level of confrontation within the United Nations and that the atmosphere of fruitful co-operation among States within the Organization become a rule.

The following measures could contribute to a greater effectiveness of the United Nations Security Council:

- Arrangements for closer interaction among the permanent members of the Council; the permanent members could study the possibility of elaborating such measures, procedures and mutual obligations in the spirit of restraint and self-limitation, and respect for the freedom of choice of the peoples, which would rule out the involvement of major Powers in confrontations through regional conflicts;

- A more active use of the mechanisms for formal and informal consultations among Security Council members with the participation of the Secretary-General as well as, if need be, of the parties directly involved;
- The holding, in some cases, of formal closed meetings by the Security Council, which will make it possible to concentrate on expanding the scope of agreement and deeper consideration of the problems where agreement is emerging, without mandatory adoption of any final documents;
- The holding by the Security Council of periodic meetings at the foreign-minister level in the course or on the eve of General Assembly sessions, which, however, should not duplicate the general debate at the sessions.

The General Assembly could tangibly increase its contribution to resolving international problems by updating and improving its methods and style of operation in the following fields:

- The preparation and adoption of a greater number of General Assembly decisions on the basis of consensus reflecting the balance of interests of States;
- The maintenance of the prestige and the prevention of political devaluation of General Assembly recommendations adopted by voting;
- Monitoring the implementation of General Assembly resolutions;
- Holding of special sessions of the General Assembly on individual concrete matters related to ensuring comprehensive security.

The Soviet Union would not oppose:

- The universalization of the Economic and Social Council;
- The elimination of some of its subsidiary bodies, provided that their functions are to be performed by the Council itself;
- The extension of the duration of the Council's sessions, holding of theme sessions, if necessary, sessions of the Council at the ministerial level to discuss practical issues of promoting international economic, scientific, technical, social and humanitarian co-operation.

The Soviet Union stands for a greater role of the Secretary-General and deems it important that a constructive approach prevail within the United Nations towards his peace-making efforts, based on the understanding that under the Charter of the United Nations and in accordance with the practice of the Organization he is within his rights to take initiative in promoting the solution of questions of ensuring international peace and security. The Secretary-General could:

- Request the convening of the Security Council;
- Inform the Council on a regular basis, including confidentially, on the developments in a conflict area or on other matters that may be of interest to the Security Council;

- More often propose to the Security Council various measures for the prevention and peaceful settlement of conflicts as well as with regard to other matters of ensuring comprehensive security;
- Submit for the consideration of the Council, on his own initiative, reports on individual matters regarding the maintenance of international peace and security including disarmament.

It would be useful to introduce a regular practice of thorough consideration by General Assembly sessions of annual reports of the Secretary-General on the activities of the Organization and of the adoption, if necessary, of decisions on the conclusions and recommendations contained therein.

The Soviet Union assumes that raising the role of the United Nations presupposes the ensuring of a sound administrative and budgetary foundation of the Organization, namely: making its intergovernmental machinery more economical; strict and full compliance by all States without exception with their financial and other obligations towards the United Nations; economical and rational use of the financial resources of the United Nations; greater efficiency of the United Nations Secretariat and streamlining of its structure.

II

The Soviet Union wants to see the positive experience and practice of United Nations peace-keeping operations consolidated and further developed and put on a more solid legal and financial basis.

These United Nations operations could be used more extensively for the implementation of Security Council decisions as well as for the prevention of emerging armed conflicts.

The following possibilities could be studied for these purposes:

- The use of United Nations personnel in situations where accusations are made of outside interference for the purpose of destabilizing existing Governments;
- The establishment by the Security Council after consultations with the appropriate regional organizations of United Nations observation posts in explosive areas of the world;
- The use by the Security Council of special missions, which would include representatives of the public as well as officials;
- The stationing of United Nations observers along frontiers within the territory of a country that seeks to protect itself from outside interference at the request of that country alone;
- The dispatch by the General Assembly of observation and fact-finding missions (civilian, military, mixed) in agreement with the Security Council and with the consent of the country (countries) to whose territory the missions would be dispatched;
- The dispatch of military observer missions on the same grounds at the initiative of the Secretary-General and as decided by him and authorized by the Security Council, above all for preventing a possible conflict.

The establishment of a reserve of military observers and armed forces of the United Nations: the USSR is prepared to participate in the formation on a mutual basis with other countries of a system of personnel training for service in the United Nations troops.

In individual cases, if need be and if United Nations Member States display such interest, the Soviet Union would be prepared to consider the question of providing for the conduct of the United Nations peace-keeping operations its military contingents as well.

The Soviet Union could take part in the logistics support for the United Nations forces; supply transportation means for moving units of the United Nations forces to the areas of their stationing; military equipment; communications means; medical personnel; medical supplies and so on.

The USSR deems acceptable various kinds of approach to the methods of solving the question of financing the operations: on a voluntary basis, at the expense of the receiving side (or sides), fully or partially from the United Nations budget. Practicality and regard for the interests and positions of the majority of the Member States should serve as criteria in this.

The activities of the Committee of 33 should be intensified and the organization of its work should be put on a regular basis. It is important to accelerate the harmonization of the procedures for peace-keeping operations on the basis of existing practice and the experience available in this field. The Committee could also consider matters related to the organization by the United Nations Secretariat of a programme of training of national military contingents detailed for possible United Nations use; summarizing the practice of United Nations force operations; standardization of agreements on the "status of United Nations forces"; setting up an international United Nations training centre for personnel to serve in United Nations troops; holding regional and international seminars on these subjects.

III

The Soviet Union stands for more extensive use of the potential of the International Court of Justice in solving outstanding international legal issues.

In the opinion of the USSR the international agreements to be developed under the auspices of the United Nations could include, where appropriate, special provisions envisaging adjudication by the International Court of Justice of disputes resulting from the interpretation and application of such agreements. The General Assembly and the Security Council could ask it more often for advisory opinions on outstanding international legal matters. The mandatory jurisdiction of the International Court of Justice must be recognized by everybody on mutually agreed terms.

The Soviet Union is convinced that the comprehensive system of security is at the same time a system of universal law and order that ensures the primacy of international law in politics.

39. The Establishment of a World Authority: Working Hypotheses

Silviu Brucan

Historically, the case for a world authority rests on the emergence of the world-system eroding the present international state-system. It logically follows that a new system of international relations requires an adequate institution to establish its corresponding world order and secure its smooth functioning during the long transition period from the old system to the new one. To be explicit in what we are talking about, by world order I mean a pattern of power relations among states capable of ensuring the functioning of various international activities according to a set of rules—written and unwritten.

Thus far, the discussion of a new international or world order has been dominated by moral, religious, ideological, and, lately, juridical and economic principles and values. Surely, none of these criteria should be overlooked since each provides some of the motivations underlying large-scale human actions so essential to such an undertaking. What is still lacking is conceptual clarity and scientific groundwork, particularly in bringing into focus the fulcrum of politics which is and remains decisive in settling the issue of world order.

A serious intellectual effort is required to fill this gap. Here are my suggestions regarding the directions of such research work and how to go about it.

1. Since the issue involved is chiefly the management of power in international society, I submit that the first thing that must be worked out is the ways and means for the establishment of an international institution wielding power of its own. In practical terms, this means that a transfer of power—a partial and gradual one, to be sure—would have to take place from nation-states to the new institution. The transfer of power to the World Authority being assumed to be gradual, it follows that during the transition period world order will be maintained by a *duality of power:* the nation-state retaining most of its sovereign prerogatives and the World Authority exercising power in international affairs to the extent of its delegated authority and competence.

2. The concept of World Authority is different from that of world government. The latter presupposes the dissolution of nation-states and the creation, instead, of a single governing body designed to run the whole world, whereas the World Authority requires the nation-state to be maintained with only a partial transfer of power to the new institution so as to enable it to operate effectively within its limited area of competence.

3. It is assumed that the World Authority will be initially entrusted with two major tasks: *peace maintenance* with a view to enforcing general disarmament and eventually abolishing war, and the *restructuring of international economic relations* with a view to overcoming the present economic crisis and eliminating the glaring inequality between the developed and developing nations. Securing peace actually means breaking the war system by halting the arms race—its specific form of

movement—and reversing its momentum. This also involves the gradual dismantling of military forces and organizations parallel with the establishment of a *world police force* and a *world tribunal,* which are needed to make sure that the decisions of the World Authority are enforced, to intervene whenever the law is violated, and for the peaceful settlement of disputes.

4. The choice of government, of its economic, social, and political system will remain the inalienable right of each nation. The World Authority will see to it that no foreign power interferes with such internal affairs of member-states. As the existence of a national police force does not prevent citizens from exercising their constitutional rights, so will the World Authority and police force not prevent nation-states from exercising their sovereignty in all spheres of domestic activity, nor will they be able to interfere with the struggle of exploited classes or oppressed minorities for a better society. Briefly, it is only the *use of force* in interstate relations that will fall within the competence of the World Authority.

5. While we live at a time when nationalism is stronger than ever and nations are extremely sensitive about their sovereign rights, experience shows that nations are nevertheless prepared to transfer some of their prerogatives, provided they are impressed by the advantages deriving therefrom. Recognizing that it is in their best interests that foreign airplanes should fly over their territory and across their frontiers, national governments have accepted the establishment of the International Civil Aviation Organization, and have abided strictly by its rules. Also, such activities as weather control, shipping, control of contagious diseases, have been entrusted to international organizations wielding some power of their own. Therefore, a thorough study should be undertaken to examine the kind of requirements to be met before governments would be willing to hand over national prerogatives to the World Authority in such activities as peace maintenance and economic relations. Since we are dealing with nations having conflicting views, both as to objectives and as to methods, such a study must find compromise solutions to accommodate everyone.

6. Confidence-building measures are essential in the case of a supranational institution, particularly on matters of national security, disarmament, and a world police force—where fears and suspicions reach their highest intensity.

7. *Economics of a warless world:* the question of conversion to a peace economy must be reexamined in the context of the present economic crisis and strategy of development.

8. *Politics of a warless world:* what kind of restrictions and pressures are necessary to apply to the nation-states, particularly great powers, in order to prevent them from using force, and eventually to abolish war. Given the dynamics of power politics, how can the World Authority contain and control it?

9. *The law of a warless world:* a totally new legal framework must be formulated, keeping in mind the conceptual novelty of a supranational institution and allowing for a gradual process toward that goal. The new constitution must spell out clearly what kind of authority and power and over what substantive areas, will be entrusted to the World Authority; also what kind of safeguards will be necessary to prevent organs of the new institution from encroaching upon areas remaining under the authority of nation-states. Finally, the jurists will also have to examine the creation of a world tribunal to establish ways and means for settling disputes.

10. *The new institutions:* The World Authority with its enforcement agencies must be conceived and spelled out functionally in terms of membership, structure, organizations, distribution of power and representation, deliberative and executive bodies, secretariat, rules of procedure, etc. Here the authors will have to devise the new institutions in such a way as to allay the fears that the World Authority once constituted may abuse its powers and become a Frankenstein monster that will terrorize us while we are unable to control it. This issue is paramount in terms of political feasibility; for, unless we assure people that they need not fear abuses from the World Authority, the political will for establishing the new institution is not likely to be forthcoming.

Equally important in this respect is to convey the feeling that in the organization of the World Authority there will be fair and equal opportunities for all nations, irrespective of size, power, and wealth. Experience has implanted in the small and poor nations fear and suspicions against misuse and manipulation of international organizations by the powerful and rich nations. A fair system of representation and distribution of power should allay such fears.

In practical terms, the UN could be instrumental in the initiation phase of the new institution, providing the proper forum for discussion of its principles, organization, and structure. What is more, the new institution will probably have to make use of the experienced staff and vast facilities of the UN, once the latter would cease to exist.

Let me frankly admit that a world authority, however rational its establishment, and however persuasive its historical case, is far ahead of present political and ideological realities and, therefore, its very idea is bound to encounter formidable resistance. Paradoxically, those who need it most, fear it most.

In fact, the changes that require the setting up of such an institution have come so rapidly in international life—quicker than a generation's span of time—that political thought and practice have been left well behind. In no other domain is there a contrast so great between the speed of change and the nature of problems, on the one hand, and the political institutions supposed to deal with them, on the other hand. And yet, horrendous problems are piling up threatening our jobs, the peace we cherish, the air we breathe, the cities we live in, the planes we fly in, and, in the last analysis, our very existence as human beings.

In a world divided by power, wealth, and ideology, probably the most difficult assignment will be the building of a model for the World Authority equally attractive and reassuring for all nations. While the citizens of great and developed nations should look at the World Authority as the safest way of avoiding a nuclear catastrophe, the citizens of the Third World should look at it as the best way of building a more democratic and equitable world order. As for the socialist nations, who are interested in both the maintenance of peace and the establishment of a more equitable economic order, surely 'peaceful coexistence,' however noble a principle, is still an "armed peace," and as such is no guarantee whatever against the outbreak of wars—not even among socialist nations themselves. It is only a world authority that can provide such a guarantee. For a Marxist, it should be clear enough that imperialism will never give up its privileged positions without resorting to the "biggest bang" at its disposal, nor will the advanced capitalist states willingly renounce their commanding positions on the world market. What could socialism mean on a radiated planet?

Apparently, with the emergence of the world-system, everybody must think anew and act anew.

40. Openings for Peace and Justice in World of Danger and Struggle

Richard A. Falk

There is a craving for a positive vision of human destiny manifest in many parts of the world. And yet, the sense of the present, the shape of the ordeal arising out of current conditions, varies greatly from place to place. Some are obsessed by the dark shadows cast by the nuclear arms race. Others are locked in a daily encounter with death through famine, disease, and physical abuse. Still others believe that the evidence is mounting that human activity is destroying the biosphere or crowding the planet beyond all thresholds of adjustments.

It is obvious that the current arrangements of power and influence can rarely provide satisfactory solutions. Especially governments, with notable exceptions, seem immobilized when it comes to the big world order issues. The most prominent states continue to seek security through strength and wealth, and do little to alter their geopolitical style, beyond on occasion acknowledging in words that the situation is dangerous.

The United Nations has also lost most of its inspirational power. There is a widespread acceptance of the Organization as a useful arena for communication, and even its helpfulness in certain limited undertakings, generally at the margins of strategic conflict. At the same time, it has become evident that those who control the purse strings of the United Nations do not want the Organization to grow very strong. Especially the two superpowers have made it plain that they prefer their freedom of action to any further endowment of global institutions with capabilities for action. The United States Government rejection of the Law of the Seas Treaty after ten years of negotiation and compromise is suggestive of the leverage that special economic interests can bring to bear on even the most moderate and mutually beneficial world order arrangements.

The beacon of socialism has also lost much of its allure. A series of revolutionary successes, going back to the victory of the Bolsheviks in October 1917, has not produced models for others to follow, especially with regard to social and political reconstruction. Even where socialist rulers have eased the rigors of the poor and cut down upon waste and gross inequity, socialism-in-power has not been a pretty thing. Repression and a sullen inefficiency has dulled the quality of life itself. Of course, there exists considerable confusion between socialism in the manner of Marx-Lenin and socialist values as the ethical foundation for a different type of social contract between the state and society. The persisting potency of revolutionary nationalist movements of liberation cannot be denied, and their mass mobilizing appeal is extended by the espousal of a socialist program for internal development. Yet, there is no longer confidence that violently wresting control of the apparatus of state power on behalf of a socialist vision is likely over time to raise the quality of human existence in a sustainable way, particularly with repect to the non-material sides of life. Those who have the clarity of will to kill on a massive scale as a tactic of struggle are likely to claim unlimited authority in post-revolutionary settings to guard the new order against enemies and defections.

Similarly, the great confidence stimulated by the breakthroughs of Western science and technology has dissipated. Earlier generations in the West believed that they were witnessing a genuine and irreversible transition over time from scarcity to abundance. With a steady increase in output the productive pie was seen as growing continuously. Even the poorest segments of society would improve their situation until eventually sharing in an overall prosperity, even if enduring cyclical setbacks due to the ebb and flow of economic forces. The debate between marxism and liberalism was carried on within this optimistic framework of assured progress. Now such names as Bhopal, Chernobyl, Challenger mock these grandiose visions of technological mastery and planetary cornucopia. At more fundamental levels, the dynamics of population growth and ecological decay make it plain that the earlier imagery of indefinite expansion and constant growth is ill-conceived in a planet of limited resources, including limited quantities of air, water, and land.

Of couse, disillusionment is not total, nor should it be. Extraordinary achievements have been recorded even by governments and even in the most recent decade: China has moderated its population growth; India has attained food self-sufficiency; New Zealand and Greece have gained some distance from nuclearism; Argentina, Brazil, Uruguay, others have made unexpected and exhilarating, yet still precarious, transitions from militarized rule to democratic forms of governance.

The United Nations continues to provide a much needed safety valve for the explosive tensions of geopolitical rivalry and ideological encounter. Beyond this, the UN General Assembly does register the conscience of humanity on such litmus issues of world policy as majority rule in South Africa and self-determination for the Palestinian people. Over the last two decades the United Nations has provided an indispensable arena for mobilizing concern, providing information and sharpening awareness about entries on the planetary agenda: environmental quality, population control, food sufficiency, resource strategies, disarmament and the status of women. Often the formal outreach of the United Nations is hampered by the bickerings and sensitivities of governments, but UN conferences stimulate counter-conferences by citizen groups that provide a wider understanding of the depth of the problems, the dependence for solutions upon value and structural changes, and evidence of the growing potency of transnational networks of concerned individuals and groups.

And while the wonders of science and technology seem unable to deliver us from the shackles of poverty, neither have their achievements been without benefit. Life expectancy has been generally extended. Many innovations have improved the quality of life, enriching our experience and enjoyments, and protecting many of us from the ravages of nature. The planet is productive beyond the wildest dreams of pre-industrial expectations, and this productivity has helped undermine social practices associated with slavery, serfdom, and servitude. And we can look ahead to incredible possibilities of citizen participation in post-industrial surroundings, computer technology enabling much more consultative patterns of popular sovereignty to be enacted in real life, at least as a possibility.

The global setting, then, is subtle and complicated. The unevenness of circumstances, outlooks, capabilities makes it difficult to generalize about conditions on the planet. Yet some patterns seem to be taking shape that permit a firmer grasp upon reality: the old frameworks for problem-solving cannot overcome several underlying challenges confronting human society; new frameworks for problem-solving are beginning to be discernable on the horizons of political action.

This chasm between the old and new is a treacherous historical interval. The social forces associated with the old struggle hard to sustain their grip on reality. Antiquated mind-sets fashion "solutions" by straining beyond the limits of the feasible, by constant reassurances about competence and by elaborate reliance on secrecy and deception to hide failures. In some ways, the Strategic Defence Initiative (SDI or Star Wars) is a perfect embodiment of these impulses at the precipice of history: conceived by a superpower government, packaged as a critique of the old (deterrence) and as a harbinger of utopia (a nuclear-free, yet secure, world) reliant upon the cultural disposition toward technological "fixes", beneficial to those bureaucratic and economic interests that profit most from the arms race, and capable of being easily diverted in militarist directions at odds with the main promotional claims.

Another revealing strategy for coping with the chasm is to revive the old ways in fierce, fundamentalist forms. The chasm between old and new is denied by retreating into the past, sanctified by claims of truth and salvation and energized by bloody images of enemies and constant strife. The Islamic Revolution, Rev. Moon's Unification Church, the Moral Majority are a few manifestations of fundamentalist "fixes". Here, too, the political choreography is revealing: the voice of a traditional leader who speaks on behalf of the virtuous, the condemnation of modern values and social practices, the reassertion of the virtues of the countryside as over against the sins of the city, and the claims that truth is accessible, not by scientific inquiry, but through revelation and a devout reading of sacred texts. Such fundamentalist passion is extremist at its core, claiming the mandate to sweep away all obstacles that lie in its paths, no matter what the human costs, and regarding its modernizing and temporizing opponents as irremediably corrupt. This kind of unconditional behavior attacks modernity from behind, so to speak, while the true historical forces are superceding modernity, shifting our axes of awareness to the decentered rhythms of post-industrial dynamics.

There are other expressions of chasm consciousness, as well. The surfacing of terrorism is an expression of nihilistic sentiments that totally repudiate any orderly process of change or adjustment. The terrorist, alienated from mass action, insists on administering shocks, gaining potency by being a gruesome form of media entertainment, even as any prospect of real influence disappears. A successful terrorism generates counter-terrorism, and engenders fear, not revolutionary solidarity, and not constructive adjustments of conflict.

A still more prevalent response is to make the leap across the chasm in restricted vehicles that can accommodate only "the fittest". Part of the world, the poor and marginalized is stranded among the reefs of the old, while those that can contribute to the post-industrial world are brought across in style. The result is a sharp break within the social fabric of every society, giving rise in the end to the conflictual imagery of "two worlds", a faultline that shatters all prospects of human solidarity, and characterizes the less successful segments of society as burdens, as dispensable.

The final tropism is an array of apathies. In many modern societies materialism through consumerist enticements itself serves as an opiate. If this is unsufficient, then drugs are often available. Narcotized escapism paralyzes the capacities we require to make the crossing from the old to the new. Indeed, as never before, humanity needs to summon its powers of imagination to envisage and embody responses that respond, cures that cure, medicines that heal. The babel of false gestures makes it especially important to interpret the promising initiatives visible on the distant shore, and give them a semblance, however preliminary, of coherence.

This statement tries to sustain its balance on this tightrope between the old and the new. This stance expresses an underlying conviction that *only such a balance* can enable activists, citizens and leaders to craft real solutions in many diverse domains of concrete challenge.

THE STATE AND POLITICAL VIOLENCE

As the old crumbles, the new emerges; the skyline alters its overall contours. New shapes and patterns become visible, especially to the attentive eye. What is especially innovative are the groupings, tactics and goals evident in relation to domains of social action, and their bearings on what we understand by politics, and what gives these developments their particular force is a fundamental reinvention of politics taking place before our eyes.

To begin with, the new patterns of action are not primarily preoccupied with the state and gaining control over the mechanisms of governmental authority. And furthermore, and perhaps more surprisingly, these initiatives directed at change, even if radical and militant, are not disposed to rely on violence. These reorientations toward *state power* and *instrumental violence* reflect a mixture of practical adjustment and principled assessment.

As a practical matter, the state seems at once too strong and too unresponsive to be a fruitful focus for the undertakings of activists. As a principled matter, control over the state by those with differing goals has generally in the past not yielded positive results, encouraging a betrayal, or at least the subordination, of the animating ideals of revolutionary struggle. Often politicans elected to leadership by large majorities report that they lacked freedom of action and felt constrained from a variety of directions.

Similarly, with political violence, recourse to violence invites violent retaliation especially by the militarized state, a governmental center of operations that specializes in coercion, and is disposed to associate "power" mainly with violence. For societal initiatives to challenge established patterns by violent means is generally to put the challenger at a big disadvantage. The old system is at its strongest when conflict is defined as an outright military encounter. Also, such a beleaguered system can present itself as the refuge of the citizenry and even a discontented people is likely to prefer an effective program of counter-terrorism to a persistence of anarchic and random violence. But there is an ethical element present also. The record of violent struggle is bloody and the results, even when the challenger prevails, are disturbing. The claim to be entitled to inflict pain and even kill opponents by violence is one that is rarely renounced once victory is achieved. New enemies are found. New occasions for violence emerge. The cycle of enemies and combat goes on.

As so the field of innovative social and political action is neither state-centric nor dominated by tales of violent exploits. At the same time, these boundaries should not be drawn too rigidly. In some circumstances of acute oppression by efficient institutions of state power, there exists an occasion where violent struggle ensues and the objective of action is access to state power, at least so as to gain relief from what currently exists. The anti-apartheid struggle in South Africa has a violent dimension and is certainly intent upon dismantling the whole state-implanted system of racialism, embodied in apartheid.

Here is our point. Discriminate violence can be justified as a last resort by the oppressed in an exceptional circumstance, and liberation from oppression may necessarily center on reshaping state power, *but this is no longer what movements for peace and justice in the world are primarily about.*

DEPICTING THE NEW

It is not easy to depict the new in general, global terms. The essence of the new is a series of local, specific, particularistic responses to the impingement of destructive forces on human society. These responses are undertaken in light of this basic tendency to forget (mostly) about gaining control over the state and to renounce violence. Such responses can be clustered into patterns, yet at some loss of specificity. What follows are some interpretations about the character and content of the new, noticing that what we call the new often has deep roots in the past, and has evolved over time as a reaction to earlier experience, and is certainly never novel.

An Emphasis on Local, Grassroots. What is happening in many places in the world is the emergence of social groups, and even movements, seeking to address a local manifestation of a wider problem. Perhaps, it is the challenge of a terrible ecological disaster, as deforestation of a river valley or the introduction at given sites of a dangerous technology such as nuclear power. Perhaps, a militarist intrusion upon nationalist strivings for autonomy, as in the form of foreign base or the harbor entry of a nuclear-powered ship.

The new tendency is toward local, grassroots initiatives based on the assumption that local, municipal authority exists, has been dormant for too long, and is entitled to act, even if these initiatives are opposed to the policies of those who head the government in the capital city and are ignored, even scorned, by central government elites.

The Realization that Information Is Power. Citizens have discovered that independent information deployed by respected voluntary associations can challenge some abuses of state power. The International Committee of the Red Cross pioneered decades ago to provide protection for various categories of special victims of war: prisoners, wounded, civilians. More recently, a series of private organizations have been relying on their capacity to disseminate trustworthy information relating to controversial issues, even if at variance with the claims and policies of powerful governments. The human rights area is illustrated. Amnesty International has been effective by issuing reports on prisoners of conscience and torture. It has deployed this information to encourage governments to reform, at least by curtailing specified abuses against specified individuals. Even if mounting a general campaign against such a practice as torture, Amnesty International never challenges the legitimacy of a government to remain in control of a given state, or even criticizes basic attitudes toward governance.

SIPRI has used information to clarify the character of the arms race. As such, it provides the grounds for other "narratives" about international security than those favored by the propaganda outlets of the main governments. It undercuts purely ideological and self-serving accounts, and influences official channels to seek greater credibility.

Environmental groups, also, throughout the world have used information to challenge the policies of government, increasing our overall appreciation that information is power. And further, it is becoming evident that citizens can often deploy this information effectively without vast resources to enable full dissemination. Their information is not tainted by connexions with partisanship and special pleading, and can be believed, although hostile power/wealth centers devote vast energy to discrediting operations if the preferred passive posture of neglect fails. Using information to attain influence depends on *trust*, and avoiding any impression that a hidden agenda exists, that the information is presented to evoke a specific impression, and has been thereby converted into propaganda.

A Discovery that Everyday Relations Is Politics. Among these new patterns and practices is the realization that how we act in "private" spheres of family, workplace, personal relationships is "politics". Adam Michnik, on behalf of Polish Solidarity, has eloquently explained how the insistence of citizens on truthfulness, openness and trust undermines and restricts the control of the most arbitrary and authoritarian government, especially if these postures struck in a militant way, that is, as defiance that at least in potentiality, expresses a commitment to honest action even at the risk of death or imprisonment.

Michel Foucault, in his writings and activities, has extended this series of insights to various domains of society, especially the treatment of deviants (criminals, mental patients, homosexuals) by formal institutions. Foucault believed that the presentation of the actualities of oppressive circumstances would stimulate corrective action. In this regard, information is a tool at the disposal of civil society, even if restraints on criticism exist. His effort to stimulate prison reform by issuing reports on the actual lives of prisoners is an expression of this sense that "politics" is everywhere that people are made to suffer as a consequence of institutional control.

Of course, also, the women's movement has exerted a huge influence in these settings. It is now a commonplace home truth that a social movement cannot hope to succeed unless men and women share control and authority on a more or less equal basis, and that a failure to share even in private space is an imitation of prevailing power structures. Action so tainted even in personal domains is understood to preclude net cumulative change of any enduring character at the scale of whole societies, or larger.

An Understanding that Religious Traditions and Institutions Can Be and Are Being Mobilized for Constructive Roles. The notion that religion was an opiate or an aspect of the ruling ideology is being repeatedly drawn into question throughout the world. Some of this new religious activism is supportive of the pursuit of peace and justice. We have become aware of "liberation theology" in diverse forms in several distinct regions. Also, the leadership of established churches is increasingly acknowledging an active responsibility to dedicate energies to the tragedies of poverty and to challenge the nuclearism of the state.

One expression of this religious awakening has been The Sanctuary Movement in the United States. Its essence consists of many churches as communities giving "sanctuary" to "aliens" who would face persecution and acute hardship if deported to Central America according to the guidelines of official United States policy. Those religious men and women granting sanctuary face prison terms for defying the state.

A more broad-based activism can be found in the collaboration between churches and democratizing social movements, as in such countries as the Philippines (in the transition from the regime of Marcos to the government of Cory Aquino), as Poland (in lending support to workers struggles) and as Chile (in the struggle of citizens against a brutal military dictatorship).

It should be stressed here that the churches and religious institutions may be deeply divided or lend support to the most repressive tendencies of a state, even when it acts violently against civilians (for instance, as in Sri Lanka in support of official violence against Tamils or in Iran to stimulate persecution of the Bahai's).

The Law and Institutions of Government Can Be Involved Positively. The new movements for radical change in various settings have discovered that law and governmental institutions can contribute to emancipation, even if dominated by a reactionary orientation. Various tactics in different settings seem appropriate.

In oppressive countries, invoking human rights treaties that have been hypocritically ratified (apparently in the belief that no active internal opposition existed to press their relevance) by oppressive governments can legitimize opposition, put the leadership on the defensive and win wider public and transnational support for dissident goals.

Nuclear activists have undertaken several initiatives. They have persuaded hundreds of local governments to endorse the nuclear freeze proposal and, a somewhat lesser number, to declare their town or city to be "a nuclear free zone". Nuclear resisters in the United States and Western Europe have claimed rights under international law to challenge symbolically the deployment of first-strike weapons (Trident, Cruise, Pershing) and to protest the continuation of nuclear testing. In trials, these citizens have invoked a defense of "necessity" and have claimed a Nuremberg right and duty to act non-violently to summon public opposition to the persistence of nuclear crimes of state.

Lawyers have organized as "professionals" to reinforce this activism by interpretations of relevant standards of international law. A London Nuclear War Tribunal was held in January 1985 to assess these contentions, the judges selected by an organizing committee of English lawyers who also arranged a parade of appropriate expert witnesses, each subject to sustained direct and cross examination. More structurally, the Permanent Peoples Tribunal has organized thirteen separate proceedings to assess the rights of peoples as over against the highly contested policies of governments.

In these latter settings, the forms of law have been reproduced without bureaucratic sanction from the state. In effect, the state is losing its monopoly over "law" and institutions. In the earlier settings discussed in this section, established rules and courts are invoked to interpret the law in favor of peace and justice initiatives and to counter the policies of the state.

Feminine Energies and Symbolic Imagination Is Contriving Alternative Images and Conceptions of Power, Authority and Order. Not women as such, but the feminine, seems capable of activating the political imagination in important ways—especially, helping organized society to disentangle its understanding of effective authority from violence; to rescue law and order, and government, from hierarchical arrangements of top-down bureaucratic structure; to separate power generally from destructive capability and military/police techniques; and to distinguish political leadership from concentrations of wealth, egoistic prestige and royalist pretensions.

Women are the leading, but not the exclusive, bearers of feminine creativity. It is evident in such peace initiatives as Greenham Common, Mutlangen and The Great Peace Journey that a feminized political dynamic is at work, reconstructing our images of power, authority, leadership and order. Some of the elements present are the following: gentle anger; shared leadership that works against cults of personality; a blurred boundary between personal relations and public agenda; disinterest in traditional authority roles; avoidance of hierarchy; reliance on song, dance, prayer as principal instruments of struggle; a softer geometry of desirable order (the circle, not the square or stage).

In Greenham Common and Mutlangen women have taken the lead in confronting state power over the deployment of cruise missiles on behalf of NATO. It bring the contrast between the old and the new into vivid relief, and emphasizes the gulf that separates and endangers.

The Great Peace Journey started two years ago in Sweden involves delegations of citizens visiting foreign political leaders to secure their affirmative response (their "yes") to a series of five questions that imply a willingness to disarm and demilitarize if some conditions are met, including a willingness by their counterparts in other governments to do the same thing. This initiative, conceived and enacted mainly by younger Swedish women without prior prominence, is an extraordinary attempt to build a bridge across the chasm separating old dying forms from new emerging ones. It builds on the impulse of even the most militarist governments to strike a virtuous pose in public and give a cheap yes to peace and justice, conceived as a ritual gesture or photo opportunity, but not as a real commitment with behaviorial consequences. The whole subversive motive of The Great Peace Journey is to initiate a dialogue, to insist that if government says yes, then to ask in subsequent initiatives why doesn't it keep its words, act with consistency, fulfill its commitment to the peoples of the world, and take action. It involves a politics of seduction, to be sure, but subtly aimed at disrobing and enfeebling the still reigning war gods.

Officials and Leaders Acting on Behalf of Governments, Corporations and Banks Are All Accountable and Personally Responsible, and Should Be Judged by Fair Legal Procedures if Guilty of Crimes. The impulse to hold officials legally accountable was given dramatic form after World War II when surviving political and military leaders, corporate officials, and prominent professionals (doctors, lawyers, judges) of the defeated Axis Powers, Germany and Japan, were prosecuted before courts set up by international agreement. These trials started at Nuremberg and

Tokyo had many flaws, but they contributed to a growing public insistence that no one is above law and morality, and that acting behind a bureaucratic cover is no excuse, even if in response to superior orders.

Recently, when the Shah was deposed in Iran, Marcos in the Philippines, Duvalier in Haiti, there was a strong popular demand that these dictatorial leaders be charged with crimes of state. In Argentina the transition to democracy has included orderly trials against the former leadership (military and civilian) that were regarded as responsible for torture, disappearances and abuses of public trust.

There is at work a slow, yet widening, process of support to extend the reach of constitutionalism to war/peace and state/society relations. As such, there is borne a correlative notion of legitimate reistance to the abuse of state power. Being a loyal citizen alters its character from unqualified obedience to one of selective defiance.

To the extent that leading governments sustain a nuclear arms race, flagrantly violate human rights, negligently ignore ecological constraints, or deprive a people of its resources by waste or corruption, there is established a strong normative pressure to be active in defiance of established power. The type of defiance may vary depending on conditions, but the foundation for such action is firm, creating the potential for a revolutionary reinterpretion of relations between the individual and the state. As Bruce Springsteen told a rock concert audience, "In 1985, blind faith in your leaders, or in anything, will get you killed".

Visions, Plans, Orientations: Toward and Away From a Positive Program. Our emphasis has been to detect emerging shapes in an early dawn indistinct light. As such, we are not inventing or prescribing, but are reporting, and interpreting, sharing concerns and hopes. Unlike many other normative enterprises, we have no blueprint hidden away. We share the widespread distrust of grandiose solutions spun out by intellectuals who are not in the trenches.

At the same time, the managers and power-wielders have their plans and programs, reinforced by an enormous capability to summon support and weaken opposition by manipulating information, by proceeding violently against adversaries, and by deploying resources and large-scale administrative technologies. It would be a mistake to underestimate the resilience of the complex networks of control and persuasion that remain at the disposal of state and market forces. These embattled hierarchies are themselves driven to adopt utopian projects to overcome the rising tide of disaffection with the old ways. The Strategic Defense Initiative and even pseudo-negotiations between the superpowers beneath the banner of total nuclear disarmament are examples of undertakings that seem neither serious nor sincere, yet respond to cultural yearnings for larger visions than emerge out of gradualist promises of incremental reform.

Gradualism no longer suffices, but neither is there a ready-made or credible vision of the future available to the forces of change. It is part of the challenge we confront to keep one's balance on the tightrope while leading the peoples of the world towards a sustainable future. Not easy, but distinctly possible.

What seems available is a coherent awareness of *normative vectors: the aggregate implications of the new tendencies that seek a non-violent, democratized, ecologically prudent, spiritually fulfilling, and joyous destiny for the species and the planet earth.* What is being set forth is an interpretation of emancipating social forces already in motion and some conjectures about how to strengthen and accelerate their effects. Part of the politics associated with the potency of information is to create broader fields of awareness about what is happening. Building coherent awareness is itself empowering; information and interpretaiton can be an empowering catalyst for existing social forces.

Something else is at stake. The old ways dominate our language, and our language shapes, if not constitutes, our feelings, thoughts, and actions about reality. A role for intellectuals sympathetic with new shapes of social action is to work at the frontiers of human expression, finding the means to express emergent strivings that concern the roots of our collective experience at this stage of history. Listening to the culture, especially to its often obscure and crazy voices at the outer frontiers of experimentation is certainly suggestive as are the envisionings of popular culture in the form of rock lyrics, graffiti, and muscial rhythms. There is much material available to anyone willing to compose a sketchbook of the promised land.

Democratic Security. There exists on all sides a terrible concern with being secure against what threatens and ravages. The old order seeks to wield even more destructive capacity via centralization of information and the intimidation of deviance. Technology in the form of computers takes on a strategic role in the overall process of tracking down and exterminating enemies of the state. Outer space is being currently prepared as an extension of this obsession with militarized control, satellites, sensing systems, and even laser guns are expressions of this desperate last gap of a colonizing mentality.

The tendencies we discern are drawn to another understanding of security, its polar twin, hardly visible to "the realist" conditioned by the prevailing old order. This reorientation of security, what we call "democratic security", is rooted in the claims of popular sovereignty and a trust in the democratizing capacities of people to participate actively in their own security arrangements. In its further reaches, democratic security seeks to embody non-violent instruments of protection, defense, and resistance for political communities seeking to sustain their separate identity and sacred places of habitation. It would put into practices certain feminist reworkings of institutional structure and practice.

Yet, the pursuit of democratic security can and must proceed by stages. It must also invent scenarios that respond to more limited priorities of time and place. Foucault's imperative "react to the intolerable!" cannot be understood as one unified directive. Famine is intolerable in Africa, communal violence in parts of India, nuclearism in the North, dreadful abuses of governmental roles by dictatorial regimes, ecological plunder by countries caught up in a vortex of capitalist and developmental greed. To fight back, from below, to recognize connections, to understand that empowering of peoples to achieve their security by democratizing practices is to repudiate the paralyzing mindset of "national security" that relies on missiles, guns, propaganda, and on the associated notion that elites (rich and strong) are the proper guardians of the future.

Positive Development. The application of human ingenuity to the use of natural resources is what we mean by "development". This interaction is guided by the centralized technologies of the state in concert with "the wisdom" of the market that allows the availability of money to shape what is done and to determine relative claims of individuals and groups on resources. If those who are deprived resent such a plan for allocations, then they are given an option to accumulate purchasing power or gain control over the apparatus of states. Change occurs but within a framework that achieves coherence, if at all, then from configurations of money, violence, and the orientations of leading states.

The new claims on resources are receptive to the unconditional importance of satisfying basic human needs. We are in solidarity with all those of any race, nationality, religion who lack food, shelter, health care, clothing, education, work, and opportunities for family, for pleasure, and for privacy. To worry about cosmetics and luxuries, but to neglect life-enabling needs of our fellow inhabitants of the planet is to rupture human identity.

Similarly, our ways of using resources must be sustainable and respectful of the beauty and diversity of nature, as it evolved over eons of mostly adaptive adjustment. Homogenizing "plans" for growth via expansion of production through the rising claims of state and market forces work against the priorities of basic needs, ecological quality, and strike at the very heart of human community, upon which all other longer ranged prospects for hope in the end depend.

Popular Governance. For many societies the essence of public concern is to alter the character of relations between the state and civil society. Frequently in our world that relationship is oppressive and exploitative either to the people as a whole or towards segments of the population. A nation or people may be held captive by the reigning elite in control of the main instruments of violence and intimidation. Minorities (or even majorities) may be persecuted. The extreme contemporary instance of systematic abuse is the treatment of the black majority by the ruling white minority in South Africa.

The problems are multi-faceted: abuses of state power; denials of human rights; absence of any mechanism of consent and participation by the citizenry; corruption and waste; intimidation and hardship as a daily routine.

Oppressive forms of governance result in poverty and jeopardy for the target groups. The whole of society can be held captive by a wily dictator. In modern time, political theories has vested in the people a right of resistance, even revolution, in the face of tyranny.

The absence of consensual government also tends to produce internal violence and raise regional tensions and provide pretexts for interventionary policies. Oppression and warfare are linked by many close ties. Governance patterns are militarized, creating pressures on the populace to fight back. The military orientation to governance spills over onto foreign policy. Warrior values of war are generally affirmed.

At the core, then, of struggles to establish a more peaceful world is the whole question of governance. As indicated earlier, this question relates to all levels of social organization starting within the inner life of individuals and in family relations between parent and child and men and women. The models for public oppression get their start in reserved or private space. Similarly, the positive models of popular governance (ample participation, consent, respect for law, fairness) can be initiated in even the most oppressive circumstances by what we do behind closed doors.

The state demoralizes the people if its patterns of oppression are internalized in human relations of the home and street. The citizenry establish their participation in "political" life to the extent that they act openly and with trust in their everyday lives at workplace and at home. Adam Michnik and others in Eastern Europe have pioneered the exercise of democratic practices in a circumstance where the formal procedures of state/society are resolutely anti-democratic.

The actuality of popular governance need not be deferred until there is a change of leadership and outlook. Nor must the victims of oppression choose to fight back violently; indeed, it is almost never helpful, especially in modern societies, to meet a militarized governmental system on its own preferred terrain of armed combat. Nor must reform depend on the will of the governing elites. By establishing popular governance at home, at work, in church and social gatherings, among friends, there is a widening zone of autonomy created.

Part of the process of reform is to expose the dishonesty and abusive practices by those "in charge". Information that is reliable is a tool of resistance. Failure to uphold norms of human rights that have been (hypocritically) accepted by the central government exposes the leadership to criticism, even ridicule. These pressures are real, just as the use of violence against dissenters in the night is real. No government is comfortable about defying the global norms of minimal decency these days. If it engages in dark practices, it seeks to hide their occurrence by keeping them as secret as possible. Effective revelations are, therefore, a form of sanction.

Also, the dynamics of popular sovereignty depend on transnational support. It is not only a matter of building international pressure, it is also learning from the exploits of others. Transnational bonding by non-violent resistance groups is mutually encouraging.

Even governments are capable of contributing to the growth of popular governance. When the government of New Zealand reflects its anti-nuclear climate of opinion in legislative action against bringing nuclear ships into ports, an alternative model of statist politics and security policy for a small country is being shaped. A small, vulnerable country is take a stand, refusing to be swept up in the geopolitical currents of nuclearism.

LINES OF ACTION

The creativity of the new social movements, the dynamics of reinventing politics and democracy, the multiple open spaces that exist in even the most closed systems of hierarchical power, make it impossible to catalogue and attach priorities to opportunities for action on behalf of a peaceful and just world. These opportunities are as numerous as the reoriented political imagination identifies.

As a transnational group concerned with the global agenda, we shall mention several "zones" of action, not with any claim that these are necessarily the most "important" options along the range of opportunity. Our specific situation encourages an overview, and seeks to establish the connectedness of many separate undertakings, each seemingly a local/grassroots response to a concrete set of provocations.

Such an acknowledgement also suggests that common conditions exist across the boundaries by which the old order draws its most critical distinctions, as well as is mutually empowering to those whose struggle viewed in isolation seems futile, as the forces arrayed by the state structure are so overwhelming.

In part, our special mission is to help establish a supportive, nurturing climate for the emergence of these new creative energies at work on the great endeavour of reconstruction. As such, our sense of political affiliation must be multiple, expressing an essential loyalty to the species as a whole and to the future as a time when the new emerging order exists as a coherent framework for human endeavour. Our citizenship can not be restricted by considerations of space and territorial law. It is a matter, above all, of ecological, biological, and spiritual solidarity and of an aspirational insistence that we must be dedicated in our lives to the creation of a benevolent polity for all peoples. We want a world, in effect, in which we can declare our identity as "world citizens", but no such world exists, as yet. For now, we can proclaim ourselves as *citizen pilgrims*, committed to a journey through time to a future as yet uncreated.

Along these pathways there are several appropriate emblematic activities to which we lend our support.

1. *Seizing opportunities for enduring the arms race between the superpowers, and generally deescalating levels of tension and armament in the various war zones of the world.* In the last few years, the Soviet Union has taken a series of initiatives to end the nuclear arms race. For seventeen months it sustained a unilateral moratorium on nuclear testing, inviting the United States to join, and proposing to establish a permanent, well-verified treaty of prohibition. Other initiatives have called for the elimination of all nuclear weapons within a decade. At the mini-summit at Reykjavik, Iceland, there appeared a brief glimmer of hope that the leaders of the two superpowers might agree in a process of total nuclear disarmament. After Iceland "wiser" heads have insisted that the Soviet initiatives were a trick or that President Reagan was poorly briefed or that security would diminish if deterrence were supplanted by a disarming process. We are left with a confirmed sense that public opinion and an active peace movement are needed to take advantage of unprecedented opportunities to move toward an ending of the nuclear arms race and toward nuclear (and other forms of) disarmament.

2. *Networks and voluntary associations that use information independently to expose intolerable dangers, lies, corruptions.* The models of the International Committee of the Red Cross, Amnesty International, Americas Watch, and the Permanent Peoples Tribunal are inspirational. The opportunities abound to counter the distorted information and disinformation of mainstream media and propaganda/public relations output of governments, fundamentalist sects.

Individuals with few resources can raise public concern by issuing reports, taking testimony, spreading awareness through seminars and meetings. Even under authoritarian conditions information may often be spread by indirection—if described as "peace studies", or undertaken under religious auspices, or addressed at apparently "safe" issues such as those overseas.

A suggestive possibility at the moment would be the formation of a Global Ozone Study Group or an AIDS Global Information Unit. In both settings, the trends are alarming, official institutions are not responding vigorously, mixed motives are at work. These initiatives are not only appropriate, they are exemplary.

3. *Encouragement of as widespread endorsement of the Nuremberg obligation by all sectors of society.* In effect, the Nuremberg Obligation commits individuals and groups to international law in areas of war and peace as a primary commitment of law and morality. This commitment extends to preparation for war, as well as participation in combat operations. Such an extended image of coverage embraces the nuclear arms race, especially any association with first-strike weaponry or first-use strategies, deployments, threats, or uses.

The Nuremberg Obligation is a reminder to leaders that they are accountable for their behavior, and criminally and individually liable for violations of international law, even if action is taken in the line of official duty and performed reluctantly. The Nuremberg Obligation is also a way of reinforcing moral and political initiatives to oppose and resist governmental policies involving militarism and repression.

It is important to encourage widespread awareness of the Nuremberg Obligation and to get diverse transnational groups to consider adopting a pledge to work for its implementation in all spheres of activity.

Peace and religious groups might also be encouraged to explore the implications of the Nuremberg Obligation for their activities, and as an anchor for both stands of conscience and patterns of justification that are trans-cultural and trans-ideological.

4. *Spreading the word; acquiring knowledge; the role of education.* Institutions of learning have overwhelming incorporated patterns of belief and outlook associated with the decaying old order. It is time to challenge this monopoly over knowledge in the name of the emergent understanding of all aspects of reality. The importance of integration, wholeness, perspective to our appreciation of reality is crucial.

But more than this, specialized research units are needed to deepen and extend our awareness and knowledge. A variety of designations can be adopted: Peace Studies; World Order Studies; Non-Violence; Human Rights and Democracy; Social and Global Concern. The possibility of careful research exploration into specific issues—air pollution near a given city—needs to be combined with inquiries into wider problem-sets: the limits of military power; arms races and war.

It would be important to examine texts in use throughout school systems, and expose biases toward violence, fear and statism. It is essential to open the mind of young people to alternative possibilities for security, development, and governance.

5. *Frameworks for a new constitutionalism.* One basic premise is the need to challenge claims by states to use violence beyond their territory. To undergird this process of challenge it is necessary to establish mechanisms by which citizens can contest foreign policy as a matter of normal legal right. The reassurance of a lawful foreign policy is as big a step towards realizing constitutional promises as has been the extension of the franchise to earlier groups such as women and racial minorities.

6. *Join the struggle against apartheid.* Apartheid has been condemned by virtually all sources of moral and political authority in the world. There is disagreement about how to translate the condemnation into policy and action. At this stage,

those who are victims of the system have formed a powerful and courageous movement of resistance. There appears to be strong grounds to defer to this movement in shaping appropriate action external to South Africa. Such an analysis tends to suggest support for sanctions, for divestment, and yet also encouragement of reconciling moves even at this late stage.

41. Struggles for a Just World Peace: A Transition Strategy

Saul H. Mendlovitz

COMMITMENT AND CALL

"There is a great disorder under heaven." It is not clear whether this condition is good or evil, but it is clear that major changes are taking place in the global political system and in the domestic structures of the majority of the states of the world, including the most powerful. The emergence of global civilization at a period of unprecedented growth rate in human population combined as it is with intensive communicative interaction amongst various societies, the demands and claims of people everywhere to tolerable material satisfaction—basic human needs, the right to be free from authoritarian abuse by governments and perhaps even to participate meaningfully in decisions which affect one's own life, are now part of the political environment of all societies and the global society. Meanings and practices of democracy and sovereignty are being challenged and questioned. Transformation— meaning fundamental change in human society—appears to be taking place and some form of global polity comprehending interdependence, integration and inter-penetration is evolving.

Whether that polity will be preceded by a "Dark Age" or Lebanonisation of the globe, whether it will be organized and run by a relatively small powerful group of individuals and states who in the name of order will impose a system, or whether the polity will be for the benefit of the vast bulk of humanity, is open. Precisely because of this openness we believe it is a moment for people who are committed to peace and justice to mobilize a transnational social movement: The Movement For A Just World Peace.

This is a commitment and call to individuals, groups, organizations, and leadership of progressive governments throughout the globe to join in a common effort in the *struggles* for a more just world peace. We are very much aware that war, hegemonic imperialism, authoritarianism, poverty, social injustice, ecological insta-bility and alienation are problems faced by human beings throughout the globe; that the interaction of these problems produces a global political system in which militarism is deeply rooted and there is an almost unquestioned component of the ideological and political doctrines of the state system. It is against this background that we commit ourselves to a set of interrelated values: peace, social justice, economic well-being, ecological balance and positive identity. We know that straight line projection or, more concretely, present structures prevent realization of these values for some 40 percent of humanity; this is intolerable.

We also know and take heart in the fact that there are a growing number of people throughout the entire globe who are concerned and ready to act to change these straight line projections and structures; there are literally hundreds, indeed thousands, of struggles attempting to create local communities and a global society providing participation, an ecologically sound environment and polity free from militarism. We recognize that the nation-state in the Third World has been a progressive force and does provide some protection and some security against imperial hegemony or domination by stronger powers. Yet it must be acknowledged that the nation-state system as it is presently constituted is incapable of dealing with a series of global crises. The structure of the present system now operates to produce the straight line projections we have just noted.

It is against this background that we announce our intention to join in the formation of the Movement For A Just World Peace. This movement must be rooted in the existential circumstances of people struggling against oppression for justice and dignity in concrete political and social conditions throughout the globe. At the same time the social reality in which we participate at this moment in history is one which involves global penetration by Western civilization and an awareness by almost everyone—no matter how confined and isolated to one's own area—that they are a part of the human society and the globe. It is the recognition of immediate struggles and the power of global political, economic, and social forces that lead us to characterize present circumstances as many worlds/one world.

Within this context it is important to establish some principles for selection of specific political and social objectives. These principles as well as objectives are intended to promote the realization of the values of peace, social justice, economic well-being, ecological balance and positive identity. Here we propose some principles which we believe would be useful as the basis for this selection.

PRINCIPLES, PROGRAM AND PRAXIS

To begin with, we must be willing, in fact invite, the possibility of transcending the images, norms, and concerns of the nation-state system as we have known it for the past 500 years. Furthermore, we must take into account the vast variety and disparity, in income, power, and influence among the many territorial groupings of human beings throughout the globe. It is important, therefore, to identify struggles, programs and projects which develop simultaneously in the following fashion:

1. To the maximum extent possible, attempt to form decentralized units of production, consumption and community participation; these units must be informed by universalist as well as local existential values and some right of appeal to some outside unit should be made part of this formation.
2. The development of unique and creative forms of transnational cooperation to promote the values of the movement.
3. Wide participation in the creation and management of global institutions for global problems.

Within a framework of these principles, images, and norms we recommend the following criteria in the selection of transformative projects:

1. Engage only in those political, social and cultural projects which benefit humanity. If that criterion proves to be too difficult, select only those projects

which directly benefit the lowest 40 percent of humanity in terms of material well-being and meaningful participation in decision-making.

2. System transformation rather than system reform should guide selection of projects.

3. Select projects which have the capacity of organizing somewhere between 5–15 percent of the polity in which you expect the project to take place.

4. The use of violence should be avoided, if at all possible. If used, it should be used only against targets which are themselves the direct source of oppression and the decision to use violence should be subjected not only to "local" people but wherever possible to a transnational group of like-minded individuals.

The images, principles and concerns just noted suggest the following actions to achieve short, intermediate, and long-run targets for a Movement For A Just World Peace.

Short-Run: Targets for 1991–93

- Establishment of cadres (national and sectoral) for a Movement For A Just World Peace (see below, Organization Program).
- Establishing links with like-minded individuals in other societies for the purpose of setting up a network for a transnational social movement.
- Establishing peace and justice agendas for local and national politics.
- Debt relief.
- Targeting human rights violations (most egregious state behavior, i.e., Iran, Iraq, Afghanistan, etc.).
- A democratic Union of South Africa.
- Initiating an annual process of five percent reductions in defense budgets over a ten-year period with savings being allocated for basic needs, domestically and globally. If necessary, initiate tax resistance movements.

Intermediate-Run: Targets for 2001–03

- Establishment of a small but permanent peacekeeping force for the UN with the authority of humanitarian intervention in civil wars.
- Establishment of a global food agency to implement the right to food.
- Vigorous implementation of Forward Looking Strategies of the 1985 UN Conference on International Women's Decade.
- Promotion of individuals for office, whether electoral or appointive, who announce a commitment to global policy as a framework in which national and local society must operate.
- Acceptance of a global code of conduct for multinational corporations, state trade associations of the socialist bloc, and the various state-owned enterprises of the Third World which would be accountable to the values of a just world peace as well as the test of profitability.
- Submission to the compulsory jurisdiction of the International Court of Justice for all treaties concluded during and after the decade of 1990.
- Establishment of a court to deal with individuals who commit crimes against humanity.

Long-Run: Targets for 2011–13

- Global tax scheme to establish and maintain a basic needs regime for global society.
- Complete and general disarmament with alternative security system in place.
- Political decision-making authority to be given to an ecological regime.
- A constitutional framework for global institutions on global matters with appropriate authoritative linkages for transnational cooperative enterprises based on the principle of maximum decentralization of production, consumption, and community participation in decision-making.
- Regional and global human rights regime with compulsory jurisdiction.

It should be noted that the 2011–13 targets are set out so as to provide standards for evaluating the work that is being done on a yearly basis from 1991–93. It should also be pointed out that, in the main, work on all of these targets would begin now; that is to say, in order to accomplish the 2001–03 and 2011–13 targets, some groups would have to begin working immediately on these tasks.

This set of targets will need to be reviewed constantly and opportunities not already mentioned can fit in while others which seem impossible to bring about in the period suggested will have to be dropped. But the first question is, can we agree—even among a small number of people who are committed to both reflection and action—on some such set of targets as these?

If that is possible, then we should move to the next question. How do we organize ourselves, catalyze, and join with others in the Movement For A Just World Peace?

ORGANIZING A GLOBAL TRANSFORMATION CADRE (GTC)
FOR THE UNITED STATES: SOME PRELIMINARY THOUGHTS

We consider essential to the validity and success of the movement that it be a transnational effort—both in practice as well as image. It is for that reason we have included transnational linkages in our short-run targets and in an organizational program. At the same time, it is important, perhaps crucial, to specify concretely the way to organize in one's own society. The exercise that follows should be undertaken by individuals in all regions of the world; that is to say some specification on the matter in which struggle movements in one's own society can relate to global processes is indispensable. It is in this spirit that we direct our attention to the United States. There is one very important additional reason to concern oneself with the United States; it is the fact that this polity is still one of the major actors in the globe. Thus, what we do or do not do in the United States will have a significant impact on the success or failure of the Movement For A Just World Peace.

The overriding organizational thrust is to develop a critical mass of individuals who are committed and dedicated to global transformation. I will call this group the Global Transformation Cadre (GTC).

The implementation of this concept should probably be initiated in the following manner: Bring together a group of intellectuals and social activists, perhaps no more than 25–35 people, whose task it would be to articulate the concerns and issues of both a political ideology and practical action program for the movement. It would be critical to ask, is the time ripe for participating in an articulate, announced social movement to bring about global transformation for the realization of a just world peace? In addition to a close scrutiny of whether or not such a movement is sensible at this time, we should probably go over some carefully prepared documents relating to all the matters noted above, i.e., theoretical, ethical, and praxis aspects for the movement.

It is difficult to assess how long it will take to reach consensus on these matters. Assume, however, that after two to ten meetings with a group of anywhere from 20 to 100 people we have worked through an ideological position and a set of targets for the next 15–20-year period, we can then move on to the organization of the movement.

Implicit in these comments is the awareness that there already exist in the United States many movements (i.e., ideological and political left; community organizing, neighborhood empowerment groups; ecological and life style change; interpersonal transformation; and spiritual transformation). These movements tend to share the same values, but have differing conceptions of praxis and somewhat competing visions of the good world. The movement, to be effective, should engage in interaction with all of these movements.

It will have to appeal as well to individuals in all categories of occupations, professions, bureaucracies. That is, we want the young executive at IBM or the associated partner in a major Wall Street firm or the foreman of a Ford Motor Company or the worker in a vineyard in California, conceiving of themselves as carrying forward the movement by the activity they are engaged in. There would have to be constant interaction between the thinking and action parts of our programming. Whether this should be done through cell meetings or through some broad-scale educational movement or through some new social invention or through some combination of these and other ways is something we need to discuss at length.

A few words about structure. As an initial matter we should make the distinction among cells, cadres, and coalitions. Cells would be groups of individuals who choose to live together and do so in such a way as to exemplify in their daily living as well as their political action the manner in which a just world peace might be brought into being and would be operated. I have in mind here such groups as the Berrigans, the Movement for a New Society, and some of the environmental, feminist, and religious communes which have been set up in various parts of the United States. Cadres are individuals who, while not living together, form a group which set up an organizational structure with concrete political targets, specific functions and responsibilities, and submit themselves to monitoring and review of their achievements with regard to these objectives by a cadre. Coalitions are broader scaled political alliances, more opportunistic and pragmatic in terms of allies around particular issues.

Undoubtedly, the GTC will have to be concerned on how much interaction and engagement it should have in coalition politics. There is, of course, a wide variety of individuals, associations, and organizations who have developed single issue, reformist, and multiple issue programs. The questions of linkages and the problems they raise may be addressed in the early stages of organization or can be left for consideration after we have developed our own cadres.

Some Additional Thoughts Concerning Organization

Perhaps it might be useful to jot down some specific organizational projects we might engage in initiating the movement.

1. First, we should attempt to ferret out the "closet" globalists in the United States. This would consist not only of the lapsed World Federalist, Planetary Citizens, as well as individuals who have been associated with the UNA, World Affairs Councils and the like, but people who, once they were asked to respond to a genuine global movement, would come out of the closet and identify themselves. The particular techniques for identifying and ferreting out these people need a good deal of discussion.

2. In addition to picking up individuals who have an inherent global policy attitude, we must begin to establish linkages at the grass-roots, local, and sectoral levels of the United States. More specifically, we need to find people in activist movements, for example, supporters of the Rainbow Coalition, other poverty and minority actors, feminists, ecologists and show the connection between the problems they are trying to solve and the global political system. At the same time, there are many difficult analytical and ethical issues involved in relating local and sectoral (labor, education, agriculture, religion) levels which will need a good deal of thought. The religious community should be one of our main targets in all of this.

3. It might be important to initiate a political process now with two kinds of specific actions: First, we should identify perhaps a half dozen Congressional candidates like Alan Cranston of California, Mark Hatfield of Oregon, and Patricia Schroeder of Colorado, who might be willing to run on a Just World Peace platform or more minimally use this kind of rhetoric in their 1990s campaigns. We should be prepared to discuss with them the movement's participation in their campaign, identifying all the risks and opportunities involved.

Second, we should make certain that people running for office at all levels of the society—and the various sectors—be questioned on their feelings towards global policy. There is no reason why we should not be asking candidates for governors, state legislators, mayors, town council people, school board people, and presidents of community colleges, heads of utility companies, chief executive officers of large industries at their annual board meetings, how they feel about disarmament policies, apartheid in South Africa, environmental spoilation, and the like.

4. It is crucial that we have a transnational link visibly operating and prepared to permit us to join them in appropriate ways in their own society. More concretely, as soon as possible we should invite a half dozen people from various parts of the world to become involved in the movement and to think through the strategy of their being part of the movement.

Finally, I should make clear that the targets which are listed for the years 1991–93, 2001–03, and 2011–13 are intended seriously and illustratively. That is to say, these are the targets and processes I would argue for within the GTC. At the same time, they are illustrative in the sense that I do not consider this particular set of projects as the only ones a social movement for A Just World Peace could center around. It is crucial, however, I believe, to attempt to set up a process which articulates concrete political goals and particular kinds of actions to achieve those goals.

BIBLIOGRAPHY

THE UNITED NATIONS—GENERAL

Abi-Saab, Georges, ed. *The Concept of International Organization* (Paris: UNESCO, 1981).

Baehr, Peter R., and Leon Gordenker. *The United Nations: Reality and Ideal* (New York: Praeger Publishers, 1984).

Claude, Inis L., Jr. *States and the Global System: Politics, Law and Organization* (New York: St. Martin's Press, 1988).

Feld, Werner J., Robert S. Jordan, and Leon Hurwitz. *International Organizations: A Comparative Approach*, 2nd ed. (New York: Praeger, 1988).

Finkelstein, Lawrence S., ed. *Politics in the United Nations System* (Durham, N.C.: Duke University Press, 1988).

Franck, Thomas M. *Nation Against Nation: What Happened to the U.N. Dream and What the U.S. Can Do About It* (New York: Oxford University Press, 1985).

Gati, Toby Trister, ed. *The US, the UN, and the Management of Global Change* (New York: New York University Press, 1983).

Harrod, Jeffrey, and Nico Schrijver, eds. *The UN Under Attack* (London: Gower, 1988).

Jacobson, Harold K. *Networks of Interdependence*, 2nd ed. (New York: Alfred A. Knopf, 1984).

MacBride, Sean, ed. *Many Voices, One World* (Paris: UNESCO, 1980).

Pitt, David, and Thomas G. Weiss, eds. *The Nature of United Nations Bureaucracies* (Boulder, Colo.: Westview Press, 1986).

Preston, William, Jr., Edward S. Herman, and Herbert I. Schiller. *Hope & Folly: The United States and UNESCO 1945–1985* (Minneapolis: University of Minnesota Press, 1989).

Rajan, M. S., V. S. Mani, and C.S.R. Murthy, eds. *The Nonaligned and the United Nations* (New Delhi: South Asian Publishers, 1987).

Ramcharan, B. G. *Keeping Faith with the United Nations* (Dordrecht: Martinus Nijhoff Publishers, 1987).

Renninger, John P., ed. *The Future Role of the United Nations in an Interdependent World* (Boston: M. Nijhoff Publishers, 1989).

Riggs, Robert E., and Jack C. Plano. *The United Nations: International Organization and World Politics* (Chicago: The Dorsey Press, 1988).

Roberts, Adam, and Benedict Kingsbury, eds. *United Nations, Divided World: The UN's Role in International Relations* (Oxford: Clarendon Press, 1988).

Saxena, J. N., Gurdip Singh, and A. K. Koul, eds. *United Nations for a Better World* (New Delhi: Lancers Books, 1986).

Taylor, Paul, and A.J.R. Groom, eds. *International Institutions at Work* (London: Pinter Publishers, 1988).

THE ROLE OF SOCIAL MOVEMENTS

Biko, Steve. *I Write What I Like* (New York: Harper, 1978).
Boyle, Francis. *Defending Civil Resistance under International Law* (Dobbs Ferry, N.Y.: Transnational Publishers, 1987).
Brandt, Willy. *Arms and Hunger* (trans. Anthea Bell) (Cambridge, Mass.: The MIT Press, 1986).
Chiang, Pei-Heng. *Non-Governmental Organizations at the United Nations* (New York: Praeger Publishers, 1981).
Falk, Richard A., Samuel S. Kim, and Saul H. Mendlovitz, eds. *Toward a Just World Order* (Boulder, Colo.: Westview Press, 1982).
Freire, Paulo. *Pedagogy of the Oppressed* (New York: Herder & Herder, 1970).
Gran, Guy. *Development by People* (New York: Praeger Publishers, 1983).
Gutierrez, Gustavo. *A Theology of Liberation* (New York: Orbis Books, 1973).
Mendlovitz, Saul H. *The Struggle for a Just World Order: An Agenda of Inquiry and Praxis for the 1980s*, WOMP Working Paper No. 20 (New York: Institute for World Order, 1981).
Mendlovitz, Saul H., and R.B.J. Walker, eds. *Towards a Just World Peace: Perspectives from Social Movements* (London: Butterworths, 1987).
Sakharov, Andrei D. *Co-existence and Intellectual Freedom* (New York: Norton, 1968).
Shariati, Ali. *On the Sociology of Islam* (Berkeley, Calif.: Mizan Press, 1979).
Sharp, Gene. *The Politics of Nonviolent Action* (Boston: Porter Sargent Publishers, 1973).

CHANGES AND CONTINUITIES

Arend, Anthony Clark. *Pursuing a Just and Durable Peace: John Foster Dulles* (New York: Greenwood Press, 1988).
Barros, James. *Trygve Lie and the Cold War: The UN Secretary-General Pursues Peace, 1946–1953* (DeKalb, Ill.: Northern Illinois University Press, 1989).
Claude, Inis L., Jr. *The Changing United Nations* (New York: Random House, 1967).
Goodrich, Leland M., Edvard Hambro, and Anne P. Simons. *United Nations Charter: Commentary and Documents*, 3rd ed. (New York: Columbia University Press, 1969).
Hilderbrand, Robert C. *Dumbarton Oaks: The Origins of the United Nations and the Search for Postwar Security* (Chapel Hill: University of North Carolina Press, 1990).
League of Nations. *The Development of International Cooperation in Economic and Social Affairs* (Geneva: League Secretariat, August 1939).
Luard, Evan. *A History of the United Nations*, Vol. I, *The Years of Western Domination, 1945–1955* (New York: St. Martin's Press, 1982).
Mangone, Gerald. *A Short History of International Organization* (New York: McGraw-Hill, 1954).
Northedge, F. S. *The League of Nations: Its Life and Times 1920–1946* (New York: Holmes & Meier, 1986).
Peterson, M. J. *The General Assembly in World Politics* (Boston, London, Sydney: Allen & Unwin, 1986).
Russell, Ruth B., and Jeanette E. Muther. *A History of the United Nations: The Role of the United States, 1945–49* (Washington, D.C.: The Brookings Institution, 1958).

Walters, F. P. A *History of the League of Nations*, 2 vols. (London: Oxford University Press, 1952).

DIVERSE NORMATIVE PERSPECTIVES

Claude, Inis L., Jr. *American Approaches to World Affairs* (Lanham, Md.: University Press of America, 1986).
Coate, Roger A. *Unilateralism, Ideology and United States Foreign Policy: The U.S. In and Out of UNESCO* (Boulder, Colo.: Lynne Rienner Publishers, 1988).
Finger, Seymour Maxwell, and Joseph R. Harbert, eds. *U.S. Policy in International Institutions*, rev. ed. (Boulder, Colo.: Westview Press, 1982).
Franck, T. M., J. P. Reninger, and V. D. Tikhomov. *Diplomatic Views on the United Nations System: An Attitude Survey* (New York: UNITAR, 1982).
Groom, A.J.R., and Paul Taylor, eds. *Functionalism: Theory and Practice in International Relations* (London: University of London Press, 1975).
Haas, Ernst B. *Beyond the Nation-State: Functionalism and International Organization* (Stanford: Stanford University Press, 1964).
Hinsley, H. F. *Power and the Pursuit of Peace* (New York: Cambridge University Press, 1978).
Hsiung, James, and Samuel Kim, eds. *China in the Global Community* (New York: Praeger Publishers, 1980).
Jackson, Richard L. *The Non-Aligned, the UN and the Superpowers* (New York: Praeger Publishers, 1983).
Kaufmann, Johan. *United Nations Decision Making* (Alphen aan den Rijn: Sijthoff & Noordhoff, 1980).
Kim, Samuel S. *China, the United Nations, and World Order* (Princeton, N.J.: Princeton University Press, 1979).
Kirkpatrick, Jeane J. *The Reagan Phenomenon—and Other Speeches on Foreign Policy* (Washington, D.C.: American Enterprise Institute, 1983).
Kubalkova, V., and A. A. Cruickshank. *Marxism-Leninism and Theory of International Relations* (London: Routledge & Kegan Paul, 1980).
Mazrui, Ali. *A World Federation of Cultures: An African Perspective* (New York: Free Press, 1976).
Mitrany, David. *A Working Peace System*, rev. ed. (Chicago: Quadrangle Books, 1966).
Mortimore, Robert. *The Third World Coalition in International Politics* (Boulder, Colo.: Westview Press, 1984).
Moynihan, Patrick. *A Dangerous Place* (New York: Berkeley Books, 1980).
Sauvant, Karl P. *The Group of 77: Evolution, Structure, Organization* (Dobbs Ferry, N.Y.: Oceana Publications, 1981).
Smith, Anthony. *The Geopolitics of Information: How Western Culture Dominates the World* (New York: Oxford University Press, 1980).
Stoessinger, John G. *The United Nations and the Superpowers*, 4th ed. (New York: Random House, 1977).

A NORMATIVE AND STRUCTURAL OVERVIEW

Bailey, Sidney D. *The Procedure of the UN Security Council*, 2nd ed. (Oxford: Clarendon Press, 1988).
Bardonnet, Daniel, ed. *The Adaptation of Structures and Methods at the United Nations* (Dordrecht, Boston, Lancaster: Martinus Nijhoff Publishers, 1986).

Barros, James. *Office without Power: Secretary-General Sir Eric Drummond, 1919–1933* (New York: Oxford University Press, 1979).

Bertrand, Maurice. *The Role of the United Nations in the Economic and Social Fields* (New York: UNA of the USA, May 1987).

Bloed, A., and P. van Dijk, eds. *Forty Years International Court of Justice: Jurisdiction, Equity and Equality* (Utrecht: Europa Instituut, 1988).

Buergenthal, Thomas. *Law-Making in the International Civil Aviation Organization* (Syracuse: Syracuse University Press, 1969).

Cassese, Antonio. *Violence and Law in the Modern Age* (Princeton, N.J.: Princeton University Press, 1988).

Codding, George A., Jr. *The Universal Postal Union* (New York: New York University Press, 1964).

Codding, George A., Jr., and Anthony M. Rutkowski. *The International Telecommunications Union in a Changing World* (Dedham, Mass.: Artech House, 1982).

Corrigan, Peter. *The World Health Organization* (Hove, Eng.: Wayland Publishers, 1979).

Cox, Robert W., Harold K. Jacobson, and others. *The Anatomy of Influence: Decision Making in International Organizations* (New Haven: Yale University Press, 1973).

Dore, Isaak I. *The International Mandate System and Namibia* (Boulder, Colo.: Westview Press, 1985).

Falk, Richard A. *Reviving the World Court* (Charlottesville, Va.: University Press of Virginia, 1986).

Falk, Richard A., Friedrich Kratochwil, and Saul H. Mendlovitz, eds., *International Law: A Contemporary Perspective* (Boulder, Colo.: Westview Press, 1985).

Franck, Thomas M. *Judging the World Court* (New York: Priority Press Publications, 1986).

Graham, Norman A., and Robert S. Jordan, eds. *The International Civil Service: Changing Role and Concepts* (New York: Pergamon Press, 1980).

Gross, Leo, ed. *The Future of the International Court of Justice*, 2 vols. (Dobbs Ferry, N.Y.: Oceana Publications, 1976).

Hazzard, Shirley. *Countenance of Truth: The United Nations and the Waldheim Case* (New York: Viking, 1990).

Higgins, Rosalyn. *The Development of International Law Through the Political Organs of the United Nations* (London: Oxford University Press, 1963).

Hill, Martin. *Towards Greater Order, Coherence, and Coordination in the United Nations System* (New York: UNITAR, 1974).

———. *The United Nations System: Coordinating Its Economic and Social Work* (Cambridge: Cambridge University Press, 1978).

Jordan, Robert S., ed. *Dag Hammarksjöld Revisited: The UN Secretary-General as a Force in World Politics* (Durham, N.C.: Carolina Academic Press, 1983).

Luard, Evan. *International Agencies: The Emerging Framework of Interdependence* (London: Macmillan, 1977).

McWhinney, Edward. *United Nations Law Making* (New York: Holmes & Meier Publishers, 1984).

———. *The International Court of Justice and the Western Tradition of International Law* (Dordrecht, Boston, Lancaster: Martinus Nijhoff Publishers, 1987).

Meron, Theodor. *The United Nations Secretariat: The Rules and the Practice* (Lexington, Mass.: D. C. Heath, 1977).

Murray, James N., Jr. *The United Nations Trusteeship System* (Urbana: University of Illinois Press, 1957).

Nicol, Davidson. *The United Nations Security Council: Towards Greater Effectiveness* (New York: UNITAR, 1982).

Peterson, M. J. *The General Assembly in World Politics* (Winchester, Mass.: Allen & Unwin, 1986).

Ramcharan, B. G. *Humanitarian Good Offices in International Law* (Hingham, Mass.: Kluwer Academic Publishers, 1983).

Reymond, Henri, and Sidney Mailick. *International Personnel Policies and Practices* (New York: Praeger Publishers, 1985).

Sebenius, James K. *Negotiating the Law of the Sea* (Cambridge, Mass.: Harvard University Press, 1984).

Sewell, James P. *UNESCO and World Politics* (Princeton, N.J.: Princeton University Press, 1975).

Sinclair, Ian. *The International Law Commission* (Cambridge: Grotius Publications, 1987).

U Thant, *View from the UN* (Garden City, N.Y.: Doubleday, 1978).

Weiss, Thomas G. *International Bureaucracy: An Analysis of the Operation of Functional and Global International Secretariats* (Lexington, Mass.: D. C. Heath, 1975).

Wells, Clare. *The UN, UNESCO and the Politics of Knowledge* (New York: St. Martin's Press, 1987).

Williams, Douglas. *The Specialized Agencies and the United Nations: The System in Crisis* (New York: St. Martin's Press, 1987).

Yemin, Edward. *Legislative Powers in the United Nations and Specialized Agencies* (Leyden: A. W. Sijthoff, 1969).

Zacher, Mark W. *Dag Hammarskjöld's United Nations* (New York: Columbia University Press, 1970).

THE UNITED NATIONS AND WORLD ORDER VALUES

Angell, Robert C. *The Quest for World Order* (Ann Arbor, Mich.: University of Michigan Press, 1979).

Bull, Hedley. *The Anarchical Society: A Study of Order in World Politics* (New York: Columbia University Press, 1977).

Dolman, Antony J. *Resources, Regimes, World Order* (New York: Pergamon Press, 1981).

Falk, Richard A. *A Global Approach to National Policy* (Cambridge, Mass.: Harvard University Press, 1975).

————. *A Study of Future Worlds* (New York: Free Press, 1975).

Galtung, Johan. *The True Worlds: A Transnational Perspective* (New York: Free Press, 1980).

Gurtov, Melvin. *Global Politics in the Human Interest* (Boulder, Colo.: Lynne Rienner Publishers, 1985).

Haas, Ernst, Mary Pat Williams, and Don Babai. *Scientists and World Order* (Berkeley, Calif.: University of California Press, 1977).

Johansen, Robert C. *The National Interest and the Human Interest* (Princeton, N.J.: Princeton University Press, 1980).

Kegley, Charles W., Jr., and Eugene R. Wittkopf. *The Global Agenda: Issues and Perspectives*, 2nd ed. (New York: Random House, 1988).

Keohane, Robert O. *After Hegemony: Cooperation and Discord in the World Political Economy* (Princeton, N.J.: Princeton University Press, 1984).

Kim, Samuel S. *The Quest for a Just World Order* (Boulder, Colo.: Westview Press, 1984).

Kothari, Rajni. *Footsteps into the Future: Diagnosis of the Present World and a Design for an Alternative* (New York: Free Press, 1974).

Kothari, Rajni, *et al. Towards a Liberating Peace* (New York: New Horizons Press, 1988).

Lagos, Gustavo, and Horacio H. Godoy. *Revolution of Being: A Latin American View of the Future* (New York: Free Press, 1977).

Soroos, Marvin S. *Beyond Sovereignty: The Challenge of Global Policy* (Columbia, S.C.: University of South Carolina Press, 1986).

THE UNITED NATIONS AND INTERNATIONAL PEACE AND SECURITY

Abi-Saab, George. *The United Nations Operation in the Congo, 1960–1964* (New York: Oxford University Press, 1978).

Bailey, Sidney D. *How Wars End: The United Nations and the Termination of Armed Conflicts, 1946–1964*, 2 vols. (New York: Oxford University Press, 1982).

Common Security: A Blueprint for Survival. Report of the Independent Commission on Disarmament and Security Issues (New York: Simon and Schuster, 1982).

De Lupis, Ingrid Detter. *The Law of War* (Cambridge and New York: Cambridge University Press, 1987).

Falk, Richard A. *Revolutionaries and Functionaries: The Dual Face of Terrorism* (New York: E. P. Dutton, 1988).

Falk, Richard A., and Samuel S. Kim, eds. *The War System: An Interdisciplinary Approach* (Boulder, Colo.: Westview Press, 1980).

Ferencz, Benjamin B. *A Common Sense Guide to World Peace* (New York: Oceana Publications, 1985).

Florini, Ann, and Nina Tannenwald. *On the Front Lines: The United Nations' Role in Preventing and Containing Conflict* (New York: UNA of the USA, 1984).

Foell, Earl W., and Richard A. Nenneman, eds. *How Peace Came to the World* (Cambridge, Mass.: The MIT Press, 1986).

Frei, Daniel. *Perceived Images* (Totowa, N.J.: Rowman and Allanheld, 1986).

Fujita, Hisakazu. *International Regulation of the Use of Nuclear Weapons* (Osaka: Kansai University Press, 1988).

Haas, Ernst B. *Why We Still Need the United Nations: The Collective Management of International Conflict, 1945–1984* (Berkeley: Institute of International Studies, University of California, 1986).

Higgins, Rosalyn. *United Nations Peacekeeping*, 4 vols. (London: Oxford University Press, 1969–1981).

Kaldor, Mary, and Asbjorn Eide, eds. *The World Military Order: The Impact of Military Technology in the Third World* (London: Macmillan, 1979).

Lall, Arthur S. *Multilateral Negotiations and Mediation* (New York: Pergamon Press, 1985).

Murphy, John F. *The United Nations and the Control of International Violence: A Legal and Political Analysis* (Totowa, N.J.: Allanheld, Osmun, 1982).

Nicol, Davidson, ed. *Paths to Peace: The UN Security Council and Its Presidency* (New York: Pergamon Press, 1981).

Pilar, Paul. *Negotiating Peace: War Termination as a Bargaining Process* (Princeton, N.J.: Princeton University Press, 1983).

Potter, William C., ed. *International Nuclear Trade and Nonproliferation: The Challenge of the Emerging Suppliers* (Lexington, Mass.: Lexington Books, 1990).

Rikhye, Indar Jit. *The Theory and Practice of Peacekeeping* (London: C. Hurst, 1984).

Rikhye, Indar Jit, and Kjell Skjelsbaek, eds. *The United Nations and Peacekeeping* (New York: Macmillan, 1990).

Singh, J. N. *Use of Force Under International Law* (New Delhi: Harnam Publications, 1984).

Skogmo, Bjorn. *UNIFIL: International Peacekeeping in Lebanon* (Boulder, Colo.: L. Rienner Publishers, 1989).

Thakur, Ramesh. *International Peacekeeping in Lebanon: United Nations Authority and Multinational Force* (Boulder, Colo.: Westview Press, 1987).
Thakur, Ramesh, ed. *International Conflict Resolution* (Boulder, Colo.: Westview Press, 1988).
UNESCO. *International Dimensions of Humanitarian Law* (Paris: UNESCO, 1988).
UNITAR. *The United Nations and the Maintenance of International Peace and Security* (Dordrecht, Boston, Lancaster: Martinus Nijhoff Publishers, 1987).
United Nations. *The Blue Helmets: A Review of United Nations Peace-keeping* (New York: United Nations, 1985).
Usachev, Igor. *A World Without Arms?* (Moscow: Progress Publishers, 1984).
Vaayrynen, Raimo, Dieter Senghaas, and Christian Schmidt, eds. *The Quest for Peace* (Beverly Hills, Calif.: Sage Publications, 1987).
Weston, Burns, ed. *Toward Nuclear Disarmament and Global Security: A Search for Alternatives* (Boulder, Colo.: Westview Press, 1984).
Wiseman, Henry, ed. *Peacekeeping: Appraisals and Proposals* (New York: Pergamon Press, 1983).
Zacher, Mark. *International Conflicts and Collective Security, 1946–77* (New York: Praeger Publishers, 1979).

THE UNITED NATIONS AND THE WORLD ECONOMY

Altschuler, Arkady. *International Monetary Law* (Moscow: Progress Publishers, 1988).
Balassa, Bela. *Change and Challenge in the World Economy* (New York: St. Martin's Press, 1985).
Bertrand, Maurice. *The Role of the United Nations in the Economic and Social Fields* (New York: UNA of the USA, May 1987).
Budhoo, Davison L. *Enough Is Enough* (New York: New Horizons Press, 1990).
Bulajic, Milan. *Principles of International Development Law* (Dordrecht, Boston, Lancaster: Martinus Nijhoff Publishers, 1986).
Dell, Sidney S. *The United Nations and International Business* (Durham, N.C.: Duke University Press, 1990).
Galtung, Johan, P. O'Brien, and R. Preiswerk, eds. *Self-Reliance: A Strategy for Development* (London: Bogle-L'Ouverture, 1980).
Gwin, Catherine. *The International Monetary Fund in a Multipolar World* (New Brunswick, N.J.: Transactions Books, 1990).
Havnevik, Kjell J., ed. *The IMF and the World Bank in Africa: Conditionality, Impact and Alternatives* (Uppsala, Sweden: Scandinavian Institute of African Studies, 1987).
Hudec, Robert E. *Developing Countries in the GATT Legal System* (Aldershot, England: Gower, 1987).
Hutchful, Eboe, ed. *The IMF and Ghana: The Confidential Record* (London: Zed Press, 1987).
Jackson, John H. *The World Trading System: Law and Policy of International Economic Relations* (Cambridge, Mass.: The MIT Press, 1989).
―――. *Restructuring the GATT System* (New York: Council on Foreign Relations Press, 1990).
Jepma, C. J., ed. *North-South Co-operation in Retrospect and Prospect* (London: Routledge, 1988).
Krasner, Stephen D. *The Third World Against Global Liberalism* (Berkeley: University of California Press, 1985).
Long, Olivier. *Law and Its Limitations in the GATT Multilateral Trade System* (Dordrecht, Boston, Lancaster: Martinus Nijhoff Publishers, 1985).

Makarczyk, Jerzy. *Principles of a New International Economic Order: A Study of International Law in the Making* (Dordrecht, Boston, London: Martinus Nijhoff Publishers, 1988).

Meagher, Robert F. *An International Redistribution of Wealth and Power: A Study of the Charter of Economic Rights and Duties of States* (New York: Pergamon Press, 1979).

Modelski, George, ed. *Transnational Corporations and World Order* (San Francisco: W. H. Freeman & Co., 1979).

North-South: A Program for Survival. Report of the Independent Commission on International Development Issues (Cambridge, Mass.: The MIT Press, 1980).

Rothstein, Robert I. *Global Bargaining: UNCTAD and the Quest for a New International Economic Order* (Princeton, N.J.: Princeton University Press, 1979).

Schachter, Oscar. *Sharing the World's Resources* (New York: Columbia University Press, 1977).

Simai, M. *Interdependence and Conflicts in the World Economy* (Budapest: Akademia Kiado, 1981).

Snyder, Francis, and Peter Slinn, eds. *International Law of Development: Comparative Perspectives* (Abingdon, England: Professional Books, 1987).

Talbot, Ross B. *The Four World Food Agencies in Rome* (Ames: Iowa State University Press, 1990).

Tinbergen, Jan, *et al. Reshaping the International Order* (New York: E. P. Dutton, 1976).

United Nations Centre on Transnational Corporations. *Transnational Corporations in World Development: Trends and Prospects* (New York: United Nations, 1988).

Weiss, Thomas G., and Anthony Jennings, *More for the Least? Prospects for Poorest Countries in the Eighties* (Lexington, Mass.: D. C. Heath, 1983).

Zartman, I. William, ed. *Positive Sum: Improving North-South Negotiations* (New Brunswick, N.J.: Transactions Books, 1987).

THE UNITED NATIONS AND SOCIAL JUSTICE

Alston, Philip, ed. *The International Dimensions of Human Rights*, 2 vols. (Westport, Conn.: Greenwood Press, 1984).

Burgers, J. Herman, and Hans Danelius, eds. *The United Nations Convention against Torture: A Handbook on the Convention against Torture and Other Cruel, Inhuman or Degrading Treatment or Punishment* (Dordrecht, Boston, Lancaster: Martinus Nijhoff Publishers, 1988).

Crawford, James, ed. *The Rights of Peoples* (Oxford: Clarendon Press, 1988).

Donnelly, Jack. *Universal Human Rights in Theory and Practice* (Ithaca, N.Y.: Cornell University Press, 1989).

Eide, Asbjorn, *et al.*, eds. *Food as a Human Right* (Tokyo: The United Nations University, 1984).

Falk, Richard A. *Human Rights and State Sovereignty* (New York: Holmes and Meier Publishers, 1981).

Ferris, Elizabeth G., ed. *Refugees and World Politics* (New York: Praeger Publishers, 1985).

Forsythe, David. *Human Rights and World Politics*, 2nd ed. (Lincoln: University of Nebraska Press, 1989).

Fraser, Arvonne S. *The U.N. Decade for Women: Documents and Dialogue* (Boulder, Colo.: Westview Press, 1987).

Henkin, Louis, ed. *The International Bill of Rights: The Covenant on Civil and Political Rights* (New York: Columbia University Press, 1981).

Hevener, Natalie Kaufman. *International Law and the Status of Women* (Boulder, Colo.: Westview Press, 1983).

Humphrey, John T. *No Distant Millennium: The International Law of Human Rights* (Paris: Unesco, 1989).

Joyce, James Avery. *World Labour Rights and Their Protection* (London: Croom Helm, 1980).

Livezey, Lowell W. *Nongovernmental Organizations and the Ideas of Human Rights* (Princeton, N.J.: Center of International Studies, Princeton University, 1988).

McDougal, Myres S., Harold D. Lasswell, and Lung-Chu Chen. *Human Rights and World Public Order* (New Haven: Yale University Press, 1980).

Meron, Theodor. *Human Rights Law-Making in the United Nations: A Critique of Instruments and Process* (New York: Oxford University Press, 1986).

Meron, Theodor, ed. *Human Rights in International Law: Legal and Policy Issues*, 2 vols. (Oxford: Clarendon Press, 1984).

Mower, Glenn, Jr. *International Cooperation for Social Justice* (Westport, Conn.: Greenwood Press, 1985).

Ramcharan, B. G., ed. *Human Rights: Thirty Years After the Universal Declaration* (The Hague: Martinus Nijhoff, 1979).

_____. *The Concept and Present Status of the International Protection of Human Rights: Forty Years After the Universal Declaration* (Boston: Martinus Nijhoff, 1989).

Sieghart, Paul. *The Lawful Rights of Mankind: An Introduction to the International Legal Code of Human Rights* (Oxford and New York: Oxford University Press, 1985).

Tolley, Howard, Jr. *The UN Commission on Human Rights* (Boulder, Colo.: Westview Press, 1987).

UNESCO. *Philosophical Foundations of Human Rights* (Paris: UNESCO, 1986).

United Nations. *The United Nations and Human Rights* (New York: United Nations, 1984).

_____. *United Nations Action in the Field of Human Rights* (New York: UIPUB, 1985).

_____. *Human Rights: Status of International Instruments* (New York: United Nations, 1987).

United Nations Children's Fund. *The State of the World's Children 1989* (New York: Oxford University Press, 1989).

Vasak, Karel, and Philip Alston, eds. *The International Dimensions of Human Rights* (Westport, Conn.: Greenwood Press, 1982).

Vincent, R. J. *Human Rights and International Relations* (New York: Cambridge University Press, 1986).

Zuijdwijk, Ton J. *Petitioning the United Nations: A Study in Human Rights* (Aldershot, Hampshire: Gower, 1982).

THE UNITED NATIONS AND ECOLOGICAL BALANCE

Borgese, Elizabeth Mann. *The Future of the Oceans: A Report to the Club of Rome* (Montreal: Harvest House, 1986).

Brown, Lester, *et al. State of the World 1989: A Worldwatch Institute Report on Progress Toward a Sustainable Society* (New York: W. W. Norton & Co., 1989).

Dupuy, Rene-Jean, ed. *The Future of the International Law of the Environment* (Dordrecht, Boston, Lancaster: Martinus Nijhoff Publishers, 1985).

Gribbin, John. *The Hole in the Sky: Man's Threat to the Ozone Layer* (London: Transworld Publishers, 1988).

Haas, Peter M. *Saving the Mediterranean: The Politics of International Environmental Cooperation* (New York: Columbia University Press, 1990).

Joyner, Christopher, and Sudhir K. Chopra, eds. *The Antarctic Legal Regime* (Dordrecht, Boston, London: Martinus Nijhoff Publishers, 1988).

Le Prestre, Philippe. *The World Bank and the Environmental Challenge* (Cranbury, N.J.: Susquehanna University Press, 1989).

M'Gonigle, Michael, and Mark W. Zacher. *Pollution, Politics and International Law* (Berkeley, Calif.: University of California Press, 1979).

Monro, R. D., ed. *Environmental Protection and Sustainable Development: Legal Principles and Recommendations* (Dordrecht, Boston, Lancaster: Martinus Nijhoff, 1987).

Ophuls, William. *Ecology and the Politics of Scarcity* (San Francisco: W. H. Freeman and Co., 1977).

Orr, David W., and Marvin S. Soroos, eds. *The Global Predicament: Ecological Perspectives on World Order* (Chapel Hill, N.C.: University of North Carolina Press, 1979).

Pearson, Charles S., ed. *Multinational Corporations, Environment, and the Third World: Business Matters* (Durham, N.C.: Duke University Press, 1987).

Ross, Lester, and Mitchell A. Silk. *Environmental Law and Policy in the People's Republic of China* (Westport, Conn.: Greenwood Press, 1987).

Sand, Peter H. *Marine Environment Law in the United Nations Environment Programme* (London and New York: Tycooly Publishing, 1988).

Schneider, Jan. *World Public Order of the Environment: Towards an International Ecological Law and Organization* (Toronto: University of Toronto Press, 1979).

Stockholm International Peace Research Institute (SIPRI). *Weapons of Mass Destruction and the Environment* (London: Taylor & Francis, 1977).

UNESCO. *Man Belongs to the Earth: UNESCO's Man and Biosphere Programme* (Paris: UNESCO, 1988).

United Nations. *Interrelations: Resources, Environment, Population and Development.* Proceedings of a United Nations Symposium held at Stockholm, August 6–10, 1979 (New York: United Nations, 1980).

Weiss, Edith Brown. *In Fairness to Future Generations: International Law, Common Patrimony, and Intergenerational Equity* (Dobbs Ferry, N.Y.: Transnational Publishers, 1989).

Westing, Arthur M., ed. *Global Resources and International Conflict: Environmental Factors in Strategic Policy and Action* (Oxford: Oxford University Press, 1986).

World Commission on Environment and Development. *Our Common Future* (New York: Oxford University Press, 1987).

World Resources Institute for Environment and Development. *World Resources, 1988–1989* (Washington, D.C.: World Resources Institute for Environment and Development, 1988).

Young, Oran R. *International Cooperation: Building Regimes for Natural Resources and the Environment* (Ithaca, N.Y.: Cornell University Press, 1989).

THE UNITED NATIONS AND THE FUTURE

Atlantic Council of the USA. *The Future of the United Nations: A Strategy for Like-Minded Nations* (Boulder, Colo.: Westview Press, 1977).

Beres, Louis Rene, and Harry R. Targ, eds. *Planning Alternative World Futures: Values, Methods, and Models* (New York: Praeger Publishers, 1975).

Falk, Richard A. *A Study of Future Worlds* (New York: Free Press, 1975).

Galtung, Johan. *The True Worlds: A Transnational Perspective* (New York: Free Press, 1980).

Herrera, Amilcar O., et al. *Catastrophe or New Society? A Latin American World Model* (Ottawa, Canada: International Development Research Center, 1976).

Kim, Samuel S. *The Quest for a Just World Order* (Boulder, Colo.: Westview Press, 1984).

Kothari, Rajni. *Footsteps into the Future: Diagnosis of the Present World and a Design for an Alternative* (New York: Free Press, 1974).

Lagos, Gustavo, and Horacio H. Godoy. *Revolution of Being: A Latin American View of the Future* (New York: Free Press, 1977).
Leontief, Wassily, *et al. The Future of the World Economy* (New York: Oxford University Press, 1977).
Ornauer, H., *et al. Images of the World in the Year 2000: A Comparative Ten Nation Study* (Atlantic Highlands, N.J.: Humanities Press, 1976).
Polak, Fred. *The Image of the Future*, 2 vols., trans. by Elise Boulding (New York: Oceana Press, 1955, 1961).
UNA of the USA. *A Successor Vision: The United Nations of Tomorrow* (New York: UNA of the USA, September 1987).

THE UNITED NATIONS AT A CROSSROADS

Baratta, Joseph Preston, comp. *Strengthening the United Nations: A Bibliography on U.N. Reform and World Federalism* (New York, Westport, London: Greenwood Press, 1987).
Behrstock, Julian. *The Eighth Case: Troubled Times at the United Nations* (Lanham, Md.: University Press of America, 1987).
Beigbeder, Yves. *Management Problems in UN Organizations* (New York: St. Martin's Press, 1987).
Bertrand, Maurice. *Reflections on Reform of the United Nations* (Geneva: U.N. Joint Inspection Unit, 1985).
_____ . *The Third Generation World Organization* (Dordrecht, the Netherlands: Martinus Nijhoff, 1989).
Clark, Grenville, and Louis B. Sohn, *World Peace through World Law*, 3rd ed. (Cambridge, Mass.: Harvard University Press, 1966).
Common Security: Blueprint for Survival. The Report of the Independent Commission on Disarmament and Security Issues (New York: Simon & Schuster, 1982).
Fromuth, Peter. *The U.N. at 40: The Problems and Opportunities* (New York: UNA of the USA, June 1986).
Galtung, Johan. *There Are Alternatives! Four Roads to Peace and Security* (Chester Springs, Pa.: Dufour Editions, 1984).
Hanrieder, Wolfram F. *Global Peace and Security: Trends and Challenges* (Boulder, Colo.: Westview Press, 1987).
Henrikson, Alan K., ed. *Negotiating World Order: The Artisanship and Architecture of Global Diplomacy* (Wilmington: Scholarly Resources Inc., 1986).
Logue, John, ed. *United Nations Reform and Restructure* (Villanova, Pa.: Villanova University Press, 1980).
M'Bow, Amadou-Mahtar. *Where the Future Begins* (Paris: UNESCO, 1982).
Mendlovitz, Saul H., ed. *On the Creation of a Just World Order* (New York: Free Press, 1975).
Mikus, Joseph. *Beyond Deterrence: From Power Politics to World Public Order* (New York, Bern, Frankfurt am Main, Paris: Peter Lang, 1988).
Nerfin, Marc, ed. *Another Development* (Uppsala, Sweden: Hammarksjöld Foundation, 1977).
North-South: A Program for Survival. Report of the Independent Commission on International Development Issues under the Chairmanship of Willy Brandt (Cambridge, Mass.: The MIT Press, 1980).
Pines, Burton Yale, ed. *A World Without a U.N.: What Would Happen if the U.N. Shut Down* (Washington, D.C.: Heritage Foundation, 1984).
Sharp, Gene. *Exploring Nonviolent Alternatives* (Boston: Porter Sargent Publishers, 1971).

Smoke, Richard, and Willis Harman, *Paths to Peace: Exploring the Feasibility of Sustainable Peace* (Boulder, Colo.: Westview Press, 1987).

Steele, David. *The Reform of the United Nations* (London: Croom Helm, 1987).

UNA of the USA. *The United Nations in World Affairs: Options for the United States* (New York: UNA of the USA, 1984).

ACRONYMS

ABM	Anti-Ballistic Missile
ACC	Administrative Committee for Coordination
ACD	Arms Control and Disarmament
AIDS	Acquired Immune Deficiency Syndrome
ASEAN	Association of Southeast Asian Nations
BIS	Bank for International Settlements
BN	Basic Needs
CBW	Chemical and Biological Warfare
CCD	Conference of the Committee On Disarmament
CD	Committee on Disarmament
CDP	Committee for Development Planning
CEMA	Council for Mutual Economic Assistance
CFCs	Chlorofluorocarbons
CEPAL	United Nations Economic Commission for Latin America
CERD	Committee on the Elimination of Racial Discrimination
CIDIE	Committee of International Development Institutions on the Environment
CMEA	Council of Mutual Economic Assistance
CND	Campaign for Nuclear Disarmament
COMECON	See CMEA
CPSU	Communist Party of the Soviet Union
CSCE	Conference on Security and Cooperation in Europe
DIEC	Director-General for International Economic Cooperation
DIESA	Department of International Economic and Social Affairs
ECB	Environment Coordination Board
ECE	(The United Nations) Economic Commission for Europe
ECOSOC	Economic and Social Council
ELC	Environment Liaison Centre
FAO	Food and Agricultural Organizations of the United Nations
GATT	General Agreement on Tariffs and Trade
GEMS	Global Environment Monitoring System
GNP	Gross National Product
GTC	Global Transformation Cadre
HCR	High Commissioner for Refugees
IAEA	International Atomic Energy Agency

IBRD	International Bank for Reconstruction and Development
ICAO	International Civil Aviation Organization
ICJ	International Court of Justice
ICSU	International Council of Scientific Unions
IDA	International Development Association
IDEP	(The United Nations) Institute for Development and Economic Planning (Dakar, Senegal)
IFAD	International Fund for Agricultural Development
IFC	International Finance Corporation
IFOR	International Fellowship of Reconciliation
IGOs	International Governmental Organizations
IGOSS	Integrated Global Ocean Stations System
ILC	International Law Commission
ILO	International Labour Organization
ILPES	(The United Nations) Instuto Latinoamericano de Planificacion Economica y Social (Santiago, Chile)
IMF	International Monetary Fund
IMO	International Maritime Organization
INF	Intermediate-Range Nuclear Forces
INFOTERRA	International Referral System for Sources of Environmental Information
INGOs	International Nongovernmental Organizations
IOC	International Oceanographic Commission
IPU	Interparliamentary Union
ISBA	International Sea Bed Authority
ISSC	International Social Science Council
ITU	International Telecommunication Union
IUCN	International Union for the Conservation of Nature and Natural Resources
LDCs	Less Developed Countries
MAB	Man and the Biosphere
MIGA	Multilateral Investment Guarantee Agency
MIRV	Multiple Independently Targeted Re-entry Vehicles
MNF	Multinational Force
MX	Missiles Experimental
NAM	Non-Aligned Movement
NATO	North Atlantic Treaty Organization
NFZs	Nuclear Free Zones
NGOs	Nongovernmental Organizations
NICs	Newly Industrialized Countries
NIEO	New International Economic Order
NPT	Non-Proliferation Treaty
OAS	Organization of American States
OAU	Organization of African Unity
ODA	Official Development Assistance
OECD	Organization for Economic Cooperation and Development
ONUC	*Operation des Nations Unies au Congo* (United Nations Operation in the Congo)
OPEC	Organization of Petroleum Exporting Countries
PAC	Programme Activity Centre
PLO	Palestine Liberation Organization
PQLI	Physical Quality of Life Index

PRC	People's Republic of China
RSS	Rashtriya Swayamsevak Sangh
SALs	Structural Adjustment Loans
SAP	Special Action Programme
SDI	Strategic Defense Initiative
SDRs	Special Drawing Rights
SIPRI	Stockholm International Peace Research Institution
SO	Special Organization
SSOD-I	First Special Session on Disarmament
SSOD-II	Second Special Session on Disarmament
START	Strategic Arms Reduction Talks
SUNFED	Special United Nations Fund for Economic Development
TCDC	Technical Cooperation Among Developing Countries (a programme of UNDP)
TNCs	Transnational Corporations
TVA	Tennessee Valley Authority
UN	United Nations
UNA	United Nations Association
UNCI	United Nations Commission for Indonesia
UNCLOS-III	United Nations Convention on the Law of the Sea
UNCTAD	United Nations Conference on Trade and Development
UNDOF	United Nations Disengagement Observer Force
UNDP	United Nations Development Programme
UNDRO	Office of the United Nations Disaster Relief Coordinator
UNEF I	United Nations Emergency Force I
UNEF II	United Nations Emergency Force II
UNEP	United Nations Environment Programme
UNESCO	United Nations Educational, Scientific, and Cultural Organization
UNFICYP	United Nations Peace-Keeping Force in Cyprus
UNFPA	United Nations Fund for Population Activities
UNGOMAP	United Nations Good Offices Mission for Afghanistan and Pakistan
UNHCR	United Nations High Commissioner for Refugees
UNICEF	United Nations Children's Fund
UNICYP	United Nations Force in Cyprus
UNIDIR	United Nations Research Institute for Disarmament
UNIDO	United Nations Industrial Development Organization
UNIFIL	United Nations Interim Force in Lebanon
UNIIMOG	United Nations Iran-Iraq Military Observer Group
UNIPOM	United Nations India-Pakistan Observation Mission
UNRISD	United Nations Research Institute on Social Development (Geneva)
UNITAR	United Nations Institute for Training and Research
UNMOGIP	United Nations Military Observer Group for India and Pakistan
UNOGIL	United Nations Observer Group in Lebanon
UNRWA	United Nations Relief and Works Agency for Palestine Refugees in the Near East
UNSCOB	United Nations Special Committee on the Balkans
UNTSO	United Nations Truce Supervision Organization in Palestine
UNU	United Nations University
UNYOM	United Nations Observer Mission in Yemen
UPU	Universal Postal Union
WFC	World Food Council

WFP	World Food Programme
WHO	World Health Organization
WICEM	World Industry Conference on Environmental Management
WIDER	World Institute for Development Economics Research
WILPF	Women's International League for Peace and Freedom
WIPO	World Intellectual Property Organization
WMO	World Meteorological Organization
WOMP	World Order Models Project
WRI	War Resisters' International
WWW	World Weather Watch

ABOUT THE BOOK
AND EDITORS

The United Nations is back—negotiating the crisis in the gulf, investigating clashes between Israelis and Palestinians, and generally participating in the shaping of the new global order as the Cold War world is transformed. This text is designed to provide a broad conceptual and theoretical base for evaluating the promise and performance of the UN.

Part One introduces perspectives on global governance and gives a structural and normative overview of the UN over the years. Part Two assesses the contributions and limitations of the UN in realizing world order values. Part Three explores contending visions of the future and competing proposals for reforming the UN.

Intended for use as a basic text in international organization, world order, and global/peace studies courses and as a supplementary text of readings in international relations and law, this anthology encourages students to deepen their understanding of the UN as a global actor and to question their own and their governments' positions toward the UN against the backdrop of a broader conception of security. The extensive original introductory essays, seminal articles and documents, and suggestions for further reading make this an invaluable text and reference for students, scholars, and citizens of the global community.

Richard A. Falk is Albert G. Milbank Professor of International Law and Practice at Princeton University and director of U.S. participation in the World Order Models Project (WOMP). **Samuel S. Kim** is a research associate at the Center of International Studies at Princeton University and is associate editor of *Alternatives: Social Transformation and Humane Governance*. **Saul H. Mendlovitz** is Dag Hammarskjöld Professor of World Order and Peace Studies at Rutgers University School of Law at Newark, director of WOMP, and editor of *Alternatives*.